bash Cookbook™

Carl Albing, JP Vossen, and Cameron Newham

Beijing · Cambridge · Farnham · Köln · Sebastopol · Tokyo

bash Cookbook™

by Carl Albing, JP Vossen, and Cameron Newham

Published by O'Reilly Media, Inc., 1005 Gravenstein Highway North, Sebastopol, CA 95472.

O'Reilly books may be purchased for educational, business, or sales promotional use. Online editions are also available for most titles (*safari.oreilly.com*). For more information, contact our corporate/institutional sales department: (800) 998-9938 or *corporate@oreilly.com*.

Editor: Mike Loukides	**Cover Designer:** Karen Montgomery
Production Editor: Laurel R.T. Ruma	**Interior Designer:** David Futato
Copyeditor: Derek Di Matteo	**Illustrators:** Robert Romano and Jessamyn Read
Production Services: Tolman Creek Design	

Printing History:

May 2007: First Edition.

ISBN: 978-0-596-52678-8
[LSI]

Table of Contents

Preface . . . . **xiii**

1. Beginning bash **1**

    1.1   Decoding the Prompt   4

    1.2   Showing Where You Are   5

    1.3   Finding and Running Commands   6

    1.4   Getting Information About Files   8

    1.5   Showing All Hidden (dot) Files in the Current Directory   10

    1.6   Using Shell Quoting   12

    1.7   Using or Replacing Built-ins and External Commands   13

    1.8   Determining If You Are Running Interactively   15

    1.9   Setting bash As Your Default Shell   16

    1.10   Getting bash for Linux   17

    1.11   Getting bash for xBSD   20

    1.12   Getting bash for Mac OS X   21

    1.13   Getting bash for Unix   22

    1.14   Getting bash for Windows   23

    1.15   Getting bash Without Getting bash   24

    1.16   Learning More About bash Documentation   25

2. Standard Output **28**

    2.1   Writing Output to the Terminal/Window   29

    2.2   Writing Output but Preserving Spacing   30

    2.3   Writing Output with More Formatting Control   31

    2.4   Writing Output Without the Newline   32

    2.5   Saving Output from a Command   33

    2.6   Saving Output to Other Files   34

2.7	Saving Output from the ls Command	35
2.8	Sending Both Output and Error Messages to Different Files	37
2.9	Sending Both Output and Error Messages to the Same File	37
2.10	Appending Rather Than Clobbering Output	39
2.11	Using Just the Beginning or End of a File	39
2.12	Skipping a Header in a File	40
2.13	Throwing Output Away	41
2.14	Saving or Grouping Output from Several Commands	41
2.15	Connecting Two Programs by Using Output As Input	43
2.16	Saving a Copy of Output Even While Using It As Input	44
2.17	Connecting Two Programs by Using Output As Arguments	46
2.18	Using Multiple Redirects on One Line	47
2.19	Saving Output When Redirect Doesn't Seem to Work	48
2.20	Swapping STDERR and STDOUT	50
2.21	Keeping Files Safe from Accidental Overwriting	52
2.22	Clobbering a File on Purpose	53

3.	**Standard Input**	**55**
3.1	Getting Input from a File	55
3.2	Keeping Your Data with Your Script	56
3.3	Preventing Weird Behavior in a Here-Document	57
3.4	Indenting Here-Documents	59
3.5	Getting User Input	60
3.6	Getting Yes or No Input	61
3.7	Selecting from a List of Options	64
3.8	Prompting for a Password	65

4.	**Executing Commands**	**67**
4.1	Running Any Executable	67
4.2	Telling If a Command Succeeded or Not	69
4.3	Running Several Commands in Sequence	71
4.4	Running Several Commands All at Once	72
4.5	Deciding Whether a Command Succeeds	74
4.6	Using Fewer if Statements	75
4.7	Running Long Jobs Unattended	76
4.8	Displaying Error Messages When Failures Occur	77
4.9	Running Commands from a Variable	78
4.10	Running All Scripts in a Directory	79

5. Basic Scripting: Shell Variables **80**

 5.1 Documenting Your Script   82

 5.2 Embedding Documentation in Shell Scripts   83

 5.3 Promoting Script Readability   85

 5.4 Separating Variable Names from Surrounding Text 86

 5.5 Exporting Variables   87

 5.6 Seeing All Variable Values   89

 5.7 Using Parameters in a Shell Script   90

 5.8 Looping Over Arguments Passed to a Script   91

 5.9 Handling Parameters with Blanks   92

 5.10 Handling Lists of Parameters with Blanks   94

 5.11 Counting Arguments   96

 5.12 Consuming Arguments   98

 5.13 Getting Default Values   99

 5.14 Setting Default Values   100

 5.15 Using null As a Valid Default Value   101

 5.16 Using More Than Just a Constant String for Default 102

 5.17 Giving an Error Message for Unset Parameters 103

 5.18 Changing Pieces of a String   105

 5.19 Using Array Variables   106

6. Shell Logic and Arithmetic **108**

 6.1 Doing Arithmetic in Your Shell Script   108

 6.2 Branching on Conditions   111

 6.3 Testing for File Characteristics   114

 6.4 Testing for More Than One Thing   117

 6.5 Testing for String Characteristics   118

 6.6 Testing for Equal   119

 6.7 Testing with Pattern Matches   121

 6.8 Testing with Regular Expressions   122

 6.9 Changing Behavior with Redirections   125

 6.10 Looping for a While   126

 6.11 Looping with a read   128

 6.12 Looping with a Count   130

 6.13 Looping with Floating-Point Values   131

 6.14 Branching Many Ways   132

 6.15 Parsing Command-Line Arguments   134

 6.16 Creating Simple Menus   137

6.17	Changing the Prompt on Simple Menus	138
6.18	Creating a Simple RPN Calculator	139
6.19	Creating a Command-Line Calculator	142

7. Intermediate Shell Tools I 144

7.1	Sifting Through Files for a String	145
7.2	Getting Just the Filename from a Search	147
7.3	Getting a Simple True/False from a Search	148
7.4	Searching for Text While Ignoring Case	149
7.5	Doing a Search in a Pipeline	149
7.6	Paring Down What the Search Finds	151
7.7	Searching with More Complex Patterns	152
7.8	Searching for an SSN	153
7.9	Grepping Compressed Files	154
7.10	Keeping Some Output, Discarding the Rest	155
7.11	Keeping Only a Portion of a Line of Output	156
7.12	Reversing the Words on Each Line	157
7.13	Summing a List of Numbers	158
7.14	Counting String Values	159
7.15	Showing Data As a Quick and Easy Histogram	161
7.16	Showing a Paragraph of Text After a Found Phrase	163

8. Intermediate Shell Tools II 165

8.1	Sorting Your Output	165
8.2	Sorting Numbers	166
8.3	Sorting IP Addresses	167
8.4	Cutting Out Parts of Your Output	170
8.5	Removing Duplicate Lines	171
8.6	Compressing Files	172
8.7	Uncompressing Files	174
8.8	Checking a tar Archive for Unique Directories	175
8.9	Translating Characters	176
8.10	Converting Uppercase to Lowercase	177
8.11	Converting DOS Files to Linux Format	178
8.12	Removing Smart Quotes	179
8.13	Counting Lines, Words, or Characters in a File	180
8.14	Rewrapping Paragraphs	181
8.15	Doing More with less	181

9. Finding Files: find, locate, slocate **184**

9.1   Finding All Your MP3 Files   184

9.2   Handling Filenames Containing Odd Characters   186

9.3   Speeding Up Operations on Found Files   187

9.4   Finding Files Across Symbolic Links   188

9.5   Finding Files Irrespective of Case   188

9.6   Finding Files by Date   189

9.7   Finding Files by Type   191

9.8   Finding Files by Size   192

9.9   Finding Files by Content   192

9.10 Finding Existing Files and Content Fast   194

9.11 Finding a File Using a List of Possible Locations   195

10. Additional Features for Scripting **199**

10.1 "Daemon-izing" Your Script   199

10.2 Reusing Code with Includes and Sourcing   200

10.3 Using Configuration Files in a Script   202

10.4 Defining Functions   203

10.5 Using Functions: Parameters and Return Values   205

10.6 Trapping Interrupts   207

10.7 Redefining Commands with alias   211

10.8 Avoiding Aliases, Functions   213

11. Working with Dates and Times **216**

11.1 Formatting Dates for Display   217

11.2 Supplying a Default Date   218

11.3 Automating Date Ranges   220

11.4 Converting Dates and Times to Epoch Seconds   222

11.5 Converting Epoch Seconds to Dates and Times   223

11.6 Getting Yesterday or Tomorrow with Perl   224

11.7 Figuring Out Date and Time Arithmetic   225

11.8 Handling Time Zones, Daylight Saving Time, and Leap Years   227

11.9 Using date and cron to Run a Script on the Nth Day 228

12. End-User Tasks As Shell Scripts **230**

12.1 Starting Simple by Printing Dashes   230

12.2 Viewing Photos in an Album   232

12.3 Loading Your MP3 Player   237

12.4 Burning a CD   242

12.5 Comparing Two Documents   244

13. Parsing and Similar Tasks **248**

13.1	Parsing Arguments for Your Shell Script	248
13.2	Parsing Arguments with Your Own Error Messages	251
13.3	Parsing Some HTML	253
13.4	Parsing Output into an Array	255
13.5	Parsing Output with a Function Call	256
13.6	Parsing Text with a read Statement	257
13.7	Parsing with read into an Array	258
13.8	Getting Your Plurals Right	259
13.9	Taking It One Character at a Time	260
13.10	Cleaning Up an SVN Source Tree	261
13.11	Setting Up a Database with MySQL	262
13.12	Isolating Specific Fields in Data	264
13.13	Updating Specific Fields in Data Files	266
13.14	Trimming Whitespace	268
13.15	Compressing Whitespace	271
13.16	Processing Fixed-Length Records	273
13.17	Processing Files with No Line Breaks	275
13.18	Converting a Data File to CSV	277
13.19	Parsing a CSV Data File	278

14. Writing Secure Shell Scripts **280**

14.1	Avoiding Common Security Problems	282
14.2	Avoiding Interpreter Spoofing	283
14.3	Setting a Secure $PATH	283
14.4	Clearing All Aliases	285
14.5	Clearing the Command Hash	286
14.6	Preventing Core Dumps	287
14.7	Setting a Secure $IFS	287
14.8	Setting a Secure umask	288
14.9	Finding World-Writable Directories in Your $PATH	289
14.10	Adding the Current Directory to the $PATH	291
14.11	Using Secure Temporary Files	292
14.12	Validating Input	296
14.13	Setting Permissions	298
14.14	Leaking Passwords into the Process List	299
14.15	Writing setuid or setgid Scripts	300
14.16	Restricting Guest Users	301
14.17	Using chroot Jails	303

14.18	Running As a Non-root User	305
14.19	Using sudo More Securely	305
14.20	Using Passwords in Scripts	307
14.21	Using SSH Without a Password	308
14.22	Restricting SSH Commands	316
14.23	Disconnecting Inactive Sessions	318

15. Advanced Scripting **320**
15.1	Finding bash Portably for #!	321
15.2	Setting a POSIX $PATH	322
15.3	Developing Portable Shell Scripts	324
15.4	Testing Scripts in VMware	326
15.5	Using for Loops Portably	327
15.6	Using echo Portably	329
15.7	Splitting Output Only When Necessary	332
15.8	Viewing Output in Hex	333
15.9	Using bash Net-Redirection	334
15.10	Finding My IP Address	335
15.11	Getting Input from Another Machine	340
15.12	Redirecting Output for the Life of a Script	342
15.13	Working Around "argument list too long" Errors	343
15.14	Logging to syslog from Your Script	345
15.15	Sending Email from Your Script	345
15.16	Automating a Process Using Phases	348

16. Configuring and Customizing bash **352**
16.1	bash Startup Options	353
16.2	Customizing Your Prompt	353
16.3	Change Your $PATH Permanently	361
16.4	Change Your $PATH Temporarily	362
16.5	Setting Your $CDPATH	367
16.6	Shortening or Changing Command Names	369
16.7	Adjusting Shell Behavior and Environment	371
16.8	Adjusting readline Behavior Using .inputrc	371
16.9	Keeping a Private Stash of Utilities by Adding ~/bin 373	
16.10	Using Secondary Prompts: $PS2, $PS3, $PS4	374
16.11	Synchronizing Shell History Between Sessions	376
16.12	Setting Shell History Options	377

16.13	Creating a Better cd Command	380
16.14	Creating and Changing into a New Directory in One Step	381
16.15	Getting to the Bottom of Things	383
16.16	Adding New Features to bash Using Loadable Built-ins	384
16.17	Improving Programmable Completion	389
16.18	Using Initialization Files Correctly	394
16.19	Creating Self-Contained, Portable RC Files	398
16.20	Getting Started with a Custom Configuration	400

17. Housekeeping and Administrative Tasks **411**

17.1	Renaming Many Files	411
17.2	Using GNU Texinfo and Info on Linux	413
17.3	Unzipping Many ZIP Files	414
17.4	Recovering Disconnected Sessions Using screen	415
17.5	Sharing a Single bash Session	417
17.6	Logging an Entire Session or Batch Job	418
17.7	Clearing the Screen When You Log Out	420
17.8	Capturing File Metadata for Recovery	421
17.9	Creating an Index of Many Files	422
17.10	Using diff and patch	422
17.11	Counting Differences in Files	426
17.12	Removing or Renaming Files Named with Special Characters	428
17.13	Prepending Data to a File	429
17.14	Editing a File in Place	432
17.15	Using sudo on a Group of Commands	434
17.16	Finding Lines in One File But Not in the Other	436
17.17	Keeping the Most Recent N Objects	439
17.18	Grepping ps Output Without Also Getting the grep Process Itself	442
17.19	Finding Out Whether a Process Is Running	443
17.20	Adding a Prefix or Suffix to Output	444
17.21	Numbering Lines	446
17.22	Writing Sequences	448
17.23	Emulating the DOS Pause Command	450
17.24	Commifying Numbers	450

18. Working Faster by Typing Less **453**

18.1	Moving Quickly Among Arbitrary Directories	453
18.2	Repeating the Last Command	455
18.3	Running Almost the Same Command	456

	18.4	Substituting Across Word Boundaries	457
	18.5	Reusing Arguments	458
	18.6	Finishing Names for You	459
	18.7	Playing It Safe	460

19. Tips and Traps: Common Goofs for Novices **462**
	19.1	Forgetting to Set Execute Permissions	462
	19.2	Fixing "No such file or directory" Errors	463
	19.3	Forgetting That the Current Directory Is Not in the $PATH	465
	19.4	Naming Your Script Test	466
	19.5	Expecting to Change Exported Variables	467
	19.6	Forgetting Quotes Leads to "command not found" on Assignments	468
	19.7	Forgetting That Pattern Matching Alphabetizes	470
	19.8	Forgetting That Pipelines Make Subshells	470
	19.9	Making Your Terminal Sane Again	473
	19.10	Deleting Files Using an Empty Variable	474
	19.11	Seeing Odd Behavior from printf	474
	19.12	Testing bash Script Syntax	476
	19.13	Debugging Scripts	477
	19.14	Avoiding "command not found" When Using Functions	479
	19.15	Confusing Shell Wildcards and Regular Expressions	480

A. Reference Lists **482**
bash Invocation	482
Prompt String Customizations	483
ANSI Color Escape Sequences	484
Built-in Commands and Reserved Words	485
Built-in Shell Variables	487
set Options	491
shopt Options	492
Adjusting Shell Behavior Using set, shopt, and Environment Variables	494
Test Operators	505
I/O Redirection	506
echo Options and Escape Sequences	508
printf	509
Date and Time String Formatting with strftime	513
Pattern-Matching Characters	514
extglob Extended Pattern-Matching Operators	515
tr Escape Sequences	515

Readline Init File Syntax   516
emacs Mode Commands   518
vi Control Mode Commands   520
Table of ASCII Values   522

B. Examples Included with bash **524**
Startup-Files Directory Examples   524

C. Command-Line Processing **532**
Command-Line Processing Steps   532

D. Revision Control **538**
CVS   539
Subversion   545
RCS   550
Other   557

E. Building bash from Source **559**
Obtaining bash   559
Unpacking the Archive   559
What's in the Archive   560
Who Do I Turn To?   564

Index **567**

Preface

Every modern operating system has at least one shell and some have many. Some shells are command-line oriented, such as the shell discussed in this book. Others are graphical, like Windows Explorer or the Macintosh Finder. Some users will interact with the shell only long enough to launch their favorite application, and then never emerge from that until they log off. But most users spend a significant amount of time using the shell. The more you know about your shell, the faster and more productive you can be.

Whether you are a system administrator, a programmer, or an end user, there are certainly occasions where a simple (or perhaps not so simple) shell script can save you time and effort, or facilitate consistency and repeatability for some important task. Even using an alias to change or shorten the name of a command you use often can have a significant effect. We'll cover this and much more.

As with any general programming language, there is more than one way to do a given task. In some cases, there is only one *best* way, but in most cases there are at least two or three equally effective and efficient ways to write a solution. Which way you choose depends on your personal style, creativity, and familiarity with different commands and techniques. This is as true for us as authors as it is for you as the reader. In most cases we will choose a single method and implement it. In a few cases we may choose a particular method and explain why we think it's the best. We may also occasionally show more than one equivalent solution so you can choose the one that best fits your needs and environment.

There is also sometimes a choice between a clever way to write some code, and a readable way. We will choose the readable way every time because experience has taught us that no matter how transparent you think your clever code is now, six or eighteen months and 10 projects from now, you will be scratching your head asking yourself what you were thinking. Trust us, write clear code, and document it—you'll thank yourself (and us) later.

Who Should Read This Book

This book is for anyone who uses a Unix or Linux system, as well as system administrators who may use several systems on any given day. With it, you will be able to create scripts that allow you to accomplish more, in less time, more easily, consistently, and repeatably than ever before.

Anyone? Yes. New users will appreciate the sections on automating repetitive tasks, making simple substitutions, and customizing their environment to be more friendly and perhaps behave in more familiar ways. Power users and administrators will find new and different solutions to common tasks and challenges. Advanced users will have a collection of techniques they can use at a moment's notice to put out the latest fire, without having to remember every little detail of syntax.

Ideal readers include:

- New Unix or Linux users who don't know much about the shell, but want to do more than point and click
- Experienced Unix or Linux users and system administrators looking for quick answers to shell scripting questions
- Programmers who work in a Unix or Linux (or even Windows) environment and want to be more productive
- New Unix or Linux sysadmins, or those coming from a Windows environment who need to come up to speed quickly
- Experienced Windows users and sysadmins who want a more powerful scripting environment

This book will only briefly cover basic and intermediate shell scripting—see *Learning the bash Shell* by Cameron Newham (O'Reilly) and *Classic Shell Scripting* by Nelson H.F. Beebe and Arnold Robbins (O'Reilly) for more in-depth coverage. Instead, our goal is to provide solutions to common problems, with a strong focus on the "how to" rather than the theory. We hope this book will save you time when figuring out solutions or trying to remember syntax. In fact, that's why we wrote this book. It's one we wanted to read through to get ideas, then refer to practical working examples when needed. That way we don't have to remember the subtle differences between the shell, Perl, C, and so forth.

This book assumes you have access to a Unix or Linux system (or see Recipe 1.15, "Getting bash Without Getting bash" and Recipe 15.4, "Testing Scripts in VMware") and are familiar with logging in, typing basic commands, and using a text editor. You do not have to be root to use the vast majority of the recipes, though there are a few, particularly dealing with installing bash, where root access will be needed.

About This Book

This book covers *bash*, the GNU Bourne Again Shell, which is a member of the Bourne family of shells that includes the original Bourne shell *sh*, the Korn shell *ksh*, and the Public Domain Korn Shell *pdksh*. While these and other shells such as *dash*, and *zsh* are not specifically covered, odds are that most of the scripts will work pretty well with them.

You should be able to read this book cover to cover, and also just pick it up and read anything that catches your eye. But perhaps most importantly, we hope that when you have a question about how to do something or you need a hint, you will be able to easily find the right answer—or something close enough—and save time and effort.

A great part of the Unix philosophy is to build simple tools that do one thing well, then combine them as needed. This combination of tools is often accomplished via a shell script because these commands, called pipelines, can be long or difficult to remember and type. Where appropriate, we'll cover the use of many of these tools in the context of the shell script as the glue that holds the pieces together to achieve the goal.

This book was written using OpenOffice.org Writer running on whatever Linux or Windows machine happened to be handy, and kept in Subversion (see Appendix D). The nature of the Open Document Format facilitated many critical aspects of writing this book, including cross-references and extracting code see Recipe 13.17, "Processing Files with No Line Breaks."

GNU Software

bash, and many of the tools we discuss in this book, are part of the GNU Project (*http://www.gnu.org/*). GNU (pronounced guh-noo, like canoe) is a recursive acronym for "GNU's Not Unix" and the project dates back to 1984. Its goal is to develop a free (as in freedom) Unix-like operating system.

Without getting into too much detail, what is commonly referred to as *Linux* is, in fact, a kernel with various supporting software as a core. The GNU tools are wrapped around it and it has a vast array of other software possibly included, depending on your distribution. However, the Linux kernel itself is not GNU software.

The GNU project argues that Linux should in fact be called "GNU/Linux" and they have a good point, so some distributions, notably Debian, do this. Therefore GNU's goal has arguably been achieved, though the result is not exclusively GNU.

The GNU project has contributed a vast amount of superior software, notably including *bash*, but there are GNU versions of practically every tool we discuss in this book. And while the GNU tools are more rich in terms of features and (usually) friendliness, they are also sometimes a little different. We discuss this in Recipe 15.3,

"Developing Portable Shell Scripts," though the commercial Unix vendors in the 1980s and 1990s are also largely to blame for these differences.

Enough (several books this size worth) has already been said about all of these aspects of GNU, Unix, and Linux, but we felt that this brief note was appropriate. See *http://www.gnu.org* for much more on the topic.

A Note About Code Examples

When we show an executable piece of shell scripting in this book, we typically show it in an offset area like this:

```
$ ls
a.out  cong.txt  def.conf  file.txt  more.txt  zebra.list
$
```

The first character is often a dollar sign ($) to indicate that this command has been typed at the *bash* shell prompt. (Remember that you can change the prompt, as in Recipe 16.2, "Customizing Your Prompt," so your prompt may look very different.) The prompt is printed by the shell; you type the remainder of the line. Similarly, the last line in such an example is often a prompt (the $ again), to show that the command has ended execution and control has returned to the shell.

The pound or hash sign (#) is a little trickier. In many Unix or Linux files, including bash shell scripts, a leading # denotes a comment, and we have used it that way in some out our code examples. But as the trailing symbol in a bash command prompt (instead of $), # means you are logged in as root. We only have one example that is running anything as root, so that shouldn't be confusing, but it's important to understand.

When you see an example without the prompt string, we are showing the contents of a shell script. For several large examples we will number the lines of the script, though the numbers are not part of the script.

We may also occasionally show an example as a session log or a series of commands. In some cases, we may cat one or more files so you can see the script and/or data files we'll be using in the example or in the results of our operation.

```
$ cat data_file
static header line1
static header line2
1 foo
2 bar
3 baz
```

Many of the longer scripts and functions are available to download as well. See the end of this Preface for details. We have chosen to use `#!/usr/bin/env bash` for these examples, where applicable, as that is more portable than the `#!/bin/bash` you will see on Linux or a Mac. See Recipe 15.1, "Finding bash Portably for #!" for more details.

Also, you may notice something like the following in some code examples:

```
# cookbook filename: snippet_name
```

That means that the code you are reading is available for download on our site (*http://www.bashcookbook.com*). The download (*.tgz* or *.zip*) is documented, but you'll find the code in something like *./chXX/snippet_name*, where *chXX* is the chapter and *snippet_name* is the name of the file.

Useless Use of cat

Certain Unix users take a positively giddy delight in pointing out inefficiencies in other people's code. Most of the time this is constructive criticism gently given and gratefully received.

Probably the most common case is the so-called "useless use of *cat* award" bestowed when someone does something like `cat file | grep foo` instead of simply `grep foo file`. In this case, *cat* is unnecessary and incurs some system overhead since it runs in a subshell. Another common case would be `cat file | tr '[A-Z]' '[a-z]'` instead of `tr '[A-Z]' '[a-z]' < file`. Sometimes using *cat* can even cause your script to fail (see Recipe 19.8, "Forgetting That Pipelines Make Subshells").

But... (you knew that was coming, didn't you?) sometimes unnecessarily using *cat* actually does serve a purpose. It might be a placeholder to demonstrate the fragment of a pipeline, with other commands later replacing it (perhaps even `cat -n`). Or it might be that placing the file near the left side of the code draws the eye to it more clearly than hiding it behind a `<` on the far right side of the page.

While we applaud efficiency and agree it is a goal to strive for, it isn't as critical as it once was. We are *not* advocating carelessness and code-bloat, we're just saying that processors aren't getting any slower any time soon. So if you like *cat*, use it.

A Note About Perl

We made a conscious decision to avoid using Perl in our solutions as much as possible, though there are still a few cases where it makes sense. Perl is already covered elsewhere in far greater depth and breadth than we could ever manage here. And Perl is generally much larger, with significantly more overhead, than our solutions. There is also a fine line between shell scripting and Perl scripting, and this is a book about shell scripting.

Shell scripting is basically glue for sticking Unix programs together, whereas Perl incorporates much of the functionality of the external Unix programs into the language itself. This makes it more efficient and in some ways more portable, at the expense of being different, and making it harder to efficiently run any external programs you still need.

The choice of which tool to use often has more to do with familiarity than with any other reason. The bottom line is always getting the work done; the choice of tools is secondary. We'll show you many of ways to do things using *bash* and related tools. When you need to get your work done, you get to choose what tools you use.

More Resources

- *Perl Cookbook*, Nathan Torkington and Tom Christiansen (O'Reilly)
- *Programming Perl,* Larry Wall et al. (O'Reilly)
- *Perl Best Practices,* Damian Conway (O'Reilly)
- *Mastering Regular Expressions,* Jeffrey E. F. Friedl (O'Reilly)
- *Learning the bash Shell*, Cameron Newham (O'Reilly)
- *Classic Shell Scripting*, Nelson H.F. Beebe and Arnold Robbins (O'Reilly)

Conventions Used in This Book

The following typographical conventions are used in this book:

Plain text
> Indicates menu titles, menu options, menu buttons, and keyboard accelerators (such as Alt and Ctrl).

Italic
> Indicates new terms, URLs, email addresses, filenames, file extensions, pathnames, directories, and Unix utilities.

Constant width
> Indicates commands, options, switches, variables, attributes, keys, functions, types, classes, namespaces, methods, modules, properties, parameters, values, objects, events, event handlers, XML tags, HTML tags, macros, the contents of files, or the output from commands.

Constant width bold
> Shows commands or other text that should be typed literally by the user.

Constant width italic
> Shows text that should be replaced with user-supplied values.

 This icon signifies a tip, suggestion, or general note.

 This icon indicates a warning or caution.

Using Code Examples

This book is here to help you get your job done. In general, you may use the code in this book in your programs and documentation. You do not need to contact us for permission unless you're reproducing a significant portion of the code. For example, writing a program that uses several chunks of code from this book does not require permission. Selling or distributing a CD-ROM of examples from O'Reilly books does require permission. Answering a question by citing this book and quoting example code does not require permission. Incorporating a significant amount of example code from this book into your product's documentation does require permission.

We appreciate, but do not require, attribution. An attribution usually includes the title, author, publisher, and ISBN. For example: "*bash Cookbook* by Carl Albing, JP Vossen, and Cameron Newham. Copyright 2007 O'Reilly Media, Inc., 978-0-596-52678-8."

If you feel your use of code examples falls outside fair use or the permission given above, feel free to contact us at *permissions@oreilly.com*.

We'd Like to Hear from You

Please address comments and questions concerning this book to the publisher:

O'Reilly Media, Inc.
1005 Gravenstein Highway North
Sebastopol, CA 95472
800-998-9938 (in the United States or Canada)
707-829-0515 (international or local)
707-829-0104 (fax)

We have a web page for this book, where we list errata, examples, and any additional information. You can access this page at:

http://www.oreilly.com/catalog/9780596526788

You can find information about this book, code samples, errata, links, *bash* documentation, and more at the authors' site:

http://www.bashcookbook.com

Please drop by for a visit to learn, contribute, or chat. The authors would love to hear from you about what you like and don't like about the book, what *bash* wonders you may have found, or lessons you have learned.

To comment or ask technical questions about this book, send email to:

bookquestions@oreilly.com

For more information about our books, conferences, Resource Centers, and the O'Reilly Network, see our web site at:

http://www.oreilly.com

Safari® Enabled

 When you see a Safari® Enabled icon on the cover of your favorite technology book, that means the book is available online through the O'Reilly Network Safari Bookshelf.

Safari offers a solution that's better than e-books. It's a virtual library that lets you easily search thousands of top tech books, cut and paste code samples, download chapters, and find quick answers when you need the most accurate, current information. Try it for free at *http://safari.oreilly.com*.

Acknowledgments

Thank you to the GNU Software Foundation and Brian Fox for writing *bash*. And thank you to Chet Ramey, who has been maintaining and improving *bash* since around version 1.14 in the early to mid-1990s. More thanks to Chet for answering our questions and for reviewing a draft of this book.

Reviewers

Many thanks to our reviewers: Yves Eynard, Chet Ramey, William Shotts, Ryan Waldron, and Michael Wang. They all provided valuable feedback, suggestions and in some cases provided alternate solutions, pointed out issues we had overlooked, and in general greatly improved the book. Any errors or omissions in this text are ours and not theirs. An excellent example of their wisdom is the correct observation, "that sentence doesn't know whether it's coming or going!"

O'Reilly

Thanks to the entire team at O'Reilly, including Mike Loukides, Derek Di Matteo, and Laurel Ruma.

From the Authors

Carl

The writing of a book is never a solitary effort, though it has its moments. Thanks to JP and Cameron for working on this project with me. Our complementary talents and time schedules have made this a better book than it could have been alone.

Thanks also to JP for his great sysadmin efforts to provide us with some infrastructure. Thanks to Mike for listening to my proposal for a *bash* cookbook and putting me in touch with JP and Cameron who were doing the same, for pushing us along when we got stuck, and reining us in when we went crazy. His steady guidance and technical input were much appreciated. My wife and children have patiently supported me through this process, giving me encouragement, motivation, as well as time and space to work. I thank them wholeheartedly.

But deeper than the immediate task of this book was the background and preparation. I'm greatly indebted to Dr. Ralph Bjork who made it possible for me to start working with Unix, back before almost anyone had ever heard of it. His vision, foresight, and guidance have paid dividends for me longer than I would ever have expected.

My work on this book is dedicated to my parents, Hank and Betty, who have given me every good thing they had to offer—life itself, Christian faith, love, an excellent education, a sense of belonging, and all those good and healthy things one hopes to pass on to one's own children. I can never thank them enough.

JP

Thanks to Cameron for writing *Learning the bash Shell*, from which I learned a lot and which was my primary reference until I started this project, and for contributing so much useful material from it. Thanks to Carl for all his work, without whom this would have taken four times as long and only been half as good. Thanks to Mike for getting the ball rolling, then keeping it rolling, and for bringing Carl on board. And thanks to both Carl and Mike for their patience with my life and time management issues.

This book is dedicated to Dad, who'd get a kick out of it. He always told me there are only two decisions that matter: what you do and who you marry. I've managed to get two for two, so I guess I'm doing pretty well. So this is also dedicated to Karen, for her incredible support, patience, and understanding during this longer than expected process and without whom even computers wouldn't be as fun. Finally, to Kate and Sam, who contributed greatly to my aforementioned life management issues.

Cameron

I'd like to thank both JP and Carl for their splendid work, without which this book probably wouldn't exist. I'd also like to thank JP for coming up with the idea of creating a bash cookbook; I'm sure he was regretting it through all those long hours at the keyboard, but with the tome complete in his hands I'm certain that he's glad he took part. Lastly, I'd like to once again thank Adam.

## CHAPTER 1

Beginning bash

What's a shell, and why should you care about it?

Any recent computer operating system (by *recent*, we mean since about 1970) has some sort of user interface—some way of specifying commands for the operating system to execute. But in lots of operating systems, that command interface was really built in and there was only one way to talk to the computer. Furthermore, an operating system's command interface would let you execute commands, but that was about all. After all, what else was there to do?

The Unix operating system popularized the notion of separating the *shell* (the part of the system that lets you type commands) from everything else: the input/output system, the scheduler, memory management, and all of the other things the operating system takes care of for you (and that most users don't want to care about). The shell was just one more program; it was a program whose job was executing other programs on behalf of users.

But that was the beginning of a revolution. The shell was just another program that ran on Unix, if you didn't like the standard one, you could create your own. So by the end of Unix's first decade, there were at least two competing shells: the Bourne Shell, *sh* (which was a descendant of the original Thomson shell), plus the C Shell, *csh*. By the end of Unix's second decade, there were a few more alternatives: the Korn shell, (*ksh*), and the first versions of the bash shell (*bash*). By the end of Unix's third decade, there were probably a dozen different shells.

You probably don't sit around saying "should I use *csh* or *bash* or *ksh* today?" You're probably happy with the standard shell that came with your Linux (or BSD or Mac OS X or Solaris or HP/UX) system. But disentangling the shell from the operating system itself made it much easier for software developers (such as Brian Fox, the creator of *bash*, and Chet Ramey, the current developer and maintainer of *bash*), to write better shells—you could create a new shell without modifying the operating system itself. It was much easier to get a new shell accepted, since you didn't have to talk some operating vendor into building the shell into their system; all you had to do was package the shell so that it could be installed just like any other program.

Still, that sounds like a lot of fuss for something that just takes commands and executes them. And you would be right—*a shell that just let you type commands wouldn't be very interesting*. However, two factors drove the evolution of the Unix shell: user convenience and programming. And the result is a modern shell that does much more than just accept commands.

Modern shells are very convenient. For example, they remember commands that you've typed, and let you re-use those commands. Modern shells also let you edit those commands, so they don't have to be the same each time. And modern shells let you define your own command abbreviations, shortcuts, and other features. For an experienced user, typing commands (e.g., with shorthand, shortcuts, command completion) is a lot more efficient and effective than dragging things around in a fancy windowed interface.

But beyond simple convenience, shells are programmable. There are many sequences of commands that you type again and again. Whenever you do anything a second time, you should ask "Can't I write a program to do this for me?" You can. A shell is also a programming language that's specially designed to work with your computer system's commands. So, if you want to generate a thousand MP3 files from WAV files, you write a shell program (or a *shell script*). If you want to compress all of your system's logfiles, you can write a shell script to do it. Whenever you find yourself doing a task repeatedly, you should try to automate it by writing a shell script. There are more powerful scripting languages, like Perl, Python, and Ruby, but the Unix shell (whatever flavor of shell you're using) is a great place to start. After all, you already know how to type commands; why make things more complex?

Why bash?

Why is this book about *bash*, and not some other shell? Because *bash* is everywhere. It may not be the newest, and it's arguably not the fanciest or the most powerful (though if not, it comes close), nor is it the only shell that's distributed as open source software, but it is ubiquitous.

The reason has to do with history. The first shells were fairly good programing tools, but not very convenient for users. The C shell added a lot of user conveniences (like the ability to repeat a command you just typed), but as a programming language it was quirky. The Korn shell, which came along next (in the early 80s), added a lot of user conveniences, and improved the programming language, and looked like it was on the path to widespread adoption. But *ksh* wasn't open source software at first; it was a proprietary software product, and was therefore difficult to ship with a free operating system like Linux. (The Korn shell's license was changed in 2000, and again in 2005.)

In the late 1980s, the Unix community decided standardization was a good thing, and the POSIX working groups (organized by the IEEE) were formed. POSIX standardized the Unix libraries and utilities, including the shell. The standard shell was primarily based on the 1988 version of the Korn Shell, with some C shell features and a bit of invention to fill in the gaps. *bash* was begun as part of the GNU project's effort to produce a complete POSIX system, which naturally needed a POSIX shell.

bash provided the programming features that shell programmers needed, plus the conveniences that command-line users liked. It was originally conceived as an alternative to the Korn shell, but as the free software movement became more important, and as Linux became more popular, *bash* quickly overshadowed *ksh*.

As a result, *bash* is the default user shell on every Linux distribution we know about (there are a few hundred Linux distros, so there are probably a few with some odd-ball default shell), as well as Mac OS X. It's also available for just about every other Unix operating system, including BSD Unix and Solaris. In the rare cases where *bash* doesn't ship with the operating system, it's easy to install. It's even available for Windows (via Cygwin). It's both a powerful programming language and a good user interface and you won't find yourself sacrificing keyboard shortcuts to get elaborate programming features.

You can't possibly go wrong by learning *bash*. The most common default shells are the old Bourne shell and *bash*, which is mostly Bourne shell compatible. One of these shells is certainly present on any modern, major Unix or Unix-like operating system. And as noted, if *bash* isn't present you can always install it. But there are other shells. In the spirit of free software, the authors and maintainers of all of these shells share ideas. If you read the *bash* change logs, you'll see many places where a feature was introduced or tweaked to match behavior on another shell. But most people won't care. They'll use whatever is already there and be happy with it. So if you are interested, by all means investigate other shells. There are many good alternatives and you may find one you like better—though it probably won't be as ubiquitous as *bash*.

The bash Shell

bash is a shell: a command interpreter. The main purpose of *bash* (or of any shell) is to allow you to interact with the computer's operating system so that you can accomplish whatever you need to do. Usually that involves launching programs, so the shell takes the commands you type, determines from that input what programs need to be run, and launches them for you. You will also encounter tasks that involve a sequence of actions to perform that are recurring, or very complicated, or both. Shell programming, usually referred to as *shell scripting*, allows you to automate these tasks for ease of use, reliability, and reproducibility.

In case you're new to *bash*, we'll start with some basics. If you've used Unix or Linux at all, you probably aren't new to *bash*—but you may not have known you were using it. *bash* is really just a language for executing commands—so the commands you've been typing all along (e.g., *ls*, *cd*, *grep*, *cat*) are, in a sense, *bash* commands. Some of these commands are built into *bash* itself; others are separate programs. For now, it doesn't make a difference which is which.

We'll end this chapter with a few recipes on getting *bash*. Most systems come with *bash* pre-installed, but a few don't. Even if your system comes with *bash*, it's always a good idea to know how to get and install it—new versions, with new features, are released from time to time.

If you're already running *bash*, and are somewhat familiar with it, you may want to go straight to Chapter 2. You are not likely to read this book in order, and if you dip into the middle, you should find some recipes that demonstrate what *bash* is really capable of. But first, the basics.

1.1 Decoding the Prompt

Problem

You'd like to know what all the punctuation on your screen means.

Solution

All command-line shells have some kind of prompt to alert you that the shell is ready to accept your input. What the prompt looks like depends on many factors including your operating system type and version, shell type and version, distribution, and how someone else may have configured it. In the Bourne family of shells, a trailing $ in the prompt generally means you are logged in as a regular user, while a trailing # means you are *root*. The *root* account is the administrator of the system, equivalent to the *System* account on Windows (which is even more powerful than the *Administrator* account), or the *Supervisor* account on Netware. *root* is all-powerful and can do anything on a typical Unix or Linux system.

Default prompts also often display the path to the directory that you are currently in; however, they usually abbreviate it. So a ~ means you are in your home directory. Some default prompts may also display your username and the name of the machine you are logged into. If that seems silly now, it won't when you're logged into five machines at once possibly under different usernames.

Here is a typical Linux prompt for a user named *jp* on a machine called *adams*, sitting in the home directory. The trailing $ indicates this is a regular user, not *root*.

```
jp@adams:~$
```

Here's the prompt after changing to the */tmp* directory. Notice how ~, which really meant */home/jp*, has changed to */tmp*.

```
jp@adams:/tmp$
```

Discussion

The shell's prompt is the thing you will see most often when you work at the command line, and there are many ways to customize it more to your liking. But for now, it's enough to know how to interpret it. Of course, your default prompt may be different, but you should be able to figure out enough to get by for now.

There are some Unix or Linux systems where the power of *root* may be shared, using commands like *su* and *sudo*. Or *root* may not even be all-powerful, if the system is running some kind of mandatory access control (MAC) system such as the NSA's SELinux.

See Also

- Recipe 1.2, "Showing Where You Are"
- Recipe 14.19, "Using sudo More Securely"
- Recipe 16.2, "Customizing Your Prompt"
- Recipe 17.15, "Using sudo on a Group of Commands"

1.2   Showing Where You Are

Problem

You are not sure what directory you are in, and the default prompt is not helpful.

Solution

Use the *pwd* built-in command, or set a more useful prompt (as in Recipe 16.2, "Customizing Your Prompt"). For example:

```
bash-2.03$ pwd
/tmp

bash-2.03$ export PS1='[\u@\h \w]$ '
[jp@solaris8 /tmp]$
```

Discussion

pwd stands for *print working directory* and takes two options. -L displays your logical path and is the default. -P displays your physical location, which may differ from your logical path if you have followed a symbolic link.

```
bash-2.03$ pwd
/tmp/dir2

bash-2.03$ pwd -L
/tmp/dir2

bash-2.03$ pwd -P
/tmp/dir1
```

See Also

- Recipe 16.2, "Customizing Your Prompt"

1.3 Finding and Running Commands

Problem

You need to find and run a particular command under *bash*.

Solution

Try the *type, which, apropos, locate, slocate, find,* and *ls* commands.

Discussion

bash keeps a list of directories in which it should look for commands in an environment variable called $PATH. The *bash* built-in *type* command searches your environment (including aliases, keywords, functions, built-ins, and files in the $PATH) for executable commands matching its arguments and displays the type and location of any matches. It has several arguments, notably the -a flag, which causes it to print all matches instead of stopping at the first one. The *which* command is similar but only searches your $PATH (and *csh* aliases). It may vary from system to system (it's usually a *csh* shell script on BSD, but a binary on Linux), and usually has a -a flag like *type*. Use these commands when you know the name of a command and need to know exactly where it's located, or to see if it's on this computer. For example:

```
$ type which
which is hashed (/usr/bin/which)

$ type ls
ls is aliased to `ls  -F -h'

$ type -a ls
ls is aliased to `ls  -F -h'
ls is /bin/ls

$ which which
/usr/bin/which
```

Almost all commands come with some form of help on how to use them. Usually there is online documentation called *manpages*, where "man" is short for manual. These are accessed using the *man* command, so man ls will give you documentation about the *ls* command. Many programs also have a built-in help facility, accessed by providing a "help me" argument such as -h or --help. Some programs, especially on other operating systems, will give you help if you don't give them arguments. Some Unix commands will also do that, but a great many of them will not. This is due to the way that Unix commands fit together into something called *pipelines*, which we'll cover later. But what if you don't know or can't remember the name of the command you need?

apropos searches manpage names and descriptions for regular expressions supplied as arguments. This is incredibly useful when you don't remember the name of the command you need. This is the same as man -k.

```
$ apropos music
cms (4) - Creative Music System device driver

$ man -k music
cms (4) - Creative Music System device driver
```

locate and *slocate* consult database files about the system (usually compiled and updated by a *cron* job) to find files or commands almost instantly. The location of the actual database files, what is indexed therein, and how often it is checked, may vary from system to system. Consult your system's manpages for details. *slocate* stores permission information (in addition to filenames and paths) so that it will not list programs to which the user does not have access. On most Linux systems, *locate* is a symbolic link to *slocate*; other systems may have separate programs, or may not have *slocate* at all.

```
$ locate apropos
/usr/bin/apropos
/usr/share/man/de/man1/apropos.1.gz
/usr/share/man/es/man1/apropos.1.gz
/usr/share/man/it/man1/apropos.1.gz
/usr/share/man/ja/man1/apropos.1.gz
/usr/share/man/man1/apropos.1.gz
```

For much more on the *find* command, see all of Chapter 9.

Last but not least, try using *ls* also. Remember if the command you wish to run is in your current directory, you must prefix it with a ./ since the current working directory is usually not in your $PATH for security reasons (see Recipe 14.3, "Setting a Secure $PATH" and Recipe 14.10, "Adding the Current Directory to the $PATH").

See Also

- help type
- man which
- man apropos
- man locate
- man slocate
- man find
- man ls
- Chapter 9
- Recipe 4.1, "Running Any Executable"
- Recipe 14.10, "Adding the Current Directory to the $PATH"

1.4 Getting Information About Files

Problem

You need more information about a file, such as what it is, who owns it, if it's executable, how many hard links it has, or when it was last accessed or changed.

Solution

Use the *ls*, *stat*, *file*, or *find* commands.

```
$ touch /tmp/sample_file


$ ls /tmp/sample_file
/tmp/sample_file

$ ls -l /tmp/sample_file
-rw-r--r--    1 jp       jp                    0 Dec 18 15:03 /tmp/sample_file


$ stat /tmp/sample_file
File: "/tmp/sample_file"
Size: 0          Blocks: 0          IO Block: 4096    Regular File
Device: 303h/771d   Inode: 2310201    Links: 1
Access: (0644/-rw-r--r--) Uid: (  501/       jp) Gid: (  501/       jp)
Access: Sun Dec 18 15:03:35 2005
Modify: Sun Dec 18 15:03:35 2005
Change: Sun Dec 18 15:03:42 2005


$ file /tmp/sample_file
/tmp/sample_file: empty

$ file -b /tmp/sample_file
empty


$ echo '#!/bin/bash -' > /tmp/sample_file


$ file /tmp/sample_file
/tmp/sample_file: Bourne-Again shell script text executable

$ file -b /tmp/sample_file
Bourne-Again shell script text executable
```

For much more on the *find* command, see all of Chapter 9.

Discussion

The command ls shows only filenames, while ls -1 provides more details about each file. *ls* has many options; consult the manpage on your system for the ones it supports. Useful options include:

-a

Do not hide files starting with . (dot)

-F

Show the type of file with one of these trailing type designators: /*@%=|

-l

Long listing

-L

Show information about the linked file, rather than the symbolic link itself

-Q

Quote names (GNU extension, not supported on all systems)

-r

Reverse sort order

-R

Recurse though subdirectories

-S

Sort by file size

-1

Short format but only one file per line

When using -F a slash (/) indicates a directory, an asterisk (*) means the file is executable, an at sign (@) indicates a symbolic link, a percent sign (%) shows a whiteout, an equal sign (=) is a socket, and a pipe or vertical bar (|) is a FIFO.

stat, *file*, and *find* all have many options that control the output format; see the manpages on your system for supported options. For example, these options produce output that is similar to ls -1:

```
$ ls -l /tmp/sample_file
-rw-r--r--    1 jp       jp                   14 Dec 18 15:04 /tmp/sample_file

$ stat -c'%A %h %U %G %s %y %n' /tmp/sample_file
-rw-r--r-- 1 jp jp 14 Sun Dec 18 15:04:12 2005 /tmp/sample_file

$ find /tmp/ -name sample_file -printf '%m %n %u %g %t %p'
644 1 jp jp Sun Dec 18 15:04:12 2005 /tmp/sample_file
```

Not all operating systems and versions have all of these tools. For example, Solaris does not include *stat* by default.

It is also worth pointing out that directories are nothing more than files that the operating system knows to treat specially. So the commands above work just fine on directories, though sometimes you may need to modify a command to get the behavior you expect. For example, using ls -d to list information about the directory, rather than just ls (listing the contents of the directory).

See Also

- man ls
- man stat
- man file
- man find
- Chapter 9

1.5   Showing All Hidden (dot) Files in the Current Directory

Problem

You want to see only hidden (dot) files in a directory to edit a file you forget the name of or remove obsolete files. ls -a shows all files, including normally hidden ones, but that is often too noisy, and ls -a .* doesn't do what you think it will.

Solution

Use ls -d along with whatever other criteria you have.

```
ls -d .*
ls -d .b*
ls -d .[!.]*
```

Or construct your wildcard in such a way that . and .. don't match.

```
$ grep -l 'PATH'  ~/.[!.]*
/home/jp/.bash_history
/home/jp/.bash_profile
```

Discussion

Due to the way the shell handles file wildcards, the sequence .* does not behave as you might expect or desire. The way *filename expansion* or *globbing* works is that any string containing the characters *, ?, or [is treated as a *pattern*, and replaced by an alphabetically sorted list of file names matching the pattern. * matches any string, including the null string, while ? matches any single character. Characters enclosed in [ ] specify a list or range of characters, any of which will match. There are also various extended pattern-matching operators that we're not going to cover here (see

"Pattern-Matching Characters" and "extglob Extended Pattern-Matching Operators" in Appendix A). So *.txt means any file ending in *.txt*, while *txt means any file ending in txt (no dot). f?o would match foo or fao but not fooo. So you'd think that .* would match any file beginning with a dot.

The problem is that .* is expanded to include . and .., which are then both displayed. Instead of getting just the dot files in the current directory, you get those files, plus all the files and directories in the current directory (.), all the files and directories in the parent directory (..), and the names and contents of any subdirectories in the current directory that start with a dot. This is very confusing, to say the least.

You can experiment with the same *ls* command with -d and without, then try echo .*. The *echo* trick simply shows you what the shell expanded your .* to. Try echo .[!.]* also.

.[!.]* is a filename expansion pattern where [ ] denotes a list of characters to match, but the leading ! negates the list. So we are looking for a dot, followed by any character that is *not* a dot, followed by any number of any characters. You may also use ^ to negate a character class, but ! is specified in the POSIX standard and thus is more portable.

.[!.]* will miss a file named ..*foo*. You could add something like .??* to match anything starting with a dot that is also at least three characters long. But ls -d .[!.]* .??* will then display anything that matches both patterns twice. Or you can use .??* alone, but that will miss files like .*a*. Which you use depends on your needs and environment; there is no good one-size-fits-all solution.

```
$ ls -a
.                    ..foo                .normal_dot_file
..                   .a                   normal_file

$ ls -d .[!.]*
.a                   .normal_dot_file

$ ls -d .??*
..foo                .normal_dot_file

..foo                .a                   .normal_dot_file
normal_dot_file

$ ls -d .[!.]* .??* | sort -u
..foo
.a
.normal_dot_file
```

You can use echo * as an emergency substitute for *ls* if the *ls* command is corrupt or not available for some reason. This works because * is expanded by the shell to everything in the current directory, which results in a list similar to what you'd get with ls.

See Also

- man ls
- *http://www.gnu.org/software/coreutils/faq/#ls-_002da-_002a-does-not-list-dot-files*
- Section 2.11 in *http://www.faqs.org/faqs/unix-faq/faq/part2*
- "Pattern Matching Characters" in Appendix A
- "extglob Extended Pattern-Matching Operators" in Appendix A

1.6   Using Shell Quoting

Problem

You need a rule of thumb for using command-line quoting.

Solution

Enclose a string in single quotes unless it contains elements that you want the shell to interpolate.

Discussion

Unquoted text and even text enclosed in double quotes is subject to shell expansion and substitution. Consider:

```
$ echo A coffee is $5?!
A coffee is ?!

$ echo "A coffee is $5?!"
-bash: !": event not found

$ echo 'A coffee is $5?!'
A coffee is $5?!
```

In the first example, $5 is treated as a variable to expand, but since it doesn't exist it is set to null. In the second example, the same is true, but we never even get there because !" is treated as a history substitution, which fails in this case because it doesn't match anything in the history. The third example works as expected.

To mix some shell expansions with some literal strings you may use the shell escape character \ or change your quoting. The exclamation point is a special case because the preceding backslash escape character is not removed. You can work around that by using single quotes or a trailing space as shown here.

```
$ echo 'A coffee is $5 for' "$USER" '?!'
A coffee is $5 for jp ?!

$ echo "A coffee is \$5 for $USER?\!"
A coffee is $5 for jp?\!
```

```
$ echo "A coffee is \$5 for $USER?! "
A coffee is $5 for jp?!
```

Also, you can't embed a single quote inside single quotes, even if using a backslash, since nothing (not even the backslash) is interpolated inside single quotes. But you can work around that by using double quotes with escapes, or by escaping a single quote *outside* of surrounding single quotes.

```
# We'll get a continuation prompt since we now have unbalanced quotes
$ echo '$USER won't pay $5 for coffee.'
> ^C

# WRONG
$ echo "$USER won't pay $5 for coffee."
jp won't pay  for coffee.

# Works
$ echo "$USER won't pay \$5 for coffee."
jp won't pay $5 for coffee.

# Also works
$ echo 'I won'\''t pay $5 for coffee.'
I won't pay $5 for coffee.
```

See Also

- Chapter 5 for more about shell variable and the $VAR syntax
- Chapter 18 for more about ! and the history commands

1.7   Using or Replacing Built-ins and External Commands

Problem

You want to replace a built-in command with your own function or external command, and you need to know exactly what your script is executing (e.g., */bin/echo* or the built-in *echo*). Or you've created a new command and it may be conflicting with an existing external or built-in command.

Solution

Use the *type* and *which* commands to see if a given command exists and whether it is built-in or external.

```
# type cd
cd is a shell builtin

# type awk
awk is /bin/awk
```

```
# which cd
/usr/bin/which: no cd in (/bin:/sbin:/usr/bin:/usr/sbin:/usr/local/bin:/usr/local/
sbin:/usr/bin/X11:/usr/X11R6/bin:/root/bin)

# which awk
/bin/awk
```

Discussion

A built-in command is just that; it is built into the shell itself, while an external command is an external file launched by the shell. The external file may be a binary, or it may be a shell script itself, and its important to understand the difference for a couple of reasons. First, when you are using a given version of a particular shell, built-ins will always be available but external programs may or may not be installed on a particular system. Second, if you give one of your own programs the same name as a built-in, you will be very confused about the results since the built-in will always take precedence (see Recipe 19.4, "Naming Your Script Test"). It is possible to use the *enable* command to turn built-in commands off and on, though we strongly recommend against doing so unless you are absolutely sure you understand what you are doing. enable -a will list all built-ins and their enabled or disabled status.

One problem with built-in commands is that you generally can't use a -h or --help option to get usage reminders, and if a manpage exists it's often just a pointer to the large *bash* manpage. That's where the *help* command, which is itself a built-in, comes in handy. *help* displays help about shell built-ins.

```
# help help
help: help [-s] [pattern ...]
    Display helpful information about builtin commands.  If PATTERN is
    specified, gives detailed help on all commands matching PATTERN,
    otherwise a list of the builtins is printed.  The -s option
    restricts the output for each builtin command matching PATTERN to
    a short usage synopsis.
```

When you need to redefine a built-in you use the *builtin* command to avoid loops. For example:

```
cd () {
    builtin cd "$@"
    echo "$OLDPWD --> $PWD"
}
```

To force the use of an external command instead of any function or built-in that would otherwise have precedence, use enable -n, which turns off shell built-ins, or *command*, which ignores shell functions. For example, to use the *test* found in $PATH instead of the shell built-in version, type **enable -n test** and then run **test**. Or, use command ls to use the native *ls* command rather than any *ls* function you may have created.

See Also

- man which
- help help
- help builtin
- help command
- help enable
- help type
- Recipe 19.4, "Naming Your Script Test"
- "Built-in Shell Variables" in Appendix A

1.8   Determining If You Are Running Interactively

Problem

You have some code you want to run only if you are (or are not) running interactively.

Solution

Use the following case statement:

```
#!/usr/bin/env bash
# cookbook filename: interactive

case "$-" in
    *i*)   # Code for interactive shell here
        ;;
    *)     # Code for non-interactive shell here
        ;;
esac
```

Discussion

$- is a string listing of all the current shell option flags. It will contain i if the shell is interactive.

You may also see code like the following (this will work, but the solution above is the preferred method):

```
if [ "$PS1" ]; then
    echo This shell is interactive
else
    echo This shell is not interactive
fi
```

See Also

- help case
- help set
- Recipe 6.14, "Branching Many Ways," for more explanation of the case statement

1.9   Setting bash As Your Default Shell

Problem

You're using a BSD system, Solaris, or some other Unix variant for which *bash* isn't the default shell. You're tired of starting *bash* explicitly all the time, and want to make *bash* your default shell.

Solution

First, make sure *bash* is installed. Try typing **bash --version** at a command line. If you get a version, it's installed:

```
$ bash --version
GNU bash, version 3.00.16(1)-release (i386-pc-solaris2.10)
Copyright (C) 2004 Free Software Foundation, Inc.
```

If you don't see a version number, you may be missing a directory from your path. chsh -l or cat /etc/shells may give you a list of valid shells on some systems. Otherwise, ask your system administrator where *bash* is, or if it can be installed.

chsh -l provides a list of valid shells on Linux, but opens an editor and allows you to change settings on BSD. -l is not a valid option to chsh on Mac OS X, but just running chsh will open an editor to allow you to change settings, and chpass -s *shell* will change your shell.

If *bash* is installed, use the chsh -s command to change your default shell. For example, chsh -s /bin/bash. If for any reason that fails try chsh, passwd -e, passwd -l chpass, or usermod -s /usr/bin/bash. If you still can't change your shell ask your system administrator, who may need to edit the */etc/passwd* file. On most systems, */etc/passwd* will have lines of the form:

```
cam:pK1Z9BCJbzCrBNrkjRUdUiTtFOh/:501:100:Cameron Newham:/home/cam:/bin/bash
cc:kfDKDjfkeDJKJySFgJFWErrElpe/:502:100:Cheshire Cat:/home/cc:/bin/bash
```

As *root*, you can just edit the last field of the lines in the password file to the full pathname of whatever shell you choose. If your system has a *vipw* command, you should use it to ensure password file consistency.

> Some systems will refuse to allow a login shell that is not listed in */etc/shells*. If *bash* is not listed in that file, you will have to have your system administrator add it.

Discussion

Some operating systems, notably the BSD Unixes, typically place *bash* in the */usr* partition. You may want to think twice about changing *root*'s shell on such systems. If the system runs into trouble while booting, and you have to work on it before */usr* is mounted, you've got a real problem: there isn't a shell for *root* to use. Therefore, it's best to leave the default shell for *root* unchanged. However, there's no reason not to make *bash* the default shell for regular user accounts. And it goes without saying that it's bad practice to use the *root* account unless it's absolutely necessary. Use your regular (user) account whenever possible. With commands like *sudo*, you should very rarely need a *root* shell.

If all else fails, you can probably replace your existing login shell with *bash* using *exec*, but this is not for the faint of heart. See "A7) How can I make bash my login shell?" in the *bash* FAQ at *ftp://ftp.cwru.edu/pub/bash/FAQ*.

See Also

- man chsh
- man passwd
- man chpass
- /etc/shells
- "A7) How can I make bash my login shell?" from *ftp://ftp.cwru.edu/pub/bash/FAQ*
- Recipe 14.19, "Using sudo More Securely"
- Recipe 14.13, "Setting Permissions"

1.10   Getting bash for Linux

Problem

You want to get *bash* for your Linux system, or you want to make sure you have the latest version.

Solution

bash is included in virtually all modern Linux distributions. To make sure you have the latest version available for your distribution, use the distribution's built-in packaging tools. You must be *root* or have the root password to upgrade or install applications.

Some Linux distributions (notably Debian) include *bash* version 2.x as plain *bash* and version 3.x as *bash3*, so you need to watch out for that. Table 1-1 lists the default versions as of early 2007 (distributions update their repositories often, so versions might have changed from this listing).

Table 1-1. Default Linux distributions

Distribution	2.x in base install	2.x in updates	3.x in base install	3.x in updates
Debian Woody	2.05a	N/A	N/A	N/A
Debian Sarge[a]	2.05b	3.1dfsg-8 (testing & unstable)	3.0-12(1)-release	3.00.16(1)-release
Fedora Core 1	bash-2.05b-31.i386.rpm	bash-2.05b-34.i386.rpm	N/A	N/A
Fedora Core 2	bash-2.05b-38.i386.rpm	N/A	N/A	N/A
Fedora Core 3	N/A	N/A	bash-3.0-17.i386.rpm	bash-3.0-18.i386.rpm
Fedora Core 4	N/A	N/A	bash-3.0-31.i386.rpm	N/A
Fedora Core 5	N/A	N/A	bash-3.1-6.2.i386.rpm	bash-3.1-9.fc5.1.i386.rpm
Fedora Core 6	N/A	N/A	bash-3.1-16.1.i386.rpm	N/A
Knoppix 3.9 & 4.0.2	N/A	N/A	3.0-15	N/A
Mandrake 9.2[b]	bash-2.05b-14mdk.i586.rpm	N/A	N/A	N/A
Mandrake 10.1[c]	bash-2.05b-22mdk.i586.rpm	N/A	N/A	N/A
Mandrake 10.2[d]	N/A	N/A	bash-3.0-2mdk.i586.rpm	N/A
Mandriva 2006.0[e]	N/A	N/A	bash-3.0-6mdk.i586.rpm	N/A
Mandriva 2007.0[f]	N/A	N/A	bash-3.1-7mdv2007.0.i586.rpm	N/A
OpenSUSE 10.0	N/A	N/A	3.00.16(1)-release	3.0.17(1)-release
OpenSUSE 10.1	N/A	N/A	3.1.16(1)-release	N/A
OpenSUSE 10.2	N/A	N/A	bash-3.1-55.i586.rpm	N/A
SLED 10 RC3	N/A	N/A	3.1.17(1)-release	N/A
RHEL 3.6, CentOS 3.6	bash-2.05b.0(1)	N/A	N/A	N/A
RHEL 4.4, CentOS 4.4	N/A	N/A	3.00.15(1)-release	N/A
MEPIS 3.3.1	N/A	N/A	3.0-14	N/A
Ubuntu 5.10[g]	N/A	N/A	3.0.16(1)	N/A
Ubuntu 6.06[g]	N/A	N/A	3.1.17(1)-release	N/A
Ubuntu 6.10[gh]	N/A	N/A	3.1.17(1)-release	N/A

[a] Debian Sarge: see also *bash-builtins, bash-doc, bash-minimal, bash-static, bash3-doc*

[b] Mandrake 9.2: bash-completion-20030821-3mdk.noarch.rpm, *bash-doc-2.05b-14mdk.i586.rpm, bash1-1.14.7-31mdk.i586.rpm*

[c] Mandrake 10.1: see also *bash-completion-20040711-1mdk.noarch.rpm, bash-doc-2.05b-22mdk.i586.rpm, bash1-1.14.7-31mdk.i586.rpm*

[d] Mandrake 10.2: see also *bash-completion-20050121-2mdk.noarch.rpm, bash-doc-3.0-2mdk.i586.rpm*

[e] Mandrake 2006.0: see also *bash-completion-20050721-1mdk.noarch.rpm, bash-doc-3.0-6mdk.i586.rpm*

[f] Mandrake 2007.0: see also *bash-completion-20060301-5mdv2007.0.noarch.rpm, bash-doc-3.1-7mdv2007.0.i586.rpm*

[g] Ubuntu: see also the *bash-builtins, bash-doc, bash-static,* and *abs-guide* packages

[h] Ubuntu 6.10 symlinks *dash* to */bin/sh* instead of *bash* as previous versions of Ubuntu and most other Linux distributions (*https://wiki.ubuntu.com/DashAsBinSh*)

For Debian and Debian-derived systems such as Knoppix, Ubuntu, and MEPIS, make sure your */etc/apt/sources.list* file is pointing at an up-to-date Debian mirror; then use the graphical Synaptic, *kpackage*, *gnome-apt*, or Add/Remove Programs tools, the terminal-based *aptitude* tool, or from the command line:

```
apt-get update && apt-get install bash bash3 bash-builtins bash-doc bash3-doc
```

For Red Hat distributions, including Fedora Core (FC) and Red Hat Enterprise Linux (RHEL), use the GUI Add/Remove Applications tool (if the GUI is missing from the menus, at a command line for RHEL3 type **redhat-config-packages &** or for RHEL4 type **system-config-packages &**). For a command line only:

```
up2date install bash
```

For Fedora Core and CentOS, you may use the above RHEL directions or from the command line:

```
yum update bash
```

For SUSE, use either the GUI or terminal version of YaST. You may also use the command-line RPM tool.

For Mandriva/Mandrake, use the GUI Rpmdrake tool or from the command line:

```
urpmi bash
```

Discussion

It's impossible to cover every Linux distribution and difficult even to cover the major ones, as they are all evolving rapidly. Fortunately, much of that evolution is in the area of ease-of-use, so it should not be very difficult to figure out how to install software on your distribution of choice.

When using Knoppix, Ubuntu, or other Live CDs, software updates and installations will most likely fail due to the read-only media. Versions of such distributions that have been installed to a hard disk should be updatable.

The apt-get update && apt-get install bash bash3 bash-builtins bash-doc bash3-doc command above will generate errors on systems that do not provide a *bash3* package. You may safely ignore such errors.

See Also

- *http://wiki.linuxquestions.org/wiki/Installing_Software*
- CentOS: *http://www.centos.org/docs/3/rhel-sag-en-3/pt-pkg-management.html*
- *http://www.centos.org/docs/4/html/rhel-sag-en-4/pt-pkg-management.html*
- Debian: *http://www.debian.org/doc/*, see the "APT HOWTO" and "dselect Documentation for Beginners"
- *http://www.debianuniverse.com/readonline/chapter/06*
- Fedora Core: *http://fedora.redhat.com/docs/yum/*

- Red Hat Enterprise Linux: *https://www.redhat.com/docs/manuals/enterprise/ RHEL-3-Manual/sysadmin-guide/pt-pkg-management.html*
- *https://www.redhat.com/docs/manuals/enterprise/RHEL-4-Manual/sysadmin-guide/ pt-pkg-management.html*
- Mandriva: *http://www.mandriva.com/en/community/users/documentation*
- *http://doc.mandrivalinux.com/MandrakeLinux/101/en/Starter.html/software-management.html*
- *http://doc.mandrivalinux.com/MandrakeLinux/101/en/Starter.html/ch19s05.html*
- MEPIS (note about installing or removing applications): *http://mepis.org/docs/*
- OpenSuSE: *http://www.opensuse.org/Documentation*
- *http://www.opensuse.org/User_Documentation*
- *http://forge.novell.com/modules/xfmod/project/?yast*
- Ubuntu: *http://www.ubuntulinux.org/support/documentation/helpcenter_view*
- Recipe 1.9, "Setting bash As Your Default Shell"

1.11   Getting bash for xBSD

Problem

You want to get *bash* for your FreeBSD, NetBSD, or OpenBSD system, or you want to make sure you have the latest version.

Solution

To see if *bash* is installed, check the */etc/shells* file. To install or update *bash*, use the pkg_add command. If you are an experienced BSD user, you may prefer using the ports collection, but we will not cover that here.

FreeBSD:

```
pkg_add -vr bash
```

For NetBSD, browse to Application Software for NetBSD at *http://netbsd.org/ Documentation/software/* and locate the latest *bash* package for your version and architecture, then use a command such as:

```
pkg_add -vu ftp://ftp.netbsd.org/pub/NetBSD/packages/pkgsrc-2005Q3/NetBSD-2.0/i386/
All/bash-3.0pl16nb3.tgz
```

For OpenBSD, you use the pkg_add -vr command. You may have to adjust the FTP path for your version and architecture. Also, there may be a statically compiled version. For example: *ftp://ftp.openbsd.org/pub/OpenBSD/3.8/packages/i386/bash-3.0. 16p1-static.tgz*.

```
pkg_add -vr ftp://ftp.openbsd.org/pub/OpenBSD/3.8/packages/i386/bash-3.0.16p1.tgz
```

Discussion

FreeBSD and OpenBSD place *bash* in */usr/local/bin/bash* while NetBSD uses */usr/pkg/bin/bash*.

Interestingly, PC-BSD 1.2, a "rock-solid Unix operating system based on FreeBSD," comes with *bash* 3.1.17(0) in */usr/local/bin/bash*, though the default shell is still *csh*.

See Also

- Recipe 1.9, "Setting bash As Your Default Shell"
- Recipe 15.4, "Testing Scripts in VMware"

1.12 Getting bash for Mac OS X

Problem

You want to get *bash* for your Mac, or you want to make sure you have the latest version.

Solution

According to Chet Ramey's *bash* page (*http://tiswww.tis.case.edu/~chet/bash/bashtop.html*), Mac OS 10.2 (Jaguar) and newer ship with *bash* as */bin/sh*. 10.4 (Tiger) has version 2.05b.0(1)-release (powerpc-apple-darwin8.0). There are also precompiled OS X packages of *bash-2.05* available from many web sites. One such package is at HMUG. Bash for Darwin (the base for Mac OS X) is available from Fink or DarwinPorts.

Discussion

It is also possible to build a more recent version of *bash* from source, but this is recommended only for experienced users.

See Also

- *http://tiswww.tis.case.edu/~chet/bash/bashtop.html*
- *http://www.hmug.org/pub/MacOS_X/BSD/Applications/Shells/bash/*
- *http://fink.sourceforge.net/pdb/package.php/bash*
- *http://darwinports.opendarwin.org/ports.php?by=name&substr=bash*

1.13   Getting bash for Unix

Problem

You want to get *bash* for your Unix system, or you want to make sure you have the latest version.

Solution

If it's not already installed or in your operating system's program repository, check Chet Ramey's *bash* page for binary downloads, or build it from source (see Appendix E).

Discussion

According to Chet Ramey's *bash* page (*http://tiswww.tis.case.edu/~chet/bash/bashtop.html*):

> Solaris 2.x, Solaris 7, and Solaris 8 users can get a precompiled version of *bash-3.0* from the Sunfreeware site. Sun ships *bash-2.03* with Solaris 8 distributions, ships *bash-2.05* as a supported part of Solaris 9, and ships *bash-3.0* as a supported part of Solaris 10 (directly on the Solaris 10 CD).

> AIX users can get precompiled versions of older releases of *bash* for various versions of AIX from Groupe Bull, and sources and binaries of current releases for various AIX releases from UCLA. IBM makes *bash-3.0* available for AIX 5L as part of the AIX toolbox for [GNU/]Linux applications. They use RPM format; you can get RPM for AIX from there, too.

> SGI users can get an installable version of *bash-2.05b* from the SGI Freeware page.

> HP-UX users can get *bash-3.0* binaries and source code from the Software Porting and Archive Center for HP-UX.

> Tru64 Unix users can get sources and binaries for *bash-2.05b* from the HP/Compaq Tru64 Unix Open Source Software Collection.

See Also

- *http://tiswww.tis.case.edu/~chet/bash/bashtop.html*
- *http://www.sun.com/solaris/freeware.html*
- *http://aixpdslib.seas.ucla.edu/packages/bash.html*
- *http://www.ibm.com/servers/aix/products/aixos/linux/index.html*
- *http://freeware.sgi.com/index-by-alpha.html*
- *http://hpux.cs.utah.edu/*
- *http://hpux.connect.org.uk/hppd/hpux/Shells/*
- *http://hpux.connect.org.uk/hppd/hpux/Shells/bash-3.00.16/*
- *http://h30097.www3.hp.com/demos/ossc/html/bash.htm*

- Recipe 1.9, "Setting bash As Your Default Shell"
- Appendix E

1.14 Getting bash for Windows

Problem

You want to get *bash* for your Windows system, or you want to make sure you have the latest version.

Solution

Use Cygwin.

Download *http://www.cygwin.com/setup.exe* and run it. Follow the prompts and choose the packages to install, including *bash*, which is located in the shells category and is selected by default. As of early 2007, *bash-3.1-6* and 3.2.9-11 are available.

Once Cygwin is installed, you will have to configure it. See the User Guide at *http://cygwin.com/cygwin-ug-net/*.

Discussion

From the Cygwin site:

> What Is Cygwin
>
> Cygwin is a Linux-like environment for Windows. It consists of two parts:
>
> - A DLL (cygwin1.dll), which acts as a Linux API emulation layer providing substantial Linux API functionality.
> - A collection of tools, which provide Linux look and feel.
>
> The Cygwin DLL works with all non-beta, non "release candidate," x86 32-bit versions of Windows since Windows 95, with the exception of Windows CE.
>
> What Isn't Cygwin
>
> - Cygwin is not a way to run native Linux apps on Windows. You have to rebuild your application from source if you want to get it running on Windows.
> - Cygwin is not a way to magically make native Windows apps aware of Unix functionality (e.g., signals, ptys). Again, you need to build your apps from source if you want to take advantage of Cygwin functionality.

Cygwin is a true Unix-like environment running on top of Windows. It is an excellent tool, but sometimes it might be overkill. For Windows native binaries of the GNU Text Utils (not including *bash*), see *http://unxutils.sourceforge.net/*.

Microsoft Services for Unix (*http://www.microsoft.com/windowsserversystem/sfu/default.mspx*) may also be of interest, but note that it is not under active development anymore, though it will be supported until at least 2011 (*http://www.eweek.com/article2/0,1895,1855274,00.asp*).

For powerful character-based and GUI command-line shells with a more consistent interface, but a DOS/Windows flavor, see *http://jpsoft.com/*. None of the authors are affiliated with this company, but one is a long-time satisfied user.

See Also

- *http://www.cygwin.com/*
- *http://unxutils.sourceforge.net/*
- *http://www.microsoft.com/windowsserversystem/sfu/default.mspx*
- *http://jpsoft.com/*
- *http://www.eweek.com/article2/0,1895,1855274,00.asp*

1.15   Getting bash Without Getting bash

Problem

You want to try out a shell or a shell script on a system you don't have the time or the resources to build or buy.

Or, you feel like reading a Zen-like recipe just about now.

Solution

Get a free or almost free shell account from HP, Polar Home, or another vendor.

Discussion

HP maintains a free "test drive" program that provides free shell accounts on many operating systems on various HP hardware. See *http://www.testdrive.hp.com/* for details.

Polar Home provides many free services and almost free shell accounts. According to their web site:

> polarhome.com is non commercial, educational effort for popularization of shell enabled operating systems and Internet services, offering shell accounts, mail and other online services on all available systems (currently on Linux, OpenVMS, Solaris, AIX, QNX, IRIX, HP-UX, Tru64, FreeBSD, OpenBSD, NetBSD and OPENSTEP).
>
> [...]
>
> **Note:** this site is continuously under construction and running on slow lines and low capacity servers that have been retired, therefore as a non commercial site user/visitor, nobody should have too high expectations in any meaning of the word. Even if polarhome.com does all to provide services on professional level, users should not expect more than "AS-IS".
>
> polarhome.com is a distributed site, but more than 90% of polarhome realm is located in Stockholm, Sweden.

See Also

- List of free shell accounts: *http://www.ductape.net/~mitja/freeunix.shtml*
- *http://www.testdrive.hp.com/os/*
- *http://www.testdrive.hp.com/faq/*
- *http://www.polarhome.com/*

1.16 Learning More About bash Documentation

Problem

You'd like to read more about *bash* but don't know where to start.

Solution

Well you're reading this book, which is a great place to start! The other O'Reilly books about *bash* and shell scripting are: *Learning the bash Shell* by Cameron Newham (O'Reilly) and *Classic Shell Scripting* by Nelson H.F. Beebe and Arnold Robbins (O'Reilly).

Unfortunately, the official *bash* documentation has not been easily accessible online—until now! Previously, you had to download several different tarballs, locate all the files that contain documentation, and then decipher the file names to find what you wanted. Now, our companion web site (*http://www.bashcookbook.com/*) has done all this work for you and provides the official *bash* reference documentation online so it's easy to refer to. Check it out, and refer others to it as needed.

Official documentation

The official *bash* FAQ is at: *ftp://ftp.cwru.edu/pub/bash/FAQ*. See especially "H2) What kind of *bash* documentation is there?" The official reference guide is also strongly recommended; see below for details.

Chet Ramey's (the current *bash* maintainer) *bash* page (called *bashtop*) contains a ton of very useful information (*http://tiswww.tis.case.edu/~chet/bash/bashtop.html*). Chet also maintains the following (listed in bashtop):

README
> A file describing *bash*: *http://tiswww.tis.case.edu/chet/bash/README*

NEWS
> A file tersely listing the notable changes between the current and previous versions: *http://tiswww.tis.case.edu/chet/bash/NEWS*

CHANGES
> A complete *bash* change history: *http://tiswww.tis.case.edu/chet/bash/CHANGES*

INSTALL
> Installation instructions: *http://tiswww.tis.case.edu/chet/bash/INSTALL*

NOTES

Platform-specific configuration and operation notes: *http://tiswww.tis.case.edu/chet/bash/NOTES*

COMPAT

Compatibility issues between *bash3* and *bash1*: *http://tiswww.tis.case.edu/~chet/bash/COMPAT*

The latest *bash* source code and documentation are always available at: *http://ftp.gnu.org/gnu/bash/*.

We highly recommend downloading both the source and the documentation even if you are using prepackaged binaries. Here is a brief list of the documentation. See Appendix B for an index of the included examples and source code. See the source tarball's *./doc* directory, for example: *http://ftp.gnu.org/gnu/bash/bash-3.1.tar.gz*, *bash-3.1/doc*:

.FAQ

A set of frequently asked questions about *bash* with answers

.INTRO

A short introduction to *bash*

article.ms

An article Chet wrote about *bash* for *The Linux Journal*

bash.1

The *bash* manpage

bashbug.1

The bashbug manpage

builtins.1

A manpage that documents the built-ins extracted from *bash.1*

bashref.texi

The "bash reference manual"

bashref.info

The "bash reference manual" processed by "makeinfo"

rbash.1

The restricted *bash* shell manpage

readline.3

The readline manpage

The *.ps* files are postscript versions of the above. The *.html* files are HTML versions of the manpage and reference manual. The *.0* files are formatted manual pages. The *.txt* versions are ASCII—the output of groff -Tascii.

In the document tarball, for example: *http://ftp.gnu.org/gnu/bash/bash-doc-3.1.tar.gz*, *bash-doc-3.1*:

.bash.0
>The *bash* manpage (formatted)(also PDF, ps, HTML)

bashbug.0
>The bashbug manpage (formatted)

bashref
>The *Bash Reference Guide* (also PDF, ps, HTML, dvi)

builtins.0
>The built-ins manpage (formatted)

.rbash.0
>The restricted *bash* shell manpage (formatted)

Other documentation

- *The Advanced Bash-Scripting Guide* at *http://www.tldp.org/LDP/abs/html/index. html* and *http://www.tldp.org/LDP/abs/abs-guide.pdf*
- Writing Shell Scripts at *http://www.linuxcommand.org/writing_shell_scripts.php*
- *BASH Programming – Introduction HOW-TO* at *http://www.tldp.org/HOWTO/ Bash-Prog-Intro-HOWTO.html*
- *Bash Guide for Beginners* at *http://www.tldp.org/LDP/Bash-Beginners-Guide/html/* and *http://www.tldp.org/LDP/Bash-Beginners-Guide/Bash-Beginners-Guide.pdf*
- *The Bash Prompt HOWTO* at *http://www.tldp.org/HOWTO/Bash-Prompt-HOWTO/index.html*
- Very old, but still useful: *UNIX shell differences and how to change your shell* at *http://www.faqs.org/faqs/unix-faq/shell/shell-differences/*
- *[Apple's] Shell Scripting Primer* at *http://developer.apple.com/documentation/ OpenSource/Conceptual/ShellScripting/*

See Also

- Appendix B

CHAPTER 2
Standard Output

No software is worth anything if there is no output of some sort. But I/O (Input/ Output) has long been one of the nastier areas of computing. If you're ancient, you remember the days most of the work involved in running a program was setting up the program's input and output. Some of the problems have gone away; for example, you no longer need to get operators to mount tapes on a tape drive (not on any laptop or desktop system that I've seen). But many of the problems are still with us.

One problem is that there are many different types of output. Writing something on the screen is different from writing something in a file—at least, it sure seems different. Writing something in a file seems different from writing it on a tape, or in flash memory, or on some other kind of device. And what if you want the output from one program to go directly into another program? Should software developers be tasked with writing code to handle all sorts of output devices, even ones that haven't been invented yet? That's certainly inconvenient. Should users have to know how to connect the programs they want to run to different kinds of devices? That's not a very good idea, either.

One of the most important ideas behind the Unix operating system was that everything looked like a *file* (an ordered sequence of bytes). The operating system was responsible for this magic. It didn't matter whether you were writing to a file on the disk, the terminal, a tape drive, a memory stick, or something else; your program only needed to know how to write to a file, and the operating system would take it from there. That approach greatly simplified the problem. The next question was, simply, "which file?" How does a program know whether to write to the file that represents a terminal window, a file on the disk, or some other kind of file? Simple: that's something that can be left to the shell.

When you run a program, you still have to connect it to output files and input files (which we'll see in the next chapter). That task doesn't go away. But the shell makes it trivially easy. A command as simple as:

```
$ dosomething < inputfile > outputfile
```

reads its input from `inputfile` and sends its output to `outputfile`. If you omit >
outputfile, the output goes to your terminal window. If you omit <inputfile, the
program takes its input from the keyboard. The program literally doesn't know
where its output is going, or where its input is coming from. You can send the output anywhere you want (including to another program) by using *bash*'s redirection
facilities.

But that's just the start. In this chapter, we'll look at ways to generate output, and
the shell's methods for sending that output to different places.

2.1 Writing Output to the Terminal/Window

Problem

You want some simple output from your shell commands.

Solution

Use the *echo* built-in command. All the parameters on the command line are printed
to the screen. For example:

```
echo Please wait.
```

produces

```
Please wait.
```

as we see in this simple session where we typed the command at the *bash* prompt
(the $ character):

```
$ echo Please wait.
Please wait.
$
```

Discussion

The *echo* command is one of the most simple of all *bash* commands. It prints the
arguments of the command line to the screen. But there are a few points to keep in
mind. First, the shell is parsing the arguments on the *echo* command line (like it does
for every other command line). This means that it does all its substitutions, wildcard
matching, and other things before handing the arguments off to the *echo* command.
Second, since they are parsed as arguments, the spacing between arguments is
ignored. For example:

```
$ echo this     was     very     widely     spaced
this was very widely spaced
$
```

Normally the fact that the shell is very forgiving about whitespace between arguments is a helpful feature. Here, with *echo*, it's a bit disconcerting.

See Also

- help echo
- help printf
- Recipe 2.3, "Writing Output with More Formatting Control"
- Recipe 15.6, "Using echo Portably"
- Recipe 19.1, "Forgetting to Set Execute Permissions"
- "echo Options and Escape Sequences" in Appendix A
- "printf" in Appendix A

2.2 Writing Output but Preserving Spacing

Problem

You want the output to preserve your spacing.

Solution

Enclose the string in quotes. The previous example, but with quotes added, will preserve our spacing.

```
$ echo "this    was    very    widely    spaced"
this    was    very    widely    spaced
$
```

or:

```
$ echo 'this    was    very    widely    spaced'
this    was    very    widely    spaced
$
```

Discussion

Since the words are enclosed in quotes, they form a single argument to the *echo* command. That argument is a string and the shell doesn't need to interfere with the contents of the string. In fact, by using the single quotes (' ') the shell is told explicitly not to interfere with the string at all. If you use double quotes ("), some shell substitutions will take place (variable and tilde expansions and command substitutions), but since we have none in this example, the shell has nothing to change. When in doubt, use the single quotes.

See Also

- help echo
- help printf
- Chapter 5 for more information about substitution

- Recipe 2.3, "Writing Output with More Formatting Control"
- Recipe 15.6, "Using echo Portably"
- Recipe 19.11, "Seeing Odd Behavior from printf"
- "echo Options and Escape Sequences" in Appendix A

2.3   Writing Output with More Formatting Control

Problem

You want more control over the formatting and placement of output.

Solution

Use the *printf* built-in command.

For example:

```
$ printf '%s = %d\n' Lines  $LINES
Lines = 24
$
```

or:

```
$ printf '%-10.10s = %4.2f\n' 'GigaHerz' 1.92735
GigaHerz   = 1.93
$
```

Discussion

The *printf* built-in command behaves like the C language library call, where the first argument is the format control string and the successive arguments are formatted according to the format specifications (%).

The numbers between the % and the format type (s or f in our example) provide additional formatting details. For the floating-point type (f), the first number (4 in the 4.2 specifier) is the width of the entire field. The second number (2) is how many digits should be printed to the right of the decimal point. Note that it rounds the answer.

For a string, the first digit is the maximum field width, and the second is the minimum field width. The string will be truncated (if longer than max) or blank padded (if less than min) as needed. When the max and min specifiers are the same, then the string is guaranteed to be that length. The negative sign on the specifier means to left-align the string (within its field width). Without the minus sign, the string would right justify, thus:

```
$ printf '%10.10s = %4.2f\n' 'GigaHerz' 1.92735
  GigaHerz = 1.93
$
```

The string argument can either be quoted or unquoted. Use quotes if you need to preserve embedded spacing (there were no spaces needed in our one-word strings), or if you need to escape the special meaning of any special characters in the string (again, our example had none). It's a good idea to be in the habit of quoting any string that you pass to *printf*, so that you don't forget the quotes when you need them.

See Also

- help printf
- *http://www.opengroup.org/onlinepubs/009695399/functions/printf.html*
- *Learning the bash Shell,* Cameron Newham (O'Reilly), page 171, or any C reference on its *printf* function
- Recipe 15.6, "Using echo Portably"
- Recipe 19.11, "Seeing Odd Behavior from printf"
- "printf" in Appendix A

2.4   Writing Output Without the Newline

Problem

You want to produce some output without the default newline that *echo* provides.

Solution

Using *printf* it's easy—just leave off the ending \n in your format string. With *echo*, use the -n option.

```
$ printf "%s %s" next prompt
next prompt$
```

or:

```
$ echo -n prompt
prompt$
```

Discussion

Since there was no newline at the end of the *printf* format string (the first argument), the prompt character ($) appears right where the *printf* left off. This feature is much more useful in shell scripts where you may want to do partial output across several statements before completing the line, or where you want to display a prompt to the user before reading input.

With the *echo* command there are two ways to eliminate the newline. First, the -n option suppresses the trailing newline. The *echo* command also has several escape sequences with special meanings similar to those in C language strings (e.g., \n for newline). To use these escape sequences, you must invoke *echo* with the -e option. One of *echo*'s escape sequences is \c, which doesn't print a character, but rather inhibits printing the ending newline. Thus, here's a third solution:

```
$ echo -e 'hi\c'
hi$
```

Because of the powerful and flexible formatting that *printf* provides, and because it is a built-in with very little overhead to invoke (unlike other shells or older versions of *bash*, where *printf* was a standalone executable), we will use *printf* for many of our examples throughout the book.

See Also

- help echo
- help printf
- *http://www.opengroup.org/onlinepubs/009695399/functions/printf.html*
- See Chapter 3, particularly Recipe 3.5, "Getting User Input"
- Recipe 2.3, "Writing Output with More Formatting Control"
- Recipe 15.6, "Using echo Portably"
- Recipe 19.11, "Seeing Odd Behavior from printf"
- "echo Options and Escape Sequences" in Appendix A
- "printf" in Appendix A

2.5   Saving Output from a Command

Problem

You want to keep the output from a command by putting it in a file.

Solution

Use the > symbol to tell the shell to redirect the output into a file. For example:

```
$ echo fill it up
fill it up
$ echo fill it up > file.txt
$
```

Just to be sure, let's look at what is inside *file.txt* to see if it captured our output:

```
$ cat file.txt
fill it up
$
```

Discussion

The first line of the example shows an *echo* command with three arguments that are printed out. The second line of code uses the > to capture that output into a file named *file.txt*, which is why no output appears after that *echo* command.

The second part of the example uses the *cat* command to display the contents of the file. We can see that the file contains what the *echo* command would have otherwise sent as output.

The *cat* command gets its name from the longer word *concatenation*. The *cat* command concatenates the output from the several files listed on its command line, as in: cat file1 filetwo anotherfile morefiles—the contents of those files would be sent, one after another, to the terminal window. If a large file had been split in half then it could be glued back together (i.e., concatenated) by capturing the output into a third file:

```
$ cat first.half second.half > whole.file
```

So our simple command, cat file.txt, is really just the trivial case of concatenating only one file, with the result sent to the screen. That is to say, while *cat* is capable of more, its primary use is to dump the contents of a file to the screen.

See Also

- man cat
- Recipe 17.21, "Numbering Lines"

2.6 Saving Output to Other Files

Problem

You want to save the output with a redirect to elsewhere in the filesystem, not in the current directory.

Solution

Use more of a pathname when you redirect the output.

```
$ echo some more data > /tmp/echo.out
```

or:

```
$ echo some more data > ../../over.here
```

Discussion

The filename that appears after the redirection character (the >) is actually a pathname. If it begins with no other qualifiers, the file will be placed in the current directory.

If that filename begins with a slash (/) then this is an *absolute* pathname, and will be placed where it specifies in the filesystem hierarchy (i.e., *tree*) beginning at the root (provided all the intermediary directories exist and have permissions that allow you to traverse them). We used */tmp* since it is a well-known, universally available scratch directory on virtually all Unix systems. The shell, in this example, will create the file named *echo.out* in the */tmp* directory.

Our second example, placing the output into *../../over.here*, uses a *relative* pathname, and the .. is the specially-named directory inside every directory that refers to the parent directory. So each reference to .. moves up a level in the filesystem tree (toward the root, not what we usually mean by up in a tree). The point here is that we can redirect our output, if we want, into a file that is far away from where we are running the command.

See Also

- *Learning the bash Shell* by Cameron Newham (O'Reilly), pages 7–10 for an introduction to files, directories, and the dot notation (i.e., . and ..)

2.7   Saving Output from the ls Command

Problem

You tried to save output from the *ls* command with a redirect, but when you look at the resulting file, the format is not what you expected.

Solution

Use the -C option on *ls* when you redirect the output.

Here's the *ls* command showing the contents of a directory:

```
$ ls
a.out  cong.txt  def.conf  file.txt  more.txt  zebra.list
$
```

But when we save the output with the > to redirect it to a file, and then show the file contents, we get this:

```
$ ls > /tmp/save.out
$ cat /tmp/save.out
a.out
cong.txt
def.conf
file.txt
more.txt
zebra.list
$
```

This time we'll use the -C option:

```
$ ls -C > /tmp/save.out
$ cat /tmp/save.out
a.out  cong.txt  def.conf  file.txt  more.txt  zebra.list
$
```

Alternatively, if we use the -1 option on *ls* when we don't redirect, then we get output like this:

```
$ ls -1
a.out
cong.txt
def.conf
file.txt
more.txt
save.out
zebra.list
$
```

Then the original attempt at redirection matches this output.

Discussion

Just when you thought that you understood redirection and you tried it on a simple *ls* command, it didn't quite work right. What's going on here?

The shell's redirection is meant to be transparent to all programs, so programs don't need special code to make their output redirect-able. The shell takes care of it when you use the > to send the output elsewhere. But it turns out that code can be added to a program to figure out when its output is being redirected. Then, the program can behave differently in those two cases—and that's what *ls* is doing.

The authors of *ls* figured that if your output is going to the screen then you probably want columnar output (-C option), as screen real estate is limited. But they assumed if you're redirecting it to a file, then you'll want one file per line (the minus one -1 option) since there are more interesting things you can do (i.e., other processing) that is easier if each filename is on a line by itself.

See Also

- man ls
- Recipe 2.6, "Saving Output to Other Files"

2.8   Sending Both Output and Error Messages to Different Files

Problem

You are expecting output from a program but you don't want it to get littered with error messages. You'd like to save your error messages, but it's harder to find them mixed among the expected output.

Solution

Redirect output and error messages to different files.

```
$ myprogram 1> messages.out  2> message.err
```

Or more commonly:

```
$ myprogram > messages.out  2> message.err
```

Discussion

This example shows two different output files that will be created by the shell. The first, *messages.out*, will get all the output from the hypothetical *myprogram* redirected into it. Any error messages from *myprogram* will be redirected into *message.err*.

In the constructs 1> and 2> the number is the file *descriptor*, so 1 is STDOUT and 2 is STDERR. When no number is specified, STDOUT is assumed.

See Also

* Recipe 2.6, "Saving Output to Other Files"
* Recipe 2.13, "Throwing Output Away"

2.9   Sending Both Output and Error Messages to the Same File

Problem

Using redirection, you can redirect output or error messages to separate files, but how do you capture all the output and error messages to a single file?

Solution

Use the shell syntax to redirect standard error messages to the same place as standard output.

Preferred:

```
$ both >& outfile
```

or:

```
$ both &> outfile
```

or older and slightly more verbose:

```
$ both > outfile 2>&1
```

where both is just our (imaginary) program that is going to generate output to both STDERR and STDOUT.

Discussion

&> or >& is a shortcut that simply sends both STDOUT and STDERR to the same place—exactly what we want to do.

In the third example, the 1 appears to be used as the target of the redirection, but the >& says to interpret the 1 as a *file descriptor* instead of a filename. In fact, the 2>& are a single entity, indicating that standard output (2) will be redirected (>) to a file descriptor (&) that follows (1). The 2>& all have to appear together without spaces, otherwise the 2 would look just like another argument, and the & actually means something completely different when it appears by itself. (It has to do with running the command in the background.)

It may help to think of all redirection operators as taking a leading number (e.g., 2>) but that the default number for > is 1, the standard output file descriptor.

You could also do the redirection in the other order, though it is slightly less readable, and redirect standard output to the same place to which you have already redirected standard error:

```
$ both 2> outfile 1>&2
```

The 1 is used to indicate standard output and the 2 for standard error. By our reasoning (above) we could have written just >&2 for that last redirection, since 1 is the default for >, but we find it more readable to write the number explicitly when redirecting file descriptors.

Note the order of the contents of the output file. Sometimes the error messages may appear sooner in the file than they do on the screen. That has to do with the unbuffered nature of standard error, and the effect becomes more pronounced when writing to a file instead of the screen.

See Also

- Recipe 2.6, "Saving Output to Other Files"
- Recipe 2.13, "Throwing Output Away"

2.10   Appending Rather Than Clobbering Output

Problem

Each time you redirect your output, it creates that output file anew. What if you want to redirect output a second (or third, or ...) time, and don't want to clobber the previous output?

Solution

The double greater-than sign (>>) is a *bash* redirector that means *append the output*:

```
$ ls > /tmp/ls.out
$ cd ../elsewhere
$ ls >> /tmp/ls.out
$ cd ../anotherdir
$ ls >> /tmp.ls.out
$
```

Discussion

The first line includes a redirect that removes the file if it exists and starts with a clean (empty) file, filling it with the output from the *ls* command.

The second and third invocations of *ls* use the double greater than sign (>>) to indicate appending to, rather than replacing, the output file.

See Also

- Recipe 2.6, "Saving Output to Other Files"
- Recipe 2.13, "Throwing Output Away"

2.11   Using Just the Beginning or End of a File

Problem

You need to display or use just the beginning or end of a file.

Solution

Use the *head* or *tail* commands. By default, *head* will output the first 10 lines and *tail* will output the last 10 lines of the given file. If more than one file is given, the appropriate lines from each of them are output. Use the -*number* switch (e.g., -5) to change the number of lines. *tail* also has the -f and -F switches, which follow the end of the file as it is written to. And it has an interesting + switch that we cover in Recipe 2.12, "Skipping a Header in a File."

Discussion

head and *tail*, along with *cat*, *grep*, *sort*, *cut*, and *uniq*, are some of the most commonly used Unix text processing tools out there. If you aren't already familiar with them, you'll soon wonder how you ever got along without them.

See Also

- Recipe 2.12, "Skipping a Header in a File"
- Recipe 7.1, "Sifting Through Files for a String"
- Recipe 8.1, "Sorting Your Output"
- Recipe 8.4, "Cutting Out Parts of Your Output"
- Recipe 8.5, "Removing Duplicate Lines"
- Recipe 17.21, "Numbering Lines"

2.12   Skipping a Header in a File

Problem

You have a file with one or more header lines and you need to process just the data, and skip the header.

Solution

Use the *tail* command with a special argument. For example, to skip the first line of a file:

```
$ tail +2 lines
Line 2

Line 4
Line 5
```

Discussion

An argument to *tail*, which is a number starting dash (-), will specify a line offset relative to the end of the file. So tail -10 *file* shows the last 10 lines of *file*, which also happens to be the default if you don't specify anything. But a number starting with a plus (+) sign is an offset relative to the top of the file. Thus, tail +1 *file* gives you the entire file, the same as *cat*. +2 skips the first line, and so on.

See Also

- man tail
- Recipe 13.11, "Setting Up a Database with MySQL"

2.13 Throwing Output Away

Problem

Sometimes you don't want to save the output into a file; in fact, sometimes you don't even want to see it at all.

Solution

Redirect the output to */dev/null* as shown in these examples:

```
$ find / -name myfile -print 2> /dev/null
```

or:

```
$ noisy >/dev/null 2>&1
```

Discussion

We could redirect the unwanted output into a file, then remove the file when we're done. But there is an easier way. Unix and Linux systems have a special device that isn't real hardware at all, just a *bit bucket* where we can dump unwanted data. It's called */dev/null* and is perfect for these situations. Any data written there is simply thrown away, so it takes up no disk space. Redirection makes it easy.

In the first example, only the output going to standard error is thrown away. In the second example, both standard output and standard error are discarded.

In rare cases, you may find yourself in a situation where */dev* is on a read-only file system (for example, certain information security appliances), in which case you are stuck with the first suggestion of writing to a file and then removing it.

See Also

- Recipe 2.6, "Saving Output to Other Files"

2.14 Saving or Grouping Output from Several Commands

Problem

You want to capture the output with a redirect, but you're typing several commands on one line.

```
$ pwd; ls; cd ../elsewhere; pwd; ls > /tmp/all.out
```

The final redirect applies only to the last command, the last *ls* on that line. All the other output appears on the screen (i.e., does not get redirected).

Solution

Use braces { } to group these commands together, then redirection applies to the output from all commands in the group. For example:

```
$ { pwd; ls; cd ../elsewhere; pwd; ls; } > /tmp/all.out
```

 There are two very subtle catches here. The braces are actually *reserved words*, so they must be surrounded by white space. Also, the trailing semicolon is required before the closing space.

Alternately, you could use parentheses ( ) to tell *bash* to run the commands in a subshell, then redirect the output of the entire subshell's execution. For example:

```
$ (pwd; ls; cd ../elsewhere; pwd; ls) > /tmp/all.out
```

Discussion

While these two solutions look very similar, there are two important differences. The first difference is syntactic, the second is semantic. Syntactically, the braces need to have whitespace around them and the last command inside the list must terminate with a semicolon. That's not required when you use parentheses. The bigger difference, though, is semantic—what these constructs mean. The braces are just a way to group several commands together, more like a shorthand for our redirecting, so that we don't have to redirect each command separately. Commands enclosed in parentheses, however, run in another instance of the shell, a child of the current shell called a *subshell*.

The subshell is almost identical to the current shell's environment, i.e., variables, including $PATH, are all the same, but traps are handled differently (for more on traps, see Recipe 10.6, "Trapping Interrupts"). Now here is the big difference in using the subshell approach: because a subshell is used to execute the *cd* commands, when the subshell exits, your main shell is back where it started, i.e., its current directory hasn't moved, and its variables haven't changed.

With the braces used for grouping, you end up in the new directory (*../elsewhere* in our example). Any other changes that you make (variable assignments, for example) will be made to your current shell instance. While both approaches result in the same output, they leave you in very different places.

One interesting thing you can do with braces is form more concise branching blocks (Recipe 6.2, "Branching on Conditions"). You can shorten this:

```
if [ $result = 1 ]; then
    echo "Result is 1; excellent."
    exit 0
else
    echo "Uh-oh, ummm, RUN AWAY! "
    exit 120
fi
```

into this:

```
[ $result = 1 ] \
    && { echo "Result is 1; excellent."  ; exit 0;   } \
    || { echo "Uh-oh, ummm, RUN AWAY! "  ; exit 120; }
```

How you write it depends on your style and what you think is readable.

See Also

- Recipe 6.2, "Branching on Conditions"
- Recipe 10.6, "Trapping Interrupts"
- Recipe 15.11, "Getting Input from Another Machine"
- Recipe 19.5, "Expecting to Change Exported Variables"
- Recipe 19.8, "Forgetting That Pipelines Make Subshells"
- "Built-in Shell Variables" in Appendix A to learn about BASH_SUBSHELL

2.15 Connecting Two Programs by Using Output As Input

Problem

You want to take the output from one program and use it as the input of another program.

Solution

You could redirect the output from the first program into a temporary file, then use that file as input to the second program. For example:

```
$ cat one.file another.file > /tmp/cat.out
$ sort < /tmp/cat.out
...
$ rm /tmp/cat.out
```

Or you could do all of that in one step by sending the output directly to the next program by using the pipe symbol | to connect them. For example:

```
$ cat one.file another.file | sort
```

You can also link a sequence of several commands together by using multiple pipes:

```
$ cat my* | tr 'a-z' 'A-Z' | uniq | awk -f transform.awk | wc
```

Discussion

By using the pipe symbol we don't have to invent a temporary filename, remember it, and remember to delete it.

Programs like *sort* can take input from standard in (redirected via the < symbol) but they can also take input as a filename—for example:

```
$ sort /tmp/cat.out
```

rather than redirecting the input into *sort*:

```
$ sort < /tmp/cat.out
```

That behavior (of using a filename if supplied, and if not, of using standard input) is a typical Unix/Linux characteristic, and a useful model to follow so that commands can be connected one to another via the pipe mechanism. If you write your programs and shell scripts that way, they will be more useful to you and to those with whom you share your work.

Feel free to be amazed at the powerful simplicity of the pipe mechanism. You can even think of the pipe as a rudimentary parallel processing mechanism. You have two commands (programs) running in parallel, sharing data—the output of one as the input to the next. They don't have to run sequentially (where the first runs to completion before the second one starts)—the second one can get started as soon as data is available from the first.

Be aware, however, that commands run this way (i.e., connected by pipes), are run in separate subshells. While such a subtlety can often be ignored, there are a few times when the implications of this are important. We'll discuss that in Recipe 19.8, "Forgetting That Pipelines Make Subshells."

Also consider a command such as svn -v log | less. If *less* exits before Subversion has finished sending data, you'll get an error like "svn: Write error: Broken pipe". While it isn't pretty, it also isn't harmful. It happens all the time when you pipe some a voluminous amount of data into a program like *less*—you often want to quit once you've found what you're looking for, even if there is more data coming down the pipe.

See Also

- Recipe 3.1, "Getting Input from a File"
- Recipe 19.8, "Forgetting That Pipelines Make Subshells"

2.16 Saving a Copy of Output Even While Using It As Input

Problem

You want to debug a long sequence of piped I/O, such as:

```
$ cat my* | tr 'a-z' 'A-Z' | uniq | awk -f transform.awk | wc
```

How can you see what is happening between uniq and awk without disrupting the pipe?

Solution

The solution to these problems is to use what plumbers call a T-joint in the pipes. For *bash*, that means using the *tee* command to split the output into two identical streams, one that is written to a file and the other that is written to standard out, so as to continue the sending of data along the pipes.

For this example where we'd like to debug a long string of pipes, we insert the *tee* command between *uniq* and *awk*:

```
$ ... uniq | tee /tmp/x.x | awk -f transform.awk ...
```

Discussion

The *tee* command writes the output to the filename specified as its parameter and also write that same output to standard out. In our example, that sends a copy to */tmp/x.x* and also sends the same data to *awk*, the command to which the output of *tee* is connected via the | pipe symbol.

Don't worry about what each different piece of the command line is doing in these examples; we just want to illustrate how *tee* can be used in any sequence of commands.

Let's back up just a bit and start with a simpler command line. Suppose you'd just like to save the output from a long-running command for later reference, while at the same time seeing it on the screen. After all, a command like:

```
find / -name '*.c' -print | less
```

could find a lot of C source files, so it will likely scroll off the window. Using *more* or *less* will let you look at the output in manageable pieces, but once completed they don't let you go back and look at that output without re-running the command. Sure, you could run the command and save it to a file:

```
find / -name '*.c' -print > /tmp/all.my.sources
```

but then you have to wait for it to complete before you can see the contents of the file. (OK, we know about `tail -f` but that's just getting off topic here.) The *tee* command can be used instead of the simple redirection of standard output:

```
find / -name '*.c' -print | tee /tmp/all.my.sources
```

In this example, since the output of *tee* isn't redirected anywhere, it will print to the screen. But the copy that is diverted into a file will be there for later use (e.g., `cat /tmp/all.my.sources`).

Notice, too, that in these examples we did not redirect standard error at all. This means that any errors, like you might expect from *find*, will be printed to the screen but won't show up in the *tee* file. We could have added a 2>&1 to the *find* command:

```
find / -name '*.c' -print 2>&1 | tee /tmp/all.my.sources
```

to include the error output in the *tee* file. It won't be neatly separated, but it will be captured.

See Also

- man tee
- Recipe 18.5, "Reusing Arguments"
- Recipe 19.13, "Debugging Scripts"

2.17 Connecting Two Programs by Using Output As Arguments

Problem

What if one of the programs to which you would like to connect with a pipe doesn't work that way? For example, you can remove files with the *rm* command, specifing the files to be removed as parameters to the command:

```
$ rm my.java your.c their.*
```

but *rm* doesn't read from standard input, so you *can't* do something like:

```
find . -name '*.c' | rm
```

Since *rm* only takes its filenames as arguments or parameters on the command line, how can we get the output of a previously-run command (e.g., *echo* or *ls*) onto the command line?

Solution

Use the command substitution feature of *bash*:

```
$ rm $(find . -name '*.class')
$
```

Discussion

The $( ) encloses a command that is run in a subshell. The output from that command is substituted in place of the $( ) phrase. Newlines in the output are replaced with a space character (actually it uses the first character of $IFS, which is a space by default, during word splitting), so several lines of output become several parameters on the command line.

The earlier shell syntax was to use back-quotes instead of $( ) for enclosing the sub-command. The $( ) syntax is preferred over the older backward quotes `` ` `` syntax because it easier to nest and arguably easier to read. However, you will probably see `` ` `` more often than $( ), especially in older scripts or from those who grew up with the original Bourne or C shells.

In our example, the output from *find*, typically a list of names, will become the arguments to the *rm* command.

Warning: be very careful when doing something like this because *rm* is very unforgiving. If your *find* command finds more than you expect, *rm* will remove it with no recourse. This is not Windows; you cannot recover deleted files from the trashcan. You can mitigate the danger with `rm -i`, which will prompt you to verify each delete. That's OK on a small number of files, but interminable on a large set.

One way to use such a mechanism in *bash* with greater safety is to run that inner command first by itself. When you can see that you are getting the results that you want, only then do you use it in the command with back-quotes.

For example:

```
$ find . -name '*.class'
First.class
Other.class
$ rm $(find . -name '*.class')
$
```

We'll see in an upcoming recipe how this can be made even more foolproof by using `!!` instead of retyping the *find* command (see Recipe 18.2, "Repeating the Last Command").

See Also

- Recipe 18.2, "Repeating the Last Command"
- Recipe 15.13, "Working Around "argument list too long" Errors"

2.18   Using Multiple Redirects on One Line

Problem

You want to redirect output to several different places.

Solution

Use redirection with file numbers to open all the files that you want to use. For example:

```
$ divert 3> file.three  4> file.four  5> file.five  6> else.where
$
```

where divert might be a shell script with various commands whose output you want to send to different places. For example, you might write *divert* to contain lines like this: `echo option $OPTSTR >&5`. That is, our *divert* shell script could direct its output to various different descriptors which the invoking program can send to different destinations.

Similarly, if *divert* was a C program executable, you could actually write to descriptors 3, 4, 5, and 6 without any need for open( ) calls.

Discussion

In an earlier recipe we explained that each file descriptor is indicated by a number, starting at 0 (zero). So standard input is 0, out is 1, and error is 2. That means that you could redirect standard output with the slightly more verbose 1> (rather than a simple >) followed by a filename, but there's no need. The shorthand > is fine. It also means that you can have the shell open up any number of arbitrary file descriptors and have them set to write various files so that the program that the shell then invokes from the command line can use these opened file descriptors without further ado.

While we don't recommend this technique, it is intriguing.

See Also

- Recipe 2.6, "Saving Output to Other Files"
- Recipe 2.8, "Sending Both Output and Error Messages to Different Files"
- Recipe 2.13, "Throwing Output Away"

2.19   Saving Output When Redirect Doesn't Seem to Work

Problem

You tried using > but some (or all) of the output still appears on the screen.

For example, the compiler is producing some error messages.

```
$ gcc bad.c
bad.c: In function `main':
bad.c:3: error: `bad' undeclared (first use in this function)
bad.c:3: error: (Each undeclared identifier is reported only once
bad.c:3: error: for each function it appears in.)
bad.c:3: error: parse error before "c"
$
```

You wanted to capture those messages, so you tried redirecting the output:

```
$ gcc bad.c > save.it
bad.c: In function `main':
bad.c:3: error: `bad' undeclared (first use in this function)
bad.c:3: error: (Each undeclared identifier is reported only once
bad.c:3: error: for each function it appears in.)
bad.c:3: error: parse error before "c"
$
```

However, it doesn't seem to have redirected anything. In fact, when you examine the file into which you were directing the output, that file is empty (zero bytes long):

```
$ ls -l save.it
-rw-r--r-- 1 albing users 0 2005-11-13 15:30 save.it
$ cat save.it
$
```

Solution

Redirect the error output, as follows:

```
$ gcc bad.c 2> save.it
$
```

The contents of *save.it* are now the error messages that we had seen before.

Discussion

So what's going on here? Every process in Unix and Linux typically starts out with three open file descriptors: one for input called *standard input* (STDIN), one for output called *standard output* (STDOUT), and one for error messages called *standard error* (STDERR). It is really up to the programmer, who writes any particular program, to stick to these conventions and write error messages to standard error and to write the normally expected output to standard out, so there is no guarantee that every error message that you ever get will go to standard error. But most of the long-established utilities are well behaved this way. That is why these compiler messages are not being diverted with a simple > redirect; it only redirects standard output, not standard error.

Each file descriptor is indicated by a number, starting at 0. So standard input is 0, output is 1, and error is 2. That means that you could redirect standard output with the slightly more verbose: 1> (rather than a simple >) followed by a filename, but there's no need. The shorthand > is fine.

One other difference between standard output and standard error: standard output is *buffered* but standard error is *unbuffered,* that is every character is written individually, not collected together and written as a bunch. This means that you see the error messages right away and that there is less chance of them being dropped when a fault occurs, but the cost is one of efficiency. It's not that standard output is unreliable, but in error situations (e.g., a program dies unexpectedly), the buffered output may not have made it to the screen before the program stops executing. That's why standard error is unbuffered: to be sure the message gets written. By contrast, standard out is buffered. Only when the buffer is full (or when the file is closed) does the output actually get written. It's more efficient for the more frequently used output. Efficiency isn't as important when an error is being reported.

What if you want to see the output as you are saving it? The *tee* command we discussed in Recipe 2.16, "Saving a Copy of Output Even While Using It As Input" seems just the thing:

```
$ gcc bad.c 2>&1 | tee save.it
```

This will take standard error and redirect it to standard out, piping them both into *tee*. The *tee* command will write its input to both the file (save.it) and *tee*'s standard out, which will go to your screen since it isn't otherwise redirected.

This is a special case of redirecting because normally the order of the redirections is important. Compare these two commands:

```
$ somecmd >my.file 2>&1
```

```
$ somecmd 2>&1 >my.file
```

In the first case, standard out is redirected to a file (my.file), and then standard error is redirected to the same place as standard out. All output will appear in *my.file*.

But that is not the case with the second command. In the second command, standard error is redirected to standard out (which at that point is connected to the screen), after which standard out is redirected to my.file. Thus only standard out messages will be put in the file and errors will still show on the screen.

However, this ordering had to be subverted for pipes, since you couldn't put the second redirect after the pipe symbol, because after the pipe comes the next command. So *bash* makes an exception when you write:

```
$ somecmd 2>&1 | othercmd
```

and recognizes that standard out is being piped. It therefore assumes that you want to include standard error in the piping when you write 2>&1 even though its normal ordering wouldn't work that way.

The other result of this, and of pipe syntax in general, is that it gives us no way to pipe just standard error and not standard out into another command—unless we first swap the file descriptors (see the next recipe).

See Also

- Recipe 2.17, "Connecting Two Programs by Using Output As Arguments
- Recipe 2.20, "Swapping STDERR and STDOUT"

2.20   Swapping STDERR and STDOUT

Problem

You need to swap STDERR and STDOUT so you can send STDOUT to a logfile, but then send STDERR to the screen and to a file using the *tee* command. But pipes only work with STDOUT.

Solution

Swap STDERR and STDOUT before the pipe redirection using a third file descriptor:

```
$ ./myscript 3>&1 1>stdout.logfile 2>&3- | tee -a stderr.logfile
```

Discussion

Whenever you redirect file descriptors, you are duplicating the open descriptor to another descriptor. This gives you a way to swap descriptors, much like how any program swaps two values—by means of a third, temporary holder. It looks like: copy A into C, copy B into A, copy C into B and then you have swapped the values of A and B. For file descriptors, it looks like this:

```
$ ./myscript  3>&1 1>&2 2>&3
```

Read the syntax 3>&1 as "give file descriptor 3 the same value as output file descriptor 1." What happens here is that it duplicates file descriptor 1 (i.e., STDOUT) into file descriptor 3, our temporary holding place. Then it duplicates file descriptor 2 (i.e., STDERR) into STDOUT, and finally duplicates file descriptor 3 into STDERR. The net effect is that STDERR and STDOUT file descriptors have swapped places.

So far so good. Now we just change this slightly. Once we've made the copy of STDOUT (into file descriptor 3), we are free to redirect STDOUT into the logfile we want to have capture the output of our script or other program. Then we can copy the file descriptor from its temporary holding place (fd 3) into STDERR. Adding the pipe will now work because the pipe connects to the (original) STDOUT. That gets us to the solution we wrote above:

```
$ ./myscript 3>&1 1>stdout.logfile 2>&3- | tee -a stderr.logfile
```

Note the trailing - on the 2>&3- term. We do that so that we close file descriptor 3 when we are done with it. That way our program doesn't have an extra open file descriptor. We are tidying up after ourselves.

See Also

- *Linux Server Hacks,* First Edition, hack #5 "n>&m: Swap STDOUT and STDERR," by Rob Flickenger (O'Reilly)
- Recipe 2.19, "Saving Output When Redirect Doesn't Seem to Work"
- Recipe 10.1, ""Daemon-izing" Your Script"

2.21   Keeping Files Safe from Accidental Overwriting

Problem

You don't want to delete the contents of a file by mistake. It can be too easy to mistype a filename and find that you've redirected output into a file that you meant to save.

Solution

Tell the shell to be more careful, as follows:

```
$ set -o noclobber
$
```

If you decide you don't want to be so careful after all, then turn the option off:

```
$ set +o noclobber
$
```

Discussion

The noclobber option tells *bash* not to overwrite any existing files when you redirect output. If the file to which you redirect output doesn't (yet) exist, everything works as normal, with *bash* creating the file as it opens it for output. If the file already exists, however, you will get an error message.

Here it is in action. We begin by turning the option off, just so that your shell is in a known state, regardless of how your particular system may be configured.

```
$ set +o noclobber
$ echo something > my.file
$ echo some more > my.file
$ set -o noclobber
$ echo something > my.file
bash: my.file: cannot overwrite existing file
$ echo some more >> my.file
$
```

The first time we redirect output to *my.file* the shell will create it for us. The second time we redirect, *bash* overwrites the file (it truncates the file to 0 bytes and starts writing from there). Then we set the noclobber option and we get an error message when we try to write to that file. As we show in the last part of this example, we can append to the file (using >>) just fine.

Beware! The noclobber option only refers to the shell's clobbering of a file when redirecting output. It will *not* stop other file manipulating actions of other programs from clobbering files (see Recipe 14.13, "Setting Permissions").

```
$ echo useless data > some.file
$ echo important data > other.file
$ set -o noclobber
$ cp some.file other.file
$
```

Notice that no error occurs; the file is copied over the top of an existing file. That copy is done via the *cp* command. The shell doesn't get involved.

If you're a good and careful typist this may not seem like an important option, but we will look at other recipes where filenames are generated with regular expressions or passed as variables. Those filenames could be used as the filename for output redirection. In such cases, having noclobber set may be an important safety feature for preventing unwanted side effects (whether goofs or malicious actions).

See Also

- A good Linux reference on the chmod command and file permissions, such as:
  - *http://www.linuxforums.org/security/file_permissions.html*
  - *http://www.comptechdoc.org/os/linux/usersguide/linux_ugfilesup.html*
  - *http://www.faqs.org/docs/linux_intro/sect_03_04.html*
  - *http://www.perlfect.com/articles/chmod.shtml*
- Recipe 14.13, "Setting Permissions"

2.22 Clobbering a File on Purpose

Problem

You like to have noclobber set, but every once in a while you do want to clobber a file when you redirect output. Can you override *bash*'s good intentions, just once?

Solution

Use >| to redirect your output. Even if noclobber is set, *bash* ignores its setting and overwrites the file.

Consider this example:

```
$ echo something > my.file
$ set -o noclobber
$ echo some more >| my.file
$ cat my.file
some more
$ echo once again > my.file
bash: my.file: cannot overwrite existing file
$
```

Notice that no error message occurs on the second *echo*, but on the third *echo*, when we are no longer using the vertical bar but just the plain > character by itself, the shell warns us and does not clobber the existing file.

Discussion

Using noclobber does not take the place of file permissions. If you don't have write permission in the directory, you won't be able to create the file, whether or not you use the >| construct. Similarly, you must have write permission on the file itself to overwrite that existing file, whether or not you use the >|.

So why the vertical bar? Perhaps because the exclamation point was already used by *bash* for other things, and the vertical bar is close, visually, to the exclamation point. But why would ! be the appropriate symbol? Well, for emphasis of course. Its use in English (with the imperative mood) fits that sense of "do it anyway!" when telling *bash* to overwrite the file if need be. Secondly, the *vi* (and *ex*) editors use the ! in that same meaning in their write (:w! *filename*) command. Without a !, the editor will complain if you try to overwrite an existing file. With it, you are telling the editor to "do it!"

See Also

- Recipe 14.13, "Setting Permissions"

## CHAPTER 3

Standard Input

Whether it is data for a program to crunch, or simple commands to direct the behavior of a script, input is as fundamental as output. The first part of any program is the beginning of the "input/output" yin and yang of computing.

3.1 Getting Input from a File

Problem

You want your shell commands to read data from a file.

Solution

Use input redirection, indicated by the < character, to read data from a file.

```
$ wc < my.file
```

Discussion

Just as the > sends output to a file, so < takes input from a file. The choice and shape of the characters was meant to give a visual clue as to what was going on with redirection. Can you see it? (Think "arrowhead.")

Many shell commands will take one or more filenames as arguments, but when no filename is given, will read from standard input. Those commands can then be invoked as either: *command filename* or as *command < filename* with the same result. That's the case here with *wc*, but also with *cat* and others.

It may look like a simple feature, and be familiar if you've used the DOS command line before, but it is a significant feature to shell scripting (which the DOS command line borrowed) and was radical in both its power and simplicity when first introduced.

See Also

- Recipe 2.6, "Saving Output to Other Files"

3.2   Keeping Your Data with Your Script

Problem

You need input to your script, but don't want a separate file.

Solution

Use a *here-document*, with the << characters, redirecting the text from the command line rather than from a file. When put into a shell script, the script file then contains the data along with the script.

Here's an example of a shell script in a file we call *ext*:

```
$ cat ext
#
# here is a "here" document
#
grep $1 <<EOF
mike x.123
joe  x.234
sue  x.555
pete x.818
sara x.822
bill x.919
EOF
$
```

It can be used as a shell script for simple phone number lookups:

```
$ ext bill
bill x.919
$
```

or:

```
$ ext 555
sue  x.555
$
```

Discussion

The *grep* command looks for occurrences of the first argument in the files that are named, or if no files are named it looks to standard input.

A typical use of *grep* is something like this:

```
$ grep somestring file.txt
```

or:

```
$ grep myvar *.c
```

In our *ext* script we've parameterized the *grep* by making the string that we're searching for be the parameter of our shell script ($1). Whereas we often think of *grep* as searching for a fixed string through various different files, here we are going to vary what we search for, but search through the same data every time.

We could have put our phone numbers in a file, say *phonenumbers.txt*, and then used that filename on the line that invokes the *grep* command:

```
grep $1 phonenumbers.txt
```

However, that requires two separate files (our script and our datafile) and raises the question of where to put them and how to keep them together.

So rather than supplying one or more filenames (to search through), we set up a here-document and tell the shell to redirect standard input to come from that (temporary) document.

The << syntax says that we want to create such a temporary input source, and the EOF is just an arbitrary string (you can choose what you like) to act as the terminator of the temporary input. It is not part of the input, but acts as the marker to show where it ends. The regular shell script (if any) resumes after the marker.

We also might add -i to the *grep* command to make our search is case-insensitive. Thus, using grep -i $1 <<EOF would allow us to search for "Bill" as well as "bill."

See Also

- man grep
- Recipe 3.3, "Preventing Weird Behavior in a Here-Document"
- Recipe 3.4, "Indenting Here-Documents"

3.3   Preventing Weird Behavior in a Here-Document

Problem

Your here-document is behaving weirdly. You tried to maintain a simple list of donors using the method described previously for phone numbers. So you created a file called *donors* that looked like this:

```
$ cat donors
#
# simple lookup of our generous donors
#
grep $1 <<EOF
# name amt
pete $100
joe  $200
sam  $ 25
bill $  9
EOF
$
```

But when you tried running it you got weird output:

```
$ ./donors bill
pete bill00
bill $  9
$ ./donors pete
pete pete00
$
```

Solution

Turn off the shell scripting features inside the here-document by escaping any or all of the characters in the ending marker:

```
# solution
grep $1 <<\EOF
pete $100
joe  $200
sam  $ 25
bill $  9
EOF
```

Discussion

It's a very subtle difference, but the <<EOF is replaced with <<\EOF, or <<'EOF' or even <<E\OF—they all work. It's not the most elegant syntax, but it's enough to tell *bash* that you want to treat the "here" data differently.

Normally (i.e., unless we use this escaping syntax), says the *bash* manpage, "…all lines of the here-document are subjected to parameter expansion, command substitution, and arithmetic expansion."

So what's happening in our original *donor* script is that the amounts are being interpreted as shell variables. For example, $100 is being seen as the shell variable $1 followed by two zeros. That's what gives us pete00 when we search for "pete" and bill00 when we search for "bill."

When we escape some or all of the characters of the EOF, *bash* knows not to do the expansions, and the behavior is the expected behavior:

```
$ ./donors pete
pete $100
$
```

Of course you may *want* the shell expansion on your data—it can be useful in the correct circumstances, but isn't what we want here. We've found it to be a useful practice to always escape the marker as in <<'EOF' or <<\EOF to avoid unexpected results, unless you know that you really want the expansion to be done on your data.

Trailing whitespace (e.g., even just a single blank space) on your closing EOF marker will cause it not to be recognized as the closing marker. *bash* will swallow up the rest of your script, treating it as input too, and looking for that EOF. Be sure there are no extra characters (especially blanks or tabs) after the EOF.

See Also

- Recipe 3.2, "Keeping Your Data with Your Script"
- Recipe 3.4, "Indenting Here-Documents"

3.4 Indenting Here-Documents

Problem

The here-document is great, but it's messing up your shell script's formatting. You want to be able to indent for readability.

Solution

Use <<- and then you can use tab characters (only!) at the beginning of lines to indent this portion of your shell script.

```
$ cat myscript.sh
...
    grep $1 <<-'EOF'
        lots of data
        can go here
        it's indented with tabs
        to match the script's indenting
        but the leading tabs are
        discarded when read
        EOF
    ls
...
$
```

Discussion

The hyphen just after the << is enough to tell *bash* to ignore the leading tab characters. This is for *tab* characters only and not arbitrary white space. This is especially important with the EOF or any other marker designation. If you have spaces there, it will not recognize the EOF as your ending marker, and the "here" data will continue through to the end of the file (swallowing the rest of your script). Therefore, you may want to always left-justify the EOF (or other marker) just to be safe, and let the formatting go on this one line.

Just as trailing whitespace of any kind on your closing EOF delimiter prevents it from being recognized as the closing delimiter (see the warning in Recipe 3.3, "Preventing Weird Behavior in a Here-Document"), so too will using a leading character other than just the tab character. If your script indents with spaces or a combination of spaces and tabs, don't use that technique on here-documents. Either use just tabs, or keep it all flush left. Also, watch out for text editors that automatically replace tabs with spaces.

See Also

- Recipe 3.2, "Keeping Your Data with Your Script"
- Recipe 3.3, "Preventing Weird Behavior in a Here-Document"

3.5   Getting User Input

Problem

You need to get input from the user.

Solution

Use the read statement:

```
read
```

or:

```
read - p "answer me this " ANSWER
```

or:

```
read PRE MID POST
```

Discussion

In its simplest form, a read statement with no arguments will read user input and place it into the shell variable REPLY.

If you want *bash* to print a prompt string before reading the input, use the -p option. The next word following the -p will be the prompt, but quoting allows you to supply multiple words for a prompt. Remember to end the prompt with punctuation and/or a blank, as the cursor will wait for input right at the end of the prompt string.

If you supply multiple variable names on the read statement, then the read will parse the input into words, assigning them in order. If the user enters fewer words, the extra variables will be set blank. If the user enters more words than there are variables on the read statement, then all of the extra words will be part of the last variable in the list.

See Also

- help read
- building robust code
- Recipe 3.8, "Prompting for a Password"
- Recipe 6.11, "Looping with a read"
- Recipe 13.6, "Parsing Text with a read Statement"
- Recipe 14.12, "Validating Input"

3.6 Getting Yes or No Input

Problem

You need to get a simple yes or no input from the user, and you want to be as user-friendly as possible. In particular, you do not want to be case sensitive, and you want to provide a useful default if the user presses the Enter key.

Solution

If the actions to take are simple, use this self-contained function:

```
# cookbook filename: func_choose

# Let the user make a choice about something and execute code based on
# the answer
# Called like: choose <default (y or n)> <prompt> <yes action> <no action>
# e.g. choose "y" \
#       "Do you want to play a game?" \
#       /usr/games/GlobalThermonucularWar \
#       'printf "%b" "See you later Professor Falkin.\n"' >&2
# Returns: nothing
function choose {

    local default="$1"
    local prompt="$2"
    local choice_yes="$3"
    local choice_no="$4"
    local answer

    read -p "$prompt" answer
    [ -z "$answer" ] && answer="$default"

    case "$answer" in
        [yY1] ) eval "$choice_yes"
            # error check
            ;;
        [nN0] ) eval "$choice_no"
```

```
                # error check
            ;;
    *       ) printf "%b" "Unexpected answer '$answer'!"  >&2 ;;
    esac
} # end of function choose
```

If the actions are complicated, use this function and handle the results in your main code.

```
# cookbook filename: func_choice.1

# Let the user make a choice about something and return a standardized
# answer.  How the default is handled and what happens next is up to
# the if/then after the choice in main
# Called like: choice <promtp>
# e.g.  choice "Do you want to play a game?"
# Returns: global variable CHOICE
function choice {

    CHOICE=''
    local prompt="$*"
    local answer

    read -p "$prompt" answer
    case "$answer" in
        [yY1] ) CHOICE='y';;
        [nNo] ) CHOICE='n';;
        *       ) CHOICE="$answer";;
    esac
} # end of function choice
```

The following code calls the choice function to prompt for and verify a package date. Assuming $THISPACKAGE is set, the function displays the date and asks for verification. If the user types y, Y, or Enter, then that date is accepted. If the user enters a new date, the function loops and verifies it (for a different treatment of this problem, see Recipe 11.7, "Figuring Out Date and Time Arithmetic"):

```
# cookbook filename: func_choice.2

CHOICE=''
until [ "$CHOICE" = "y" ]; do
    printf "%b" "This package's date is $THISPACKAGE\n" >&2
    choice "Is that correct? [Y/,<New date>]: "
    if [ -z "$CHOICE" ]; then
        CHOICE='y'
    elif [ "$CHOICE" != "y" ]; then
        printf "%b" "Overriding $THISPACKAGE with ${CHOICE}\n"
        THISPACKAGE=$CHOICE
    fi
done

# Build the package here
```

Next we'll show different ways to handle some "yes or no" questions. Carefully read the prompts and look at the defaults. In both cases the user can simply hit the Enter key, and the script will then take the default the programmer intended.

```
# If the user types anything except a case insensitive 'n', they will
# see the error log
choice "Do you want to look at the error log file? [Y/n]: "
if [ "$choice" != "n" ]; then
    less error.log
fi

# If the user types anything except a case insensitive 'y', they will
# not see the message log
choice "Do you want to look at the message log file? [y/N]: "
if [ "$choice" = "y" ]; then
    less message.log
fi
```

Finally, this function asks for input that might not exist:

```
# cookbook filename: func_choice.3

choice "Enter your favorite color, if you have one: "
if [ -n "$CHOICE" ]; then
    printf "%b" "You chose: $CHOICE\n"
else
    printf "%b" "You do not have a favorite color.\n"
fi
```

Discussion

Asking the user to make a decision is often necessary in scripting. For getting arbitrary input, see Recipe 3.5, "Getting User Input." For choosing an option from a list, see Recipe 3.7, "Selecting from a List of Options."

If the possible choices and the code to handle them are fairly straightforward, the first self-contained function is easier to use, but it's not always flexible enough. The second function is flexible at the expense of having to do more in the main code.

Note that we've sent the user prompts to STDERR so that the main script output on STDOUT may be redirected without the prompts cluttering it up.

See Also

- Recipe 3.5, "Getting User Input"
- Recipe 3.7, "Selecting from a List of Options"
- Recipe 11.7, "Figuring Out Date and Time Arithmetic"

3.7   Selecting from a List of Options

Problem

You need to provide the user with a list of options to choose from and you don't want to make them type any more than necessary.

Solution

Use *bash*'s built-in select construct to generate a menu, then have the user choose by typing the number of the selection:

```
# cookbook filename: select_dir

directorylist="Finished $(for i in /*;do [ -d "$i" ] && echo $i; done)"

PS3='Directory to process? ' # Set a useful select prompt
until [ "$directory" == "Finished" ]; do

    printf "%b" "\a\n\nSelect a directory to process:\n" >&2
    select directory in $directorylist; do

        # User types a number which is stored in $REPLY, but select
        # returns the value of the entry
        if [ "$directory" = "Finished" ]; then
            echo "Finished processing directories."
            break
        elif [ -n "$directory" ]; then
            echo "You chose number $REPLY, processing $directory ..."
            # Do something here
            break
        else
            echo "Invalid selection!"
        fi # end of handle user's selection

    done # end of select a directory
done # end of while not finished
```

Discussion

The select function makes it trivial to present a numbered list to the user on STDERR, from which they may make a choice. Don't forget to provide an "exit" or "finished" choice.

The number the user typed is returned in $REPLY, and the value of that entry is returned in the variable you specified in the select construct.

See Also

- help select
- help read
- Recipe 3.6, "Getting Yes or No Input"

3.8 Prompting for a Password

Problem

You need to prompt the user for a password, but you don't want it echoed on the screen.

Solution

```
read -s -p "password: " PASSWD
printf "%b" "\n"
```

Discussion

The -s option tells the read command not to echo the characters typed (s is for silent) and the -p option says that the next argument is the prompt to be displayed prior to reading input.

The line of input that is read from the user is put into the environment variable named $PASSWD.

We follow read with a printf to print out a newline. The printf is necessary because read -s turns off the echoing of characters. With echoing disabled, when the user presses the Enter key, no newline is echoed and any subsequent output would appear on the same line as the prompt. Printing the newline gets us to the next line, as you would expect. It may even be handy for you to write the code all on one line to avoid intervening logic; putting it on one line also prevents mistakes should you cut and paste this line elsewhere:

```
read -s -p "password: " PASSWD ; printf "%b" "\n"
```

Be aware that if you read a password into an environment variable it is in memory in plain text, and thus may be accessed via a core dump or *proc/core*. It is also in the process environment, which may be accessible by other processes. You may be better off using certificates with SSH, if possible. In any case, it is wise to assume that *root* and possibly other users on the machine may gain access to the password, so you should handle the situation accordingly.

Some older scripts may use s to disable the screen echo while a password is being entered. The problem with that is this if the user breaks the script, echo will still be off. Experienced users will know to type stty sane to fix it, but it's very confusing. If you still need to use this method, set a trap to turn echo back on when the script terminates. See Recipe 10.6, "Trapping Interrupts."

See Also

- help read
- Recipe 10.6, "Trapping Interrupts"
- Recipe 14.14, "Leaking Passwords into the Process List"
- Recipe 14.20, "Using Passwords in Scripts"
- Recipe 14.21, "Using SSH Without a Password"
- Recipe 19.9, "Making Your Terminal Sane Again"

## CHAPTER 4

Executing Commands

The main purpose of *bash* (or of any shell) is to allow you to interact with the computer's operating system so that you can accomplish whatever you need to do. Usually that involves launching programs, so the shell takes the commands you type, determines from that input what programs need to be run, and launches them for you.

Let's take a look at the basic mechanism for launching jobs and explore some of the features *bash* offers for launching programs in the foreground or the background, sequentially or in parallel, indicating whether programs succeeded and more.

4.1 Running Any Executable

Problem

You need to run a command on a Linux or Unix system.

Solution

Use *bash* and type the name of the command at the prompt.

```
$ someprog
```

Discussion

This seems rather simple, and in a way it is, but a lot goes on behind the scenes that you never see. What's important to understand about *bash* is that its basic operation is to load and execute programs. All the rest is just window dressing to get ready to run programs. Sure there are shell variables and control statements for looping and if/then/else branching, and there are ways to control input and output, but they are all icing on the cake of program execution.

So where does it get the program to run?

bash will use a shell variable called $PATH to locate your executable. The $PATH variable is a list of directories. The directories are separated by colons (:). *bash* will search in each of those directories for a file with the name that you specified. The order of the directories is important—*bash* looks at the order in which the directories are listed in the variable, and takes the first executable found.

```
$ echo $PATH
/bin:/usr/bin:/usr/local/bin:.
$
```

In the $PATH variable shown above, four directories are included. The last directory in that list is just a single dot (called the *dot directory*, or just *dot*), which represents the current directory. The dot is the name of the directory found within every directory on a Linux or Unix file system—wherever you are, that's the directory to which dot refers. For example, when you copy a file from someplace to dot (i.e., cp /other/ place/file .), you are copying the file into the current directory. By having the dot directory listed in our path, *bash* will look for commands not just in those other directories, but also in the current directory (.).

Many people feel that putting dot on your $PATH is too great a security risk—someone could trick you and get you to run their own (malicious) version of a command in place of one that you were expecting. Now if dot were listed first, then someone else's version of *ls* would supersede the normal *ls* command and you might unwittingly run that command. Don't believe us? Try this:

```
$ bash
$ cd
$ touch ls
$ chmod 755 ls
$ PATH=".:$PATH"
$ ls
$
```

Suddenly, the *ls* appears not to work in your home directory. You get no output. When you *cd* to some other location (e.g., cd /tmp), then *ls* will work, but not in your home directory. Why? Because in that directory there is an empty file called *ls* that is run (and does nothing—it's empty) instead of the normal *ls* command located at */bin/ls*. Since we started this example by running a new copy of *bash*, you can exit from this mess by exiting this subshell; but you might want to remove the bogus *ls* command first:

```
$ cd
$ rm ls
$ exit
$
```

Can you see the mischief potential of wandering into a strange directory with your path set to search the dot directory before anywhere else?

If you put dot as the last directory in your $PATH variable, at least you won't be tricked that easily. Of course, if you leave it off altogether it is arguably even safer and you can still run commands in your local directory by typing a leading dot and slash character, as in:

```
$ ./myscript
```

The choice is yours.

 Never allow a dot or writable directories in *root*'s $PATH. For more, see Recipe 14.9, "Finding World-Writable Directories in Your $PATH" and Recipe 14.10, "Adding the Current Directory to the $PATH."

Don't forget to set the file's permissions to execute permission before you invoke your script:

```
$ chmod a+x ./myscript
$ ./myscript
```

You only need to set the permissions once. Thereafter you can invoke the script as a command.

A common practice among some *bash* experts is to create a personal *bin* directory, analogous to the system directories */bin* and */usr/bin* where executables are kept. In your personal *bin* you can put copies of your favorite shell scripts and other customized or private commands. Then add your home directory to your $PATH, even to the front (PATH=~/bin:$PATH). That way, you can still have your own customized favorites without the security risk of running commands from strangers.

See Also

- Chapter 16 for more on customizing your environment
- Recipe 1.3, "Finding and Running Commands"
- Recipe 14.9, "Finding World-Writable Directories in Your $PATH"
- Recipe 14.10, "Adding the Current Directory to the $PATH"
- Recipe 16.9, "Keeping a Private Stash of Utilities by Adding ~/bin"
- Recipe 19.1, "Forgetting to Set Execute Permissions"

4.2   Telling If a Command Succeeded or Not

Problem

You need to know whether the command you ran succeeded.

Solution

The shell variable $? will be set with a non-zero value if the command fails—provided that the programmer who wrote that command or shell script followed the established convention:

```
$ somecommand
it works...
$ echo $?
0
$ badcommand
it fails...
$ echo $?
1
$
```

Discussion

The *exit status* of a command is kept in the shell variable referenced with $?. Its value can range from 0 to 255. When you write a shell script, it's a good idea to have your script exit with a non-zero value if you encounter an error condition. (Just keep it below 255, or the numbers will wrap around.) You return an exit status with the exit statement (e.g., exit 1 or exit 0). But be aware that you only get one shot at reading the exit status:

```
$ badcommand
it fails...
$ echo $?
1
$ echo $?
0
$
```

Why does the second time give us 0 as a result? Because the second time is reporting on the status of the immediately preceding *echo* command. The first time we typed echo $? it returned a 1, which was the return value of *badcommand*. But the *echo* command itself succeeds, therefore the new, most-recent status is success (i.e., a 0 value). So you only get one chance to check it. Therefore, many shell scripts will immediately assign the status to another shell variable, as in:

```
$ badcommand
it fails...
$ STAT=$?
$ echo $STAT
1
$ echo $STAT
1
$
```

We can keep the value around in the variable $STAT and check its value later on.

Although we're showing this in command-line examples, the real use of variables like $? comes in writing scripts. You can usually see if a command worked or not if you are watching it run on your screen. But in a script, the commands may be running unattended.

One of the great features of *bash* is that the scripting language is identical to commands as you type them at a prompt in a terminal window. This makes it much easier to check out syntax and logic as you write your scripts.

The exit status is more often used in scripts, and often in `if` statements, to take different actions depending on the success or failure of a command. Here's a simple example for now, but we will revisit this topic in future recipes:

```
$ somecommand
...
$ if (( $? )) ; then echo failed ; else echo OK; fi
```

See Also

- Recipe 4.5, "Deciding Whether a Command Succeeds"
- Recipe 4.8, "Displaying Error Messages When Failures Occur"
- Recipe 6.2, "Branching on Conditions"

4.3   Running Several Commands in Sequence

Problem

You need to run several commands, but some take a while and you don't want to wait for the last one to finish before issuing the next command.

Solution

There are three solutions to this problem, although the first is rather trivial: just keep typing. A Linux or Unix system is advanced enough to be able to let you type while it works on your previous commands, so you can simply keep typing one command after another.

Another rather simple solution is to type those commands into a file and then tell *bash* to execute the commands in the file—i.e., a simple shell script.

Assume that we want to run three commands: *long*, *medium*, and *short*, each of whose execution time is reflected in its name. We need to run them in that order, but don't want to wait around for *long* to finish before starting the other commands. We could use a shell script (aka *batch file*). Here's a primitive way to do that:

```
$ cat > simple.script
long
medium
```

```
    short
    ^D                            # Ctrl-D, not visible
    $ bash ./simple.script
```

The third, and arguably best, solution is to run each command in sequence. If you want to run each program, regardless if the preceding ones fail, separate them with semicolons:

```
    $ long ; medium ; short
```

If you only want to run the next program if the preceding program worked, and all the programs correctly set exit codes, separate them with double-ampersands:

```
    $ long && medium && short
```

Discussion

The *cat* example was just a very primitive way to enter text into a file. We redirect the output from the command into the file named *simple.script* (for more on redirecting output, see Chapter 3). Better you should use a real editor, but such things are harder to show in examples like this. From now on, when we want to show a script, we'll just either show the text as disembodied text not on a command line, or we will start the example with a command like cat filename to dump the contents of the file to the screen (rather than redirecting output from our typing into the file), and thus display it in the example.

The main point of this simple solution is to demonstrate that more than one command can be put on the *bash* command line. In the first case the second command isn't run until the first command exits, and the third doesn't execute until the second exits and so on, for as many commands as you have on the line. In the second case the second command isn't run unless the first command succeeds, and the third doesn't execute until the second succeeds and so on, for as many commands as you have on the line.

4.4   Running Several Commands All at Once

Problem

You need to run three commands, but they are independent of each other, and don't need to wait for each other to complete.

Solution

You can run a command in the background by putting an ampersand (&) at the end of the command line. Thus, you could fire off all three jobs in rapid succession as follows:

```
    $ long &
    [1] 4592
    $ medium &
```

```
[2] 4593
$ short
$
```

Or better yet, you can do it all on one command line:

```
$ long & medium & short
[1] 4592
[2] 4593
$
```

Discussion

When we run a command in the *background* (there really is no such place in Linux), all that really means is that we disconnect keyboard input from the command and the shell doesn't wait for the command to complete before it gives another prompt and accepts more command input. Output from the job (unless we take explicit action to do otherwise) will still come to the screen, so all three jobs will be interspersing output to the screen.

The odd bits of numerical output are the job number in square brackets, followed by the process ID of the command that we just started in the background. In our example, job 1 (process 4592) is the *long* command, and job 2 (process 4593) is *medium*.

We didn't put *short* into the background since we didn't put an ampersand at the end of the line, so *bash* will wait for it to complete before giving us the shell prompt (the $).

The job number or process ID can be used to provide limited control over the job. You can kill the *long* job with kill %1 (since its job number was 1). Or you could specify the process number (e.g., kill 4592) with the same deadly results.

You can also use the job number to reconnect to a background job. Connect it back to the foreground with fg %1. But if you only had one job running in the background, you wouldn't even need the job number, just fg by itself.

If you start a job and then realize it will take longer to complete than you thought, you can pause it using Ctrl-Z, which will return you to a prompt. You can then type bg to un-pause the job so it will continue running in the background. This is basically adding a trailing & after the fact.

See Also

- Chapter 2 on redirecting output

4.5 Deciding Whether a Command Succeeds

Problem

You need to run some commands, but you only want to run certain commands if certain other ones succeed. For example, you'd like to change directories (using the *cd* command) into a temporary directory and remove all the files. However, you don't want to remove any files if the *cd* fails (e.g., if permissions don't allow you into the directory, or if you spell the directory name wrong).

Solution

We can use the exit status ($?) of the *cd* command in combination with an if statement to do the *rm* only if the *cd* was successful.

```
cd mytmp
if (( $? == 0 )); then rm * ; fi
```

Discussion

Obviously, you wouldn't need to do this if you were typing the commands by hand. You would see any error messages from the *cd* command, and thus you wouldn't type the *rm* command. But scripting is another matter, and this test is very well worth doing to make sure that you don't accidentally erase all the files in the directory where you are running.

Let's say you ran that script from the wrong directory, one that didn't have a subdirectory named *mytmp*. When it runs, the *cd* would fail, so the current directory remains unchanged. Without the if check (the *cd* having failed) the script would just continue on to the next statement. Running the rm * would remove all the files in your current directory. Ouch. The if is worth it.

So how does $? get its value? It is the exit code of the command. For C Language programmers, you'll recognize this as the value of the argument supplied to the exit( ) function; e.g., exit(4); would return a 4. For the shell, zero is considered success and a non-zero value means failure.

If you're writing *bash* scripts, you'll want to be sure that your *bash* scripts explicitly set return values, so that $? is set properly from your script. If you don't, the value set will be the value of the last command run, which you may not want as your result.

See Also

- Recipe 4.2, "Telling If a Command Succeeded or Not"
- Recipe 4.6, "Using Fewer if Statements"

4.6   Using Fewer if Statements

Problem

As a conscientious programmer, you took to heart what we described in the previous recipe, Recipe 4.5, "Deciding Whether a Command Succeeds." You applied the concept to your latest shell script, and now you find that the shell script is unreadable, if with all those if statements checking the return code of every command. Isn't there an alternative?

Solution

Use the double-ampersand operator in *bash* to provide conditional execution:

```
$ cd mytmp && rm *
```

Discussion

Two commands separated by the double ampersands tells *bash* to run the first command and then to run the second command only if the first command succeeds (i.e., its exit status is 0). This is very much like using an if statement to check the exit status of the first command in order to protect the running of the second command:

```
cd mytmp
if (( $? == 0 )); then rm * ; fi
```

The double ampersand syntax is meant to be reminiscent of the logical *and* operator in C Language. If you know your logic (and your C) then you'll recall that if you are evaluating the logical expression A AND B, then the entire expression can only be true if both (sub)expression A and (sub)expression B evaluate to true. If either one is false, the whole expression is false. C Language makes use of this fact, and when you code an expression like if (A && B) { ... }, it will evaluate expression A first. If it is false, it won't even bother to evaluate B since the overall outcome (false) has already been determined (by A being false).

So what does this have to do with *bash*? Well, if the exit status of the first command (the one to the left of the &&) is non-zero (i.e., failed) then it won't bother to evaluate the second expression—i.e., it won't run the other command at all.

If you want to be thorough about your error checking, but don't want if statements all over the place, you can have *bash* exit any time it encounters a failure (i.e., a non-zero exit status) from every command in your script (except in while loops and if statements where it is already capturing and using the exit status) by setting the -e flag.

```
set -e
cd mytmp
rm *
```

Setting the -e flag will cause the shell to exit when a command fails. If the *cd* fails, the script will exit and never even try to execute the rm * command. We don't recommend doing this on an interactive shell, because when the shell exits it will make your shell window go away.

See Also

- Recipe 4.8, "Displaying Error Messages When Failures Occur" for an explanation of the || syntax, which is similar in some ways, but also quite different from the && construct

4.7   Running Long Jobs Unattended

Problem

You ran a job in the background, then exited the shell and went for coffee. When you came back to check, the job was no longer running and it hadn't completed. In fact, your job hadn't progressed very far at all. It seems to have quit as soon as you exited the shell.

Solution

If you want to run a job in the background and expect to exit the shell before the job completes, then you need to *nohup* the job:

```
$ nohup long &
nohup: appending output to `nohup.out'
$
```

Discussion

When you put the job in the background (via the &), it is still a child process of the *bash* shell. When you exit an instance of the shell, *bash* sends a *hangup* (hup) signal to all of its child processes. That's why your job didn't run for very long. As soon as you exited *bash*, it killed your background job. (Hey, you were leaving; how was it supposed to know?)

The *nohup* command simply sets up the child process to ignore hang-up signals. You can still kill a job with the *kill* command, because *kill* sends a SIGTERM signal not a SIGHUP signal. But with *nohup*, *bash* won't inadvertently kill your job when you exit.

The message that *nohup* gives about appending your output is just *nohup* trying to be helpful. Since you are likely to exit the shell after issuing a *nohup* command, your output destination will likely go away—i.e., the *bash* session in your terminal window would no longer be active. So, where would the job be able to write? More importantly, writing to a non-existent destination would cause a failure. So *nohup* redirects the output for you, appending it (not overwriting, but adding at the end) to a file named *nohup.out* in the current directory. You can explicitly redirect the output elsewhere on the command line and *nohup* is smart enough to detect that this has happened and doesn't use *nohup.out* for your output.

See Also

- Chapter 2 for various recipes on redirecting output, since you probably want to do that for a background job
- Recipe 10.1, ""Daemon-izing" Your Script"
- Recipe 17.4, "Recovering Disconnected Sessions Using screen"

4.8   Displaying Error Messages When Failures Occur

Problem

You need your shell script to be verbose about failures. You want to see error messages when commands don't work, but if statements tend to distract from the visual flow of statements.

Solution

A common idiom among some shell programmers is to use the || with commands to spit out debug or error messages. Here's an example:

```
cmd || printf "%b" "cmd failed. You're on your own\n"
```

Discussion

Similar to how the && didn't bother to evaluate the second expression if the first was false, the || tells the shell not to bother to evaluate the second expression if the first one is true (i.e., succeeds). As with &&, the || syntax harkens back to logic and C Language where the outcome is determined (as true) if the first expression in A OR B evaluates to true—so there's no need to evaluate the second expression. In *bash*, if the first expression returns 0 (i.e., succeeds) then it just continues on. Only if the first expression (i.e., exit value of the command) returns a non-zero value must it evaluate the second part, and thus run the other command.

Warning—don't be fooled by this:

```
cmd || printf "%b" "FAILED.\n" ; exit 1
```

The exit will be executed in either case! The OR is only between those two commands. If we want to have the *exit* happen only on error, we need to group it with the *printf* so that both are considered as a unit. The desired syntax would be:

```
cmd || { printf "%b" "FAILED.\n" ; exit 1 ; }
```

Due to an oddity of *bash* syntax, the semicolon after the last command and just before the } is required, and that closing brace must be separated by whitespace from the surrounding text.

See Also

- Recipe 2.14, "Saving or Grouping Output from Several Commands"
- Recipe 4.6, "Using Fewer if Statements" for an explanation of && syntax

4.9 Running Commands from a Variable

Problem

You want to run different commands in your script depending on circumstances. How can you vary which commands run?

Solution

There are many solutions to this problem—it's what scripting is all about. In coming chapters we'll discuss various programming logic that can be used to solve this problem, such as if/then/else, case statements, and more. But here's a slightly different approach that reveals something about *bash*. We can use the contents of a variable (more on those in Chapter 5) not just for parameters, but also for the command itself.

```
FN=/tmp/x.x
PROG=echo
$PROG $FN
PROG=cat
$PROG $FN
```

Discussion

We can assign the program name to a variable (here we use $PROG), and then when we refer to that variable in the place where a command name would be expected, it uses the value of that variable ($PROG) as the command to run. The *bash* shell parses the command line, substitutes the values of its variables and takes the result of all the substitutions and then treats that as the command line, as if it had been typed that way verbatim.

 Be careful about the variable names you use. Some programs such as InfoZip use environment variables such as $ZIP and $UNZIP to pass settings to the program itself. So if you do something like ZIP='/usr/bin/zip', you can spend days pulling your hair out wondering why it works fine from the command line, but not in your script. Trust us. We learned this one the hard way. Also, RTFM.

See Also

- Chapter 11
- Recipe 14.3, "Setting a Secure $PATH"
- Recipe 16.19, "Creating Self-Contained, Portable RC Files"
- Recipe 16.20, "Getting Started with a Custom Configuration"
- Appendix C for a descripton of all the various substitutions that are preformed on a command line; you'll want to read a few more chapters before tackling that subject

4.10 Running All Scripts in a Directory

Problem

You want to run a series of scripts, but the list keeps changing; you're always adding new scripts, but you don't want to continuously modify a master list.

Solution

Put the scripts you want to run in a directory, and let *bash* run everything that it finds. Instead of keeping a master list, simply look at the contents of that directory. Here's a script that will run everything it finds in a directory:

```
for SCRIPT in /path/to/scripts/dir/*
do
    if [ -f $SCRIPT -a -x $SCRIPT ]
    then
        $SCRIPT
    fi
done
```

Discussion

We will discuss the for loop and the if statement in greater detail in Chapter 6, but this gives you a taste. The variable $SCRIPT will take on successive values for each file that matches the wildcard pattern *, which matches everything in the current directory (except invisible dot files, which begin with a period). If it is a file (the -f test) and has execute permissions set (the -x test), the shell will then try to run that script.

In this simple example, we have provided no way to specify any arguments to the scripts as they are executed. This simple script may work well for your personal needs, but wouldn't be considered robust; some might consider it downright dangerous. But we hope it gives you an idea of what lies ahead: some programming-language-style scripting capabilities.

See Also

- Chapter 6 for more about for loops and if statements

CHAPTER 5
Basic Scripting: Shell Variables

bash shell programming is a lot like any kind of programming, and that includes having variables—containers that hold strings and numbers, which can be changed, compared, and passed around. *bash* variables have some very special operators that can be used when you refer to the variable. *bash* also has some important built-in variables, ones that provide important information about the other variables in your script. This chapter takes a look at *bash* variables and some special mechanisms for referencing variables, and shows how they can be put to use in your scripts.

Variables in a *bash* script are often written as all-uppercase names, though that is not required—just a common practice. You don't need to declare them; just use them where you want them. They are basically all of type string, though some *bash* operations can treat their contents as a number. They look like this in use:

```
# trivial script using shell variables
# (but at least it is commented!)
MYVAR="something"
echo $MYVAR
# similar but with no quotes
MY_2ND=anotherone
echo $MY_2ND
# quotes are needed here:
MYOTHER="more stuff to echo"
echo $MYOTHER
```

There are two significant aspects of *bash* variable syntax that may not be intuitively obvious regarding shell variables. First, on the assignment, the name=value syntax is straightforward enough, but there cannot be any spaces around the equal sign.

Let's consider for a moment why this is the case. Remember that the basic semantics of the shell is to launch programs—you name the program on the command line and that is the program that gets launched. Any words of text that follow after it on the command line are passed along as arguments to the program. For example when you type:

```
$ ls filename
```

the word `ls` is the name of the command and `filename` is the first and only argument in this example.

Why is that relevant? Well, consider what a variable assignment in *bash* would look like if you allowed spaces around the equal sign, like this:

```
MYVAR = something
```

Can you see that the shell would have a hard time distinguishing between the name of a command to invoke (like the *ls* example) and the assignment of a variable? This would be especially true for commands that can use = symbols as one or more of their arguments (e.g., *test*). So to keep it simple, the shell doesn't allow spaces around the equal sign in an assignment. Otherwise it would see them just as separate words. The flip side of this is also worth noting—don't use an equal sign in a filename, especially not one for a shell script (it is possible, just not recommended).

The second aspect of shell variable syntax worth noting is the use of the dollar sign when referring to the variable. You don't use the dollar sign on the variable name to assign it a value, but you do use the dollar sign to get the value of the variable. (The exception to this is using variables inside a $((...)) expression.) In compiler jargon, this difference in syntax for assigning and retrieving the value is the difference between the L-value and the R-value of the variable (for Left and Right side of an assignment operator).

Once again, the reason for this is for simple disambiguation. Consider the following:

```
MYVAR=something
echo MYVAR is now MYVAR
```

As this example tries to point out, how would one distinguish between the literal string "MYVAR" and the value of the $MYVAR variable? Use quotes, you say? If you were to require quoting around literal strings then everything would get a lot messier—you would have to quote every non-variable name, which includes commands! Who wants to type:

```
$ "ls" "-l" "/usr/bin/xmms"
```

(Yes, for those of you who thought about trying it, it does work.) So rather than have to put quotes around everything, the onus is put on the variable reference by using the R-value syntax. Put a dollar sign on a variable name when you want to get at the value associated with that variable name.

```
MYVAR=something
echo MYVAR is now $MYVAR
```

Just remember that since everything in *bash* is strings, we need the dollar sign to show a variable reference.

5.1 Documenting Your Script

Problem

Before we say one more word about shell scripts or variables, we have to say something about documenting your scripts. After all, you need to be able to understand your script even when several months have passed since you wrote it.

Solution

Document your script with comments. The # character denotes the beginning of a comment. All the characters after it on that line are ignored by the shell.

```
#
# This is a comment.
#
# Use comments frequently.
# Comments are your friends.
```

Discussion

Some people have described shell syntax, regular expressions, and other parts of shell scripting as *write only* syntax, implying that it is nearly impossible to understand the intricacies of many shell scripts.

One of your best defenses against letting your shell scripts fall into this trap is the liberal use of comments (another is the use of meaningful variable names). It helps to put a comment before strange syntax or terse expressions.

```
# replace the semi with a blank
NEWPATH=${PATH/;/ }
#
# switch the text on either side of a semi
sed -e 's/^\(.*\);\(.*\)$/\2;\1/' < $FILE
```

Comments can even be typed in at the command prompt with an interactive shell. This can be turned off, but it is on by default. There may be a few occasions when it is useful to make interactive comments.

See Also

- "shopt Options" in Appendix A gives the option for turning interactive comments on or off

5.2 Embedding Documentation in Shell Scripts

Problem

You want a simple way to provide formatted end-user documentation (e.g., man or html pages) for your script. You want to keep both code and documentation markup in the same file to simplify updates, distribution, and revision control.

Solution

Embed documentation in the script using the "do nothing" built-in (a colon) and a here-document:

```
#!/usr/bin/env bash
# cookbook filename: embedded_documentation

echo 'Shell script code goes here'

# Use a : NOOP and here document to embed documentation,
: <<'END_OF_DOCS'

Embedded documentation such as Perl's Plain Old Documentation (POD),
or even plain text here.

Any accurate documentation is better than none at all.

Sample documentation in Perl's Plain Old Documentation (POD) format adapted  from
CODE/ch07/Ch07.001_Best_Ex7.1 and 7.2 in Perl Best Practices.

=head1 NAME

MY~PROGRAM--One line description here

=head1 SYNOPSIS

  MY~PROGRAM [OPTIONS] <file>

=head1 OPTIONS

  -h = This usage.
  -v = Be verbose.
  -V = Show version, copyright and license information.


=head1 DESCRIPTION

A full description of the application and its features.
May include numerous subsections (i.e. =head2, =head3, etc.)


[...]
```

```
=head1 LICENSE AND COPYRIGHT

=cut

END_OF_DOCS
```

Then to extract and use that POD documentation, try these commands.

```
# To read on-screen, automatically paginated
$ perldoc myscript


# Just the "usage" sections
$ pod2usage myscript


# Create an HTML version
$ pod2html myscript > myscript.html


# Create a man page
$ pod2man myscript > myscript.1
```

Discussion

Any plain text documentation or mark-up can be used this way, either interspersed throughout the code or better yet collected at the end of the script. Since computer systems that have *bash* will probably also have Perl, its Plain Old Documentation (POD) may be a good choice. Perl usually comes with *pod2** programs to convert POD to HTML, LaTeX, man, text, and usage files.

Damian Conway's *Perl Best Practices* (O'Reilly) has some excellent library module and application documentation templates that could be easily translated into any documentation format including plain text. In that book, see *CODE/ch07/Ch07.001_ Best_Ex7.1* and 7.2 in the examples tarball (*http://examples.oreilly.com/perlbp/PBP_ code.tar.gz*).

If you keep all of your embedded documentation at the very bottom of the script, you could also add an exit 0 right before the documentation begins. That will simply exit the script rather than force the shell to parse each line looking for the end of the here-document, so it will be a little faster. Thought, you need to be careful not to do that if you intersperse code and embedded documentation in the body of the script.

See Also

- *http://examples.oreilly.com/perlbp/PBP_code.tar.gz*
- "Embedding manpages in Shell Scripts with kshdoc" at *http://www.unixlabplus. com/unix-prog/kshdoc/kshdoc.html*

5.3 Promoting Script Readability

Problem

You'd like to make your script as readable as possible for ease of understanding and future maintenance.

Solution

- Document your script as noted in Recipe 5.1, "Documenting Your Script" and Recipe 5.2, "Embedding Documentation in Shell Scripts"
- Indent and use vertical whitespace wisely
- Use meaningful variable names
- Use functions, and give them meaningful names
- Break lines at meaningful places at less than 76 characters or so
- Put the most meaningful bits to the left

Discussion

Document your intent, not the trivial details of the code. If you follow the rest of the points, the code should be pretty clear. Write reminders, provide sample data layouts or headers, and make a note of all the details that are in your head now, as you write the code. But document the code itself too if it is subtle or obscure.

We recommend indenting using four spaces per level, with no tabs and especially no mixed tabs. There are many reasons for this, though it often is a matter of personal preference or company standards. After all, four spaces is always four spaces, no matter how your editor (excepting proportional fonts) or printer is set. Four spaces is big enough to be easily visible as you glance across the script but small enough that you can have several levels of indenting without running the lines off the right side of your screen or printed page. We also suggest indenting continued lines with two additional spaces, or as needed, to make the code the most clear.

Use vertical white space, with separators if you like them, to create blocks of similar code. Of course you'll do that with functions as well.

Use meaningful names for variables and functions, and spell them out. The only time $i or $x is *ever* acceptable is in a for loop. You may think that short, cryptic names are saving you time and typing now, but we guarantee that you will lose that time 10- or 100-fold somewhere down the line when you have to fix or modify that script.

Break long lines at around 76 characters. Yes, we know that most of the screens (or rather terminal programs) can do a lot more than that. But 80 character paper and screens are still the default, and it never hurts to have some white space to the right of the code. Constantly having to scroll to the right or having lines wrap on the screen or printout is annoying and distracting. Don't cause it.

Unfortunately, there are sometimes exceptions to the long line rule. When creating lines to pass elsewhere, perhaps via Secure Shell (SSH), and in certain other cases, breaking up the line can cause many more code headaches than it solves. But in most cases, it makes sense.

Try to put the most meaningful bits to the left when you break a line because we read shell code left-to-right, so the unusual fact of a continued line will stand out more. It's also easier to scan down the left edge of the code for continued lines, should you need to find them. Which is more clear?

```
# Good
[ $results ] \
  && echo "Got a good result in $results" \
  || echo 'Got an empty result, something is wrong'


# Also good
[ $results ] && echo "Got a good result in $results" \
             || echo 'Got an empty result, something is wrong'


# OK, but not ideal
[ $results ] && echo "Got a good result in $results" \
  || echo 'Got an empty result, something is wrong'


# Bad
[ $results ] && echo "Got a good result in $results" || echo 'Got an empty result,
something is wrong'


# Bad
[ $results ] && \
  echo "Got a good result in $results" || \
  echo 'Got an empty result, something is wrong'
```

See Also

- Recipe 5.1, "Documenting Your Script"
- Recipe 5.2, "Embedding Documentation in Shell Scripts"

5.4   Separating Variable Names from Surrounding Text

Problem

You need to print a variable along with other text. You are using the dollar sign in referring to the variable. But how do you distinguish the end of the variable name from other text that follows? For example, say you wanted to use a shell variable as part of a filename, as in:

```
for FN in 1 2 3 4 5
do
    somescript /tmp/rep$FNport.txt
done
```

How will the shell read that? It will think that the variable name starts with the $ and ends with the punctuation. In other words, it will think that $FNport is the variable name, not the intended $FN.

Solution

Use the full syntax for a variable reference, which includes not just the dollar sign, but also braces around the variable name:

```
somescript /tmp/rep${SUM}bay.txt
```

Discussion

Because shell variables are only alphanumeric characters, there are many instances where you won't need to use the braces. Any whitespace or punctuation (except underscore) provides enough of a clue to where the variable name ends. But when in doubt, use the braces.

See Also

- Recipe 1.6, "Using Shell Quoting"

5.5   Exporting Variables

Problem

You defined a variable in one script, but when you called another script it didn't know about the variable.

Solution

Export variables that you want to pass on to other scripts:

```
export MYVAR
export NAME=value
```

Discussion

Sometimes it's a good thing that one script doesn't know about the other script's variables. If you called a shell script from within a for loop in the first script, you wouldn't want the second script messing up the iterations of your for loop.

But sometimes you do want the information passed along. In those cases, you can export the variable so that its value is passed along to any other program that it invokes.

If you want to see a list of all the exported variables, just type the built-in command *env* (or export -p) for a list of each variable and its value. All of these are available for your script when it runs. Many have already been set up by the *bash* startup scripts (see Chapter 16 for more on configuring and customizing *bash*).

You can have the export statement just name the variable that will be exported. Though the export statement can be put anywhere prior to where you need the value to be exported, script writers often group these export statements together like variable declarations at the front of a script. You can also make the export part of any variable assignment, though that won't work in old versions of the shell.

Once exported, you can assign repeatedly to the variable without exporting it each time. So, sometimes you'll see statements like:

```
export FNAME
export SIZE
export MAX
...
MAX=2048
SIZE=64
FNAME=/tmp/scratch
```

and at other times you'll see:

```
export FNAME=/tmp/scratch
export SIZE=64
export MAX=2048
...
FNAME=/tmp/scratch2
...
FNAME=/tmp/stillexported
```

One word of caution: the exported variables are, in effect, *call by value*. Changing the value of the exported value in the called script does not change that variable's value back in the calling script.

This begs the question: "How would you pass back a changed value from the called script?" Answer: you can't.

Is there a better answer? Unfortunately, there isn't. You can only design your scripts so that they don't need to do this. What mechanisms have people used to cope with this limitation?

One approach might be to have the called script echo its changed value as output from the script, letting you read the output with the resulting changed value. For example, suppose one script exports a variable $VAL and then calls another script that modifies $VAL. To get the new value returned, you have to write the new value to standard out and capture that value and assign it to $VAL, as in:

```
VAL=$(anotherscript)
```

in order to change the value of $VAL (see Recipe 10.5, "Using Functions: Parameters and Return Values"). You could even change multiple values and echo them each in turn to standard out. The calling program could then use a shell read to capture each line of output one at a time into the appropriate variables. This requires that the called script produce no other output to standard out (at least not before or among the variables), and sets up a very strong interdependency between the scripts (not good from a maintenance standpoint).

See Also

- help export
- Chapter 16 for more information on configuring and customizing bash
- Recipe 5.6, "Seeing All Variable Values"
- Recipe 10.5, "Using Functions: Parameters and Return Values"
- Recipe 19.5, "Expecting to Change Exported Variables"

5.6   Seeing All Variable Values

Problem

How can I see which variables have been exported and what values they have? Do I have to *echo* each one by hand? How would I tell if they are exported?

Solution

Use the *set* command to see the value of all variables and function definitions in the current shell.

Use the *env* (or export -p) command to see only those variables that have been exported and would be available to a subshell.

Discussion

The *set* command, with no other arguments, produces (on standard out) a list of all the shell variables currently defined along with their values, in a `name=value` format. The *env* command is similiar. If you run either, you will find a rather long list of variables, many of which you might not recognize. Those variables have been created for you, as part of the shell's startup process.

The list produced by *env* is a subset of the list produced by *set*, since not all variables are exported.

If there are particular variables or values that are of interest, and you don't want the entire list, just pipe it into a *grep* command. For example:

```
$ set | grep MY
```

will show only those variables whose name or value has the two-character sequence MY somewhere in it.

See Also

- help set
- help export
- man env
- Chapter 16 for more on configuring and customizing bash
- Appendix A for reference lists for all of the built-in shell variables

5.7   Using Parameters in a Shell Script

Problem

You also want users to be able to invoke your script with a parameter. You could require that users set a shell variable, but that seems clunky. You also need to pass data to another script. You could agree on environment variables, but that ties the two scripts together too closely.

Solution

Use command-line parameters. Any words put on the command line of a shell script are available to the script as numbered variables:

```
# simple shell script
echo $1
```

The script will echo the first parameter supplied on the command line when it is invoked. Here it is in action:

```
$ cat simplest.sh
# simple shell script
echo ${1}
$ ./simplest.sh you see what I mean
you
$ ./simplest.sh one more time
one
$
```

Discussion

The other parameters are available as ${2}, ${3}, ${4}, ${5}, and so on. You don't need the braces for the single-digit numbers, except to separate the variable name from the surrounding text. Typical scripts have only a handful of parameters, but when you get to ${10} you better use the braces or else the shell will interpret that as ${1} followed immediately by the literal string 0 as we see here:

```
$ cat tricky.sh
echo $1 $10 ${10}
$ ./tricky.sh I II III IV V VI VII VIII IX X XI
I I0 X
$
```

The tenth argument has the value X but if you write $10 in your script, then the shell will give you $1, the first parameter, followed immediately by a zero, the literal character that you put next to the $1 in your echo statement.

See Also

- Recipe 5.4, "Separating Variable Names from Surrounding Text"

5.8   Looping Over Arguments Passed to a Script

Problem

You want to take some set of actions for a given list of arguments. You could write your shell script to do that for one argument and use $1 to reference the parameter. But what if you'd like to do this for a whole bunch of files? You would like to be able to invoke your script like this:

```
actall  *.txt
```

knowing that the shell will pattern match and build a list of filenames that match the *.txt pattern (any filename ending with .txt).

Solution

Use the shell special variable $* to refer to all of your arguments, and use that in a for loop like this:

```
#!/usr/bin/env bash
# cookbook filename: chmod_all.1
#
# change permissions on a bunch of files
#
for FN in $*
do
    echo changing $FN
    chmod 0750 $FN
done
```

Discussion

The variable $FN is our choice; we could have used any shell variable name we wanted there. The $* refers to all the arguments supplied on the command line. For example, if the user types:

```
$ ./actall abc.txt another.txt allmynotes.txt
```

the script will be invoked with $1 equal to *abc.txt* and $2 equal to *another.txt* and $3 equal to *allmynotes.txt*, but $* will be equal to the entire list. In other words, after the shell has substituted the list for $* in the for statement, it will be as if the script had read:

```
for FN in abc.txt another.txt allmynotes.txt
do
  echo changing $FN
  chmod 0750 $FN
done
```

The for loop will take one value at a time from the list, assign it to the variable $FN and proceed through the list of statements between the do and the done. It will then repeat that loop for each of the other values.

But you're not finished yet! This script works fine when filenames have no spaces in them, but sometimes you encounter filenames with spaces. Read the next two recipes to see how this script can be improved.

See Also

- help for
- Recipe 6.12, "Looping with a Count"

5.9 Handling Parameters with Blanks

Problem

You wrote a script that took a filename as a parameter and it seemed to work, but then one time your script failed. The filename, it turns out, had an embedded blank.

Solution

You'll need to be careful to quote any shell parameters that might contain filenames. When referring to a variable, put the variable reference inside double quotes.

Discussion

Thanks a lot, Apple! Trying to be user friendly, they popularized the concept of space characters as valid characters in filenames, so users could name their files with names like *My Report* and *Our Dept Data* instead of the ugly and unreadable

MyReport and *Our_Dept_Data*. (How could anyone possibly understand what those old-fashioned names meant?) Well, that makes life tough for the shell, because the space is the fundamental separator between words, and so filenames were always kept to a single word. Not so anymore.

So how do we handle this?

Where a shell script once had simply `ls -l $1`, it is better to write `ls -l "$1"` with quotes around the parameter. Otherwise, if the parameter has an embedded blank, it will be parsed into separate words, and only part of the name will be in `$1`. Let's show you how this *doesn't* work:

```
$ cat simpls.sh
# simple shell script
ls -l ${1}
$
$ ./simple.sh Oh the Waste
ls: Oh: No such file or directory
$
```

When we don't put any quotes around the filename as we invoke the script, then *bash* sees three arguments and substitutes the first argument (Oh) for `$1`. The *ls* command runs with Oh as its only argument and can't find that file.

So now let's put quotes around the filename when we invoke the script:

```
$ ./simpls.sh "Oh the Waste"
ls: Oh: No such file or directory
ls: the: No such file or directory
ls: Waste: No such file or directory
$
```

Still not good. *bash* has taken the three-word filename and substituted it for `$1` on the *ls* command line in our script. So far so good. Since we don't have quotes around the variable reference in our script, however, *ls* sees each word as a separate argument, i.e., as separate filenames. It can't find any of them.

Let's try a script that quotes the variable reference:

```
$ cat quoted.sh
# note the quotes
ls -l "${1}"
$
$ ./quoted.sh "Oh the Waste"
-rw-r--r--  1 smith users 28470 2007-01-11 19:22 Oh the Waste
$
```

When we quoted the reference "{$1}" it was treated as a single word (a single filename), and the *ls* then had only one argument—the filename—and it could complete its task.

See Also

- Chapter 19 for common goofs
- Recipe 1.6, "Using Shell Quoting"
- Appendix C for more information on command-line processing

5.10   Handling Lists of Parameters with Blanks

Problem

OK, you have quotes around your variable as the previous recipe recommended. But you're still getting errors. It's just like the script from the Recipe 5.8, "Looping Over Arguments Passed to a Script," but it fails when a file has a blank in its name:

```
#
for FN in $*
do
    chmod 0750 "$FN"
done
```

Solution

It has to do with the $* in the script, used in the for loop. For this case we need to use a different but related shell variable, $@. When it is quoted, the resulting list has quotes around each argument separately. The shell script should be written as follows:

```
#!/usr/bin/env bash
# cookbook filename: chmod_all.2
#
# change permissions on a bunch of files
# with better quoting in case of filenames with blanks
#
for FN in "$@"
do
    chmod 0750 "$FN"
done
```

Discussion

The parameter $* expands to the list of arguments supplied to the shell script. If you invoke your script like this:

```
$ myscript these are args
```

then $* refers to the three arguments these are args. And when used in a for loop, such as:

```
for FN in $*
```

then the first time through the loop, $FN is assigned the first word (these) and the second time, the second word (are), etc.

If the arguments are filenames and they are put on the command line by pattern matching, as when you invoke the script this way:

```
$ myscript *.mp3
```

then the shell will match all the files in the current directory whose names end with the four characters .mp3, and they will be passed to the script. So consider an example where there are three MP3 files whose names are:

```
vocals.mp3
cool music.mp3
tophit.mp3
```

The second song title has a blank in the filename between cool and music. When you invoke the script with:

```
$ myscript  *.mp3
```

you'll get, in effect:

```
$ myscript  vocals.mp3 cool music.mp3 tophit.mp3
```

If your script contains the line:

```
for FN in $*
```

that will expand to:

```
for FN in vocals.mp3 cool music.mp3 tophit.mp3
```

which has four words in its list, not three. The second song title has a blank as the fifth character (cool music.mp3), and the blank causes the shell to see that as two separate words (cool and music.mp3), so $FN will be cool on the second iteration through the for loop. On the third iteration, $FN will have the value music.mp3 but that, too, is not the name of your file. You'll get file-not-found error messages.

It might seem logical to try quoting the $* but

```
for FN in "$*"
```

will expand to:

```
for FN in  "vocals.mp3 cool music.mp3 tophit.mp3"
```

and you will end up with a single value for $FN equal to the entire list. You'll get an error message like this:

```
chmod: cannot access 'vocals.mp3 cool music.mp3 tophit.mp3': No such file or
directory
```

Instead you need to use the shell variable $@ and quote it. Unquoted, $* and $@ give you the same thing. But when quoted, *bash* treats them differently. A reference to $* inside of quotes gives the entire list inside one set of quotes, as we just saw. But a reference to $@ inside of quotes returns not one string but a list of quoted strings, one for each argument.

In our example using the MP3 filenames:

```
for FN in "$@"
```

will expand to:

```
for FN in "vocals.mp3" "cool music.mp3" "tophit.mp3"
```

and you can see that the second filename is now quoted so that its blank will be kept as part of its name and not considered a separator between two words.

The second time through this loop, $FN will be assigned the value cool music.mp3, which has an embedded blank. So be careful how you refer to $FN—you'll probably want to put it in quotes too, so that the space in the filename is kept as part of that string and not used as a separator. That is, you'll want to use "$FN" as in:

```
$ chmod 0750 "$FN"
```

Shouldn't you always use "$@" in your for loop? Well, it's a lot harder to type, so for quick-and-dirty scripts, when you know your filenames don't have blanks, it's probably OK to keep using the old-fashioned $* syntax. For more robust scripting though, we recommend "$@" as the safer way to go. We'll probably use them interchangeably throughout this book, because even though we know better, old habits die hard—and some of us never use blanks in our filenames! (Famous last words.)

See Also

- Recipe 5.8, "Looping Over Arguments Passed to a Script"
- Recipe 5.9, "Handling Parameters with Blanks"
- Recipe 5.12, "Consuming Arguments"
- Recipe 6.12, "Looping with a Count"

5.11 Counting Arguments

Problem

You need to know with how many parameters the script was invoked.

Solution

Use the shell built-in variable ${#}. Here's some scripting to enforce an exact count of three arguments:

```
#!/usr/bin/env bash
# cookbook filename: check_arg_count
#
# Check for the correct # of arguments:
# Use this syntax or use: if [ $# -lt 3 ]
if (( $# < 3 ))
then
```

```
        printf "%b" "Error. Not enough arguments.\n" >&2
        printf "%b" "usage: myscript file1 op file2\n" >&2
        exit 1
elif (( $# > 3 ))
then
        printf "%b" "Error. Too many arguments.\n" >&2
        printf "%b" "usage: myscript file1 op file2\n" >&2
        exit 2
else
        printf "%b" "Argument count correct.  Proceeding...\n"
fi
```

And here is what it looks like when we run it, once with too many arguments and once with the correct number of arguments:

```
$ ./myscript myfile is copied into yourfile
Error. Too many arguments.
usage: myscript file1 op file2

$ ./myscript myfile copy yourfile
Argument count correct.  Proceeding...
```

Discussion

After the opening comments (always a helpful thing to have in a script), we have the if test to see whether the number of arguments supplied (found in $#) is greater than three. If so, we print an error message, remind the user of the correct usage, and exit.

The output from the error messages are redirected to standard error. This is in keeping with the intent of standard error as the channel for all error messages.

The script also has a different return value depending on the error that was detected. While not that significant here, it is useful for any script that might be invoked by other scripts, so that there is a programmatic way not only to detect failure (non-zero exit value), but to distinguish between error types.

One word of caution: don't confuse ${#} with ${#VAR} or even ${VAR#alt} just because they all use the # inside of braces. The first gives the number of arguments the second gives the length of the value in the variable VAR, and the third does a certain kind of substitution.

See Also

- Recipe 4.2, "Telling If a Command Succeeded or Not"
- Recipe 5.1, "Documenting Your Script"
- Recipe 5.12, "Consuming Arguments"
- Recipe 5.18, "Changing Pieces of a String"
- Recipe 6.12, "Looping with a Count"

5.12   Consuming Arguments

Problem

For any serious shell script, you are likely to have two kinds of arguments—options that modify the behavior of the script and the real arguments with which you want to work. You need a way to get rid of the option argument(s) after you've processed them.

Remember this script:

```
for FN in "$@"
do
     echo changing $FN
     chmod 0750 "$FN"
done
```

It's simple enough—it echoes the filename that it is working on, then it changes that file's permissions. What if you want it to work quietly sometimes, not echoing the filename? How would we add an option to turn off this verbose behavior while pre-serving the for loop?

Solution

```
#!/usr/bin/env bash
# cookbook filename: use_up_option
#
# use and consume an option
#
# parse the optional argument
VERBOSE=0;
if [[ $1 = -v ]]
then
     VERBOSE=1;
     shift;
fi
#
# the real work is here
#
for FN in "$@"
do
     if (( VERBOSE == 0 ))
     then
          echo changing $FN
     fi
     chmod 0750 "$FN"
done
```

Discussion

We add a flag variable, $VERBOSE, to tell us whether or not to echo the filename as we work. But once the shell script has seen the -v and set the flag, we don't want the -v in the argument list any more. The shift statement tells *bash* to shift its arguments down one position, getting rid of the first argument ($1) as $2 becomes $1, and $3 becomes $2, and so on.

That way, when the for loop runs, the list of parameters (in $@) no longer contains the -v but starts with the next parameter.

This approach of parsing arguments is alright for handling a single option. But if you want more than one option, you need a bit more logic. By convention, options to a shell script (usually) are not dependent on position; e.g., myscript -a -p should be the same as myscript -p -a. Moreover, a robust script should be able to handle repeated options and either ignore them or report an error. For more robust parsing, see the recipe on *bash*'s getopts built-in (Recipe 13.1, "Parsing Arguments for Your Shell Script").

See Also

- help shift
- Recipe 5.8, "Looping Over Arguments Passed to a Script"
- Recipe 5.11, "Counting Arguments"
- Recipe 5.12, "Consuming Arguments"
- Recipe 6.15, "Parsing Command-Line Arguments"
- Recipe 13.1, "Parsing Arguments for Your Shell Script"
- Recipe 13.2, "Parsing Arguments with Your Own Error Messages"

5.13   Getting Default Values

Problem

You have a shell script that takes arguments supplied on the command line. You'd like to provide default values so that the most common value(s) can be used without needing to type them every time.

Solution

Use the ${:-} syntax when referring to the parameter, and use it to supply a default value:

```
FILEDIR=${1:-"/tmp"}
```

Discussion

There are a series of special operators available when referencing a shell variable. This one, the :- operator, says that if $1 is not set or is null then it will use what follows, /tmp in our example, as the value. Otherwise it will use the value that is already set in $1. It can be used on any shell variable, not just the positional parameters (1, 2, 3, etc.), but they are probably the most common use.

Of course you could do this the long way by constructing an if statement and checking to see if the variable is null or unset (we leave that as an exercise to the reader), but this sort of thing is so common in shell scripts that this syntax has been welcomed as a convenient shorthand.

See Also

- *bash* manpage on parameter substitution
- *Learning the bash Shell* by Cameron Newham (O'Reilly), pages 91–92
- *Classic Shell Scripting* by Nelson H.F. Beebe and Arnold Robbins (O'Reilly), pages 113–114
- Recipe 5.14, "Setting Default Values"

5.14   Setting Default Values

Problem

Your script may rely on certain environment variables, either widely used ones (e.g., $USER) or ones specific to your own business. If you want to build a robust shell script, you should make sure that these variables do have a reasonable value. You want to guarantee a reasonable default value. How?

Solution

Use the assignment operator in the shell variable reference the first time you refer to it to assign a value to the variable if it doesn't already have one, as in:

```
cd ${HOME:=/tmp}
```

Discussion

The reference to $HOME in the example above will return the current value of $HOME unless it is empty or not set at all. In those cases (empty or not set), it will return the value /tmp, which will also be assigned to $HOME so that further references to $HOME will have this new value.

We can see this in action here:

```
$ echo ${HOME:=/tmp}
/home/uid002
$ unset HOME     # generally not wise to do
$ echo ${HOME:=/tmp}
/tmp
$ echo $HOME
```

```
/tmp
$ cd ; pwd
/tmp
$
```

Once we unset the variable it no longer had any value. When we then used the `:=` operator as part of our reference to it, the new value (`/tmp`) was substituted. The subsequent references to `$HOME` returned its new value.

One important exception to keep in mind about the assignment operator: this mechanism will not work with positional parameter arguments (e.g., `$1` or `$*`). For those cases, use `:-` in expressions like `${1:-default}`, which will return the value without trying to do the assignment.

As an aside, it might help you to remember some of these crazy symbols if you think of the visual difference between `${VAR:=value}` and `${VAR:-value}`. The `:=` will do an assignment as well as return the value on the right of the operator. The `:-` will do half of that—it just returns the value but doesn't do the assignment—so its symbol is only half of an equal sign (i.e., one horizontal bar, not two). If this doesn't help, forget that we mentioned it.

See Also

- Recipe 5.13, "Getting Default Values"

5.15   Using null As a Valid Default Value

Problem

You need to set a default value, but you want to allow an empty string as a valid value. You only want to substitute the default in the case where the value is unset.

The `${:=}` operator has two cases where the new value will be used: first, when the value of the shell variable has previously not been set (or has been explicitly unset); and second, where the value has been set but is empty, as in `HOME=""` or `HOME=$OTHER` (where `$OTHER` had no value).

Solution

The shell can distinguish between these two cases, and omitting the colon (`:`) indicates that you want to make the substitution only if the value is unset. If you write only `${HOME=/tmp}` without the colon, the assignment will take place only in the case where the variable is not set (never set or explicitly unset).

Discussion

Let's play with the $HOME variable again, but this time without the colon in the operator:

```
$ echo ${HOME=/tmp}  # no substitution needed
/home/uid002
$ HOME=""       # generally not wise
$ echo ${HOME=/tmp}  # will NOT substitute

$ unset HOME     # generally not wise
$ echo ${HOME=/tmp}     # will substitute
/tmp
$ echo $HOME
/tmp
$
```

In the case where we simply made the $HOME variable an empty string, the = operator didn't do the substitution since $HOME did have a value, albeit null. But when we unset the variable, the substitution occurs. If you want to allow for empty strings, use just the = with no colon. Most times, though, the := is used because you can do little with an empty value, deliberate or not.

See Also

- Recipe 5.13, "Getting Default Values"
- Recipe 5.14, "Setting Default Values"

5.16   Using More Than Just a Constant String for Default

Problem

You need something more than just a constant string as the default value for the variable.

Solution

You can use quite a bit more on the righthand side of these shell variable references. For example:

```
cd ${BASE:="$(pwd)"}
```

Discussion

As the example shows, the value that will be substituted doesn't have to be just a string constant. Rather it can be the result of a more complex shell expression, including running commands in a subshell (as in the example). In our example, if

$BASE is not set, the shell will run the *pwd* built-in command (to get the current directory) and use the string that it returns as the value.

So what can you do on the righthand side of this (and the other similar) operators? The *bash* manpage says that what we put to the right of the operator "is subject to tilde expansion, parameter expansion, command substitution, and arithmetic expansion."

Here is what that means:

- Parameter expansion means that we could use other shell variables in this expression, as in: ${BASE:=${HOME}}.
- Tilde expansion means that we can use expressions like ~bob and it will expand that to refer to the home directory of the username bob. Use ${BASE:=~uid17} to set the default value to the home directory for user uid17, but don't put quotes around this string, as that will defeat the tilde expansion.
- Command substitution is what we used in the example; it will run the commands and take their output as the value for the variable. Commands are enclosed in the single parentheses syntax, $(cmds).
- Arithmetic expansion means that we can do integer arithmetic, using the $((...)) syntax in this expression. Here's an example:

    ```
    echo ${BASE:=/home/uid$((ID+1))}
    ```

See Also

- Recipe 5.13, "Getting Default Values"

5.17   Giving an Error Message for Unset Parameters

Problem

Those shorthands for giving a default value are cool, but maybe you need to force the users to give you a value, otherwise you don't want to proceed. Perhaps if they left off a parameter, they don't really understand how to invoke your script. You want to leave nothing to guesswork. Is there anything shorter than lots of if statements to check each of your several parameters?

Solution

Use the ${:?} syntax when referring to the parameter. *bash* will print an error message and then exit if the parameter is unset or null.

```
#!/usr/bin/env bash
# cookbook filename: check_unset_parms
#
```

```
USAGE="usage: myscript scratchdir sourcefile conversion"
FILEDIR=${1:?"Error. You must supply a scratch directory."}
FILESRC=${2:?"Error. You must supply a source file."}
CVTTYPE=${3:?"Error. ${USAGE}"}
```

Here's what happens when we run that script with insufficient arguments:

```
$ ./myscript /tmp /dev/null
./myscript: line 5: 3: Error. usage: myscript scracthdir sourcefile conversion
$
```

Discussion

The check is made to see if the first parameter is set (or null) and if not, it will print an error message and exit.

The third variable uses another shell variable in its message. You can even run another command inside it:

```
CVTTYPE=${3:?"Error. $USAGE. $(rm $SCRATCHFILE)"}
```

If parameter three is not set, then the error message will contain the phrase "Error.", along with the value of the variable named $USAGE and then any output from the command which removes the filename named by the variable $SCRATCHFILE. OK, so we're getting carried away. You can make your shell script awfully compact, and we do mean *awfully*. It is better to waste some whitespace and a few bytes to make the logic ever so much more readable, as in:

```
if [ -z "$3" ]
then
    echo "Error. $USAGE"
    rm $SCRATCHFILE
fi
```

One other consideration: the error message produced by the ${:?} feature comes out with the shell script filename and line number. For example:

```
./myscript: line 5: 3: Error. usage: myscript scracthdir sourcefile conversion
```

Because you have no control over this part of the message, and since it looks like an error in the shell script itself, combined with the issue of readability, this technique is not so popular in commercial-grade shell scripts. (It is handy for debugging, though.)

See Also

- Recipe 5.13, "Getting Default Values"
- Recipe 5.14, "Setting Default Values"
- Recipe 5.16, "Using More Than Just a Constant String for Default"

5.18 Changing Pieces of a String

Problem

You want to rename a number of files. The filenames are almost right, but they have the wrong suffix.

Solution

Use a *bash* parameter expansion feature that will remove text that matches a pattern.

```
#!/usr/bin/env bash
# cookbook filename: suffixer
#
# rename files that end in .bad to be .bash

for FN in *.bad
do
    mv "${FN}" "${FN%bad}bash"
done
```

Discussion

The for loop will iterate over a list of filenames in the current directory that all end in .bad. The variable $FN will take the value of each name one at a time. Inside the loop, the mv command will rename the file (move it from the old name to the new name). We need to put quotes around each filename in case the filename contains embedded spaces.

The crux of this operation is the reference to $FN that includes an automatic deletion of the trailing bad characters. The ${ } delimit the reference so that the bash adjacent to it is just appended right on the end of the string.

Here it is broken down into a few more steps:

```
NOBAD="${FN%bad}"
NEWNAME="${NOBAD}bash"
mv "${FN}" "${NEWNAME}"
```

This way you can see the individual steps of stripping off the unwanted suffix, creating the new name, and then renaming the files. Putting it all on one line isn't so bad though, once you get used to the special operators.

Since we are not just removing a substring from the variable but are replacing the bad with bash, we could have used the substitution operator for variable references, the slash (/). Similar to editor commands (e.g., those found in *vi* and *sed*) that use the slash to delimit substitutions, we could have written:

```
mv "${FN}" "${FN/.bad/.bash}"
```

(Unlike the editor commands, you don't use a final slash—the right-brace serves that function.)

However, one reason that we didn't do it this way is because the substitution isn't anchored, and will make the substitution anywhere in the variable. If, for example, we had a file named *subaddon.bad* then the substitution would leave us with *subashdon.bad*, which is not what we want. If we used a double slash for the first slash, it would substitute every occurrence within the variable. That would result in *subashdon.bash*, which isn't what we want either.

There are several operators that do various sorts of manipulation on the string values of variables when referenced. Table 5-1 summarizes them.

Table 5-1. String-manipulation operators

inside ${ ... }	Action taken
name:number:number	Substring starting character, length
#name	Return the length of the string
name#pattern	Remove (shortest) front-anchored pattern
name##pattern	Remove (longest) front-anchored pattern
name%pattern	Remove (shortest) rear-anchored pattern
name%%pattern	Remove (longest) rear-anchored pattern
name/pattern/string	Replace first occurrence
name//pattern/string	Replace all occurrences

Try them all. They are very handy.

See Also

- man rename
- Recipe 12.5, "Comparing Two Documents"

5.19   Using Array Variables

Problem

There have been plenty of scripts so far with variables, but can *bash* deal with an array of variables?

Solution

Yes. *bash* now has an array syntax for single-dimension arrays.

Description

Arrays are easy to initialize if you know the values as you write the script. The format is simple:

```
MYRA=(first second third home)
```

Each element of the array is a separate word in the list enclosed in parentheses. Then you can refer to each this way:

```
echo runners on ${MYRA[0]} and ${MYRA[2]}
```

This output is the result:

```
runners on first and third
```

If you write only $MYRA, you will get only the first element, just as if you had written ${MYRA[0]}.

See Also

- *Learning the bash Shell* by Cameron Newham (O'Reilly), pages 157–161 for more information about arrays

CHAPTER 6

Shell Logic and Arithmetic

One of the big improvements that modern versions of *bash* have when compared with the original Bourne shell is in the area of arithmetic. Early versions of the shell had no built-in arithmetic; it had to be done by invoking a separate executable, even just to add 1 to a variable. In a way it's a tribute to how useful and powerful the shell was and is—that it can be used for so many tasks despite that awful mechanism for arithmetic. Maybe no one expected the shell to be so useful and so well used but, after a while, the simple counting useful for automating repetitive tasks needed simple, straightforward syntax. The lack of such capability in the original Bourne shell contributed to the success of the C shell (*csh*) when it introduced C Language-like syntax for shell programming, including numeric variables. Well, that was then and this is now. If you haven't looked at shell arithmetic in *bash* for a while, you're in for a big surprise.

Beyond arithmetic, there are the control structures familiar to any programmer. There is an if/then/else construct for decision making. There are while loops and for loops, but you will see some *bash* peculiarities to all of these. There is a case statement made quite powerful by its string pattern matching, and an odd construct called select. After discussing these features we will end the chapter by using them to build two simple command-line calculators.

6.1 Doing Arithmetic in Your Shell Script

Problem

You need to do some simple arithmetic in your shell script.

Solution

Use $(( )) or let for integer arithmetic expressions.

```
COUNT=$((COUNT + 5 + MAX * 2))
let COUNT+=5+MAX*2
```

Discussion

As long as you keep to integer arithmetic, you can use all the standard (i.e., C-like) operators inside of $(( )) for arithmetic. There is one additional operator—you can use ** for raising to a power, as in MAX=$((2**8)), which yields 256.

Spaces are not needed nor are they prohibited around operators and arguments (though ** must be together) within a $(( )) expression. But you must not have spaces around the equals sign, as with any *bash* variable assignment. If you wrote:

```
COUNT = $((COUNT + 5))   # not what you think!
```

then *bash* will try to run a program named *COUNT* and its first argument would be an equal sign, and its second argument would be the number you get adding 5 to the value of $COUNT. Remember not to put spaces around the equal sign.

Another oddity to these expressions is that the $ that we normally put in front of a shell variable to say we want its value (as in $COUNT or $MAX) is not needed inside the double parentheses. For example, $((COUNT +5 MAX * 2)) needs no dollar sign on the shell variables—in effect, the outer $ applies to the entire expression.

We do need the dollar sign, though, if we are using a positional parameter (e.g., $2) to distinguish it from a numeric constant (e.g., "2"). Here's an example:

```
COUNT=$((COUNT + $2 + OFFSET))
```

There is a similar mechanism for integer arithmetic with shell variables using the *bash* built-in let statement. It uses the same arithmetic operators as the $(( )) construct:

```
let COUNT=COUNT+5
```

When using let, there are some fancy assignment operators we can use such as this (which will accomplish the same thing as the previous line):

```
let COUNT+=5
```

(This should look familiar to programmers of C/C++ and Java.)

Table 6-1 shows a list of those special assignment operators.

Table 6-1. Explanation of assignment operators in bash

Operator	Operation with assignment	Use	Meaning
=	Simple assignment	a=b	a=b
*=	Multiplication	a*=b	a=(a*b)
/=	Division	a/=b	a=(a/b)
%=	Remainder	a%=b	a=(a%b)
+=	Addition	a+=b	a=(a+b)
-=	Subtraction	a-=b	a=(a-b)
<<=	Bit-shift left	a<<=b	a=(a<<b)

Table 6-1. Explanation of assignment operators in bash (continued)

Operator	Operation with assignment	Use	Meaning
>>=	Bit-shift right	a>>=b	a=(a>>b)
&=	Bitwise "and"	a&=b	a=(a&b)
^=	Bitwise "exclusive or"	a^=b	a=(a^b)
| =	Bitwise "or"	a|=b	a=(a|b)

These assignment operators are also available with $(( )) provided they occur inside the double parentheses. The outermost assignment is still just plain old shell variable assignment.

The assignments can also be cascaded, through the use of the comma operator:

```
echo $(( X+=5 , Y*=3 ))
```

which will do both assignments and then echo the result of the second expression (since the comma operator returns the value of its second expression). If you don't want to echo the result, the more common usage would be with the let statement:

```
let  X+=5  Y*=3
```

The comma operator is not needed here, as each word of a let statement is its own arithmetic expression.

Unlike many other places in *bash* scripts where certain characters have special meanings (like the asterisk for wildcard patterns or parentheses for subshell execution), in these expressions we don't need to use quotes or backslashes to escape them since they don't have their special meaning in let statements or inside of the $(( )) construct:

```
let Y=(X+2)*10

Y=$(( ( X + 2 ) * 10 ))
```

One other important difference between the let statement and the $(( )) syntax deals with the rather minor issue of the whitespace (i.e., the space character). The let statement requires that there be no spaces around not only the assignment operator (the equal sign), but around any of the other operators as well; it must all be packed together into a single word.

The $(( )) syntax, however, can be much more generous, allowing all sorts of whitespace within the parentheses. For that reason, it is both less prone to errors and makes the code much more readable and is, therefore, our preferred way of doing *bash* integer arithmetic. However, an exception can be made for the occasional += assignment or ++ operator, or when we get nostalgic for the early days of BASIC programming (which had a LET statement).

Remember; this is integer arithmetic, not floating point. Don't expect much out of an expression like 2/3, which in integer arithmetic evaluates to 0 (zero). The division is integer division, which will truncate any fractional result.

See Also

- help let
- bash manpage

6.2   Branching on Conditions

Problem

You want to check if you have the right number of arguments and take actions accordingly. You need a branching construct.

Solution

The if statement in *bash* is similar in appearance to that in other programming languages:

```
if [ $# -lt 3 ]
then
    printf "%b" "Error. Not enough arguments.\n"
    printf "%b" "usage: myscript file1 op file2\n"
    exit 1
fi
```

or alternatively:

```
if (( $# < 3 ))
then
    printf "%b" "Error. Not enough arguments.\n"
    printf "%b" "usage: myscript file1 op file2\n"
    exit 1
fi
```

Here's a full-blown if with an elif (*bash*-talk for else-if) and an else clause:

```
if (( $# < 3 ))
then
    printf "%b" "Error. Not enough arguments.\n"
    printf "%b" "usage: myscript file1 op file2\n"
    exit 1
elif (( $# > 3 ))
then
    printf "%b" "Error. Too many arguments.\n"
    printf "%b" "usage: myscript file1 op file2\n"
    exit 2
```

```
    else
        printf "%b" "Argument count correct.   Proceeding...\n"
    fi
```

You can even do things like this:

```
[ $result = 1 ] \
    && { echo "Result is 1; excellent."  ; exit 0;   } \
    || { echo "Uh-oh, ummm, RUN AWAY! "  ; exit 120; }
```

(For a discussion of this last example, see Recipe 2.14, "Saving or Grouping Output from Several Commands.")

Discussion

We have two things we need to discuss: the basic structure of the if statement and how it is that we have different syntax (parentheses or brackets, operators or options) for the if expression. The first may help explain the second. The general form for an if statement, from the manpage for *bash*, is:

```
if list; then list; [ elif list; then list; ] ... [ else list; ] fi
```

The [and] in our description here are used to delineate optional parts of the statement (e.g., some if statements have no else clause). So let's look for a moment at the if without any optional elements.

The simplest form for an if statement would be:

```
if list; then list; fi
```

 In bash, the semicolon serves the same purpose as a newline—it ends a statement. So in the first examples of the Solution section we could have crammed the example onto fewer lines by using the semicolons, but it is more readable to use newlines.

The then *list* seems to make sense—it's the statement or statements that will be executed provided that the if condition is true—or so we would surmise from other programming languages. But what's with the if *list*? Wouldn't you expect it to be if *expression*?

You might, except that this is a shell—a command processor. Its primary operation is to execute commands. So the list after the if is a place where you can put a list of commands. What, you ask, will be used to determine the branching—the alternate paths of the then or the else? It will be determined by the return value of the last command in the list. (The return value, you might remember, is also available as the value of the variable $?.)

Let's take a somewhat strange example to make this point:

```
$ cat trythis.sh
if ls; pwd; cd $1;
then
    echo success;
```

```
else
    echo failed;
fi
pwd

$ bash ./trythis.sh /tmp
...
$ bash ./trythis.sh /nonexistant
...
$
```

In this strange script, the shell will execute three commands (an *ls*, a *pwd*, and a *cd*) before doing any branching. The argument to the cd is the first argument supplied on the shell script invocation. If there is no argument supplied, it will just execute cd, which returns you to your home directory.

So what happens? Try it yourself and find out. The result showing "success" or "failed" will depend on whether or not the cd command succeeds. In our example, the cd is the last command in the if list of commands. If the cd fails, the else clause is taken, but if it succeeds, the then clause is taken.

Properly written commands and built-ins will return a value of 0 (zero) when they encounter no errors in their execution. If they detect a problem (e.g., bad parameters, I/O errors, file not found), they will return some non-zero value (often a different value for each different kind of error they detect).

This is why it is important for both shell script writers and C (and other language) programmers to be sure to return sensible values upon exiting from their scripts and programs. Someone's if statement may be depending on it!

OK, so how do we get from this strange if construct to something that looks like a real if statement—the kind that you are used to seeing in programs? What's going on with the examples that began this recipe? After all, they don't look like lists of statements.

Let's try this on for size:

```
if test $# -lt 3
then
    echo try again.
fi
```

Do you see something that looks like, if not an entire list, then at least like a single shell command—the built-in command *test*, which will take its arguments and compares their values? The *test* command will return a 0 if true or a 1 otherwise. To see this yourself, try the *test* command on a line by itself, and then echo $? to see its return value.

The first example we gave that began if [$# -lt 3] looks a lot like the *test* statement—because the [is actually the *test* command—with just a different name for the same command. (When invoked with the name [it also requires a trailing] as the last parameter, for readability and aesthetic reasons.) So that explains the first syntax—the expression on the if statement is actually a list of only one command, a *test* command.

 In the early days of Unix, *test* was its own separate executable and [was just a link to the same executable. They still exist as executables used by other shells, but *bash* implements them as a built-in command.

Now what about the if (($# < 3)) expression in our list of examples in the Solution section? The double parentheses are one of several types of *compound commands*. This kind is useful for if statements because it performs an arithmetic evaluation of the expression between the double parentheses. This is a more recent *bash* improvement, added for just such an occasion as its use in if statements.

The important distinctions to make with the two kinds of syntax that can be used with the if statement are the ways to express the tests, and the kinds of things for which they test. The double parentheses are strictly arithmetic expressions. The square brackets can also test for file characteristics, but its syntax is much less streamlined for arithmetic expressions. This is particularly true if you need to group larger expressions with parentheses (which need to be quoted or escaped).

See Also

- help if
- help test
- man test
- Recipe 2.14, "Saving or Grouping Output from Several Commands"
- Recipe 4.2, "Telling If a Command Succeeded or Not"
- Recipe 6.3, "Testing for File Characteristics"
- Recipe 6.5, "Testing for String Characteristics"
- Recipe 15.11, "Getting Input from Another Machine"

6.3   Testing for File Characteristics

Problem

You want to make your script robust by checking to see if your input file is there before reading from it; you would like to see if your output file has write permissions before writing to it; you would like to see if there is a directory there before you attempt to *cd* into it. How do you do all that in *bash* scripts?

Solution

Use the various file characteristic tests in the *test* command as part of your `if` statements. Your specific problems might be solved with scripting that looks something like this:

```
#!/usr/bin/env bash
# cookbook filename: checkfile
#
DIRPLACE=/tmp
INFILE=/home/yucca/amazing.data
OUTFILE=/home/yucca/more.results

if [ -d "$DIRPLACE" ]
then
    cd $DIRPLACE
    if [ -e "$INFILE" ]
    then
        if [ -w "$OUTFILE" ]
        then
            doscience < "$INFILE" >> "$OUTFILE"
        else
            echo "can not write to $OUTFILE"
        fi
    else
        echo "can not read from $INFILE"
    fi
else
    echo "can not cd into $DIRPLACE"
fi
```

Discussion

We put all the references to the various filenames in quotes in case they have any embedded spaces in the pathnames. There are none in this example, but if you change the script you might use other pathnames.

We tested and executed the *cd* before we tested the other two conditions. In this example it wouldn't matter, but if *INFILE* or *OUTFILE* were relative pathnames (not beginning from the root of the file system, i.e., with a leading "/"), then the test might evaluate true before the *cd* and not after, or vice versa. This way, we test right before we use the files.

We use the double-greater-than operator >> to concatenate output onto our results file, rather than wiping it out. You wouldn't really care if the file had write permissions if you were going to obliterate it. (Then you would only need write permission on its containing directory.)

The several tests could be combined into one large `if` statement using the -a (read "and") operator, but then if the test failed you couldn't give a very helpful error message since you wouldn't know which test it didn't pass.

There are several other characteristics for which you can test. Three of them are tested using binary operators, each taking two filenames:

FILE1 -nt *FILE2*

> Is newer than (it checks the modification date)

FILE1 -ot *FILE2*

> Is older than

FILE1 -ef *FILE2*

> Have the same device and inode numbers (identical file, even if pointed to by different links)

Table 6-2 shows the other tests related to files (see "Test Operators" in Appendix A for a more complete list). They all are unary operators, taking the form *option filename* as in if [-e myfile].

Table 6-2. Unary operators that check file characteristics

Option	Description
-b	File is block special device (for files like */dev/hda1*)
-c	File is character special (for files like */dev/tty*)
-d	File is a directory
-e	File exists
-f	File is a regular file
-g	File has its set-group-ID bit set
-h	File is a symbolic link (same as -L)
-G	File is owned by the effective group ID
-k	File has its sticky bit set
-L	File is a symbolic link (same as -h)
-O	File is owned by the effective user ID
-p	File is a named pipe
-r	File is readable
-s	File has a size greater than zero
-S	File is a socket
-u	File has its set-user-ID bit set
-w	File is writable
-x	File is executable

See Also

- Recipe 2.10, "Appending Rather Than Clobbering Output"
- Recipe 4.6, "Using Fewer if Statements"
- "Test Operators" in Appendix A

6.4   Testing for More Than One Thing

Problem

What if you want to test for more than one characteristic? Do you have to nest your if statements?

Solution

Use the operators for logial AND (-a) and OR (-o) to combine more than one test in an expression. For example:

```
if [ -r $FILE -a -w $FILE ]
```

will test to see that the file is both readable *and* writable.

Discussion

All the file test conditions include an implicit test for existence, so you don't need to test if a file exists and is readable. It won't be readable if it doesn't exist.

These conjunctions (-a for AND and -o for OR) can be used for all the various test conditions. They aren't limited to just the file conditions.

You can make several and/or conjunctions on one statement. You might need to use parentheses to get the proper precedence, as in a and (b or c), but if you use parentheses, be sure to escape their special meaning from the shell by putting a backslash before each or by quoting each parenthesis. Don't try to quote the entire expression in one set of quotes, however, as that will make your entire expression a single term that will be treated as a test for an empty string (see Recipe 6.5, "Testing for String Characteristics").

Here's an example of a more complex test with the parentheses properly escaped:

```
if [ -r "$FN" -a \( -f "$FN" -o  -p "$FN" \) ]
```

Don't make the assumption that these expressions are evaluated in quite the same order as in Java or C language. In C and Java, if the first part of the AND expression is false (or the first part true in an OR expression), the second part of the expression won't be evaluated (we say the expression *short-circuited*). However, because the shell makes multiple passes over the statement while preparing it for evaluation (e.g., doing parameter substitution, etc.), both parts of the joined condition may have been partially evaluated. While it doesn't matter in this simple example, in more complicated situations it might. For example:

```
if [ -z "$V1" -o -z "${V2:=YIKES}" ]
```

Even if $V1 is empty, satisfying enough of the if statement that the second part of the condition (checking if $V2 is empty) need not occur, the value of $V2 may have already been modified (as a side-effect of the parameter substitution for $V2). The parameter substitution step occurs before the -z tests are made. Confused? Don't be…just don't count on short circuits in your conditionals. If you need that kind of behavior, just break the if statement into two nested if statements.

See Also

- Recipe 6.5, "Testing for String Characteristics"
- Appendix C for more on command-line processing

6.5   Testing for String Characteristics

Problem

You want your script to check the value of some strings before using them. The strings could be user input, read from a file, or environment variables passed to your script. How do you do that with *bash* scripts?

Solution

There are some simple tests that you can do with the built-in *test* command, using the single bracket if statements. You can check to see whether a variable has any text, and you can check to see whether two variables are equal as strings.

Discussion

For example:

```
#!/usr/bin/env bash
# cookbook filename: checkstr
#
# if statement
# test a string to see if it has any length
#
# use the command line argument
VAR="$1"
#
if [ "$VAR" ]
then
    echo has text
else
    echo zero length
fi
#
if [ -z "$VAR" ]
then
    echo zero length
else
    echo has text
fi
```

We use the phrase "has any length" deliberately. There are two types of variables that will have no length—those that have been set to an empty string and those that have not been set at all. This test does not distinguish between those two cases. All it asks is whether there are some characters in the variable.

It is important to put quotes around the "$VAR" expression because without them your syntax could be disturbed by odd user input. If the value of $VAR were x -a 7 -lt 5 and if there were no quotes around the $VAR, then the expression:

```
if [ -z $VAR ]
```

would become (after variable substitution):

```
if [ -z  x -a 7 -lt 5 ]
```

which is legitimate syntax for a more elaborate test, but one that will yield a result that is not what you wanted (i.e., one not based on whether the string has characters).

See Also

- Recipe 6.7, "Testing with Pattern Matches"
- Recipe 6.8, "Testing with Regular Expressions"
- Recipe 14.2, "Avoiding Interpreter Spoofing"
- "Test Operators" in Appendix A

6.6 Testing for Equal

Problem

You want to check to see if two shell variables are equal, but there are two different test operators: -eq and = (or ==). So which one should you use?

Solution

The type of comparison you need determines which operator you should use. Use the -eq operator for numeric comparisons and the equality primary = (or ==) for string comparisons.

Discussion

Here's a simple script to illustrate the situation:

```
#!/usr/bin/env bash
# cookbook filename: strvsnum
#
# the old string vs. numeric comparison dilemma
#
VAR1=" 05 "
VAR2="5"
```

```
    printf "%s" "do they -eq as equal? "
    if [ "$VAR1" -eq "$VAR2" ]
    then
        echo YES
    else
        echo NO
    fi

    printf "%s" "do they = as equal? "
    if [ "$VAR1" = "$VAR2" ]
    then
        echo YES
    else
        echo NO
    fi
```

When we run the script, here is what we get:

```
$ bash strvsnum
do they -eq as equal? YES
do they = as equal? NO
$
```

While the numeric value is the same (5) for both variables, characters such as leading zeros and whitespace can mean that the strings are not equal as strings.

Both = and == are accepted, but the single equal sign follows the POSIX standard and is more portable.

It may help you to remember which comparison to use if you can recognize that the -eq operator is similar to the FORTRAN .eq. operator. (FORTRAN is a very numbers-oriented language, used for scientific computation.) In fact, there are several numerical comparison operators, each similar to an old FORTRAN operator. The abbreviations, all listed in Table 6-3, are rather mnemonic-like and easy to figure out.

Table 6-3. bash's comparison operators

Numeric	String	Meaning
-lt	<	Less than
-le	<=	Less than or equal to
-gt	>	Greater than
-ge	>=	Greater than or equal to
-eq	=, ==	Equal to
-ne	!=	Not equal to

On the other hand, these are the opposite of Perl, in which eq, ne, etc. are the string operators, while ==, !=, etc. are numeric.

See Also

- Recipe 6.7, "Testing with Pattern Matches"
- Recipe 6.8, "Testing with Regular Expressions"
- Recipe 14.12, "Validating Input"
- "Test Operators" in Appendix A

6.7   Testing with Pattern Matches

Problem

You want to test a string not for a literal match, but to see if it fits a pattern. For example, you want to know if a file is named like a JPEG file might be named.

Solution

Use the double-bracket compound statement in an if statement to enable shell-style pattern matches on the righthand side of the equals operator:

```
if [[ "${MYFILENAME}" == *.jpg ]]
```

Discussion

The double-brackets is a newer syntax (*bash* version 2.01 or so). It is not the old-fashioned [of the *test* command, but a newer *bash* mechanism. It uses the same operators that work with the single bracket form, but in the double-bracket syntax the equal sign is a more powerful string comparator. The equal sign operator can be a single equal sign or a double equals as we have used here. They are the same semantically. We prefer to use the double equals (especially when using the pattern matching) to emphasize the difference, but it is not the reason that we get pattern matching—that comes from the double-bracket compound statement.

The standard pattern matching includes the * to match any number of characters, the question mark (?) to match a single character, and brackets for including a list of possible characters. Note that these resemble shell file wildcards, and are not regular expressions.

Don't put quotes around the pattern if you want it to behave as a pattern. If our string had been quoted, it would have only matched strings with a literal asterisk as the first character.

There are more powerful pattern matching capabilities available by turning on some additional options in *bash*. Let's expand our example to look for filenames that end in either *.jpg* or *.jpeg*. We could do that with this bit of code:

```
shopt -s extglob
if [[ "$FN" == *.@(jpg|jpeg) ]]
then
    # and so on
```

The shopt -s command is the way to turn on shell options. The extglob is the option dealing with extended pattern matching (or *globbing*). With this extended pattern matching we can have several patterns, separated by the | character and grouped by parentheses. The first character preceding the parentheses says whether the list should match just one occurrence of a pattern in the list (using a leading @) or some other criteria. Table 6-4 lists the possibilities (see also "extglob Extended Pattern-Matching Operators" in Appendix A).

Table 6-4. Grouping symbols for extended pattern-matching

Grouping	Meaning
@(...)	Only one occurrence
*(...)	Zero or more occurrences
+(...)	One or more occurrences
?(...)	Zero or one occurrences
!(...)	Not these occurrences, but anything else

Matches are case sensitive, but you may use shopt -s nocasematch (in *bash* versions 3.1+) to change that. This option affects case and [[commands.

See Also

- Recipe 14.2, "Avoiding Interpreter Spoofing"
- Recipe 16.7, "Adjusting Shell Behavior and Environment"
- "Pattern-Matching Characters" in Appendix A
- "extglob Extended Pattern-Matching Operators" in Appendix A
- "shopt Options" in Appendix A

6.8   Testing with Regular Expressions

Problem

Sometimes even the extended pattern matching of the extglob option isn't enough. What you really need are regular expressions. Let's say that you rip a CD of classical music into a directory, *ls* that directory, and see these names:

```
$ ls
Ludwig Van Beethoven - 01 - Allegro.ogg
Ludwig Van Beethoven - 02 - Adagio un poco mosso.ogg
Ludwig Van Beethoven - 03 - Rondo - Allegro.ogg
```

```
Ludwig Van Beethoven - 04 - "Coriolan" Overture, Op. 62.ogg
Ludwig Van Beethoven - 05 - "Leonore" Overture, No. 2 Op. 72.ogg
$
```

You'd like to write a script to rename these files to something simple, such as just the track number. How can you do that?

Solution

Use the regular expression matching of the =~ operator. Once it has matched the string, the various parts of the pattern are available in the shell variable $BASH_REMATCH. Here is the part of the script that deals with the pattern match:

```
#!/usr/bin/env bash
# cookbook filename: trackmatch
#
for CDTRACK in *
do
    if [[ "$CDTRACK" =~ "([[:alpha:][:blank:]]*)- ([[:digit:]]*) - (.*)$" ]]
    then
        echo Track ${BASH_REMATCH[2]} is ${BASH_REMATCH[3]}
        mv "$CDTRACK" "Track${BASH_REMATCH[2]}"
    fi
done
```

Caution: this requires *bash* version 3.0 or newer because older versions don't have the =~ operator. In addition, *bash* version 3.2 unified the handling of the pattern in the == and =~ conditional command operators but introduced a subtle quoting bug that was corrected in 3.2 patch #3. If the solution above fails, you may be using *bash* version 3.2 without that patch. You might want to upgrade to a newer version. You might also avoid the bug with a less readable version of the regular expression by removing the quotes around the regex and escaping each parenthesis and space character individually, which gets ugly quickly:

```
    if [[ "$CDTRACK" =~ \([[:alpha:][:blank:]]*\)-\ \([[:digit:
    ]]*\)\ -\ \(.*\)\$ ]]
```

Discussion

If you are familiar with regular expressions from *sed*, *awk*, and older shells, you may notice a few slight differences with this newer form. Most noticeable are the character classes such as [:alpha:] and that the grouping parentheses don't need to be escaped—we don't write \(here as we would in *sed*. Here \(would mean a literal parenthesis.

The subexpressions, each enclosed in parentheses, are used to populate the *bash* built-in array variable $BASH_REMATCH. The zeroth element ($BASH_REMATCH[0]) is the entire string matched by the regular expression. Any subexpressions are available as $BASH_REMATCH[1], $BASH_REMATCH[2], and so on. Any time a regular expression is used this way, it will populate the variable $BASH_REMATCH. Since other *bash* functions may want to use regular expression matching, you may want to assign this variable to one of your own naming as soon as possible, so as to preserve the values for your later use. In our example we use the values right away, inside our if/then clause, so we don't bother to save them for use elsewhere.

Regular expressions have often been described as *write-only* expressions because they can be very difficult to decipher. We'll build this one up in several steps to show how we arrived at the final expression. The general layout of the filenames given to our datafiles, as in this example, seems to be like this:

```
Ludwig Van Beethoven - 04 - "Coriolan" Overture, Op. 62.ogg
```

i.e., a composer's name, a track number, and then the title of the piece, ending in .ogg (these were saved in Ogg Vorbis format, for smaller space and higher fidelity).

Beginning at the left-hand side of the expression is an opening (or left) parenthesis. That begins our first subexpression. Inside it, we will write an expression to match the first part of the filename, the composer's name—marked in bold here:

([[:alpha:][:blank:]]*)- ([[:digit:]]*) - (.*)$

The composer's name consists of any number of alphabetic characters and blanks. We use the square brackets to group the set of characters that will make up the name. Rather than write [A-Za-z0-9], we use the character class names [:alpha:] and [:blank:] and put them inside the square brackets. This is followed by an asterisk to indicate "0 or more" repetitions. The right parenthesis closes off the first subexpression, followed by a literal hyphen and a blank.

The second subexpression (marked in bold here) will attempt to match the track number:

([[:alpha:][:blank:]]*)- **([[:digit:]]*)** - (.*)$

The second subexpression begins with another left parenthesis. The track numbers are integers, composed of digits (the character class [:digit:]), which we write inside another pair of brackets followed by an asterisk as [[:digit:]]* to indicate "0 or more" of what is in the brackets (i.e., digits). Then our pattern has the literals blank, hyphen, and blank.

The final subexpression will catch everything else, including the track name and the file extension.

([[:alpha:][:blank:]]*)- ([[:digit:]]*) - **(.*)$**

The third and final subexpression is the common and familiar .* regular expression, which means any number (*) of any character (.). We end the expression with a dollar sign, which matches the end of the string. Matches are case-sensitive, but you may use shopt -s nocasematch (available in *bash* versions 3.1+) to change that. This option affects case and [[commands.

See Also

- man regex (Linux, Solaris, HP-UX) or man re_format (BSD, Mac) for the details of your regular expression library
- *Mastering Regular Expressions* by Jeffrey E. F. Friedl (O'Reilly)
- Recipe 7.7, "Searching with More Complex Patterns"
- Recipe 7.8, "Searching for an SSN"
- Recipe 19.15, "Confusing Shell Wildcards and Regular Expressions"

6.9   Changing Behavior with Redirections

Problem

Normally you want a script to behave the same regardless of whether input comes from a keyboard or a file, or whether output is going to the screen or a file. Occasionally, though, you want to make that distinction. How do you do that in a script?

Solution

Use the test -t option in an if statement to branch between the two desired behaviors.

Discussion

Think long and hard before you do this. So much of the power and flexibility of *bash* scripting comes from the fact that scripts can be pipelined together. Be sure you have a really good reason to make your script behave oddly when input or output is redirected.

See Also

- Recipe 2.18, "Using Multiple Redirects on One Line"
- Recipe 2.19, "Saving Output When Redirect Doesn't Seem to Work"
- Recipe 2.20, "Swapping STDERR and STDOUT"
- Recipe 10.1, ""Daemon-izing" Your Script"
- Recipe 15.9, "Using bash Net-Redirection"
- Recipe 15.12, "Redirecting Output for the Life of a Script"
- "I/O Redirection" in Appendix A

6.10 Looping for a While

Problem

You want your shell script to perform some actions repeatedly as long as some condition is met.

Solution

Use the while looping construct for arithmetic conditions:

```
while (( COUNT < MAX ))
do
    some stuff
    let COUNT++
done
```

for filesystem-related conditions:

```
while [ -z "$LOCKFILE" ]
do
    some things
done
```

or for reading input:

```
while read lineoftext
do
    process $lineoftext
done
```

Discussion

The double parentheses in our first while statement are just arithmetic expressions, very much like the $(( )) expression for shell variable assignment. They bound an arithmetic expression and assume that variable names mentioned inside the parentheses are meant to be dereferenced. That is, you don't write $VAR, and instead use VAR inside the parentheses.

The use of the square brackets in while [-z "$LOCKFILE"] is the same as with the if statement—the single square bracket is the same as using the test statement.

The last example, while read lineoftext, doesn't have any parentheses, brackets, or braces. The syntax of the while statement in *bash* is defined such that the condition of the while statement is a list of statements to be executed (just like the if statement), and the exit status of the last one determines whether the condition is true or false. An exit status of zero, and the condition is considered true, otherwise false.

A read statement returns a 0 on a successful read and a -1 on end-of-file, which means that the while will find it true for any successful read, but when the end of file is reached (and -1 returned) the while condition will be false and the looping will end. At that point, the next statement to be executed will be the statement after the done statement.

This logic of "keep looping while the statement returns zero" might seem a bit flipped—most C-like languages use the opposite, namely, "loop while nonzero." But in the shell, a zero return value means everything went well; non-zero return values indicate an error exit.

This explains what happens with the (( )) construct, too. Any expression inside the parentheses is evaluated, and if the result is nonzero, then the result of the (( )) is to return a zero; similarly, a zero result returns a one. This means we can write expressions like Java or C programmers would, but the while statement still works as always in *bash*, expecting a zero result to be true.

In practical terms, it means we can write an infinite loop like this:

```
while (( 1 ))
{
...
}
```

which "feels right" to a C programmer. But remember that the while statement is looking for a zero return—which it gets because (( )) returns 0 for a true (i.e., non-zero) result.

Before we leave the while loop, let's take one more look at that while read example, which is reading from standard input (i.e., the keyboard), and see how it might get modified in order to read input from a file instead of the keyboard.

This is typically done in one of three ways. The first requires no real modifications to the statements at all. Rather, when the script is invoked, standard input is redirected from a file like this:

```
$ myscript <file.name
```

But suppose you don't want to leave it up to the caller. If you know what file you want to process, or if it was supplied as a command-line argument to your script, then you can use this same while loop as is, but redirect the input from the file as follows:

```
while read lineoftext
do
    process that line
done < file.input
```

As a third way you might do this, you could begin by *cat*-ing the file to dump it to standard output, and then connect the standard output of that program to the standard input for the while statement:

```
cat file.input | \
while read lineoftext
do
    process that line
done
```

Because of the pipe, both the cat command and the while loop (including the *process that line* part), are each executing in their own separate subshells. This means that if you use this method, the script commands inside the while loop cannot affect the other parts of the script outside the loop. For example, any variables that you set within the while loop will no longer have those values after the loop ends. Such is not the case however if you use while read ... done < file.input, because that isn't a pipeline.

In the last example, the trailing backslash has no characters after it, just a newline. Therefore it escapes the newline, telling the shell to continue onto the next line without terminating the line. This is a more readable way to highlight the two different actions—the cat command and the while statement.

See Also

- Recipe 6.2, "Branching on Conditions"
- Recipe 6.3, "Testing for File Characteristics"
- Recipe 6.4, "Testing for More Than One Thing"
- Recipe 6.5, "Testing for String Characteristics"
- Recipe 6.6, "Testing for Equal"
- Recipe 6.7, "Testing with Pattern Matches"
- Recipe 6.8, "Testing with Regular Expressions"
- Recipe 6.11, "Looping with a read"
- Recipe 19.8, "Forgetting That Pipelines Make Subshells"

6.11 Looping with a read

Problem

What can you do with a while loop? One common technique is to read the output of previous commands. Let's say you're using the Subversion revision control system, which is executable as *svn*. (This example is very similar to what you would do for *cvs* as well.) When you check the status of a directory subtree to see what files have been changed, you might see something like this:

```
$ svn status bcb
M       bcb/amin.c
?       bcb/dmin.c
?       bcb/mdiv.tmp
A       bcb/optrn.c
M       bcb/optson.c
?       bcb/prtbout.4161
?       bcb/rideaslist.odt
?       bcb/x.maxc
$
```

The lines that begin with question marks are files about which Subversion has not been told; in this case they're scratch files and temporary copies of files. The lines that begin with an A are newly added files, and those that begin with M have been modified since the last changes were committed.

To clean up this directory it would be nice to get rid of all the scratch files, which are those files named in lines that begin with a question mark.

Solution

Try:

```
svn status mysrc | grep '^?' | cut -c8- | \
    while read FN; do echo "$FN"; rm -rf "$FN"; done
```

or:

```
svn status mysrc | \
while read TAG FN
do
    if [[ $TAG == \? ]]
    then
        echo $FN
        rm -rf "$FN"
    fi
done
```

Discussion

Both scripts will do the same thing—remove files that *svn* reports with a question mark.

The first approach uses several subprograms to do its work (not a big deal in these days of gigahertz processors), and would fit on a single line in a typical terminal window. It uses *grep* to select only the lines that begin (signified by the ^) with a question mark. The expression '^?' is put in single quotes to avoid any special meanings that those characters have for *bash*. It then uses *cut* to take only the characters beginning in column eight (through the end of the line). That leaves just the filenames for the while loop to read.

The read will return a nonzero value when there is no more input, so at that point the loop will end. Until then, the read will assign the line of text that it reads each time into the variable "$FN", and that is the filename that we remove. We use the -rf options in case the unknown file is actually a directory of files, and to remove even read-only files. If you don't want/need to be so drastic in what you remove, leave those options off.

The second script can be described as more shell-like, since it doesn't need *grep* to do its searching (it uses the if statement) and it doesn't need *cut* to do its parsing (it uses the read statement). We've also formatted it more like you would format a script in a file. If you were typing this at a command prompt, you could collapse the indentation, but for our use here the readability is much more important than saving a few keystrokes.

The read in this second script is reading into two variables, not just one. That is how we get *bash* to parse the line into two pieces—the leading character and the filename. The read statement parses its input into words, like words on a shell command line. The first word on the input line is assigned to the first word in the list of variables on the read statement, the second word to the second variable, and so on. The last variable in the list gets the entire remainder of the line, even if it's more than a single word. In our example, $TAG gets the first word, which is the character (an M, A, or ?) that the whitespace defines the end of that word and the beginning of the next. The variable $FN gets the remainder of the line as the filename, which is significant here in case the filenames have embedded spaces. (We wouldn't want just the first word of the filename.) The script removes the filename and the loop continues.

See Also

- Appendix D

6.12   Looping with a Count

Problem

You need to loop a fixed number of times. You could use a while loop and do the counting and testing, but programming languages have for loops for such a common idiom. How does one do this in *bash* ?

Solution

Use a special case of the for syntax, one that looks a lot like C Language, but with double parentheses:

```
$ for (( i=0 ; i < 10 ; i++ )) ; do echo $i ; done
```

Discussion

In early versions of the shell, the original syntax for the for loop only included iterating over a fixed list of items. It was a neat innovation for such a word-oriented language as shell scripts, dealing with filenames and such. But when users needed to count, they sometimes found themselves writing:

```
for i in 1 2 3 4 5 6 7 8 9 10
do
    echo $i
done
```

Now that's not too bad, especially for small loops, but let's face it—that's not going to work for 500 iterations. (Yes, you could nest loops 5×10, but come on!) What you really need is a for loop that can count.

The special case of the for loop with C-like syntax is a relatively recent addition to *bash* (appearing in version 2.04). Its more general form can be described as:

```
for (( expr1 ; expr2 ; expr3 )) ; do list ; done
```

The use of double parentheses is meant to indicate that these are arithmetic expressions. You don't need to use the $ construct (as in $i, except for arguments like $1) when referring to variables inside the double parentheses (just like the other places where double parentheses are used in *bash*). The expressions are integer arithmetic expressions and offer a rich variety of operators, including the use of the comma to put multiple operations within one expression:

```
for (( i=0, j=0 ; i+j < 10 ; i++, j++ ))
do
    echo $((i*j))
done
```

That for loop initializes two variables (i and j), then has a more complex second expression adding the two together before doing the less-than comparison. The comma operator is used again in the third expression to increment both variables.

See Also

- Recipe 6.13, "Looping with Floating-Point Values"
- Recipe 17.22, "Writing Sequences"

6.13   Looping with Floating-Point Values

Problem

The for loop with arithmetic expressions only does integer arithmetic. What do I do for floating-point values?

Solution

Use the *seq* command to generate your floating-point values, if your system provides it:

```
for fp in $(seq 1.0 .01 1.1)
do
    echo $fp; other stuff too
done
```

or:

```
seq 1.0 .01 1.1 | \
while read fp
do
```

```
        echo $fp; other stuff too
    done
```

Discussion

The *seq* command will generate a sequence of floating-point numbers, one per line.
The arguments to *seq* are the starting value, the increment, and the ending value.
This is *not* the intuitive order if you are used to the C language for loop, or if you
learned your looping from BASIC (e.g., FOR I=4 TO 10 STEP 2). With *seq* the increment
is the *middle* argument.

In the first example, the $( ) runs the command in a subshell and returns the result with
the newlines replaced by just whitespace, so each value is a string value for the for loop.

In the second example, *seq* is run as a command with its output piped into a while
loop that reads each line and does something with it. This would be the preferred
approach for a really long sequence, as it can run the *seq* command in parallel with
the while. The for loop version has to run *seq* to completion and put all of its output
on the command line for the for statement. For very large sequences, this could be
time- and memory-consuming.

See Also

* Recipe 6.12, "Looping with a Count"
* Recipe 17.22, "Writing Sequences"

6.14 Branching Many Ways

Problem

You have a series of comparisons to make, and the if/then/else is getting pretty long
and repetitive. Isn't there an easier way?

Solution

Use the case statement for a multiway branch:

```
case $FN in
    *.gif) gif2png $FN
        ;;
    *.png) pngOK $FN
        ;;
    *.jpg) jpg2gif $FN
        ;;
    *.tif | *.TIFF) tif2jpg $FN
        ;;
    *) printf "File not supported: %s" $FN
        ;;
esac
```

The equivalent to this using if/then/else statements is:

```
if [[ $FN == *.gif ]]
then
    gif2png $FN
elif [[ $FN == *.png ]]
then
    pngOK $FN
elif [[ $FN == *.jpg ]]
then
    jpg2gif $FN
elif [[ $FN == *.tif || $FN == *.TIFF ]]
then
    tif2jpg $FN
else
    printf "File not supported: %s" $FN
fi
```

Discussion

The case statement will expand the word (including parameter substitution) between the case and the in keywords. It will then try to match the word with the patterns listed in order. This is a very powerful feature of the shell. It is not just doing simple value comparisons, but string pattern matches. We have simple patterns in our example: *.gif matches any character sequence (signified by the *) that ends with the literal characters .gif.

Use |, a vertical bar meaning logical OR, to separate different patterns for which you want to take the same action. In the example above, if $FN ends either with .tif or .TIFF then the pattern will match and the (fictional) *tif2jpg* command will be executed.

Use the double semicolon to end the set of statements or else *bash* will continue executing into the next set of statements.

There is no else or default keyword to indicate the statements to execute if no pattern matches. Instead, use * as the last pattern—since that pattern will match anything. Placing it last makes it act as the default and match anything that hasn't already been matched.

An aside to C/C++ and Java programmers: the bash case is similar to the switch statement, and each pattern corresponds to a case. Notice though, the variable on which you can switch/case is a shell variable (typically a string value) and the cases are patterns (not just constant values). The patterns end with a right parenthesis (not a colon). The equivalent to the break in C/C++ and Java switch statements is, in *bash*, a double semicolon. The equivalent to their default keyword is, in *bash*, the * pattern.

Matches are case-sensitive, but you may use shopt -s nocasematch (available in *bash* versions 3.1+) to change that. This option affects case and [[commands.

We end the case statement with an esac (that's "c-a-s-e" spelled backwards; "end-case" was too long, we suppose, just like using elif instead of "elseif" to be shorter).

See Also

- help case
- help shopt
- Recipe 6.2, "Branching on Conditions"

6.15   Parsing Command-Line Arguments

Problem

You want to write a simple shell script to print a line of dashes, but you want to parameterize it so that you can specify different line lengths and specify a character to use other than just a dash. The syntax would look like this:

```
dashes          # would print out 72 dashes
dashes 50       # would print out 50 dashes
dashes -c= 50   # would print out 50 equal signs
dashes -cx      # would print out 72 x characters
```

What's an easy way to parse those simple arguments?

Solution

For serious scripting, you should use the getopts built-in. But we would like to show you the case statement in action, so for this simple situation we'll use case for argument parsing.

Here's the beginning of the script (see Recipe 12.1, "Starting Simple by Printing Dashes" for a complete remove):

```
#!/usr/bin/env bash
# cookbook filename: dashes
#
# dashes - print a line of dashes
#
# options: # how many (default 72)
#          -c X  use char X instead of dashes
#

LEN=72
CHAR='-'
while (( $# > 0 ))
do
    case $1 in
        [0-9]*) LEN=$1
            ;;
        -c) shift;
```

```
            CHAR=${1:--}
            ;;
    *)      printf 'usage: %s [-c X] [#]\n' $(basename $0) >&2
            exit 2
            ;;
    esac
    shift
done
#
# more...
```

Discussion

The default length (72) and the default character (-) are set at the beginning of the script (after some useful comments). The while loop allows us to parse more than one parameter. It will keep looping while the number of arguments ($#) is above zero.

The case statement matches three different patterns. First, the [0-9]* will match any digit followed by any other characters. We could have used a more elaborate expression to allow only pure numbers, but we'll assume that any argument that begins with a digit is a number. If that isn't true (e.g., the user types 1T4), then the script will error when it tries to use $LEN. We can live with that for now.

The second pattern is a literal -c. There is no pattern to this, just an exact match. In that case, we use the shift built-in command to throw away that argument (now that we know what it is) and we take the next argument (which has now become the first argument, so it is referenced as $1) and save that as the new character choice. We use :- when referencing $1 (as in ${1:-x}) to specify a default value if the parameter isn't set. That way, if the user types -c but fails to specify an argument, it will use the default, specified as the character immediately following the :-. In the expression ${1:-x} it would be x. For our script, we wrote ${1:--} (note the two minus signs), so the character taken as default is the (second) minus sign.

The third pattern is the wildcard pattern (*), which matches everything, so that any argument unmatched by the previous patterns will be matched here. By placing it last in the case statement, it is the catch-all that notifies the user of an error (since it wasn't one of the prescribed parameters) and it issues an error message.

That printf error message probably needs explaining if you're new to *bash*. There are four sections of that statement to look at. The first is simply the command name, printf. The second is the format string that printf will use (see Recipe 2.3, "Writing Output with More Formatting Control" and "printf" in Appendix A). We use single quotes around the string so that the shell doesn't try to interpret any of the string. The last part of the line (>&2) tells the shell to redirect that output to standard error. Since this is an error message, that seems appropriate. Many script writers are casual about this and often neglect this redirection on error messages. We think it is a good habit to always redirect error messages to standard error.

The third part of the line invokes a subshell to run the basename command on $0, and then returns the output of the command as text on the command line. This is a common idiom used to strip off any leading path part of how the command was invoked. For example, consider what would happen if we used only $0. Here are two different but erroneous invocations of the same script. Notice the error messages:

```
$ dashes -g
usage: dashes [-c X] [#]

$ /usr/local/bin/dashes -g
usage: /usr/local/bin/dashes [-c X] [#]
```

In the second invocation, we used the full pathname. The error message then also contained the full pathname. Some people find this annoying. So we strip $0 down to just the script's base name (using the basename command). Then the error messages look the same regardless of how the script is invoked:

```
$ dashes -g
usage: dashes [-c X] [#]

$ /usr/local/bin/dashes -g
usage: dashes [-c X] [#]
```

While this certainly takes a bit more time than just hardcoding the script name or using $0 without trimming it, the extra time isn't that vital since this is an error message and the script is about to exit anyway.

We end the case statement with an esac and then do a shift so as to consume the argument that we just matched in our case statement. If we didn't do that, we'd be stuck in the while loop, parsing the same argument over and over. The shift will cause the second argument ($2) to become the first ($1) and the third to become the second, and so on, but also $# to be one smaller. On some iteration of the loop $# finally reaches zero (when there are no more arguments) and the loop terminates.

The actual printing of the dashes (or other character) is not shown here, as we wanted to focus on the case statement and related actions. You can see the complete script, with a function for the usage message, in its entirety, in Recipe 12.1, "Starting Simple by Printing Dashes."

See Also

- help case
- help getopts
- help getopt
- Recipe 2.3, "Writing Output with More Formatting Control"
- Recipe 5.8, "Looping Over Arguments Passed to a Script"
- Recipe 5.11, "Counting Arguments"
- Recipe 5.12, "Consuming Arguments"

- Recipe 6.15, "Parsing Command-Line Arguments"
- Recipe 12.1, "Starting Simple by Printing Dashes"
- Recipe 13.1, "Parsing Arguments for Your Shell Script"
- Recipe 13.2, "Parsing Arguments with Your Own Error Messages"
- "printf" in Appendix A

6.16   Creating Simple Menus

Problem

You have a simple SQL script that you would like to run against different databases to reset them for tests that you want to run. You could supply the name of the database on the command line, but you want something more interactive. How can you write a shell script to choose from a list of names?

Solution

Use the select statement to create simple character-based screen menus. Here's a simple example:

```
#!/usr/bin/env bash
# cookbook filename: dbinit.1
#
DBLIST=$(sh ./listdb | tail +2)
select DB in $DBLIST
do
    echo Initializing database: $DB
    mysql -uuser -p $DB <myinit.sql
done
```

Ignore for a moment how $DBLIST gets its values; just know that it is a list of words (like the output from *ls* would give). The select statement will display those words, each preceded by a number, and the user will be prompted for input. The user makes a choice by typing the number and the corresponding word is assigned to the variable specified after the keyword select (in this case DB).

Here's what the running of this script might look like:

```
$ ./dbinit
1) testDB
2) simpleInventory
3) masterInventory
4) otherDB
#? 2
Initializing database: simpleInventory
#?
$
```

Discussion

When the user types "2" the variable DB is assigned the word simpleInventory. If you really want to get at the user's literal choice, the variable $REPLY will hold it, in this case it would be "2".

The select statement is really a loop. When you have entered a choice it will execute the body of the loop (between the do and the done) and then re-prompt you for the next value.

It doesn't redisplay the list every time, only if you make no choice and just press the Enter key. So whenever you want to see the list again, just press Enter.

It does not re-evaluate the code after the in, that is, you can't alter the list once you've begun. If you modified $DBLIST inside the loop, it wouldn't change your list of choices.

The looping will stop when it reaches the end of the file, which for interactive use means when you type Ctrl-D. (If you piped a series of choices into a select loop, it would end when the input ends.)

There isn't any formatting control over the list. If you're going to use select, you have to be satisfied with the way it displays your choices. You can, however, alter the prompt on the select.

See Also

- Recipe 3.7, "Selecting from a List of Options"
- Recipe 16.2, "Customizing Your Prompt"
- Recipe 16.10, "Using Secondary Prompts: $PS2, $PS3, $PS4"

6.17   Changing the Prompt on Simple Menus

Problem

You just don't like that prompt in the select menus. How can it be changed?

Solution

The *bash* environment variable $PS3 is the prompt used by select. Set it to a new value and you'll get a new prompt.

Discussion

This is the third of the *bash* prompts. The first ($PS1) is the prompt you get before most commands. (We've used $ in our examples, but it can be much more elaborate than that, including user ID or directory names.) If a line of command input needs to be continued, the second prompt is used ($PS2).

For select loops, the third prompt, $PS3, is used. Set it before the select statement to make the prompt be whatever you want. You can even modify it within the loop to have it change as the loop progresses.

Here's a script similar to the previous recipe, but one that counts how many times it has handled a valid input:

```
#!/usr/bin/env bash
# cookbook filename: dbinit.2
#
DBLIST=$(sh ./listdb | tail +2)

PS3="0 inits >"

select DB in $DBLIST
do
    if [ $DB ]
    then
        echo Initializing database: $DB

        PS3="$((i++)) inits >"

        mysql -uuser -p $DB <myinit.sql
    fi
done
$
```

We've added some extra whitespace to make the setting of $PS3 stand out more. The if statement assures us that we're only counting the times when the user entered a valid choice. Such a check would be useful in the previous version, but we were keeping it simple.

See Also

- Recipe 3.7, "Selecting from a List of Options"
- Recipe 6.17, "Changing the Prompt on Simple Menus"
- Recipe 16.2, "Customizing Your Prompt"
- Recipe 16.10, "Using Secondary Prompts: $PS2, $PS3, $PS4"

6.18 Creating a Simple RPN Calculator

Problem

You may be able to convert binary to decimal, octal, or hex in your head but it seems that you can't do simple arithmetic anymore and you can never find a calculator when you need one. What to do?

Solution

Create a calculator using shell arithmetic and RPN notation:

```
#!/usr/bin/env bash
# cookbook filename: rpncalc
#
# simple RPN command line (integer) calculator
#
# takes the arguments and computes with them
# of the form a b op
# allow the use of x instead of *
#
# error check our argument counts:
if [ \( $# -lt 3 \) -o  \( $(($# % 2)) -eq 0 \) ]
then
    echo "usage: calc number number op [ number op ] ..."
    echo "use x or '*' for multiplication"
    exit 1
fi

ANS=$(($1 ${3//x/*} $2))
shift 3
while [ $# -gt 0 ]
do
    ANS=$((ANS ${2//x/*} $1))
    shift 2
done
echo $ANS
```

Discussion

 Any arithmetic done within $(( )) is integer arithmetic only.

The idea of RPN (or *postfix*) style of notation puts the operands (the numbers) first, followed by the operator. If we are using RPN, we don't write 5 + 4 but rather 5 4 + as our expression. If you want to multiply the result by 2, then you just put 2 * on the end, so the whole expression would be 5 4 + 2 *, which is great for computers to parse because you can go left to right and never need parentheses. The result of any operation becomes the first operand for the next expression.

In our simple *bash* calculator we will allow the use of lowercase x as a substitute for the multiplication symbol since * has special meaning to the shell. But if you escape that special meaning by writing '*' or * we want that to work, too.

How do we error check the arguments? We will consider it an error if there are less than three arguments (we need two operands and one operator, e.g., 6 3 /). There can be more than three arguments, but in that case there will always be an odd number (since we start with three and add two more, a second operand and the next operator, and so on, always adding two more; the valid number of arguments would be 3 or 5 or 7 or 9 or ...). We check that with the expression:

```
$(($# % 2)) -eq 0
```

to see if the result is zero. The $(( )) says we're doing some shell arithmetic inside. We are using the % operator (called the *remainder operator*) to see if $# (which is the number of arguments) is divisible by 2 with no remainder (i.e., -eq 0).

Now that we know there are the right number of arguments, we can use them to compute the result. We write:

```
ANS=$(($1 ${3//x/*} $2))
```

which will compute the result and substitute the asterisk for the letter x at the same time. When you invoke the script you give it an RPN expression on the command line, but the shell syntax for arithmetic is our normal (*infix*) notation. So we can evaluate the expression inside of $(( )) but we have to switch the arguments around. Ignoring the x-to-* substitution for the moment, you can see it is just:

```
ANS=$(($1 $3 $2))
```

which just moves the operator between the two operands. *bash* will substitute the parameters before doing the arithmetic evaluation, so if $1 is 5 and $2 is 4 and $3 is a + then after parameter substitution *bash* will have:

```
ANS=$((5 + 4))
```

and it will evaluate that and assign the result, 9, to ANS. Done with those three arguments, we shift 3 to toss them and get the new arguments into play. Since we've already checked that there are an odd number of arguments, if we have any more arguments to process, we will have at least two more (only 1 more and it would be an even number, since 3+1=4).

From that point on we loop, taking two arguments at a time. The previous answer is the first operand, the next argument (now $1 as a result of the shift) is our second operand, and we put the operator inside $2 in between and evaluate it all much like before. Once we are out of arguments, the answer is what we have in ANS.

One last word, about the substitution. ${2} would be how we refer to the second argument. Though we often don't bother with the {} and just write $2, we need them here for the additional operations we will ask *bash* to perform on the argument. We write ${2//x/*} to say that we want to replace or substitute (//) an x with (indicated by the next /) an * before returning the value of $2. We could have written this in two steps by creating an extra variable:

```
OP=${2//x/*}
ANS=$((ANS OP $1))
```

That extra variable can be helpful as you first begin to use these features of *bash*, but once you are familiar with these common expressions, you'll find yourself putting them all together on one line (even though it'll be harder to read).

Are you wondering why we didn't write $ANS and $OP in the expression that does the evaluation? We don't have to use the $ on variable names inside of $(( )) expressions, except for the positional parameters (e.g., $1, $2). The positional parameters need it to distinguish them from regular numbers (e.g., 1, 2).

See Also

- Chapter 5
- Recipe 6.19, "Creating a Command-Line Calculator"

6.19   Creating a Command-Line Calculator

Problem

You need more than just integer arithmetic, and you've never been very fond of RPN notation. How about a different approach to a command-line calculator?

Solution

Create a trivial command-line calculator using *awk*'s built-in floating-point arithmetic expressions:

```
# cookbook filename: func_calc

# Trivial command line calculator
function calc
{
    awk "BEGIN {print \"The answer is: \" $* }";
}
```

Discussion

You may be tempted to try echo The answer is: $(($*)), which will work fine for integers, but will truncate the results of floating-point operations.

We use a function because *aliases* do not allow the use of arguments.

You will probably want to add this function to your global */etc/bashrc* or local */.bashrc*

The operators are what you'd expect and are the same as in C:

```
$ calc 2 + 3 + 4
The answer is: 9

$ calc 2 + 3 + 4.5
The answer is: 9.5
```

Watch out for shell meta characters. For example:

```
$ calc (2+2-3)*4
-bash: syntax error near unexpected token `2+2-3'
```

You need to escape the special meaning of the parentheses. You can put the expression inside single quotes, or just use the backslash in front of any special (to the shell) character to escape its meaning. For example:

```
$ calc '(2+2-3)*4'
The answer is: 4

$ calc \(2+2-3\)\*4
The answer is: 4

$ calc '(2+2-3)*4.5'
The answer is: 4.5
```

We need to escape the multiplication symbol too, since that has special meaning to *bash* as the wildcard for filenames. This is especially true if you like to put whitespace around your operators, as in 17 + 3 * 21, because then * will match all the files in the current directory, putting their names on the command line in place of the asterisk—definitely not what you want.

See Also

- man awk
- "ARITHMETIC EVALUATION" in the bash(1) manpage
- Recipe 6.18, "Creating a Simple RPN Calculator"
- Recipe 16.6, "Shortening or Changing Command Names"

CHAPTER 7
Intermediate Shell Tools I

It is time to expand our repertoire. This chapter's recipes use some utilities that are not part of the shell, but which are so useful that it is hard to imagine using the shell without them.

One of the over-arching philosophies of Unix (and thus Linux) is that of small (i.e., limited in scope) program pieces that can be fit together to provide powerful results. Rather than have one program do everything, we have many different programs that each do one thing well.

That is true of *bash* as well. While *bash* is getting big and feature-rich, it still doesn't try to do everything, and there are times when it is easier to use other commands to accomplish a task even if *bash* can be stretched to do it.

A simple example of this is the *ls* command. You needn't use *ls* to see the contents of your current directory. You could just type **echo *** to have filenames displayed. Or you could even get fancier, using the *bash* printf command and some formatting, etc. But that's not really the purpose of the shell, and someone has already provided a listing program (*ls*) to deal with all sorts of variations on filesystem information.

Perhaps more importantly, by not expecting *bash* to provide more filesystem listing features, we avoid additional feature creep pressures on *bash* and instead give it some measure of independence; *ls* can be released with new features without requiring that we all upgrade our *bash* versions.

But enough philosophy—back to the practical.

What we have here are three of the most useful text-related utilities: *grep*, *sed*, and *awk*.

The *grep* program searches for strings, the *sed* program provides a way to edit text as it passes through a pipeline, and *awk*, well, *awk* is its own interesting beast, a precursor to *perl* and a bit of a chameleon—it can look quite different depending on how it is used.

These utilities, and a few more that we will discuss in an upcoming chapter, become very much a part of most shell scripts and most sessions spent typing commands to *bash*. If your shell script requires a list of files on which to operate, it is likely that either *find* or *grep* will be used to supply that list of files, and that *sed* and/or *awk* will be used to parse the input or format the output at some stage of the shell script.

To say it another way, if our scripting examples are going to tackle real-world problems, they need to use the wider range of tools that are actually used by real-world *bash* users and programmers.

7.1 Sifting Through Files for a String

Problem

You need to find all occurrences of a string in one or more files.

Solution

The *grep* command searches through files looking for the expression you supply:

```
$ grep printf *.c
both.c:    printf("Std Out message.\n", argv[0], argc-1);
both.c:    fprintf(stderr, "Std Error message.\n", argv[0], argc-1);
good.c:    printf("%s: %d args.\n", argv[0], argc-1);
somio.c:        // we'll use printf to tell us what we
somio.c:        printf("open: fd=%d\n", iod[i]);
$
```

The files we searched through in this example were all in the current directory. We just used the simple shell pattern *.c to match all the files ending in *.c* with no preceding pathname.

Not all the files through which you want to search may be that conveniently located. Of course, the shell doesn't care how much pathname you type, so we could have done something like this:

```
$ grep printf ../lib/*.c ../server/*.c ../cmd/*.c *.c
```

Discussion

When more than one file is searched, *grep* begins its output with the filename, followed by a colon. The text after the colon is what actually appears in the files that *grep* searched.

The search matches any occurrence of the characters, so a line that contained the string "fprintf" was returned, since "printf" is contained within "fprintf".

The first (non-option) argument to *grep* can be just a simple string, as in this example, or it can be a more complex regular expression (RE). These REs are not the same as the shell's pattern matching, though they can look similar at times. Pattern matching is so powerful that you may find yourself relying on it to the point where you'll start using "grep" as a verb, and wishing you could make use of it everywhere, as in "I wish I could grep my desk for that paper you wanted."

You can vary the output from *grep* using options on the command line. If you don't want to see the specific filenames, you may turn this off using the -h switch to *grep*:

```
$ grep -h printf *.c
  printf("Std Out message.\n", argv[0], argc-1);
  fprintf(stderr, "Std Error message.\n", argv[0], argc-1);
  printf("%s: %d args.\n", argv[0], argc-1);
    // we'll use printf to tell us what we
    printf("open: fd=%d\n", iod[i]);
$
```

If you don't want to see the actual lines from the file, but only a count of the number of times the expression is found, then use the -c option:

```
$ grep -c printf *.c
both.c:2
good.c:1
somio.c:2
$
```

 A common mistake is to forget to provide *grep* with a source of input. For example grep *myvar*. In this case *grep* assumes you will provide input from STDIN, but you think it will get it from a file. So it just sits there forever, seemingly doing nothing. (In fact, it is waiting for input from your keyboard.) This is particularly hard to catch when you are grepping a large amount of data and expect it to take a while.

See Also

- man grep
- man regex (Linux, Solaris, HP-UX) or man re_format (BSD, Mac) for the details of your regular expression library
- *Mastering Regular Expressions* by Jeffrey E. F. Friedl (O'Reilly)
- *Classic Shell Scripting* by Nelson H.F. Beebe and Arnold Robbins (O'Reilly), Sections 3.1 and 3.2
- Chapter 9 and the *find* utility, for more far-reaching searches
- Recipe 19.5, "Expecting to Change Exported Variables"

7.2 Getting Just the Filename from a Search

Problem

You need to find the files in which a certain string appears. You don't want to see the line of text that was found, just the filenames.

Solution

Use the -l option of *grep* to get just the filenames:

```
$ grep -l printf *.c
both.c
good.c
somio.c
```

Discussion

If *grep* finds more than one match per file, it still only prints the name once. If *grep* finds no matches, it gives no output.

This option is handy if you want to build a list of files to be operated on, based on the fact that they contain the string that you're looking for. Put the *grep* command inside $( ) and those filenames can be used on the command line.

For example, to remove the files that contain the phrase "This file is obsolete," you could use this shell command combination:

```
$ rm -i $(grep -l 'This file is obsolete' * )
```

We've added the -i option to *rm* so that it will ask you before it removes each file. That's obviously a safer way to operate, given the power of this combination of commands.

bash expands the * to match every file in the current directory (but does not descend into sub-directories) and passes them as the arguments to *grep*. Then *grep* produces a list of filenames that contain the given string. This list then is handed to the *rm* command to remove each file.

See Also

- man grep
- man rm
- man regex (Linux, Solaris, HP-UX) or man re_format (BSD, Mac) for the details of your regular expression library
- *Mastering Regular Expressions* by Jeffrey E. F. Friedl (O'Reilly)
- Recipe 2.15, "Connecting Two Programs by Using Output As Input"
- Recipe 19.5, "Expecting to Change Exported Variables"

7.3 Getting a Simple True/False from a Search

Problem

You need to know whether a certain string is in a particular file. However, you don't want any output, just a yes or no sort of answer.

Solution

Use -q, the "quiet" option for *grep*. Or, for maximum portability, just throw the output away by redirecting it into */dev/null*. Either way, your answer is in the *bash* return status variable $? so you can use it in an if-test like this:

```
$ grep -q findme bigdata.file
$ if [ $? -eq 0 ] ; then echo yes ; else  echo nope ; fi
nope
$
```

Discussion

In a shell script, you often don't want the results of the search displayed in the output; you just want to know whether there is a match so that your script can branch accordingly.

As with most Unix/Linux commands, a return value of 0 indicates successful completion. In this case, success is defined as having found the string in at least one of the given files (in this example, we searched in only one file). The return value is stored in the shell variable $?, which we can then use in an if statement.

If we list multiple filenames after grep -q, then *grep* stops searching after the very first occurrence of the search string being found. It doesn't search all the files, as you really just want to know whether it found any occurrence of the string. If you really need to read through all the files (why?), then rather than use -q you can do this:

```
$ grep findme bigdata.file >/dev/null
$ if [ $? -eq 0 ] ; then echo yes ; else  echo nope ; fi
nope
$
```

The redirecting to */dev/null* sends the output to a special kind of device, a *bit bucket*, that just throws everything you give it away.

The */dev/null* technique is also useful if you want to write shell scripts that are portable across the various flavors of *grep* that are available on Unix and Linux systems, should you find one that doesn't support the -q option.

See Also

- man grep
- man regex (Linux, Solaris, HP-UX) or man re_format (BSD, Mac) for the details of your regular expression library

---

- *Mastering Regular Expressions* by Jeffrey E. F. Friedl (O'Reilly)
- Recipe 19.5, "Expecting to Change Exported Variables"

7.4   Searching for Text While Ignoring Case

Problem

You need to search for a string (e.g., "error") in a log file, and you want to do it case-insensitively to catch all occurrences.

Solution

Use the -i option on *grep* to ignore case:

```
$ grep -i error logfile.msgs
```

Discussion

A case-insensitive search finds messages written "ERROR", "error", "Error," as well as ones like "ErrOR" and "eRrOr." This option is particularly useful for finding words anywhere that you might have mixed-case text, including words that might be capitalized at the beginning of a sentence or email addresses.

See Also

- man grep
- man regex (Linux, Solaris, HP-UX) or man re_format (BSD, Mac) for the details of your regular expression library
- *Mastering Regular Expressions* by Jeffrey E. F. Friedl (O'Reilly)
- Chapter 9's discussion of the *find* command and its -iname option
- Recipe 19.5, "Expecting to Change Exported Variables"

7.5   Doing a Search in a Pipeline

Problem

You need to search for some text, but the text you're searching for isn't in a file; instead, it's in the output of a command or perhaps even the output of a pipeline of commands.

Solution

Just pipe your results into *grep*:

```
$ some pipeline | of commands | grep
```

Discussion

When no filename is supplied to *grep*, it reads from standard input. Most well-designed utilities meant for shell scripting will do this. It is one of the things that makes them so useful as building blocks for shell scripts.

If you also want to have *grep* search error messages that come from the previous command, be sure to redirect its error output into standard output before the pipe:

```
$ gcc bigbadcode.c 2>&1 | grep -i error
```

This command attempts to compile some hypothetical, hairy piece of code. We redirect standard error into standard output (2>&1) before we proceed to pipe (|) the output into *grep*, where it will search case-insensitively (-i) looking for the string error.

Don't overlook the possibility of grepping the output of *grep*. Why would you want to do that? To further narrow down the results of a search. Let's say you wanted to find out Bob Johnson's email address:

```
$ grep -i johnson mail/*
... too much output to think about; there are lots of Johnsons in the world ...
$ !! | grep -i robert
grep -i johnson mail/* | grep -i robert
... more manageable output ...
$ !! | grep -i "the bluesman"
grep -i johnson mail/* | grep -i robert | grep -i "the bluesman"
Robert M. Johnson, The Bluesman <rmj@noplace.org>
```

You could have re-typed the first *grep*, but this example also shows the power of the !! history operator. The !! let's you repeat the previous command without retyping it. You can then continue adding to the command line after the !! as we show here. The shell will display the command that it runs, so that you can see what you got as a result of the !! substitution (see Recipe 18.2, "Repeating the Last Command").

You can build up a long *grep* pipeline very quickly and simply this way, seeing the results of the intermediate steps as you go, and deciding how to refine your search with additional *grep* expressions. You could also accomplish the same task with a single *grep* and a clever regular expression, but we find that building up a pipeline incrementally is easier.

See Also

- man grep
- man regex (Linux, Solaris, HP-UX) or man re_format (BSD, Mac) for the details of your regular expression library
- *Mastering Regular Expressions* by Jeffrey E. F. Friedl (O'Reilly)
- Recipe 2.15, "Connecting Two Programs by Using Output As Input"
- Recipe 18.2, "Repeating the Last Command"
- Recipe 19.5, "Expecting to Change Exported Variables"

7.6   Paring Down What the Search Finds

Problem

Your search is returning way more than you expected, including many results you don't want.

Solution

Pipe the results into grep -v with an expression that describes what you don't want to see.

Let's say you were searching for messages in a log file, and you wanted all the messages from the month of December. You know that your logfile uses the 3-letter abbreviation for December as Dec, but you're not sure if it's always written as Dec, so to be sure to catch them all you type:

```
$ grep -i dec logfile
```

but you find that you also get phrases like these:

```
...
error on Jan 01: not a decimal number
error on Feb 13: base converted to Decimal
warning on Mar 22: using only decimal numbers
error on Dec 16 : the actual message you wanted
error on Jan 01: not a decimal number
...
```

A quick and dirty solution in this case is to pipe the first result into a second *grep* and tell the second *grep* to ignore any instances of "decimal":

```
$ grep -i dec logfile | grep -vi decimal
```

It's not uncommon to string a few of these together (as new, unexpected matches are also discovered) to filter down the search results to what you're really looking for:

```
$ grep -i dec logfile | grep -vi decimal | grep -vi decimate
```

Discussion

The "dirty" part of this "quick and dirty" solution is that the solution here might also get rid of some of the December log messages, ones that you wanted to keep—if they have the word "decimal" in them, they'll be filtered out by the grep -v.

The -v option can be handy if used carefully; you just have to keep in mind what it might exclude.

For this particular example, a better solution would be to use a more powerful regular expression to match the December date, one that looked for "Dec" followed by a space and two digits:

```
$ grep 'Dec [0-9][0-9]' logfile
```

But that often won't work either because *syslog* uses a space to pad single digit dates, so we add a space in the first list [0-9]:

```
$ grep 'Dec [0-9 ][0-9]' logfile
```

We used single quotes around the expression because of the embedded spaces, and to avoid any possible shell interpretation of the bracket characters (not that there would be, but just as a matter of habit). It's good to get into the habit of using single quotes around anything that might possibly be confusing to the shell. We could have written:

```
$ grep Dec\ [0-9\ ][0-9] logfile
```

escaping the space with a backslash, but in that form it's harder to see where the search string ends and the filename begins.

See Also

- man grep
- man regex (Linux, Solaris, HP-UX) or man re_format (BSD, Mac) for the details of your regular expression library
- *Mastering Regular Expressions* by Jeffrey E. F. Friedl (O'Reilly)
- Recipe 19.5, "Expecting to Change Exported Variables"

7.7   Searching with More Complex Patterns

The regular expression mechanism of *grep* provides for some very powerful patterns that can fit most of your needs.

A *regular expression* describes patterns for matching against strings. Any alphabetic character just matches that character in the string. "A" matches "A", "B" matches "B"; no surprise there. But regular expressions define other special characters that can be used by themselves or in combination with other characters to make more complex patterns.

We already said that any character without some special meaning simply matches itself—"A" to "A" and so on. The next important rule is to combine letters just by position, so "AB" matches "A" followed by "B". This, too, seems obvious.

The first special character is (.). A period (.) matches any single character. Therefore .... matches any four characters; A. matches an "A" followed by any character; and .A. matches any character, then an "A", then any character (not necessarily the same character as the first).

An asterisk (*) means to repeat zero or more occurrences of the previous character. So A* means zero or more "A" characters, and .* means zero or more characters of any sort (such as "abcdefg", "aaaabc", "sdfgf ;lkjhj", or even an empty line).

So what does ..* mean? Any single character followed by zero or more of any character (i.e., one or more characters) but not an empty line.

Speaking of lines, the caret ^ matches the beginning of a line of text and the dollar sign $ matches the end of a line; hence ^$ matches an empty line (the beginning followed by the end, with nothing in between).

What if you want to match an actual period, caret, dollar sign, or any other special character? Precede it by a backslash (\). So ion. matches the letters "ion" followed by any other letter, but ion\. matches "ion" bounded by a period (e.g., at the end of a sentence or wherever else it appears with a trailing dot).

A set of characters enclosed in square brackets (e.g., [abc]) matches any one of those characters (e.g., "a" or "b" or "c"). If the first character inside the square brackets is a caret, then it matches any character that is *not* in that set.

For example, [AaEeIiOoUu] matches any of the vowels, and [^AaEeIiOoUu] matches any character that is not a vowel. This last case is not the same as saying that it matches consonants because [^AaEeIiOoUu] also matches punctuation and other special characters that are neither vowels nor consonants.

Another mechanism we want to introduce is a repetition mechanism written as \{n,m\} where n is the minimum number of repetitions and m is the maximum. If it is written as \{n\} it means "exactly n times," and when written as "\{n,\}" then "at least n times."

For example, the regular expression A\{5\} means five capital A letters in a row, whereas A\{5,\} means five or more capital A letters.

7.8   Searching for an SSN

Problem

You need a regular expression to match a Social Security number. These numbers are nine digits long, typically grouped as three digits, then two digits, then a final four digits (e.g., 123-45-6789). Sometimes they are written without hyphens, so you need to make hyphens optional in the regular expression.

Solution

```
$ grep '[0-9]\{3\}-\{0,1\}[0-9]\{2\}-\{0,1\}[0-9]\{4\}' datafile
```

Discussion

These kinds of regular expressions are often jokingly referred to as *write only* expressions, meaning that they can be difficult or impossible to read. We'll take this one apart to help you understand it. In general, though, in any *bash* script that you write using regular expressions, be sure to put comments nearby explaining what you intended the regular expression to match.

If we added some spaces to the regular expression we would improve its readability, making visual comprehension easier, but it would change the meaning—it would say that we'd need to match space characters at those points in the expression. Ignoring that for the moment, let's insert some spaces into the previous regular expression so that we can read it more easily:

```
[0-9]\{3\}   -\{0,1\}   [0-9]\{2\}  -\{0,1\} [0-9]\{4\}
```

The first grouping says "any digit" then "exactly 3 times." The next grouping says "a dash" then "0 or 1 time." The third grouping says "any digit" then "exactly 2 times." The next grouping says "a dash" then "0 or 1 time." The last grouping says "any digit" then "exactly 4 times."

See Also

- man regex (Linux, Solaris, HP-UX) or man re_format (BSD, Mac) for the details of your regular expression library
- *Classic Shell Scripting* by Nelson H.F. Beebe and Arnold Robbins (O'Reilly) Section 3.2, for more about regular expressions and the tools that use them
- *Mastering Regular Expressions* by Jeffrey E. F. Friedl (O'Reilly)
- Recipe 19.5, "Expecting to Change Exported Variables"

7.9   Grepping Compressed Files

Problem

You need to grep some compressed files. Do you have to uncompress them first?

Solution

Not if you have *zgrep, zcat*, or *gzcat* on your system.

zgrep is simply a *grep* that understands various compressed and uncompressed files (which types are understood varies from system to system). You will commonly run into this when searching *syslog* messages on Linux, since the log rotation facilities leave the current log file uncompressed (so it can be in use), but *gzip* archival logs:

```
$ zgrep 'search term' /var/log/messages*
```

zcat is simply a *cat* that understands various compressed and uncompressed files (which types are understood varies from system to system). It might understand more formats than *zgrep*, and it might be installed on more systems by default. It is also used in recovering damaged compressed files, since it will simply output everything it possibly can, instead of erroring out as *gunzip* or other tools might.

gzcat is similar to *zcat*, the differences having to do with commercial versus free Unix variants, and backward compatibility:

```
$ zcat /var/log/messages.1.gz
```

Discussion

The *less* utility may also be configured to transparently display various compressed files, which is very handy. See Recipe 8.15, "Doing More with less."

See Also

* Recipe 8.6, "Compressing Files"
* Recipe 8.7, "Uncompressing Files"
* Recipe 8.15, "Doing More with less"

7.10   Keeping Some Output, Discarding the Rest

Problem

You need a way to keep some of your output and discard the rest.

Solution

The following code prints the first word of every line of input:

```
$ awk '{print $1}' myinput.file
```

Words are delineated by whitespace. The *awk* utility reads data from the filename supplied on the command line, or from standard input if no filename is given. Therefore, you can redirect the input from a file, like this:

```
$ awk '{print $1}' < myinput.file
```

or even from a pipe, like this:

```
$ cat myinput.file | awk '{print $1}'
```

Discussion

The *awk* program can be used in several different ways. Its easiest, simplest use is just to print one or more selected fields from its input.

Fields are delineated by whitespace (or specified with the -F option) and are numbered starting at 1. The field $0 represents the entire line of input.

awk is a complete programming language; *awk* scripts can become extremely complex. This is only the beginning.

See Also

* man awk
* *http://www.faqs.org/faqs/computer-lang/awk/faq/*
* *Effective awk Programming* by Arnold Robbins (O'Reilly)
* *sed & awk* by Arnold Robbins and Dale Dougherty (O'Reilly)

7.11 Keeping Only a Portion of a Line of Output

Problem

You want to keep only a portion of a line of output, such as just the first and last words. For example, you would like *ls* to list just filenames and permissions, without all of the other information provided by ls -l. However, you can't find any options to *ls* that would limit the output in that way.

Solution

Pipe *ls* into *awk*, and just pull out the fields that you need:

```
$ ls -l | awk '{print $1, $NF}'
total 151130
-rw-r--r-- add.1
drwxr-xr-x art
drwxr-xr-x bin
-rw-r--r-- BuddyIcon.png
drwxr-xr-x CDs
drwxr-xr-x downloads
drwxr-sr-x eclipse
...
$
```

Discussion

Consider the output from the ls -l command. One line of it looks like this:

```
drwxr-xr-x  2 username group     176 2006-10-28 20:09 bin
```

so it is convenient for *awk* to parse (by default, whitespace delineates fields in *awk*). The output from ls -l has the permissions as the first field and the filename as the last field.

We use a bit of a trick to print the filename. Since the various fields are referenced in *awk* using a dollar sign followed by the field number (e.g., $1, $2, $3), and since *awk* has a built-in variable called NF that holds the number of fields found on the current line, $NF always refers to the last field. (For example, the *ls* output line has eight fields, so the variable NF contains 8, so $NF refers to the eighth field of the input line, which in our example is the filename.)

Just remember that you don't use a $ to read the value of an *awk* variable (unlike *bash* variables). NF is a valid variable reference by itself. Adding a $ before it changes its meaning from "the number of fields on the current line" to "the last field on the current line."

See Also

- man awk
- *http://www.faqs.org/faqs/computer-lang/awk/faq/*
- *Effective awk Programming* by Arnold Robbins (O'Reilly)
- *sed & awk* by Arnold Robbins and Dale Dougherty (O'Reilly)

7.12   Reversing the Words on Each Line

Problem

You want to print the input lines with words in the reverse order.

Solution

```
$ awk '{
>       for (i=NF; i>0; i--) {
>            printf "%s ", $i;
>       }
>       printf "\n"
>   }'
```

You don't type the > characters; the shell will print those as a prompt to say that you haven't ended your command yet (it is looking for the matching single-quote mark). Because the *awk* program is enclosed in single quotes, the *bash* shell lets us type multiple lines, prompting us with the secondary prompt > until we supply the matching end quote. We spaced out the program for readability, even though we could have stuffed it all onto one line like this:

```
$ awk '{for (i=NF; i>0; i--) {printf "%s ", $i;} printf "\n" }'
```

Discussion

The *awk* program has syntax for a for loop, very much in the C language style. It even supports a printf mechanism for formatted output, again modeled after the C language version (or the *bash* version, too). We use the for loop to count down from the last to the first field, and print each field as we go. We deliberately don't put a \n on that first printf because we want to keep the several fields on the same line of output. When the loop is done, we add a newline to terminate the line of output.

The reference to $i is very different in *awk* compared to *bash*. In *bash*, when we write $i we are getting at the value stored in the variable named i. But in *awk*, as with most programming languages, we simply reference the value in i by naming it—that is by just writing i. So what is meant by $i in *awk*? The value of the variable i is resolved to a number, and then the dollar-number expression is understood as a reference to a field (or word) of input—that is, the i-th field. So as i counts down from the last field to the first, this loop will print the fields in that reversed order.

See Also

- man printf(1)
- man awk
- *http://www.faqs.org/faqs/computer-lang/awk/faq/*
- *Effective awk Programming* by Arnold Robbins (O'Reilly)
- *sed & awk* by Arnold Robbins and Dale Dougherty (O'Reilly)
- "printf" in Appendix A

7.13 Summing a List of Numbers

Problem

You need to sum a list of numbers, including numbers that don't appear on lines by themselves.

Solution

Use *awk* both to isolate the field to be summed and to do the summing. Here we'll sum up the numbers that are the file sizes from the output of an ls -l command:

```
$ ls -l | awk '{sum += $5} END {print sum}'
```

Discussion

We are summing up the fifth field of the ls -l output. The output of ls -l looks like this:

```
-rw-r--r--  1 albing users 267 2005-09-26 21:26 lilmax
```

and the fields are: permissions, links, owner, group, size (in bytes), date, time, and filename. We're only interested in the size, so we use $5 in our *awk* program to reference that field.

We enclose the two bodies of our *awk* program in braces ({}); note that there can be more than one body (or block) of code in an *awk* program. A block of code preceded by the literal keyword END is only run once, when the rest of the program has finished. Similarly, you can prefix a block of code with BEGIN and supply some code that will be run before any input is read. The BEGIN block is useful for initializing variables, and we could have used one here to initialize sum, but *awk* guarantees that variables will start out empty.

If you look at the output of an ls -l command, you will notice that the first line is a total, and doesn't fit our expected format for the other lines.

We have two choices for dealing with that. We can pretend it's not there, which is the approach taken above. Since that undesired line doesn't have a fifth field, then our reference to $5 will be empty, and our sum won't change.

The more conscientious approach would be to eliminate that field. We could do so before we give the output to *awk* by using *grep*:

```
$ ls -l | grep -v '^total' | awk '{sum += $5} END {print sum}'
```

or we could do a similar thing within *awk*:

```
$ ls -l | awk '/^total/{getline} {sum += $5} END {print sum}'
```

The ^total is a regular expression (regex); it means "the letters t-o-t-a-l occurring at the beginning of a line" (the leading ^ anchors the search to the beginning of a line). For any line of input matching that regex, the associated block of code will be executed. The second block of code (the sum) has no leading text, the absence of which tells *awk* to execute it for every line of input (meaning this will happen regardless of whether the line matches the regex).

Now, the whole point of adding the special case for "total" was to exclude such a line from our summing. Therefore in the ^total block we add a getline command, which reads in the next line of input. Thus, when the second block of code is reached, it is with a new line of input. The getline does not re-match all the patterns from the top, only the ones from there on down. In *awk* programming, the order of the blocks of code matters.

See Also

- man awk
- *http://www.faqs.org/faqs/computer-lang/awk/faq/*
- *Effective awk Programming* by Arnold Robbins (O'Reilly)
- *sed & awk* by Arnold Robbins and Dale Dougherty (O'Reilly)

7.14   Counting String Values

Problem

You need to count all the occurrences of several different strings, including some strings whose values you don't know beforehand. That is, you're not trying to count the occurrences of a pre-determined set of strings. Rather, you are going to encounter some strings in your data and you want to count these as-yet-unknown strings.

Solution

Use *awk*'s associative arrays (also known as hashes) for your counting.

For our example, we'll count how many files are owned by various users on our system. The username shows up as the third field in an ls -l output. So we'll use that field ($3) as the index of the array, and increment that member of the array:

```
#
# cookbook filename: asar.awk
#
NF > 7 {
        user[$3]++
      }
END {
        for (i in user)
        {
            printf "%s owns %d files\n", i, user[i]
        }
      }
```

We invoke *awk* a bit differently here. Because this *awk* script is a bit more complex, we've put it in a separate file. We use the -f option to tell *awk* where to get the script file:

```
$ ls -lR /usr/local | awk -f asar.awk
bin owns 68 files
albing owns 1801 files
root owns 13755 files
man owns 11491 files
$
```

Discussion

We use the condition NF > 7 as a qualifier to part of the *awk* script to weed out the lines that do not contain filenames, which appear in the ls -lR output and are useful for readability because they include blank lines to separate different directories as well as total counts for each subdirectory. Such lines don't have as many fields (or words). The expression NF>7 that precedes the opening brace is not enclosed in slashes, which is to say that it is not a regular expression. It's a logical expression, much like you would use in an if statement, and it evaluates to true or false. The NF variable is a special built-in variable that refers to the number of fields for the current line of input. So only if a line of input has more than seven fields (words of text) will it be processed by the statements within the braces.

The key line, however, is this one:

```
user[$3]++
```

Here the username (e.g., *bin*) is used as the index to the array. It's called an *associative array*, because a hash table (or similar mechanism) is being used to associate each unique string with a numerical index. *awk* is doing all that work for you behind the scenes; you don't have to write any string comparisons and lookups and such.

Once you've built such an array it might seem difficult to get the values back out. For this, *awk* has a special form of the for loop. Instead of the numeric for(i=0; i<max; i++) that *awk* also supports, there is a particular syntax for associative arrays:

```
for (i in user)
```

In this expression, the variable i will take on successive values (in no particular order) from the various values used as indexes to the array user. In our example, this means that i will take on the values (i.e., bin, albing, man, root), one each iteration of the loop. If you haven't seen associative arrays before, then we hope that you're surprised and impressed. It is a very powerful feature of *awk* (and Perl).

See Also

- man awk
- *http://www.faqs.org/faqs/computer-lang/awk/faq/*
- *Effective awk Programming* by Arnold Robbins (O'Reilly)
- *sed & awk* by Arnold Robbins and Dale Dougherty (O'Reilly)

7.15   Showing Data As a Quick and Easy Histogram

Problem

You need a quick screen-based histogram of some data.

Solution

Use the associative arrays of *awk*, as discussed in the previous recipe:

```awk
#
# cookbook filename: hist.awk
#
function max(arr,  big)
{
    big = 0;
    for (i in user)
    {
        if (user[i] > big) { big=user[i];}
    }
    return big
}

NF > 7 {
        user[$3]++
    }
END {
        # for scaling
        maxm = max(user);
        for (i in user)
        {
```

```
            #printf "%s owns %d files\n", i, user[i]
            scaled = 60 * user[i] / maxm ;
            printf "%-10.10s  [%8d]:", i, user[i]
            for (i=0; i<scaled; i++) {
                printf "#";
            }
            printf "\n";
        }
    }
```

When we run it with the same input as the previous recipe, we get:

```
$ ls -lR /usr/local | awk -f hist.awk
bin        [      68]:#
albing     [    1801]:#######
root       [   13755]:#################################################
man        [   11491]:#########################################
$
```

Discussion

We could have put the code for max as the first code inside the END block, but we wanted to show you that you can define functions in *awk*. We are using a bit of fancier printf. The string format %-10.10s will left justify and pad to 10 characters but also truncate at 10 characters. The integer format %8d will assure that the integer is printed in an 8 character field. This gives each histogram the same starting point, by using the same amount of space regardless of the username or the size of the integer.

Like all arithmetic in *awk*, the scaling calculation is done with floating point unless we explicitly truncate the result with a call to the built-in int( ) function. We don't do so, which means that the for loop will execute at least once, so that even the smallest amount of data will still display a single hash mark.

The order of data returned from the for (i in user) loop is in no particular order, probably based on some convenient ordering of the underlying hash table. If you wanted the histogram displayed in a sorted order, either numeric by count or alphabetical by username, you would have to add some sorting. One way to do this is to break this program apart into two pieces, sending the output from the first part into the *sort* command and then piping that output into the second piece to print the histogram.

See Also

- man awk
- *http://www.faqs.org/faqs/computer-lang/awk/faq/*
- *Effective awk Programming* by Arnold Robbins (O'Reilly)
- *sed & awk* by Arnold Robbins and Dale Dougherty (O'Reilly)
- Recipe 8.1, "Sorting Your Output"

7.16   Showing a Paragraph of Text After a Found Phrase

Problem

You are searching for a phrase in a document, and want to show the paragraph after the found phrase.

Solution

We're assuming a simple text file, where *paragraph* means all the text between blank lines, so the occurrence of a blank line implies a paragraph break. Given that, it's a pretty short *awk* program:

```
$ cat para.awk
/keyphrase/ { flag=1 }
{ if (flag == 1) { print $0 } }
/^$/ { flag=0 }
$
$ awk -f para.awk < searchthis.txt
```

Discussion

There are just three simple code blocks. The first is invoked when a line of input matches the regular expression (here just the word "keyphrase"). If "keyphrase" occurs anywhere within a line of input, that is a match and this block of code will be executed. All that happens in this block is that the flag is set.

The second code block is invoked for every line of input, since there is no regular expression preceding its open brace. Even the input that matches "keyphrase" will also be applied to this code block (if we didn't want that effect, we could use a `continue` statement in the first block). All this second block does is print the entire input line, but only if the flag is set.

The third block has a regular expression that, if satisfied, will simply reset (turn off) the flag. That regular expression uses two characters with special meaning—the caret (^), when used as the first character of a regular expression, matches the beginning of the line; the dollar sign ($), when used as the last character, matches the end of the line. So the regular expression ^$ means "an empty line" because it has no characters between the beginning and end of the line.

We could have used a slightly more complicated regular expression for an empty line to let it handle any line with just whitespace rather than a completely blank line. That would make the third line look like this:

```
/^[:blank:]*$/ { flag=0 }
```

Perl programmers love the sort of problem and solution discussed in this recipe, but we've implemented it with *awk* because Perl is (mostly) beyond the scope of this book. If you know Perl, by all means use it. If not, *awk* might be all you need.

See Also

- man awk
- *http://www.faqs.org/faqs/computer-lang/awk/faq/*
- *Effective awk Programming* by Arnold Robbins (O'Reilly)
- *sed & awk* by Arnold Robbins and Dale Dougherty (O'Reilly)

Intermediate Shell Tools II

Once again, we have some useful utilities that are not part of the shell but are used in so many shell scripts that you really should know about them.

Sorting is such a common task, and so useful for readability reasons, that it's good to know about the *sort* command. In a similar vein, the *tr* command will translate or map from one character to another, or even just delete characters.

One common thread here is that these utilities are written not just as standalone commands, but also as *filters* that can be included in a pipeline of commands. These sorts of commands will typically take one to many filenames as parameters (or arguments), but in the absence of any filenames they will read from standard input. They also write to standard output. That combination makes it easy to connect to the command with pipes, as in *something* | sort | *even more*.

That makes them especially useful, and avoids the clutter and confusion of a myriad of temporary files.

8.1 Sorting Your Output

Problem

You would like output in a sorted order, but you don't want to write (yet again) a custom sort function for your program or shell script. Hasn't this been done already?

Solution

Use the *sort* utility. You can sort one or more files by putting the file names on the command line:

```
$ sort file1.txt file2.txt myotherfile.xyz
```

With no filenames on the command, *sort* will read from standard input so you can pipe the output from a previous command into *sort*:

```
$ somecommands | sort
```

Discussion

It can be handy to have your output in sorted order, and handier still not to have to add sorting code to every program you write. The shell's piping allows you to hook up *sort* to any program's standard output.

There a few options to *sort*, but two of the three most worth remembering are:

```
$ sort -r
```

to reverse the order of the sort (where, to borrow a phrase, the last shall be first and the first, last); and

```
$ sort -f
```

to "fold" lower- and uppercase characters together; i.e., to ignore the case differences. This can be done either with the -f option or with a GNU long-format option:

```
$ sort --ignore-case
```

We decided to keep you in suspense, so see the next recipe, Recipe 8.2, "Sorting Numbers," for the third coolest *sort* option.

See Also

- man sort
- Recipe 8.2, "Sorting Numbers"

8.2   Sorting Numbers

Problem

When sorting numeric data you notice that the order doesn't seem right:

```
$ sort somedata
2
200
21
250
$
```

Solution

You need to tell *sort* that the data should be sorted as numbers. Specify a numeric sort with the -n option:

```
$ sort -n somedata
2
21
200
250
$
```

Discussion

There is nothing wrong with the original (if odd) sort order if you realize that it is an alphabetic sort on the data (i.e., 21 comes after 200 because 1 comes after 0 in an alphabetic sort). Of course, what you probably want is numeric ordering, so you need to use the -n option.

sort -rn can be very handy in giving you a descending frequency list of something when combined with uniq -c. For example, let's display the most popular shells on this system:

```
$ cut -d':' -f7 /etc/passwd | sort | uniq -c | sort -rn
    20 /bin/sh
    10 /bin/false
     2 /bin/bash
     1 /bin/sync
```

cut -d':' -f7 /etc/passwd isolates the shell from the */etc/passwd* file. Then we have to do an initial sort so that *uniq* will work. uniq -c counts consecutive, duplicate lines, which is why we need the pre-sort. Then sort -rn gives us a reverse, numerical sort, with the most popular shell at the top.

If you don't need to count the occurrences and just want a unique list of values—i.e., if you want *sort* to remove duplicates—then you can use the -u option on the *sort* command (and omit the *uniq* command). So to find just the list of different shells on this system:

```
cut -d':' -f7 /etc/passwd | sort -u
```

See Also

- man sort
- man uniq
- man cut

8.3   Sorting IP Addresses

Problem

You want to sort a list of numeric IP address, but you'd like to sort by the last portion of the number or by the entire address logically.

Solution

To sort by the last octet only (old syntax):

```
$ sort -t. -n +3.0 ipaddr.list
10.0.0.2
192.168.0.2
```

```
192.168.0.4
10.0.0.5
192.168.0.12
10.0.0.20
$
```

To sort the entire address as you would expect (POSIX syntax):

```
$ sort -t . -k 1,1n -k 2,2n -k 3,3n -k 4,4n ipaddr.list
10.0.0.2
10.0.0.5
10.0.0.20
192.168.0.2
192.168.0.4
192.168.0.12
$
```

Discussion

We know this is numeric data, so we use the -n option. The -t option indicates the character to use as a *separator* between *fields* (in our case, a period) so that we can also specify which fields to sort first. In the first example, we start sorting with the third field (zero-based) from the left, and the very first character (again, zero-based) of that field, so +3.0.

In the second example, we used the new POSIX specification instead of the traditional (but obsolete) +pos1 -pos2 method. Unlike the older method, it is not zero-based, so fields start at 1.

```
$ sort -t . -k 1,1n -k 2,2n -k 3,3n -k 4,4n ipaddr.list
```

Wow, that's ugly. Here it is in the old format: sort -t. +0n -1 +1n -2 +2n -3 +3n -4, which is just as bad.

Using -t. to define the field delimiter is the same, but the sort-key fields are given quite differently. In this case, -k 1,1n means "start sorting at the beginning of field one (1) and (,) stop sorting at the end of field one (1) and do a numerical sort (n). Once you get that, the rest is easy. When using more than one field, it's very important to tell *sort* where to stop. The default is to go to the end of the line, which is often not what you want and which will really confuse you if you don't understand what it's doing.

 The order that *sort* uses is affected by your locale setting. If your results are not as expected, that's one thing to check.

Your sort order will vary from system to system depending on whether your *sort* command defaults to using a *stable* sort. A stable sort preserves the original order in the sorted data when the sort fields are equal. Linux and Solaris do not default to a stable sort, but NetBSD does. And while -S turns off the stable sort on NetBSD, it sets the buffer size on other versions of *sort*.

If we run this *sort* command on a Linux or Solaris system:

```
$ sort -t. -k4n ipaddr.list
```

or this command on a NetBSD system

```
$ sort -t. -S -k4n ipaddr.list
```

we will get the data sorted as shown in the 1st column of Table 8-1. Remove the -S on a NetBSD system, and *sort* will produce the ordering as shown in the second column.

Table 8-1. Sort ordering comparison of Linux, Solaris, and NetBSD

Linux and Solaris (default) and NetBSD (with -S)		NetBSD stable (default) sort ordering	
10.0.0.2	# sluggish	192.168.0.2	# laptop
192.168.0.2	# laptop	10.0.0.2	# sluggish
10.0.0.4	# mainframe	192.168.0.4	# office
192.168.0.4	# office	10.0.0.4	# mainframe
192.168.0.12	# speedy	192.168.0.12	# speedy
10.0.0.20	# lanyard	10.0.0.20	# lanyard

If our input file, *ipaddr.list*, had all the 192.168 addresses first, followed by all the 10. addresses, then the stable sort would leave the 192.168 address first when there is a tie, that is when two elements in our sort have the same value. We can see in Table 8-1 that this situation exists for laptop and sluggish, since each has a 2 as its fourth field, and also for mainframe and office, which tie with 4. In the default Linux sort (and NetBSD with the -S option specified), the order is not guaranteed.

To get back to something easy, and just for practice, let's sort by the text in our IP address list. This time we want our separator to be the # character and we want an alphabetic sort on the second field, so we get:

```
$ sort -t'#' -k2 ipaddr.list
10.0.0.20        # lanyard
192.168.0.2      # laptop
10.0.0.5         # mainframe
192.168.0.4      # office
10.0.0.2         # sluggish
192.168.0.12     # speedy
$
```

The sorting will start with the second key, and in this case, go through the end of the line. With just the one separator (#) per line, we didn't need to specify the ending, though we could have written -k2,2 .

See Also

- man sort
- Appendix B's example *./functions/inetaddr*, as provided in the *bash* tarball

8.4   Cutting Out Parts of Your Output

Problem

You need to look at only part of your fixed-width or column-based data. You'd like to take a subset of it, based on the column position.

Solution

Use the *cut* command with the -c option to take particular columns: Note that our example 'ps' command only works with certain systems; e.g., CentOS-4, Fedora Core 5, and Ubuntu work, but Red Hat 8, NetBSD, Solaris, and Mac OS X all garble the output due to using different columns:

```
$ ps -l | cut -c12-15
 PID
5391
7285
7286
$
```

or:

```
$ ps -elf | cut -c58-
(output not shown)
```

Discussion

With the *cut* command we specify what portion of the lines we want to keep. In the first example, we are keeping columns 12 (starting at column one) through 15, inclusive. In the second case, we specify starting at column 58 but don't specify the end of the range so that *cut* will take from column 58 on through the end of the line.

Most of the data manipulation we've looked at has been based on *fields*, relative positions separated by characters called *delimiters*. The *cut* command can do that too, but it is one of the few utilities that you'll use with *bash* that can also easily deal with fixed-width, columnar data (via the -c option).

Using *cut* to print out fields rather than columns is possible, though more limited than other choices such as *awk*. The default delimiter between fields is the Tab character, but you can specify a different delimiter with the -d option. Here is an example of a *cut* command using fields:

```
$ cut -d'#' -f2 < ipaddr.list
```

and an equivalent *awk* command:

```
$ awk -F'#' '{print $2}' < ipaddr.list
```

You can even use *cut* to handle non-matching delimiters by using more than one *cut*. You may be better off using a regular expression with *awk* for this, but sometimes a couple of quick and dirty cuts are faster to figure out and type.

Here is how you can get the field out from between square brackets. Note that the first *cut* uses a delimiter of open square bracket (-d'[') and field 2 (-f2 starting at 1). Because the first *cut* has already removed part of the line, the second *cut* uses a delimiter of closed square bracket (-d']') and field 1 (-f1).

```
$ cat delimited_data
Line [11].
Line [12].
Line [13].

$ cut -d'[' -f2 delimited_data | cut -d']' -f1
11
12
13
```

See Also

- man cut
- man awk

8.5   Removing Duplicate Lines

Problem

After selecting and/or sorting some data you notice that there are many duplicate lines in your results. You'd like to get rid of the duplicates, so that you can see just the unique values.

Solution

You have two choices available to you. If you've just been sorting your output, add the -u option to the *sort* command:

```
$ somesequence | sort -u
```

If you aren't running *sort*, just pipe the output into *uniq*—provided, that is, that the output is sorted, so that identical lines are adjacent:

```
$ somesequence > myfile
$ uniq myfile
```

Discussion

Since *uniq* requires the data to be sorted already, we're more likely to just add the -u option to *sort* unless we also need to count the number of duplicates (-c, see Recipe 8.2, "Sorting Numbers"), or see only the duplicates (-d), which *uniq* can do.

Don't accidentally overwrite a valuable file by mistake; the *uniq* command is a bit odd in its parameters. Whereas most Unix/Linux commands take multiple input files on the command line, *uniq* does not. In fact, the first (non-option) argument is taken to be the (one and only) input file and any second argument, if supplied, is taken as the *output* file. So if you supply two filenames on the command line, the second one will get clobbered without warning.

See Also

- man sort
- man uniq
- Recipe 8.2, "Sorting Numbers"

8.6   Compressing Files

Problem

You need to compress some files and aren't sure of the best way to do it.

Solution

First, you need to understand that in traditional Unix, archiving (or combining) and compressing files are two different operations using two different tools, while in the DOS and Windows world it's typically one operation with one tool. A "tarball" is created by combining several files and/or directories using the *tar* (tape archive) command, then compressed using the *compress*, *gzip*, or *bzip2* tools. This results in files like *tarball.tar.Z*, *tarball.tar.gz*, *tarball.tgz*, or *tarball.tar.bz2*. Having said that, many other tools, including *zip*, are supported.

In order to use the correct format, you need to understand where your data will be used. If you are simply compressing some files for yourself, use whatever you find easiest. If other people will need to use your data, consider what platform they will be using and what they are comfortable with.

The Unix traditional tarball was *tarball.tar.Z*, but *gzip* is now much more common and *bzip2* (which offers better compression than *gzip*) is gaining ground. There is also a tool question. Some versions of *tar* allow you to use the compression of your choice automatically while creating the archive. Others don't.

The universally accepted Unix or Linux format would be a *tarball.tar.gz* created like this:

```
$ tar cf tarball_name.tar directory_of_files
$ gzip tarball_name.tar
```

If you have GNU *tar*, you could use -Z for *compress* (don't, this is obsolete), -z for *gzip* (safest), or -j for *bzip2* (highest compression). Don't forget to use an appropriate filename, this is not automatic.

```
$ tar czf tarball_name.tgz directory_of_files
```

While *tar* and *gzip* are available for many platforms, if you need to share with Windows you are better off using *zip*, which is nearly universal. *zip* and *unzip* are supplied by the InfoZip packages on Unix and almost any other platform you can possibly think of. Unfortunately, they are not always installed by default. Run the command by itself for some helpful usage information, since these tools are not like most other Unix tools. And note the -l option to convert Unix line endings to DOS line endings, or -ll for the reverse.

```
$ zip -r zipfile_name directory_of_files
```

Discussion

There are far too many compression algorithms and tools to talk about here; others include: AR, ARC, ARJ, BIN, BZ2, CAB, CAB, JAR, CPIO, DEB, HQX, LHA, LZH, RAR, RPM, UUE, and ZOO.

When using *tar*, we *strongly* recommend using a relative directory to store all the files. If you use an absolute directory, you might overwrite something on another system that you shouldn't. If you don't use any directory, you'll clutter up whatever directory the user is in when they extract the files (see Recipe 8.8, "Checking a tar Archive for Unique Directories"). The recommended use is the name and possibly version of the data you are processing. Table 8-2 shows some examples.

Table 8-2. Good and bad examples of naming files for the tar utility

Good	Bad
./myapp_1.0.1	myapp.c
	myapp.h
	myapp.man
./bintools	/usr/local/bin

It is worth noting that Red Hat Package Manager (RPM) files are actually CPIO files with a header. You can get a shell or Perl script called *rpm2cpio* (*http://fedora.redhat. com/docs/drafts/rpm-guide-en/ch-extra-packaging-tools.html*) to strip that header and then extract the files like this:

```
$ rpm2cpio some.rpm | cpio -i
```

Debian's *.deb* files are actually *ar* archives containing gzipped or bzipped *tar* archives. They may be extracted with the standard *ar*, *gunzip*, or *bunzip2* tools.

Many of the Windows-based tools such as WinZip, PKZIP, FilZip, and 7-Zip can handle many or all of the above formats and more (including tarballs and RPMs).

See Also

- man tar
- man gzip
- man bzip2
- man compress
- man zip
- man rpm
- man ar
- man dpkg
- *http://www.info-zip.org/*
- *http://fedora.redhat.com/docs/drafts/rpm-guide-en/ch-extra-packaging-tools.html*
- *http://en.wikipedia.org/wiki/Deb_(file_format)*
- *http://www.rpm.org/*
- *http://en.wikipedia.org/wiki/RPM_Package_Manager*
- Recipe 7.9, "Grepping Compressed Files"
- Recipe 8.7, "Uncompressing Files"
- Recipe 8.8, "Checking a tar Archive for Unique Directories"
- Recipe 17.3, "Unzipping Many ZIP Files"

8.7   Uncompressing Files

Problem

You need to uncompress one or more files ending in extensions like tar, tar.gz, gz, tgz, Z, or zip.

Solution

Figure out what you are dealing with and use the right tool. Table 8-3 maps common extensions to programs capable of handling them.

Table 8-3. Common file extensions and compression utilities

File extension	Command
.tar	tar tf (list contents), tar xf (extract)
.tar.gz, .tgz	GNU tar: tar tzf (list contents), tar xzf (extract)
	else: gunzip *file* && tar xf *file*
.tar.bz2	GNU tar: tar tjf (list contents), tar xjf (extract)
	else: gunzip2 *file* && tar xf *file*

Table 8-3. Common file extensions and compression utilities (continued)

File extension	Command
`.tar.Z`	GNU tar: `tar tZf` (list contents), `tar xZf` (extract)
	else: `uncompress` *file* && `tar xf` *file*
`.zip`	`unzip` (often not installed by default)

You should also try the *file* command:

```
$ file what_is_this.*
what_is_this.1: GNU tar archive
what_is_this.2: gzip compressed data, from Unix

$ gunzip what_is_this.2
gunzip: what_is_this.2: unknown suffix -- ignored

$ mv what_is_this.2 what_is_this.2.gz

$ gunzip what_is_this.2.gz

$ file what_is_this.2
what_is_this.2: GNU tar archive
```

Discussion

If the file extension matches none of those listed in Table 8-3 and the *file* command doesn't help, but you are sure it's an archive of some kind, then you should do a web search for it.

See Also

- Recipe 7.9, "Grepping Compressed Files"
- Recipe 8.6, "Compressing Files"

8.8   Checking a tar Archive for Unique Directories

Problem

You want to untar an archive, but you want to know beforehand into which directories it is going to write. You can look at the table of contents of the tarfile by using `tar -t`, but this output can be very large and it's easy to miss something.

Solution

Use an *awk* script to parse off the directory names from the tar archive's table of contents, then use `sort -u` to leave you with just the unique directory names:

```
$ tar tf some.tar | awk -F/ '{print $1}' | sort -u
```

Discussion

The t option will produce the table of contents for the file specified with the f option whose filename follows. The *awk* command specifies a non-default field separator by using -F/ to specify a slash as the separator between fields. Thus, the print $1 will print the first directory name in the pathname.

Finally, all the directory names will be sorted and only unique ones will be printed.

If a line of the output contains a single period then some files will be extracted into the current directory when you unpack this *tar* file, so be sure to be in the directory you desire.

Similarly, if the filenames in the archive are all local and without a leading ./ then you will get a list of filenames that will be created in the current directory.

If the output contains a blank line, that means that some of the files are specified with absolute pathnames (i.e., beginning with /), so again be careful, as extracting such an archive might clobber something that you don't want replaced.

See Also

- man tar
- man awk
- Recipe 8.1, "Sorting Your Output"
- Recipe 8.2, "Sorting Numbers"
- Recipe 8.3, "Sorting IP Addresses"

8.9   Translating Characters

Problem

You need to convert one character to another in all of your text.

Solution

Use the *tr* command to translate one character to another. For example:

```
$ tr ';' ',' <be.fore >af.ter
```

Discussion

In its simplest form, a *tr* command replaces occurrences of the first (and only) character of the first argument with the first (and only) character of the second argument.

In the example solution, we redirected input from the file named *be.fore* and sent the output into the file named *af.ter* and we translated all occurrences of a semicolon into a comma.

Why do we use the single quotes around the semicolon and the comma? Well, a semicolon has special meaning to *bash*, so if we didn't quote it *bash* would break our command into two commands, resulting in an error. The comma has no special meaning, but we quote it out of habit to avoid any special meaning we may have forgotten about—i.e., it's safer always to use the quotes, then we never forget to use them when we need them.

The *tr* command can do more that one translation at a time by putting the several characters to be translated in the first argument and their corresponding resultant characters in the second argument. Just remember, it's a one-for-one substitution. For example:

```
$ tr ';:.!?' ',' <other.punct >commas.all
```

will translate all occurrences of the punctuation symbols of semicolon, colon, period, exclamation point and question mark to commas. Since the second argument is shorter than the first, its last (and here, its only) character is repeated to match the length of the first argument, so that each character has a corresponding character for the translation.

Now this kind of translation could be done with the *sed* command, though *sed* syntax is a bit trickier. The *tr* command is not as powerful, since it doesn't use regular expressions, but it does have some special syntax for ranges of characters—and that can be quite useful as we'll see in Recipe 8.10, "Converting Uppercase to Lowercase."

See Also

* man tr

8.10   Converting Uppercase to Lowercase

Problem

You need to eliminate case distinctions in a stream of text.

Solution

You can translate all uppercase characters (A–Z) to lowercase (a–z) using the *tr* command and specifying a range of characters, as in:

```
$ tr 'A-Z' 'a-z' <be.fore >af.ter
```

There is also special syntax in *tr* for specifying this sort of range for upper- and lowercase conversions:

```
$ tr '[:upper:]' '[:lower:]' <be.fore >af.ter
```

Discussion

Although *tr* doesn't support regular expressions, it does support a range of characters. Just make sure that both arguments end up with the same number of characters. If the second argument is shorter, its last character will be repeated to match the length of the first argument. If the first argument is shorter, the second argument will be truncated to match the length of the first.

Here's a very simplistic encoding of a text message using a simple substitution cypher that offsets each character by 13 places (i.e., ROT13). An interesting characteristic of ROT13 is that the same process is used to both encipher and decipher the text:

```
$ cat /tmp/joke
Q: Why did the chicken cross the road?
A: To get to the other side.

$ tr 'A-Za-z' 'N-ZA-Mn-za-m' < /tmp/joke
D: Jul qvq gur puvpxra pebff gur ebnq?
N: Gb trg gb gur bgure fvqr.

$ tr 'A-Za-z' 'N-ZA-Mn-za-m' < /tmp/joke | tr 'A-Za-z' 'N-ZA-Mn-za-m'
Q: Why did the chicken cross the road?
A: To get to the other side.
```

See Also

- man tr
- *http://en.wikipedia.org/wiki/Rot13*

8.11 Converting DOS Files to Linux Format

Problem

You need to convert DOS formatted text files to the Linux format. In DOS, each line ends with a pair of characters—the return and the newline. In Linux, each line ends with a single newline. So how can you delete that extra DOS character?

Solution

Use the -d option on *tr* to delete the character(s) in the supplied list. For example, to delete all DOS carriage returns (\r), use the command:

```
$ tr -d '\r' <file.dos >file.txt
```

 This will delete all \r characters in the file, not just those at the end of a line. Typical text files rarely have characters like that inline, but it is possible. You may wish to look into the *dos2unix* and *unix2dos* programs if you are worried about this.

Discussion

The *tr* utility has a few special escape sequences that it recognizes, among them \r for carriage return and \n for newline. The other special backslash sequences are listed in Table 8-4.

Table 8-4. The special escape sequences of the tr utility

Sequence	Meaning
\ooo	Character with octal value ooo (1-3 octal digits)
\\	A backslash character (i.e., escapes the backslash itself)
\a	"audible" bell, the ASCII BEL character (since "b" was taken for backspace)
\b	Backspace
\f	Form feed
\n	Newline
\r	Return
\t	Tab (sometimes called a "horizontal" tab)
\v	Vertical tab

See Also

* man tr

8.12   Removing Smart Quotes

Problem

You want simple ASCII text out of a document in MS Word, but when you save it as text some odd characters still remain.

Solution

Translate the odd characters back to simple ASCII like this:

```
$ tr '\221\222\223\224\226\227' '\047\047""--' <odd.txt >plain.txt
```

Discussion

Such "smart quotes" come from the Windows-1252 character set, and may also show up in email messages that you save as text. To quote from Wikipedia on this subject:

> A few mail clients send curved quotes using the Windows-1252 codes but mark the text as ISO-8859-1 causing problems for decoders that do not make the dubious assumption that C1 control codes in ISO-8859-1 text were meant to be Windows-1252 printable characters.

To clean up such text, we can use the *tr* command. The 221 and 222 (octal) curved single-quotes will be translated to simple single quotes. We specify them in octal (047) to make it easier on us, since the shell uses single quotes as a delimiter. The 223 and 224 (octal) are opening and closing curved quotes, and will be translated to simple double quotes. The double quotes can be typed within the second argument since the single quotes protect them from shell interpretation. The 226 and 227 (octal) are dash characters and will be translated to hyphens (and no, that second hyphen in the second argument is not technically needed, since *tr* will repeat the last character to match the length of the first argument, but it's better to be specific).

See Also

- man tr
- *http://en.wikipedia.org/wiki/Curved_quotes* for way more than you might ever have wanted to know about quotation marks and related character set issues

8.13   Counting Lines, Words, or Characters in a File

Problem

You need to know how many lines, words, or characters are in a given file.

Solution

Use the *wc* (word count) command with *awk* in a command substitution.

The normal output of *wc* is something like this:

```
$ wc data_file
      5      15      60 data_file

# Lines only
$ wc -l data_file
      5 data_file

# Words only
$ wc -w data_file
     15 data_file

# Characters (often the same as bytes) only
$ wc -c data_file
     60 data_file

# Note 60B
$ ls -l data_file
-rw-r--r--  1 jp  users   60B Dec  6 03:18 data_file
```

You may be tempted to just do something like this:

```
data_file_lines=$(wc -l "$data_file")
```

That won't do what you expect, since you'll get something like "5 data_file" as the value. Instead, try this:

```
data_file_lines=$(wc -l "$data_file" | awk '{print $1}')
```

Discussion

If your version of *wc* is locale aware, the number of characters will not equal the number of bytes in some character sets.

See Also

- man wc
- Recipe 15.7, "Splitting Output Only When Necessary"

8.14   Rewrapping Paragraphs

Problem

You have some text with lines that are too long or too short, so you'd like to re-wrap them to be more readable.

Solution

Use the *fmt* command, optionally with a goal and maximum line length:

```
$ fmt mangled_text
$ fmt 55 60 mangled_text
```

Discussion

One tricky thing about *fmt* is that it expects blank lines to separate headers and paragraphs. If your input file doesn't have those blanks, it has no way to tell the difference between different paragraphs and extra newlines inside the same paragraph. So you will end up with one giant paragraph, with the correct line lengths.

The *pr* command might also be of some interest for formatting text.

See Also

- man fmt
- man pr

8.15   Doing More with less

"*less* is more!"

Problem

You'd like to take better advantage of the features of the *less* pager.

Solution

Read the *less* manpage and use the $LESS variable with *~/.lessfilter* and *~/.lesspipe* files.

less takes options from the $LESS variable, so rather than creating an alias with your favorite options, put them in that variable. It takes both long and short options, and any command-line options will override the variable. We recommend using the long options in the $LESS variable since they are easy to read. For example:

```
export LESS="--LONG-PROMPT --LINE-NUMBERS --ignore-case --QUIET"
```

But that is just the beginning. *less* is expandable via *input preprocessors*, which are simply programs or scripts that pre-process the file that *less* is about to display. This is handled by setting the $LESSOPEN and $LESSCLOSE environment variables appropriately.

You could build your own, but save yourself some time and look into Wolfgang Friebel's *lesspipe.sh* available at *http://www-zeuthen.desy.de/~friebel/unix/lesspipe.html* (but see the discussion below first). The script works by setting and exporting the $LESSOPEN environment variable when run by itself:

```
$ ./lesspipe.sh
LESSOPEN="|./lesspipe.sh %s"
export LESSOPEN
```

So you simply run it in an *eval* statement, like eval $(/path/to/lessfilter.sh) or eval `/path/to/lessfilter.sh`, and then use *less* as usual. The list of supported formats for version 1.53 is:

> gzip, compress, bzip2, zip, rar, tar, nroff, ar archive, pdf, ps, dvi, shared library, executable, directory, RPM, Microsoft Word, OpenOffice 1.x and OASIS (OpenDocument) formats, Debian, MP3 files, image formats (png, gif, jpeg, tiff, ...), utf-16 text, iso images and filesystems on removable media via /dev/xxx

But there is a catch. These formats require various external tools, so not all features in the example *lesspipe.sh* will work if you don't have them. The package also contains *./configure* (or *make*) scripts to generate a version of the filter that will work on your system, given the tools that you have available.

Discussion

less is unique in that it is a GNU tool that was already installed by default on every single test system we tried—every one. Not even bash can say this. And version differences aside, it works the same on all of them. Quite a claim to fame.

However, the same cannot be said for *lesspipe** and less open filters. We found other versions, with wildly variable capabilities, besides the ones listed above.

- Red Hat has a */usr/bin/lesspipe.sh* that can't be used like eval \`lesspipe\`.
- Debian has a */usr/bin/lesspipe* that can be *eval*'ed and also supports additional filters via a *~/.lessfilter* file.
- SUSE Linux has a */usr/bin/lessopen.sh* that can't be *eval*'ed.
- FreeBSD has a trivial */usr/bin/lesspipe.sh* (no *eval*, *.Z*, *.gz*, or *.bz2*).
- Solaris, HP-UX, the other BSDs, and the Mac have nothing by default.

To see if you already have one of these, try this on your systems. This Debian system has the Debian *lesspipe* installed but not in use (since $LESSOPEN is not defined):

```
$ type lesspipe.sh; type lesspipe; set | grep LESS
-bash3: type: lesspipe.sh: not found
lesspipe is /usr/bin/lesspipe
```

This Ubuntu system has the Debian *lesspipe* installed and in use:

```
$ type lesspipe.sh; type lesspipe; set | grep LESS
-bash: type: lesspipe.sh: not found
lesspipe is hashed (/usr/bin/lesspipe)
LESSCLOSE='/usr/bin/lesspipe %s %s'
LESSOPEN='| /usr/bin/lesspipe %s'
```

We recommend that you download, configure, and use Wolfgang Friebel's *lesspipe. sh* because it's the most capable. We also recommend that you read the *less* manpage because it's very interesting.

See Also

- man less
- man lesspipe
- man lesspipe.sh
- *http://www.greenwoodsoftware.com/less/*
- *http://www-zeuthen.desy.de/~friebel/unix/lesspipe.html*

Finding Files: find, locate, slocate

How easy is it for you to search for files throughout your filesystem?

For the first few files that you created, it was easy enough just to remember their names and where you kept them. Then when you got more files, you created subdirectories (or *folders* in GUI-speak) to clump your files into related groups. Soon there were subdirectories inside of subdirectories, and now you are having trouble remembering where you put things. Of course, with larger and larger disks it is getting easier to just keep creating and never deleting any files (and for some of us, this getting older thing isn't helping either).

But how do you find that file you were just editing last week? Or the attachment that you saved in a subdirectory (it seemed such a logical choice at the time). Or maybe your filesystem has become cluttered with MP3 files scattered all over it.

Various attempts have been made to provide graphical interfaces to help you search for files, which is all well and good—but how do you use the results from a GUI-style search as input to other commands?

bash and the GNU tools can help. They provide some very powerful search capabilities that enable you to search by filename, dates of creation or modification, even content. They send the results to standard output, perfect for use in other commands or scripts.

So stop your wondering—here's the information you need.

9.1   Finding All Your MP3 Files

Problem

You have MP3 audio files scattered all over your filesystem. You'd like to move them all into a single location so that you can organize them and then copy them onto a music player.

Solution

The *find* utility can locate all of those files and then execute a command to move them where you want. For example:

```
$ find . -name '*.mp3' -print -exec mv '{}' ~/songs \;
```

Discussion

The syntax for the *find* utility is unlike other Unix tools. It doesn't use options in the typical way, with dash and single-letter collections up front followed by several words of arguments. Rather, the options look like short words, and are ordered in a logical sequence describing the logic of which files are to be found, and what to do with them, if anything, when they are found. These word-like options are often called *predicates*.

A *find* command's first arguments are the directory or directories in which to search. A typical use is simply (.) for the current directory. But you can provide a whole list of directories, or even search the entire filesystem (permissions allowing) by specifying the root of the filesystem (/) as the starting point.

In our example the first option (the -name predicate) specifies the pattern we will search for. Its syntax is like the *bash* pattern matching syntax, so *.mp3 will match all filenames that end in the characters ".mp3". Any file that matches this pattern is considered to return true and will thus continue to the next predicate of the command.

Think of it this way: *find* will climb around on the filesystem and each filename that it finds it will present to this gauntlet of conditions that must be run. Any condition that is true is passed. Encounter a false and that filename's turn is immediately over, and the next filename is processed.

Now the -print condition is easy. It is always true and it has the side effect of printing the name to standard output. So any file that has made it this far in the sequence of conditions will have its name printed.

The -exec is a bit odd. Any filename making it this far will become part of a command that is executed. The remainder of the lineup to the \; is the command to be executed. The {} is replaced by the name of the file that was found. So in our example, if *find* encounters a file named *mhsr.mp3* in the *./music/jazz* subdirectory, then the command that will be executed will be:

```
mv ./music/jazz/mhsr.mp3 ~/songs
```

The command will be issued for each file that matches the pattern. If lots and lots of matching files are found, lots and lots of commands will be issued. Sometimes this is too demanding of system resources and it can be a better idea to use *find* just to find the files and print the filenames into a datafile and issue fewer commands by consolidating arguments several to a line. (But with machines getting faster all the time, this is less and less of an issue. It might even be something worthwhile for your dual core or quad core processor to do.)

See Also

- man find
- Recipe 1.3, "Finding and Running Commands"
- Recipe 1.4, "Getting Information About Files"
- Recipe 9.2, "Handling Filenames Containing Odd Characters"

9.2   Handling Filenames Containing Odd Characters

Problem

You used a *find* command like the one in Recipe 9.1, "Finding All Your MP3 Files" but the results were not what you intended because many of your filenames contain odd characters.

Solution

First, understand that to Unix folks, odd means "anything not a lowercase letter, or maybe a number." So uppercase, spaces, punctuation, and character accents are all odd. But you'll find all of those and more in the names of many songs and bands.

Depending on the oddness of the characters, your system, tools, and goal, it might be enough to simply quote the replacement string (i.e., put single quotes around the {}, as in '{}') . You did test your command first, right?

If that's no good, try using the -print0 argument to *find* and the -0 argument to *xargs*. -print0 tells *find* to use the null character (\0) instead of whitespace as the output delimiter between pathnames found. -0 then tells *xargs* the input delimiter. These will always work, but they are not supported on every system.

The *xargs* command takes whitespace delimited (except when using -0) pathnames from standard input and executes a specified command on as many of them as possible (up to a bit less than the system's ARG_MAX value; see Recipe 15.13, "Working Around "argument list too long" Errors"). Since there is a lot of overhead associated with calling other commands, using *xargs* can drastically speed up operations because you are calling the other command as few times as possible, rather than each time a pathname is found.

So, to rewrite the solution from Recipe 9.1, "Finding All Your MP3 Files" to handle odd characters:

```
$ find . -name '*.mp3' -print0 | xargs -i -0 mv '{}' ~/songs
```

Here is a similar example demonstrating how to use *xargs* to work around spaces in a path or filename when locating and then coping files:

```
$ locate P1100087.JPG PC220010.JPG PA310075.JPG PA310076.JPG | xargs -i cp '{}' .
```

Discussion

There are two problems with this approach. One is that not all versions of *xargs* support the -i option, and the other is that the -i option eliminates argument grouping, thus negating the speed increase we were hoping for. The problem is that the *mv* command needs the destination directory as the final argument, but traditional *xargs* will simply take its input and tack it onto the end of the given command until it runs out of space or input. The results of that behavior applied to an *mv* command would be very, very ugly. So some versions of *xargs* provide a -i switch that defaults to using {} (like *find*), but using -i requires that the command be run one at a time. So the only benefit over using *find*'s -exec is the odd character handling.

However, the *xargs* utility is most effective when used in conjunction with *find* and a command like *chmod* that just wants a list of arguments to process. You can really see a vast speed improvement when handling large numbers of pathnames. For example:

```
$ find some_directory -type f -print0 | xargs -0 chmod 0644
```

See Also

- man find
- man xargs
- Recipe 9.1, "Finding All Your MP3 Files"
- Recipe 15.13, "Working Around "argument list too long" Errors"

9.3   Speeding Up Operations on Found Files

Problem

You used a *find* command like the one in Recipe 9.1, "Finding All Your MP3 Files" and the resulting operations take a long time because you found a lot of files, so you want to speed it up.

Solution

See the discussion on *xargs* Recipe 9.2, "Handling Filenames Containing Odd Characters."

See Also

- Recipe 9.1, "Finding All Your MP3 Files"
- Recipe 9.2, "Handling Filenames Containing Odd Characters"

9.4 Finding Files Across Symbolic Links

Problem

You issued a *find* command to find your *.mp3* files but it didn't find all of them—it missed all those that were part of your filesystem but were mounted via a *symbolic link*. Is *find* unable to cross that kind of boundary?

Solution

Use the -follow predicate. The example we used before becomes:

```
$ find . -follow -name '*.mp3' -print0 | xargs -i -0 mv '{}' ~/songs
```

Discussion

Sometimes you don't want find to cross over onto other filesystems, which is where symbolic links originated. So the default for *find* is not to follow a symbolic link. If you do want it to do so, then use the -follow option as the first option in the list on your *find* command.

See Also

- man find

9.5 Finding Files Irrespective of Case

Problem

Some of your MP3 files end with *.MP3* rather than *.mp3*. How do you find those?

Solution

Use the -iname predicate (if your version of *find* supports it) to run a case-insensitive search, rather than just -name. For example:

```
$ find . -follow -iname '*.mp3' -print0 | xargs -i -0 mv '{}' ~/songs
```

Discussion

Sometimes you care about the case of the filename and sometimes you don't. Use the -iname option when you don't care, in situations like this, where *.mp3* or *.MP3* both indicate that the file is probably an MP3 file. (We say *probably* because on Unix-like systems you can name a file anything that you want. It isn't forced to have a particular extension.)

One of the most common places where you'll see the upper- and lowercase issue is when dealing with Microsoft Windows-compatible filesystems, especially older or "lowest common denominator" filesystems. A digital camera that we use stores its files with filenames like *PICT001.JPG*, incrementing the number with each picture. If you were to try:

```
$ find . -name '*.jpg' -print
```

you wouldn't find many pictures. In this case you could also try:

```
$ find . -name '*.[Jj][Pp][Gg]' -print
```

since that regular expression will match either letter in brackets, but that isn't as easy to type, especially if the pattern that you want to match is much longer. In practice, -iname is an easier choice. The catch is that not every version of *find* supports the -iname predicate. If your system doesn't support it, you could try tricky regular expressions as shown above, use multiple -name options with the case variations you expect, or install the GNU version of *find*.

See Also

- man find

9.6   Finding Files by Date

Problem

Suppose someone sent you a JPEG image file that you saved on your filesystem a few months ago. Now you don't remember where you put it. How can you find it?

Solution

Use a *find* command with the -mtime predicate, which checks the date of last modification. For example:

```
find . -name '*.jpg' -mtime +90 -print
```

Discussion

The -mtime predicate takes an argument to specify the timeframe for the search. The 90 stands for 90 days. By using a plus sign on the number (+90) we indicate that we're looking for a file modified *more than* 90 days ago. Write -90 (using a minus sign) for *less than* 90 days. Use neither a plus nor minus to mean exactly 90 days.

There are several predicates for searching based on file modification times and each take a quantity argument. Using a plus, minus, or no sign indicates greater than, less than, or equals, respectively, for all of those predicates.

The *find* utility also has logical AND, OR, and NOT constructs so if you know that the file was at least one week old (7 days) but not more than 14 days old, you can combine the predicates like this:

```
$ find . -mtime +7 -a -mtime -14 -print
```

You can get even more complicated using OR as well as AND and even NOT to combine conditions, as in:

```
$ find . -mtime +14 -name '*.text' -o \( -mtime -14 -name '*.txt' \) -print
```

This will print out the names of files ending in .text that are older than 14 days, as well as those that are newer than 14 days but have .txt as their last 4 characters.

You will likely need parentheses to get the precedence right. Two predicates in sequence are like a logical AND, which binds tighter than an OR (in *find* as in most languages). Use parentheses as much as you need to make it unambiguous.

Parentheses have a special meaning to *bash*, so we need to escape that meaning, and write them as \(and \) or inside of single quotes as '(' and ')'. You cannot use single quotes around the entire expression though, as that will confuse the *find* command. It wants each predicate as its own word.

See Also

- man find

9.7 Finding Files by Type

Problem

You are looking for a directory with the word "java" in it. When you tried:

```
$ find . -name '*java*' -print
```

you got way too many files—including all the Java source files in your part of the filesystem.

Solution

Use the -type predicate to select only directories:

```
$ find . -type d -name '*java*' -print
```

Discussion

We put the -type d first followed by the -name *java*. Either order would have found the same set of files. By putting the -type d first in the list of options, though, the search will be slightly more efficient: as each file is encountered, the test will be made to see if it is a directory and then only directories will have their names checked against the pattern. All files have names; relatively few are directories. So this ordering eliminates most files from further consideration before we ever do the string comparison. Is it a big deal? With processors getting faster all the time, it matters less so. With disk sizes getting bigger all the time, it matters more so. There are several types of files for which you can check, not just directories. Table 9-1 lists the single characters used to find these types of files.

Table 9-1. Characters used by find's -type predicate

Key	Meaning
b	block special file
c	character special file
d	directory
p	pipe (or "fifo")
f	plain ol' file
l	symbolic link
s	socket
D	(Solaris only) "door"

See Also

- man find

9.8   Finding Files by Size

Problem

You want to do a little housecleaning, and to get the most out of your effort you are going to start by finding your largest files and deciding if you need to keep them around. But how do you find your largest files?

Solution

Use the -size predicate in the *find* command to select files above, below, or exactly a certain size. For example:

```
find . -size +3000k -print
```

Discussion

Like the numeric argument to -mtime, the -size predicate's numeric argument can be preceded by a minus sign, plus sign, or no sign at all to indicate less than, greater than, or exactly equal to the numeric argument. So we've indicated, in our example, that we're looking for files that are greater than the size indicated.

The size indicated includes a unit of k for kilobytes. If you use c for the unit, that means just bytes (or characters). If you use b, or don't put any unit, that indicates a size in blocks. (The block is a 512-byte block, historically a common unit in Unix systems.) So we're looking for files that are greater than 3 MB in size.

See Also

- man find
- man du

9.9   Finding Files by Content

Problem

How do you find a file of some known content? Let's say that you had written an important letter and saved it as a text file, putting *.txt* on the end of the filename. Beyond that, the only thing you remember about the content of the letter is that you had used the word "portend."

Solution

If you are in the vicinity of that file, say within the current directory, you can start with a simple *grep*:

```
grep -i portend *.txt
```

With the -i option, *grep* will ignore upper- and lowercase difference. This command may not be sufficient to find what you're looking for, but start simply. Of course, if you think the file might be in one of your many subdirectories, you can try to reach all the files that are in subdirectories of the current directory with this command:

```
grep -i portend */*.txt
```

Let's face it, though, that's not a very thorough search.

If that doesn't do it, let's use a more complete solution: the *find* command. Use the -exec option on *find* so that if the predicates are true up to that point, it will execute a command for each file it finds. You can invoke *grep* or other utilities like this:

```
find . -name '*.txt' -exec grep -Hi portend '{}' \;
```

Discussion

We use the -name '*.txt' construct to help narrow down the search. Any such test will help, since having to run a separate executable for each file that it finds is costly in time and CPU horsepower. Maybe you have a rough idea of how old the file is (e.g., -mdate -5 or some such).

The '{}' is where the filename is put when executing the command. The \; indicates the end of the command, in case you want to continue with more predicates. Both the braces and the semicolon need to be escaped, so we quote one and use the backslash for the other. It doesn't matter which way we escape them, only that we do escape them, so that *bash* doesn't misinterpret them.

On some systems, the -H option will print the name of the file if *grep* finds something. Normally, with only one filename on the command, *grep* won't bother to name the file, it just prints out the matching line that it finds. Since we're searching through many files, we need to know which file was grepped.

If you're running a version of *grep* that doesn't have the -H option, then just put */dev/ null* as one of the filenames on the *grep* command. The *grep* command will then have more than one file to open, and will print out the filename if it finds the text.

See Also

- man find

9.10   Finding Existing Files and Content Fast

Problem

You'd like to be able to find files without having to wait for a long *find* command to complete, or you need to find a file with some specific content.

Solution

If your system has *locate*, *slocate*, Beagle, Spotlight or some other indexer, you are already set. If not, look into them.

As we discussed in Recipe 1.3, "Finding and Running Commands", *locate* and *slocate* consult database files about the system (usually compiled and updated by a *cron* job) to find file or command names almost instantly. The location of the actual database files, what is indexed therein, and how often, may vary from system to system. Consult your system's manpages for details.

```
$ locate apropos
/usr/bin/apropos
/usr/share/man/de/man1/apropos.1.gz
/usr/share/man/es/man1/apropos.1.gz
/usr/share/man/it/man1/apropos.1.gz
/usr/share/man/ja/man1/apropos.1.gz
/usr/share/man/man1/apropos.1.gz
```

locate and *slocate* don't index content though, so see Recipe 9.9, "Finding Files by Content" for that.

Beagle and Spotlight are examples of a fairly recent technology known as *desktop search* engines or indexers. Google Desktop Search and Copernic Desktop Search are two examples from the Microsoft Windows world. Desktop search tools use some kind of indexer to crawl, parse, and index the names *and contents* of all of the files (and usually email messages) in your personal file space; i.e., your home directory on a Unix or Linux system. This information is then almost instantly available to you when you look for it. These tools are usually very configurable, graphical, operate on a per-user basis, and index the contents of your files.

Discussion

slocate stores permission information (in addition to filenames and paths) so that it will not list programs to which the user does not have access. On most Linux systems *locate* is a symbolic link to *slocate*; other systems may have separate programs, or may not have *slocate* at all. Both of these are command-line tools that crawl and index the entire filesystem, more or less, but they only contain filenames and locations.

See Also

- man locate
- man slocate
- *http://beagle-project.org/*
- *http://www.apple.com/macosx/features/spotlight/*
- *http://desktop.google.com/*
- *http://www.copernic.com/en/products/desktop-search/*
- Recipe 1.3, "Finding and Running Commands"
- Recipe 9.9, "Finding Files by Content"

9.11 Finding a File Using a List of Possible Locations

Problem

You need to execute, source, or read a file, but it may be located in a number of different places in or outside of the $PATH.

Solution

If you are going to source the file and it's located somewhere on the $PATH, just source it. *bash*'s built-in *source* command (also known by the shorter-to-type but harder-to-read POSIX name ".") will search the $PATH if the sourcepath shell option is set, which it is by default:

```
$ source myfile
```

If you want to execute a file only if you know it exists in the $PATH and is executable, and you have *bash* version 2.05b or higher, use type -P to search the $PATH. Unlike the *which* command, type -P only produces output when it finds the file, which makes it much easier to use in this case:

```
LS=$(type -P ls)
[ -x $LS ] && $LS

# --OR--

LS=$(type -P ls)
if [ -x $LS ]; then
    : commands involving $LS here
fi
```

If you need to look in a variety of locations, possibly including the $PATH, use a for loop. To search the $PATH, use the variable substitution operator ${*variable/pattern/ replacement*} to replace the : separator with a space, and then use for as usual. To search the $PATH and other possible locations, just list them:

```
for path in ${PATH//:/ }; do
    [ -x "$path/ls" ] && $path/ls
done

# --OR--

for path in ${PATH//:/ } /opt/foo/bin /opt/bar/bin; do
    [ -x "$path/ls" ] && $path/ls
done
```

If the file is not in the $PATH, but could be in a list of locations, possibly even under different names, list the entire path and name:

```
for file in /usr/local/bin/inputrc /etc/inputrc ~/.inputrc; do
    [ -f "$file" ] && bind -f "$file" && break   # Use the first one found
done
```

Perform any additional tests as needed. For example, you may wish to use *screen* when logging in if it's present on the system:

```
for path in ${PATH//:/ }; do
    if [ -x "$path/screen" ]; then
        # If screen(1) exists and is executable:
        for file in /opt/bin/settings/run_screen ~/settings/run_screen; do
            [ -x "$file" ] && $file && break  # Execute the first one found
        done
    fi
done
```

See Recipe 16.20, "Getting Started with a Custom Configuration" for more details on this code fragment.

Discussion

Using for to iterate through each possible location may seem like overkill, but it's actually very flexible and allows you to search wherever you need to, apply whatever other tests are appropriate, and then do whatever you want with the file if found. By replacing : with a space in the $PATH, we turn it into the kind of space-delimited list for expects (but as we also saw, any space delimited list will work). Adapting this technique as needed will allow you to write some very flexible and portable shell scripts that can be very tolerant of file locations.

You may be tempted to set $IFS=':' to directly parse the $PATH, rather than preparsing it into $path. That will work, but involves extra work with variables and isn't as flexible.

You may also be tempted to do something like the following:

```
[ "$(which myfile)" ] && bind -f $(which myfile)
```

The problem here is not when the file exists, but when it doesn't. The *which* utility behaves differently on different systems. The Red Hat *which* is also aliased to provide details when the argument is an alias, and to set various command-line switches; and it returns a not found message (while *which* on Debian or FreeBSD do not). But if you try that line on NetBSD you could end up trying to bind `no myfile` in /sbin /usr/sbin /bin /usr/bin /usr/pkg/sbin /usr/pkg/bin /usr/X11R6/bin /usr/local/sbin /usr/local/bin, which is not what you meant.

The *command* command is also interesting in this context. It's been around longer than type -P and may be useful under some circumstances.

Red Hat Enterprise Linux 4.x behaves like this:

```
$ alias which
alias which='alias | /usr/bin/which --tty-only --read-alias --show-dot --show-tilde'

$ which rd
alias rd='rmdir'
        /bin/rmdir

$ which ls
alias ls='ls --color=auto -F -h'
        /bin/ls

$ which cat
/bin/cat

$ which cattt
/usr/bin/which: no cattt in (/usr/kerberos/bin:/usr/local/bin:/bin:/usr/bin:/usr/
X11R6/bin:/home/jp/bin)

$ command -v rd
alias rd='rmdir'

$ command -v ls
alias ls='ls --color=auto -F -h'

$ command -v cat
/bin/cat
```

Debian and FreeBSD (but not NetBSD or OpenBSD) behave like this:

```
$ alias which
-bash3: alias: which: not found

$ which rd

$ which ls
/bin/ls

$ which cat
/bin/cat

$ which cattt

$ command -v rd
-bash: command: rd: not found
```

```
$ command -v ls
/bin/ls

$ command -v cat
/bin/cat

$ command -v ll
alias ll='ls -l'
```

See Also

- help type
- man which
- help source
- man source
- Recipe 16.20, "Getting Started with a Custom Configuration"
- Recipe 17.4, "Recovering Disconnected Sessions Using screen"

## CHAPTER 10

Additional Features for Scripting

Many scripts are written as simple one-off scripts that are only used by their author, consisting of only a few lines, perhaps only a single loop, if that. But some scripts are heavy-duty scripts that will see a lot of use from a variety of users. Such scripts will often need to take advantage of features that allow for better sharing and reuse of code. These advanced scripting tips and techniques can be useful for many kinds of scripts, and are often found in larger systems of scripts such as the */etc/init.d* scripts on many Linux systems. You don't have to be a system administrator to appreciate and use these techniques. They will prove themselves on any large scripting effort.

10.1 "Daemon-izing" Your Script

Problem

Sometimes you want a script to run as a *daemon*, i.e., in the background and never ending. To do this properly you need to be able to detach your script from its controlling *tty*, that is from the terminal session used to start the daemon. Simply putting an ampersand on the command isn't enough. If you start your daemon script on a remote system via an SSH (or similar) session, you'll notice that when you log out, the SSH session doesn't end and your window is hung until that script ends (which, being a daemon, it won't).

Solution

Use the following to invoke your script, run it in the background, and still allow yourself to log out:

```
nohup mydaemonscript 0<&-  1>/dev/null  2>&1  &
```

or:

```
nohup mydaemonscript  >>/var/log/myadmin.log  2>&1  <&-  &
```

Discussion

You need to close the controlling *tty*, which is connected in three ways to your (or any) job: standard input (STDIN), standard output (STDOUT), and standard error (STDERR). We can close STDOUT and STDERR by pointing them at another file—typically either a log file, so that you can retrieve their output at a later time, or at the file */dev/null* to throw away all their output. We use the redirecting operator > to do this.

But what about STDIN? The cleanest way to deal with STDIN is to close the file descriptor. The *bash* syntax to do that is like a redirect, but with a dash for the filename (0<&- or <&-).

We use the *nohup* command so that the script is run without being interrupted by a hangup signal when we log off.

In the first example, we use the file descriptor numbers (i.e., 0, 1, 2) explicitly in all three redirections. They are optional in the case of STDIN and STDOUT, so in our second example we don't use them explicitly. We also put the input redirect at the end of the second command rather than at the beginning, since the order here is not important. (However, the order is important and the file descriptor numbers are necessary in redirecting STDERR.)

See Also

- Chapters 2 and 3 for more on redirecting input and redirecting output

10.2   Reusing Code with Includes and Sourcing

Problem

There are a set of shell variable assignments that you would like to have common across a set of scripts that you are writing. You tried putting this configuration information in its own script. But when you run that script from within another script, the values don't stick; e.g., your configuration is running in another shell, and when that shell exits, so do your values. Is there some way to run that configuration script within the current shell?

Solution

Use the *bash* shell's *source* command or POSIX single period (.) to read in the contents of that configuration file. The lines of that file will be processed as if encountered in the current script.

Here's an example of some configuration data:

```
$ cat myprefs.cfg
SCRATCH_DIR=/var/tmp
```

```
IMG_FMT=png
SND_FMT=ogg
$
```

It is just a simple script consisting of three assignments. Here's another script, one that will use these values:

```
#
# use the user prefs
#
source $HOME/myprefs.cfg
cd ${SCRATCH_DIR:-/tmp}
echo You prefer $IMG_FMT image files
echo You prefer $SND_FMT sound files
```

and so forth.

Discussion

The script that is going to use the configuration file uses the *source* command to read in the file. It can also use a dot (.) in place of the word *source*. A dot is easy and quick to type, but hard to notice in a script or screen shot:

```
. $HOME/myprefs.cfg
```

You wouldn't be the first person to look right past the dot and think that the script was just being executed.

bash also has a third syntax, one that comes from the input processor *readline*, a topic we will not get into here. We'll just say that an equivalent action can occur with this syntax:

```
$include $HOME/myprefs.cfg
```

provided that the file is in your search path (or else specify an explicit path) and that the file has execute permissions and, of course, read permission, too. That dollar sign is not the command prompt, but part of the directive $include.

Sourcing is both a powerful and a dangerous feature of *bash* scripting. It gives you a way to create a configuration file and then share that file among several scripts. With that mechanism, you can change your configuration by editing one file, not several scripts.

The contents of the configuration file are not limited to simple variable assignment, however. Any valid shell command is legal syntax, because when you source a file like this, it is simply getting its input from a different source, but it is still the *bash* shell processing *bash* commands. Regardless of what shell commands are in that sourced file, for example loops or invoking other commands, it is all legitimate shell input and will be run as if it were part of your script.

Here's a modified configuration file:

```
$ cat myprefs.cfg
SCRATCH_DIR=/var/tmp
```

```
IMG_FMT=$(cat $HOME/myimage.pref)
if [ -e /media/mp3 ]
then
    SND_FMT=mp3
else
    SND_FMT=ogg
fi
echo config file loaded
$
```

This configuration file is hardly what one thinks of as a passive list of configured variables. It can run other commands (e.g., *cat*) and use if statements to vary its choices. It even ends by echoing a message. Be careful when you source something, as it's a wide open door into your script.

One of the best uses of sourcing scripts comes when you can define *bash* functions (as we will show you in Recipe 10.3, "Using Configuration Files in a Script"). These functions can then be shared as a common library of functions among all the scripts that source the script of function definitions.

See Also

- The *bash* manpage for more about *readline*
- Recipe 10.3, "Using Configuration Files in a Script"
- Recipe 10.4, "Defining Functions"

10.3   Using Configuration Files in a Script

Problem

You want to use one or more external configuration files for one or more scripts.

Solution

You could write a lot of code to parse some special configuration file format. Do yourself a favor and don't do that. Just make the config file a shell script and use the solution in Recipe 10.2, "Reusing Code with Includes and Sourcing."

Discussion

This is just a specific application of sourcing a file. However, it's worth noting that you may need to give a little thought as to how you can reduce all of your configuration needs to *bash*-legal syntax. In particular, you can make use of Boolean flags, and optional variables (see Chapter 5 and Recipe 15.11, "Getting Input from Another Machine").

```
# In config file
VERBOSE=0                # '' for off, 1 for on
SSH_USER='jbagadonutz@'  # Note trailing @, set to '' to use the current user
```

```
# In script
[ "$VERBOSE" ] || echo "Verbose msg from $) goes to STDERR" >&2
[...]
ssh $SSH_USER$REMOTE_HOST [...]
```

Of course, depending on the user to get the configuration file correct can be chancy, so instead of requiring the user to read the comment and add the trailing @, we could do it in the script:

```
# If $SSH_USER is set and doesn't have a trailing @ add it:
[ -n "$SSH_USER" -a "$SSH_USER" = "${SSH_USER%@}" ] && SSH_USER="$SSH_USER@"
```

Or just use:

```
ssh ${SSH_USER:+${SSH_USER}@}${REMOTE_HOST} [...]
```

to make that same substitution right in place. The *bash* variable operator :+ will do the following: if $SSH_USER has a value, it will return the value to the right of the :+ (in this case we specified the variable itself along with an extra @); otherwise, if unset or empty, it will return nothing.

See Also

- Chapter 5
- Recipe 10.2, "Reusing Code with Includes and Sourcing"
- Recipe 15.11, "Getting Input from Another Machine"

10.4   Defining Functions

Problem

There are several places in your shell script where you would like to give the user a *usage message* (a message describing the proper syntax for the command), but you don't want to keep repeating the code for the same *echo* statement. Isn't there a way to do this just once and have several references to it? If you could make the usage message its own script, then you could just invoke it anywhere in your original script—but that requires two scripts, not one. Besides, it seems odd to have the message for how to use one script be the output of a different script. Isn't there a better way to do this?

Solution

You need a *bash* function. At the beginning of your script put something like this:

```
function usage ()
{
    printf "usage: %s  [ -a | - b ]  file1 ... filen\n" $0  > &2
}
```

Then later in your script you can write code like this:

```
if [ $# -lt 1 ]
then
    usage
fi
```

Discussion

Functions may be defined in several ways ([function] *name* ( ) *compound-command*
[*redirections*]). We could write a function definition any of these ways:

```
function usage ( )
{
    printf "usage: %s  [ -a | - b ]  file1 ... filen\n" $0  > &2
}
```

```
function usage {
    printf "usage: %s  [ -a | - b ]  file1 ... filen\n" $0  > &2
}
```

```
usage ( )
{
    printf "usage: %s  [ -a | - b ]  file1 ... filen\n" $0  > &2
}
```

```
usage ( ) {
    printf "usage: %s  [ -a | - b ]  file1 ... filen\n" $0  > &2
}
```

Either the reserved word function or the trailing ( ) must be present. If function is
used, the ( ) are optional. We like using the word *function* because it is very clear and
readable, and it is easy to grep for; e.g., grep '^function' *script* will list the functions in your *script*.

This function definition should go at the front of your shell script, or at least somewhere before you need to invoke it. The definition is, in a sense, just another *bash*
statement. But once it has been executed, then the function is defined. If you invoke
the function before it is defined you will get a "command not found" error. That's
why we always put our function definitions first before any other commands in our
script.

Our function does very little; it is just a *printf* statement. Because we only have one
usage message, if we ever add a new option, we don't need to modify several statements, just this one.

The only argument to *printf* beyond the format string is $0, the name by which the
shell script was invoked. You might even want to use the expression $(basename $0)
so that only the last part of any pathname is included.

Since the usage message is an error message, we redirect the output of the *printf* to standard error. We could also have put that redirection on the outside of the function definition, so that all output from the function would be redirected:

```
function usage ()
{
    printf "usage: %s  [ -a | - b ]  file1 ... filen\n" $0

} > &2
```

See Also

- Recipe 7.1, "Sifting Through Files for a String"
- Recipe 16.13, "Creating a Better cd Command"
- Recipe 16.14, "Creating and Changing into a New Directory in One Step"
- Recipe 19.14, "Avoiding "command not found" When Using Functions"

10.5   Using Functions: Parameters and Return Values

Problem

You want to use a function and you need to get some values into the function. How do you pass in parameters? How do you get values back?

Solution

You don't put parentheses around the arguments like you might expect from some programming languages. Put any parameters for a *bash* function right after the function's name, separated by whitespace, just like you were invoking any shell script or command. Don't forget to quote them if necessary!

```
# define the function:
function max ()
{ ... }
#
# call the function:
#
max    128   $SIM
max    $VAR  $CNT
```

You have two ways to get values back from a function. You can assign values to variables inside the body of your function. Those variables will be global to the whole script unless they are explicitly declared local within the function:

```
# cookbook filename: func_max.1

# define the function:
function max ()
{
```

```
    local HIDN
    if [ $1 -gt $2 ]
    then
        BIGR=$1
    else
        BIGR=$2
    fi
    HIDN=5
}
```

For example:

```
# call the function:
max    128    $SIM
# use the result:
echo $BIGR
```

The other way is to use *echo* or *printf* to send output to standard output. Then you must invoke the function inside a $( ), capturing the output and using the result, or it will be wasted on the screen:

```
# cookbook filename: func_max.2

# define the function:
function max ( )
{
    if [ $1 -gt $2 ]
    then
        echo $1
    else
        echo $2
    fi
}
```

For example:

```
# call the function:
BIGR=$(max    128    $SIM)
# use the result
echo $BIGR
```

Discussion

Putting parameters on the invocation of the function is just like calling any shell script. The parameters are just the other words on the command line.

Within the function, the parameters are referred to as if they were command-line arguments by using $1, $2, etc. However, $0 is left alone. It remains the name by which the entire script was invoked. On return from the function, $1, $2, etc. are back to referring to the parameters with which the script was invoked.

Also of interest is the $FUNCNAME array. $FUNCNAME all by itself references the zeroth element of the array, which is the name of the currently executing function. In other words, $FUNCNAME is to a function as $0 is to a script, except without all the path information. The rest of the array elements is hat amounts to a call stack, with "main" as the bottom or last element. This variable only exists while a function is executing.

We included the useless variable $HIDN just to show that it is local to the function definition. Even though we can assign it values inside the function, any such value would not be available elsewhere in the script. It is a variable whose value is local to that function; it comes into existence when the function is called, and is gone once the function returns.

Returning values by setting variables is more efficient, and can handle lots of data—many variables can be set—but the approach has its drawbacks. It requires that the function and the rest of the script agree on variable names for the information hand-off. This kind of coupling has maintenance issues. The other approach, using the output as the way to return values, does reduce this coupling, but is limited in its usefulness—it is limited in how much data it can return before your script has to spend lots of effort parsing the results of the function. So which to use? As with much of engineering, this, too, is a trade-off and you have to decide based on your specific needs.

See Also

- Recipe 1.6, "Using Shell Quoting"
- Recipe 16.4, "Change Your $PATH Temporarily"

10.6 Trapping Interrupts

Problem

You are writing a script that needs to be able to trap signals and respond accordingly.

Solution

Use the *trap* utility to set signal handlers. First, use trap -l (or kill -l) to list the signals you may trap. They vary from system to system:

```
# NetBSD
$ trap -l
 1) SIGHUP       2) SIGINT       3) SIGQUIT      4) SIGILL
 5) SIGTRAP      6) SIGABRT      7) SIGEMT       8) SIGFPE
 9) SIGKILL     10) SIGBUS      11) SIGSEGV     12) SIGSYS
13) SIGPIPE     14) SIGALRM     15) SIGTERM     16) SIGURG
17) SIGSTOP     18) SIGTSTP     19) SIGCONT     20) SIGCHLD
21) SIGTTIN     22) SIGTTOU     23) SIGIO       24) SIGXCPU
25) SIGXFSZ     26) SIGVTALRM   27) SIGPROF     28) SIGWINCH
29) SIGINFO     30) SIGUSR1     31) SIGUSR2     32) SIGPWR
```

```
# Linux
$ trap -l
 1) SIGHUP        2) SIGINT       3) SIGQUIT      4) SIGILL
 5) SIGTRAP       6) SIGABRT      7) SIGBUS       8) SIGFPE
 9) SIGKILL      10) SIGUSR1     11) SIGSEGV     12) SIGUSR2
13) SIGPIPE      14) SIGALRM     15) SIGTERM     17) SIGCHLD
18) SIGCONT      19) SIGSTOP     20) SIGTSTP     21) SIGTTIN
22) SIGTTOU      23) SIGURG      24) SIGXCPU     25) SIGXFSZ
26) SIGVTALRM    27) SIGPROF     28) SIGWINCH    29) SIGIO
30) SIGPWR       31) SIGSYS      33) SIGRTMIN    34) SIGRTMIN+1
35) SIGRTMIN+2   36) SIGRTMIN+3  37) SIGRTMIN+4  38) SIGRTMIN+5
39) SIGRTMIN+6   40) SIGRTMIN+7  41) SIGRTMIN+8  42) SIGRTMIN+9
43) SIGRTMIN+10 44) SIGRTMIN+11 45) SIGRTMIN+12 46) SIGRTMIN+13
47) SIGRTMIN+14 48) SIGRTMIN+15 49) SIGRTMAX-15 50) SIGRTMAX-14
51) SIGRTMAX-13 52) SIGRTMAX-12 53) SIGRTMAX-11 54) SIGRTMAX-10
55) SIGRTMAX-9  56) SIGRTMAX-8  57) SIGRTMAX-7  58) SIGRTMAX-6
59) SIGRTMAX-5  60) SIGRTMAX-4  61) SIGRTMAX-3  62) SIGRTMAX-2
63) SIGRTMAX-1  64) SIGRTMAX
```

Next, set your trap(s) and signal handlers. Note that the exit status of your script will be 128+*signal number* if the command was terminated by signal *signal number*. Here is a simple case where we only care that we got a signal and don't care what it was. If our trap had been trap '' ABRT EXIT HUP INT TERM QUIT, this script would be rather hard to kill because any of those signals would just be ignored.

```
$ cat hard_to_kill
#!/bin/bash -
trap ' echo "You got me! $?" ' ABRT EXIT HUP INT TERM QUIT
trap ' echo "Later... $?"; exit ' USR1
sleep 120

$ ./hard_to_kill
^CYou got me! 130
You got me! 130

$ ./hard_to_kill &
[1] 26354

$ kill -USR1 %1
User defined signal 1
Later... 158
You got me! 0
[1]+  Done                    ./hard_to_kill

$ ./hard_to_kill &
[1] 28180

$ kill %1
You got me! 0
[1]+  Terminated              ./hard_to_kill
```

This is a more interesting example:

```
#!/usr/bin/env bash
# cookbook filename: hard_to_kill
```

```
function trapped {
    if [ "$1" = "USR1" ]; then
        echo "Got me with a $1 trap!"
        exit
    else
        echo "Received $1 trap--neener, neener"
    fi
}

trap "trapped ABRT" ABRT
trap "trapped EXIT" EXIT
trap "trapped HUP"  HUP
trap "trapped INT"  INT
trap "trapped KILL" KILL    # This won't actually work
trap "trapped QUIT" QUIT
trap "trapped TERM" TERM
trap "trapped USR1" USR1    # This one is special

# Just hang out and do nothing, without introducing "third-party"
# trap behavior, such as if we used 'sleep'
while (( 1 )); do
    :   # : is a NOOP
done
```

Here we invoke this example then try to kill it:

```
$ ./hard_to_kill
^CReceived INT trap--neener, neener
^CReceived INT trap--neener, neener
^CReceived INT trap--neener, neener
^Z
[1]+  Stopped                 ./hard_to_kill

$ kill -TERM %1

[1]+  Stopped                 ./hard_to_kill
Received TERM trap--neener, neener

$ jobs
[1]+  Stopped                 ./hard_to_kill

$ bg
[1]+ ./hard_to_kill &

$ jobs
[1]+  Running                 ./hard_to_kill &

$ kill -TERM %1
Received TERM trap--neener, neener

$ kill -HUP %1
Received HUP trap--neener, neener
```

```
$ kill -USR1 %1
Got me with a USR1 trap!
Received EXIT trap--neener, neener

[1]+  Done                    ./hard_to_kill
```

Discussion

First, we should mention that you can't actually trap -SIGKILL (-9). That signal kills processes dead immediately, so they have no chance to trap anything. So maybe our examples weren't really so hard to kill after all. But remember that this signal does not allow the script or program to clean up or shut down gracefully at any time. That's often a bad thing, so try to avoid using kill -KILL unless you have no other choice.

Usage for *trap* is as follows:

```
trap [-lp] [arg] [signal [signal]]
```

The first nonoption argument to *trap* is the code to execute when the given signal is received. As shown above, that code can be self-contained, or a call to a function. For most nontrivial uses a call to one or more error handling functions is probably best, since that lends itself well to cleanup and graceful termination features. If this argument the null string, the given signal or signals will be ignored. If the argument is - or missing, but one or more signals are listed, they will be reset to the shell defaults. -l lists the signal names as show above, while -p will print any current traps and their handlers.

When using more than one trap handler, we recommend you take the extra time to alphabetize signal names because that makes them easier to read and find later on.

As noted above, the exit status of your script will be 128+*signal number* if the command was terminated by signal *signal number*.

There are three pseudosignals for various special purposes. The DEBUG signal is similar to EXIT but is used before every command for debugging purposes. The RETURN signal is triggered when execution resumes after a function or *source* (.) call. And the ERR signal is triggered after a simple command fails. Consult the *bash Reference* for more specific details and caveats, especially dealing with functions using the *declare* built-in or the set -o functrace option.

Note there are some POSIX differences that affect *trap*. As noted in the *bash Reference*, "starting *bash* with the --posix command-line option or executing set -o posix while *bash* is running will cause *bash* to conform more closely to the POSIX 1003.2 standard by changing the behavior to match that specified by POSIX in areas where the *bash* default differs." In particular, this will cause *kill* and *trap* to display signal names without the leading SIG and the output of kill -l will be different. And *trap* will handle its argument somewhat more strictly, in particular it will require a leading - in order to reset the trap to shell default. In other words it requires trap - USR1, not just trap USR1. We recommend that you always include the - even when not necessary, because it makes your intent clearer in the code.

See Also

- help trap
- Recipe 1.16, "Learning More About bash Documentation"
- Recipe 10.1, ""Daemon-izing" Your Script"
- Recipe 14.11, "Using Secure Temporary Files"
- Recipe 17.7, "Clearing the Screen When You Log Out"

10.7 Redefining Commands with alias

Problem

You'd like to slightly alter the definition of a command, perhaps so that you always use a particular option on a command (e.g., always using -a on the *ls* command or -i on the *rm* command).

Solution

Use the *alias* feature of *bash* for interactive shells (only). The *alias* command is smart enough not to go into an endless loop when you say something like:

```
alias ls='ls -a'
```

In fact, just type alias with no other arguments and you can see a list of aliases that are already defined for you in your *bash* session. Some installations may already have several available for you.

Discussion

The alias mechanism is a straightforward text substitution. It occurs very early in the command-line processing, so other substitutions will occur after the alias. For example, if you want to define the single letter "h" to be the command that lists your home directory, you can do it like this:

```
alias h='ls $HOME'
```

or like this:

```
alias h='ls ~'
```

The use of single quotes is significant in the first instance, meaning that the variable $HOME will not be evaluated when the definition of the alias is made. Only when you run the command will the (string) substitution be made, and only then will the $HOME variable be evaluated. That way if you change the definition of $HOME the alias will move with it, so to speak.

If, instead, you used double quotes, then the substitution of the variable's value would be made right away and the alias would be defined with the value of $HOME substituted. You can see this by typing alias with no arguments so that *bash* lists all the alias definitions. You would see something like this:

```
...
alias h='ls /home/youracct'
...
```

If you don't like what your alias does and want to get rid of it, just use *unalias* and the name of the alias that you no longer want. For example:

```
unalias h
```

will remove the definition that we just made above. If you get really messed up, you can use unalias -a to remove all the alias definitions in your current shell session. But what if someone has created an alias for *unalias*? Simple, if you prefix it with a backslash, alias expansion is not performed. So use \unalias -a instead.

Aliases do not allow arguments. For example, you cannot do this:

```
# Does NOT work, arguments NOT allowed
$ alias='mkdir $1 && cd $1'
```

The difference between $1 and $HOME is that $HOME is defined (one way or another) when the alias itself is defined, while you'd expect $1 to be passed in at runtime. Sorry, that doesn't work. Use a function instead.

See Also

- Appendix C for more on command-line processing
- Recipe 10.4, "Defining Functions"
- Recipe 10.5, "Using Functions: Parameters and Return Values"

- Recipe 14.4, "Clearing All Aliases"
- Recipe 16.14, "Creating and Changing into a New Directory in One Step"

10.8 Avoiding Aliases, Functions

Problem

You've written an alias or function to override a real command, and now you want to execute the real command.

Solution

Use the *bash* shell's *builtin* command to ignore shell functions and aliases to run the actual built-in command.

Use the *command* command to ignore shell functions and aliases to run the actual external command.

If you only want to avoid alias expansion, but still allow function definitions to be considered, then prefix the command with \ to just prevent alias expansion.

Use the *type* command (also with -a) to figure out what you've got.

Here are some examples:

```
$ alias echo='echo ~~~'

$ echo test
~~~ test

$ \echo test
test

$ builtin echo test
test

$ type echo
echo is aliased to `echo ~~~'

$ unalias echo

$ type echo
echo is a shell builtin

$ type -a echo
echo is a shell builtin
echo is /bin/echo

$ echo test
test
```

Here is a function definition that we will discuss:

```
function cd ( )
{
    if [[ $1 = "..." ]]
    then
        builtin cd ../..
    else
        builtin cd $1
    fi
}
```

Discussion

The *alias* command is smart enough not to go into an endless loop when you say something like alias ls='ls -a' or alias echo='echo ~~~', so in our first example we need to do nothing special on the righthand side of our alias definition to refer to the actual *echo* command.

When we have *echo* defined as an alias, then the *type* command will tell us not only that this is an alias, but will show us the alias definition. Similarly with function definitions, we would be shown the actual body of the function. type -a *some_command* will show us all of the places (aliases, built-ins, functions, and external) that contain *some_command* (as long as you are not also using -p).

In our last example, the function overrides the definition of *cd* so that we can add a simple shortcut. We want our function to understand that cd ... means to go up two directories; i.e., cd ../.. (see Recipe 16.13, "Creating a Better cd Command"). All other arguments will be treated as normal. Our function simply looks for a match with ... and substitutes the real meaning. But how, within (or without) the function, do you invoke the underlying *cd* command so as to actually change directories? The *builtin* command tells *bash* to assume that the command that follows is a shell built-in command and not to use any alias or function definition. We use it within the function, but it can be used at any time to refer, unambiguously, to the actual command, avoiding any function name that might be overriding it.

If your function name was that of an executable, like *ls*, and not a built-in command, then you can override any alias and/or function definition by just referring to the full path to the executable, such as */bin/ls* rather than just *ls* as the command. If you don't know its full path name, just prefix the command with the keyword *command* and *bash* will ignore any alias and function definitions with that name and use the actual command. Please note, however, that the $PATH variable will still be used to determine the location of the command. If you are running the wrong *ls* because your $PATH has some unexpected values, adding a *command* will not help in that situation.

See Also

- help builtin
- help command
- help type
- Recipe 14.4, "Clearing All Aliases"
- Recipe 16.13, "Creating a Better cd Command"

CHAPTER 11

Working with Dates and Times

Working with dates and times should be simple, but it's not. Regardless of whether you're writing a shell script or a much larger program, time keeping is full of complexities: different formats for displaying the time and date, Daylight Saving Time, leap years, leap seconds, and all of that. For example, imagine that you have a list of contracts and the dates on which they were signed. You'd like to compute expiration dates for all of those contracts. It's not a trivial problem: does a leap year get in the way? Is it the sort of contract where daylight saving time is likely to be a problem? And how do you format the output so that it's unambiguous? Does 7/4/07 mean July 4, 2007, or does it mean April 7?

Dates and times permeate every aspect of computing. Sooner or later you are going to have to deal with them: in system, application, or transaction logs; in data processing scripts; in user or administrative tasks; and more. This chapter will help you deal with them as simply and cleanly as possible. Computers are very good at keeping time accurately, particularly if they are using the Network Time Protocol (NTP) to keep themselves synced with national and international time standards. They're also great at understanding the variations in Daylight Saving Time from locale to locale. To work with time in a shell script, you need the Unix *date* command (or even better, the GNU version of the *date* command, which is standard on Linux). *date* is capable of displaying dates in different formats and even doing date arithmetic correctly.

Note that *gawk* (the GNU version of *awk*), has the same *strftime* formatting as the GNU *date* command. We're not going to cover *gawk* usage here except for one trivial example. We recommend sticking with GNU *date* because it's much easier to use and it has the very useful -d argument. But keep *gawk* in mind should you ever encounter a system that has *gawk* but not GNU *date*.

11.1 Formatting Dates for Display

Problem

You need to format dates or time for output.

Solution

Use the *date* command with a *strftime format specification*. See "Date and Time String Formatting with strftime" in Appendix A or the *strftime* manpage for the list of format specifications supported.

```
# Setting environment variables can be helpful in scripts:
$ STRICT_ISO_8601='%Y-%m-%dT%H:%M:%S%z'   # http://greenwichmeantime.com/info/iso.htm
$ ISO_8601='%Y-%m-%d %H:%M:%S %Z'         # Almost ISO-8601, but more human-readable
$ ISO_8601_1='%Y-%m-%d %T %Z'             # %T is the same as %H:%M:%S
$ DATEFILE='%Y%m%d%H%M%S'                 # Suitable for use in a file name

$ date "+$ISO_8601"
2006-05-08 14:36:51 CDT

gawk "BEGIN {print strftime(\"$ISO_8601\")}"
2006-12-07 04:38:54 EST

# Same as previous $ISO_8601
$ date '+%Y-%m-%d %H:%M:%S %Z'
2006-05-08 14:36:51 CDT

$ date -d '2005-11-06' "+$ISO_8601"
2005-11-06 00:00:00 CST

$ date "+Program starting at: $ISO_8601"
Program starting at: 2006-05-08 14:36:51 CDT

$ printf "%b" "Program starting at: $(date '+$ISO_8601')\n"
Program starting at: $ISO_8601

$ echo "I can rename a file like this: mv file.log file_$(date +$DATEFILE).log"
I can rename a file like this: mv file.log file_20060508143724.log
```

Discussion

You may be tempted to place the + in the environment variable to simplify the later command. On some systems the date command is more picky about the existence and placement of the + than on others. Our advice is to explicitly add it to the *date* command itself.

Many more formatting options are available, see the *date* manpage or the C strftime( ) function (man 3 strftime) on your system for a full list.

Unless otherwise specified, the time zone is assumed to be local time as defined by your system. The %z format is a nonstandard extension used by the GNU *date* command; it may not work on your system.

ISO 8601 is the recommended standard for displaying dates and times and should be used if at all possible. It offers a number of advantages over other display formats:

- It is a recognized standard
- It is unambiguous
- It is easy to read while still being easy to parse programmatically (e.g., using *awk* or *cut*)
- It sorts as expected when used in columnar data or in filenames

Try to avoid MM/DD/YY or DD/MM/YY or even worse M/D/YY or D/M/YY formats. They do not sort well and they are ambiguous, since either the day or the month may come first depending on geographical location, which also makes them hard to parse. Likewise, use 24-hour time when possible to avoid even more ambiguity and parsing problems.

See Also

- man date
- *http://www.cl.cam.ac.uk/~mgk25/iso-time.html*
- *http://www.qsl.net/g1smd/isopdf.htm*
- *http://greenwichmeantime.com/info/iso.htm*
- "Date and Time String Formatting with strftime" in Appendix A

11.2   Supplying a Default Date

Problem

You want your script to provide a useful default date, and perhaps prompt the user to verify it.

Solution

Using the GNU *date* command, assign the most likely date to a variable, then allow the user to change it:

```
#!/usr/bin/env bash
# cookbook filename: default_date

# Use Noon time to prevent a script running around midnight and a clock a
# few seconds off from causing off by one day errors.
START_DATE=$(date -d 'last week Monday 12:00:00' '+%Y-%m-%d')
```

```
while [ 1 ]; do
    printf "%b" "The starting date is $START_DATE, is that correct? (Y/new date) "
    read answer

    # Anything other than ENTER, "Y" or "y" is validated as a new date
    # could use "[Yy]*" to allow the user to spell out "yes"...
    # validate the new date format as: CCYY-MM-DD
    case "$answer" in
        [Yy]) break
            ;;
        [0-9][0-9][0-9][0-9]-[0-9][0-9]-[0-9][0-9])
            printf "%b" "Overriding $START_DATE with $answer\n"
            START_DATE="$answer"
            ;;

        *)  printf "%b" "Invalid date, please try again...\n"
            ;;
    esac
done

END_DATE=$(date -d "$START_DATE +7 days" '+%Y-%m-%d')

echo "START_DATE: $START_DATE"
echo "END_DATE:   $END_DATE"
```

Discussion

Not all *date* commands support the -d option, but the GNU version does. Our advice is to obtain and use the GNU *date* command if at all possible.

Leave out the user verification code if your script is running unattended or at a known time (e.g., from *cron*).

See Recipe 11.1, "Formatting Dates for Display" for information about how to format the dates and times.

We use code like this in scripts that generate SQL queries. The script runs at a given time and creates a SQL query for a specific date range to generate a report.

See Also

- man date
- Recipe 11.1, "Formatting Dates for Display"
- Recipe 11.3, "Automating Date Ranges"

11.3   Automating Date Ranges

Problem

You have one date (perhaps from Recipe 11.2, "Supplying a Default Date") and you would like to generate the other automatically.

Solution

The GNU *date* command is very powerful and flexible, but the power of -d isn't documented well. Your system may document this under *getdate* (try the *getdate* manpage). Here are some examples:

```
$ date '+%Y-%m-%d %H:%M:%S %z'
2005-11-05 01:03:00 -0500

$ date -d 'today' '+%Y-%m-%d %H:%M:%S %z'
2005-11-05 01:04:39 -0500

$ date -d 'yesterday' '+%Y-%m-%d %H:%M:%S %z'
2005-11-04 01:04:48 -0500

$ date -d 'tomorrow' '+%Y-%m-%d %H:%M:%S %z'
2005-11-06 01:04:55 -0500

$ date -d 'Monday' '+%Y-%m-%d %H:%M:%S %z'
2005-11-07 00:00:00 -0500

$ date -d 'this Monday' '+%Y-%m-%d %H:%M:%S %z'
2005-11-07 00:00:00 -0500

$ date -d 'last Monday' '+%Y-%m-%d %H:%M:%S %z'
2005-10-31 00:00:00 -0500

$ date -d 'next Monday' '+%Y-%m-%d %H:%M:%S %z'
2005-11-07 00:00:00 -0500

$ date -d 'last week' '+%Y-%m-%d %H:%M:%S %z'
2005-10-29 01:05:24 -0400

$ date -d 'next week' '+%Y-%m-%d %H:%M:%S %z'
2005-11-12 01:05:29 -0500

$ date -d '2 weeks' '+%Y-%m-%d %H:%M:%S %z'
2005-11-19 01:05:42 -0500

$ date -d '-2 weeks' '+%Y-%m-%d %H:%M:%S %z'
2005-10-22 01:05:47 -0400

$ date -d '2 weeks ago' '+%Y-%m-%d %H:%M:%S %z'
2005-10-22 01:06:00 -0400
```

```
$ date -d '+4 days' '+%Y-%m-%d %H:%M:%S %z'
2005-11-09 01:06:23 -0500

$ date -d '-6 days' '+%Y-%m-%d %H:%M:%S %z'
2005-10-30 01:06:30 -0400

$ date -d '2000-01-01 +12 days' '+%Y-%m-%d %H:%M:%S %z'
2000-01-13 00:00:00 -0500

$ date -d '3 months 1 day' '+%Y-%m-%d %H:%M:%S %z'
2006-02-06 01:03:00 -0500
```

Discussion

The -d option allows you to specify a specific date instead of using *now*, but not all *date* commands support it. The GNU version supports it and our advice is to obtain and use that version if at all possible.

Using -d can be tricky. These arguments work as expected:

```
$ date '+%a %Y-%m-%d'
Sat 2005-11-05

$ date -d 'today' '+%a %Y-%m-%d'
Sat 2005-11-05

$ date -d 'Saturday' '+%a %Y-%m-%d'
Sat 2005-11-05

$ date -d 'last Saturday' '+%a %Y-%m-%d'
Sat 2005-10-29

$ date -d 'this Saturday' '+%a %Y-%m-%d'
Sat 2005-11-05
```

But if you run this on Saturday you would expect to see *next* Saturday, but instead you get today:

```
$ date -d 'next Saturday' '+%a %Y-%m-%d'
Sat 2005-11-05
```

Also watch out for this week or *DAY* because as soon as that is in the past, this week becomes *next* week. So if you run this on Saturday 2005-11-05, you get these results, which may not be what you were thinking:

```
$ date -d 'this week Friday' '+%a %Y-%m-%d'
Fri 2005-11-11
```

The -d options can be incredibly useful, but be sure to thoroughly test your code and provide appropriate error checking.

If you don't have GNU *date*, you may find the shell functions presented in "Shell Corner: Date-Related Shell Functions" in the September 2005 issue of *UnixReview* to be very useful. The article presents five shell functions:

pn_month
>   Previous and next *x* months relative to the given month

end_month
>   End of month of the given month

pn_day
>   Previous and next *x* days of the given day

cur_weekday
>   Day of week for the given day

pn_weekday
>   Previous and next *x* day of weeks relative to the given day

And these were added not long before this book went to press:

pn_day_nr
>   (Non-recursive) Previous and next *x* days of the given day

days_between
>   Number of days between two dates

Note that pn_month, end_month, and cur_weekday are independent of the rest of the functions. However, pn_day is built on top of pn_month and end_month, and pn_weekday is built on top of pn_day and cur_weekday.

See Also

- man date
- man getdate
- *http://www.unixreview.com/documents/s=9884/ur0509a/ur0509a.html*
- *http://www.unixlabplus.com/unix-prog/date_function/*
- Recipe 11.2, "Supplying a Default Date"

11.4   Converting Dates and Times to Epoch Seconds

Problem

You want to convert a date and time to Epoch seconds to make it easier to do date and time arithmetic.

Solution

Use the GNU *date* command with the nonstandard -d option and a standard %s format:

```
# "Now" is easy
$ date '+%s'
1131172934
```

```
# Some other time needs the non-standard -d
$ date -d '2005-11-05 12:00:00 +0000' '+%s'
1131192000
```

Discussion

If you do not have the GNU *date* command available, this is a harder problem to solve. Our advice is to obtain and use the GNU *date* command if at all possible. If that is not possible you might be able to use Perl. Here are three ways to print the time right now in Epoch seconds:

```
$ perl -e 'print time, qq(\n);'
1154158997

# Same as above
$ perl -e 'use Time::Local; print timelocal(localtime()) . qq(\n);'
1154158997

$ perl -e 'use POSIX qw(strftime); print strftime("%s", localtime()) . qq(\n);'
1154159097
```

Using Perl to convert a specific day and time instead of *right now* is even harder due to Perl's date/time data structure. Years start at 1900 and months (but not days) start at zero instead of one. The format of the command is: timelocal(*sec, min, hour, day, month-1, year-1900*). So to convert 2005-11-05 06:59:49 to Epoch seconds:

```
# The given time is in local time
$ perl -e 'use Time::Local; print timelocal("49", "59", "06", "05", "10", "105") .
qq(\n);'
1131191989

# The given time is in UTC time
$ perl -e 'use Time::Local; print timegm("49", "59", "06", "05", "10", "105") . qq(\
n);'
1131173989
```

See Also

- man date
- Recipe 11.5, "Converting Epoch Seconds to Dates and Times"
- "Date and Time String Formatting with strftime" in Appendix A

11.5 Converting Epoch Seconds to Dates and Times

Problem

You need to convert Epoch seconds to a human-readable date and time.

Solution

Use the GNU date command with your desired format from Recipe 11.1, "Formatting Dates for Display":

```
EPOCH='1131173989'

$ date -d "1970-01-01 UTC $EPOCH seconds" +"%Y-%m-%d %T %z"
2005-11-05 01:59:49 -0500

$ date --utc --date "1970-01-01 $EPOCH seconds" +"%Y-%m-%d %T %z"
2005-11-05 06:59:49 +0000
```

Discussion

Since Epoch seconds are simply the number of seconds since the Epoch (which is Midnight on January 1, 1970, also known as 1970-01-01T00:00:00), this command starts at the Epoch, adds the Epoch seconds, and displays the date and time as you wish.

If you don't have GNU *date* on your system you can try one of these Perl one-liners:

```
EPOCH='1131173989'

$ perl -e "print scalar(gmtime($EPOCH)), qq(\n);"     # UTC
Sat Nov  5 06:59:49 2005

$ perl -e "print scalar(localtime($EPOCH)), qq(\n);"  # Your local time
Sat Nov  5 01:59:49 2005

$ perl -e "use POSIX qw(strftime); print strftime('%Y-%m-%d %H:%M:%S',
localtime($EPOCH)), qq(\n);"
2005-11-05 01:59:49
```

See Also

- man date
- Recipe 11.1, "Formatting Dates for Display"
- Recipe 11.4, "Converting Dates and Times to Epoch Seconds"
- "Date and Time String Formatting with strftime" in Appendix A

11.6   Getting Yesterday or Tomorrow with Perl

Problem

You need to get yesterday or tomorrow's date, and you have Perl but not GNU *date* on your system.

Solution

Use this Perl one-liner, adjusting the number of seconds added to or subtracted from time:

```
# Yesterday at this same time (note subtraction)
$ perl -e "use POSIX qw(strftime); print strftime('%Y-%m-%d', localtime(time -
86400)), qq(\n);"

# Tomorrow at this same time (note addition)
$ perl -e "use POSIX qw(strftime); print strftime('%Y-%m-%d', localtime(time +
86400)), qq(\n);"
```

Discussion

This is really just a specific application of the recipes above, but is so common that it's worth talking about by itself. See Recipe 11.7, "Figuring Out Date and Time Arithmetic" for a handy table of values that may be of use.

See Also

- Recipe 11.2, "Supplying a Default Date"
- Recipe 11.3, "Automating Date Ranges"
- Recipe 11.4, "Converting Dates and Times to Epoch Seconds"
- Recipe 11.5, "Converting Epoch Seconds to Dates and Times"
- Recipe 11.7, "Figuring Out Date and Time Arithmetic"
- "Date and Time String Formatting with strftime" in Appendix A

11.7 Figuring Out Date and Time Arithmetic

Problem

You need to do some kind of arithmetic with dates and times.

Solution

If you can't get the answer you need using the *date* command (see Recipe 11.3, "Automating Date Ranges"), convert your existing dates and times to Epoch seconds using Recipe 11.4, "Converting Dates and Times to Epoch Seconds," perform your calculations, then convert the resulting Epoch seconds back to your desired format using Recipe 11.5, "Converting Epoch Seconds to Dates and Times."

> If you don't have GNU *date*, you may find the shell functions presented in "Shell Corner: Date-Related Shell Functions" in the September 2005 issue of *Unix Review* to be very useful. See Recipe 11.3, "Automating Date Ranges."

For example, suppose you have log data from a machine where the time was badly off. Everyone should already be using the Network Time Protocol (NTP) so this doesn't happen, but just suppose:

```
CORRECTION='172800'    # 2 days worth of seconds

# Code to extract the date portion from the data
# into $bad_date go here

# Suppose it's this:
bad_date='Jan  2 05:13:05'  # syslog formated date

# Convert to Epoch using GNU date
bad_epoch=$(date -d "$bad_date" '+%s')

# Apply correction
good_epoch=$(( bad_epoch + $CORRECTION ))

# Make corrected date human-readable
good_date=$(date -d "1970-01-01 UTC $good_epoch seconds")    # GNU Date
good_date_iso=$(date -d "1970-01-01 UTC $good_epoch seconds" +'%Y-%m-%d %T') # GNU
Date

echo "bad_date:       $bad_date"
echo "bad_epoch:      $bad_epoch"
echo "Correction:     +$CORRECTION"
echo "good_epoch:     $good_epoch"
echo "good_date:      $good_date"
echo "good_date_iso:  $good_date_iso"

# Code to insert the $good_date back into the data goes here
```

 Watch out for years! Some Unix commands like *ls* and *syslog* try to be easy to read and omit the year under certain conditions. You may need to take that into account when calculating your correction factor. If you have data from a large range of dates or from different time zones, you will have to find some way to break it into separate files and process them individually.

Discussion

Dealing with any kind of date arithmetic is much easier using Epoch seconds than any other format of which we are aware. You don't have to worry about hours, days, weeks, or years, you just do some simple addition or subtraction and you're all set. Using Epoch seconds also avoids all the convoluted rules about leap years and seconds, and if you standardize on one time zone (usually UTC, which used to be called GMT) you can even avoid time zones.

Table 11-1 lists values that may be of use.

Table 11-1. Conversion table of common Epoch time values

Seconds	Minutes	Hours	Days
60	1		
300	5		
600	10		
3,600	60	1	
18,000	300	5	
36,000	600	10	
86,400	1,440	24	1
172,800	2,880	48	2
604,800	10,080	168	7
1,209,600	20,160	336	14
2,592,000	43,200	720	30
31,536,000	525,600	8,760	365

See Also

- *http://www.jpsdomain.org/networking/time.html*
- Recipe 11.3, "Automating Date Ranges"
- Recipe 11.4, "Converting Dates and Times to Epoch Seconds"
- Recipe 11.5, "Converting Epoch Seconds to Dates and Times"
- Recipe 13.12, "Isolating Specific Fields in Data"

11.8 Handling Time Zones, Daylight Saving Time, and Leap Years

Problem

You need to account for time zones, Daylight Saving Time, and leap years or seconds.

Solution

Don't. This is a lot trickier than it sounds. Leave it to code that's already been in use and debugged for years, and just use a tool that can handle your needs. Odds are high that one of the other recipes in this chapter has covered what you need, probably using GNU *date*. If not, there is almost certainly another tool out there that can do the job. For example, there are a number of excellent Perl modules that deal with dates and times.

Really, we aren't kidding. This is a real nightmare to get right. Save yourself a lot of agony and just use a tool.

See Also

- Recipe 11.1, "Formatting Dates for Display"
- Recipe 11.3, "Automating Date Ranges"
- Recipe 11.4, "Converting Dates and Times to Epoch Seconds"
- Recipe 11.5, "Converting Epoch Seconds to Dates and Times"
- Recipe 11.7, "Figuring Out Date and Time Arithmetic"

11.9 Using date and cron to Run a Script on the Nth Day

Problem

You need to run a script on the Nth weekday of the month (e.g., the second Wednesday), and most *crons* will not allow that.

Solution

Use a bit of shell code in the command to be run. In your Linux Vixie Cron *crontab* adapt one of the following lines. If you are using another *cron* program, you may need to convert the day of the week names to numbers according to the schedule your *cron* uses (0–6 or 1–7) and use +%w (day of week as number) in place of +%a (*locale*'s abbreviated weekday name):

```
# Vixie Cron
# Min   Hour DoM   Mnth DoW Program
# 0-59 0-23 1-31 1-12 0-7

# Run the first Wednesday @ 23:00
00 23 1-7 * Wed [ "$(date '+%a')" == "Wed" ] && /path/to/command args to command

# Run the second Thursday @ 23:00
00 23 8-14 * Thu [ "$(date '+%a')" == "Thu" ] && /path/to/command

# Run the third Friday @ 23:00
00 23 15-21 * Fri [ "$(date '+%a')" == "Fri" ] && /path/to/command

# Run the fourth Saturday @ 23:00
00 23 22-27 * Sat [ "$(date '+%a')" == "Sat" ] && /path/to/command

# Run the fifth Sunday @ 23:00
00 23 28-31 * Sun [ "$(date '+%a')" == "Sun" ] && /path/to/command
```

 Note that any given day of the week doesn't always happen five times during one month, so be sure you really know what you are asking for if you schedule something for the fifth week of the month.

Discussion

Most versions of *cron* (including Linux's Vixie Cron) do not allow you to schedule a job on the Nth day of the month. To get around that, we schedule the job to run during the *range of days* when the Nth day we need occurs, then check to see if it is the correct day on which to run. The "second Wednesday of the month" must occur somewhere in the range of the 8th to 14th day of the month. So we simply run every day and see if it's Wednesday. If so, we execute our command.

Table 11-2 shows the ranges noted above.

Table 11-2. Day ranges for each week of a month

Week	Day range
First	1 to 7
Second	8 to 14
Third	15 to 21
Fourth	22 to 27
Fifth (see previous warning note)	28 to 31

We know this almost seems too simplistic; check a calendar if you don't believe us:

```
$ cal 10 2006
    October 2006
 S  M Tu  W Th  F  S
 1  2  3  4  5  6  7
 8  9 10 11 12 13 14
15 16 17 18 19 20 21
22 23 24 25 26 27 28
29 30 31
```

See Also

- man 5 crontab
- man cal

CHAPTER 12

End-User Tasks As Shell Scripts

You have seen a lot of smaller scripts and syntax up to now. Our examples have, of necessity, been small in scale and scope. Now we would like to show you a few larger (though not large) examples. They are meant to give you useful, real world examples of actual uses of shell scripts beyond just system administration tasks. We hope you find them useful or usable. More than that, we hope you learn something about *bash* by reading through them and maybe trying them yourself or even tweaking them for your own use.

12.1 Starting Simple by Printing Dashes

Problem

To print a line of dashes with a simple command might sound easy—and it is. But as soon as you think you've got a simple script, it begins to grow. What about varying the length of the line of dashes? What about changing the character from a dash to a user-supplied character? Do you see how easily *feature creep* occurs? Can we write a simple script that takes those extensions into account without getting too complex?

Solution

Consider this script:

```
 1   #!/usr/bin/env bash
 2   # cookbook filename: dash
 3   # dash - print a line of dashes
 4   # options: # how many (default 72)
 5   #          -c X  use char X instead of dashes
 6   #
 7   function usagexit ( )
 8   {
 9       printf "usage: %s [-c X] [#]\n" $(basename $0)
10       exit 2
11   } >&2
```

```
12  LEN=72
13  CHAR='-'
14  while (( $# > 0 ))
15  do
16      case $1 in
17      [0-9]*) LEN=$1;;
18      -c) shift
19          CHAR=$1;;
20      *) usagexit;;
21      esac
22      shift
23  done

24  if (( LEN > 4096 ))
25  then
26      echo "too large" >&2
27      exit 3

28  fi
29  # build the string to the exact length
30  DASHES=""
31  for ((i=0; i<LEN; i++))
32  do
33      DASHES="${DASHES}${CHAR}"
34  done
35  printf "%s\n" "$DASHES"
```

Discussion

The basic task is accomplished by building a string of the required number of dashes (or an alternate character) and then printing that string to standard output (STD-OUT). That takes only the six lines from 30–35. Lines 12 and 13 set the default values. All the other lines are spent on argument parsing, error checking, user messages, and comments.

You will find that it's pretty typical for a robust, end-user script. Less than 20 percent of the code does more than 80 percent of the work. But that 80 percent of the code is what makes it usable and "friendly" for your users.

In line 9 we use basename to trim off any leading pathname characters when displaying this script's name. That way no matter how the user invokes the script (for example, *./dashes*, */home/username/bin/dashes*, or even *../../over/there/dashes*), it will still be referred to as just *dashes* in the usage message.

The argument parsing is done while there are some arguments to parse (line 14). As arguments are handled, each shift built-in will decrement the number of arguments and eventually get us out of the while loop. There are only two possible allowable arguments: specifying a number for the length (line 17), and a -c option followed by a number (see lines 18–19). Anything else (line 20) will result in the usage message and an early exit.

We could be more careful in parsing the -c and its argument. By not using more sophisticated parsing (e.g., *getopt* Recipe 13.1, "Parsing Arguments for Your Shell Script"), the option and it's argument must be separated by whitespace. (In running the script one must type -c n and not -cn.) We don't even check to see that the second argument is supplied at all. Furthermore, it could be not just a single letter but a whole string. (Can you think of a simple way to limit this, by just taking the first character of the argument? Do you need/want to? Why not let the user specify a string instead of a single character?)

The parsing of the numerical argument could also use some more sophisticated techniques. The patterns in a case statement follow the rules of *pathname expansion* and are not regular expressions. It might be tempting to assume that the case pattern [0-9]* means only digits, but that would be the regular expression meaning. In the case statement it means any string that begins with a digit. Not catching erroneous input like 9.5 or 612more will result in errors in the script later on. The use of an if statement with its more sophisticated regular expression matching might be useful here.

As a final comment on the code: at line 24 the script enforces a maximum length, though it is completely arbitrary. Would you keep or remove such a restriction?

You can see from this example that even simple scripts can be come quite involved, mostly due to error checking, argument parsing, and the like. For scripts that you write for yourself, such techniques are often glossed over or skipped entirely—after all, as the only user of the script you know the proper usage and are willing to use it correctly or have it fail in an ugly display of error messages. For scripts that you want to share, however, such is not the case, and much care and effort will likely be put into toughening up your script.

See Also

- Recipe 5.8, "Looping Over Arguments Passed to a Script"
- Recipe 5.11, "Counting Arguments"
- Recipe 5.12, "Consuming Arguments"
- Recipe 6.15, "Parsing Command-Line Arguments"
- Recipe 13.1, "Parsing Arguments for Your Shell Script"

12.2   Viewing Photos in an Album

Problem

You have a directory full of images like the ones you just downloaded from your digital camera. You want a quick and easy way to view them all, so that you can pick out the good ones.

Solution

Write a shell script that will generate a set of html pages so that you can view your photos with a browser. Call it *mkalbum* and put it somewhere like your *~/bin* directory.

On the command line, *cd* into the directory where you want your album created (typically where your photos are located). Then run some command that will generate the list of photos that you want included in this album (e.g., ls *.jpg, but see also Recipe 9.5, "Finding Files Irrespective of Case"), and pipe this output into the *mkalbum* shell script, which we will explain later. You need to put the name of the album (i.e., the name of a directory that will be created by the script) on the command line as the only argument to the shell script. It might look something like this:

```
$ ls *.jpg | mkalbum rugbymatch
```

Figure 12-1 shows a sample of the generated web page.

Figure 12-1. Sample mkalbum web page

The large title is the photo (i.e., the filename); there are hyperlinks to other pages for first, last, next, and previous.

The fpllowing is the shell script (*mkalbum*) that will generate a set of html pages, one page per image (the line numbers are not part of the script, but are put here to make it easier to discuss):

```
 1  #!/usr/bin/env bash
 2  # cookbook filename: mkalbum
 3  # mkalbum - make an html "album" of a pile of photo files.
 4  # ver. 0.2
 5  #
 6  # An album is a directory of html pages.
 7  # It will be created in the current directory.
 8  #
 9  # An album page is the html to display one photo, with
10  # a title that is the filename of the photo, along with
11  # hyperlinks to the first, previous, next, and last photos.
12  #
13  # ERROUT
14  ERROUT()
15  {
16      printf "%b" "$@"
17  } >&2
18
19  #
20  # USAGE
21  USAGE()
22  {
23      ERROUT "usage: %s <newdir>\n" $(basename $0)
24  }
25
26  # EMIT(thisph, startph, prevph, nextph, lastph)
27  EMIT()
28  {
29    THISPH="../$1"
30    STRTPH="${2%.*}.html"
31    PREVPH="${3%.*}.html"
32    NEXTPH="${4%.*}.html"
33    LASTPH="${5%.*}.html"
34    if [ -z "$3" ]
35    then
36       PREVLINE='<TD> Prev </TD>'
37    else
38       PREVLINE='<TD> <A HREF="'$PREVPH'"> Prev </A> </TD>'
39    fi
40    if [ -z "$4" ]
41    then
42        NEXTLINE='<TD> Next </TD>'
43    else
44        NEXTLINE='<TD> <A HREF="'$NEXTPH'"> Next </A> </TD>'
45    fi
46  cat <<EOF
47  <HTML>
48  <HEAD><TITLE>$THISPH</TITLE></HEAD>
49  <BODY>
50    <H2>$THISPH</H2>
51  <TABLE WIDTH="25%">
52    <TR>
53    <TD> <A HREF="$STRTPH"> First </A> </TD>
54    $PREVLINE
```

```
55      $NEXTLINE
56      <TD> <A HREF="$LASTPH"> Last </A> </TD>
57      </TR>
58   </TABLE>
59      <IMG SRC="$THISPH" alt="$THISPH"
60      BORDER="1" VSPACE="4" HSPACE="4"
61      WIDTH="800" HEIGHT="600"/>
62   </BODY>
63   </HTML>
64   EOF
65   }
66
67   if (( $# != 1 ))
68   then
69        USAGE
70        exit -1
71   fi
72   ALBUM="$1"
73   if [ -d "${ALBUM}" ]
74   then
75        ERROUT "Directory [%s] already exists.\n" ${ALBUM}
76        USAGE
77        exit -2
78   else
79        mkdir "$ALBUM"
80   fi
81   cd "$ALBUM"
82
83   PREV=""
84   FIRST=""
85   LAST="last"
86
87   while read PHOTO
88   do
89        # prime the pump
90        if [ -z "${CURRENT}" ]
91        then
92            CURRENT="$PHOTO"
93            FIRST="$PHOTO"
94            continue
95        fi
96
97        PHILE=$(basename "${CURRENT}")
98        EMIT "$CURRENT" "$FIRST" "$PREV" "$PHOTO" "$LAST" > "${PHILE%.*}.html"
99
100  1     # set up for next iteration
101        PREV="$CURRENT"
102        CURRENT="$PHOTO"
103
104  done
105
106  PHILE=$(basename ${CURRENT})
107  EMIT "$CURRENT" "$FIRST" "$PREV"     ""    "$LAST" > "${PHILE%.*}.html"
108
```

```
109  # make the symlink for "last"
110  ln -s "${PHILE%.*}.html" ./last.html
111
112  # make a link for index.html
113  ln -s "${FIRST%.*}.html" ./index.html
114
```

Discussion

While there are plenty of free or inexpensive photo viewers, using *bash* to build a simple photo album helps to illustrate the power of shell programming, and gives us a meatier example to discuss.

The shell script begins (line 1) with the special comment that defines which executable to use to run this script. Then follows some comments describing the script. Let's just put in one more word encouraging you to be sure to comment your script. Even the sparsest comments are worth something 3 days or 13 months from now when you wish you could remember what this script was all about.

After the comments we have put our function definitions. The ERROUT function (lines 14–17) will act very much like *printf* (since all it does is invoke *printf*) but with the added twist that it redirects its output to standard error. This saves you from having to remember to redirect the output on every *printf* of error messages.

While normally we put the redirection at the end of a command, here (line 17) it is put at the end of a function definition to tell *bash* to redirect all output that emanates from this function.

The USAGE function (lines 21–24), while not strictly necessary as a separate function, is a handy way to document up front how you expect your script to be invoked. Rather than hard-coding the name of the script in our usage message, we like to use the $0 special variable in case the script is renamed. Since $0 is the name of the script as it was invoked, if the script is invoked with its full pathname (e.g., */usr/local/bin/ mkalbum*) then $0 is the full pathname and the usage message would include the full pathname. By taking the basename (line 23) we get rid of all that path noise.

The EMIT function (lines 27–65) is a larger function. Its purpose is to emit the HTML for each page of the album. Each page is its own (static) web page, with hyperlinks to the previous and next image as well as links to the first and last image. The EMIT function doesn't know much; it is given the names of all the images to which to link. It takes those names and converts them to page names, which for our script are the same as the image name but with the file extension changed to html. So for example if $2 held the filename *pict001.jpg*, the result of ${2%.*}.html would be *pict001.html*.

Since there is so much HTML to emit, rather than have *printf* after *printf* statement, we use the *cat* command and a here-document (line 46) to allow us to type the literal HTML in the script, line after line, along with shell variable expansion being applied to the lines. The *cat* command is simply copying (concatenating) the STDIN to the STDOUT. In our script we redirect STDIN to take its input from the succeeding lines

---

of text, i.e., a here-document. By *not* quoting the end-of-input word (just EOF and not 'EOF' or \EOF), *bash* will continue to do variable substitution on our input lines, enabling us to use variable names based on our parameters for various titles and hyperlinks.

We could have passed in a filename to the EMIT function, and have had EMIT redirect its own output to that file. But such redirection was not really logically a part of the emit idea (c.f. ERROUT whose whole purpose *was* the redirection). The purpose of EMIT was to create the HTML; where we send that HTML is another matter. Because *bash* allows us to redirect output so easily, it is possible to make that a separate step. Besides, it was easier to debug when the method just wrote its output to STDOUT.

The last two commands in the script (lines 110 and 113) create symbolic links as short cuts to the first and last photos. This way the script doesn't need to figure out the name of the first and last pages of the album, it just uses the hardcoded names *index.html* and *last.html*, respectively, when generating all the other album pages. Then as a last step, since the last filename processed is the last photo in our album, it creates the link to it. Similarly with the first page, although we know that name right away, we waited until the end to put it with the other symbolic link, just as a matter of style—to keep the two similar operations in proximity.

See Also

- *http://www.w3schools.com/*
- *HTML & XHTML: The Definitive Guide* by Chuch Musciano and Bill Kennedy (O'Reilly)
- Recipe 3.2, "Keeping Your Data with Your Script"
- Recipe 3.3, "Preventing Weird Behavior in a Here-Document"
- Recipe 3.4, "Indenting Here-Documents"
- Recipe 5.13, "Getting Default Values"
- Recipe 5.14, "Setting Default Values"
- Recipe 5.18, "Changing Pieces of a String"
- Recipe 5.19, "Using Array Variables"
- Recipe 9.5, "Finding Files Irrespective of Case"
- Recipe 16.9, "Keeping a Private Stash of Utilities by Adding ~/bin"

12.3   Loading Your MP3 Player

Problem

You have a collection of MP3 files that you would like to put in your MP3 player. But you have more music than can fit on your MP3 player. How can you load your player with music without having to baby-sit it by dragging and dropping files until it is full?

Solution

Use a shell script to keep track of the available space as it copies files onto the MP3 player, quitting when it is full.

```
1   #!/usr/bin/env bash
2   # cookbook filename: load_mp3
3   # Fill up my mp3 player with as many songs as will fit.
4   # N.B.: This assumes that the mp3 player is mounted on /media/mp3
5   #
6
7   #
8   # determine the size of a file
9   #
10  function FILESIZE ( )
11  {
12      FN=${1:-/dev/null}
13      if [[ -e $FN ]]
14      then
15          # FZ=$(ls -s $FN | cut -d ' ' -f 1)
16              set -- $(ls -s "$FN")
17              FZ=$1
18          fi
19  }
20
21  #
22  # compute the freespace on the mp3 player
23  #
24  function FREESPACE
25  {
26      # FREE=$(df /media/mp3 | awk '/^\/dev/ {print $4}')
27      set -- $(df /media/mp3 | grep '^/dev/')
28      FREE=$4
29  }
30
31  # subtract the (given) filesize from the (global) freespace
32  function REDUCE ( )
33  (( FREE-=${1:-0}))
34
35  #
36  # main:
37  #
38  let SUM=0
39  let COUNT=0
40  export FZ
41  export FREE
42  FREESPACE
43  find . -name '*.mp3' -print | \
44  (while read PATHNM
45  do
46      FILESIZE "$PATHNM"
47      if ((FZ <= FREE))
48      then
49          echo loading $PATHNM
```

```
50      cp "$PATHNM" /media/mp3
51      if (( $? == 0 ))
52      then
53          let SUM+=FZ
54          let COUNT++
55          REDUCE $FZ
56      else
57          echo "bad copy of $PATHNM to /media/mp3"
58          rm -f /media/mp3/$(basename "$PATHNM")
59          # recompute because we don't know how far it got
60          FREESPACE
61      fi
62      # any reason to go on?
63      if (( FREE <= 0 ))
64      then
65          break
66      fi
67      else
68          echo skipping $PATHNM
69      fi
70  done
71  printf "loaded %d songs (%d blocks)"  $COUNT $SUM
72  printf " onto /media/mp3 (%d blocks free)\n" $FREE
73  )
74  # end of script
```

Discussion

Invoke this script and it will copy any MP3 file that it finds from the current directory on down (toward the leaf nodes of the tree) onto an MP3 player (or other device) mounted on */media/mp3*. The script will try to determine the freespace on the device before it begins its copying, and then it will subtract the disk size of copied items so as to know when to quit (i.e., when the device is full, or as full as we can get it).

The script is simple to invoke:

```
$ fillmp3
```

and then you can watch as it copies files, or you can go grab a cup of coffee—it depends on how fast your disk and your MP3 memory writes go.

Let's look at some *bash* features used in this script, referencing them by line number.

Let's start at line 35, after the opening comments and the function definitions. (We'll return to the function definitions later.) The main body of the shell script starts by initializing some variables (lines 38–39) and exporting some variables so they will be available globally. At line 42 we call the FREESPACE function to determine how much free space is available on the MP3 player before we begin copying files.

Line 43 has the *find* command that will locate all the MP3 files (actually only those files whose names end in ".mp3"). This information is piped into a while loop that begins on line 44.

Why is the while loop wrapped inside of parentheses? The parentheses mean that the statements inside it will be run inside of a subshell. But what we're concerned about here is that we group the while statement with the *printf* statements that follow (lines 71 and 72). Since each statement in a pipeline is run in its own subshell, and since the *find* pipes its output into the while loop, then none of the counting that we do inside the while loop will be available outside of that loop. By putting the while and the *printfs* inside of a subshell, they are now both executing in the same shell environment and can share variables.

Let's look inside the while loop and see what it's doing:

```
46        FILESIZE "$PATHNM"
47        if (( FZ <= FREE))
48        then
49            echo loading $PATHNM
50            cp "$PATHNM" /media/mp3
51            if (( $? == 0 ))
52            then
```

For each filename that it reads (from the *find* command's output) it will use the FILESIZE function to determine the size of that file (see below for a discussion of that function). Then it checks (line 47) to see if the file is smaller than the remaining disk space, i.e., whether there is room for this file. If so, it will *echo* the filename so we can see what it's doing and then it will copy (line 50) the file onto the MP3 player.

It's important to check and see if the copy command completed successfully (line 51). The $? is the result of the previous command, so it represents the result of the the *cp* command. If the copy is successful, then we can deduct its size from the space available on the MP3 player. But if the copy failed, then we need to try to remove the copy (since, if it is there at all, it will be incomplete). We use the -f option on *rm* so as to avoid error messages if the file never got created. Then we recalculate the free space to be sure that we have the count right. (After all, the copy might have failed because somehow our estimate was wrong and we really are out of space.)

In the main part of the script, all three of our if statements (lines 47, 51, and 63) use the double parentheses around the expression. All three are numerical if statements, and we wanted to use the familiar operators (vis. <= and ==). These same if conditions could have been checked using the square bracket ([) form of the if statement, but then the operators would be -le and -eq. We do use a different form of the if statement in line 13, in the FILESIZE function. There we need to check the existence of the file (whose name is in the variable $FN). That is simple to write with the -e operator, but that is not available to the arithmetic-style if statement (i.e., when using parentheses instead of square brackets).

Speaking of arithmetic expressions, lets take a look at the REDUCE function and see what's going on there:

```
32  function REDUCE ( )
33  (( FREE-=${1:-0}))
```

Most people write functions using curly braces to delimit the body of the function. However, in *bash*, any compound statement will work. In this case we chose the double-parentheses of arithmetic evaluation, since that is all we need the function to do. Whatever value is supplied on the command line that invokes REDUCE will be the first (positional) parameter (i.e., $1). We simply subtract that value from $FREE to get the new value for $FREE. That is why we used the arithmetic expression syntax—so that we can use the -= operator.

While we are looking at the functions, let's look at two lines in the FILESIZE function. Take a close look at these lines:

```
16      set -- $(ls -s "$FN")
17      FZ=$1
```

There is a lot going on in those few characters. First, the *ls* command is run inside of a subshell (the $( ) construct). The -s option on *ls* gives us the size, in blocks, of the file along with the file name. The output of the command is returned as words on the command line for the set command. The purpose of the set command here is to parse the words of the *ls* output. Now there are lots of ways we could do that, but this approach is a useful technique to remember.

The set -- will take the remaining words on the command line and make them the new positional parameters. If you write set -- this is a test, then $1 is this and $3 is a. The previous values for $1, $2, etc are lost, but in line 12 we saved into $FN the only parameter that gets passed in to this function. Having done so, we are free to reuse the positional parameters, and we use them by having the shell do the parsing for us. We can then get at the file size as $1, as you see in line 17. (By the way, in this case, since this is inside a function, it is only the function's positional parameters that are changed, not those from the invoking of the script.)

We use this technique of having the shell do our parsing for us, again on line 27 in the other function:

```
27      set -- $(df /media/mp3 | grep '^/dev/')
28      FREE=$4
```

The output of the *df* command will report on the size, in blocks, available on the device. We pipe the output through *grep*, since we only want the one line with our device's information and we don't want the heading line that *df* produces. Once *bash* has set our arguments, we can grab the free space on the device as $4.

The comment on line 26 shows an alternative way to parse the output of the *df* command. We could just pipe the output into *awk* and let it parse the output from *df* for us:

```
26      # FREE=$(df /media/mp3 | awk '/^\/dev/ {print $4}')
```

By using the expression in slashes, we tell *awk* to pay attention only to lines with a leading */dev*. (The caret anchors the search to the beginning of the line and the backslash escapes the meaning of the slash, so as not to end the search expression at that point and to include a slash as the first character to find.)

So which approach to use? They both involve invoking an external program, in one case *grep* and in the other *awk*. There are usually several ways to accomplish the same thing (in *bash* as in life), so the choice is yours. In our experience, it usually comes down to which one you think of first.

See Also

- man df
- man grep
- man awk
- Recipe 10.4, "Defining Functions"
- Recipe 10.5, "Using Functions: Parameters and Return Values"
- Recipe 19.8, "Forgetting That Pipelines Make Subshells"

12.4 Burning a CD

Problem

You have a directory full of files on your Linux system that you would like to burn to a CD. Do you need an expensive CD burning program, or can you do it with the shell and some open source programs?

Solution

You can do it with two open source programs called *mkisofs* and *cdrecord*, and a *bash* script to help you keep all the options straight.

Start by putting all the files that you want to copy to CD into a directory structure. The script will take that directory, make an ISO filesystem image from those files, then burn the ISO image. All it takes is a bunch of disk space and a bit of time—but you can get up and wander while the *bash* script runs.

 This script may not work on your system. We include it here as an example of shell scripting, not as a workable CD recording and backup mechanism.

```
1   #!/usr/bin/env bash
2   # cookbook filename: cdscript
3   # cdscript - prep and burn a CD from a dir.
4   #
5   # usage: cdscript dir [ cddev ]
6   #
7   if [[ $# < 1 || $# > 2 ]]
8   then
9       echo 'usage: cdscript dir [ cddev ]'
```

```
10     exit 2
11  fi
12
13  # set the defaults
14  RCDIR=$1
15  # your device might be "ATAPI:0,0,0" or other digits
16  CDDEV=${2:-"ATAPI:0,0,0"}
17  ISOIMAGE=/tmp/cd$$.iso
18
19  echo "building ISO image..."
20  #
21  # make the ISO fs image
22  #
23  mkisofs $ISOPTS -A "$(cat ~/.cdAnnotation)" \
24      -p "$(hostname)" -V "$(basename $SRCDIR)" \
25      -r -o "$ISOIMAGE" $SRCDIR
26  STATUS=$?
27  if [ $STATUS -ne 0 ]
28  then
29      echo "Error. ISO image failed."
30      echo "Investigate then remove $ISOIMAGE"
31      exit $STATUS
32  fi
33
34  echo "ISO image built; burning to cd..."
35  exit
36
37  # burn the CD
38  SPD=8
39  OPTS="-eject -v fs=64M driveropts=burnproof"
40  cdrecord $OPTS -speed=$SPD dev=${CDDEV} $ISOImage
41  STATUS=$?
42  if [ $STATUS -ne 0 ]
43  then
44      echo "Error. CD Burn failed."
45      echo "Investigate then remove $ISOIMAGE"
46      exit $STATUS
47  fi
48
49  rm -f $ISOIMAGE
50  echo "Done."
```

Discussion

Here is a quick look at some of the odder constructs in this script.

At line 17:

```
17  ISOIMAGE=/tmp/cd$$.iso
```

we construct a temporary filename by using the $$ variable, which gives us our process number. As long as this script is running, it will be the one and only process of that number, so it gives us a name that is unique among all other running processes. (See Recipe 14.11, "Using Secure Temporary Files" for a better way.)

In line 26, we save the status of the *mkisofs* command. Well-written Unix and Linux commands (and *bash* shell scripts) will return 0 on success (i.e., nothing went wrong) and a nonzero value if they fail. We could have just used the $? in the if statement on line 27 except that we want to preserve the status from the *mkisofs* command so that, in the event of failure, we can pass that back out as the return value of this script (line 31). We do the same with the *cdrecord* command and its return value on lines 41–47.

It may take a bit of thought to unpack lines 23–25:

```
23    mkisofs $ISOPTS -A "$(cat ~/.cdAnnotation)" \
24        -p "$(hostname)" -V "$(basename $SRCDIR)" \
25        -r -o "$ISOIMAGE" $SRCDIR
```

All three lines are just a single line of input to *bash* which has been separated across lines by putting the backslash as the very last character on the line in order to escape the normal meaning of an end of line. Be sure you don't put a space after the trailing \. But that's just the tip of the iceberg here. There are three subshells that are invoked whose output is used in the construction of the final command line that invokes *mkisofs*.

First there is an invocation of the *cat* program to dump the contents of a file called *.cdAnnotation* located in the home directory (~/) of the user invoking this script. The purpose is to provide a string to the -A option, which the manpage describes as "a text string that will be written into the volume header." Similarly, the -p option wants another such string, this time indicating the preparer of the image. For our script it seemed like it might be handy to put the hostname where the script is run as the preparer, so we run *hostname* in a subshell. Finally, the volume name is specified with the -V parameter, and for that we will use the name of the directory where all the files are found. Since that directory is specified on the command line to our script, but will likely be a full pathname, we use *basename* in a subshell to peel off the leading directory pathname, if any (so, for example, */usr/local/stuff* becomes just *stuff*).

See Also

- Recipe 14.11, "Using Secure Temporary Files"

12.5   Comparing Two Documents

Problem

It is easy to compare two text files (see Recipe 17.10, "Using diff and patch"). But what about documents produced by your suite of office applications? They are not stored as text, so how can you compare them? If you have two versions of the same document, and you need to know what the content changes are (if any) between the two versions, is there anything you can do besides printing them out and comparing page after page?

Solution

First, use an office suite that will let you save your documents in Open Document Format (ODF). This is the case for packages like OpenOffice.org while other commercial packages have promised to add support soon. Once you have your files in ODF, you can use a shell script to compare just the content of the files. We stress the word *content* here because the formatting differences are another issue, and it is (usually) the content that is the most important determinant of which version is new or more important to the end user.

Here is a *bash* script that can be used to compare two OpenOffice.org files, which are saved in ODF (but use the conventional suffix *odt* to indicate a text-oriented document, as opposed to a spreadsheet or a presentation file).

```
1  #!/usr/bin/env bash
2  # cookbook filename: oodiff
3  # oodiff -- diff the CONTENTS of two OpenOffice.org files
4  # works only on .odt files
5  #
6  function usagexit ( )
7  {
8      echo "usage: $0 file1 file2"
9      echo "where both files must be .odt files"
10     exit $1
11 } >&2
12
13 # assure two readable arg filenames which end in .odt
14 if (( $# != 2 ))
15 then
16     usagexit 1
17 fi
18 if [[ $1 != *.odt || $2 != *.odt ]]
19 then
20     usagexit 2
21 fi
22 if [[ ! -r $1 || ! -r $2 ]]
23 then
24     usagexit 3
25 fi
26
27 BAS1=$(basename "$1" .odt)
28 BAS2=$(basename "$2" .odt)
29
30 # unzip them someplace private
31 PRIV1="/tmp/${BAS1}.$$_1"
32 PRIV2="/tmp/${BAS2}.$$_2"
33
34 # make absolute
35 HERE=$(pwd)
36 if [[ ${1:0:1} == '/' ]]
37 then
38     FULL1="${1}"
```

```
39   else
40       FULL1="${HERE}/${1}"
41   fi
42
43   # make absolute
44   if [[ ${2:0:1} == '/' ]]
45   then
46       FULL2="${2}"
47   else
48       FULL2="${HERE}/${2}"
49   fi
50
51   # mkdir scratch areas and check for failure
52   # N.B. must have whitespace around the { and } and
53   #       must have the trailing ; in the {} lists
54   mkdir "$PRIV1" || { echo Unable to mkdir $PRIV1 ; exit 4; }
55   mkdir "$PRIV2" || { echo Unable to mkdir $PRIV2 ; exit 5; }
56
57   cd "$PRIV1"
58   unzip -q "$FULL1"
59   sed -e 's/>/>\
60   /g' -e 's/</\
61   </g' content.xml > contentwnl.xml
62
63   cd "$PRIV2"
64   unzip -q "$FULL2"
65   sed -e 's/>/>\
66   /g' -e 's/</\
67   </g' content.xml > contentwnl.xml
68
69   cd $HERE
70
71   diff "${PRIV1}/contentwnl.xml" "${PRIV2}/contentwnl.xml"
72
73   rm -rf $PRIV1 $PRIV2
```

Discussion

Underlying this script is the knowledge that OpenOffice.org files are stored like ZIP files. Unzip them and there are a collection of XML files that define your document. One of those files contains the content of your document, that is, the paragraphs of text without any formatting (but with XML tags to tie each snippet of text to its for-matting). The basic idea behind the script is to *unzip* the two documents and com-pare the content pieces using *diff*, and then clean up the mess that we've made.

One other step is taken to make the *diff*s easier to read. Since the content is all in XML and there aren't a lot of newlines, the script will insert a newline after every tag and before every end-tag (tags that begin with a slash, as in </ ... >). While this introduces a lot of blank lines, it also enables *diff* to focus on the real differences: the textual content.

As far as shell syntax goes, you have seen all this in other recipes in the book, but it may be worth explaining a few pieces of syntax just to be sure you can tell what is going on in the script.

Line 11 redirects all the output from this shell function to STDERR. That seems appropriate since this is a help message, not the normal output of this program. By putting the redirect on the function definition, we don't need to remember to redirect every output line separately.

Line 36 contains the terse expression if [[${1:0:1} == '/']], which checks to see whether the first argument begins with a slash character. The ${1:0:1} is the syntax for a substring of a shell variable. The variable is ${1}, the first positional parameter. The :0:1 syntax says to start at an offset of zero and that the substring should be one character long.

Lines 59–60 and 60–61 may be a little hard to read because they involve escaping the newline character so that it becomes part of the *sed* substitution string. The substitution expression takes each > in the first substitution and each < in the second, and replaces it with itself *plus* a newline. We do this to our content file in order to spread out the XML and get the content on lines by itself. That way the *diff* doesn't show any XML tags, just content text.

See Also

- Recipe 8.7, "Uncompressing Files"
- Recipe 13.3, "Parsing Some HTML"
- Recipe 14.11, "Using Secure Temporary Files"
- Recipe 17.3, "Unzipping Many ZIP Files"
- Recipe 17.10, "Using diff and patch"

CHAPTER 13

Parsing and Similar Tasks

This is a chapter of tasks that programmers might recognize. It's not necessarily more advanced than other *bash* script recipes in the book, but if you are not a programmer, these tasks might seem obscure or irrelevant to your use of *bash*. We won't do much explaining of the reasons why you'd find yourself in these situations (as a programmer, you'll recognize some if not all of them). Even if you don't recognize the situation, you should read them for what you can learn about *bash*.

Some of the recipes in this chapter include the parsing of command-line arguments. Recall that the typical way to specify options on a shell script is to have a leading minus sign and a single letter. For example, an option for your script to give fewer messages might use -q as a flag to mean quiet mode. Sometimes an option might take an argument. For example, a user option where you need to specify a username might use -u followed by the username. This distinction will be made clear in this chapter's first recipe.

13.1 Parsing Arguments for Your Shell Script

Problem

You want to have some options on your shell script, some flags that you can use to alter its behavior. You could do the parsing directly, using ${#} to tell you how many arguments have been supplied, and testing ${1:0:1} to test the first character of the first argument to see if it is a minus sign. You would need some if/then or case logic to identify which option it is and whether it takes an argument. What if the user doesn't supply a required argument? What if the user calls your script with two options combined (e.g., -ab)? Will you also parse for that? The need to parse options for a shell script is a common situation. Lots of scripts have options. Isn't there a more standard way to do this?

Solution

Use *bash*'s built-in *getopts* command to help parse options.

Here is an example, based largely on the example in the manpage for *getopts*:

```
#!/usr/bin/env bash
# cookbook filename: getopts_example
#
# using getopts
#
aflag=
bflag=
while getopts 'ab:' OPTION
do
  case $OPTION in
  a)    aflag=1
        ;;
  b)    bflag=1
        bval="$OPTARG"
        ;;
  ?)    printf "Usage: %s: [-a] [-b value] args\n" $(basename $0) >&2
        exit 2
        ;;
  esac
done
shift $(($OPTIND - 1))

if [ "$aflag" ]
then
  printf "Option -a specified\n"
fi
if [ "$bflag" ]
then
  printf 'Option -b "%s" specified\n' "$bval"
fi
printf "Remaining arguments are: %s\n" "$*"
```

Discussion

There are two kinds of options supported here. The first and simpler kind is an option that stands alone. It typically represents a flag to modify a command's behavior. An example of this sort of option is the -l option on the *ls* command. The second kind of option requires an argument. An example of this is the *mysql* command's -u option, which requires that a username be supplied, as in `mysql -u sysadmin`. Let's look at how *getopts* supports the parsing of both kinds.

The use of getopts has two arguments.

```
getopts 'ab:' OPTION
```

The first is a list of option letters. The second is the name of a shell variable. In our example, we are defining -a and -b as the only two valid options, so the first argument in getopts has just those two letters…and a colon. What does the colon signify? It indicates that -b needs an argument, just like -u *username* or -f *filename* might be used. The colon needs to be adjacent to any option letter taking an argument. For example, if only -a took an argument we would need to write 'a:b' instead.

The *getopts* built-in will set the variable named in the second argument to the value that it finds when it parses the shell script's argument list ($1, $2, etc). If it finds an argument with a leading minus sign, it will treat that as an option argument and put the letter into the given variable ($OPTION in our example). Then it returns true (i.e., 0) so that the while loop will process the option then continue to parse options by repeated calls to *getopts* until it runs out of arguments (or encounters a double minus -- to allow users to put an explicit end to the options). Then *getopts* returns false (i.e., non-zero) and the while loop ends.

Inside the loop, when the parsing has found an option letter for processing, we use a case statement on the variable $OPTION to set flags or otherwise take action when the option is encountered. For options that take arguments, that argument is placed in the shell variable $OPTARG (a fixed name not related to our use of $OPTION as our variable). We need to save that value by assigning it to another variable because as the parsing continues to loop, the variable $OPTARG will be reset on each call to *getopts*.

The third case of our case statement is a question mark, a shell pattern that matches any single character. When *getopts* finds an option that is not in the set of expected options ('ab:' in our example) then it will return a literal question mark in the variable ($OPTION in our example). So we could have made our case statement read \?) or '?') for an exact match, but the ? as a pattern match of any single character provides a convenient default for our case statement. It will match a literal question mark as well as matching any other single character.

In the usage message that we print, we have made two changes from the example script in the manpage. First, we use $(basename $0) to give the name of the script without all the extra pathnames that may have been part of how it was invoked. Secondly, we redirect this message to standard error (>&2) because that is really where such messages belong. All of the error messages from *getopts* that occur when an unknown option or missing argument is encountered are always written to standard error. We add our usage message to that chorus.

When the while loop terminates, we see the next line to be executed is:

```
shift $(($OPTIND - 1))
```

which is a shift statement used to move the positional parameters of the shell script from $1, $2, etc. down a given number of positions (tossing the lower ones). The variable $OPTIND is an index into the arguments that *getopts* uses to keep track of where it is when it parses. Once we are done parsing, we can toss all the options that we've processed by doing this shift statement. For example, if we had this command line:

```
myscript -a -b alt plow harvest reap
```

then after parsing for options, $OPTIND would be set to 4. By doing a shift of three ($OPTIND-1) we would get rid of the options and then a quick echo $* would give this:

```
plow harvest reap
```

So, the remaining (non-option) arguments are ready for use in your script (in a for loop perhaps). In our example script, the last line is a *printf* showing all the remaining arguments.

See Also

- help case
- help getopts
- help getopt
- Recipe 5.8, "Looping Over Arguments Passed to a Script"
- Recipe 5.11, "Counting Arguments"
- Recipe 5.12, "Consuming Arguments"
- Recipe 6.10, "Looping for a While"
- Recipe 6.14, "Branching Many Ways"
- Recipe 6.15, "Parsing Command-Line Arguments"
- Recipe 13.2, "Parsing Arguments with Your Own Error Messages"

13.2 Parsing Arguments with Your Own Error Messages

Problem

You are using *getopts* to parse your options for your shell script. But you don't like the error messages that it writes when it encounters bad input. Can you still use *getopts* but write your own error handling?

Solution

If you just want *getopts* to be quiet and not report any errors at all, just assign $OPTERR=0 before you begin parsing. But if you want *getopts* to give you more information without the error messages, then just begin the option list with a colon. (The v--- in the comments below is meant to be an arrow pointing to a particular place in the line below it, to show that special colon.)

```
#!/usr/bin/env bash
# cookbook filename: getopts_custom
#
# using getopts - with custom error messages
#
```

```
aflag=
bflag=
# since we don't want getopts to generate error
# messages, but want this script to issue its
# own messages, we will put, in the option list, a
# leading ':' v---here    to silence getopts.
while getopts :ab: FOUND
do
    case $FOUND in
    a)      aflag=1
            ;;
    b)      bflag=1
            bval="$OPTARG"
            ;;
    \:)     printf "argument missing from -%s option\n" $OPTARG
            printf "Usage: %s: [-a] [-b value] args\n" $(basename $0)
            exit 2
            ;;
    \?)     printf "unknown option: -%s\n" $OPTARG
            printf "Usage: %s: [-a] [-b value] args\n" $(basename $0)
            exit 2
            ;;

    esac >&2

done
shift $(($OPTIND - 1))

if [ "$aflag" ]
then
    printf "Option -a specified\n"
fi
if [ "$bflag" ]
then
    printf 'Option -b "%s" specified\n' "$bval"
fi
printf "Remaining arguments are: %s\n" "$*"
```

Discussion

The script is very much the same as the recipe Recipe 13.1, "Parsing Arguments for Your Shell Script." See that discussion for more background. One difference here is that *getopts* may now return a colon. It does so when an option is missing (e.g., you invoke the script with -b but without an argument for it). In that case, it puts the option letter into $OPTARG so that you know what option it was that was missing its argument.

Similarly, if an unsupported option is given (e.g., if you tried -d when invoking our example) *getopts* returns a question mark as the value for $FOUND, and puts the letter (the d in this case) into $OPTARG so that it can be used in your error messages.

We put a backslash in front of both the colon and the question mark to indicate that these are literals and not any special patterns or shell syntax. While not necessary for the colon, it looks better to have the parallel construction with the two punctuations both being escaped.

We added an I/O redirection on the esac (the end of the case statement), so that all output from the various *printf* statements will be redirected to standard error. This is in keeping with the purpose of standard error and is just easier to put it here than remembering to put it on each *printf* individually.

See Also

- help case
- help getopts
- help getopt
- Recipe 5.8, "Looping Over Arguments Passed to a Script"
- Recipe 5.11, "Counting Arguments"
- Recipe 5.12, "Consuming Arguments"
- Recipe 6.15, "Parsing Command-Line Arguments"
- Recipe 13.1, "Parsing Arguments for Your Shell Script"

13.3   Parsing Some HTML

Problem

You want to pull the strings out of some HTML. For example, you'd like to get at the href="*urlstringstuff*" type strings from the <a> tags within a chunk of HTML.

Solution

For a quick and easy shell parse of HTML, provided it doesn't have to be foolproof, you might want to try something like this:

```
cat $1 | sed -e 's/>/>\
/g' | grep '<a' | while IFS='"' read a b c ; do echo $b; done
```

Discussion

Parsing HTML from *bash* is pretty tricky, mostly because *bash* tends to be very line oriented whereas HTML was designed to treat newlines like whitespace. So it's not uncommon to see tags split across two or more lines as in:

```
<a href="blah...blah...blah
  other stuff >
```

There are also two ways to write <a> tags, one with a separate ending </a> tag, and one without, where instead the singular <a> tag itself ends with a /> . So, with multiple tags on a line and the last tag split across lines, it's a bit messy to parse, and our simple *bash* technique for this is often not foolproof.

Here are the steps involved in our solution. First, break the multiple tags on one line into at most one line per tag:

```
cat file | sed -e 's/>/>\
/g'
```

Yes, that's a newline right after the backslash so that it substitutes each end-of-tag character (i.e., the >) with that same character and then a newline. That will put tags on separate lines with maybe a few extra blank lines. The trailing g tells *sed* to do the search and replace *globally*, i.e., multiple times on a line if need be.

Then you can pipe that output into *grep* to grab just the <a tag lines or maybe just lines with double quotes:

```
cat file | sed -e 's/>/>\
/g' | grep '<a'
```

or:

```
cat file | sed -e 's/>/>\
/g' | grep '".*"'
```

(that's g r e p ' ". * " '). The single quotes tell the shell to take the inner characters literally and not do any shell expansion on them; the rest is a regular expression to match a double quote followed by any character (.) any number of times (*) followed by another double quote. (This won't work if the string itself is split across lines.)

To parse out the contents of what's inside the double quotes, one trick is to use the shell's Internal Field Separator ($IFS) to tell it to use the double quote (") as the separator; or you can do a similar thing with *awk* and its -F option (*F* for field separator). For example:

```
cat $1 | sed -e 's/>/>\
/g' | grep '".*"' | awk -F'"' '{ print $2}'
```

(Or use the grep '<a' if you just want <a tags and not all quoted strings.)

If you want to use the $IFS shell trick, rather than *awk*, it would be:

```
cat $1 | sed -e 's/>/>\
/g' | grep '<a' | while IFS='"' read PRE URL POST ; do echo $URL; done
```

where the *grep* output is piped into a while loop and the while loop will read the input into three fields (PRE, URL, and POST). By preceding the read command with the IFS='"', we set that environment variable just for the read command, not for the entire script. Thus, for the line of input that it reads, it will parse with the quotes as its notion of what separates the words of the input line. It will set PRE to be everything up to the first quote, URL to be everything from there to the next quote, and POST to be everything thereafter. Then the script just echoes the second variable, URL. That's all the characters between the quotes.

See Also

- man sed
- man grep

13.4   Parsing Output into an Array

Problem

You want the output of some program or script to be put into an array.

Solution

```
#!/usr/bin/env bash
# cookbook filename: parseViaArray
#
# find the file size
# use an array to parse the ls -l output into words

LSL=$(ls -ld $1)

declare -a MYRA
MYRA=($LSL)

echo the file $1 is ${MYRA[4]} bytes.
```

Discussion

In our example, we take the output from the ls -l command and parse the words by putting them into an array. Then we can just refer to each array element to get at each word. The typical output from the ls -l command looks like this (yours may vary due to locale):

```
-rw-r--r--  1 albing users 113 2006-10-10 23:33 mystuff.txt
```

Arrays are easy to initialize if you know the values as you write the script. The format is simple. We begin by declaring the variable to be an array, and then we assign it values:

```
declare -a MYRA
MYRA=(first second third home)
```

The same can be done by using a variable inside those parentheses. Just be sure *not* to use quotes around the variable. Writing MYRA=$("$LSL") will put the entire string into the first argument, since it is all contained as one quoted string. Then ${MYRA[0]} will be the only array element, and it will contain the entire string, which is not what you wanted.

We also could have shortened this script by combining the steps, and it would look like this:

```
declare -a MYRA
MYRA=($(ls -ld $1))
```

If you want to know how many elements you have in your new array, just reference the variable ${#MYRA[*]} or ${#MYRA[@]}, either of which is a lot of special characters to type.

See Also

- Recipe 5.19, "Using Array Variables"

13.5   Parsing Output with a Function Call

Problem

You want to parse the output of some program into various variables to be used elsewhere in your program. Arrays are great when you are looping through the values, but not very readable if you want to refer to each separately, rather than by an index.

Solution

Use a function call to parse the words:

```
#!/usr/bin/env bash
# cookbook filename: parseViaFunc
#
# parse ls -l via function call
# an example of output from ls -l follows:
# -rw-r--r--  1 albing users 126 2006-10-10 22:50 fnsize

function lsparts ()
{
    PERMS=$1
    LCOUNT=$2
    OWNER=$3
    GROUP=$4
    SIZE=$5
    CRDATE=$6
    CRDAY=$7
    CRTIME=$8
    FILE=$9
}

lsparts $(ls -l "$1")

echo $FILE has $LCOUNT 'link(s)' and is $SIZE bytes long.
```

Here's what it looks like when it runs:

```
$ ./fnsize fnsize
fnsize has 1 link(s) and is 311 bytes long.
$
```

Discussion

We can let *bash* do the work of parsing by putting the text to be parsed on a function call. Calling a function is much like calling a shell script. *bash* parses the words into separate variables and assigns them to $1, $2, etc. Our function can just assign each positional parameter to a separate variable. If the variables are not declared locally then they are available outside as well as inside the function.

We put quotes around the reference to $1 in the *ls* command in case the filename supplied has spaces in its name. The quotes keep it all together so that *ls* sees it as a single filename and not as a series of separate filenames.

We use quotes in the expression 'link(s)' to avoid special treatment of the parentheses by *bash*. Alternatively, we could have put the entire phrase (except for the echo itself) inside of double quotes—double, not single, quotes so that the variable substitution (for $FILE, etc.) still occurs.

See Also

- Recipe 10.4, "Defining Functions"
- Recipe 10.5, "Using Functions: Parameters and Return Values"
- Recipe 13.8, "Getting Your Plurals Right"
- Recipe 17.7, "Clearing the Screen When You Log Out"

13.6   Parsing Text with a read Statement

Problem

The are many ways to parse text with *bash*. What if I don't want to use a function? Is there another way?

Solution

Use the read statement.

```
#!/usr/bin/env bash
# cookbook filename: parseViaRead
#
# parse ls -l with a read statement
# an example of output from ls -l follows:
# -rw-r--r--  1 albing users 126 2006-10-10 22:50 fnsize
```

```
ls -l "$1" | { read PERMS LCOUNT OWNER GROUP SIZE CRDATE CRTIME FILE ;
               echo $FILE has $LCOUNT 'link(s)' and is $SIZE bytes long. ;
             }
```

Discussion

Here we let read do all the parsing. It will break apart the input into *words*, where words are separated by whitespace, and assign each word to the variables named on the read command. Actually, you can even change the separator, by setting the *bash* variable $IFS (which means Internal Field Separator) to whatever character you want for parsing; just remember to set it back!

As you can see from the sample output of ls -l, we have tried to choose names that get at the meaning of each word in that output. Since FILE is the last word, any extra fields will also be part of that variable. That way if the name has whitespace in it like "Beethoven Fifth Symphony" then all three words will end up in $FILE.

See Also

- Recipe 2.14, "Saving or Grouping Output from Several Commands"
- Recipe 19.8, "Forgetting That Pipelines Make Subshells"

13.7   Parsing with read into an Array

Problem

You've got a varying number of words on each line of input, so you can't just assign each word to a predetermined variable.

Solution

Use the -a option on the read statement, and the words will be read into an array variable.

```
read -a MYRAY
```

Discussion

Whether coming from user input or a pipeline, read will parse the input into words, putting each word in its own array element. The variable does not need to be declared as an array—using it in this fashion is enough to make it into an array. Each element can be referenced with the *bash* array syntax, which is a zero-based array. So the second word on a line of input will be put into ${MYRAY[1]} in our example. The number of words will determine the size of the array. In our example, the size of the array is ${#MYRAY[@]}.

See Also

- Recipe 3.5, "Getting User Input"
- Recipe 13.6, "Parsing Text with a read Statement"

13.8 Getting Your Plurals Right

Problem

You want to use a plural noun when you have more than one of an object. But you don't want to scatter if statements all through your code.

Solution

```
#!/usr/bin/env bash
# cookbook filename: pluralize
#
# A function to make words plural by adding an s
# when the value ($2) is != 1 or -1
# It only adds an 's'; it is not very smart.
#
function plural ()
{
    if [ $2 -eq 1 -o $2 -eq -1 ]
    then
        echo ${1}
    else
        echo ${1}s
    fi
}

while read num name
do
    echo $num $(plural "$name" $num)
done
```

Discussion

The function, though only set to handle the simple addition of an s, will do fine for many nouns. The function doesn't do any error checking of the number or contents of the arguments. If you wanted to use this script in a serious application, you might want to add those kinds of checks.

We put the name in quotes when we call the plural function in case there are embedded blanks in the name. It did, after all, come from the read statement, and the last variable on a read statement gets all the remaining text from the input line. You can see that in the following example.

We put the solution script into a file named *pluralize* and ran it against the following data:

```
$ cat input.file
1 hen
2 duck
3 squawking goose
4 limerick oyster
5 corpulent porpoise

$ ./pluralize < input.file
1 hen
2 ducks
3 squawking gooses
4 limerick oysters
5 corpulent porpoises
$
```

"Gooses" isn't correct English, but the script did what was intended. If you like the C-like syntax better, you could write the if statement like this:

```
if (( $2 == 1 || $2 == -1 ))
```

The square bracket (i.e., the test built-in) is the older form, more common across the various versions of *bash*, but either should work. Use whichever form's syntax is easiest for you to remember.

We don't expect you would keep a file like *pluralize* around, but the plural function might be handy to have as part of a larger scripting project. Then whenever you report on the count of something you could use the plural function as part of the reference, as shown in the while loop above.

See Also

- Recipe 6.11, "Looping with a read"

13.9 Taking It One Character at a Time

Problem

You have some parsing to do and for whatever reason nothing else will do—you need to take your strings apart one character at a time.

Solution

The substring function for variables will let you take things apart and another feature tells you how long a string is:

```
#!/usr/bin/env bash
# cookbook filename: onebyone
#
```

```
# parsing input one character at a time

while read ALINE
do
    for ((i=0; i < ${#ALINE}; i++))
    do
        ACHAR=${ALINE:i:1}
        # do something here, e.g. echo $ACHAR
    done
done
```

Discussion

The read will take input from standard in and put it, a line at a time, into the variable $ALINE. Since there are no other variables on the read command, it takes the entire line and doesn't divvy it up.

The for loop will loop once for each character in the $ALINE variable. We can compute how many times to loop by using ${#ALINE}, which returns the length of the contents of $ALINE.

Each time through the loop we assign ACHAR the value of the one-character substring of ALINE that begins at the ith position. That's simple enough. Now, what was it you needed to parse this way?

See Also

- Check out the other parsing techniques in this chapter to see if you can avoid working at this low level

13.10 Cleaning Up an SVN Source Tree

Problem

Subversion's svn status command shows all the files that have been modified, but if you have scratch files or other garbage lying around in your source tree, *svn* will list those, too. It would be useful to have a way to clean up your source tree, removing those files unknown to Subversion.

 Subversion won't know about new files unless and until you do an svn add command. *Don't* run this script until you've added any new source files, or they'll be gone for good.

Solution

```
svn status src | grep '^\?' | cut -c8- | \
while read fn; do echo "$fn"; rm -rf "$fn"; done
```

Discussion

The svn status output lists one file per line. It puts an M as the first character of a line for files that have been modified, an A for newly added (but not yet committed) files, and a question mark for those about which it knows nothing. We just *grep* for those lines beginning with a question mark and cut off the leading eight columns of each line of output so that we are left with just the filename on each line. We read those filenames with a read statement in a while loop. The echo isn't strictly necessary, but it's useful to see what's being removed, just in case there is a mistake or an error. You can at least see that it's gone for good. When we do the remove, we use the -rf options in case the file is a directory, but mostly just to keep the remove quiet. Problems encountered with permissions and such are squelched by the -f option. It just removes the file as best as your permissions allow. We put the reference to the filename in quotes "$fn" in case there are special characters (like spaces) in the filename.

See Also

- Recipe 6.11, "Looping with a read"
- Appendix D

13.11 Setting Up a Database with MySQL

Problem

You want to create and initialize several databases using MySQL. You want them all to be initialized using the same SQL commands. Each database needs its own name, but each database will have the same contents, at least at initialization. You may need to do this setup over and over, as in the case where these databases are used as part of a test suite that needs to be reset when tests are rerun.

Solution

A simple *bash* script can help with this administrative task:

```
#!/usr/bin/env bash
# cookbook filename: dbiniter
#
# initialize databases from a standard file
# creating databases as needed.

DBLIST=$(mysql -e "SHOW DATABASES;" | tail +2)
select DB in $DBLIST "new..."
do
    if [[ $DB == "new..." ]]
    then
        printf "%b" "name for new db: "
        read DB rest
        echo creating new database $DB
```

```
        mysql -e "CREATE DATABASE IF NOT EXISTS $DB;"
    fi

    if [ "$DB" ]
    then
        echo Initializing database: $DB
        mysql $DB < ourInit.sql
    fi
done
```

Discussion

The `tail +2` is added to remove the heading from the list of databases (see Recipe 2.12, "Skipping a Header in a File").

The `select` creates the menus showing the existing databases. We added the literal `"new..."` as an additional choice (see Recipe 3.7, "Selecting from a List of Options" and Recipe 6.16, "Creating Simple Menus").

When the user wants to create a new database, we prompt for and read a new name, but we use two fields on the `read` command as a bit of error handling. If the user types more than one name on the line, we only use the first name—it gets put into the variable $DB while the rest of the input is put into $rest and ignored. (We could add an error check to see if $rest is null.)

Whether created anew or chosen from the list of extant databases, if the $DB variable is not empty, it will invoke *mysql* one more time to feed it the set of SQL statements that we've put into the file *ourInit.sql* as our standardized initialization sequence.

If you're going to use a script like this, you might need to add parameters to your *mysql* command, such as `-u` and `-p` to prompt for username and password. It will depend on how your database and its permissions are configured or whether you have a file named *.my.cnf* with your MySQL defaults.

We could also have added an error check after the creation of the new database to see if it succeeded; if it did not succeed, we could unset DB thereby bypassing the initialization. However, as many a math textbook has said, "we leave that as an exercise for the reader."

See Also

- Recipe 2.12, "Skipping a Header in a File"
- Recipe 3.7, "Selecting from a List of Options"
- Recipe 6.16, "Creating Simple Menus for more about the `select` command"
- Recipe 14.20, "Using Passwords in Scripts"

13.12 Isolating Specific Fields in Data

Problem

You need to extract one or more fields from each line of output.

Solution

Use *cut* if there are delimiters you can easily pick out, even if they are different for the beginning and end of the field you need:

```
# Here's an easy one, what users, home directories and shells do
# we have on this NetBSD system
$ cut -d':' -f1,6,7 /etc/passwd
root:/root:/bin/csh
toor:/root:/bin/sh
daemon:/:/sbin/nologin
operator:/usr/guest/operator:/sbin/nologin
bin:/:/sbin/nologin
games:/usr/games:/sbin/nologin
postfix:/var/spool/postfix:/sbin/nologin
named:/var/chroot/named:/sbin/nologin
ntpd:/var/chroot/ntpd:/sbin/nologin
sshd:/var/chroot/sshd:/sbin/nologin
smmsp:/nonexistent:/sbin/nologin
uucp:/var/spool/uucppublic:/usr/libexec/uucp/uucico
nobody:/nonexistent:/sbin/nologin
jp:/home/jp:/usr/pkg/bin/bash


# What is the most popular shell on the system?
$ cut -d':' -f7 /etc/passwd | sort | uniq -c | sort -rn
  10 /sbin/nologin
   2 /usr/pkg/bin/bash
   1 /bin/csh
   1 /bin/sh
   1 /usr/libexec/uucp/uucico


# Now let's see the first two directory levels
$ cut -d':' -f6 /etc/passwd | cut -d'/' -f1-3 | sort -u
/
/home/jp
/nonexistent
/root
/usr/games
/usr/guest
/var/chroot
/var/spool
```

Use *awk* to split on multiples of whitespace, or if you need to rearrange the order of the output fields. Note the → denotes a tab character in the output. The default is space but you can change that using $OFS:

```
# Users, home directories and shells, but swap the last two
# and use a tab delimiter
$ awk 'BEGIN {FS=":"; OFS="\t"; } { print $1,$7,$6; }' /etc/passwd
root → /bin/csh → /root
toor → /bin/sh → /root
daemon → /sbin/nologin → /
operator → /sbin/nologin → /usr/guest/operator
bin → /sbin/nologin → /
games → /sbin/nologin → /usr/games
postfix → /sbin/nologin → /var/spool/postfix
named → /sbin/nologin → /var/chroot/named
ntpd → /sbin/nologin → /var/chroot/ntpd
sshd → /sbin/nologin → /var/chroot/sshd
smmsp → /sbin/nologin → /nonexistent
uucp → /usr/libexec/uucp/uucico → /var/spool/uucppublic
nobody → /sbin/nologin → /nonexistent
jp → /usr/pkg/bin/bash → /home/jp


# Multiples of whitespace and swapped, first field removed
$ grep '^# [1-9]' /etc/hosts | awk '{print $3,$2}'
10.255.255.255 10.0.0.0
172.31.255.255 172.16.0.0
192.168.255.255 192.168.0.0
```

Use grep -o to display just the part that matched your pattern. This is particularly handy when you can't express delimiters in a way that lends itself to the above solutions. For example, say you need to extract all IP addresses from a file, no matter where they are. Note we use *egrep* because of the regular expression (regex), but -o should work with whichever GNU *grep* flavor you use, but it is probably not supported on non-GNU versions. Check your documentation.

```
$ cat has_ipas
This is line 1 with 1 IPA: 10.10.10.10
Line 2 has 2; they are 10.10.10.11 and 10.10.10.12.
Line three is ftp_server=10.10.10.13:21.

$ egrep -o '[0-9]{1,3}\.[0-9]{1,3}\.[0-9]{1,3}\.[0-9]{1,3}' has_ipas
10.10.10.10
10.10.10.11
10.10.10.12
10.10.10.13
```

Discussion

The possibilities are endless, and we haven't even scratched the surface here. This is the very essence of what the Unix toolchain idea is all about. Take a number of small tools that do one thing well and combine them as needed to solve problems.

Also, the regex we used for IP addresses is naive and could match other things, including invalid addresses. For a much better pattern, use the Perl Compatible Regular Expressions (PCRE) regex from *Mastering Regular Expressions* by Jeffrey E. F. Friedl (O'Reilly), if your *grep* supports -P. Or use Perl.

```
$ grep -oP '([01]?\d\d?|2[0-4]\d|25[0-5])\.([01]?\d\d?|2[0-4]\d|25[0-5])\.([01]?\d\
d?|2[0-4]\d|25[0-5])\.([01]?\d\d?|2[0-4]\d|25[0-5])' has_ipas
10.10.10.10
10.10.10.11
10.10.10.12
10.10.10.13


$ perl -ne 'while ( m/([01]?\d\d?|2[0-4]\d|25[0-5])\.([01]?\d\d?|2[0-4]\d|25[0-5])\.
([01]?\d\d?|2[0-4]\d|25[0-5])\.([01]?\d\d?|2[0-4]\d|25[0-5])/g ) { print qq($1.$2.$3.
$4\n); }' has_ipas
10.10.10.10
10.10.10.11
10.10.10.12
10.10.10.13
```

See Also

- man cut
- man awk
- man grep
- *Mastering Regular Expressions* by Jeffrey E. F. Friedl (O'Reilly)
- Recipe 8.4, "Cutting Out Parts of Your Output"
- Recipe 13.14, "Trimming Whitespace"
- Recipe 15.10, "Finding My IP Address"
- Recipe 17.16, "Finding Lines in One File But Not in the Other"

13.13 Updating Specific Fields in Data Files

Problem

You need to extract certain parts (fields) of a line (record) and update them.

Solution

In the simple case, you want to extract a single field from a line, then perform some operation on it. For that, you can use *cut* or *awk*. See Recipe 13.12, "Isolating Specific Fields in Data" for details.

For the more complicated case, you need to modify a field in a data file without extracting it. If it's a simple search and replace, use *sed*.

For example, let's switch everyone from *csh* to *sh* on this NetBSD system.

```
$ grep csh /etc/passwd
root:*:0:0:Charlie &:/root:/bin/csh

$ sed 's/csh$/sh/' /etc/passwd | grep '^root'
root:*:0:0:Charlie &:/root:/bin/sh
```

You can use *awk* if you need to do arithmetic on a field or modify a string only in a certain field:

```
$ cat data_file
Line 1 ends
Line 2 ends
Line 3 ends
Line 4 ends
Line 5 ends


$ awk '{print $1, $2+5, $3}' data_file
Line 6 ends
Line 7 ends
Line 8 ends
Line 9 ends
Line 10 ends


# If the second field contains '3', change it to '8' and mark it
$ awk '{ if ($2 == "3") print $1, $2+5, $3, "Tweaked" ; else  print $0; }' data_file
Line 1 ends
Line 2 ends
Line 8 ends Tweaked
Line 4 ends
Line 5 ends
```

Discussion

The possibilities here are as endless as your data, but hopefully the examples above will give you enough of a start to easily modify your data.

See Also

- man awk
- man sed
- *http://sed.sourceforge.net/sedfaq.html*
- *http://sed.sourceforge.net/sed1line.txt*
- Recipe 11.7, "Figuring Out Date and Time Arithmetic"
- Recipe 13.12, "Isolating Specific Fields in Data"

13.14 Trimming Whitespace

Problem

You need to trim leading and/or trailing whitespace from lines for fields of data.

Solution

These solutions rely on a *bash*-specific treatment of read and $REPLY. See the end of the discussion for an alternate solution.

First, we'll show a file with some leading and trailing whitespace. Note we add ~~ to show the whitespace. Note the → denotes a literal tab character in the output:

```
# Show the whitespace in our sample file
$ while read; do echo ~~"$REPLY"~~; done < whitespace
~~ This line has leading spaces.~~
~~This line has trailing spaces. ~~
~~ This line has both leading and trailing spaces. ~~
~~ → Leading tab.~~
~~Trailing tab. → ~~
~~ → Leading and trailing tab. → ~~
~~      → Leading mixed whitespace.~~
~~Trailing mixed whitespace.      → ~~
~~      → Leading and trailing mixed whitespace.      → ~~
```

To trim both leading and trailing whitespace use $IFS add the built-in REPLY variable (see the discussion for why this works):

```
$ while read REPLY; do echo ~~"$REPLY"~~; done < whitespace
~~This line has leading spaces.~~
~~This line has trailing spaces.~~
~~This line has both leading and trailing spaces.~~
~~Leading tab.~~
~~Trailing tab.~~
~~Leading and trailing tab.~~
~~Leading mixed whitespace.~~
~~Trailing mixed whitespace.~~
~~Leading and trailing mixed whitespace.~~
```

To trim only leading or only trailing *spaces*, use a simple pattern match:

```
# Leading spaces only
$ while read; do echo "~~${REPLY## }~~"; done < whitespace
~~This line has leading spaces.~~
~~This line has trailing spaces. ~~
~~This line has both leading and trailing spaces. ~~
~~ → Leading tab.~~
~~Trailing tab. ~~
~~ → Leading and trailing tab. → ~~
~~ → Leading mixed whitespace.~~
~~Trailing mixed whitespace.      → ~~
~~ → Leading and trailing mixed whitespace.      → ~~
```

```
# Trailing spaces only
$ while read; do echo "~~${REPLY%% }~~"; done < whitespace
~~ This line has leading spaces.~~
~~This line has trailing spaces.~~
~~ This line has both leading and trailing spaces.~~
~~ → Leading tab.~~
~~Trailing tab. ~~
~~ → Leading and trailing tab. → ~~
~~     → Leading mixed whitespace.~~
~~Trailing mixed whitespace.     → ~~
~~     → Leading and trailing mixed whitespace.     → ~~
```

Trimming only leading or only trailing *whitespace* (including tab) is a bit more complicated:

```
# You need this either way
$ shopt -s extglob

# Leading whitespaces only
$ while read; do echo "~~${REPLY##+([[:space:]])}~~"; done < whitespace
~~This line has leading spaces.~~
~~This line has trailing spaces. ~~
~~This line has both leading and trailing spaces. ~~
~~Leading tab.~~
~~Trailing tab. ~~
~~Leading and trailing tab. → ~~
~~Leading mixed whitespace.~~
~~Trailing mixed whitespace.     → ~~
~~Leading and trailing mixed whitespace.     → ~~


# Trailing whitespaces only
$ while read; do echo "~~${REPLY%%+([[:space:]])}~~"; done < whitespace
~~ This line has leading spaces.~~
~~This line has trailing spaces.~~
~~ This line has both leading and trailing spaces.~~
~~ → Leading tab.~~
~~Trailing tab.~~
~~ → Leading and trailing tab.~~
~~     → Leading mixed whitespace.~~
~~Trailing mixed whitespace.~~
~~     → Leading and trailing mixed whitespace.~~
```

Discussion

OK, at this point you are probably looking at these lines and wondering how we're going to make this comprehensible. It turns out there's a simple, if subtle explanation.

Here we go. The first example used the default $REPLY variable that read uses when you do not supply your own variable name(s). Chet Ramey (maintainer of *bash*) made a design decision that, "[if] there are no variables, save the text of the line read to the variable $REPLY [unchanged, else parse using $IFS]."

```
$ while read; do echo ~~"$REPLY"~~; done < whitespace
```

But when we supply one or more variable names to read, it does parse the input, using the values in $IFS (which are space, tab, and newline by default). One step of that parsing process is to trim leading and trailing whitespace—just what we want:

```
$ while read REPLY; do echo ~~"$REPLY"~~; done < whitespace
```

To trim leading or trailing (but not both) spaces is easy using the ${##} or ${%%} operators (see Recipe 6.7, "Testing with Pattern Matches"):

```
$ while read; do echo "~~${REPLY## }~~"; done < whitespace
$ while read; do echo "~~${REPLY%% }~~"; done < whitespace
```

But covering tabs is a little harder. If we had only tabs, we could use the ${##} or ${%%} operators and insert literal tabs using the Ctrl-V Ctrl-I key sequence. But that's risky since it's probable there's a mix of spaces and tabs, and some text editors or unwary users may strip out the tabs. So we turn on extended globbing and use a character class to make our intent clear. The [:space:] character class would work without extglob, but we need to say "one or more occurrences" using +( ) or else it will trim a single space or tabs, but not multiples or both on the same line.

```
# This works, need extglob for +( ) part
$ shopt -s extglob
$ while read; do echo "~~${REPLY##+([[:space:]])}~~"; done < whitespace
$ while read; do echo "~~${REPLY%%+([[:space:]])}~~"; done < whitespace


# This doesn't
$ while read; do echo "~~${REPLY##[[:space:]]}~~"; done < whitespace
~~This line has leading spaces.~~
~~This line has trailing spaces. ~~
~~This line has both leading and trailing spaces. ~~
~~Leading tab.~~
~~Trailing tab. ~~
~~Leading and trailing tab.          ~~
~~    → Leading mixed whitespace.~~
~~Trailing mixed whitespace.     → ~~
~~    → Leading and trailing mixed whitespace.     → ~~
```

Here's a different take, exploiting the same $IFS parsing, but to parse out fields (or words) instead of records (or lines):

```
$ for i in $(cat white_space); do echo ~~$i~~; done
~~This~~
~~line~~
~~has~~
~~leading~~
~~white~~
~~space.~~
~~This~~
~~line~~
~~has~~
~~trailing~~
~~white~~
~~space.~~
```

```
~~This~~
~~line~~
~~has~~
~~both~~
~~leading~~
~~and~~
~~trailing~~
~~white~~
~~space.~~
```

Finally, although the original solutions rely on Chet's design decision about read and $REPLY, this solution does not:

```
shopt -s extglob

while IFS= read -r line; do
    echo "None: ~~$line~~"                      # preserve all whitespaces
    echo "Ld:   ~~${line##+([[:space:]])}~~"    # trim leading whitespace
    echo "Tr:   ~~${line%%+([[:space:]])}~~"    # trim trailing whitespace
    line="${line##+([[:space:]])}"              # trim leading and...
    line="${line%%+([[:space:]])}"              # ...trailing whitespace
    echo "All:  ~~$line~~"                      # Show all trimmed
done < whitespace
```

See Also

- Recipe 6.7, "Testing with Pattern Matches"
- Recipe 13.6, "Parsing Text with a read Statement"

13.15 Compressing Whitespace

Problem

You have runs of whitespace in a file (perhaps it is fixed length, space padded) and you need to compress the spaces down to a single character or delimiter.

Solution

Use *tr* or *awk* as appropriate.

Discussion

If you are trying to compress runs of whitespace down to a single character, you can use *tr*, but be aware that you may damage the file if it is not well formed. For example, if fields are delimited by multiple whitespace characters but internally have spaces, compressing multiple spaces down to one space will remove that distinction. Imagine if the _ characters in the following example were spaces instead. Note the → denotes a literal tab character in the output.

```
$ cat data_file
Header1                  Header2                  Header3
Rec1_Field1              Rec1_Field2              Rec1_Field3
Rec2_Field1              Rec2_Field2              Rec2_Field3
Rec3_Field1              Rec3_Field2              Rec3_Field3

$ cat data_file | tr -s ' ' '\t'
Header1 → Header2 → Header3
Rec1_Field1 → Rec1_Field2 → Rec1_Field3
Rec2_Field1 → Rec2_Field2 → Rec2_Field3
Rec3_Field1 → Rec3_Field2 → Rec3_Field3
```

If your field delimiter is more than a single character, *tr* won't work since it translates *single characters* from its first set into the *matching single character* in the second set. You can use *awk* to combine or convert field separators. *awk*'s internal field separator FS accepts regular expressions, so you can separate on pretty much anything. There is a handy trick to this as well. An assignment to any field causes *awk* to reassemble the record using the output field separator OFS. So assigning field one to itself and then printing the record has the effect of translating FS to OFS without you having to worry about how many records there are in the data.

In this example, multiple spaces delimit fields, but fields also have internal spaces, so the more simple case of awk 'BEGIN { OFS = "\t" } { $1 = $1; print }' data_file1 won't work. Here is a data file:

```
$ cat data_file1
Header1                  Header2                  Header3
Rec1 Field1              Rec1 Field2              Rec1 Field3
Rec2 Field1              Rec2 Field2              Rec2 Field3
Rec3 Field1              Rec3 Field2              Rec3 Field
```

In the next example, we assign two spaces to FS and tab to OFS. We then make an assignment ($1 = $1) so *awk* rebuilds the record, but that results in strings of tabs replacing the double spaces, so we use *gsub* to squash the tabs, then we print. Note the → denotes a literal tab character in the output. The output is a little hard to read, so there is a hex dump as well. Recall that ASCII tab is 09 while ASCII space is 20.

```
$ awk 'BEGIN { FS = "  "; OFS = "\t" } { $1 = $1; gsub(/\t+/, "\t"); print }' data_
file1
Header1 → Header2 → Header3
Rec1 Field1 → Rec1 Field2 → Rec1 Field3
Rec2 Field1 → Rec2 Field2 → Rec2 Field3
Rec3 Field1 → Rec3 Field2 → Rec3 Field3

$ awk 'BEGIN { FS = "  "; OFS = "\t" } { $1 = $1; gsub(/\t+/, "\t"); print }' data_
file1 | hexdump -C
00000000  48 65 61 64 65 72 31 09  48 65 61 64 65 72 32 09  |Header1.Header2.|
00000010  48 65 61 64 65 72 33 0a  52 65 63 31 20 46 69 65  |Header3.Rec1 Fie|
00000020  6c 64 31 09 52 65 63 31  20 46 69 65 6c 64 32 09  |ld1.Rec1 Field2.|
00000030  52 65 63 31 20 46 69 65  6c 64 33 0a 52 65 63 32  |Rec1 Field3.Rec2|
```

```
00000040  20 46 69 65 6c 64 31 09  52 65 63 32 20 46 69 65  | Field1.Rec2 Fie|
00000050  6c 64 32 09 52 65 63 32  20 46 69 65 6c 64 33 0a  |ld2.Rec2 Field3.|
00000060  52 65 63 33 20 46 69 65  6c 64 31 09 52 65 63 33  |Rec3 Field1.Rec3|
00000070  20 46 69 65 6c 64 32 09  52 65 63 33 20 46 69 65  | Field2.Rec3 Fie|
00000080  6c 64 0a                                          |ld.|
00000083
```

You can also use *awk* to trim leading and trailing whitespace in the same way, but as noted previously, this will replace your field separators unless they are already spaces:

```
# Remove leading and trailing whitespace,
# but also replace TAB field separators with spaces
$ awk '{ $1 = $1; print }' white_space
```

See Also

- *Effective awk Programming* by Arnold Robbins (O'Reilly)
- *sed & awk* by Arnold Robbins and Dale Dougherty (O'Reilly)
- Recipe 13.16, "Processing Fixed-Length Records"
- "tr Escape Sequences" in Appendix A
- "Table of ASCII Values" in Appendix A

13.16 Processing Fixed-Length Records

Problem

You need to read and process data that is in a fixed-length (also called fixed-width) form.

Solution

Use Perl or *gawk* 2.13 or greater. Given a file like:

```
$ cat fixed-length_file
Header1----------Header2------------------------Header3---------
Rec1 Field1     Rec1 Field2               Rec1 Field3
Rec2 Field1     Rec2 Field2               Rec2 Field3
Rec3 Field1     Rec3 Field2               Rec3 Field3
```

You can process it using GNU's *gawk*, by setting FIELDWIDTHS to the correct field lengths, setting OFS as desired, and making an assignment so *gawk* rebuilds the record (see the *awk* trick in Recipe 13.14, "Trimming Whitespace"). However, *gawk* does not remove the spaces used in padding the original record, so we use two *gsubs* to do that, one for all the internal fields and the other for the last field in each record. Finally, we just print. Note the → denotes a literal tab character in the output. The output is a little hard to read, so there is a hex dump as well. Recall that ASCII tab is 09 while ASCII space is 20.

```
$ gawk ' BEGIN { FIELDWIDTHS = "18 32 16"; OFS = "\t" } { $1 = $1; gsub(/ +\t/, "\
t"); gsub(/ +$/, ""); print }' fixed-length_file
Header1-----------  → Header2------------------------  → Header3---------
Rec1 Field1 → Rec1 Field2 → Rec1 Field3
Rec2 Field1 → Rec2 Field2 → Rec2 Field3
Rec3 Field1 → Rec3 Field2 → Rec3 Field3


$ gawk ' BEGIN { FIELDWIDTHS = "18 32 16"; OFS = "\t" } { $1 = $1; gsub(/ +\t/, "\
t"); gsub(/ +$/, ""); print }' fixed-length_file | hexdump -C
00000000  48 65 61 64 65 72 31 2d  2d 2d 2d 2d 2d 2d 2d 2d  |Header1---------|
00000010  2d 2d 09 48 65 61 64 65  72 32 2d 2d 2d 2d 2d 2d  |--.Header2------|
00000020  2d 2d 2d 2d 2d 2d 2d 2d  2d 2d 2d 2d 2d 2d 2d 2d  |----------------|
00000030  2d 2d 2d 09 48 65 61 64  65 72 33 2d 2d 2d 2d 2d  |---.Header3-----|
00000040  2d 2d 2d 2d 0a 52 65 63  31 20 46 69 65 6c 64 31  |----.Rec1 Field1|
00000050  09 52 65 63 31 20 46 69  65 6c 64 32 09 52 65 63  |.Rec1 Field2.Rec|
00000060  31 20 46 69 65 6c 64 33  0a 52 65 63 32 20 46 69  |1 Field3.Rec2 Fi|
00000070  65 6c 64 31 09 52 65 63  32 20 46 69 65 6c 64 32  |eld1.Rec2 Field2|
00000080  09 52 65 63 32 20 46 69  65 6c 64 33 0a 52 65 63  |.Rec2 Field3.Rec|
00000090  33 20 46 69 65 6c 64 31  09 52 65 63 33 20 46 69  |3 Field1.Rec3 Fi|
000000a0  65 6c 64 32 09 52 65 63  33 20 46 69 65 6c 64 33  |eld2.Rec3 Field3|
000000b0  0a                                                |.|
000000b1
```

If you don't have *gawk*, you can use Perl, which is more straightforward anyway. We use a non-printing while input loop (-n), unpack each record ($_) as it's read, and turn the resulting list back into a scalar by joining the elements with a tab. We then print each record, adding a newline at the end:

```
$ perl -ne 'print join("\t", unpack("A18 A32 A16", $_) ) . "\n";' fixed-length_file
Header1-----------  → Header2------------------------  → Header3---------
Rec1 Field1 → Rec1 Field2 → Rec1 Field3
Rec2 Field1 → Rec2 Field2 → Rec2 Field3
Rec3 Field1 → Rec3 Field2 → Rec3 Field3


$ perl -ne 'print join("\t", unpack("A18 A32 A16", $_) ) . "\n";' fixed-length_file |
hexdump -C
00000000  48 65 61 64 65 72 31 2d  2d 2d 2d 2d 2d 2d 2d 2d  |Header1---------|
00000010  2d 2d 09 48 65 61 64 65  72 32 2d 2d 2d 2d 2d 2d  |--.Header2------|
00000020  2d 2d 2d 2d 2d 2d 2d 2d  2d 2d 2d 2d 2d 2d 2d 2d  |----------------|
00000030  2d 2d 2d 09 48 65 61 64  65 72 33 2d 2d 2d 2d 2d  |---.Header3-----|
00000040  2d 2d 2d 2d 0a 52 65 63  31 20 46 69 65 6c 64 31  |----.Rec1 Field1|
00000050  09 52 65 63 31 20 46 69  65 6c 64 32 09 52 65 63  |.Rec1 Field2.Rec|
00000060  31 20 46 69 65 6c 64 33  0a 52 65 63 32 20 46 69  |1 Field3.Rec2 Fi|
00000070  65 6c 64 31 09 52 65 63  32 20 46 69 65 6c 64 32  |eld1.Rec2 Field2|
00000080  09 52 65 63 32 20 46 69  65 6c 64 33 0a 52 65 63  |.Rec2 Field3.Rec|
00000090  33 20 46 69 65 6c 64 31  09 52 65 63 33 20 46 69  |3 Field1.Rec3 Fi|
000000a0  65 6c 64 32 09 52 65 63  33 20 46 69 65 6c 64 33  |eld2.Rec3 Field3|
000000b0  0a                                                |.|
000000b1
```

See the Perl documentation for the pack and unpack template formats.

Discussion

Anyone with any Unix background will automatically use some kind of delimiter in output, since the *textutils* toolchain is never far from mind, so fixed-length (also called fixed-width) records are rare in the Unix world. They are very common in the mainframe world however, so they will occasionally crop up in large applications that originated on big iron, such as some applications from SAP. As we've just seen, it's no problem to handle.

One caveat to this recipe is that it requires each record to end in a newline. Many old mainframe record formats don't, in which case you can use Recipe 13.17, "Processing Files with No Line Breaks" to add newlines to the end of each record before processing.

See Also

- man gawk
- *http://www.faqs.org/faqs/computer-lang/awk/faq/*
- *http://perldoc.perl.org/functions/unpack.html*
- *http://perldoc.perl.org/functions/pack.html*
- Recipe 13.14, "Trimming Whitespace"
- Recipe 13.17, "Processing Files with No Line Breaks"

13.17 Processing Files with No Line Breaks

Problem

You have a large file with no line breaks, and you need to process it.

Solution

Pre-process the file and add line breaks in appropriate places. For example, Open-Office.org's Open Document Format (ODF) files are basically zipped XML files. It is possible to *unzip* them and *grep* the XML, which we did a lot while writing this book. See Recipe 12.5, "Comparing Two Documents" for a more comprehensive treatment of ODF files. In this example, we insert a newline after every closing angle bracket (>). That makes it much easier to process the file using *grep* or other *textutils*. Note that we must enter a backslash followed immediately by the Enter key to embed an escaped newline in the *sed* script:

```
$ wc -l content.xml
       1 content.xml

$ sed -e 's/>/>\
/g' content.xml | wc -l
    1687
```

If you have fixed-length records with no newlines, do this instead, where *48* is the length of the record.

```
$ cat fixed-length
Line_1__aaaaaaaaaaaaaaaaaaaaaaaaaaaaaaaaaaaaaZZZLine_2__
aaaaaaaaaaaaaaaaaaaaaaaaaaaaaaaaaaaaaaaZZZLine_3__
aaaaaaaaaaaaaaaaaaaaaaaaaaaaaaaaaaaaaaaZZZLine_4__
aaaaaaaaaaaaaaaaaaaaaaaaaaaaaaaaaaaaaaaZZZLine_5__
aaaaaaaaaaaaaaaaaaaaaaaaaaaaaaaaaaaaaaaZZZLine_6__
aaaaaaaaaaaaaaaaaaaaaaaaaaaaaaaaaaaaaaaZZZLine_7__
aaaaaaaaaaaaaaaaaaaaaaaaaaaaaaaaaaaaaaaZZZLine_8__
aaaaaaaaaaaaaaaaaaaaaaaaaaaaaaaaaaaaaaaZZZLine_9__
aaaaaaaaaaaaaaaaaaaaaaaaaaaaaaaaaaaaaaaZZZLine_10_
aaaaaaaaaaaaaaaaaaaaaaaaaaaaaaaaaaaaaaaZZZLine_11_
aaaaaaaaaaaaaaaaaaaaaaaaaaaaaaaaaaaaaaaZZZLine_12_
aaaaaaaaaaaaaaaaaaaaaaaaaaaaaaaaaaaaaaaZZZ


$ wc -l fixed-length
       1 fixed-length

$ sed 's/.\{48\}/&\
/g;' fixed-length
Line_1__aaaaaaaaaaaaaaaaaaaaaaaaaaaaaaaaaaaaaZZZ
Line_2__aaaaaaaaaaaaaaaaaaaaaaaaaaaaaaaaaaaaaZZZ
Line_3__aaaaaaaaaaaaaaaaaaaaaaaaaaaaaaaaaaaaaZZZ
Line_4__aaaaaaaaaaaaaaaaaaaaaaaaaaaaaaaaaaaaaZZZ
Line_5__aaaaaaaaaaaaaaaaaaaaaaaaaaaaaaaaaaaaaZZZ
Line_6__aaaaaaaaaaaaaaaaaaaaaaaaaaaaaaaaaaaaaZZZ
Line_7__aaaaaaaaaaaaaaaaaaaaaaaaaaaaaaaaaaaaaZZZ
Line_8__aaaaaaaaaaaaaaaaaaaaaaaaaaaaaaaaaaaaaZZZ
Line_9__aaaaaaaaaaaaaaaaaaaaaaaaaaaaaaaaaaaaaZZZ
Line_10_aaaaaaaaaaaaaaaaaaaaaaaaaaaaaaaaaaaaaZZZ
Line_11_aaaaaaaaaaaaaaaaaaaaaaaaaaaaaaaaaaaaaZZZ
Line_12_aaaaaaaaaaaaaaaaaaaaaaaaaaaaaaaaaaaaaZZZ


$ perl -pe 's/(.{48})/$1\n/g;' fixed-length
Line_1__aaaaaaaaaaaaaaaaaaaaaaaaaaaaaaaaaaaaaZZZ
Line_2__aaaaaaaaaaaaaaaaaaaaaaaaaaaaaaaaaaaaaZZZ
Line_3__aaaaaaaaaaaaaaaaaaaaaaaaaaaaaaaaaaaaaZZZ
Line_4__aaaaaaaaaaaaaaaaaaaaaaaaaaaaaaaaaaaaaZZZ
Line_5__aaaaaaaaaaaaaaaaaaaaaaaaaaaaaaaaaaaaaZZZ
Line_6__aaaaaaaaaaaaaaaaaaaaaaaaaaaaaaaaaaaaaZZZ
Line_7__aaaaaaaaaaaaaaaaaaaaaaaaaaaaaaaaaaaaaZZZ
Line_8__aaaaaaaaaaaaaaaaaaaaaaaaaaaaaaaaaaaaaZZZ
Line_9__aaaaaaaaaaaaaaaaaaaaaaaaaaaaaaaaaaaaaZZZ
Line_10_aaaaaaaaaaaaaaaaaaaaaaaaaaaaaaaaaaaaaZZZ
Line_11_aaaaaaaaaaaaaaaaaaaaaaaaaaaaaaaaaaaaaZZZ
Line_12_aaaaaaaaaaaaaaaaaaaaaaaaaaaaaaaaaaaaaZZZ
```

Discussion

This happens often when people create output programatically, especially using canned modules and especially with HTML or XML output.

Note the *sed* substitutions have an odd construct that allows an embedded newline. In *sed*, a literal ampersand (&) on the righthand side (RHS) of a substitution is replaced by the entire expression matched on the lefthand side (LHS), and the trailing \ on the first line escapes the newline so the shell accepts it, but it's still in the *sed* RHS substitution. This is because *sed* doesn't recognize \n as a metacharacter on the RHS of s///.

See Also

* *http://sed.sourceforge.net/sedfaq.html*
* *Effective awk Programming* by Arnold Robbins (O'Reilly)
* *sed & awk* by Arnold Robbins and Dale Dougherty (O'Reilly)
* Recipe 12.5, "Comparing Two Documents"
* Recipe 13.16, "Processing Fixed-Length Records"

13.18 Converting a Data File to CSV

Problem

You have a data file that you need to convert to a Comma Separated Values (CSV) file.

Solution

Use *awk* to convert the data into CSV format:

```
$ awk 'BEGIN { FS="\t"; OFS="\",\"" } { gsub(/"/, "\"\""); $1 = $1; printf "\"%s\"\
n", $0}' tab_delimited
"Line 1","Field 2","Field 3","Field 4","Field 5 with ""internal"" double-quotes"
"Line 2","Field 2","Field 3","Field 4","Field 5 with ""internal"" double-quotes"
"Line 3","Field 2","Field 3","Field 4","Field 5 with ""internal"" double-quotes"
"Line 4","Field 2","Field 3","Field 4","Field 5 with ""internal"" double-quotes"
```

You can do the same thing in Perl also:

```
$ perl -naF'\t' -e 'chomp @F; s/"/""/g for @F; print q(").join(q(","), @F).qq("\n);'
tab_delimited
"Line 1","Field 2","Field 3","Field 4","Field 5 with ""internal"" double-quotes"
"Line 2","Field 2","Field 3","Field 4","Field 5 with ""internal"" double-quotes"
"Line 3","Field 2","Field 3","Field 4","Field 5 with ""internal"" double-quotes"
"Line 4","Field 2","Field 3","Field 4","Field 5 with ""internal"" double-quotes"
```

Discussion

First of all, it's tricky to define exactly what CSV really means. There is no formal specification, and various vendors have implemented various versions. Our version here is very simple, and should hopefully work just about anywhere. We place double quotes around all fields (some implementations only quote strings, or strings with internal commas), and we double internal double quotes.

To do that, we have *awk* split up the input fields using a tab as the field separator, and set the output field separator (OFS) to ",". We then globally replace any double quotes with two double quotes, make an assignment so *awk* rebuilds the record (see the *awk* trick in Recipe 13.14, "Trimming Whitespace") and print out the record with leading and trailing double quotes. We have to escape double quotes in several places, which looks a little cluttered, but otherwise this is very straightforward.

See Also

- awk FAQ
- Recipe 13.14, "Trimming Whitespace"
- Recipe 13.19, "Parsing a CSV Data File"

13.19 Parsing a CSV Data File

Problem

You have a Comma Separated Values (CSV) data file that you need to parse.

Solution

Unlike the previous recipe for converting to CSV, there is no easy way to do this, since it's tricky to define exactly what CSV really means.

Possible solutions for you to explore are:

- sed: *http://sed.sourceforge.net/sedfaq4.html#s4.12*
- awk: *http://lorance.freeshell.org/csv/*
- Perl: *Mastering Regular Expressions* by Jeffrey E. F. Friedl (O'Reilly) has a regex to do this
- Perl: See the CPAN (*http://www.cpan.org/*) for various modules
- Load the CSV file into a spreadsheet (OpenOffice.org's Calc and Microsoft's Excel both work), then copy and paste into a text editor and you should get tab delimited output that you can now use easily

Discussion

As noted in Recipe 13.18, "Converting a Data File to CSV," there is no formal specification for CSV, and that fact, combined with data variations, makes this task much harder than it sounds.

See Also

- Recipe 13.18, "Converting a Data File to CSV"

CHAPTER 14

Writing Secure Shell Scripts

Writing secure shell scripts?! How can shell scripts be secure when you can read the source code?

Any system that depends on concealing implementation details is attempting to use *security by obscurity*, and that is no security at all. Just ask the major software manufacturers whose source code is a closely guarded trade secret, yet whose products are incessantly vulnerable to exploits written by people who have never seen that source code. Contrast that with the code from OpenSSH and OpenBSD, which is totally open, yet very secure.

Security by obscurity will never work for long, though some forms of it can be a useful *additional* layer of security. For example, having daemons assigned to listen on nonstandard port numbers will keep a lot of the so-called script-kiddies away. But security by obscurity must never be the *only* layer of security because sooner or later, someone is going to discover whatever you've hidden.

As Bruce Schneier says, security is a process. It's not a product, object, or technique, and it is never finished. As technology, networks, attacks and defenses evolve, so must your security process. So what does it mean to write *secure* shell scripts?

Secure shell scripts will reliably do what they are supposed to do, and only what they are supposed to do. They won't lend themselves to being exploited to gain root access, they won't accidentally `rm -rf /`, and they won't leak information, such as passwords. They will be robust, but will fail gracefully. They will tolerate inadvertent user mistakes and sanitize all user input. They will be as simple as possible, and contain only clear, readable code and documentation so that the intention of each line is unambiguous.

That sounds a lot like any well-designed, robust program, doesn't it? Security should be part of any good design process from the start—it shouldn't be tacked on at the end. In this chapter we've highlighted the most common security weaknesses and questions, and shown you how to tackle them.

A lot has been written about security over the years. If you're interested, *Practical UNIX & Internet Security* by Gene Spafford et al. (O'Reilly) is a good place to start. Chapter 15 of *Classic Shell Scripting* by Nelson H.F. Beebe and Arnold Robbins (O'Reilly), is another excellent resource. There are also many good online references, such as "A Lab engineer's check list for writing secure Unix code" at *http://www.auscert.org.au/render.html?it=1975*.

The following listing collects the most universal of the secure shell programming techniques, so they are all in one place as a quick reference when you need them or to copy into a script template. Be sure to read the full recipe for each technique so you understand it.

```
#!/usr/bin/env bash
# cookbook filename: security_template

# Set a sane/secure path
PATH='/usr/local/bin:/bin:/usr/bin'
# It's almost certainly already marked for export, but make sure
\export PATH

# Clear all aliases.  Important: leading \ inhibits alias expansion
\unalias -a

# Clear the command path hash
hash -r

# Set the hard limit to 0 to turn off core dumps
ulimit -H -c 0 --

# Set a sane/secure IFS (note this is bash & ksh93 syntax only--not portable!)
IFS=$' \t\n'

# Set a sane/secure umask variable and use it
# Note this does not affect files already redirected on the command line
# 002 results in 0774 perms, 077 results in 0700 perms, etc...
UMASK=002
umask $UMASK

until [ -n "$temp_dir" -a ! -d "$temp_dir" ]; do
    temp_dir="/tmp/meaningful_prefix.${RANDOM}${RANDOM}${RANDOM}"
done
mkdir -p -m 0700 $temp_dir \
  || (echo "FATAL: Failed to create temp dir '$temp_dir': $?"; exit 100)

# Do our best to clean up temp files no matter what
# Note $temp_dir must be set before this, and must not change!
cleanup="rm -rf $temp_dir"
trap "$cleanup" ABRT EXIT HUP INT QUIT
```

14.1   Avoiding Common Security Problems

Problem

You want to avoid common security problems in your scripting.

Solution

Validate all external input, including interactive input and that from configuration files and interactive use. In particular, never eval input that you have not checked very thoroughly.

Use secure temporary files, ideally in secure temporary directories.

Make sure you are using trusted external executables.

Discussion

In a way, this recipe barely scratches the surface of scripting and system security. Yet it also covers the most common security problems you'll find.

Data validation, or rather the lack of it, is a huge deal in computer security right now. This is the problem that leads to buffer overflows, which are by far the most common class of exploit going around. *bash* doesn't suffer from this issue in the same way that C does, but the concepts are the same. In the *bash* world it's more likely that unvalidated input will contain something like ; rm -rf / than a buffer over-flow; however, neither is welcome. Validate your data!

Race conditions are another big issue, closely tied to the problem of an attacker gaining an ability to write over unexpected files. A *race condition* exists when two or more separate events must occur in the correct order at the correct time without external interference. They often result in providing an unprivileged user with read and/or write access to files they shouldn't be able to access, which in turn can result in so-called privilege escalation, where an ordinary user can gain root access. Insecure use of temporary files is a very common factor in this kind of attack. Using secure temporary files, especially inside secure temporary directories, will eliminate this attack vector.

Another common attack vector is trojaned utilities. Like the Trojan horse, these appear to be one thing while they are in fact something else. The canonical example here is the trojaned *ls* command that works just like the real *ls* command except when run by *root*. In that case it creates a new user called *r00t*, with a default password known to the attacker and deletes itself. Using a secure $PATH is about the best you can do from the scripting side. From the systems side there are many tools such as Tripwire and AIDE to help you assure system integrity.

See Also

- *http://www.tripwiresecurity.com/*
- *http://www.cs.tut.fi/~rammer/aide.html*
- *http://osiris.shmoo.com/*

14.2   Avoiding Interpreter Spoofing

Problem

You want to avoid certain kinds of *setuid root* spoofing attacks.

Solution

Pass a single trailing dash to the shell, as in:

```
#!/bin/bash -
```

Discussion

The first line of a script is a magic line (often called the *shebang* line) that tells the kernel what interpreter to use to process the rest of the file. The kernel will also look for a single option to the specified interpreter. There are some attacks that take advantage of this fact, but if you pass an argument along, they are avoided. See *http://www.faqs.org/faqs/unix-faq/faq/part4/section-7.html* for details.

However, hard-coding the path to *bash* may present a portability issue. See Recipe 15.1, "Finding bash Portably for #!" for details.

See Also

- Recipe 14.15, "Writing setuid or setgid Scripts"
- Recipe 15.1, "Finding bash Portably for #!"

14.3   Setting a Secure $PATH

Problem

You want to make sure you are using a secure path.

Solution

Set $PATH to a known good state at the beginning of every script:

```
# Set a sane/secure path
PATH='/usr/local/bin:/bin:/usr/bin'
# It's almost certainly already marked for export, but make sure
export PATH
```

Or use the *getconf* utility to get a path guaranteed by POSIX to find all of the standard utilities:

```
export PATH=$(getconf PATH)
```

Discussion

There are two portability problems with the example above. First, `` is more portable (but less readable) than $( ). Second, having the export command on the same line as the variable assignment won't always work. var='foo'; export var is more portable than export var='foo'. Also note that the export command need only be used once to flag a variable to be exported to child processes.

If you don't use *getconf*, our example is a good default path for starters, though you may need to adjust it for your particular environment or needs. You might also use the less portable version:

```
export PATH='/usr/local/bin:/bin:/usr/bin'
```

Depending on your security risk and needs, you should also consider using absolute paths. This tends to be cumbersome and can be an issue where portability is concerned, as different operating systems put tools in different places. One way to mitigate these issues to some extent is to use variables. If you do this, sort them so you don't end up with the same command three times because you missed it scanning the unsorted list.

One other advantage of this method is that it makes it very easy to see exactly what tools your script depends on, and you can even add a simple function to make sure that each tool is available and executable before your script really gets going.

```
#!/usr/bin/env bash
# cookbook filename: finding_tools

# export may or may not also be needed, depending on what you are doing

# These are fairly safe bets
_cp='/bin/cp'
_mv='/bin/mv'
_rm='/bin/rm'

# These are a little trickier
case $(/bin/uname) in
    'Linux')
        _cut='/bin/cut'
        _nice='/bin/nice'
        # [...]
    ;;
    'SunOS')
        _cut='/usr/bin/cut'
        _nice='/usr/bin/nice'
```

```
     # [...]
  ;;
  # [...]
esac
```

 Be careful about the variable names you use. Some programs like InfoZip use environment variables such as $ZIP and $UNZIP to pass settings to the program itself. So if you do something like ZIP='/usr/bin/zip', you can spend days pulling your hair out wondering why it works fine from the command line, but not in your script. Trust us. We learned this one the hard way. Also RTFM.

See Also

- Recipe 6.14, "Branching Many Ways"
- Recipe 6.15, "Parsing Command-Line Arguments"
- Recipe 14.9, "Finding World-Writable Directories in Your $PATH"
- Recipe 14.10, "Adding the Current Directory to the $PATH"
- Recipe 15.2, "Setting a POSIX $PATH"
- Recipe 16.3, "Change Your $PATH Permanently"
- Recipe 16.4, "Change Your $PATH Temporarily"
- Recipe 19.3, "Forgetting That the Current Directory Is Not in the $PATH"
- "Built-in Commands and Reserved Words" in Appendix A

14.4   Clearing All Aliases

Problem

You need to make sure that there are no malicious aliases in your environment for security reasons.

Solution

Use the \unalias -a command to unalias any existing aliases.

Discussion

If an attacker can trick *root* or even another user into running a command, they will be able to gain access to data or privileges they shouldn't have. One way to trick another user into running a malicious program is to create an alias to some other common program (e.g., *ls*).

The leading \, which suppresses alias expansion, is very important because without it you can do evil things like this:

```
$ alias unalias=echo
$ alias builtin=ls

$ builtin unalias vi
ls: unalias: No such file or directory
ls: vi: No such file or directory

$ unalias -a
-a
```

See Also

- Recipe 10.7, "Redefining Commands with alias"
- Recipe 10.8, "Avoiding Aliases, Functions"
- Recipe 16.6, "Shortening or Changing Command Names"

14.5 Clearing the Command Hash

Problem

You need to make sure that your command hash has not been subverted.

Solution

Use the hash -r command to clear entries from the command hash.

Discussion

On execution, *bash* "remembers" the location of most commands found in the $PATH to speed up subsequent invocations.

If an attacker can trick *root* or even another user into running a command, they will be able to gain access to data or privileges they shouldn't have. One way to trick another user into running a malicious program is to poison the hash so that the wrong program may be run.

See Also

- Recipe 14.9, "Finding World-Writable Directories in Your $PATH"
- Recipe 14.10, "Adding the Current Directory to the $PATH"
- Recipe 15.2, "Setting a POSIX $PATH"
- Recipe 16.3, "Change Your $PATH Permanently"
- Recipe 16.4, "Change Your $PATH Temporarily"
- Recipe 19.3, "Forgetting That the Current Directory Is Not in the $PATH"

14.6   Preventing Core Dumps

Problem

You want to prevent your script from dumping core in the case of an unrecoverable error, since core dumps may contain sensitive data from memory such as passwords.

Solution

Use the *bash* built-in *ulimit* to set the core file size limit to 0, typically in your *.bashrc* file:

```
ulimit -H -c 0 --
```

Discussion

Core dumps are intended for debugging and contain an image of the memory used by the process at the time it failed. As such, the file will contain anything the process had stored in memory (e.g., user-entered passwords).

Set this in a system-level file such as */etc/profile* or */etc/bashrc* to which users have no write access if you don't want them to be able to change it.

See Also

- help ulimit

14.7   Setting a Secure $IFS

Problem

You want to make sure your Internal Field Separator environment variable is clean.

Solution

Set it to a known good state at the beginning of every script using this clear (but not POSIX-compliant) syntax:

```
# Set a sane/secure IFS (note this is bash & ksh93 syntax only--not portable!)
IFS=$' \t\n'
```

Discussion

As noted, this syntax is not portable. However, the canonical portable syntax is unreliable because it may easily be inadvertently stripped by editors that trim whitespace. The values are traditionally space, tab, newline—and the order is important. $*, which returns all positional parameters, the special ${!prefix@} and ${!prefix*} parameter expansions, and programmable completion, all use the *first* value of $IFS as their separator.

The typical method for writing that leaves a trailing space and tab on the first line:

```
1  IFS='• → &#182;¶
2  '
```

Newline, space, tab is less likely to be trimmed, but changes the default order, which may result in unexpected results from some commands.

```
1  IFS='&#182;¶
2  • → '
```

See Also

* Recipe 13.14, "Trimming Whitespace"

14.8   Setting a Secure umask

Problem

You want to make sure you are using a secure umask.

Solution

Use the *bash* built-in *umask* to set a known good state at the beginning of every script:

```
# Set a sane/secure umask variable and use it
# Note this does not affect files already redirected on the command line
# 002 results in 0774 perms, 077 results in 0700 perms, etc...
UMASK=002
umask $UMASK
```

Discussion

We set the $UMASK variable in case we need to use different masks elsewhere in the program. You could just as easily do without it; it's not a big deal.

```
umask 002
```

 Remember that umask is a mask that specifies the bits to be *taken away* from the default permissions of 777 for directories and 666 for files. When in doubt, test it out:

```
# Run a new shell so you don't affect your current
environment
/tmp$ bash

# Check the current settings
/tmp$ touch um_current

# Check some other settings
/tmp$ umask 000 ; touch um_000
/tmp$ umask 022 ; touch um_022
```

```
/tmp$ umask 077 ; touch um_077

/tmp$ ls -l um_*
-rw-rw-rw-    1 jp          jp            0 Jul 22 06:05 um000
-rw-r--r--    1 jp          jp            0 Jul 22 06:05 um022
-rw-------    1 jp          jp            0 Jul 22 06:05 um077
-rw-rw-r--    1 jp          jp            0 Jul 22 06:05 umcurrent

# Clean up and exit the sub-shell
/tmp$ rm um_*
/tmp$ exit
```

See Also

- help umask
- *http://linuxzoo.net/page/sec_umask.html*

14.9   Finding World-Writable Directories in Your $PATH

Problem

You want to make sure that there are no world-writable directories in *root*'s $PATH. To see why, read Recipe 14.10, "Adding the Current Directory to the $PATH."

Solution

Use this simple script to check your $PATH. Use it in conjunction with su - or *sudo* to check paths for other users:

```
#!/usr/bin/env bash
# cookbook filename: chkpath.1
# Check your $PATH for world-writable or missing directories

exit_code=0

for dir in ${PATH//:/ }; do
    [ -L "$dir" ] && printf "%b" "symlink, "
    if [ ! -d "$dir" ]; then
        printf "%b" "missing\t\t"
        (( exit_code++ ))
    elif [ "$(ls -lLd $dir | grep '^d.......w. ')" ]; then
            printf "%b" "world writable\t"
            (( exit_code++ ))
    else
            printf "%b" "ok\t\t"
    fi
    printf "%b" "$dir\n"
done
exit $exit_code
```

For example:

```
# ./chkpath
ok              /usr/local/sbin
ok              /usr/local/bin
ok              /sbin
ok              /bin
ok              /usr/sbin
ok              /usr/bin
ok              /usr/X11R6/bin
ok              /root/bin
missing         /does_not_exist
world writable  /tmp
symlink, world writable /tmp/bin
symlink, ok     /root/sbin
```

Discussion

We convert the $PATH to a space-delimited list using the technique from Recipe 9.11, "Finding a File Using a List of Possible Locations," test for symbolic links (-L), and make sure the directory actually exists (-d). Then we get a long directory listing (-l), dereferencing symbolic links (-L), and listing the directory name only (-d), not the directory's contents. Then we finally get to *grep* for world-writable directories.

As you can see, we spaced out the ok directories, while directories with a problem may get a little cluttered. We also broke the usual rule of Unix tools being quiet unless there's a problem, because we felt it was a useful opportunity to see exactly what is in your path and give it a once-over in addition to the automated check.

We also provide an exit code of zero on success with no problems detected in the $PATH, or the count of errors found. With a little more tweaking, we can add the file's mode, owner, and group into the output, which might be even more valuable to check:

```
#!/usr/bin/env bash
# cookbook filename: chkpath.2
# Check your $PATH for world-writable or missing directories, with 'stat'

exit_code=0

for dir in ${PATH//:/ }; do
    [ -L "$dir" ] && printf "%b" "symlink, "
    if [ ! -d "$dir" ]; then
        printf "%b" "missing\t\t\t\t"
        (( exit_code++ ))
    else
        stat=$(ls -lHd $dir | awk '{print $1, $3, $4}')
        if [ "$(echo $stat | grep '^d.......w. ')" ]; then
            printf "%b" "world writable\t$stat "
            (( exit_code++ ))
        else
            printf "%b" "ok\t\t$stat "
```

```
        fi
    fi
    printf "%b" "$dir\n"

done
exit $exit_code
```

For example:

```
# ./chkpath ; echo $?
ok              drwxr-xr-x root root /usr/local/sbin
ok              drwxr-xr-x root root /usr/local/bin
ok              drwxr-xr-x root root /sbin
ok              drwxr-xr-x root root /bin
ok              drwxr-xr-x root root /usr/sbin
ok              drwxr-xr-x root root /usr/bin
ok              drwxr-xr-x root root /usr/X11R6/bin
ok              drwx------ root root /root/bin
missing                          /does_not_exist
world writable  drwxrwxrwt root root /tmp
symlink, ok            drwxr-xr-x root root /root/sbin
2
```

See Also

- Recipe 9.11, "Finding a File Using a List of Possible Locations"
- Recipe 14.10, "Adding the Current Directory to the $PATH"
- Recipe 15.2, "Setting a POSIX $PATH"
- Recipe 16.3, "Change Your $PATH Permanently"
- Recipe 16.4, "Change Your $PATH Temporarily"
- Recipe 19.3, "Forgetting That the Current Directory Is Not in the $PATH"

14.10 Adding the Current Directory to the $PATH

Problem

Having to type ./script is tedious and you'd rather just add . (or an empty directory, meaning a leading or trailing : or a :: in the middle) to your $PATH.

Solution

We advise against doing this for any user, but we strongly advise against doing this for *root*. If you absolutely must do this, make sure . comes last. Never do it as *root*.

Discussion

As you know, the shell searches the directories listed in $PATH when you enter a command name without a path. The reason not to add . is the same reason not to allow world-writable directories in your $PATH.

Say you are in *tmp* and have . as the first thing in your $PATH. If you type *ls* and there happens to be a file called */tmp/ls*, you will run that file instead of the */bin/ls* you meant to run. Now what? Well, it depends. It's possible (even likely given the name) that */tmp/ls* is a malicious script, and if you have just run it as *root* there is no telling what it could do, up to and including deleting itself when it's finished to remove the evidence.

So what if you put it last? Well, have you ever typed *mc* instead of *mv*? We have. So unless Midnight Commander is installed on your system, you could accidentally run *./mc* when you meant */bin/mv*, with the same results as above.

Just say no to dot!

See Also

- Section 2.13 of *http://www.faqs.org/faqs/unix-faq/faq/part2/*
- Recipe 9.11, "Finding a File Using a List of Possible Locations"
- Recipe 14.3, "Setting a Secure $PATH"
- Recipe 14.9, "Finding World-Writable Directories in Your $PATH"
- Recipe 15.2, "Setting a POSIX $PATH"
- Recipe 16.3, "Change Your $PATH Permanently"
- Recipe 16.4, "Change Your $PATH Temporarily"
- Recipe 19.3, "Forgetting That the Current Directory Is Not in the $PATH"

14.11 Using Secure Temporary Files

Problem

You need to create a temporary file or directory, but are aware of the security implications of using a predictable name.

Solution

The easy and "usually good enough" solution is to just use $RANDOM inline in your script. For example:

```
# Make sure $TMP is set to something
[ -n "$TMP" ] || TMP='/tmp'

# Make a "good enough" random temp directory
until [ -n "$temp_dir" -a ! -d "$temp_dir" ]; do
    temp_dir="/tmp/meaningful_prefix.${RANDOM}${RANDOM}${RANDOM}"
done
mkdir -p -m 0700 $temp_dir
   || { echo "FATAL: Failed to create temp dir '$temp_dir': $?"; exit 100 }
```

```
# Make a "good enough" random temp file
until [ -n "$temp_file" -a ! -e "$temp_file" ]; do
    temp_file="/tmp/meaningful_prefix.${RANDOM}${RANDOM}${RANDOM}"
done
touch $temp_file && chmod 0600 $temp_file
    || { echo "FATAL: Failed to create temp file '$temp_file': $?"; exit 101 }
```

Even better, use both a random temporary directory and a random filename!

```
# cookbook filename: make_temp

# Make a "good enough" random temp directory
until [ -n "$temp_dir" -a ! -d "$temp_dir" ]; do
    temp_dir="/tmp/meaningful_prefix.${RANDOM}${RANDOM}${RANDOM}"
done
mkdir -p -m 0700 $temp_dir \
    || { echo "FATAL: Failed to create temp dir '$temp_dir': $?"; exit 100 }

# Make a "good enough" random temp file in the temp dir
temp_file="$temp_dir/meaningful_prefix.${RANDOM}${RANDOM}${RANDOM}"
touch $temp_file && chmod 0600 $temp_file \
    || { echo "FATAL: Failed to create temp file '$temp_file': $?"; exit 101 }
```

No matter how you do it, don't forget to set a trap to clean up. As noted, $temp_dir must be set before this trap is declared, and its value must not change. If those things aren't true, rewrite the logic to account for your needs.

```
# cookbook filename: clean_temp

# Do our best to clean up temp files no matter what
# Note $temp_dir must be set before this, and must not change!
cleanup="rm -rf $temp_dir"
trap "$cleanup" ABRT EXIT HUP INT QUIT
```

Discussion

$RANDOM has been available since at least *bash-2.0*, and using it is probably good enough. Simple code is better and easier to secure than complicated code, so using $RANDOM may make your code more secure than having to deal with the validation and error-checking complexities of *mktemp* or */dev/urandom*. You may also tend to use it more because it is so simple. However, $RANDOM provides only numbers, while *mktemp* provides numbers and upper- and lowercase letters, and *urandom* provides numbers and lowercase letters, thus vastly increasing the key space.

However you create it, using a temporary directory in which to work has the following advantages:

- `mkdir -p -m 0700 $temp_dir` avoids the race condition inherent in `touch $temp_file && chmod 0600 $temp_file`.
- Files created inside the directory are not even visible to a non-*root* attacker outside the directory when 0700 permissions are set.

- A temporary directory makes it easy to ensure all of your temporary files are removed at exit. If you have temp files scattered about, there's always a chance of forgetting one when cleaning up.

- You can choose to use meaningful names for temp files inside such a directory, which may make development and debugging easier, and thus improve script security and robustness.

- Use of a meaningful prefix in the path makes it clear what scripts are running (this may be good or bad, but consider that *ps* or */proc* do the same thing). More importantly, it might highlight a script that has failed to clean up after itself, which could possibly lead to an information leak.

The code above advises using a *meaningful_prefix* in the path name you are creating. Some people will undoubtedly argue that since that is predictable, it reduces the security. It's true that part of the path is predictable, but we still feel the advantages above outweigh this objection. If you still disagree, simply omit the meaningful prefix.

Depending on your risk and security needs, you may want to use random temporary files inside the random temporary directory, as we did above. That will probably not do anything to materially increase security, but if it makes you feel better, go for it.

We talked about a race condition in touch $temp_file && chmod 0600 $temp_file. One way to avoid that is to do this:

```
saved_umask=$(umask)
umask 077
touch $temp_file
umask $saved_umask
unset saved_umask
```

We recommended using both a random temporary directory and a random (or semi-random) filename since it provides more overall benefits.

If the numeric-only nature of $RANDOM really bothers you, consider combining some other sources of pseudo-unpredictable and pseudorandom data and a hash function:

```
nice_long_random_string=$( (last ; who ; netstat -a ; free ; date \
  ; echo $RANDOM) | md5sum | cut -d' ' -f1 )
```

 We do not recommend using the fallback method shown here because the additional complexity is probably a cure that is worse than the disease. But it's an interesting look at a way to make things a lot harder than they need to be.

A theoretically more secure approach is to use the *mktemp* utility present on many modern systems, with a fallback to */dev/urandom*, also present on many modern systems, or even $RANDOM. The problem is that *mktemp* and */dev/urandom* are not always available, and dealing with that in practice in a portable way is much more complicated than our solution.

```
#+++++++++++++++++++++++++++++++++++++++++++++++++++++++++++++++++++++++++++++
# Try to create a secure temp file name or directory
# Called like: $temp_file=$(MakeTemp <file|dir> [path/to/name-prefix])
# Returns the name of an a ra it in TEMP_NAME
# For example:
#         $temp_dir=$(MakeTemp dir /tmp/$PROGRAM.foo)
#         $temp_file=$(MakeTemp file /tmp/$PROGRAM.foo)
#
function MakeTemp {

    # Make sure $TMP is set to something
    [ -n "$TMP" ] || TMP='/tmp'

    local type_name=$1
    local prefix=${2:-$TMP/temp} # Unless prefix is defined, use $TMP + temp
    local temp_type=''
    local sanity_check=''

    case $type_name in
        file )
              temp_type=''
              ur_cmd='touch'
              #                      Regular file    Readable      Writable
Owned by me
              sanity_check='test -f $TEMP_NAME -a -r $TEMP_NAME -a -w $TEMP_NAME -a
-O $TEMP_NAME'
              ;;
        dir|directory )
              temp_type='-d'
              ur_cmd='mkdir -p -m0700'
              #                       Directory      Readable      Writable
Searchable      Owned by me
              sanity_check='test -d $TEMP_NAME -a -r $TEMP_NAME -a -w $TEMP_NAME -a
-x $TEMP_NAME -a -O $TEMP_NAME'
            ;;
        * ) Error "\nBad type in $PROGRAM:MakeTemp!  Needs file|dir." 1 ;;
    esac

    # First try mktemp
    TEMP_NAME=$(mktemp $temp_type ${prefix}.XXXXXXXXX)

    # If that fails try urandom, if that fails give up
    if [ -z "$TEMP_NAME" ]; then
        TEMP_NAME="${prefix}.$(cat /dev/urandom | od -x | tr -d ' ' | head -1)"
        $ur_cmd $TEMP_NAME
    fi

    # Make sure the file or directory was actually created, or DIE
    if ! eval $sanity_check; then
        Error "\aFATAL ERROR: can't create temp $type_name with '$0:MakeTemp
$*'!\n" 2
```

```
        else
            echo "$TEMP_NAME"
        fi

    } # end of function MakeTemp
```

See Also

- man mktemp
- Recipe 14.13, "Setting Permissions"
- Appendix B, particularly *./scripts.noah/mktmp.bash*

14.12 Validating Input

Problem

You've asked for input (e.g., from a user or a program) and to ensure security or data integrity you need to make sure you got what you asked for.

Solution

There are various ways to validate your input, depending on what the input is and how strict you need to be.

Use pattern matching for simple "it matches or it doesn't" situations (see Recipe 6.6, "Testing for Equal," Recipe 6.7, "Testing with Pattern Matches," and Recipe 6.8, "Testing with Regular Expressions").

```
[[ "$raw_input" == *.jpg ]] && echo "Got a JPEG file."
```

Use a case statement when there are various things that might be valid (see Recipe 6. 14, "Branching Many Ways" and Recipe 6.15, "Parsing Command-Line Arguments").

```
# cookbook filename: validate_using_case

case $raw_input in
    *.company.com      ) # Probably a local hostname
        ;;
    *.jpg              ) # Probably a JPEG file
        ;;
    *.[jJ][pP][gG]     ) # Probably a JPEG file, case insensitive
        ;;
    foo | bar          ) # entered 'foo' or 'bar'
        ;;
    [0-9][0-9][0-9]    ) # A 3 digit number
        ;;
    [a-z][a-z][a-z][a-z] ) # A 4 lower-case char word
        ;;
    *                  ) # None of the above
        ;;
esac
```

Use a regular expression when pattern matching isn't specific enough and you have *bash* version 3.0+ (see Recipe 6.8, "Testing with Regular Expressions"). This example is looking for a three to six alphanumeric character filename with a `.jpg` extension (case sensitive):

```
[[ "$raw_input" =~ [[:alpha:]]{3,6}\.jpg ]] && echo "Got a JPEG file."
```

Discussion

For a larger and more detailed example, see the *examples/scripts/shprompt* in a recent *bash* tarball. Note this was written by Chet Ramey, who maintains *bash*:

```
# shprompt -- give a prompt and get an answer satisfying certain criteria
#
# shprompt [-dDfFsy] prompt
#    s = prompt for string
#    f = prompt for filename
#    F = prompt for full pathname to a file or directory
#    d = prompt for a directory name
#    D = prompt for a full pathname to a directory
#    y = prompt for y or n answer
#
# Chet Ramey
# chet@ins.CWRU.Edu
```

For a similar example, see *examples/scripts.noah/y_or_n_p.bash* written circa 1993 by Noah Friedman and later converted to *bash* version 2 syntax by Chet Ramey. Also in the examples see: *./functions/isnum.bash*, *./functions/isnum2*, and *./functions/isvalidip*.

See Also

- Recipe 3.5, "Getting User Input"
- Recipe 3.6, "Getting Yes or No Input"
- Recipe 3.7, "Selecting From a List of Options"
- Recipe 3.8, "Prompting for a Password"
- Recipe 6.6, "Testing for Equal"
- Recipe 6.7, "Testing with Pattern Matches"
- Recipe 6.8, "Testing with Regular Expressions"
- Recipe 6.14, "Branching Many Ways"
- Recipe 6.15, "Parsing Command-Line Arguments"
- Recipe 11.2, "Supplying a Default Date"
- Recipe 13.6, "Parsing Text with a read Statement"
- Recipe 13.7, "Parsing with read into an Array"
- Appendix B for *bash* examples

14.13 Setting Permissions

Problem

You want to set permissions in a secure manner.

Solution

If you need to set exact permissions for security reasons (or you are *sure* that you don't care what is already there, you just need to change it), use *chmod* with 4-digit octal modes.

```
$ chmod 0755 some_script
```

If you only want to add or remove permissions, but need to leave other existing permissions unchanged, use the + and - operations in symbolic mode.

```
$ chmod +x some_script
```

If you try to recursively set permissions on all the files in a directory structure using something like chmod -R 0644 *some_directory* then you'll regret it because you've now rendered any subdirectories non-executable, which means you won't be able to access their content, *cd* into them, or traverse below them. Use *find* and *xargs* with *chmod* to set the files and directories individually.

```
$ find some_directory -type f | xargs chmod 0644  # File perms
$ find some_directory -type d | xargs chmod 0755  # Dir. perms
```

Of course, if you only want to set permissions on the files in a single directory (non-recursive), just *cd* in there and set them.

When creating a directory, use `mkdir -m mode new_directory` since you not only accomplish two tasks with one command, but you avoid any possible race condition between creating the directory and setting the permissions.

Discussion

Many people are in the habit of using three-digit octal modes, but we like to use all four possible digits to be explicit about what we mean to do with all attributes. We also prefer using octal mode when possible because it's very clear what permissions you are going to end up with. You may also use the absolute operation (=) in symbolic mode if you like, but we're traditionalists who like the old octal method best.

Ensuring the final permissions when using the symbolic mode and the + or - operations is trickier since they are relative and not absolute. Unfortunately, there are many cases where you can't simply arbitrarily replace the existing permissions using octal mode. In such cases you have no choice but to use symbolic mode, often using + to add a permission while not disturbing other existing permissions. Consult your specific system's *chmod* for details, and verify that your results are as you expect.

```
$ ls -l
-rw-r--r--  1 jp  users  0 Dec  1 02:09 script.sh
```

```
# Make file read, write and executable for the owner using octal
$ chmod 0700 script.sh

$ ls -l
-rwx------  1 jp  users  0 Dec  1 02:09 script.sh

# Make file read and executable for everyone using symbolic
$ chmod ugo+rx *.sh

$ ls -l
-rwxr-xr-x  1 jp  users  0 Dec  1 02:09 script.sh
```

Note in the last example that although we added (+) rx to everyone (ugo), the owner still has write (w). That's what we wanted to do here, and that is often the case. But do you see how, in a security setting, it might be easy to make a mistake and allow an undesirable permission to slip through the cracks? That's why we like to use the absolute octal mode if possible, and of course we always check the results of our command.

In any case, before you adjust the permissions on a large group of files, thoroughly test your command. You may also want to backup the permissions and owners of the files. See Recipe 17.8, "Capturing File Metadata for Recovery" for details.

See Also

- man chmod
- man find
- man xargs
- Recipe 17.8, "Capturing File Metadata for Recovery"

14.14 Leaking Passwords into the Process List

Problem

ps may show passwords entered on the command line in the clear. For example:

```
$ ./cheesy_app -u user -p password &
[1] 13301

$ ps
  PID TT STAT    TIME COMMAND
 5280 p0 S    0:00.08 -bash
 9784 p0 R+   0:00.00 ps
13301 p0 S    0:00.01 /bin/sh ./cheesy_app -u user -p password
```

Solution

Try really hard not to use passwords on the command line.

Discussion

Really. Don't do that.

Many applications that provide a -p or similar switch will also prompt you if a password required and you do not provide it on the command line. That's great for interactive use, but not so great in scripts. You may be tempted to write a trivial "wrapper" script or an alias to try and encapsulate the password on the command line. Unfortunately, that won't work since the command is eventually run and so ends up in the process list anyway. If the command can accept the password on STDIN, you may be able to pass it in that way. That creates other problems, but at least avoids displaying the password in the process list.

```
$ ./bad_app ~.hidden/bad_apps_password
```

If that won't work, you'll need to either find a new app, patch the one you are using, or just live with it.

See Also

- Recipe 3.8, "Prompting for a Password"
- Recipe 14.20, "Using Passwords in Scripts"

14.15 Writing setuid or setgid Scripts

Problem

You have a problem you think you can solve by using the *setuid* or *setgid* bit on a shell script.

Solution

Use Unix groups and file permissions and/or *sudo* to grant the appropriate users the least privilege they need to accomplish their task.

Using the *setuid* or *setgid* bit on a shell script will create more problems—especially security problems—than it solves. Some systems (such as Linux) don't even honor the *setuid* bit on shell scripts, so creating *setuid* shell scripts creates an unnecessary portability problem in addition to the security risks.

Discussion

setuid root scripts are especially dangerous, so don't even think about it. Use *sudo*.

setuid and *setgid* have a different meaning when applied to directories than they do when applied to executable files. When one of these is set on a directory it causes any newly created files or subdirectories to be owned by the directory's owner or group, respectively.

Note you can check a file to see if it is *setuid* by using test -u or *setgid* by using test -g.

```
$ mkdir suid_dir sgid_dir

$ touch suid_file sgid_file

$ ls -l
total 4
drwxr-xr-x  2 jp  users  512 Dec  9 03:45 sgid_dir
-rw-r--r--  1 jp  users    0 Dec  9 03:45 sgid_file
drwxr-xr-x  2 jp  users  512 Dec  9 03:45 suid_dir
-rw-r--r--  1 jp  users    0 Dec  9 03:45 suid_file

$ chmod 4755 suid_dir suid_file

$ chmod 2755 sgid_dir sgid_file

$ ls -l
total 4
drwxr-sr-x  2 jp  users  512 Dec  9 03:45 sgid_dir
-rwxr-sr-x  1 jp  users    0 Dec  9 03:45 sgid_file
drwsr-xr-x  2 jp  users  512 Dec  9 03:45 suid_dir
-rwsr-xr-x  1 jp  users    0 Dec  9 03:45 suid_file

$ [ -u suid_dir ] && echo 'Yup, suid' || echo 'Nope, not suid'
Yup, suid

$ [ -u sgid_dir ] && echo 'Yup, suid' || echo 'Nope, not suid'
Nope, not suid

$ [ -g sgid_file ] && echo 'Yup, sgid' || echo 'Nope, not sgid'
Yup, sgid

$ [ -g suid_file ] && echo 'Yup, sgid' || echo 'Nope, not sgid'
Nope, not sgid
```

See Also

- man chmod
- Recipe 14.18, "Running As a Non-root User"
- Recipe 14.19, "Using sudo More Securely"
- Recipe 14.20, "Using Passwords in Scripts"
- Recipe 17.15, "Using sudo on a Group of Commands"

14.16 Restricting Guest Users

The material concerning the restricted shell in this recipe also appears in *Learning the bash Shell* by Cameron Newman (O'Reilly).

Problem

You need to allow some guest users on your system and need to restrict what they can do.

Solution

Avoid using shared accounts if possible, since you lose accountability and create logistical headaches when users leave and you need to change the password and inform the other users. Create separate accounts with the least possible permissions necessary to do whatever is needed. Consider using:

- A *chroot* jail, as discussed in Recipe 14.17, "Using chroot Jails"
- SSH to allow non-interactive access to commands or resources, as discussed in Recipe 14.21, "Using SSH Without a Password"
- *bash*'s restricted shell

Discussion

The *restricted shell* is designed to put the user into an environment where their ability to move around and write files is severely limited. It's usually used for guest accounts. You can make a user's login shell restricted by putting *rbash* in the user's */etc/passwd* entry if this option was included when *bash* was compiled.

The specific constraints imposed by the restricted shell disallow the user from doing the following:

- Changing working directories: *cd* is inoperative. If you try to use it, you will get the error message from *bash* cd: restricted.
- Redirecting output to a file: the redirectors >, >|, <>, and >> are not allowed.
- Assigning a new value to the environment variables $ENV, $BASH_ENV, $SHELL, or $PATH.
- Specifying any commands with slashes (/) in them. The shell will treat files outside of the current directory as "not found."
- Using the *exec* built-in.
- Specifying a filename containing a / as an argument to the . (*source*) built-in command.
- Importing function definitions from the shell environment at startup.
- Adding or deleting built-in commands with the -f and -d options to the *enable* built-in command.
- Specifying the -p option to the *command* built-in command.
- Turning off restricted mode with **set +r**.

These restrictions go into effect after the user's *.bash_profile* and environment files are run. In addition, it is wise to change the owner of the users' *.bash_profile* and *.bashrc* to *root*, and make these files read-only. The user's home directory should also be made read-only.

This means that the restricted shell user's entire environment is set up in */etc/profile* and *.bash_profile*. Since the user can't access */etc/profile* and can't overwrite *.bash_profile*, this lets the system administrator configure the environment as he sees fit.

Two common ways of setting up such environments are to set up a directory of safe commands and have that directory be the only one in PATH, and to set up a command menu from which the user can't escape without exiting the shell.

 The restricted shell is not proof against a determined attacker. It can also be difficult to lock down as well as you think you have, since many common applications such as Vi and Emacs allow shell escapes that might bypass the restricted shell entirely.

Used wisely it can be a valuable additional layer of security, but it should not be the only layer.

Note that the original Bourne shell has a restricted version called *rsh*, which may be confused with the so-called r-tools (*rsh*, *rcp*, *rlogin*, etc.) Remote Shell program, which is also *rsh*. The very insecure Remote Shell *rsh* has been mostly replaced (we most sincerely hope) by SSH (the Secure Shell).

See Also

- Recipe 14.17, "Using chroot Jails"
- Recipe 14.21, "Using SSH Without a Password"

14.17 Using chroot Jails

Problem

You have to use a script or application that you don't trust.

Solution

Consider placing it in a so-called *chroot jail*. The *chroot* command changes the root directory of the current process to the directory you specify, then returns a shell or *exec*'s a given command. That has the effect of placing the process, and thus the program, into a jail from which it theoretically can't escape to the parent directory. So if that application is compromised or otherwise does something malicious, it can only affect the small portion of the file system you restricted it to. In conjunction with running as a user with very limited rights, this is a very useful layer of security to add.

Unfortunately, covering all the details of *chroot* is beyond the scope of this recipe, since it would probably require a whole separate book. We present it here to promote awareness of the functionality.

Discussion

So why doesn't everything run in *chroot* jails? Because many applications need to interact with other applications, files, directories, or sockets all over the file system. That's the tricky part about using *chroot* jails; the application can't see outside of its walls, so everything it needs must be inside those walls. The more complicated the application, the more difficult it is to run in a jail.

Some applications that must inherently be exposed to the Internet, such as DNS (e.g., BIND), web, and mail (e.g., Postfix) servers, may be configured to run in *chroot* jails with varying degrees of difficulty. See the documentation for the distribution and specific applications you are running for details.

Another interesting use of *chroot* is during system recovery. Once you have booted from a Live CD and mounted the root filesystem on your hard drive, you may need to run a tool such as Lilo or Grub which, depending on your configuration, might need to believe it's really running onto the damaged system. If the Live CD and the installed system are not too different, you can usually *chroot* into the mount point of the damaged system and fix it. That works because all the tools, libraries, configuration files, and devices already exist in the jail, since they really are a complete (if not quite working) system. You might have to experiment with your $PATH in order to find things you need once you've chrooted though (that's an aspect of the "if the Live CD and the installed system are not too different" caveat).

On a related note, the NSA's Security Enhanced Linux (SELinux) implementation of Mandatory Access Controls (MAC) may be of interest. MAC provides a very granular way to specify at a system level what is and is not allowed, and how various components of the system may interact. The granular definition is called a *security policy* and it has a similar effect to a jail, in that a given application or process can do only what the policy allows it to do.

Red Hat Linux has incorporated SELinux into its enterprise product. Novell's SUSE product has a similar MAC implementation called AppArmor, and there are similar implementations for Solaris, BSD, and OS X.

See Also

- man chroot
- *http://www.nsa.gov/selinux/*
- *http://en.wikipedia.org/wiki/Mandatory_access_control*
- *http://olivier.sessink.nl/jailkit/*
- *http://www.jmcresearch.com/projects/jail/*

14.18 Running As a Non-root User

Problem

You'd like to run your scripts as a non-*root* user, but are afraid you won't be able to do the things you need to do.

Solution

Run your scripts under non-*root* user IDs, either as you or as dedicated users, and run interactively as non-*root*, but configure *sudo* to handle any tasks that require elevated privileges.

Discussion

sudo may be used in a script as easily as it may be used interactively. See the sudoers NOPASSWD option especially. See Recipe 14.19, "Using sudo More Securely."

See Also

- man sudo
- man sudoers
- Recipe 14.15, "Writing setuid or setgid Scripts"
- Recipe 14.19, "Using sudo More Securely"
- Recipe 14.20, "Using Passwords in Scripts"
- Recipe 17.15, "Using sudo on a Group of Commands"

14.19 Using sudo More Securely

Problem

You want to use *sudo* but are worried about granting too many people too many privileges.

Solution

Good! You should be worrying about security. While using *sudo* is much more secure than not using it, the default settings may be greatly improved.

Take the time to learn a bit about *sudo* itself and the */etc/sudoers* file. In particular, learn that in most cases you should not be using the ALL=(ALL) ALL specification! Yes, that will work, but it's not even remotely secure. The only difference between that and just giving everyone the *root* password is that they don't know the *root* password. They can still do everything *root* can do. *sudo* logs the commands it runs, but that's trivial to avoid by using sudo bash.

Second, give your needs some serious thought. Just as you shouldn't be using the ALL=(ALL) ALL specification, you probably shouldn't be managing users one by one either. The *sudoers* utility allows for very granular management and we strongly recommend using it. man sudoers provides a wealth of material and examples, especially the section on preventing shell escapes.

sudoers allows for four kinds of aliases: user, runas, host, and command. Judicious use of them as roles or groups will significantly reduce the maintenance burden. For instance, you can set up a User_Alias for *BUILD_USERS*, then define the machines those users need to run on with Host_Alias and the commands they need to run with Cmnd_Alias. If you set a policy to only edit */etc/sudoers* on one machine and copy it around to all relevant machines periodically using *scp* with public-key authentication, you can set up a very secure yet usable system of least privilege.

 When *sudo* asks for your password, it's really asking for your password. As in, your user account. Not *root*. For some reason people often get confused by this at first.

Discussion

Unfortunately, *sudo* is not installed by default on every system. It is usually installed on Linux and OpenBSD; other systems will vary. You should consult your system documentation and install it if it's not already there.

 You should always use *visudo* to edit your */etc/sudoers* file. Like *vipw*, *visudo* locks the file so that only one person can edit it at a time, and it performs some syntax sanity checks before replacing the production file so that you don't accidentally lock yourself out of your system.

See Also

- man sudo
- man sudoers
- man visudo
- *SSH, The Secure Shell: The Definitive Guide* by Daniel J. Barrett (O'Reilly)
- Recipe 14.15, "Writing setuid or setgid Scripts"
- Recipe 14.18, "Running As a Non-root User"
- Recipe 14.20, "Using Passwords in Scripts"
- Recipe 17.15, "Using sudo on a Group of Commands"

14.20 Using Passwords in Scripts

Problem

You need to hardcode a password in a script.

Solution

This is obviously a bad idea and should be avoided whenever possible. Unfortunately, sometimes it isn't possible to avoid it.

The first way to try to avoid doing this is to see if you can use *sudo* with the NOPASSWD option to avoid having to hardcode a password anywhere. This obviously has its own risks, but is worth checking out. See Recipe 14.19, "Using sudo More Securely" for more details.

Another alternative may be to use SSH with public keys and ideally restricted commands. See Recipe 14.21, "Using SSH Without a Password."

If there is no other way around it, about the best you can do is put the user ID and password in a separate file that is readable only by the user who needs it, then source that file when necessary (Recipe 10.3, "Using Configuration Files in a Script"). Leave that file out of revision control, of course.

Discussion

Accessing data on remote machines in a secure manner is relatively easy using SSH (see Recipe 14.21, "Using SSH Without a Password" and Recipe 15.11, "Getting Input from Another Machine"). It may even be possible to use that SSH method to access other data on the same host, but it's probably much more efficient to use *sudo* for that. But what about accessing data in a remote database, perhaps using some SQL command? There is not much you can do in that case.

Yes, you say, but what about *crypt* or the other password hashes? The problem is that the secure methods for storing passwords all involve using what's known as a one-way hash. The password checks in, but it can't check out. In other words, given the hash, there is theoretically no way to get the plain-text password back out. And that plain-text password is the point—we need it to access our database or whatever. So secure storage is out.

That leaves insecure storage, but the problem here is that it may actually be worse than plain text because it might give you a false sense of security. If it really makes you feel better, and you promise not to get a false sense of security, go ahead and use ROT13 or something to obfuscate the password. ROT13 only handles ASCII letters, so you could also use ROT47 to handle some punctuation as well.

```
$ ROT13=$(echo password | tr 'A-Za-z' 'N-ZA-Mn-za-m')
```

```
$ ROT47=$(echo password | tr '!-~' 'P-~!-O')
```

We really can't stress enough that ROT13 or ROT47 are nothing more than "security by obscurity" and thus are not security at all. They are better than nothing, if and only if, you (or your management) do not get a false sense that you are "secure" when you are not. Just be aware of your risks. Having said that, the reality is, sometimes the benefit outweighs the risk.

See Also

- *http://en.wikipedia.org/wiki/ROT13*
- Recipe 10.3, "Using Configuration Files in a Script"
- Recipe 14.15, "Writing setuid or setgid Scripts"
- Recipe 14.18, "Running As a Non-root User"
- Recipe 14.19, "Using sudo More Securely"
- Recipe 14.21, "Using SSH Without a Password"
- Recipe 15.11, "Getting Input from Another Machine"
- Recipe 17.15, "Using sudo on a Group of Commands"

14.21 Using SSH Without a Password

Problem

You need to use SSH or *scp* in a script and would like to do so without using a password. Or you're using them in a *cron* job and can't have a password.[*]

SSH1 (the protocol) and SSH1 (the executables) are deprecated and considered less secure than the newer SSH2 protocol as implemented by OpenSSH and SSH Communications Security. We strongly recommend using SSH2 with OpenSSH and will not cover SSH1 here.

Solution

There are two ways to use SSH without a password, the wrong way and the right way. The wrong way is to use a public-key that is not encrypted by a passphrase. The right way is to use a passphrase protected public-key with *ssh-agent* or *keychain*.

We assume you are using OpenSSH; if not, consult your documentation (the commands and files will be similar).

---

[*] We thank Richard Silverman and Daniel Barrett for their inspiration and excellent work in *SSH, The Secure Shell: The Definitive Guide* (especially Chapters 2, 6, and 11) and *Linux Security Cookbook*, without which this recipe would be a mere shadow of itself.

First, you need to create a key pair if you don't already have one. Only one key pair is necessary to authenticate you to as many machines as you configure, but you may decide to use more than one key pair, perhaps for personal and work reasons. The pair consists of a *private key* that you should protect at all costs, and a *public key* (*.pub*) that you can post on a billboard if you like. The two are related in a complex mathematical way such that they can identify each other, but you can't derive one from the other.

Use *ssh-keygen* (might be *ssh-keygen2* if you're not using OpenSSH) to create a key pair. -t is mandatory and its arguments are rsa or dsa. -b is optional and specifies the number of bits in the new key (1024 is the default at the time of this writing). -C allows you to specify a comment, but it defaults to *user@hostname* if you omit it. We recommend at least using -t dsa -b 2048 and we recommend strongly against using no passphrase. *ssh-keygen* also allows you to change your key file's passphrase or comment.

```
$ ssh-keygen
You must specify a key type (-t).
Usage: ssh-keygen [options]
Options:
  -b bits     Number of bits in the key to create.
  -c          Change comment in private and public key files.
  -e          Convert OpenSSH to IETF SECSH key file.
  -f filename Filename of the key file.
  -g          Use generic DNS resource record format.
  -i          Convert IETF SECSH to OpenSSH key file.
  -l          Show fingerprint of key file.
  -p          Change passphrase of private key file.
  -q          Quiet.
  -y          Read private key file and print public key.
  -t type     Specify type of key to create.
  -B          Show bubblebabble digest of key file.
  -H          Hash names in known_hosts file
  -F hostname Find hostname in known hosts file
  -C comment  Provide new comment.
  -N phrase   Provide new passphrase.
  -P phrase   Provide old passphrase.
  -r hostname Print DNS resource record.
  -G file     Generate candidates for DH-GEX moduli
  -T file     Screen candidates for DH-GEX moduli

$ ssh-keygen -t dsa -b 2048 -C 'This is my new key'
Generating public/private dsa key pair.
Enter file in which to save the key (/home/jp/.ssh/id_dsa):
Enter passphrase (empty for no passphrase):
Enter same passphrase again:
Your identification has been saved in /home/jp/.ssh/id_dsa.
Your public key has been saved in /home/jp/.ssh/id_dsa.pub.
The key fingerprint is:
84:6f:45:fc:08:3b:ce:b2:4f:2e:f3:5e:b6:9f:65:63 This is my new key
```

```
$ ls -l id_dsa*
-rw-------  1 jp   jp   1264 Dec 13 23:39 id_dsa
-rw-r--r--  1 jp   jp   1120 Dec 13 23:39 id_dsa.pub

$ cat id_dsa.pub
ssh-dss
AAAAB3NzaC1kc3MAAAEBANpgvvTslst2moZJA0ayhh1Mqa3aWwU3kfvOm9+myFZ9veFsxM7IVxIjWfAlQh3jp
lY+Q78fMzCTiG+ZrGZYn8adZ9yg5/
wACO3KXm2vKt8LfTx6I+qkMR7v15NI7tZyhxGah5qHNehReFWLuk7JXCtRrzRvWMdsHc/
L2SA1Y4fJ9Y9FfVlBdE1Er+ZIuc5xIlO6D1HFjKjt3wjbAal+oJxwZJaupZOQ7N47uwMslmc5ELQBRNDsaoqF
RKlerZASPQ5P+AH/+Cxa/fCGYwsogXSJJOH5S7+QJJHFze35YZI/
+A1D3BIa4JBf1KvtoaFr5bMdhVAkChdAdMjo96xhbdEAAAAVAJSKzCEsrUo3KAvyUO8KVD6eOB/NAAAA/3u/
Ax2TIB/M9MmPqjeH67Mh5Y5NaVWuMqwebDIXuvKQQDMUU4EPjRGmS89Hl8UKANOCq/C1T+OGzn4zrbEO6CO/
Sm3SRMP24HyIbElhlWV49sfLRO5Qmh9fRl1s7ZdcUrxkDkr2J6on5cMVB9M2nIl9OIhRVLd5RxPO1u81yqvhv
E610RdA6IMjzXcQ8ebuD2R733037oGFD7e2O7DaabKKkHZIduL/zFbQkzMDK6uAMP8ylRJNOfUsqIhHhtc//
16OT2H6nMUO9MccxZTFUfqF8xIOndElP6um4jXYk5Q30i/CtU3TZyvNeWVwyGwDi4wg2jeVeOYHU2Rh/
ZcZpwAAAQEAv2O86701U9sIuRijp8sO4h13eZrsE5rdn6aul/mkm+xAlO+WQeDXR/
ONm9BwVSrNEmIJB74tEJL3qQTMEFoCoN9KpOOYa7Qt8n4gZOvcZlI5u+cgyd1mKaggS2SnoorsRlb2Lh/
Hpe6mXus8pUTf5QT8apgXM3TgFsLDT+3rCt40IdGCZLaP+UDBuNUSKfFwCru6uGoXEwxaLO8Nv1wZOc19qrcO
Yzp7i33m6i3aOZ9Pu+TPHqYC74QmBbWq8U9DAo+7yhRIhq/
fdJzk3vIKSLbCxg4PbMwx2Qfh4dLk+L7wOasKnl5//W+RWBUrOlaZ1ZP1/azsKONcygno/OF1ew== This is
my new key
```

Once you have a key pair, add your public key to the *~/.ssh/authorized_keys* file in your home directory on any other machines to which you wish to connect using this key pair. You can use *scp*, *cp* with a floppy or USB key, or simple cut-and-paste from terminal sessions to do that. The important part is that it all ends up on a single line. While you can do it all in one command (e.g., scp id_dsa.pub remote_host:.ssh/ authorized_keys), we don't recommend that even when you're "absolutely sure" that *authorized_keys* doesn't exist. Instead, you can use a slightly more complicated but much safer command, shown in bold:

```
$ ssh remote_host "echo $(cat ~/.ssh/id_dsa.pub) >> ~/.ssh/authorized_keys"
jp@remote_host's password:

$ ssh remote_host
Last login: Thu Dec 14 00:02:52 2006 from openbsd.jpsdomai
NetBSD 2.0.2 (GENERIC) #0: Wed Mar 23 08:53:42 UTC 2005

Welcome to NetBSD!

-bash-3.00$ exit
logout
Connection to remote_host closed.
```

As you can see, we were prompted for a password for the initial *scp*, but after that *ssh* just worked. What isn't shown above is the use of the *ssh-agent*, which cached the passphrase to the key so that we didn't have to type it.

The command above also assumes that *~/.ssh* exists on both machines. If not, create it using mkdir -m 0700 -p ~/.ssh. Your *~/.ssh* directory must be mode 0700 or OpenSSH will complain. It's not a bad idea to use chmod 0600 ~/.ssh/authorized_keys as well.

It's also worth noting that we've just set up a one-way relationship. We can SSH from our local host to our remote host with no password, but the same is not true in reverse, due to both lack of the private key and lack of the agent on the remote host. You can simply copy your private key all over the place to enable a "web of passwordless SSH," but that complicates matters when you want to change your passphrase and it makes it harder to secure your private key. If possible, you are better off having one well protected and trusted machine from which you ssh out to remote hosts as needed.

The SSH agent is clever and subtle in its use. We might argue it's too clever. The way it is intended to be used in practice is via an *eval* and command substitution: eval `ssh-agent`. That creates two environment variables so that *ssh* or *scp* can find the agent and ask it about your identities. That's very slick, and it's well documented in many places. The only problem is that this is unlike any other program in common use (except some of the features of less, see Recipe 8.15, "Doing More with less")and is totally obtuse to a new or uninformed user.

If you just run the agent, it prints out some details and looks like it worked. And it did, in that it's now running. But it won't actually do anything, because the necessary environment variables were never actually set. We should also mention in passing that the handy -k switch tells the agent to exit.

```
# The Wrong Way to use the Agent

# Nothing in the environment
$ set | grep SSH
$
$ ssh-agent
SSH_AUTH_SOCK=/tmp/ssh-bACKp27592/agent.27592; export SSH_AUTH_SOCK;
SSH_AGENT_PID=24809; export SSH_AGENT_PID;
echo Agent pid 24809;

# Still nothing
$ set | grep SSH
$
# Can't even kill it, because -k needs $SSH_AGENT_PID
$ ssh-agent -k
SSH_AGENT_PID not set, cannot kill agent

# Is it even running?  Yes
$ ps x
  PID TT   STAT       TIME COMMAND
24809 ??   Is      0:00.01 ssh-agent
22903 p0   I       0:03.05 -bash (bash)
11303 p0   R+      0:00.00 ps -x

$ kill 24809

$ ps x
  PID TT   STAT       TIME COMMAND
```

```
22903 p0  I         0:03.06 -bash (bash)
30542 p0  R+        0:00.00 ps -x


# Still the Wrong Way to use the Agent
This is correct
$ eval `ssh-agent`
Agent pid 21642

# Hey, it worked!
$ set | grep SSH
SSH_AGENT_PID=21642
SSH_AUTH_SOCK=/tmp/ssh-ZfEsa28724/agent.28724

# Kill it - The wrong way
$ ssh-agent -k
unset SSH_AUTH_SOCK;
unset SSH_AGENT_PID;
echo Agent pid 21642 killed;

# Oops, the process is dead but it didn't clean up after itself
$ set | grep SSH
SSH_AGENT_PID=21642
SSH_AUTH_SOCK=/tmp/ssh-ZfEsa28724/agent.28724


# The Right Way to use the Agent
$ eval `ssh-agent`
Agent pid 19330

$ set | grep SSH
SSH_AGENT_PID=19330
SSH_AUTH_SOCK=/tmp/ssh-fwxMfj4987/agent.4987

$ eval `ssh-agent -k`
Agent pid 19330 killed

$ set | grep SSH
$
```

Intuitive isn't it? Not. Very slick, very efficient, very subtle, yes. User friendly, not so much.

OK, so once we have the agent running as expected we have to load our identities using the *ssh-add* command. That's very easy, we just run it, optionally with a list of key files to load. It will prompt for all the passphrases needed. In this example we did not list any keys, so it just used the default as set in the main SSH configuration file:

```
$ ssh-add
Enter passphrase for /home/jp/.ssh/id_dsa:
Identity added: /home/jp/.ssh/id_dsa (/home/jp/.ssh/id_dsa)
```

So now we can use SSH interactively, in this particular shell session, to log in to any machine we've previously configured, without a password or passphrase. So what about other sessions, scripts, or cron?

Use Daniel Robbins' *keychain* (*http://www.gentoo.org/proj/en/keychain/*) script, which:

> [acts] as a front-end to ssh-agent, allowing you to easily have one long-running ssh-agent process per system, rather than per login session. This dramatically reduces the number of times you need to enter your passphrase from once per new login session to once every time your local machine is rebooted.
>
> [...]
>
> keychain also provides a clean, secure way for cron jobs to take advantage of RSA/DSA keys without having to use insecure unencrypted private keys.

keychain is a clever, well-written and well-commented shell script that automates and manages the otherwise tedious process of exporting those environment variables we discussed above into other sessions. It also makes them available to scripts and *cron*. But you're probably saying to yourself, wait a second here, you want me to leave all my keys in this thing forever, until the machine reboots? Well, yes, but it's not as bad as it sounds.

First of all, you can always kill it, though that will also prevent scripts or *cron* from using it. Second, there is a --clean option that flushes cached keys when you log in. Sound backward? It actually makes sense. Here are the details, from *keychain's* author (first published by IBM developerWorks at *http://www.ibm.com/developerworks/*, see *http://www.ibm.com/developerworks/linux/library/l-keyc2/*):

> I explained that using unencrypted private keys is a dangerous practice, because it allows someone to steal your private key and use it to log in to your remote accounts from any other system without supplying a password. Well, while keychain isn't vulnerable to this kind of abuse (as long as you use encrypted private keys, that is), there is a potentially exploitable weakness directly related to the fact that keychain makes it so easy to "hook in" to a long-running ssh-agent process. What would happen, I thought, if some intruder were somehow able to figure out my password or passphrase and log into my local system? If they were somehow able to log in under my username, keychain would grant them instant access to my decrypted private keys, making it a no-brainer for them to access my other accounts.
>
> Now, before I continue, let's put this security threat in perspective. If some malicious user were somehow able to log in as me, keychain would indeed allow them to access my remote accounts. Yet, even so, it would be very difficult for the intruder to steal my decrypted private keys since they are still encrypted on disk. Also, gaining access to my private keys would require a user to actually log in as me, not just read files in my directory. So, abusing ssh-agent would be a much more difficult task than simply stealing an unencrypted private key, which only requires that an intruder somehow gain access to my files in ~/.ssh, whether logged in as me or not. Nevertheless, if an intruder were successfully able to log in as me, they could do quite a bit of additional damage by using my decrypted private keys. So, if you happen to be using keychain on a server that you don't log into very often or don't actively monitor for security breaches, then consider using the --clear option to provide an additional layer of security.

The --clear option allows you to tell keychain to assume that every new login to your account should be considered a potential security breach until proven otherwise. When you start keychain with the --clear option, keychain immediately flushes all your private keys from ssh-agent's cache when you log in, before performing its normal duties. Thus, if you're an intruder, keychain will prompt you for passphrases rather than giving you access to your existing set of cached keys. However, even though this enhances security, it does make things a bit more inconvenient and very similar to running ssh-agent all by itself, without keychain. Here, as is often the case, one can opt for greater security or greater convenience, but not both.

Despite this, using keychain with --clear still has advantages over using ssh-agent all by itself; remember, when you use keychain --clear, your cron jobs and scripts will still be able to establish passwordless connections; this is because your private keys are flushed at login, not logout. Since a logout from the system does not constitute a potential security breach, there's no reason for keychain to respond by flushing ssh-agent's keys. Thus, the --clear option is an ideal choice for infrequently accessed servers that need to perform occasional secure copying tasks, such as backup servers, firewalls, and routers.

To actually use the *keychain*-wrapped *ssh-agent* from a script or *cron*, simply source the file *keychain* creates from your script. *keychain* can also handle GPG keys:

```
[ -r ~/.ssh-agent ] && source ~/.ssh-agent \
|| { echo "keychain not runnin" >&2 ; exit 1; }
```

Discussion

When using SSH in a script, you don't want to be prompted to authenticate or have extraneous warnings displayed. The -q option will turn on quiet mode and suppress warnings, while -o 'BatchMode yes' will prevent user prompts. Obviously if there is no way for SSH to authenticate itself, it will fail, since it can't even fall back to prompting for a password. But that shouldn't be a problem since you've made it this far in this recipe.

SSH is an amazing, wonderful tool and there is a lot to it, so much that it fills another book about this size. We highly recommend *SSH, The Secure Shell: The Definitive Guide* by Richard E. Silverman and Daniel J. Barrett (O'Reilly) and for everything you ever wanted to know (and more) about SSH.

Using public keys between OpenSSH and SSH2 Server from SSH Communications Security can be tricky; see Chapter 6 in *Linux Security Cookbook* by Daniel J. Barrett et al. (O'Reilly).

The IBM developerWorks articles on SSH by *keychain* author (and Gentoo Chief Architect) Daniel Robbins are also a great reference (*http://www.ibm.com/developerworks/linux/library/l-keyc.html*, *http://www.ibm.com/developerworks/linux/library/l-keyc2/*, *http://www.ibm.com/developerworks/linux/library/l-keyc3/*).

If *keychain* doesn't seem to be working, or if it works for a while then seems to stop, you may have another script somewhere else re-running *ssh-agent* and getting things out of sync. Check the following and make sure the PIDs and socket all agree.

Depending on your operating system, you may have to adjust your *ps* command; if
-ef doesn't work, try -eu.

```
$ ps -ef | grep [s]sh-agent
jp        17364  0.0  0.0  3312 1132 ?          S    Dec16    0:00 ssh-agent

$ cat ~/.keychain/$HOSTNAME-sh
SSH_AUTH_SOCK=/tmp/ssh-UJc17363/agent.17363; export SSH_AUTH_SOCK;
SSH_AGENT_PID=17364; export SSH_AGENT_PID;

$ set | grep SSH_A
SSH_AGENT_PID=17364
SSH_AUTH_SOCK=/tmp/ssh-UJc17363/agent.17363
```

Key Fingerprints

All flavors of SSH support fingerprints to facilitate key comparison and verification for
both user and host keys. As you may guess, bit-by-bit verification of long, seemingly
random data is tedious and error prone at best, and virtually impossible (say, over the
phone) at worst. Fingerprints provide an easier way to perform this verification. You
may have seen fingerprints in other applications, especially PGP/GPG keys.

The reason to verify keys in the first place is to prevent so-called *man in the middle*
attacks. If Alice sends her key to Bob, he must make sure that the key he receives is
actually from Alice, and that Eve has not intercepted it and sent her own key instead.
This requires an out-of-band communications channel, such as a telephone.

There are two fingerprint formats, the traditional hex format from PGP and a newer,
supposedly easier to read format called *bubblebabble*. When Bob receives Alice's key,
he calls her up and reads her the fingerprint. If they match, they both know he has the
correct key.

```
$ ssh-keygen -l -f ~/.ssh/id_dsa
2048 84:6f:45:fc:08:3b:ce:b2:4f:2e:f3:5e:b6:9f:65:63 /home/jp/.ssh/id_dsa.pub

$ ssh-keygen -l -f ~/.ssh/id_dsa.pub
2048 84:6f:45:fc:08:3b:ce:b2:4f:2e:f3:5e:b6:9f:65:63 /home/jp/.ssh/id_dsa.pub

$ ssh-keygen -B -f ~/.ssh/id_dsa
2048 xosev-kytit-rakyk-tipos-bocuh-kotef-mupyc-hozok-zalip-pezad-nuxox /home/
jp/.ssh/id_dsa.pub

$ ssh-keygen -B -f ~/.ssh/id_dsa.pub
2048 xosev-kytit-rakyk-tipos-bocuh-kotef-mupyc-hozok-zalip-pezad-nuxox /home/
jp/.ssh/id_dsa.pub
```

See Also

- *http://www.gentoo.org/proj/en/keychain/*
- *http://www.ibm.com/developerworks/linux/library/l-keyc2/*

- *SSH, The Secure Shell: The Definitive Guide* by Richard E. Silverman and Daniel J. Barrett (O'Reilly)
- *Linux Security Cookbook* by Daniel J. Barrett et al. (O'Reilly)
- *Practical Cryptography* by Niels Ferguson and Bruce Schneier (Wiley)
- *Applied Cryptography* by Bruce Schneier (Wiley)
- Recipe 8.15, "Doing More with less"

14.22 Restricting SSH Commands

Problem

You'd like to restrict what an incoming SSH user or script can do.[*]

Solution

Edit the *~/.ssh/authorized_keys* file, use SSH *forced commands*, and optionally disable unnecessary SSH features. For example, suppose you want to allow an *rsync* process without also allowing interactive use.

First, you need to figure out exactly what command is being run on the remote side. Create a key (Recipe 14.21, "Using SSH Without a Password") and add a forced command to tell you. Edit the *~/.ssh/authorized_keys* file and add:

```
command="/bin/echo Command was: $SSH_ORIGINAL_COMMAND"
```

before the key. It will look something like this, all on one line:

```
command="/bin/echo Command was: $SSH_ORIGINAL_COMMAND" ssh-dss
AAAAB3NzaC1kc3MAAAEBANpgvvTslst2mOZJAOayhh1Mqa3aWwU3kfvOm9+myFZ9veFsxM7IVxIjWfAlQh3jp
lY+Q78fMzCTiG+ZrGZYn8adZ9yg5/
wACO3KXm2vKt8LfTx6I+qkMR7v15NI7tZyhxGah5qHNehReFWLuk7JXCtRrzRvWMdsHc/
L2SA1Y4fJ9Y9FfVlBdE1Er+ZIuc5xIl06D1HFjKjt3wjbAal+oJxwZJaupZOQ7N47uwMslmc5ELQBRNDsaoqF
RKlerZASPQ5P+AH/+Cxa/fCGYwsogXSJJOH5S7+QJJHFze35YZI/
+A1D3BIa4JBf1KvtoaFr5bMdhVAkChdAdMjo96xhbdEAAAAVAJSKzCEsrUo3KAvyUO8KVD6eOB/NAAAA/3u/
Ax2TIB/M9MmPqjeH67Mh5Y5NaVWuMqwebDIXuvKQQDMUU4EPjRGmS89Hl8UKANOCq/C1T+OGzn4zrbEO6CO/
Sm3SRMP24HyIbElhlWV49sfLROSQmh9fRl1s7ZdcUrxkDkr2J6on5cMVB9M2nIl9OIhRVLd5RxPO1u81yqvhv
E610RdA6IMjzXcQ8ebuD2R733O37oGFD7e2O7DaabKKkHZIduL/zFbQkzMDK6uAMP8ylRJNOfUsqIhHhtc//
16OT2H6nMUO9MccxZTFUfqF8xIOndElP6um4jXYk5Q30i/CtU3TZyvNeWVwyGwDi4wg2jeVeOYHU2Rh/
ZcZpwAAAQEAv2086701U9sIuRijp8sO4h13eZrsE5rdn6aul/mkm+xAlO+WQeDXR/
ONm9BwVSrNEmIJB74tEJL3qQTMEFoCoN9KpOOYa7Qt8n4gZOvcZlI5u+cgyd1mKaggS2SnoorsRlb2Lh/
Hpe6mXus8pUTf5QT8apgXM3TgFsLDT+3rCt4OIdGCZLaP+UDBuNUSKfFwCru6uGoXEwxaLO8Nv1wZOc19qrcO
Yzp7i33m6i3aOZ9Pu+TPHqYC74QmBbWq8U9DAo+7yhRIhq/
fdJzk3vIKSLbCxg4PbMwx2Qfh4dLk+L7wOasKnl5//W+RWBUrOlaZ1ZP1/azsKONcygno/OF1ew== This is
my new key
```

---

[*] We thank Richard Silverman and Daniel Barrett for their inspiration and excellent work in *SSH, The Secure Shell: The Definitive Guide* (especially Chapters 2, 6, and 11) and *Linux Security Cookbook* without which this recipe would be a mere shadow of itself.

Now execute your command and see what the result is.

```
$ ssh remote_host 'ls -l /etc'
Command was: ls -l /etc
```

Now, the problem with this approach is that it will break a program like *rsync* that depends on having the STDOUT/STDIN channel all to itself.

```
$ rsync -avzL -e ssh remote_host:/etc .
protocol version mismatch -- is your shell clean?
(see the rsync man page for an explanation)
rsync error: protocol incompatibility (code 2) at compat.c(64)
```

But we can work around that by modifying our forced command as follows:

```
command="/bin/echo Command was: $SSH_ORIGINAL_COMMAND >> ~/ssh_command"
```

So on the client side we try again:

```
$ rsync -avzL -e ssh 192.168.99.56:/etc .
rsync: connection unexpectedly closed (0 bytes received so far) [receiver]
rsync error: error in rsync protocol data stream (code 12) at io.c(420)
```

And on the remote host side we now have:

```
$ cat ../ssh_command
Command was: rsync --server --sender -vlLogDtprz . /etc
```

So we can update our forced command as necessary.

Two other things we can do are to set a *from host restriction* and disable SSH commands. The host restriction specifies the hostname or IP address of the source host. Disabling commands is also pretty intuitive:

```
no-port-forwarding,no-X11-forwarding,no-agent-forwarding,no-pty
```

So when we put it all together, it looks like this (still all on one giant line):

```
no-port-forwarding,no-X11-forwarding,no-agent-forwarding,no-pty,from="local_
client",command="rsync --server --sender -vlLogDtprz . /etc" ssh-dss
AAAAB3NzaC1kc3MAAAEBANpgvvTslst2mOZJAOayhh1Mqa3aWwU3kfvOm9+myFZ9veFsxM7IVxIjWfAlQh3jp
lY+Q78fMzCTiG+ZrGZYn8adZ9yg5/
wACO3KXm2vKt8LfTx6I+qkMR7v15NI7tZyhxGah5qHNehReFWLuk7JXCtRrzRvWMdsHc/
L2SA1Y4fJ9Y9FfVlBdE1Er+ZIuc5xIlO6D1HFjKjt3wjbAal+oJxwZJaupZOQ7N47uwMslmc5ELQBRNDsaoqF
RKlerZASPQ5P+AH/+Cxa/fCGYwsogXSJJOH5S7+QJJHFze35YZI/
+A1D3BIa4JBf1KvtoaFr5bMdhVAkChdAdMjo96xhbdEAAAAVAJSKzCEsrUo3KAvyUO8KVD6eOB/NAAAA/3u/
Ax2TIB/M9MmPqjeH67Mh5Y5NaVWuMqwebDIXuvKQQDMUU4EPjRGmS89Hl8UKANOCq/C1T+OGzn4zrbEO6CO/
Sm3SRMP24HyIbElhlWV49sfLRO5Qmh9fRl1s7ZdcUrxkDkr2J6on5cMVB9M2nIl9OIhRVLd5RxPO1u81yqvhv
E61ORdA6IMjzXcQ8ebuD2R733037oGFD7e2O7DaabKKkHZIduL/zFbQkzMDK6uAMP8ylRJNOfUsqIhHhtc//
16OT2H6nMUO9MccxZTFUfqF8xIOndElP6um4jXYk5Q30i/CtU3TZyvNeWVwyGwDi4wg2jeVeOYHU2Rh/
ZcZpwAAAQEAv2086701U9sIuRijp8sO4h13eZrsE5rdn6aul/mkm+xAlO+WQeDXR/
ONm9BwVSrNEmIJB74tEJL3qQTMEFoCoN9KpOOYa7Qt8n4gZOvcZlI5u+cgyd1mKaggS2SnoorsRlb2Lh/
Hpe6mXus8pUTf5QT8apgXM3TgFsLDT+3rCt4OIdGCZLaP+UDBuNUSKfFwCru6uGoXEwxaLO8Nv1wZOc19qrcO
Yzp7i33m6i3aOZ9Pu+TPHqYC74QmBbWq8U9DAo+7yhRIhq/
fdJzk3vIKSLbCxg4PbMwx2Qfh4dLk+L7wOasKnl5//W+RWBUrOlaZ1ZP1/azsKONcygno/OF1ew== This is
my new key
```

Discussion

If you have any problems with *ssh*, the -v option is very helpful. `ssh -v` or `ssh -v -v` will almost always give you at least a clue about what's going wrong. Give them a try when things are working to get an idea of what their output looks like.

If you'd like to be a little more open about what the key can and can't do, look into the OpenSSH Restricted Shell *rssh* (*http://www.pizzashack.org/rssh/*), which supports *scp*, *sftp*, *rdist*, *rsync*, and *cvs*.

You'd think restrictions like these would be very easy, but it turns out they are not. The problem has to do with the way SSH (and the r-commands before it) actually work. It's a brilliant idea and it works very well, except that it's hard to limit. To vastly oversimplify it, you can think of SSH as connecting your local STDOUT to STDIN on the remote side and the remote STDOUT to your local STDIN. So all things like *scp* or *rsync* do is stream bytes from the local machine to the remote machine as if over a pipe. But that very flexibility precludes SSH from being able to restrict interactive access while allowing *scp*. There's no difference. And that's why you can't put lots of *echo* and debugging statements in your *bash* configuration files (see Recipe 16.19, "Creating Self-Contained, Portable RC Files"); that output will intermingle with the byte stream and cause havoc.

So how does *rssh* work? It provides a wrapper that you use instead of a default login shell (like *bash*) in */etc/passwd*. That wrapper determines what it will and will not allow, but with much more flexibility than a plain old SSH-restricted command.

See Also

- *SSH, The Secure Shell: The Definitive Guide* by Richard E. Silverman and Daniel J. Barrett (O'Reilly)
- *Linux Security Cookbook* by Daniel J. Barrett et al. (O'Reilly)
- Recipe 14.21, "Using SSH Without a Password"
- Recipe 16.19, "Creating Self-Contained, Portable RC Files"

14.23 Disconnecting Inactive Sessions

Problem

You'd like to be able to automatically log out inactive users, especially *root*.

Solution

Set the $TMOUT environment variable in */etc/bashrc* or *~/.bashrc* to the number of seconds of inactivity before ending the session. In interactive mode, once a prompt is issued, if the user does not enter a command in $TMOUT seconds, *bash* will exit.

Discussion

$TMOUT is also used in the read built-in and the select command in scripts.

Don't forget to set this as a read-only variable in a system-level file such as */etc/profile* or */etc/bashrc* to which users have no write access if you don't want them to be able to change it.

```
declare -r TMOUT=3600

# Or:
readonly TMOUT=3600
```

 Since the user has control over their own environment, you cannot totally rely on $TMOUT, even if you set it as read-only, since the user could just run a different shell. Think of it as a helpful reminder to cooperative users, especially knowledgeable and interrupt-driven system administrators who may get distracted (constantly).

See Also

- Recipe 16.19, "Creating Self-Contained, Portable RC Files"

CHAPTER 15
Advanced Scripting

Unix and POSIX have long promised compatibility and portability, and long struggled to deliver it; thus, one of the biggest problems for advanced scripters is writing scripts that are *portable*, i.e., that can work on any machine that has *bash* installed. Writing scripts that run well on a wide variety of platforms is much more difficult than we wish it were. There are many variations from one system to another that can get in the way; for example, *bash* itself isn't always installed in the same place, and many common Unix commands have slightly different options (or give slightly different output) depending on the operating system. In this chapter, we'll look at several of those problems, and show you how to solve them.

Many of other things that are periodically needed are not as simple as we'd like them to be, either. So, we'll also cover solutions for additional advanced scripting tasks, such as automating processes using phases, sending email from your script, logging to syslog, using your network resources, and a few tricks for getting input and redirecting output.

Although this chapter is about advanced scripting, we'd like to stress the need for clear code, written as simply as possible, and documented. Brian Kernighan, one of the first Unix developers, put it well:

> Debugging is twice as hard as writing the code in the first place. Therefore, if you write the code as cleverly as possible, you are, by definition, not smart enough to debug it.

It's easy to write very clever shell scripts that are very difficult, if not impossible, to understand. The more clever you think you're being now, as you solve the *problem de jour*, the more you'll regret it 6, 12, or 18 months from now when you (or worse yet, someone else) have to figure out what you did and why it broke. If you have to be clever, at least document how the script works (see Recipe 5.1, "Documenting Your Script")!

15.1 Finding bash Portably for #!

Problem

You need to run a *bash* script on several machines, but *bash* is not always in the same place. See Recipe 1.11, "Getting bash for xBSD."

Solution

Use the */usr/bin/env* command in the shebang line, as in `#!/usr/bin/env bash`. If your system doesn't have *env* in */usr/bin*, ask your system administrator to install it, move it, or create a symbolic link because this is the required location. For example, Red Hat inexplicably uses */bin/env*, but they at least create a symlink to the correct location.

You could also create symbolic links for *bash* itself, but using *env* is the canonical and correct solution.

Discussion

env's purpose is to "run a program in a modified environment," but since it will search the path for the command it is given to run, it works very well for this use.

You may be tempted to use `#!/bin/sh` instead. Don't. If you are using *bash*-specific features in your script, they will not work on machines that do not use *bash* in Bourne shell mode for */bin/sh* (e.g., BSD, Solaris, Ubuntu 6.10+). And even if you aren't using *bash*-specific features now, you may forget about that in the future. If you are committed to using only POSIX features, by all means use `#!/bin/sh` (and don't develop on Linux, see Recipe 15.3, "Developing Portable Shell Scripts"), but otherwise be specific.

You may sometimes see a space between `#!` and `/bin/whatever`. Historically there were some systems that required the space, though in practice we haven't seen one in a long time. It's very unlikely any system running *bash* will require the space, and the lack of the space seems to be the most common usage now. But for the utmost historical compatibility, use the space.

We have chosen to use `#!/usr/bin/env bash` in the longer scripts and functions we've made available to download (see the end of the Preface for details), because that will run unchanged on most systems. However, since *env* uses the $PATH to find *bash*, this is arguably a security issue (see Recipe 14.2, "Avoiding Interpreter Spoofing"), albeit a minor one in our opinion.

Ironically, since we're trying to use *env* for portability, shebang line processing is not consistent across systems. Many, including Linux, allow only a single argument to the interpreter. Thus `#!/usr/bin/env bash -` will result in the error:

```
/usr/bin/env: bash -: No such file or directory
```

This is because the interpreter is `/usr/bin/env` and the single allowed argument is `bash -`. Other systems, such as BSD and Solaris, don't have this restriction.

Since the trailing - is a common security practice (see Recipe 14.2, "Avoiding Interpreter Spoofing") and since this is supported on some systems but not others, this is a security and portability problem.

You can use the trailing - for a tiny bit more security at a cost of portability, or omit it for portability at a cost of a tiny potential security risk. Since *env* is searching the path anyway, using it should probably be avoided if you have security concerns; thus the inability to portably use the trailing - is tolerable.

Therefore, our advice is to omit the trailing - when using *env* for portability, and to hard-code the interpreter and trailing - when security is critical.

See Also

- The following web pages for information on shebang (*/usr/bin/env*):
  - *http://srfi.schemers.org/srfi-22/mail-archive/msg00069.html*
  - *http://www.in-ulm.de/~mascheck/various/shebang/*
  - *http://homepages.cwi.nl/~aeb/std/hashexclam-1.html*
  - *http://www.faqs.org/faqs/unix-faq/faq/part3/*, section 3.16: Why do some scripts start with #! ... ?
- Recipe 1.11, "Getting bash for xBSD"
- Recipe 15.2, "Setting a POSIX $PATH"
- Recipe 15.3, "Developing Portable Shell Scripts"
- Recipe 15.6, "Using echo Portably"

15.2 Setting a POSIX $PATH

Problem

You are on a machine that provides older or proprietary tools (e.g., Solaris) and you need to set your PATH so that you get POSIX-compliant tools.

Solution

Use the *getconf* utility:

```
PATH=$(PATH=/bin:/usr/bin getconf PATH)
```

Here are some default and POSIX paths on several systems:

```
# Red Hat Enterprise Linux (RHEL) 4.3
$ echo $PATH
/usr/kerberos/bin:/usr/local/bin:/bin:/usr/bin:/usr/X11R6/bin:/home/$USER/bin

$ getconf PATH
/bin:/usr/bin


# Debian Sarge
$ echo $PATH
/usr/local/bin:/usr/bin:/bin:/usr/bin/X11:/usr/games

$ getconf PATH
/bin:/usr/bin


# Solaris 10
$ echo $PATH
/usr/bin:

$ getconf PATH
/usr/xpg4/bin:/usr/ccs/bin:/usr/bin:/opt/SUNWspro/bin


# OpenBSD 3.7
$ echo $PATH
/home/$USER/bin:/bin:/sbin:/usr/bin:/usr/sbin:/usr/X11R6/bin:/usr/local/bin:/usr/
local/sbin:/usr/games

$ getconf PATH
/usr/bin:/bin:/usr/sbin:/sbin:/usr/X11R6/bin:/usr/local/bin
```

Discussion

getconf reports various system configuration variables, so you can use it to set a default path. However, unless *getconf* itself is a built-in, you will need a minimal path to find it, hence the PATH=/bin:/usr/bin part of the solution.

In theory, the variable you use should be CS_PATH. In practice, PATH worked everywhere we tested while CS_PATH failed on the BSDs.

See Also

- *http://www.unixreview.com/documents/s=7781/uni1042138723500/*
- Recipe 9.11, "Finding a File Using a List of Possible Locations"

- Recipe 14.3, "Setting a Secure $PATH"
- Recipe 14.9, "Finding World-Writable Directories in Your $PATH"
- Recipe 14.10, "Adding the Current Directory to the $PATH"
- Recipe 16.3, "Change Your $PATH Permanently"
- Recipe 16.4, "Change Your $PATH Temporarily"
- Recipe 19.3, "Forgetting That the Current Directory Is Not in the $PATH"

15.3 Developing Portable Shell Scripts

Problem

You are writing a shell script that will need to run on multiple versions of multiple Unix or POSIX operating systems.

Solution

First, try using the *command* built-in with its -p option to find the POSIX version of *program*, e.g., in */usr/xpg4* or */usr/xpg6* on Solaris:

```
$ command -p program args
```

Then, if possible, find the oldest or least capable Unix machine and develop the script on that platform. If you aren't sure what the least capable platform is, use a BSD variant or Solaris (and the older a version you can find, the better).

Discussion

command -p uses a default path that is guaranteed to find all of the POSIX-standard utilities. If you're sure your script will only ever run on Linux (famous last words), then don't worry about it; otherwise, avoid developing cross-platform scripts on Linux or Windows (e.g., via Cygwin).

The problems with writing cross-platform shell scripts on Linux are:

1. */bin/sh* is not the Bourne shell, it's really */bin/bash* in Bourne mode, except when it's */bin/dash* (for example Ubuntu 6.10). Both are very good, but not perfect, and none of the three work exactly the same, which can be very confusing. In particular, the behavior of *echo* can change.
2. Linux uses the GNU tools instead of the original Unix tools.

Don't get us wrong, we love Linux and use it every day. But it isn't really Unix: it does some things differently, and it has the GNU tools. The GNU tools are great, and that's the problem. They have a lot of switches and features that aren't present on other platforms, and your script *will* break in odd ways no matter how careful you are about that. Conversely, Linux is so compatible with everything that scripts written for any other Unix-like systems will almost always run on it. They may not be perfect (e.g., *echo*'s default behavior is to display \n instead of printing a newline), but are often good enough.

There is an ironic Catch-22 here—the more shell features you use, the less you have to depend on external programs that may or may not be there or work as expected. While *bash* is far more capable than *sh*, it's also one of the tools that may or may not be there. Some form of *sh* will be on virtually any Unix or Unix-like system, but it isn't always quite what you think it is.

Another Catch-22 is that the GNU long options are much more readable in shell code, but are often not present on other systems. So instead of being able to say sort --field-separator=, unsorted_file > sorted_file, you have to use sort -t, unsorted_file > sorted_file for portability.

But take heart: developing on a non-Linux system is easier than it's ever been. If you already have and use such systems then this is obviously a nonissue. But if you don't have such systems in-house, it's now trivial to get them for free. Solaris and the BSDs all run in virtual environments such as the free VMware Player or Server, which run on Windows or Linux (and soon the Mac).

If you have a Mac running OS X, then you already have BSD—so you're all set.

You can also easily test scripts using a virtualization environment like VMware. See Recipe 15.4, "Testing Scripts in VMware." The flaw in this solution is the systems such as AIX and HP-UX that don't run on an x86 architecture, and thus don't run under VMware. Again, if you have these systems, use them. If not, see Recipe 1.15, "Getting bash Without Getting bash."

See Also

- help command
- *http://en.wikipedia.org/wiki/Debian_Almquist_shell*
- *http://en.wikipedia.org/wiki/Bash*
- *http://www.opensolaris.org/os/article/2006-02-27_getting_started_with_opensolaris_using_vmware/*
- *http://www.testdrive.hp.com/os/*
- *http://www.testdrive.hp.com/faq/*
- *http://www.polarhome.com/*
- *http://www.faqs.org/faqs/hp/hpux-faq/preamble.html*
- History of Unix, at *http://www.levenez.com/unix/*
- Recipe 1.15, "Getting bash Without Getting bash
- Recipe 15.4, "Testing Scripts in VMware
- Recipe 15.6, "Using echo Portably
- "echo Options and Escape Sequences" in Appendix A

15.4 Testing Scripts in VMware

Problem

You need to develop cross-platform scripts but do not have the appropriate systems or hardware.

Solution

If the target platforms run on the x86 architecture, download the free VMware Server and build your own. Or search for prebuilt virtual machines on the VMware site, the OS vendor or distributor's site, or the Internet.

The flaw in this solution is the systems such as AIX and HP-UX that don't run on an x86 architecture, and thus don't run under VMware. Again, if you have these systems, use them. If not, see the recipe Recipe 1.15, "Getting bash Without Getting bash."

Discussion

Testing shell scripts is usually not very resource intensive, so even moderate hardware capable of running VMware or a similar virtualization package should be fine. We mention VMware specifically because the Server and Player products are without cost, they run on Linux and Windows (and soon the Mac), and are very easy to use; but there are certainly other alternatives available.

If you install VMware Server on a Linux server, you don't even need the overhead of a GUI on the host machine—you can use the VNC-based VMware Console from another Linux or Windows machine with a GUI. Minimal virtual machines with 128 MB of RAM, or sometimes even less, should be more than enough for a shell environment for testing. Set up an NFS share to store your test scripts and data, and then simply telnet or ideally SSH to the test system.

To get you started, here's a trivial example using VMware player:

1. Get the free VMware Player for Windows or Linux from *http://www.vmware. com/player/*.
2. Get a pre-built virtual machine image:
   a. Ubuntu Linux 5.10 (Debian derivative), Firefox 1.0.7, and Gnome 2.12.1 form the basis for VMware's "Browser Appliance v1.0.0" (258M at *http:// www.vmware.com/vmtn/appliances/directory/browserapp.html*).
   b. PC-BSD is a BSD and KDE-based desktop distribution (609M at *http://www. pcbsd.org/?p=download#vmware*).
3. Unzip whichever one you selected and open it in Player, creating a new VMware UUID if prompted.

Once you boot, which takes a while, you will have either an Ubuntu 5.10 Gnome-based desktop with *bash* 3.0 or a BSD and KDE-based GUI desktop complete with *bash* 3.1 (as of this writing). You could also run two instances of Player (or run Server) and have both environments. Note these are both GUI distributions and so require much more memory and CPU time than a minimal shell-only install; thus, they are presented here as examples and quick and dirty solutions to get you started. Despite the overhead, they are useful in that they are "official" images rather than community-based images with widely variable code assurance and quality control.

 VMware's Browser Appliance has the VMware tools installed, while PC-BSD does not, so they will behave a little differently with respect to capturing and releasing your host machine's keyboard and mouse input. Pay careful attention to the bottom-left corner of Player's window for status.

Full details for the wide variety of VMware implementation possibilities are readily available via the VMware Forums and Google.

See Also

- *http://www.vmware.com/*
- *http://www.vmware.com/player/*
- *http://www.vmware.com/vmtn/appliances/*
- *http://www.vmware.com/support/ws55/doc/new_guest_tools_ws.html*
- *http://www.ubuntu.org/*
- *http://www.pcbsd.org/*
- Recipe 1.11, "Getting bash for xBSD"
- Recipe 1.15, "Getting bash Without Getting bash"

15.5   Using for Loops Portably

Problem

You need to do a for loop but want it to work on older versions of *bash*.

Solution

This method is portable back to *bash-2.04+*:

```
$ for ((i=0; i<10; i++)); do echo $i; done
0
1
2
3
```

```
4
5
6
7
8
9
```

Discussion

There are nicer ways of writing this loop in newer versions of *bash*, but they are not backwards compatible. As of *bash-3.0+* you can use the syntax for {x..y}, as in:

```
$ for i in {1..10}; do echo $i; done
1
2
3
4
5
6
7
8
9
10
```

If your system has the *seq* command, you could also do this:

```
$ for i in $(seq 1 10); do echo $i; done
1
2
3
4
5
6
7
8
9
10
```

See Also

- help for
- man seq
- Recipe 6.12, "Looping with a Count"
- Recipe 6.13, "Looping with Floating-Point Values"
- Recipe 17.22, "Writing Sequences"

15.6   Using echo Portably

Problem

You are writing a script that will run on multiple versions of Unix and Linux and you need *echo* to behave consistently even if it is not running on *bash*.

Solution

Use `printf "%b"` *whatever*, or test for the system and set `xpg_echo` using `shopt -s xpg_echo` as needed.

If you omit the `"%b"` format string (for example, `printf` *whatever*), then *printf* will try to interpret any % characters in *whatever*, which is probably not what you want. The `"%b"` format is an addition to the standard *printf* format that will prevent that misinterpretation and also expand backslash escape sequences in *whatever*.

Setting `xpg_echo` is less consistent since it only works on *bash*. It can be effective if you are sure that you'll only every run under *bash*, and not under *sh* or another similar shell that doesn't use xpg_echo.

Using *printf* requires changes to how you write echo statements, but it's defined by POSIX and should be consistent across any POSIX shell anywhere. Specifically, you have to write `printf "%b"` instead of just echo.

If you automatically type $b instead of %b you will be unhappy because that will print a blank line, since you have specified a null format. That is unless $b is actually defined, in which case the results depend on the value of $b. Either way, this can be a very difficult bug to find since $b and %b look very similar:

```
$ printf "%b" "Works"
Works

$ printf "$b" "Broken"

$
```

Discussion

In some shells, built-in *echo* behaves differently than the external *echo* used on other systems. This is not always obvious when running on Linux since */bin/sh* is actually *bash* (usually; it could also be *dash* on Ubuntu 6.10+), and there are similar circumstances on some BSDs. The difference is in how *echo* does or does not expand backslash-escape sequences. Shell built-in versions tend not to expand, while external versions (e.g., */bin/echo* and */usr/bin/echo*) tend to expand; but again, that can change from system to system.

Typical Linux (*/bin/bash*):

```
$ type -a echo
echo is a shell builtin
echo is /bin/echo

$ builtin echo "one\ttwo\nthree"
one\ttwo\nthree\n

$ /bin/echo "one\ttwo\nthree"
one\ttwo\nthree\n

$ echo -e "one\ttwo\nthree"
one  →  two
three

$ /bin/echo -e "one\ttwo\nthree"
one  →  two
three
```

$ shopt -s xpg_echo

```
$ builtin echo "one\ttwo\nthree"
one  →  two
three

$ shopt -u xpg_echo

$ builtin echo "one\ttwo\nthree"
one\ttwo\nthree\n
```

Typical BSD (*/bin/csh*, then */bin/sh*):

```
$ which echo
echo: shell built-in command.

$ echo "one\ttwo\nthree"
one\ttwo\nthree\n

$ /bin/echo "one\ttwo\nthree"
one\ttwo\nthree\n

$ echo -e "one\ttwo\nthree"
-e one\ttwo\nthree\n

$ /bin/echo -e "one\ttwo\nthree"
-e one\ttwo\nthree\n

$ printf "%b" "one\ttwo\nthree"
one  →  two
three
```

```
$ /bin/sh

$ echo "one\ttwo\nthree"
one\ttwo\nthree\n

$ echo -e "one\ttwo\nthree"
one  →  two
three

$ printf "%b" "one\ttwo\nthree"
one  →  two
three
```

Solaris 10 (/bin/sh):

```
$ which echo
/usr/bin/echo

$ type echo
echo is a shell builtin

$ echo "one\ttwo\nthree"
one  →    two
three

$ echo -e "one\ttwo\nthree"
-e one  →  two
three

$ printf "%b" "one\ttwo\nthree"
one  →  two
three
```

See Also

- help printf
- man 1 printf
- *http://www.opengroup.org/onlinepubs/009695399/functions/printf.html*
- Recipe 2.3, "Writing Output with More Formatting Control"
- Recipe 2.4, "Writing Output Without the Newline"
- Recipe 15.1, "Finding bash Portably for #!"
- Recipe 15.3, "Developing Portable Shell Scripts"
- Recipe 19.11, "Seeing Odd Behavior from printf"
- "printf" in Appendix A

15.7 Splitting Output Only When Necessary

Problem

You want to split output only if the input exceeds your limit, but the *split* command always creates at least one new file.

Solution

```
# cookbook filename: func_split

#+++++++++++++++++++++++++++++++++++++++++++++++++++++++++++++++++++++++++++++++
# Output fixed-size pieces of input ONLY if the limit is exceeded
# Called like:  Split <file> <prefix> <limit option> <limit argument>
# e.g. Split $output ${output}_ --lines 100
# See split(1) and wc(1) for option details
function Split {
    local file=$1
    local prefix=$2
    local limit_type=$3
    local limit_size=$4
    local wc_option

    # Sanity Checks
    if [ -z "$file" ]; then
        printf "%b" "Split: requires a file name!\n"
        return 1
    fi
    if [ -z "$prefix" ]; then
        printf "%b" "Split: requires an output file prefix!\n"
        return 1
    fi
    if [ -z "$limit_type" ]; then
        printf "%b" "Split: requires a limit option (e.g. --lines), see 'man split'!\
n"
        return 1
    fi
    if [ -z "$limit_size" ]; then
        printf "%b" "Split: requires a limit size (e.g. 100), see 'man split'!\n"
        return 1
    fi

    # Convert split options to wc options.  Sigh.
    # Not all options supported by all wc/split on all systems
    case $limit_type in
        -b|--bytes)      wc_option='-c';;
        -C|--line-bytes) wc_option='-L';;
        -l|--lines)      wc_option='-l';;
    esac

    # If whatever limit is exceeded
    if [ "$(wc $wc_option $file | awk '{print $1}')" -gt $limit_size ]; then
```

```
        # actually do something
        split --verbose $limit_type $limit_size $file $prefix
    fi
} # end of function Split
```

Discussion

Depending on your system, some options (e.g., -C) may not be available in *split* or *wc*.

See Also

- Recipe 8.13, "Counting Lines, Words, or Characters in a File"

15.8   Viewing Output in Hex

Problem

You need to see output in hex mode to verify that a certain whitespace or unprintable character is as expected.

Solution

Pipe the output though *hexdump* using the -C option for canonical output:

```
$ hexdump -C filename
00000000  4c 69 6e 65 20 31 0a 4c  69 6e 65 20 32 0a 0a 4c  |Line 1.Line 2..L|
00000010  69 6e 65 20 34 0a 4c 69  6e 65 20 35 0a 0a        |ine 4.Line 5..|
0000001e
```

For example, *nl* uses spaces (ASCII 20), then the line number, then a tab (ASCII 09) in its output:

```
$ nl -ba filename | hexdump -C
00000000  20 20 20 20 20 31 09 4c  69 6e 65 20 31 0a 20 20  |     1.Line 1.  |
00000010  20 20 20 32 09 4c 69 6e  65 20 32 0a 20 20 20 20  |   2.Line 2.    |
00000020  20 33 09 0a 20 20 20 20  20 34 09 4c 69 6e 65 20  | 3..     4.Line |
00000030  34 0a 20 20 20 20 20 35  09 4c 69 6e 65 20 35 0a  |4.     5.Line 5.|
00000040  20 20 20 20 20 36 09 0a                           |     6..|
00000048
```

Discussion

hexdump is a BSD utility that also comes with many Linux distributions. Other systems, notably Solaris, do not have it by default. You can use the octal dump command *od*, but it's a lot harder to read:

```
$ nl -ba filename | od -x
0000000 2020 2020 3120 4c09 6e69 2065 0a31 2020
0000020 2020 3220 4c09 6e69 2065 0a32 2020 2020
0000040 3320 0a09 2020 2020 3420 4c09 6e69 2065
0000060 0a34 2020 2020 3520 4c09 6e69 2065 0a35
0000100 2020 2020 3620 0a09
0000110
```

```
$ nl -ba filename | od -tx1
0000000 20 20 20 20 20 31 09 4c 69 6e 65 20 31 0a 20 20
0000020 20 20 20 32 09 4c 69 6e 65 20 32 0a 20 20 20 20
0000040 20 33 09 0a 20 20 20 20 20 34 09 4c 69 6e 65 20
0000060 34 0a 20 20 20 20 20 35 09 4c 69 6e 65 20 35 0a
0000100 20 20 20 20 20 36 09 0a
0000110
```

There is also a simple Perl script available at *http://www.khngai.com/perl/bin/ hexdump.txt* that might work:

```
$ ./hexdump.pl filename

        /0 /1 /2 /3 /4 /5 /6 /7 /8 /9/ A /B /C /D /E /F   0123456789ABCDEF
0000 : 4C 69 6E 65 20 31 0A 4C 69 6E 65 20 32 0A 0A 4C   Line 1.Line 2..L
0010 : 69 6E 65 20 34 0A 4C 69 6E 65 20 35 0A 0A         ine 4.Line 5..
```

See Also

- man hexdump
- man od
- *http://www.khngai.com/perl/bin/hexdump.txt*
- *http://gnuwin32.sourceforge.net/packages/hextools.htm*
- "Table of ASCII Values" in Appendix A

15.9   Using bash Net-Redirection

Problem

You need to send or receive very simple network traffic but you do not have a tool such as *netcat* installed.

Solution

If you have *bash* version 2.04+ compiled with --enable-net-redirections (it isn't compiled this way in Debian and derivatives), you can use *bash* itself. The following example is also used in Recipe 15.10, "Finding My IP Address":

```
$ exec 3<> /dev/tcp/www.ippages.com/80
$ echo -e "GET /simple/?se=1 HTTP/1.0\n" >&3
$ cat <&3
HTTP/1.1 200 OK
Date: Tue, 28 Nov 2006 08:13:08 GMT
Server: Apache/2.0.52 (Red Hat)
X-Powered-By: PHP/4.3.9
Set-Cookie: smipcomID=6670614; expires=Sun, 27-Nov-2011 08:13:09 GMT; path=/
Pragma: no-cache
Cache-Control: no-cache, must-revalidate
Content-Length: 125
```

```
Connection: close
Content-Type: text/plain; charset=ISO-8859-1

72.NN.NN.225 (US-United States) http://www..com Tue, 28 Nov 2006 08:13:09 UTC/GMT
flagged User Agent - reduced functionality
```

 As noted, this recipe will probably not work under Debian and derivatives such as Ubuntu since they expressly do not compile *bash* with `--enable-net-redirections`.

Discussion

As noted in Recipe 15.12, "Redirecting Output for the Life of a Script," it is possible to use *exec* to permanently redirect file handles within the current shell session, so the first command sets up input and output on file handle 3. The second line sends a trivial command to a path on the web server defined in the first command. Note that the user agent will appear as `"-"` on the web server side, which is what is causing the "flagged User Agent" warning. The third command simply displays the results.

Both TCP and UDP are supported. Here is a trivial way to send syslog messages to a remote server (although in production we recommend using the *logger* utility, which is much more user friendly and robust):

```
echo "<133>$0[$$]: Test syslog message from bash" > /dev/udp/loghost.example.com/514
```

Since UDP is connectionless, this is actually much easier to use than the previous TCP example. `<133>` is the *syslog priority* value for *local0.notice*, calculated according to RFC 3164. See the RFC "4.1.1 PRI Part" and *logger* manpage for details. $0 is the name and $$ is the process ID of the current program. The name will be -bash for a login shell.

See Also

- man logger
- RFC 3164: The BSD Syslog Protocol, at *http://www.faqs.org/rfcs/rfc3164.html*
- Recipe 15.10, "Finding My IP Address"
- Recipe 15.12, "Redirecting Output for the Life of a Script"
- Recipe 15.14, "Logging to syslog from Your Script"
- Appendix B, particularly *./functions/gethtml*

15.10 Finding My IP Address

Problem

You need to know the IP address of the machine you are running on.

Solution

There is no good way to do this that will work on all systems in all situations, so we will present several possible solutions.

First, you can parse output from *ifconfig* to look for IP addresses. These examples will either return the first IP address that is not a *loopback* or nothing if there are no interfaces configured or up.

```
# cookbook filename: finding_ipas

# IPv4 Using awk, cut and head
$ /sbin/ifconfig -a | awk '/(cast)/ { print $2 }' | cut -d':' -f2 | head -1

# IPv4 Using Perl, just for fun
$ /sbin/ifconfig -a | perl -ne 'if ( m/^\s*inet (?:addr:)?([\d.]+).*?cast/ ) { print
qq($1\n); exit 0; }'



# IPv6 Using awk, cut and head
$ /sbin/ifconfig -a | egrep 'inet6 addr: |address: ' | cut -d':' -f2- | cut -d'/' -f1
| head -1 | tr -d ' '

# IPv6 Using Perl, just for fun
$ /sbin/ifconfig -a | perl -ne 'if ( m/^\s*(?:inet6)? \s*addr(?:ess)?: ([0-9A-Fa-f:
]+)/ ) { print qq($1\n); exit 0; }'
```

Second, you can get your hostname and resolve back to an IP address. This is often unreliable because today's systems (especially workstations) might have incomplete or incorrect hostnames and/or might be on a dynamic network that lacks proper reverse lookup. Use at your own risk and test well.

```
$ host $(hostname)
```

Third, you may be more interested in your host's external, routable address than its internal RFC 1918 address. In that case you can use an external host such as *http://www.ippages.com/* or "FollowMeIP" (see below) to learn the address of your firewall or NAT device. The catch here is that non-Linux systems often have no command-line tool like *wget* installed by default. *lynx* or *curl* will also work, but they aren't usually installed by default either (although Mac OS X 10.4 has *curl*). Note the IP address is deliberately obscured in the following examples:

```
$ wget -q0 - http://www.ippages.com/simple/
72.NN.NN.225 (US-United States) http://www.ippages.com Mon, 27 Nov 2006 21:02:23 UTC/
GMT
(5 of 199 allowed today)
alternate access in XML format at: http://www.ippages.com/xml
alternate access via SOAP at: http://www.ippages.com/soap/server.php
alternate access via RSS feed at: http://www.ippages.com/rss.php
alternate access in VoiceXML format at: http://www.ippages.com/voicexml

$ wget -q0 - http://www.ippages.com/simple/?se=1
```

```
72.NN.NN.225 (US-United States) http://www.ippages.com Tue, 28 Nov 2006 08:11:36 UTC/
GMT

$ wget -qO - http://www.ippages.com/simple/?se=1 | cut -d' ' -f1
72.NN.NN.225


$ lynx -dump http://www.ippages.com/simple/?se=1 | cut -d' ' -f1
72.NN.NN.225

$ curl -s http://www.ippages.com/simple/?se=1 | cut -d' ' -f1
72.NN.NN.225
```

If you do not have any of the programs used above, but you do have *bash* version 2.04+ compiled with --enable-net-redirections (it isn't compiled this way in Debian and derivatives), you can use *bash* itself. See Recipe 15.9, "Using bash Net-Redirection" for details.

```
$ exec 3<> /dev/tcp/www.ippages.com/80
$ echo -e "GET /simple/?se=1 HTTP/1.0\n" >&3
$ cat <&3
HTTP/1.1 200 OK
Date: Tue, 28 Nov 2006 08:13:08 GMT
Server: Apache/2.0.52 (Red Hat)
X-Powered-By: PHP/4.3.9
Set-Cookie: smipcomID=6670614; expires=Sun, 27-Nov-2011 08:13:09 GMT; path=/
Pragma: no-cache
Cache-Control: no-cache, must-revalidate
Content-Length: 125
Connection: close
Content-Type: text/plain; charset=ISO-8859-1

72.NN.NN.225 (US-United States) http://www..com Tue, 28 Nov 2006 08:13:09 UTC/GMT
flagged User Agent - reduced functionality


$ exec 3<> /dev/tcp/www.ippages.com/80
$ echo -e "GET /simple/?se=1 HTTP/1.0\n" >&3
$ egrep '^[0-9.]+ ' <&3 | cut -d' ' -f1
72.NN.NN.225
```

"FollowMeIP" is a little different. It provides a client at *http://ipserver.fmip.org/* but you don't actually need it. Note the use of a nonstandard port, so this won't work at sites with strict egress filtering (i.e., outgoing firewall rules).

```
# Using telnet
$ telnet ipserver.fmip.org 42750 2>&1 | egrep '^[0-9]+'
72.NN.NN.225


# Using native bash (easier, if it works for you)
$ exec 3<> /dev/tcp/ipserver.fmip.org/42750 && cat <&3
72.NN.NN.225
```

Discussion

The *awk* and Perl code in the first solution above is interesting because of the operating system variations we will note here. But it turns out that the lines we're interested in all contain either Bcast or broadcast (or inet6 addr: or address:), so once we get those lines it's just a matter of parsing out the field we want. Of course Linux makes that harder by using a different format, but we've dealt with that too.

Not all systems require the path (if you aren't *root*) or -a argument to *ifconfig*, but all accept it, so it's best to use /sbin/ifconfig -a and be done with it.

Here are *ifconfig* output examples from different machines:

```
# Linux
$ /sbin/ifconfig
eth0      Link encap:Ethernet  HWaddr 00:C0:9F:0B:8F:F6
          inet addr:192.168.99.11  Bcast:192.168.99.255  Mask:255.255.255.0
          UP BROADCAST RUNNING MULTICAST  MTU:1500  Metric:1
          RX packets:33073511 errors:0 dropped:0 overruns:0 frame:827
          TX packets:52865023 errors:0 dropped:0 overruns:1 carrier:7
          collisions:12922745 txqueuelen:100
          RX bytes:2224430163 (2121.3 Mb)  TX bytes:51266497 (48.8 Mb)
          Interrupt:11 Base address:0xd000

lo        Link encap:Local Loopback
          inet addr:127.0.0.1  Mask:255.0.0.0
          UP LOOPBACK RUNNING  MTU:16436  Metric:1
          RX packets:659102 errors:0 dropped:0 overruns:0 frame:0
          TX packets:659102 errors:0 dropped:0 overruns:0 carrier:0
          collisions:0 txqueuelen:0
          RX bytes:89603190 (85.4 Mb)  TX bytes:89603190 (85.4 Mb)

$ /sbin/ifconfig
eth0      Link encap:Ethernet  HWaddr 00:06:29:33:4D:42
          inet addr:192.168.99.144  Bcast:192.168.99.255  Mask:255.255.255.0
          inet6 addr: fe80::206:29ff:fe33:4d42/64 Scope:Link
          UP BROADCAST RUNNING MULTICAST  MTU:1500  Metric:1
          RX packets:1246774 errors:14 dropped:0 overruns:0 frame:14
          TX packets:1063160 errors:0 dropped:0 overruns:0 carrier:5
          collisions:65476 txqueuelen:1000
          RX bytes:731714472 (697.8 MiB)  TX bytes:942695735 (899.0 MiB)

lo        Link encap:Local Loopback
          inet addr:127.0.0.1  Mask:255.0.0.0
          inet6 addr: ::1/128 Scope:Host
          UP LOOPBACK RUNNING  MTU:16436  Metric:1
          RX packets:144664 errors:0 dropped:0 overruns:0 frame:0
          TX packets:144664 errors:0 dropped:0 overruns:0 carrier:0
          collisions:0 txqueuelen:0
          RX bytes:152181602 (145.1 MiB)  TX bytes:152181602 (145.1 MiB)

sit0      Link encap:IPv6-in-IPv4
          inet6 addr: ::127.0.0.1/96 Scope:Unknown
```

```
          UP RUNNING NOARP  MTU:1480  Metric:1
          RX packets:0 errors:0 dropped:0 overruns:0 frame:0
          TX packets:0 errors:101910 dropped:0 overruns:0 carrier:0
          collisions:0 txqueuelen:0
          RX bytes:0 (0.0 b)  TX bytes:0 (0.0 b)
```

NetBSD
```
$ /sbin/ifconfig -a
pcn0: flags=8843<UP,BROADCAST,RUNNING,SIMPLEX,MULTICAST> mtu 1500
        address: 00:0c:29:31:eb:19
        media: Ethernet autoselect (autoselect)
        inet 192.168.99.56 netmask 0xffffff00 broadcast 192.168.99.255
        inet6 fe80::20c:29ff:fe31:eb19%pcn0 prefixlen 64 scopeid 0x1
lo0: flags=8009<UP,LOOPBACK,MULTICAST> mtu 33196
        inet 127.0.0.1 netmask 0xff000000
        inet6 ::1 prefixlen 128
        inet6 fe80::1%lo0 prefixlen 64 scopeid 0x2
ppp0: flags=8010<POINTOPOINT,MULTICAST> mtu 1500
ppp1: flags=8010<POINTOPOINT,MULTICAST> mtu 1500
sl0: flags=c010<POINTOPOINT,LINK2,MULTICAST> mtu 296
sl1: flags=c010<POINTOPOINT,LINK2,MULTICAST> mtu 296
strip0: flags=0 mtu 1100
strip1: flags=0 mtu 1100
```

OpenBSD, FreeBSD
```
$ /sbin/ifconfig
lo0: flags=8049<UP,LOOPBACK,RUNNING,MULTICAST> mtu 33224
        inet 127.0.0.1 netmask 0xff000000
        inet6 ::1 prefixlen 128
        inet6 fe80::1%lo0 prefixlen 64 scopeid 0x5
le1: flags=8863<UP,BROADCAST,NOTRAILERS,RUNNING,SIMPLEX,MULTICAST> mtu 1500
        address: 00:0c:29:25:df:00
        inet6 fe80::20c:29ff:fe25:df00%le1 prefixlen 64 scopeid 0x1
        inet 192.168.99.193 netmask 0xffffff00 broadcast 192.168.99.255
pflog0: flags=0<> mtu 33224
pfsync0: flags=0<> mtu 2020
```

Solaris
```
$ /sbin/ifconfig -a
lo0: flags=1000849<UP,LOOPBACK,RUNNING,MULTICAST,IPv4> mtu 8232 index 1
        inet 127.0.0.1 netmask ff000000
pcn0: flags=1004843<UP,BROADCAST,RUNNING,MULTICAST,DHCP,IPv4> mtu 1500 index 2
        inet 192.168.99.159 netmask ffffff00 broadcast 192.168.99.255
```

Mac
```
$ /sbin/ifconfig
lo0: flags=8049<UP,LOOPBACK,RUNNING,MULTICAST> mtu 16384
        inet 127.0.0.1 netmask 0xff000000
        inet6 ::1 prefixlen 128
        inet6 fe80::1%lo0 prefixlen 64 scopeid 0x1
gif0: flags=8010<POINTOPOINT,MULTICAST> mtu 1280
stf0: flags=0<> mtu 1280
```

```
en0: flags=8863<UP,BROADCAST,SMART,RUNNING,SIMPLEX,MULTICAST> mtu 1500
        inet6 fe80::20d:93ff:fe65:f720%en0 prefixlen 64 scopeid 0x4
        inet 192.168.99.155 netmask 0xffffff00 broadcast 192.168.99.255
        ether 00:0d:93:65:f7:20
        media: autoselect (100baseTX <half-duplex>) status: active
        supported media: none autoselect 10baseT/UTP <half-duplex> 10baseT/UTP <full-
duplex> 10baseT/UTP <full-duplex,hw-loopback> 100baseTX <half-duplex> 100baseTX
<full-duplex> 100baseTX <full-duplex,hw-loopback>
fw0: flags=8863<UP,BROADCAST,SMART,RUNNING,SIMPLEX,MULTICAST> mtu 2030
        lladdr 00:0d:93:ff:fe:65:f7:20
        media: autoselect <full-duplex> status: inactive
        supported media: autoselect <full-duplex>
```

See Also

- man awk
- man curl
- man cut
- man head
- man lynx
- man perl
- man wget
- *http://www.ippages.com/ or http://www.showmyip.com/*
- *http://ipserver.fmip.org/*
- *http://www.faqs.org/rfcs/rfc1918.html*
- Recipe 15.9, "Using bash Net-Redirection"
- Recipe 15.12, "Redirecting Output for the Life of a Script"

15.11 Getting Input from Another Machine

Problem

Your script needs to get input from another machine, perhaps to check if a file exists or a process is running.

Solution

Use SSH with public keys and command substitution. To do this, set up SSH so that you do not need a password, as described in Recipe 14.21, "Using SSH Without a Password." Next, tailor the command that SSH runs to output exactly what your script needs as input. Then simply use command substitution.

```
#!/usr/bin/env bash
# cookbook filename: command_substitution

REMOTE_HOST='host.example.com'  # Required
```

```
REMOTE_FILE='/etc/passwd'        # Required
SSH_USER='user@'                 # Optional, set to '' to not use
#SSH_ID='-i ~/.ssh/foo.id'        # Optional, set to '' to not use
SSH_ID=''

result=$(
    ssh $SSH_ID $SSH_USER$REMOTE_HOST \
        "[ -r $REMOTE_FILE ] && echo 1 || echo 0"
) || { echo "SSH command failed!" >&2; exit 1; }

if [ $result = 1 ]; then
    echo "$REMOTE_FILE present on $REMOTE_HOST"
else
    echo "$REMOTE_FILE not present on $REMOTE_HOST"
fi
```

Discussion

We do a few interesting things here. First, notice how both $SSH_USER and $SSH_ID work. They have an effect when they have a value, but when they are empty they interpolate to the empty set and are ignored. This allows us to abstract the values in the code, which lends itself to putting those values in a configuration file, putting the code into a function, or both.

```
# Interpolated line of the variables have values:
ssh -i ~/.ssh/foo.id user@host.example.com [...]

# No values:
ssh host.example.com [...]
```

Next, we set up the command that SSH runs so that there is always output (0 or 1), then check that $result is not empty. That's one way to make sure that the SSH command runs (see also Recipe 4.2, "Telling If a Command Succeeded or Not"). If $result is empty, we group commands using a { } *code block* to issue an error message and exit. But since we're always getting output from the SSH command, we have to test the value; we can't just use if [$result]; then.

If we didn't use the code block, we'd only issue the warning if the SSH command returned an empty $result, but we'd *always* exit. Read the code again until you understand why, because this is an easy way to get bitten. Likewise, if we'd tried to use a ( ) subshell instead of the { } code block, our intent would fail because the exit 1 would exit the subshell, not the script. The script would then continue even after the SSH command had failed—but the code would look *almost* correct, so this might be tricky to debug.

We could have written the last test case as follows. Which form to use depends on your style and the number of statements to execute in each situation. In this case it doesn't matter.

```
[ $result = 1 ] && echo "$REMOTE_FILE present on $REMOTE_HOST" \
               || echo "$REMOTE_FILE not present on $REMOTE_HOST"
```

Finally, we've also been careful about formatting so that no lines are too long, but the code is still readable and our intent is clear.

See Also

- Recipe 2.14, "Saving or Grouping Output from Several Commands"
- Recipe 4.2, "Telling If a Command Succeeded or Not"
- Recipe 14.21, "Using SSH Without a Password"
- Recipe 17.18, "Grepping ps Output Without Also Getting the grep Process Itself"
- Recipe 17.19, "Finding Out Whether a Process Is Running"

15.12 Redirecting Output for the Life of a Script

Problem

You'd like to redirect output for an entire script and you'd rather not have to edit every *echo* or *printf* statement.

Solution

Use a little known feature of the *exec* command to redirect STDOUT or STDERR:

```
# Optional, save the "old" STDERR
exec 3>&2

# Redirect any output to STDERR to an error log file instead
exec 2> /path/to/error_log

# script with "globally" redirected STDERR goes here

# Turn off redirect by reverting STDERR and closing FH3
exec 2>&3-
```

Discussion

Usually *exec* replaces the running shell with the command supplied in its arguments, destroying the original shell. However, if no command is given, it can manipulate redirection in the current shell. You are not limited to redirecting STDOUT or STDERR, but they are the most common targets for redirection in this case.

See Also

- help exec
- Recipe 15.9, "Using bash Net-Redirection"

15.13 Working Around "argument list too long" Errors

Problem

You get an "argument list too long" error while trying to do an operation involving shell wildcard expansion.

Solution

Use the *xargs* command, possibly in conjunction with *find*, to break up your argument list.

For simple cases, just use a for loop or *find* instead of *ls*:

```
$ ls /path/with/many/many/files/*e*
-/bin/bash: /bin/ls: Argument list too long


# Short demo, surrounding ~ are for illustration only
$ for i in ./some_files/*e*; do echo "~$i~"; done
~./some_files/A file with (parens)~
~./some_files/A file with [brackets]~
~./some_files/File with embedded
newline~
~./some_files/file with = sign~
~./some_files/file with spaces~
~./some_files/file with |~
~./some_files/file with:~
~./some_files/file with;~
~./some_files/regular_file~


$ find ./some_files -name '*e*' -exec echo ~{}~ \;
~./some_files~
~./some_files/A file with [brackets]~
~./some_files/A file with (parens)~
~./some_files/regular_file~
~./some_files/file with spaces~
~./some_files/file with = sign~
~./some_files/File with embedded
newline~
~./some_files/file with;~
~./some_files/file with:~
~./some_files/file with |~


$ for i in /path/with/many/many/files/*e*; do echo "$i"; done
[This works, but the output is too long to list]


$ find /path/with/many/many/files/ -name '*e*'
[This works, but the output is too long to list]
```

The example above works correctly with the *echo* command, but when you feed that "$i" into other programs, especially other shell constructs, $IFS and other parsing may come into play. The GNU *find* and *xargs* take that into account with find -print0 and xargs -0. (No, we don't know why it's -print0 and -0 instead of being consistent.) These arguments cause *find* to use the null character (which can't appear in a filename) instead of whitespace as an output record separator, and *xargs* to use null as its input record separator. That will correctly parse files containing odd characters.

```
$ find /path/with/many/many/files/ -name '*e*' -print0 | xargs -0 proggy
```

Discussion

Note that the default behavior of *bash* (and *sh*) is to return unmatched patterns unchanged. That means you could end up with your for loop setting $i to ./some_ files/*e* if no files match the wildcard pattern. You can set the shopt -s nullglob option to cause filename patterns that match no files to expand to a null string, rather than expand to themselves.

You might assume that the for loop solution in the simple case would run into the same problem as the *ls* command, but it doesn't. Chet Ramey tells us:

> ARG_MAX bounds the total space requirement of the *exec** family of system calls, so the kernel knows the largest buffer it will have to allocate. This is all three arguments to *execve*: program name, argument vector, and environment.

> The [*ls* command] fails because the total bytes taken up by the arguments to *execve* exceeds ARG_MAX. The [for loop] succeeds because everything is done internally: though the entire list is generated and stored, *execve* is never called.

Be careful that *find* doesn't find too many files, since it will recursively descend into all subdirectories by default while *ls* will not. Some versions of *find* have a -d option to control how deep it goes. Using the for loop is probably easier.

Use the getconf ARG_MAX command to see what the limit is on your system. It varies wildly (see also getconf LINE_MAX; see Table 15-1).

Table 15-1. System limits

System	ARG_MAX limits (bytes)
HP-UX 11	2048000
Solaris (8, 9, 10)	1048320
NetBSD 2.0.2, OpenBSD 3.7, OS/X	262144
Linux (Red Hat, Debian, Ubuntu)	131072
FreeBSD 5.4	65536

See Also

- *http://www.gnu.org/software/coreutils/faq/coreutils-faq.html#Argument-list-too-long*
- Recipe 9.2, "Handling File Names Containing Odd Characters"

15.14 Logging to syslog from Your Script

Problem

You'd like your script to be able to log to *syslog*.

Solution

Use *logger*, Netcat, or *bash*'s built-in network redirection features.

logger is installed by default on most systems and is an easy way to send messages to the local *syslog* service. However, it does not send *syslog* to remote hosts by itself. If you need to do that, you can use *bash* or Netcat.

```
$ logger -p local0.notice -t $0[$$] test message
```

Netcat is known as the "TCP/IP Swiss Army knife" and is usually not installed by default. It may also be prohibited as a hacking tool by some security policies, though *bash*'s net-redirection features do pretty much the same thing. See the discussion in Recipe 15.9, "Using bash Net-Redirection" for details on the <133>$0[$$] part.

```
# Netcat
$ echo "<133>$0[$$]: Test syslog message from Netcat" | nc -w1 -u loghost 514
```

```
# bash
$ echo "<133>$0[$$]: Test syslog message from bash" \
  > /dev/udp/loghost.example.com/514
```

Discussion

logger and Netcat have many more features than we include here. See the respective manpages for details.

See Also

- man logger
- man nc
- Recipe 15.9, "Using bash Net-Redirection"

15.15 Sending Email from Your Script

Problem

You'd like your script to be able to send email, optionally with attachments.

Solution

These solutions depend on a compatible mailer such as *mail*, *mailx*, or *mailto*, an Message Transfer Agent (MTA) being installed and running, and proper configuration of your email environment. Unfortunately, you can't always count on all of that, so these solutions must be well tested in your intended environment.

The first way to send mail from your script is to write some code to generate and send a message, as follows:

```
# Simple
cat email_body | mail -s "Message subject" recipient1@example.com recipient2@example.com
```

or:

```
# Attachment only
$ uuencode /path/to/attachment_file attachment_name | mail -s "Message Subject"
recipient1@example.com recipient2@example.com
```

or:

```
# Attachment and body
$ (cat email_body ; uuencode /path/to/attachment_file attachment_name) | mail -s
"Message Subject" recipient1@example.com recipient2@example.com
```

In practice, it's not always that easy. For one thing, while *uuencode* will probably be there, *mail* and friends may or may not, or their capabilities may vary. In some cases *mail* and *mailx* are even the same program, hard- or soft-linked together. In production, you will want to use some abstraction to allow for portability. For example, *mail* works on Linux and the BSDs, but *mailx* is required for Solaris since its *mail* lacks support for -s. *mailx* works on some Linux distributions (e.g., Debian), but not others (e.g., Red Hat). We're choosing the mailer based on hostname here, but depending on your environment using uname -o might make more sense.

```
# cookbook filename: email_sample

# Define some mail settings.  Use a case statement with uname or hostname
# to tweak settings as required for your environment.
case $HOSTNAME in
    *.company.com       ) MAILER='mail'   ;;  # Linux and BSD
    host1.*             ) MAILER='mailx'  ;;  # Solaris, BSD and some Linux
    host2.*             ) MAILER='mailto' ;;  # Handy, if installed
esac
RECIPIENTS='recipient1@example.com recipient2@example.com'
SUBJECT="Data from $0"

[...]
# Create the body as a file or variable using echo, printf, or a here-document
# Create or modify $SUBJECT and/or $RECIPIENTS as needed
[...]

( echo $email_body ; uuencode $attachment $(basename $attachment) ) \
  | $MAILER -s "$SUBJECT" "$RECIPIENTS"
```

We should also note that sending attachments in this way depends somewhat on the client you use to read the resulting message, too. Modern clients like Thunderbird (and Outlook) will detect a uuencoded message and present it as an attachment. Other clients may not. You can always save the message and *uudecode* it (*uudecode* is smart enough to skip the message part and just handle the attachment part), but that's a pain.

The second way to send mail from your scripts is to outsource the task to *cron*. While the exact feature set of *cron* varies from system to system, one thing in common is that any output from a *cron* job is mailed to the job's owner or the user defined using the MAILTO variable. So you can take advantage of that fact to get emailing for free, assuming that your email infrastructure works.

The proper way to design a script intended to run from *cron* (and many would argue any script or Unix tool at all) is to make it silent unless it encounters a warning or error. If necessary, use a -v argument to optionally allow a more verbose mode, but don't run it that way from *cron*, at least after you've finished testing. The reason for this is as noted: *cron* emails you all the output. If you get an email message from *cron* every time your script runs, you'll soon start ignoring them. But if your script is silent except when there's a problem, you'll only get a notification when there is a problem, which is ideal.

Discussion

Note that *mailto* is intended to be a multimedia and *MIME*-aware update to *mail*, and thus you could avoid using *uuencode* for sending attachments, but it's not as widely available as *mail* or *mailx*. If all else fails, *elm* or *mutt* may be used in place of *mail*, *mailx*, or *mailto*, thought they are even less likely to be installed by default than *mail**. Also, some versions of these programs support a -r option to supply a return address in case you want to supply one. *mutt* also has a -a option that makes sending attachments a breeze.

```
cat "$message_body" | mutt -s "$subject" -a "$attachment_file" "$recipients"
```

mpack is another tool worth looking into, but it is very unlikely to be installed by default. Check your system's software repository or download the source from *ftp:// ftp.andrew.cmu.edu/pub/mpack/*. From the manpage:

> The mpack program encodes the named file in one or more MIME messages. The resulting messages are mailed to one or more recipients, written to a named file or set of files, or posted to a set of newsgroups.

Another way to handle the various names and locations of mail clients is shown in Chapter 8 of *Classic Shell Scripting* by Nelson H.F. Beebe and Arnold Robbins (O'Reilly):

```
# cookbook filename: email_sample_css
# From Chapter 8 of Classic Shell Scripting
```

```
for MAIL in /bin/mailx /usr/bin/mailx /usr/sbin/mailx /usr/ucb/mailx /bin/mail /usr/
bin/mail; do
    [ -x $MAIL ] && break
done
[ -x $MAIL ] || { echo 'Cannot find a mailer!' >&2; exit 1; }
```

uuencode is an old method for translating binary data into ASCII text for transmission over links that could not support binary, which is to say most of the Internet before it became *the Internet* and the Web. We have it on good authority that at least some such links still remain, but even if you never encounter one it's still useful to be able to convert an attachment into an otherwise ASCII medium in such a way that modern mail clients will recognize it. See also *uudecode* and *mimencode*. Note that uuencoded files are about one-third larger than their binary equivalent, so you probably want to compress the file before uuencoding it.

The problem with email, aside from the differing front-end Mail User Agent (MUA) programs like *mail* and *mailx*, is that there are a lot of moving parts that must all work together. This is exacerbated by the spam problem because mail administrators have had to so severely lock down mail servers that it can easily affect your scripts. All we can say here is to fully test your solution, and talk to your system and mail administrators if necessary.

One other problem you might see is that some workstation-oriented Linux distributions, such as Ubuntu, don't install or run an MTA by default since they assume you will be using a full-featured GUI client such as Evolution or Thunderbird. If that's the case, command-line MUAs and email from *cron* won't work either. Consult your distribution's support groups for help with this as needed.

See Also

- man mail
- man mailx
- man mailto
- man mutt
- man uuencode
- man cron
- man 5 crontab

15.16 Automating a Process Using Phases

Problem

You have a long job or process you need to automate, but it may require manual intervention and you need to be able to restart at various points in the progress. You might use a GOTO to jump around, but *bash* doesn't have that.

Solution

Use a case statement to break your script up into sections or *phases*.

First, we'll define a standardized way to get answers from the user:

```
# cookbook filename: func_choice

function choice {
    # Let the user make a choice about something and return a standardized
    # answer.  How the default is handled and what happens next is up to
    # the if/then after the choice in main

    local answer
    printf "%b" "\a"          # Ring the bell
    read -p "$*" answer
    case "$answer" in
        [yY1] ) choice='y';;
        [nN0] ) choice='n';;
        *     ) choice="$answer";;
    esac
} # end of function choice
```

Then, we'll set up our phases:

```
# cookbook filename: using_phases

# Main Loop
until [ "$phase" = "Finished." ]; do

    case $phase in

        phase0 )
            ThisPhase=0
            NextPhase="$(( $ThisPhase + 1 ))"
            echo '#########################################'
            echo "Phase$ThisPhase  = Initialization of FooBarBaz build"
            # Things that should only be initialized at the beginning of a
            # new build cycle go here
# ...
            echo "Phase${ThisPhase}=Ending"
            phase="phase$NextPhase"
            ;;


# ...


        phase20 )
            ThisPhase=20
            NextPhase="$(( $ThisPhase + 1 ))"
            echo '#########################################'
            echo "Phase$ThisPhase = Main processing for FooBarBaz build"
```

```
# ...

        choice "[P$ThisPhase] Do we need to stop and fix anything? [y/N]: "
        if [ "$choice" = "y" ]; then
            echo "Re-run '$MYNAME phase${ThisPhase}' after handling this."
            exit $ThisPhase
        fi

        echo "Phase${ThisPhase}=Ending"
        phase="phase$NextPhase"
        ;;


# ...


    * )
            echo "What the heck?!?  We should never get HERE!  Gonna croak!"
            echo "Try $0 -h"
            exit 99
            phase="Finished."
            ;;
    esac
    printf "%b" "\a"           # Ring the bell
done
```

Discussion

Since exit codes only go up to 255, the exit $ThisPhase line limits you to that many phases. And our exit 99 line limits you even more, although that one is easily adjusted. If you require more than 254 phases (plus 255 as the *error* code), you have our sympathy. You can either come up with a different exit code scheme, or chain several scripts together.

You should probably set up a usage and/or summary routine that lists the various phases:

```
Phase0  = Initialization of FooBarBaz build
...
Phase20 = Main processing for FooBarBaz build
...
Phase28 ...
```

You can probably grep most of the text out of the code with something like grep 'Phase$ThisPhase' *my_script*.

You may also want to log to a local flat file, *syslog*, or some other mechanism. In that case, define a function like logmsg and use it as appropriate in the code. It could be as simple as:

```
function logmsg {
    # Write a timestamped log message to the screen and logfile
    # Note tee -a to append
    printf "%b" "`date '+%Y-%m-%d %H:%M:%S'`: $*" | tee -a $LOGFILE
} # end of function logmsg
```

You may note that this script violates our usual standard of being silent unless it encounters a problem. Since it is designed to be interactive, we're OK with that.

See Also

- Recipe 3.5, "Getting User Input"
- Recipe 3.6, "Getting Yes or No Input"
- Recipe 15.14, "Logging to syslog from Your Script"

CHAPTER 16

Configuring and Customizing bash

Would you want to work in an environment where you couldn't adjust things to your liking? Imagine not being able to adjust the height of your chair, or being forced to walk the long way to the lunchroom, just because someone else thought that was the "right way." That sort of inflexibility wouldn't be acceptable for long; however, that's what most users expect, and accept, from their computing environments. But if you're used to thinking of your user interface as something inflexible and unchangeable, relax—the user interface is not carved in stone. *bash* lets you customize it so that it works with you, rather than against you.

bash gives you a very powerful and flexible environment. Part of that flexibility is the extent to which it can be customized. If you're a casual Unix user, or if you're used to a less flexible environment, you might not be aware of what's possible. This chapter shows you how to configure *bash* to suit your individual needs and style. If you think the Unix *cat* command has a ridiculous name (most non-Unix people would agree), you can define an alias that renames it. If you use a few commands all the time, you can assign abbreviations to them, too—or even misspellings that correspond to your favorite typing errors (e.g., "mroe" for the *more* command). You can create your own commands, which can be used the same way as standard Unix commands. You can alter the prompt so that it contains useful information (like the current directory). And you can alter the way *bash* behaves; for example, you can make it case-insensitive, so that it doesn't care about the difference between upper- and lowercase. You will be surprised and pleased at how much you can improve your productivity with a few simple *bash* tweaks, especially to *readline*.

For more information about customizing and configuring *bash*, see Chapter 3 of *Learning the bash Shell* by Cameron Newham (O'Reilly).

16.1   bash Startup Options

Problem

You'd like to understand the various options you can use when starting *bash*, but bash --help is not helping you.

Solution

In addition to bash --help, try bash -c "help set" and bash -c help, or just helpset and help if you are already running in a bash shell.

Discussion

bash sometimes has several different ways to set the same option, and this is an example of that. You can set options on startup (for example, bash -x), then later turn the same option off interactively using set +x.

See Also

- Appendix A
- Recipe 19.12, "Testing bash Script Syntax"

16.2   Customizing Your Prompt

Problem

The default *bash* prompt is usually something uninformative that ends with $ and doesn't tell you much, so you would like to customize it to show information you find useful.

Solution

Customize the $PS1 and $PS2 variables as you desire.

The default prompt varies depending on your system. *bash* itself will show its major and minor version (\s-\v\$), for example, bash-3.00$. However, your operating system may have its own default, such as [*user@host* ~]$ ([\u@\h \W]\$) for Fedora Core 5. This solution presents eight basic prompts and three fancier prompts.

Basic prompts

Here are eight examples of more useful prompts that will work with *bash-1.14.7* or newer. The trailing \$ displays # if the effective UID is zero (i.e., you are *root*) and $ otherwise:

1. Username@hostname, the date and time, and the current working directory:

```
$ export PS1='[\u@\h \d \A] \w \$ '
[jp@freebsd Wed Dec 28 19:32] ~ $ cd /usr/local/bin/
[jp@freebsd Wed Dec 28 19:32] /usr/local/bin $
```

2. Username@long-hostname, the date and time in ISO 8601 format, and the base-name of the current working directory (\W):

```
$ export PS1='[\u@\H \D{%Y-%m-%d %H:%M:%S%z}] \W \$ '
[jp@freebsd.jpsdomain.org 2005-12-28 19:33:03-0500] ~ $ cd /usr/local/bin/
[jp@freebsd.jpsdomain.org 2005-12-28 19:33:06-0500] bin $
```

3. Username@hostname, *bash* version, and the current working directory (\w):

```
$ export PS1='[\u@\h \V \w] \$ '
[jp@freebsd 3.00.16] ~ $ cd /usr/local/bin/
[jp@freebsd 3.00.16] /usr/local/bin $
```

4. New line, username@hostname, base PTY, shell level, history number, newline, and full working directory name ($PWD):

```
$ export PS1='\n[\u@\h \l:$SHLVL:\!]\n$PWD\$ '

[jp@freebsd ttyp0:3:21]
/home/jp$ cd /usr/local/bin/

[jp@freebsd ttyp0:3:22]
/usr/local/bin$
```

PTY is the number of the pseudoterminal (in Linux terms) to which you are connected. This is useful when you have more than one session and are trying to keep track of which is which. Shell level is the depth of subshells you are in. When you first log in it's 1, and as you run subprocesses (for example, *screen*) it increments, so after running *screen* it would normally be 2. The history line is the number of the current command in the command history.

5. Username@hostname, the exit status of the last command, and the current working directory. Note the exit status will be reset (and thus useless) if you execute any commands from within the prompt:

```
$ export PS1='[\u@\h $? \w \$ '
[jp@freebsd 0 ~ $ cd /usr/local/bin/
[jp@freebsd 0 /usr/local/bin $ true
[jp@freebsd 0 /usr/local/bin $ false
[jp@freebsd 1 /usr/local/bin $ true
[jp@freebsd 0 /usr/local/bin $
```

6. One other interesting example is showing the number of jobs the shell is currently managing. This can be useful if you run a lot of background jobs and forget that they are there:

```
$ export PS1='\n[\u@\h jobs:\j]\n$PWD\$ '

[jp@freebsd jobs:0]
/tmp$ ls -lar /etc > /dev/null &
[1] 96461
```

```
[jp@freebsd jobs:1]
/tmp$
[1]+  Exit 1                    ls -lar /etc >/dev/null

[jp@freebsd jobs:0]
/tmp$
```

7. Let's go really crazy and show everything. Username@hostname, tty, level, history, jobs, version, and full working directory:

```
$ export PS1='\n[\u@\h t:\l l:$SHLVL h:\! j:\j v:\V]\n$PWD\$ '

[jp@freebsd t:ttyp1 l:2 h:91 j:0 v:3.00.16]
/home/jp$
```

8. The next prompt is one you will either love or hate. It shows username@hostname, T for ptty, L for shell level, C for command number, and the date and time in ISO 8601:

```
$ export PS1='\n[\u@\h:T\l:L$SHLVL:C\!:\D{%Y-%m-%d_%H:%M:%S_%Z}]\n$PWD\$ '

[jp@freebsd:Tttyp1:L1:C337:2006-08-13_03:47:11_EDT]
/home/jp$ cd /usr/local/bin/

[jp@freebsd:Tttyp1:L1:C338:2006-08-13_03:47:16_EDT]
/usr/local/bin$
```

This prompt shows very clearly who did what, when, and where and is great for documenting steps you took for some task via a simple copy and paste from a scroll-back buffer. But some people find it much too cluttered and distracting.

Fancy prompts

Here are three fancy prompts that use ANSI escape sequences for colors, or to set the title bar in an xterm. But be aware that these will not always work. There is a bewildering array of variables in system settings, xterm emulation, and SSH and telnet clients, all of which can affect these prompts.

Also, such escape sequences should be surrounded by \[and \], which tells *bash* that the enclosed characters are non-printing. Otherwise, *bash* will be confused about line lengths and wrap lines in the wrong place.

1. Username@hostname, and the current working directory in light blue (color not shown in print):

```
$ export PS1='\[\033[1;34m\][\u@\h:\w]\$\[\033[0m\] '
[jp@freebsd:~]$
[jp@freebsd:~]$ cd /tmp
[jp@freebsd:/tmp]$
```

2. Username@hostname, and the current working directory in both the xterm title bar and in the prompt itself. If you are not running in an xterm this may produce garbage in your prompt:

```
$ export PS1='\[\033]0;\u@\h:\w\007\][\u@\h:\w]\$ '
[jp@ubuntu:~]$
[jp@ubuntu:~]$ cd /tmp
[jp@ubuntu:/tmp]$
```

3. Both color and xterm updates:

```
$ export PS1='\[\033]0;\u@\h:\w\007\]\[\033[1;34m\][\u@\h:\w]\$\[\033[0m\] '
[jp@ubuntu:~]$
[jp@ubuntu:~]$ cd /tmp
[jp@ubuntu:/tmp]$
```

To save some tedious typing, the prompts from above are in the *bash Cookbook* download (*http://www.bashcookbook.com*), in the file *./ch16/prompts*, shown here:

```
# cookbook filename: prompts

# User name @ short hostname, the date and time and the current working
# directory (CWD):
export PS1='[\u@\h \d \A] \w \$ '


# User name @ long hostname, the date and time in ISO 8601 format and the
# basename of the current working directory (\W):
export PS1='[\u@\H \D{%Y-%m-%d %H:%M:%S%z}] \W \$ '


# User name @ short hostname, bash version, and the current working
# directory (\w):
export PS1='[\u@\h \V \w] \$ '


# New line, user name @ hostname, base PTY, shell level, history number, new
# line, and full working directory name ($PWD).
export PS1='\n[\u@\h \l:$SHLVL:\!]\n$PWD\$ '


# User name @ short hostname, the exit status of the last command and the
# current working directory.
export PS1='[\u@\h $? \w \$ '


# Number of jobs in the background
export PS1='\n[\u@\h jobs:\j]\n$PWD\$ '


# User, short hostname, tty, level, history, jobs, version and full
# working directory name:
export PS1='\n[\u@\h t:\l l:$SHLVL h:\! j:\j v:\V]\n$PWD\$ '


# user@host, T for ptty, L for shell level, C for command number, and the
# date and time in ISO 8601.
export PS1='\n[\u@\h:T\l:L$SHLVL:C\!:\D{%Y-%m-%d_%H:%M:%S_%Z}]\n$PWD\$ '
```

```
# User name @ short hostname, and the current working directory in light
# blue:
export PS1='\[\033[1;34m\][\u@\h:\w]\$\[\033[0m\] '


# User name @ short hostname, and the current working directory in both the
# xterm title bar and in the prompt itself.
export PS1='\[\033]0;\u@\h:\w\007\][\u@\h:\w]\$ '


# Both color and xterm updates:
export PS1='\[\033]0;\u@\h:\w\007\]\[\033[1;34m\][\u@\h:\w]\$\[\033[0m\] '
```

Discussion

Note that the *export* command need only be used once to flag a variable to be exported to child processes.

Assuming the promptvars shell option is set, which it is by default, prompt strings are decoded, expanded via parameter expansion, command substitution, and arithmetic expansion, quotes are removed, and they are finally displayed. Prompt strings are $PS1, $PS2, $PS3, and $PS4. The command prompt is $PS1. The $PS2 prompt is the secondary prompt displayed when *bash* needs more information to complete a command. It defaults to > but you may use anything you like. $PS3 is the *select* prompt (see Recipe 16.16, "Adding New Features to bash Using Loadable Built-ins" and Recipe 16.17, "Improving Programmable Completion"), which defaults to "#?", and $PS4 is the *xtrace* (debugging) prompt, with a default of "+". Note that the first character of $PS4 is replicated as many times as needed to denote levels of indirection in the currently executing command:

```
$ export PS2='Secondary> '

$ for i in *
Secondary> do
Secondary> echo $i
Secondary> done
cheesy_app
data_file
hard_to_kill
mcd
mode


$ export PS3='Pick me: '

$ select item in 'one two three'; do echo $item; done
1) one two three
Pick me: ^C


$ export PS4='+ debugging> '
```

```
$ set -x

$ echo $( echo $( for i in *; do echo $i; done ) )
+++ debugging> for i in '*'
+++ debugging> echo cheesy_app
+++ debugging> for i in '*'
+++ debugging> echo data_file
+++ debugging> for i in '*'
+++ debugging> echo hard_to_kill
+++ debugging> for i in '*'
+++ debugging> echo mcd
+++ debugging> for i in '*'
+++ debugging> echo mode
++ debugging> echo cheesy_app data_file hard_to_kill mcd mode
+ debugging> echo cheesy_app data_file hard_to_kill mcd mode
cheesy_app data_file hard_to_kill mcd mode
```

Since the prompt is only useful when you are running *bash* interactively, the best place to set it is globally in */etc/bashrc* or locally in *~/.bashrc.*

As a style note, we recommend putting a space character as the last character in the $PS1 string. It makes it easier to read what is on your screen by separating the prompt string from the commands that you type. For this, and because your string may contain other spaces or special characters, it is a good idea to use double or even single quotes to quote the string when you assign it to $PS1.

There are at least three easy ways to display your current working directory (CWD) in your prompt: \w, \W, and $PWD. \W will print the *basename* or last part of the directory, while \w will print the entire path; note that both will print ~ instead of whatever $HOME is set to when you are in your home directory. That drives some people crazy, so to print the entire CWD, use $PWD. Printing the entire CWD will cause the prompt to change length, and can even wrap in deep directory structures. That can drive other people crazy. Here is a function to truncate it and a prompt to use the function:

```
# cookbook filename: func_trunc_PWD

function trunc_PWD {
    # $PWD truncation code adapted from The Bash Prompt HOWTO:
    # 11.10. Controlling the Size and Appearance of $PWD
    # http://www.tldp.org/HOWTO/Bash-Prompt-HOWTO/x783.html

    # How many characters of the $PWD should be kept
    local pwdmaxlen=30
    # Indicator that there has been directory truncation:
    local trunc_symbol='...'
    # Temp variable for PWD
    local myPWD=$PWD

    # Replace any leading part of $PWD that matches $HOME with '~'
    # OPTIONAL, comment out if you want the full path!
```

```
    myPWD=${PWD/$HOME/~}

    if [ ${#myPWD} -gt $pwdmaxlen ]; then
        local pwdoffset=$(( ${#myPWD} - $pwdmaxlen ))
        echo "${trunc_symbol}${myPWD:$pwdoffset:$pwdmaxlen}"
    else
        echo "$myPWD"
    fi
}
```

And a demonstration:

```
$ source file/containing/trunc_PWD

[jp@freebsd ttyp0:3:60]
~/this is a bunch/of really/really/really/long directories/did I mention really/
really/long$ export PS1='\n[\u@\h \l:$SHLVL:\!]\n$(trunc_PWD)\$ '

[jp@freebsd ttyp0:3:61]
...d I mention really/really/long$
```

You will notice that the prompts above are single quoted so that $ and other special characters are taken literally. The prompt string is evaluated at display time, so the variables are expanded as expected. Double quotes may also be used, though in that case you must escape shell metacharacters, e.g., by using \$ instead of $.

The command number and the history number are usually different: the history number of a command is its position in the history list, which may include commands restored from the history file, while the command number is the position in the sequence of commands executed during the current shell session.

There is also a special variable called $PROMPT_COMMAND, which if set is interpreted as a command to execute before the evaluation and display of $PS1. The issue with that, and with using command substitution from within the $PS1 prompt, is that these commands are executed every time the prompt is displayed, which is often. For example, you could embed a command substitution such as $(ls -1 | wc -1) in your prompt to give you a count of files in the current working directory. But on an old or heavily utilized system in a large directory, that may result in significant delays before the prompt is presented and you can get on with your work. Prompts are best left short and simple (notwithstanding some of the monsters shown in the Solutions section). Define functions or aliases to easily run on demand instead of cluttering up and slowing down your prompt.

To work around ANSI or xterm escapes that produce garbage in your prompt if they are not supported, you can use something like this in your *rc* file:

```
case $TERM in
    xterm*) export PS1='\[\033]0;\u@\h:\w\007\]\[\033[1;34m\][\u@\h:\w]\$\[\033[0m\]
' ;;
        *) export PS1='[\u@\h:\w]\$ ' ;;
esac
```

See the section "Prompt String Customizations" in Appendix A.

Colors

In the ANSI example we just discussed, 1;34m means "set the character attribute to light, and the character color to blue." 0m means "clear all attributes and set no color." See the section "ANSI Color Escape Sequences" in Appendix A for the codes. The trailing m indicates a color escape sequence.

Here is a script that displays all the possible combinations. If this does not display colors on your terminal, then ANSI color is not enabled or supported.

```
#!/usr/bin/env bash
# cookbook filename: colors
#
# Daniel Crisman's ANSI color chart script from
# The Bash Prompt HOWTO: 6.1. Colours
# http://www.tldp.org/HOWTO/Bash-Prompt-HOWTO/x329.html.
#
# This file echoes a bunch of color codes to the
#   terminal to demonstrate what's available.  Each
#   line is the color code of one foreground color,
#   out of 17 (default + 16 escapes), followed by a
#   test use of that color on all nine background
#   colors (default + 8 escapes).
#

T='gYw' # The test text

echo -e "\n                 40m     41m     42m     43m\
     44m     45m     46m     47m";

for FGs in '    m' '   1m' ' 30m' '1;30m' '  31m' '1;31m' '  32m' \
           '1;32m' '  33m' '1;33m' '  34m' '1;34m' '  35m' '1;35m' \
           '  36m' '1;36m' '  37m' '1;37m';
  do FG=${FGs// /}
  echo -en " $FGs \033[$FG  $T  "
  for BG in 40m 41m 42m 43m 44m 45m 46m 47m;
    do echo -en "$EINS \033[$FG\033[$BG  $T  \033[0m";
  done
  echo;
done
echo
```

See Also

- Bash Reference Manual
- *./examples/scripts.noah/prompt.bash* in the *bash* source tarball
- *http://www.tldp.org/HOWTO/Bash-Prompt-HOWTO/index.html*
- *http://sourceforge.net/projects/bashish*
- Recipe 1.1, "Decoding the Prompt"
- Recipe 3.7, "Selecting from a List of Options"

- Recipe 16.10, "Using Secondary Prompts: $PS2, $PS3, $PS4"
- Recipe 16.16, "Adding New Features to bash Using Loadable Built-ins"
- Recipe 16.17, "Improving Programmable Completion"
- Recipe 16.18, "Using Initialization Files Correctly"
- Recipe 16.19, "Creating Self-Contained, Portable RC Files"
- Recipe 16.20, "Getting Started with a Custom Configuration"
- "Prompt String Customizations" in Appendix A
- "ANSI Color Escape Sequences" in Appendix A

16.3   Change Your $PATH Permanently

Problem

You need to permanently change your path.

Solution

First you need to discover where the path is set, and then update it. For your local account, it's probably set in *~/.profile* or *~/.bash_profile*. Find the file with grep -l PATH ~/.[^.]* and edit it with your favorite editor; then *source* the file to have the change take effect immediately.

If you are *root* and you need to set the path for the entire system, the basic procedure is the same, but there are different files in */etc* where the $PATH may be set, depending on your operating system and version. The most likely file is */etc/profile*, but */etc/bashrc*, */etc/rc*, */etc/default/login*, *~/.ssh/environment*, and the PAM */etc/environment* files are also possible.

Discussion

The grep -l PATH ~/.[^.]* command is interesting because of the nature of shell wildcard expansion and the existence of the */.* and */..* directories. See Recipe 1.5, "Showing All Hidden (dot) Files in the Current Directory," for details.

The locations listed in the $PATH have security implications, especially when you are *root*. If a world-writable directory is in *root*'s path before the typical directories (i.e., */bin*, */sbin*), then a local user can create files that *root* might execute, doing arbitrary things to the system. This is the reason that the current directory (.) should not be in *root*'s path either.

To be aware of this issue and avoid it:

- Make *root*'s path as short as possible, and never use relative paths.
- Avoid having world-writable directories in *root*'s path.

- Consider setting explicit paths in shell scripts run by *root*.
- Consider hardcoding absolute paths to utilities used in shell scripts run by *root*.
- Put user or application directories last in the $PATH, and then only for unprivileged users.

See Also

- Recipe 1.5, "Showing All Hidden (dot) Files in the Current Directory"
- Recipe 4.1, "Running Any Executable"
- Recipe 14.3, "Setting a Secure $PATH"
- Recipe 14.9, "Finding World-Writable Directories in Your $PATH"
- Recipe 14.10, "Adding the Current Directory to the $PATH"
- Recipe 16.4, "Change Your $PATH Temporarily"

16.4   Change Your $PATH Temporarily

Problem

You want to easily add or remove a directory to or from your $PATH for this session only.

Solution

There are several ways to handle this problem.

You can prepend or append the new directory, using PATH="*newdir*:$PATH" or PATH="$PATH:*newdir*", though you should make sure the directory isn't already in the $PATH.

If you need to edit something in the middle of the path, you can *echo* the path to the screen, then use your terminal's kill and yank (copy and paste) facility to duplicate it on a new line and edit it. Or, you can add the "Macros that are convenient for shell interaction" from the *readline* documentation at *http://tiswww.tis.case.edu/php/chet/ readline/readline.html#SEC12*, specifically:

```
# edit the path
"\C-xp": "PATH=${PATH}\e\C-e\C-a\ef\C-f"
# [...]
# Edit variable on current line.
"\M-\C-v": "\C-a\C-k$\C-y\M-\C-e\C-a\C-y="
```

Then pressing Ctrl-X P will display the $PATH on the current line for you to edit, while typing any variable name and pressing Meta Ctrl-V will display that variable for editing. Very handy.

For simple cases you can use this quick function (adapted slightly from Red Hat Linux's */etc/profile*):

```
# cookbook filename: func_pathmunge

# Adapted from Red Hat Linux

function pathmunge {
    if ! echo $PATH | /bin/egrep -q "(^|:)$1($|:)" ; then
        if [ "$2" = "after" ] ; then
            PATH="$PATH:$1"
        else
            PATH="$1:$PATH"
        fi
    fi
}
```

The *egrep* pattern looks for the value in $1 between two : or (|) at the beginning (^) or end ($) of the $PATH string. We chose to use a case statement in our function, and to force a leading and trailing : to do the same thing. Ours is theoretically faster since it uses a shell built-in, but the Red Hat version is more concise. Our version is also an excellent illustration of the fact that the if command works on *exit codes*, so the first if works by using the exit code set by *grep*, while the second requires the use of the test operator ([ ]).

For more complicated cases when you'd like a lot of error checking you can source and then use the following more generic functions:

```
# cookbook filename: func_tweak_path

#++++++++++++++++++++++++++++++++++++++++++++++++++++++++++++++++++++++++++
# Add a directory to the beginning or end of your path as long as it's not
# already present.  Does not take into account symbolic links!
# Returns:  1 or sets the new $PATH
# Called like:  add_to_path <directory> (pre|post)
function add_to_path {
    local location=$1
    local directory=$2

    # Make sure we have something to work with
    if [ -z "$location" -o  -z "$directory" ]; then
        echo "$0:$FUNCNAME: requires a location and a directory to add" >&2
        echo "e.g. add_to_path pre /bin" >&2
        return 1
    fi

    # Make sure the directory is not relative
    if [ $(echo $directory | grep '^/') ]; then
        : echo "$0:$FUNCNAME: '$directory' is absolute" >&2
    else
        echo "$0:$FUNCNAME: can't add relative directory '$directory' to the \$PATH"
>&2
        return 1
    fi
```

```
    # Make sure the directory to add actually exists
    if [ -d "$directory" ]; then
        : echo "$0:$FUNCNAME: directory exists" >&2
    else
        echo "$0:$FUNCNAME: '$directory' does not exist--aborting" >&2
        return 1
    fi

    # Make sure it's not already in the PATH
    if [ $(contains "$PATH" "$directory") ]; then
        echo "$0:$FUNCNAME: '$directory' already in \$PATH--aborting" >&2
    else
        : echo "$0:$FUNCNAME: adding directory to \$PATH" >&2
    fi

    # Figure out what to do
    case $location in
        pre*  ) PATH="$directory:$PATH" ;;
        post* ) PATH="$PATH:$directory" ;;
        *     ) PATH="$PATH:$directory" ;;
    esac

    # Clean up the new path, then set it
    PATH=$(clean_path $PATH)

} # end of function add_to_path


#+++++++++++++++++++++++++++++++++++++++++++++++++++++++++++++++++++++++++++++
# Remove a directory from your path, if present.
# Returns:  sets the new $PATH
# Called like:  rm_from_path <directory>
function rm_from_path {
    local directory=$1

    # Remove all instances of $directory from $PATH
    PATH=${PATH//$directory/}

    # Clean up the new path, then set it
    PATH=$(clean_path $PATH)

} # end of function rm_from_path


#+++++++++++++++++++++++++++++++++++++++++++++++++++++++++++++++++++++++++++++
# Remove leading/trailing or duplicate ':', remove duplicate entries
# Returns:  echos the "cleaned up" path
# Called like:  cleaned_path=$(clean_path $PATH)
function clean_path {
    local path=$1
    local newpath
    local directory
```

```
    # Make sure we have something to work with
    [ -z "$path" ] && return 1

    # Remove duplicate directories, if any
    for directory in ${path//:/ }; do
        contains "$newpath" "$directory" && newpath="${newpath}:${directory}"
    done

    # Remove any leading ':' separators
    # Remove any trailing ':' separators
    # Remove any duplicate ':' separators
    newpath=$(echo $newpath | sed 's/^:*//; s/:*$//; s/::/:/g')

    # Return the new path
    echo $newpath

} # end of function clean_path


#+++++++++++++++++++++++++++++++++++++++++++++++++++++++++++++++++++++++++++++
# Determine if the path contains a given directory
# Return 1 if target is contained within pattern, 0 otherwise
# Called like:  contains $PATH $dir
function contains {
    local pattern=":$1:"
    local target=$2

    # This will be a case-sensitive comparison unless nocasematch is set
    case $pattern in
        *:$target:* ) return 1;;
        *            ) return 0;;
    esac
} # end of function contains
```

Use as follows:

```
$ source chpath

$ echo $PATH
/bin:/usr/bin:/usr/local/bin:/usr/bin/X11:/usr/X11R6/bin:/home/jp/bin

$ add_to_path pre foo
-bash:add_to_path: can't add relative directory 'foo' to the $PATH

$ add_to_path post ~/foo
-bash:add_to_path: '/home/jp/foo' does not exist--aborting

$ add_to_path post '~/foo'
-bash:add_to_path: can't add relative directory '~/foo' to the $PATH

$ rm_from_path /home/jp/bin

$ echo $PATH
/bin:/usr/bin:/usr/local/bin:/usr/bin/X11:/usr/X11R6/bin
```

```
$ add_to_path /home/jp/bin
-bash:add_to_path: requires a location and a directory to add
e.g. add_to_path pre /bin

$ add_to_path post /home/jp/bin

$ echo $PATH
/bin:/usr/bin:/usr/local/bin:/usr/bin/X11:/usr/X11R6/bin:/home/jp/bin

$ rm_from_path /home/jp/bin

$ add_to_path pre /home/jp/bin

$ echo $PATH
/home/jp/bin:/bin:/usr/bin:/usr/local/bin:/usr/bin/X11:/usr/X11R6/bin
```

Discussion

There are four interesting things about this problem and the functions presented in *func_tweak_path* in the Solution.

First, if you try to modify your path or other environment variables in a shell script, it won't work because scripts run in subshells that go away when the script terminates, taking any modified environment variables with them. So instead, we source the functions into the current shell and run them from there.

Second, you may notice that add_to_path post ~/foo returns "does not exist" while add_to_path post '~/foo' returns "can't add relative directory." That's because *~/foo* is expanded by the shell to */home/jp/foo* before the function ever sees it. Not accounting for shell expansion is a common mistake. Use the *echo* command to see what the shell will actually pass to your scripts and functions.

Next, you may note the use of lines such as echo "$0:$FUNCNAME: requires a directory to add" >&2. $0:$FUNCNAME is a handy way to identify exactly where an error message is coming from. $0 is always the name of the current program (-bash in the solution's example, and the name of your script or program in other cases). Adding the function name makes it easier to track down problems when debugging. Echoing to >&2 sends the output to STDERR, where runtime user feedback, especially including warnings or errors, should go.

Finally, you can argue that the functions have inconsistent interfaces, since add_to_path and remove_from_path actually set $PATH, while clean_path displays the cleaned up path and contains returns true or false. We might not do it that way in production either, but it makes this example more interesting and shows different ways to do things. And we might argue that the interfaces make sense given what the functions do.

See Also

- For similar but much more concise, if less clear, $PATH manipulation functions, see *./examples/functions/pathfuncs* in any recent bash tarball
- Recipe 10.5, "Using Functions: Parameters and Return Values"
- Recipe 14.3, "Setting a Secure $PATH"
- Recipe 14.9, "Finding World-Writable Directories in Your $PATH"
- Recipe 14.10, "Adding the Current Directory to the $PATH"
- Recipe 16.3, "Change Your $PATH Permanently"
- Recipe 16.20, "Getting Started with a Custom Configuration"
- Appendix B

16.5   Setting Your $CDPATH

Problem

You want to make it easier to switch between several directories in various locations.

Solution

Set your $CDPATH appropriately. Your commonly used directories will likely be unique, so for a contrived example, suppose you spend a lot of time working with *init*'s *rc* directories:

```
/home/jp$ cd rc3.d
bash: cd: rc3.d: No such file or directory

/home/jp$ export CDPATH='.:/etc'

/home/jp$ cd rc3.d
/etc/rc3.d

/etc/rc3.d$ cd rc5.d
/etc/rc5.d

/etc/rc5.d$

/etc/rc5.d$ cd games
bash: cd: games: No such file or directory

/etc/rc5.d$ export CDPATH='.:/etc:/usr'

/etc/rc5.d$ cd games
/usr/games

/usr/games$
```

Discussion

According to the bash Reference, $CDPATH is "a colon-separated list of directories used as a search path for the *cd* built-in command." Think of it as $PATH for *cd*. It's a little subtle, but can be very handy.

If the argument to *cd* begins with a slash, $CDPATH will not be used. If $CDPATH is used, the absolute pathname to the new directory is printed to STDOUT, as in the example above.

Watch out when running bash in POSIX mode (e.g., as */bin/sh* or with --posix). As the bash Reference notes:

"If $CDPATH is set, the *cd* built-in will not implicitly append the current directory to it. This means that *cd* will fail if no valid directory name can be constructed from any of the entries in $CDPATH, even if a directory with the same name as the name given as an argument to *cd* exists in the current directory."

To avoid this, explicitly include **.** in $CDPATH. However, if you do that, then another subtle point noted in the bash Reference comes into play:

"If a nonempty directory name from $CDPATH is used, or if '-' is the first argument, and the directory change is successful, the absolute pathname of the new working directory is written to the standard output."

In other words, pretty much every time you use *cd* it will echo the new path to STDOUT, which is not the standard behavior.

Common directories to include in $CDPATH are:

.

The current directory (see the warning above)

~/

Your home directory

..

The parent directory

../..

The grandparent directory

~/.dirlinks

A hidden directory containing nothing but symbolic links to other commonly used directories

The above suggestions result in this:

```
export CDPATH='.:~/:..:../..:~/.dirlinks'
```

See Also

- help cd
- Recipe 16.13, "Creating a Better cd Command"
- Recipe 16.20, "Getting Started with a Custom Configuration"
- Recipe 18.1, "Moving Quickly Among Arbitrary Directories"

16.6 Shortening or Changing Command Names

Problem

You'd like to shorten a long or complex command you use often, or you'd like to rename a command you can't remember or find awkward to type.

Solution

Do not manually rename or move executable files, as many aspects of Unix and Linux depend on certain commands existing in certain places; instead, you should use aliases, functions, and possibly symbolic links.

According to the bash Reference, "Aliases allow a string to be substituted for a word when it is used as the first word of a simple command. The shell maintains a list of aliases that may be set and unset with the *alias* and *unalias* built-in commands." This means that you can rename commands, or create a macro, by listing many commands in one alias. For example, alias copy='cp' or alias ll.='ls -ld .*'.

Aliases are only expanded once, so you can change how a command works, as with alias ls='ls -F', without going into an endless loop. In most cases only the first word of the command line is checked for alias expansion, and aliases are strictly text substitutions; they *cannot use arguments* to themselves. In other words, you can't do alias='mkdir $1 && cd $1' because that doesn't work.

Functions are used in two different ways. First, they can be sourced into your interactive shell, where they become, in effect, shell scripts that are always held in memory. They are usually small, and are very fast since they are already in memory and are executed in the current process, not in a spawned subshell. Second, they may be used within a script as subroutines. Functions do allow arguments. For example:

```
# cookbook filename: func_calc

# Trivial command line calculator
function calc {
    # INTEGER ONLY! --> echo The answer is: $(( $* ))
    # Floating point
    awk "BEGIN {print \"The answer is: \" $* }";
} # end of calc
```

For personal or system-wide use, you are probably better off using aliases or functions to rename or tweak commands, but symbolic links are very useful in allowing a command to be in more than one place at a time. For example, Linux systems almost always use */bin/bash* while other systems may use */usr/bin/bash*, */usr/local/bin/bash*, or */usr/pkg/bin/bash*. While there is a better way to handle this particular issue (using *env*; see Recipe 15.1, "Finding bash Portably for #!"), in general symbolic links may be used as a workaround. We do not recommend using hard links, as they are harder to see if you are not looking for them, and they are more easily disrupted by badly behaved editors and such. Symbolic links are just more obvious and intuitive.

Discussion

Usually, only the first word of a command line is checked for alias expansion. However, if the last character of the value of that alias is a space, the next word will be checked as well. In practice, this is rarely an issue.

Since aliases can't use arguments (unlike in *csh*), you'll need to use a function if you need to pass in arguments. Since both aliases and functions reside in memory, this is not a big difference.

Unless the expand_aliases shell option is set, aliases are not expanded when the shell is not interactive. Best practices for writing scripts dictate that you not use aliases, since they may not be present on another system. You also need to define functions inside your script, or explicitly source them before use (see Recipe 19.14, "Avoiding "command not found" When Using Functions"). Thus, the best place to define them is in your global */etc/bashrc* or your local *~/.bashrc*.

See Also

- Recipe 10.4, "Defining Functions"
- Recipe 10.5, "Using Functions: Parameters and Return Values"
- Recipe 10.7, "Redefining Commands with alias"
- Recipe 14.4, "Clearing All Aliases"
- Recipe 15.1, "Finding bash Portably for #!"
- Recipe 16.18, "Using Initialization Files Correctly"
- Recipe 16.19, "Creating Self-Contained, Portable RC Files"
- Recipe 16.20, "Getting Started with a Custom Configuration"
- Recipe 19.14, "Avoiding "command not found" When Using Functions"

16.7 Adjusting Shell Behavior and Environment

Problem

You want to adjust your shell environment to account for the way you work, your physical location, your language, and more.

Solution

See the table in the section "Adjusting Shell Behavior Using set, shopt, and Environment Variables" in Appendix A.

Discussion

There are three ways to adjust various aspects of your environment. *set* is standardized in POSIX and uses one-letter options. *shopt* is specifically for *bash* shell options. And there are many environment variables in use for historical reasons, as well as for compatibility with many third-party applications. How you adjust what and where, can be be very confusing. The table in the section "Adjusting Shell Behavior Using set, shopt, and Environment Variables" in Appendix A will help you sort it out, but it's too big to duplicate here.

See Also

- help set
- help shopt
- Bash Docs (*http://www.bashcookbook.com*)
- "Adjusting Shell Behavior Using set, shopt, and Environment Variables" in Appendix A

16.8 Adjusting readline Behavior Using .inputrc

Problem

You'd like to adjust the way *bash* handles input, especially command completion. For example, you'd like it to be case-insensitive.

Solution

Edit or create a *~/.inputrc* or */etc/inputrc* file as appropriate. There are many parameters you can adjust to your liking. To have *readline* use your file when it initializes, set $INPUTRC; for example, set INPUTRC='~/.inputrc'. To re-read the file and apply or test after making changes, use bind -f *filename*.

We recommend you explore the *bind* command and the *readline* documentation, especially bind -v, bind -l, bind -s, and bind -p, though the last one is rather long and cryptic.

Some useful settings for users from other environments, notably Windows, are (see the section "Readline Init File Syntax" in Appendix A):

```
# settings/inputrc:  # readline settings
# To re-read (and implement changes to this file) use:
# bind -f $SETTINGS/inputrc

# First, include any systemwide bindings and variable
# assignments from /etc/inputrc
# (fails silently if file doesn't exist)
$include /etc/inputrc

$if Bash
  # Ignore case when doing completion
    set completion-ignore-case on
  # Completed dir names have a slash appended
    set mark-directories on
  # Completed names which are symlinks to dirs have a slash appended
    set mark-symlinked-directories on
  # List ls -F for completion
    set visible-stats on
  # Cycle through ambiguous completions instead of list
    "\C-i": menu-complete
  # Set bell to audible
    set bell-style audible
  # List possible completions instead of ringing bell
    set show-all-if-ambiguous on

  # From the readline documentation at
  # http://tiswww.tis.case.edu/php/chet/readline/readline.html#SEC12
  # Macros that are convenient for shell interaction
  # edit the path
    "\C-xp": "PATH=${PATH}\e\C-e\C-a\ef\C-f"
  # prepare to type a quoted word -- insert open and close double quotes
  # and move to just after the open quote
    "\C-x\"": "\"\"\C-b"
  # insert a backslash (testing backslash escapes in sequences and macros)
    "\C-x\\": "\\"
  # Quote the current or previous word
    "\C-xq": "\eb\"\ef\""
  # Add a binding to refresh the line, which is unbound
    "\C-xr": redraw-current-line
  # Edit variable on current line.
    #"\M-\C-v": "\C-a\C-k$\C-y\M-\C-e\C-a\C-y="
    "\C-xe": "\C-a\C-k$\C-y\M-\C-e\C-a\C-y="
$endif
```

You will want to experiment with these and other settings. Also note the $include to use the system settings, but make sure you can change them if you like. See Recipe 16.20, "Getting Started with a Custom Configuration," for the downloadable file.

Discussion

Many people are not aware of how customizable, not to mention powerful and flexible, the GNU Readline library is. Having said that, there is no "one size fits all" approach. You should work out a configuration that suits your needs and habits.

Note the first time readline is called it performs its normal startup file processing, including looking at $INPUTRC, or defaulting to ~/.inputrc if that's not set.

See Also

- help bind
- Readline docs at *http://www.bashcookbook.com*
- Recipe 16.19, "Creating Self-Contained, Portable RC Files"
- Recipe 16.20, "Getting Started with a Custom Configuration"

16.9 Keeping a Private Stash of Utilities by Adding ~/bin

Problem

You have a stash of personal utilities you like to use, but you are not *root* on the system and can't place them into the normal locations like */bin* or */usr/local/bin*, or there is some other reason to separate them.

Solution

Create a *~/bin* directory, place your utilities in it and add it to your path:

```
$ PATH="$PATH:~/bin"
```

You'll want to make this change in one of your shell initialization files, such as *~/.bashrc*. Some systems already add $HOME/bin as the last directory in a nonprivileged user account by default, so check first.

Discussion

As a fully qualified shell user (well, you bought this book), you'll certainly be creating lots of scripts. It's inconvenient to invoke scripts with their full pathname. By collecting your scripts in a *~/bin* directory, you can make your scripts look like regular Unix programs—at least to you.

For security reasons, don't put your *bin* directory at the start of your path. Starting your path with *~/bin* makes it easy to override system commands—which is inconvenient, if it happens accidentally (we've all done it), and dangerous if it's done maliciously.

See Also

- Recipe 14.9, "Finding World-Writable Directories in Your $PATH"
- Recipe 14.10, "Adding the Current Directory to the $PATH"
- Recipe 16.3, "Change Your $PATH Permanently"
- Recipe 16.4, "Change Your $PATH Temporarily"
- Recipe 16.6, "Shortening or Changing Command Names"
- Recipe 19.4, "Naming Your Script Test"

16.10 Using Secondary Prompts: $PS2, $PS3, $PS4

Problem

You'd like to understand what the $PS2, PS3, and PS4 prompts do.

Solution

$PS2 is called the *secondary prompt string* and is used when you are interactively entering a command that you have not completed yet. It is usually set to "> " but you can redefine it. For example:

```
[jp@freebsd jobs:0]
/home/jp$ export PS2='Secondary: '

[jp@freebsd jobs:0]
/home/jp$ for i in $(ls)
Secondary: do
Secondary: echo $i
Secondary: done
colors
deepdir
trunc_PWD
```

$PS3 is the *select* prompt, and is used by the *select* statement to prompt the user for a value. It defaults to #?, which isn't very intuitive. You should change it before using the *select* command; for example:

```
[jp@freebsd jobs:0]
/home/jp$ select i in $(ls)
Secondary: do
Secondary: echo $i
Secondary: done
```

```
1) colors
2) deepdir
3) trunc_PWD
#? 1
colors
#? ^C

[jp@freebsd jobs:0]
/home/jp$ export PS3='Choose a directory to echo: '

[jp@freebsd jobs:0]
/home/jp$ select i in $(ls); do echo $i; done
1) colors
2) deepdir
3) trunc_PWD
Choose a directory to echo: 2
deepdir
Choose a directory to echo: ^C
```

$PS4 is displayed during trace output. Its first character is shown as many times as necessary to denote the nesting depth. The default is "+ ". For example:

```
[jp@freebsd jobs:0]
/home/jp$ cat demo
#!/usr/bin/env bash

set -o xtrace

alice=girl
echo "$alice"

ls -l $(type -path vi)

echo line 10
echO line 11
echo line 12

[jp@freebsd jobs:0]
/home/jp$ ./demo
+ alice=girl
+ echo girl
girl
++ type -path vi
+ ls -l /usr/bin/vi
-r-xr-xr-x  6 root  wheel  285108 May  8  2005 /usr/bin/vi
+ echo line 10
line 10
+ echO line 11
./demo: line 11: echO: command not found
+ echo line 12
line 12

[jp@freebsd jobs:0]
/home/jp$ export PS4='+xtrace $LINENO: '
```

```
[jp@freebsd jobs:0]
/home/jp$ ./demo
+xtrace 5: alice=girl
+xtrace 6: echo girl
girl
++xtrace 8: type -path vi
+xtrace 8: ls -l /usr/bin/vi
-r-xr-xr-x  6 root  wheel  285108 May  8  2005 /usr/bin/vi
+xtrace 10: echo line 10
line 10
+xtrace 11: echO line 11
./demo: line 11: echO: command not found
+xtrace 12: echo line 12
line 12
```

Discussion

The $PS4 prompt uses the $LINENO variable, which when used in a function under versions of *bash* prior to 2.0 returns the number of simple commands executed, rather than the actual line number in the function. Also note the single quotes, which defer expansion of the variable until display time.

See Also

- Recipe 1.1, "Decoding the Prompt"
- Recipe 3.7, "Selecting from a List of Options"
- Recipe 6.16, "Creating Simple Menus"
- Recipe 6.17, "Changing the Prompt on Simple Menus"
- Recipe 16.2, "Customizing Your Prompt"
- Recipe 19.13, "Debugging Scripts"

16.11 Synchronizing Shell History Between Sessions

Problem

You run more than one *bash* session at a time and you would like to have a shared history between them. You'd also like to prevent the last session closed from clobbering the history from any other sessions.

Solution

Use the *history* command to synchronize your history between sessions manually or automatically.

Discussion

Using default settings, the last shell to gracefully exit will overwrite your history file, so unless it is synchronized with any other shells you had open at the same time, it will clobber their histories. Using the shell option shown in Recipe 16.12, "Setting Shell History Options," to append rather than overwrite the history file helps, but keeping your history in sync across sessions may offer additional benefits.

Manually synchronizing history involves writing an alias to append the current history to the history file, then re-reading anything new in that file into the current shell's history:

```
$ history -a
$ history -n

# OR, 'history sync'
alias hs='history -a ; history -n'
```

The disadvantage to this approach is that you must manually run the commands in each shell when you want to synchronize your history.

To automate that approach, you could use the $PROMPT_COMMAND variable:

```
PROMPT_COMMAND='history -a ; history -n'
```

The value of $PROMPT_COMMAND is interpreted as a command to execute each time the default interactive prompt $PS1 is displayed. The disadvantage to that approach is that it runs those commands *every time* $PS1 is displayed. That is very often, and on a heavily loaded or slower system that can cause it significant slowdown in your shell, especially if you have a large history.

See Also

- help history
- Recipe 16.12, "Setting Shell History Options"

16.12 Setting Shell History Options

Problem

You'd like more control over your command-line history.

Solution

Set the $HIST* variables and shell options as desired.

Discussion

The $HISTFILESIZE variable sets the number of lines permitted in the $HISTFILE. The default for $HISTSIZE is 500 lines, and $HISTFILE is *~/.bash_history* unless you are in POSIX mode, in which case it's *~/.sh_history*. Increasing $HISTSIZE may be useful, and unsetting it causes the $HISTFILE length to be unlimited. Changing $HISTFILE probably isn't necessary, except that if it is not set or the file is not writable, no history will be written to disk. The $HISTSIZE variable sets the number of lines permitted in the history stack in memory.

$HISTIGNORE and $HISTCONTROL control what goes into your history in the first place. $HISTIGNORE is more flexible since it allows you to specify patterns to decide what command lines to save to the history. $HISTCONTROL is more limited in that it supports only the few keywords listed here (any other value is ignored):

ignorespace
> Command lines that begin with a space character are not saved in the history list.

ignoredups
> Command lines that match the previous history entry are not saved in the history list.

ignoreboth
> Shorthand for both ignorespace and ignoredups.

erasedups
> All previous command lines that match the current line are removed from the history list before that line is saved.

If $HISTCONTROL is not set, or does not contain any of these keywords, all commands are saved to the history list, subject to processing $HISTIGNORE. The second and subsequent lines of a multiline compound command are not tested, and are added to the history regardless of the value of $HISTCONTROL.

(Material in the preceding paragraphs has been adapted from Edition 2.5b of *The GNU Bash Reference Manual* for *bash* Version 2.05b, last updated July 15, 2002; *http://www.gnu.org/software/bash/manual/bashref.html*.)

As of *bash* version 3, there is a fascinating new variable called $HISTTIMEFORMAT. If set and non-null, it specifies an *strftime* format string to use when displaying or writing the history. If you don't have *bash* version 3, but you do use a terminal with a scrollback buffer, adding a date and time stamp to your prompt can also be very helpful. See Recipe 16.2, "Customizing Your Prompt." Watch out because stock *bash* does not put a trailing space after the format, but some systems (e.g., Debian) have patched it to do so:

```
bash-3.00# history
    1  ls -la
    2  help history
```

```
    3  help fc
    4  history

# Ugly
bash-3.00# export HISTTIMEFORMAT='%Y-%m-%d_%H:%M:%S'

bash-3.00# history
    1  2006-10-25_20:48:04ls -la
    2  2006-10-25_20:48:11help history
    3  2006-10-25_20:48:14help fc
    4  2006-10-25_20:48:18history
    5  2006-10-25_20:48:39export HISTTIMEFORMAT='%Y-%m-%d_%H:%M:%S'
    6  2006-10-25_20:48:41history

# Better
bash-3.00# HISTTIMEFORMAT='%Y-%m-%d_%H:%M:%S; '

bash-3.00# history
    1  2006-10-25_20:48:04; ls -la
    2  2006-10-25_20:48:11; help history
    3  2006-10-25_20:48:14; help fc
    4  2006-10-25_20:48:18; history
    5  2006-10-25_20:48:39; export HISTTIMEFORMAT='%Y-%m-%d_%H:%M:%S'
    6  2006-10-25_20:48:41; history
    7  2006-10-25_20:48:47; HISTTIMEFORMAT='%Y-%m-%d_%H:%M:%S; '
    8  2006-10-25_20:48:48; history

# Getting tricky now
bash-3.00# HISTTIMEFORMAT=': %Y-%m-%d_%H:%M:%S; '

bash-3.00# history
    1  : 2006-10-25_20:48:04; ls -la
    2  : 2006-10-25_20:48:11; help history
    3  : 2006-10-25_20:48:14; help fc
    4  : 2006-10-25_20:48:18; history
    5  : 2006-10-25_20:48:39; export HISTTIMEFORMAT='%Y-%m-%d_%H:%M:%S'
    6  : 2006-10-25_20:48:41; history
    7  : 2006-10-25_20:48:47; HISTTIMEFORMAT='%Y-%m-%d_%H:%M:%S; '
    8  : 2006-10-25_20:48:48; history
```

The last example uses the : built-in with the ; metacharacter to encapsulate the date stamp into a "do nothing" command (e.g., : 2006-10-25_20:48:48;). This allows you to reuse a literal line from the history file without having to bother parsing out the date stamp. Note the space after the : is required.

There are also shell options to configure history-file handling. If histappend is set, the shell appends to the history file; otherwise it overwrites the history file. Note that it is still truncated to $HISTSIZE. If cmdhist is set, multiline commands are saved as a single line, with semicolons added as needed. If lithist is set, multiline commands are saved with embedded newlines.

See Also

- help history
- help fc
- Recipe 16.2, "Customizing Your Prompt"
- Recipe 16.7, "Adjusting Shell Behavior and Environment"
- Recipe 16.11, "Synchronizing Shell History Between Sessions"

16.13 Creating a Better cd Command

Problem

You *cd* into a lot of deep directories and would like to type cd ..... instead of cd ../
../../.. to move up four levels.

Solution

Use this function:

```
# cookbook filename: func_cd

# Allow use of 'cd ...' to cd up 2 levels, 'cd ....' up 3, etc. (like 4NT/4DOS)
# Usage: cd ..., etc.
function cd {

    local option= length= count= cdpath= i= # Local scope and start clean

    # If we have a -L or -P sym link option, save then remove it
    if [ "$1" = "-P" -o "$1" = "-L" ]; then
        option="$1"
        shift
    fi

    # Are we using the special syntax?  Make sure $1 isn't empty, then
    # match the first 3 characters of $1 to see if they are '...' then
    # make sure there isn't a slash by trying a substitution; if it fails,
    # there's no slash.  Both of these string routines require Bash 2.0+
    if [ -n "$1" -a "${1:0:3}" = '...' -a "$1" = "${1%/*}" ]; then
        # We are using special syntax
        length=${#1}  # Assume that $1 has nothing but dots and count them
        count=2       # 'cd ..' still means up one level, so ignore first two

        # While we haven't run out of dots, keep cd'ing up 1 level
        for ((i=$count;i<=$length;i++)); do
            cdpath="${cdpath}../" # Build the cd path
        done

        # Actually do the cd
        builtin cd $option "$cdpath"
    elif [ -n "$1" ]; then
```

```
        # We are NOT using special syntax; just plain old cd by itself
        builtin cd $option "$*"
    else
        # We are NOT using special syntax; plain old cd by itself to home dir
        builtin cd $option
    fi
} # end of cd
```

Discussion

The *cd* command takes an optional -L or -P argument that respectively follow symbolic links or follow the physical directory structure. Either way, we have to take them into account if we want to redefine how *cd* works.

Then, we make sure $1 isn't empty and match the first three characters of $1 to see if they are '...'. We then make sure there isn't a slash by trying a substitution; if it fails, there's no slash. Both of these string routines require *bash* version 2.0+. After that, we build the actual cd command using a portable for loop and finally use the *builtin* command to use the shell *cd* and not create an endless loop by recursively calling our cd function. We also pass in the -L or -P argument if present.

See Also

- help cd
- *http://jpsoft.com* for the 4NT shell, which is the source of this idea
- Recipe 15.5, "Using for Loops Portably"
- Recipe 16.5, "Setting Your $CDPATH"
- Recipe 16.14, "Creating and Changing into a New Directory in One Step"
- Recipe 16.15, "Getting to the Bottom of Things"
- Recipe 16.20, "Getting Started with a Custom Configuration"
- Recipe 18.1, "Moving Quickly Among Arbitrary Directories"

16.14 Creating and Changing into a New Directory in One Step

Problem

You often create new directories and immediately change into them for some operation, and all that typing is tedious.

Solution

Add the following function to an appropriate configuration file such as your *~/.bashrc* file and source it:

```
# cookbook filename: func_mcd

# mkdir newdir then cd into it
# usage: mcd (<mode>) <dir>
function mcd {
    local newdir='_mcd_command_failed_'
    if [ -d "$1" ]; then          # Dir exists, mention that...
        echo "$1 exists..."
        newdir="$1"
    else
        if [ -n "$2" ]; then      # We've specified a mode
            command mkdir -p -m $1 "$2" && newdir="$2"
        else                      # Plain old mkdir
            command mkdir -p "$1" && newdir="$1"
        fi
    fi
    builtin cd "$newdir"          # No matter what, cd into it
} # end of mcd
```

For example:

```
$ source mcd

$ pwd
/home/jp

$ mcd 0700 junk

$ pwd
/home/jp/junk

$ ls -ld .
drwx------  2 jp  users  512 Dec  6 01:03 .
```

Discussion

This function allows you to optionally specify a mode for the *mkdir* command to use when creating the directory. If the directory already exists, it will mention that fact but still *cd* into it. We use the *command* command to make sure that we ignore any shell functions for *mkdir*, and the *builtin* command to make sure we only use the shell *cd*.

We also assign _mcd_command_failed_ to a local variable in case the *mkdir* fails. If it works, the correct new directory is assigned. If it fails, when the *cd* tries to execute it will display a reasonably useful message, assuming you don't have a lot of *_mcd_ command_failed_* directories lying around:

```
$ mcd /etc/junk
mkdir: /etc/junk: Permission denied
-bash: cd: _mcd_command_failed_: No such file or directory
```

You might think that we could easily improve this using break or exit if the mkdir fails. break only works in a for, while, or until loop and exit will actually exit our shell, since a sourced function runs in the same process as the shell. We could, however, use return, which we will leave as an exercise for the reader.

```
command mkdir -p "$1" && newdir="$1" || exit 1  # This will exit our shell
command mkdir -p "$1" && newdir="$1" || break   # This will fail
```

You could also place the following in a trivial function, but we obviously prefer the more robust version given in the solution:

```
function mcd { mkdir "$1" && cd "$1"; }
```

See Also

- man mkdir
- help cd
- help function
- Recipe 16.13, "Creating a Better cd Command"
- Recipe 16.18, "Using Initialization Files Correctly"
- Recipe 16.19, "Creating Self-Contained, Portable RC Files"
- Recipe 16.20, "Getting Started with a Custom Configuration"

16.15 Getting to the Bottom of Things

Problem

You work in a lot of narrow but deep directory structures, where all the content is at the bottom and you're tired of having to manually *cd* so many levels.

Solution

```
alias bot='cd $(dirname $(find . | tail -1))'
```

Discussion

This use of *find* in a large directory structure such as */usr* could take a while and isn't recommended.

Depending on how your directory structure is set up, this may not work for you; you'll have to try it and see. The find . will simply list all the files and directories in the current directory and below, the tail -1 will grab the last line, dirname will extract just the path, and cd will take you there. It may be possible for you to tweak the command to get it to put you in the right place. For example:

```
alias bot='cd $(dirname $(find . | sort -r | tail -5 | head -1))'
alias bot='cd $(dirname $(find . | sort -r | grep -v 'X11' | tail -3 | head -1))'
```

Keep trying the part in the inner-most parentheses, especially tweaking the *find* command, until you get the results you need. Perhaps there is a key file or directory at the bottom of the structure, in which case the following function might work:

```
function bot { cd $(dirname $(find . | grep -e "$1" | head -1)); }
```

Note that aliases can't use arguments, so this must be a function. We use *grep* rather than a -name argument to *find* because *grep* is much more flexible. Depending on your structure, you might want to use *tail* instead of *head*. Again, test the *find* command first.

See Also

- man find
- man dirname
- man head
- man tail
- man grep
- man sort
- Recipe 16.13, "Creating a Better cd Command"
- Recipe 16.14, "Creating and Changing into a New Directory in One Step"

16.16 Adding New Features to bash Using Loadable Built-ins

The material in this recipe also appears in *Learning the bash Shell* by Cameron Newham (O'Reilly).

Problem

You have something that you'd like *bash* to do, but there's no built-in command for it. For efficiency reasons, you want it to be built-in to the shell rather than an external program. Or, you already have the code in C and don't want to or can't rewrite it.

Solution

Use the dynamically loadable built-ins introduced in *bash* version 2.0. The *bash* archive contains a number of pre-written built-ins in the directory *./examples/loadables/*, especially the canonical *hello.c*. You can build them by uncommenting the lines in the file *Makefile* that are relevant to your system, and typing *make*. We'll take one of these built-ins, *tty*, and use it as a case study for built-ins in general.

The following is a list of the built-ins provided in *bash* version 3.2's *./examples/ loadables/*:

basename.c	id.c	push.c	truefalse.c
cat.c	ln.c	realpath.c	tty.c
cut.c	logname.c	rmdir.c	uname.c
dirname.c	mkdir.c	sleep.c	unlink.c
finfo.c	necho.c	strftime.c	whoami.c
getconf.c	pathchk.c	sync.c	perl/bperl.c
head.c	print.c	tee.c	perl/iperl.c
hello.c	printenv.c	template.c	

Discussion

On systems that support dynamic loading, you can write your own built-ins in C, compile them into shared objects, and load them at any time from within the shell with the *enable* built-in.

We will discuss briefly how to go about writing a built-in and loading it in *bash*. The discussion assumes that you have experience with writing, compiling, and linking C programs.

tty will mimic the standard Unix command *tty*. It will print the name of the terminal that is connected to standard input. The built-in will, like the command, return true if the device is a TTY and false if it isn't. In addition, it will take an option, -s, which specifies that it should work silently (i.e., print nothing and just return a result).

The C code for a built-in can be divided into three distinct sections: the code that implements the functionality of the built-in, a help text message definition, and a structure describing the built-in so that *bash* can access it.

The description structure is quite straightforward and takes the form:

```
struct builtin builtin_name_struct = {
    "builtin_name",
    function_name,
    BUILTIN_ENABLED,
    help_array,
    "usage",
    0
};
```

The trailing _struct is required on the first line to give the *enable* built-in a way to find the symbol name. *builtin_name* is the name of the built-in as it appears in *bash*. The next field, *function-name*, is the name of the C function that implements the built-in. We'll look at this in a moment. BUILTIN_ENABLED is the initial state of the built-in, whether it is enabled or not. This field should always be set to BUILTIN_ ENABLED. *help_array* is an array of strings that are printed when *help* is used on the built-in. *usage* is the shorter form of help: the command and its options. The last field in the structure should be set to 0.

In our example we'll call the built-in tty, the C function tty_builtin, and the help array tty_doc. The usage string will be tty [-s]. The resulting structure looks like this:

```
struct builtin tty_struct = {
    "tty",
    tty_builtin,
    BUILTIN_ENABLED,
    tty_doc,
    "tty [-s]",
    0
};
```

The next section is the code that does the work. It looks like this:

```
tty_builtin (list)
    WORD_LIST *list;
{
    int opt, sflag;
    char *t;

    reset_internal_getopt ( );
    sflag = 0;
    while ((opt = internal_getopt (list, "s")) != -1)
    {
      switch (opt)
      {
          case 's':
              sflag = 1;
              break;
          default:
              builtin_usage ( );
              return (EX_USAGE);
      }
    }
    list = loptend;

    t = ttyname (0);
    if (sflag == 0)
        puts (t ? t : "not a tty");
    return (t ? EXECUTION_SUCCESS : EXECUTION_FAILURE);
}
```

Built-in functions are always given a pointer to a list of type WORD_LIST. If the built-in doesn't actually take any options, you must call no_options(list) and check its return value before any further processing. If the return value is nonzero, your function should immediately return with the value EX_USAGE.

You must always use internal_getopt rather than the standard C library getopt to process the built-in options. Also, you must reset the option processing first by calling reset_internal_getopt.

Option processing is performed in the standard way, except if the options are incorrect, in which case you should return EX_USAGE. Any arguments left after option processing are pointed to by loptend. Once the function is finished, it should return the value EXECUTION_SUCCESS or EXECUTION_FAILURE.

In the case of our *tty* built-in, we then just call the standard C library routine ttyname, and if the -s option wasn't given, print out the name of the TTY (or "not a tty" if the device wasn't). The function then returns success or failure, depending upon the result from the call to ttyname.

The last major section is the help definition. This is simply an array of strings, the last element of the array being NULL. Each string is printed to standard output when help is run on the built-in. You should, therefore, keep the strings to 76 characters or less (an 80-character standard display minus a 4-character margin). In the case of tty, our help text looks like this:

```
char *tty_doc[] = {
    "tty writes the name of the terminal that is opened for standard",
    "input to standard output.  If the `-s' option is supplied, nothing",
    "is written; the exit status determines whether or not the standard",
    "input is connected to a tty.",
    (char *)NULL
};
```

The last things to add to our code are the necessary C header files. These are *stdio.h* and the *bash* header files *config.h*, *builtins.h*, *shell.h*, and *bashgetopt.h*.

Here is the C program in its entirety:

```
# cookbook filename: builtin_tty.c

#include "config.h"
#include <stdio.h>
#include "builtins.h"
#include "shell.h"
#include "bashgetopt.h"


extern char *ttyname ( );

tty_builtin (list)
    WORD_LIST *list;
{
    int opt, sflag;
    char *t;

    reset_internal_getopt ( );
    sflag = 0;
    while ((opt = internal_getopt (list, "s")) != -1)
```

```
    {
        switch (opt)
        {
            case 's':
                sflag = 1;
                break;
            default:
                builtin_usage ( );
                return (EX_USAGE);
        }
    }
    list = loptend;

    t = ttyname (0);
    if (sflag == 0)
        puts (t ? t : "not a tty");
    return (t ? EXECUTION_SUCCESS : EXECUTION_FAILURE);
}

char *tty_doc[] = {
    "tty writes the name of the terminal that is opened for standard",
    "input to standard output.  If the `-s' option is supplied, nothing",
    "is written; the exit status determines whether or not the standard",
    "input is connected to a tty.",
    (char *)NULL
};

struct builtin tty_struct = {
    "tty",
    tty_builtin,
    BUILTIN_ENABLED,
    tty_doc,
    "tty [-s]",
    0
};
```

We now need to compile and link this as a dynamic shared object. Unfortunately, different systems have different ways to specify how to compile dynamic shared objects.

The *configure* script should put the correct commands into the *Makefile* automatically. If for some reason it doesn't, Table 16-1 lists some common systems and the commands needed to compile and link *tty.c*. Replace *archive* with the path of the top level of the *bash* archive.

Table 16-1. Common systems and commands to compile and link tty.c

System	Commands
SunOS 4	cc -pic -I*archive* -I*archive*/builtins -I*archive*/lib -c tty.c ld -assert pure-text -o tty tty.o
SunOS 5	cc -K pic -I*archive* -I*archive*/builtins -I*archive*/lib -c tty.c cc -dy -z text -G -i -h tty -o tty tty.o
SVR4, SVR4.2, Irix	cc -K PIC -I*archive* -I*archive*/builtins -I*archive*/lib -c tty.c ld -dy -z text -G -h tty -o tty tty.o

System	Commands
AIX	cc -K -Iarchive -Iarchive/builtins -Iarchive/lib -c tty.c ld -bdynamic -bnoentry -bexpall -G -o tty tty.o
Linux	cc -fPIC -Iarchive -Iarchive/builtins -Iarchive/lib -c tty.c ld -shared -o tty tty.o
NetBSD, FreeBSD	cc -fpic -Iarchive -Iarchive/builtins -Iarchive/lib -c tty.c ld -x -Bshareable -o tty tty.o

After you have compiled and linked the program, you should have a shared object called *tty*. To load this into *bash*, just type enable -f tty tty. You can remove a loaded built-in at any time with the -d option, e.g., enable -d tty.

You can put as many built-ins as you like into one shared object as long as the three main sections for each built-in are in the same C file. It is best, however, to keep the number of built-ins per shared object small. You will also probably find it best to keep similar built-ins, or built-ins that work together (e.g., *pushd*, *popd*, *dirs*), in the same shared object.

bash loads a shared object as a whole, so if you ask it to load one built-in from a shared object that has 20 built-ins, it will load all 20 (but only one will be enabled). For this reason, keep the number of built-ins small to save loading memory with unnecessary things, and group similar built-ins so that if the user enables one of them, all of them will be loaded and ready in memory for enabling.

See Also

- *./examples/loadables* in any *bash* tarball newer than 2.0

16.17 Improving Programmable Completion

This recipe was adapted directly from *Learning the bash Shell* by Cameron Newham (O'Reilly).

Problem

You love *bash*'s programmable completion but wish it could be more aware of context, especially for commands that you use often.

Solution

Find and install additional programmable completion libraries, or write your own. Some examples are provided in the *bash* tarball in *./examples/complete*. Some distributions (e.g., SUSE) have their own version in */etc/profile.d/complete.bash*. However, the largest and most well known of the third-party libraries is certainly Ian Macdonald's, which you may download as a tarball or RPM from *http://www.caliban.org/bash/index.shtml#completion* or *http://freshmeat.net/projects/bashcompletion/*. This library is already included in Debian (and derivatives like Ubuntu and MEPIS), and it is present in Fedora Extras as well as other third-party repositories.

 According to Ian's *README*: "Many of the completion functions assume GNU versions of the various text utilities that they call (e.g., *grep*, *sed*, and *awk*). Your mileage may vary."

At the time of this writing there are 103 modules provided by the *bash-completion-20060301.tar.gz* library. The following is an excerpted list:

```
# bash alias completion
# bash export completion
# bash shell function completion
# chown(1) completion
# chgrp(1) completion
# RedHat & Debian GNU/Linux if{up,down} completion
# cvs(1) completion
# rpm(8) completion
# chsh(1) completion
# chkconfig(8) completion
# ssh(1) completion
# GNU make(1) completion
# GNU tar(1) completion
# jar(1) completion
# Linux iptables(8) completion
# tcpdump(8) completion
# ncftp(1) bookmark completion
# Debian dpkg(8) completion
# Java completion
# PINE address-book completion
# mutt completion
# Python completion
# Perl completion
# FreeBSD package management tool completion
# mplayer(1) completion
# gpg(1) completion
# dict(1) completion
# cdrecord(1) completion
# yum(8) completion
# smartctl(8) completion
# vncviewer(1) completion
# svn completion
```

Discussion

Programmable completion is a feature that was introduced in *bash* version 2.04. It extends the built-in textual completion by providing hooks into the completion mechanism. This means that it is possible to write virtually any form of completion desired. For instance, if you were typing the *man* command, wouldn't it be nice to be able to hit Tab and have the manual sections listed for you. Programmable completion allows you to do this and much more.

This recipe will only look at the basics of programmable completion. If you need to delve into the inner depths and actually write your own completion code, first check the libraries of completion commands developed by other people to see if what you want has already been done or is available for use as an example. We'll just outline the basic commands and procedures needed to use the completion mechanism, should you ever need to work on it yourself.

In order to be able to do textual completion in a particular way, you first have to tell the shell how to do it when you press the Tab key. This is done via the *complete* command.

The main argument of *complete* is a name that can be the name of a command or anything else that you want textual completion to work with. As an example we will look at the *gunzip* utility that allows compressed archives of various types to be uncompressed. Normally, if you were to type:

```
$ gunzip [TAB][TAB]
```

you would get a list of filenames from which to complete. This list will include all kinds of things that are unsuitable for *gunzip*. What we really would like is the subset of those files that are suitable for the utility to work on. We can set this up by using *complete*:

```
complete -A file -X '!*.@(Z|gz|tgz)' gunzip
```

Note that in order for @(Z|gz|tgz) to work, you will need extended pattern matching switched on via shopt -s extglob.

Here we are telling the completion mechanism that when the *gunzip* command is typed in we want it to do something special. The -A flag is an action and takes a variety of arguments. In this case we provide file as the argument, which asks the mechanism to provide a list of files as possible completions. The next step is to cut this down by selecting only the files that we know will work with *gunzip*. We've done this with the -X option, which takes as its argument a filter pattern. When applied to the completion list, the filter removes anything matching the pattern, i.e., the result is everything that *doesn't* match the pattern. *gunzip* can uncompress a number of file types, including those with the extensions *.Z*, *.gz*, and *.tgz*. We want to match all filenames with extensions that have one of these three patterns. We then have to negate this with a ! (remember, the filter removes the patterns that match).

We can actually try this out first and see what completions would be returned without having to use *complete to* install the completion. We can do this via the *compgen* command:

```
compgen -A file -X '!*.@(Z|gz|tgz)'
```

This produces a list of completion strings (assuming you have some files in the current directory with these extensions). *compgen* is useful for trying out filters to see what completion strings are produced. It is also needed when more complex completion is required. We'll see an example of this later in the recipe.

Once we install the *complete* command above, either by sourcing a script that contains it or executing it on the command line, we can use the augmented completion mechanism with the *gunzip* command:

```
$gunzip [TAB][TAB]
archive.tgz  archive1.tgz  file.Z
$gunzip
```

You can probably see that there are other things we could do. What about providing a list of possible arguments for specific options to a command? For instance, the *kill* command takes a process ID, but can optionally take a signal name preceded by a dash (-) or a signal name following the option -n. We could complete with PIDs but, if there is a dash or a -n, it'll have to be done with signal names.

This is slightly more complex than the one-line example above. Here we will need some code to distinguish what has already been typed in. We'll also need to get the PIDs and the signal names. We'll put the code in a function and call the function via the completion mechanism. Here's the code to call our function, which we'll name _kill:

```
complete -F _kill kill
```

The -F option to complete tells it to call the function named _kill when it is performing textual completion for the *kill* command. The next step is to code the function:

```
# cookbook filename: func_kill

_kill() {
    local cur
        local sign

    COMPREPLY=( )
    cur=${COMP_WORDS[COMP_CWORD]}

    if (($COMP_CWORD == 2)) && [[ ${COMP_WORDS[1]} == -n ]]; then
       # return list of available signals
          _signals
    elif (($COMP_CWORD == 1 )) && [[ "$cur" == -* ]]; then
       # return list of available signals
       sign="-"
       _signals
        else
```

```
        # return list of available PIDs
        COMPREPLY=( $( compgen -W '$( command ps axo pid | sed 1d )' $cur ) )
    fi
}
```

The code is fairly standard, apart from the use of some special environment variables and a call to a function called _signals, which we'll come to shortly.

The variable $COMPREPLY is used to hold the result that is returned to the completion mechanism. It is an array that holds a set of completion strings. Initially this is set to an empty array.

The local variable $cur is a convenience variable to make the code more readable because the value is used in several places. Its value is derived from an element in the array $COMP_WORDS. This array holds the individual words on the current command line. $COMP_CWORD is an index into the array; it gives the word containing the current cursor position. The value of $cur is the word currently containing the cursor.

The first if statement tests for the condition where the *kill* command is followed by the -n option. If the first word was -n and we are on the second word, then we need to provide a list of signal names for the completion mechanism.

The second if statement is similar, except this time we are looking to complete on the current word, which starts with a dash and is followed by anything else. The body of this if again calls _signals but this time it sets the sign variable to a dash. The reason for this will become obvious when we look at the _signals function.

The remaining part in the else block returns a list of process IDs. This uses the *compgen* command to help create the array of completion strings. First it runs the *ps* command to obtain a list of PIDs and then pipes the result through *sed* to remove the first line (which is the heading "PID"). This is then given as an argument to the -W option of *compgen*, which takes a word list. *compgen* then returns all completion strings that match the value of the variable $cur and the resulting array is assigned to $COMPREPLY.

compgen is important here because we can't just return the complete list of PIDs provided by *ps*. The user may have already typed part of a PID and then attempted completion. As the partial PID will be in the variable $cur, *compgen* restricts the results to those that match or partially match that value. For example if $cur had the value 5 then *compgen* would return only values beginning with a "5", such as 5, 59, or 562.

The last piece of the puzzle is the _signals function:

```
# cookbook filename: func_signals

_signals() {
    local i

    COMPREPLY=( $( compgen -A signal SIG${cur#-} ))

    for (( i=0; i < ${#COMPREPLY[@]}; i++ )); do
```

```
        COMPREPLY[i]=$sign${COMPREPLY[i]#SIG}
    done
}
```

While we can get a list of signal names by using complete's -A signal, the names are unfortunately not in a form that is very usable and so we can't use this to directly generate the array of names. The names generated begin with the letters "SIG", while the names needed by the *kill* command don't. The *_signal* function should assign an array of signal names to $COMPREPLY, optionally preceded by a dash.

First we generate the list of signal names with *compgen*. Each name starts with the letters "SIG". In order to get *complete* to provide the correct subset if the user has begun to type a name, we add "SIG" to the beginning of the value in $cur. We also take the opportunity to remove any preceding dash that the value has so it will match.

We then loop on the array, removing the letters "SIG" and adding a dash if needed (the value of the variable sign) to each entry.

Both *complete* and *compgen* have many other options and actions; far more than we can cover here. If you are interested in taking programmable completion further, we recommend looking in the *bash* manual and downloading some of the many examples that are available on the Internet or in the *bash* tarball in *./examples/complete*.

See Also

- help complete
- help compgen
- *./examples/complete* in any *bash* tarball newer than 2.04
- *http://www.caliban.org/bash/index.shtml#completion*
- *http://freshmeat.net/projects/bashcompletion*

16.18 Using Initialization Files Correctly

Problem

You'd like to know just what the heck is with all the initialization, or *rc*, files.

Solution

Here's the cheat sheet for files and what do with them. Some or all of these files may be missing from your system, depending on how it is set up. Systems that use *bash* by default (e.g., Linux) tend to have a complete set; systems that use some other shell by default are usually missing at least some of them.

/etc/profile

Global login environment file for Bourne and similar login shells. We recommend you leave this alone unless you are the system administrator and know what you are doing.

/etc/bashrc (Red Hat) /etc/bash.bashrc (Debian)

Global environment file for interactive *bash* subshells. We recommend you leave this alone unless you are the system administrator and know what you are doing.

/etc/bash_completion

If this exists, it's almost certainly the configuration file for Ian Macdonald's programmable completion library (see Recipe 16.17, "Improving Programmable Completion"). We recommend looking into it—it's pretty cool.

/etc/inputrc

Global GNU Readline configuration. We recommend tweaking this as desired for the entire system (if you are the administrator), or tweaking *~/.inputrc* for just you (Recipe 16.20, "Getting Started with a Custom Configuration"). This is not executed or sourced but read in via Readline and $INPUTRC, and $include (or bind -f). Note that it may contain include statements to other Readline files.

~/.bashrc

Personal environment file for interactive *bash* subshells. We recommend that you place your aliases, functions, and fancy prompts here.

~/.bash_profile

Personal profile for *bash* login shells. We recommend that you make sure this sources *~/.bashrc*, then ignore it.

~/.bash_login

Personal profile file for Bourne login shells; only used by *bash* if *~/.bash_profile* is not present. We recommend you ignore this.

~/.profile

Personal profile file for Bourne login shells; only used by *bash* if *~/.bash_profile* and *~/.bash_login* are not present. We recommend you ignore this unless you also use other shells that use it.

~/.bash_history

Default storage file for your shell command history. We recommend you use the history tools (Recipe 16.12, "Setting Shell History Options") to manipulate it instead of trying to directly edit it. This is not executed or sourced, it's just a data file.

~/.bash_logout

Executed when you logout. We recommend you place any cleanup routines, (e.g., Recipe 17.7, "Clearing the Screen When You Log Out") here. This is only executed on a clean logout (i.e., not if your session dies due to a dropped WAN link).

~/.inputrc

Personal customizations for GNU Readline. We recommend tweaking this as desired (Recipe 16.20, "Getting Started with a Custom Configuration"). This is not executed or sourced but read in via Readline and $INPUTRC, and $include (or bind -f) and note that it may contain include statements to other Readline files.

We realize this list is a bit is tricky to follow, however, each OS or distribution may differ, since it's up the the vendor exactly how these files are written. To really understand how your system works, read each of the files listed above. You can also temporarily add echo *name_of_file* >&2 to the very first line of any of them that are executed or sourced (i.e., skip */etc/inputrc*, *~/.inputrc*, and *~/.bash_history*). Note that may interfere with some programs (notably *scp* and *rsync*) that are confused by extra output on STDOUT or STDERR, so remove these statements when you are finished. See the warning in Recipe 16.19, "Creating Self-Contained, Portable RC Files" for more details.

Use Table 16-2 as a guideline only, since it's not necessarily how your system will work. (In addition to the login-related rc files listed in Table 16-2, the *~/.bash_logout* rc file is used when you log out cleanly from an interactive session.)

Table 16-2. bash login rc files on Ubuntu 6.10 and Fedora Core 5

Interactive login shell	Interactive non-login shell (bash)	Noninteractive shell (script) (bash /dev/null)	Noninteractive (bash -c ':')
Ubuntu 6.10:	**Ubuntu 6.10:**	**Ubuntu 6.10:**	**Ubuntu 6.10:**
/etc/profile		N/A	N/A
/etc/bash.bashrc	*/etc/bash.bashrc*		
~/.bash_profile[a]			
~/.bashrc	*~/.bashrc*		
/etc/bash_completion	*/etc/bash_completion*		
Fedora Core 5:	**Fedora Core 5:**	**Fedora Core 5:**	**Fedora Core 5:**
/etc/profile[b][c]		N/A	N/A
/etc/profile.d/colorls.sh			
/etc/profile.d/glib2.sh			
/etc/profile.d/krb5.sh			
/etc/profile.d/lang.sh			
/etc/profile.d/less.sh			
/etc/profile.d/vim.sh			
/etc/profile.d/which-2.sh			
~/.bash_profile[a]			
~/.bashrc	*~/.bashrc*		
/etc/bashrc	*/etc/bashrc*		

[a] If *~/.bash_profile* is not found, then *~/.bash_login* or *~/.profile* will be attempted in that order.
[b] If $INPUTRC is not set and *~/.inputrc* does not exist, set $INPUTRC to */etc/inputrc*.
[c] Red Hat */etc/profile* also sources */etc/profile.d/*.sh* files; see Recipe 4.10, "Running All Scripts in a Directory" for details.

For more detail see the "Bash Startup Files" section in the Bash Reference Manual (*http://www.gnu.org/software/bash/manual/bashref.html*).

Discussion

One of the tricky things in Unix or Linux is figuring out where to change something like the $PATH or prompt on the rare occasions when you do want to do it for the whole system. Different operating systems and even versions can put things in different places. This command has a pretty good chance of finding out where your system $PATH is set, for example:

```
$ grep 'PATH=' /etc/{profile,*bash*,*csh*,rc*}
```

If that doesn't work, the only thing you can really do is *grep* all of */etc.*, as in:

```
# find /etc -type f | xargs grep 'PATH='
```

Note that unlike most of the code in this book, this is better run as *root*. You can run it as a regular user and get some results, but you may miss something and you'll almost certainly get some "Permission denied" errors.

One of the other tricky things is figuring out what you can tweak and where to do that for your personal account. We hope this chapter has given you a lot of great ideas in that regard.

See Also

- man grep
- man find
- man xargs
- The "Bash Startup Files" section in the Bash Reference Manual (*http://www.gnu. org/software/bash/manual/bashref.html*)
- Recipe 16.3, "Change Your $PATH Permanently"
- Recipe 16.12, "Setting Shell History Options"
- Recipe 16.17, "Improving Programmable Completion"
- Recipe 16.19, "Creating Self-Contained, Portable RC Files"
- Recipe 16.20, "Getting Started with a Custom Configuration"
- Recipe 17.7, "Clearing the Screen When You Log Out"

16.19 Creating Self-Contained, Portable RC Files

Problem

You work on a number of machines, some of which you have limited or full *root* control over, and some of which you do not, and you want to replicate a consistent *bash* environment while still allowing custom settings by operating system, machine, or other (e.g., work, home) criteria.

Solution

Put all of your customizations in files in a *settings* subdirectory, copy or *rsync* that directory to a location such as ~/ or */etc*, and use includes and symbolic links (e.g., ln -s ~/settings/screenrc ~/.screenrc) as necessary. Use logic in your customization files to account for criteria such as operating system, location, etc.

You may also choose not to use leading dots in the filenames to make it a little easier to manage the files. As you saw in Recipe 1.5, "Showing All Hidden (dot) Files in the Current Directory," the leading dot causes *ls* not to show the file by default, thus eliminating some clutter in your home directory listing. But since we'll be using a directory that exists only to hold configuration files, using the dot is not necessary. Note that dot files are usually not used in */etc* either, for the same reason.

See Recipe 16.20, "Getting Started with a Custom Configuration" for a sample to get you started.

Discussion

Here are the assumptions and criteria we used in developing this solution:

Assumptions

- You have a complex environment in which you control some, but not all, of the machines you use.
- For machines you control, one machine exports */opt/bin* and all other machines NFS-mount it, so all configuration files reside there. We used */opt/bin* because it's short and less likely to collide with existing directories than */usr/local/bin*, but feel free to use whatever makes sense.
- For some machines with partial control, a system-wide configuration in */etc* is used.
- For machines on which you have no administrative control, dot files are used in ~/.
- You have settings that will vary from machine to machine, and in different environments (e.g., home or work).

Criteria

- Require as few changes as possible when moving configuration files between operating systems and environments.

- Supplement, but do not replace, operating system default or system administrator supplied configurations.

- Provide enough flexibility to handle the demands made by conflicting settings (e.g., work and home CVS).

 While it may be tempting to put *echo* statements in your configuration files to see what's going on, be careful. If you do that, *scp*, *rsync*, and probably any other *rsh*-like programs will fail with mysterious errors such as:

```
scp
protocol error: bad mode

rsync
protocol version mismatch - is your shell clean?
(see the rsync manpage for an explanation)
rsync error: protocol incompatibility (code 2) at compat.
c(62)
```

ssh itself works since it is actually interactive and the output is displayed on the screen rather than confusing the data stream. See the discussion in Recipe 14.22, "Restricting SSH Commands," for details on why this happens.

For debugging, put these two lines near the top of */etc/profile* or *~/.bash_profile*, but see our warning note about confusing the data stream:

```
export PS4='+xtrace $LINENO: '
set -x
```

As an alternative (or in addition) to using set -x, you can add lines such as the following to any or all of your configuration files:

```
# E.g. in ~/.bash_profile
case "$-" in
    *i*) echo "$(date '+%Y-%m-%d_%H:%M:%S_%Z') Interactive" \
            "~/.bash_profile ssh=$SSH_CONNECTION" >> ~/rc.log ;;
    *  ) echo "$(date '+%Y-%m-%d_%H:%M:%S_%Z') Non-interactive" \
            "~/.bash_profile ssh=$SSH_CONNECTION" >> ~/rc.log ;;
esac

# In ~/.bashrc
case "$-" in
    *i*) echo "$(date '+%Y-%m-%d_%H:%M:%S_%Z') Interactive" \
            "~/.bashrc ssh=$SSH_CONNECTION" >> ~/rc.log ;;
    *  ) echo "$(date '+%Y-%m-%d_%H:%M:%S_%Z') Non-interactive" \
            "~/.bashrc ssh=$SSH_CONNECTION" >> ~/rc.log ;;
esac
```

Since there is no output to the terminal, this will not interfere with commands as we note in the warning. Run a `tail -f ~/rc.log` command in one session and run your troublesome command (e.g., *scp*, *cvs*) from elsewhere to determine which configuration files are in use. You can then more easily track down the problem.

When making any changes to your configuration files, we *strongly* advise that you open two sessions. Make all your changes in one session and then log it out and back in. If you broke something so that you can't log back in, fix it from the second session and then try again from the first one. Do not log out of both terminals until you are absolutely sure you can log back in again. This goes triple if any changes you're making could affect *root*.

You really do need to log out and back in again. Sourcing the changed files is a help, but leftovers from the previous environment may allow things to work temporarily, until you start clean and then things are broken. Make changes to the running environment as necessary, but don't change the files until you are ready to test; otherwise you'll forget and possibly be locked out if something is wrong.

See Also

- Recipe 1.5, "Showing All Hidden (dot) Files in the Current Directory"
- Recipe 14.23, "Disconnecting Inactive Sessions"
- Recipe 16.18, "Using Initialization Files Correctly"
- Recipe 16.20, "Getting Started with a Custom Configuration"

16.20 Getting Started with a Custom Configuration

Problem

You'd like to tweak your environment but aren't quite sure where to start.

Solution

Here are some samples to give you an idea of what you can do. We follow the suggestion in Recipe 16.19, "Creating Self-Contained, Portable RC Files" to keep customizations separate for easy back-outs and portability between systems.

For system-wide profile settings, add the following to */etc/profile*. Since that file is also used by the true Bourne shell, be careful not to use any *bash*-only features (e.g., *source* instead of .) if you do this on a non-Linux system. Linux uses *bash* as the default shell for both */bin/sh* and */bin/bash* (except when it doesn't, as in Ubuntu 6–10+, which uses *dash*). For user-only settings, add it to only one of *~/.bash_profile*, *~/.bash_login*, or *~/.profile*, in that order, whichever exists first:

```
# cookbook filename: add_to_bash_profile

# If we're running in bash, search for then source our settings
# You can also just hard code $SETTINGS, but this is more flexible
if [ -n "$BASH_VERSION" ]; then
    for path in /opt/bin /etc ~ ; do
        # Use the first one found
        if [ -d "$path/settings" -a -r "$path/settings" -a -x "$path/settings" ]
        then
            export SETTINGS="$path/settings"
        fi
    done
    source "$SETTINGS/bash_profile"
    #source "$SETTINGS/bash_rc"          # If necessary
fi
```

For system-wide environment settings, add the following to */etc/bashrc* (or */etc/bash.bashrc*):

```
# cookbook filename: add_to_bashrc

# If we're running in bash, and it isn't already set,
# search for then source our settings
# You can also just hard code $SETTINGS, but this is more flexible
if [ -n "$BASH_VERSION"  ]; then
    if [ -z "$SETTINGS" ]; then
        for path in /opt/bin /etc ~ ; do
            # Use the first one found
            if [ -d "$path/settings" -a -r "$path/settings" -a -x "$path/settings" ]
            then
                export SETTINGS="$path/settings"
            fi
        done
    fi
    source "$SETTINGS/bashrc"
fi
```

Sample *bash_profile*:

```
# cookbook filename: bash_profile

# settings/bash_profile: Login shell environment settings
# To re-read (and implement changes to this file) use:
# source $SETTINGS/bash_profile

# Fail-safe.  This should be set when we're called, but if not, the
# "not found" error messages should be pretty clear.
# Use leading ':' to prevent this from being run as a program after
# it is expanded.
: ${SETTINGS:='SETTINGS_variable_not_set'}

# DEBUGGING only--will break scp, rsync
# echo "Sourcing $SETTINGS/bash_profile..."
# export PS4='+xtrace $LINENO: '
# set -x
```

```
# Debugging/logging--will not break scp, rsync
#case "$-" in
#    *i*) echo "$(date '+%Y-%m-%d_%H:%M:%S_%Z') Interactive" \
#            "$SETTINGS/bash_profile ssh=$SSH_CONNECTION" >> ~/rc.log ;;
#    *  ) echo "$(date '+%Y-%m-%d_%H:%M:%S_%Z') Non-interactive" \
#            "$SETTINGS/bash_profile ssh=$SSH_CONNECTION" >> ~/rc.log ;;
#esac

# Use the keychain (http://www.gentoo.org/proj/en/keychain/) shell script
# to manage ssh-agent, if it's available.  If it's not, you should look
# into adding it.
for path in $SETTINGS ${PATH//:/ }; do
    if [ -x "$path/keychain" ]; then
        # Load default id_rsa and/or id_dsa keys, add others here as needed
        # See also --clear --ignore-missing --noask --quiet --time-out
        $path/keychain ~/.ssh/id_?sa
        break
    fi
done


# Apply interactive subshell customizations to login shells too.
# The system profile file in /etc probably already does this.
# If not, it's probably better to do in manually in wherever you:
# source "$SETTINGS/bash_profile"
# But just in case...
#for file in /etc/bash.bashrc /etc/bashrc ~/.bashrc; do
#    [ -r "$file" ] && source $file && break  # Use the first one found
#done


# Do site or host specific things here
case $HOSTNAME in
    *.company.com       ) # source $SETTINGS/company.com
                        ;;
    host1.*             ) # host1 stuff
                        ;;
    host2.company.com   ) # source .bashrc.host2
                        ;;
    drake.*             ) # echo DRAKE in bash_profile.jp!
                        ;;
esac


# Do this last because we basically fork off from here.  If we exit screen
# we return to a fully configured session.  The screen session gets configured
# as well, and if we never leave it, well, this session isn't that bloated.

# Only run if we are not already running screen AND '~/.use_screen' exists.
if [ $TERM != "screen" -a "$USING_SCREEN" != "YES" -a -f ~/.use_screen ]; then
    # We'd rather use 'type -P' here, but that was added in bash-2.05b and we
    # use systems we don't control with versions older than that.  We can't
    #  easily use 'which' since on some systems that produces output whether
```

```
            # the file is found or not.
            for path in ${PATH//:/ }; do
                if [ -x "$path/screen" ]; then
                    # If screen(1) exists and is executable, run our wrapper
                    [ -x "$SETTINGS/run_screen" ] && $SETTINGS/run_screen
                fi
            done
    fi
```

Sample *bashrc* (we know this is long, but read it for ideas):

```
# cookbook filename: bashrc

# settings/bash_profile: subshell environment settings
# To re-read (and implement changes to this file) use:
# source $SETTINGS/bashrc

# Fail-safe.  This should be set when we're called, but if not, the
# "not found" error messages should be pretty clear.
# Use leading ':' to prevent this from being run as a program after
# it is expanded.
: ${SETTINGS:='SETTINGS_variable_not_set'}


# DEBUGGING only--will break scp, rsync
# echo "Sourcing $SETTINGS/bash_profile..."
# export PS4='+xtrace $LINENO: '
# set -x

# Debugging/logging--will not break scp, rsync
#case "$-" in
#   *i*) echo "$(date '+%Y-%m-%d_%H:%M:%S_%Z') Interactive" \
#            "$SETTINGS/bashrc ssh=$SSH_CONNECTION" >> ~/rc.log ;;
#   *  ) echo "$(date '+%Y-%m-%d_%H:%M:%S_%Z') Non-interactive" \
#            "$SETTINGS/bashrc ssh=$SSH_CONNECTION" >> ~/rc.log ;;
#esac

# In theory this is also sourced from /etc/bashrc (/etc/bash.bashrc )
# or ~/.bashrc to apply all these settings to login shells too.  In practice
# if these settings only work sometimes (like in subshells), verify that.

# Set some more useful prompts
# Interactive command line prompt.
# ONLY set one of these if we really are interactive, since lots of people
# (even use sometimes) test to see if a shell is interactive using
# something like:  if [ "$PS1" ]; then
case "$-" in
    *i*)
        #export PS1='\n[\u@\h t:\l l:$SHLVL h:\! j:\j v:\V]\n$PWD\$ '
        #export PS1='\n[\u@\h:T\l:L$SHLVL:C\!:\D{%Y-%m-%d_%H:%M:%S_%Z}]\n$PWD\$ '
        export PS1='\n[\u@\h:T\l:L$SHLVL:C\!:J\j:\D{%Y-%m-%d_%H:%M:%S_%Z}]\n$PWD\$ '
        #export PS2='> '                           # Secondary (i.e. continued)
    prompt
```

```
        #export PS3='Please make a choice: '            # Select prompt
        export PS4='+xtrace $LINENO: '                  # xtrace (debug) prompt
    ;;
esac

# Make sure custom inputrc is handled, if we can find it, note different
# names. Also note different order, since for this one we probably want
# our custom settings to over-ride the system file, if present.
for file in $SETTINGS/inputrc ~/.inputrc /etc/inputrc; do
    [ -r "$file" ] && export INPUTRC="$file" && break # Use first found
done

# No core files by default
# See also /etc/security/limits.conf on many Linux systems.
ulimit -S -c 0 > /dev/null 2>&1

# Don't let CTRL-D exit the shell
set -o ignoreeof

# Set various aspects of the bash history
export HISTSIZE=5000        # Num. of commands in history stack in memory
export HISTFILESIZE=5000    # Num. of commands in history FILE
export HISTCONTROL=ignoreboth # bash < 3, omit dups & lines starting with space
export HISTIGNORE='&:[ ]*'  # bash >= 3, omit dups & lines starting with space
#export HISTTIMEFORMAT='%Y-%m-%d_%H:%M:%S_%Z=' # bash >= 3, time-stamp hist file
shopt -s histappend         # Append rather than overwrite history on exit
shopt -q -s cdspell         # Auto-fix minor typos in interactive use of 'cd'
shopt -q -s checkwinsize    # Update the values of LINES and COLUMNS
shopt -q -s cmdhist         # Make multi-line commands 1 line in history
set -o notify   # (or set -b) # Immediate notification of bckgrnd job termintn.

# Other bash settings
export LC_COLLATE='C'       # Set traditional C sort order (e.g. UC first)
export HOSTFILE='/etc/hosts' # Use /etc/hosts for host name completion
export CDPATH='~/:..:...:../..' # Similar to $PATH, but for use by 'cd'
# Note that the '.' in $CDPATH is needed so that cd will work under POSIX mode
# but this will also cause cd to echo the new directory to STDOUT!

# Import bash completion settings, if they exist in the default location.
# This can take a second or two on a slow system, so you may not always
# want to do it, even if it does exist (which it doesn't by default on many
# systems, e.g. Red Hat).
# [ -r /etc/bash_completion ] && source /etc/bash_completion

# Use a lesspipe filter, if we can find it.  This sets the $LESSOPEN variable
# Globally replace the $PATH ':' delimiter with space for use in a list
for path in $SETTINGS /opt/bin ~/ ${PATH//:/ }; do
    # Use first one found of 'lesspipe.sh' (preferred) or 'lesspipe' (Debian)
    [ -x "$path/lesspipe.sh" ] && eval $("$path/lesspipe.sh") && break
    [ -x "$path/lesspipe" ]    && eval $("$path/lesspipe")    && break
done

# Set other less & editor prefs (overkill)
export LESS="--LONG-PROMPT --LINE-NUMBERS --QUIET"
```

```
export VISUAL='vi'  # Set a default that should always work
# We'd rather use 'type -P' here, but that was added in bash-2.05b and we use
# systems we don't control with versions older than that.  We can't easily
# use 'which' since that produces output whether the file is found or not.
for path in ${PATH//:/ }; do
    # Overwrite VISUAL if we can find nano
    [ -x "$path/nano" ] \
      && export VISUAL='nano --smooth --const --nowrap --suspend' && break
done
# See above notes re: nano for why we're using this for loop
for path in ${PATH//:/ }; do
    # Alias vi to vim in binary mode if we can
    [ -x "$path/vim" ] && alias vi='vim -b' && break
done
export EDITOR="$VISUAL"       # Yet Another Possibility
export SVN_EDITOR="$VISUAL"   # Subversion
alias edit=$VISUAL            # Provide a command to use on all systems

# Set ls options and aliases
# Note all the colorizing may or may not work depending on your terminal
# emulation and settings, esp. ANSI color. But it shouldn't hurt to have.
# See above notes re: nano for why we're using this for loop
for path in ${PATH//:/ }; do
    [ -r "$path/dircolors" ] && eval "$(dircolors)" \
      && LS_OPTIONS='--color=auto' && break
done
export LS_OPTIONS="$LS_OPTIONS -F -h"
# Using dircolors may cause csh scripts to fail with an
# "Unknown colorls variable `do'." error.  The culprit is the ":do=01;35:"
# part in the LS_COLORS environment variable.  For a possible solution see
# http://forums.macosxhints.com/showthread.php?t=7287
# eval "$(dircolors)"
alias ls="ls $LS_OPTIONS"
alias ll="ls $LS_OPTIONS -l"
alias ll.="ls $LS_OPTIONS -ld"  # Usage: ll. ~/.*
alias la="ls $LS_OPTIONS -la"

# Useful aliases
alias bot='cd $(dirname $(find . | tail -1))'
alias clr='cd ~/ && clear'   # Clear and return $HOME
alias cls='clear'            # DOS-ish for clear
alias copy='cp'             # DOS-ish for cp
#alias cp='cp -i'            # Annoying Red Hat default from /root/.bashrc
alias cvsst='cvs -qn update' # Hack to get concise CVS status (like svn st)
alias del='rm'              # DOS-ish for rm
alias diff='diff -u'        # Make unified diffs the default
alias jdiff="diff --side-by-side --ignore-case --ignore-blank-lines\
 --ignore-all-space --suppress-common-lines" # Useful GNU diff command
alias dir='ls'             # DOS-ish for ls
alias hr='history -a && history -n' # Append current, then re-read history
alias ipconfig='ifconfig'  # Windows-ish for ifconfig
alias md='mkdir'           # DOS-ish for mkdir
alias move='mv'            # DOS-ish for mv
#alias mv='mv -i'           # Annoying Red Hat default from /root/.bashrc
```

```
alias ntsysv='rcconf'           # Debian rcconf is pretty close to Red Hat ntsysv
alias pathping='mtr'            # mtr - a network diagnostic tool
alias r='fc -s'                 # Recall and execute 'command' starting with...
alias rd='rmdir'                # DOS-ish for rmdir
alias ren='mv'                  # DOS-ish for mv/rename
#alias rm='rm -i'               # Annoying Red Hat default from /root/.bashrc
alias svnpropfix='svn propset svn:keywords "Id URL"'
alias tracert='traceroute'      # DOS-ish for traceroute
alias vzip='unzip -lvM'         # View contents of ZIP file
alias wgetdir="wget --non-verbose --recursive --no-parent --no-directories\
 --level=1"                     # Grab a whole directory using wget
alias zonex='host -l'           # Extract (dump) DNS zone

# if the script exists and is executable, create an alias to get
# web server headers
for path in ${PATH//:/ }; do
    [ -x "$path/lwp-request" ] && alias httpdinfo='lwp-request -eUd' && break
done

# Try to use kbdrate to make the keyboard go faster, but don't complain if
# it's not there.  Easier/faster to throw out error if it's not there...
kbdrate -r 30.0 -d 250 &> /dev/null


# Useful functions

# mkdir newdir then cd into it
# usage: mcd (<mode>) <dir>
function mcd {
    local newdir='_mcd_command_failed_'
    if [ -d "$1" ]; then        # Dir exists, mention that...
        echo $1 exists...
    else
        if [ -n "$2" ]; then    # We've specified a mode
            command mkdir -p -m $1 "$2" && newdir="$2"
        else                    # Plain old mkdir
            command mkdir -p "$1" && newdir="$1"
        fi
    fi
    builtin cd "$newdir"        # No matter what, cd into it
} # end of mcd


# Trivial command line calculator
function calc {
    # INTEGER ONLY! --> echo The answer is: $(( $* ))
    # Floating point
    awk "BEGIN {print \"The answer is: \" $* }";
} # end of calc


# Allow use of 'cd ...' to cd up 2 levels, 'cd ....' up 3, etc. (like 4NT/4DOS)
# Usage: cd ..., etc.
function cd {
```

```
    local option= length= count= cdpath= i= # Local scope and start clean

    # If we have a -L or -P sym link option, save then remove it
    if [ "$1" = "-P" -o "$1" = "-L" ]; then
        option="$1"
        shift
    fi

    # Are we using the special syntax?  Make sure $1 isn't empty, then
    # match the first 3 characters of $1 to see if they are '...' then
    # make sure there isn't a slash by trying a substitution; if it fails,
    # there's no slash.  Both of these string routines require Bash 2.0+
    if [ -n "$1" -a "${1:0:3}" = '...' -a "$1" = "${1%/*}" ]; then
        # We are using special syntax
        length=${#1}  # Assume that $1 has nothing but dots and count them
        count=2       # 'cd ..' still means up one level, so ignore first two

        # While we haven't run out of dots, keep cd'ing up 1 level
        for ((i=$count;i<=$length;i++)); do
            cdpath="${cdpath}../" # Build the cd path
        done

        # Actually do the cd
        builtin cd $option "$cdpath"
    elif [ -n "$1" ]; then
        # We are NOT using special syntax; just plain old cd by itself
        builtin cd $option "$*"
    else
        # We are NOT using special syntax; plain old cd by itself to home dir
        builtin cd $option
    fi
} # end of cd


# Do site or host specific things here
case $HOSTNAME in
    *.company.com        ) # source $SETTINGS/company.com
                         ;;
    host1.*              ) # host1 stuff
                         ;;
    host2.company.com )  # source .bashrc.host2
                         ;;
    drake.*              ) # echo DRAKE in bashrc.jp!
                           export TAPE=/dev/tape
                         ;;
esac
```

Sample *inputrc*:

```
# cookbook filename: inputrc

# settings/inputrc:  # readline settings
# To re-read (and implement changes to this file) use:
# bind -f $SETTINGS/inputrc
```

```
# First, include any systemwide bindings and variable
# assignments from /etc/inputrc
# (fails silently if file doesn't exist)
$include /etc/inputrc

$if Bash
  # Ignore case when doing completion
    set completion-ignore-case on
  # Completed dir names have a slash appended
    set mark-directories on
  # Completed names which are symlinks to dirs have a slash appended
    set mark-symlinked-directories on
  # List ls -F for completion
    set visible-stats on
  # Cycle through ambiguous completions instead of list
    "\C-i": menu-complete
  # Set bell to audible
    set bell-style audible
  # List possible completions instead of ringing bell
    set show-all-if-ambiguous on


  # From the readline documentation at
  # http://tiswww.tis.case.edu/php/chet/readline/readline.html#SEC12
  # Macros that are convenient for shell interaction
  # edit the path
    "\C-xp": "PATH=${PATH}\e\C-e\C-a\ef\C-f"
  # prepare to type a quoted word -- insert open and closed double quotes
  # and move to just after the open quote
    "\C-x\"": "\"\"\C-b"
  # insert a backslash (testing backslash escapes in sequences and macros)
    "\C-x\\": "\\"
  # Quote the current or previous word
    "\C-xq": "\eb\"\ef\""
  # Add a binding to refresh the line, which is unbound
    "\C-xr": redraw-current-line
  # Edit variable on current line.
    #"\M-\C-v": "\C-a\C-k$\C-y\M-\C-e\C-a\C-y="
    "\C-xe": "\C-a\C-k$\C-y\M-\C-e\C-a\C-y="
$endif
```

Sample *bash_logout*:

```
# cookbook filename: bash_logout

# settings/bash_logout:  execute on shell logout

# Clear the screen on logout to prevent information leaks, if not already
# set as an exit trap elsewhere
[ "$PS1" ] && clear
```

Sample *run_screen* (for GNU *screen*, which you may need to install):

```
#!/usr/bin/env bash
# cookbook filename: run_screen
```

```
# run_screen--Wrapper script intended to run from a "profile" file to run
# screen at login time with a friendly menu.

# Sanity check
if [ "$TERM" == "screen" ]; then
    printf "%b" "According to \$TERM = '$TERM' we're *already* using" \
      " screen.\nAborting...\n"
    exit 1
elif [ "$USING_SCREEN" == "YES" ]; then
    printf "%b" "According to \$USING_SCREEN = '$USING_SCREEN' we're" \
      " *already* using screen.\nAborting...\n"
    exit 1
fi

# The "$USING_SCREEN" variable is for the rare cases when screen does NOT set
# $TERM=screen.  This can happen when 'screen' in not in TERMCAP or friends,
# as is the case on a Solaris 9 box we use but don't control.  If we don't
# have some way to tell when we're inside screen, this wrapper goes into an
# ugly and confusing endless loop.

# Seed list with Exit and New options and see what screens are already running;
# The select list is white space delimited, and we only want actual screen
# sessions, so use awk to filter for those, then remove any tabs from
# 'screen -ls' output.
available_screens="Exit New $(screen -ls | awk '/\)$/ { print $1$2$3 }' \
  | tr -d ' ')"

# Print a warning if using run time feedback
run_time_feedback=0
[ "$run_time_feedback" == 1 ] && printf "%b" "
+++++++++++++++++++++++++++++++++++++++++++++++++++++++++++++++++++++++++++++++
'screen' Notes:

1) If you reconnect to a screen that is already Attached, you will 'steal'
that existing screen.

2) A session marked 'multi' is in multi-user mode, so be careful about
re-attaching to it.

3) Sessions marked 'unreachable' or 'dead' should be investigated and
removed with the -wipe option if appropriate.\n\n"


# Present a list of choices
PS3='Choose a screen for this session: '
select selection in $available_screens; do
    if [ "$selection" == "Exit" ]; then
        break
    elif [ "$selection" == "New" ]; then
        export USING_SCREEN=YES
        exec screen -c $SETTINGS/screenrc -a \
                    -S $USER.$(date '+%Y-%m-%d_%H:%M:%S%z')
        break
    elif [ "$selection" ]; then
```

```
        # Pull out just the part we need using cut
        # We'd rather use a 'here string' [$(cut -d'(' -f1 <<< $selection)]
        # than this echo, but they are only in bash-2.05b+.
        screen_to_use=$(echo $selection | cut -d'(' -f1)
        exec screen -dr $screen_to_use
        break
    else
        printf "%b" "Invalid selection.\n"
    fi
done
```

Discussion

See the code and the code's comments for details.

Something interesting happens if you set $PS1 at inappropriate times, or if you set traps using clear. Many people use code like this to test to see if the current shell is interactive:

```
if [ "$PS1" ]; then
    : Interactive code here
fi
```

If you arbitrarily set $PS1 if the shell isn't interactive, or if you set a trap using just clear instead of ["$PS1"] && clear, you'll get errors like this when using *scp* or *ssh* non-interactively:

```
# e.g. from tput
No value for $TERM and no -T specified

# e.g. from clear
TERM environment variable not set.
```

See Also

- Chapters 17–19
- Recipe 16.18, "Using Initialization Files Correctly"
- Recipe 16.19, "Creating Self-Contained, Portable RC Files"
- Recipe 17.5, "Sharing a Single bash Session"
- Appendix C

## CHAPTER 17

Housekeeping and Administrative Tasks

These recipes cover tasks that come up in the course of using or administering computers. They are presented here because they don't fit well anywhere else in the book.

17.1 Renaming Many Files

Problem

You want to rename many files, but mv *.foo *.bar doesn't work. Or, you want to rename a group of files in arbitrary ways.

Solution

We presented a simple loop to change file extensions in Recipe 5.18, "Changing Pieces of a String"; see that recipe for more details. Here is a for loop example:

```
for FN in *.bad
do
    mv "${FN}" "${FN%bad}bash"
done
```

What about more arbitrary changes? For example, say you are writing a book and want the chapter file names to follow a certain format, but the publisher has a conflicting format. You could name the files like *chNN=Title=Author.odt*, then use a simple for loop and *cut* in a command substitution to rename them.

```
$ for i in *.odt; do mv "$i" "$(echo $i | cut -d'=' -f1,3)"; done
```

Discussion

You should always use quotes around file arguments in case there's a space. While testing the code in the solution we also used *echo* and angle brackets to make it very clear what the arguments are (using set -x is also helpful).

Once we were very sure our command worked, we removed the angle brackets and replaced *echo* with *mv*.

```
# Testing
$ for i in *.odt; do echo "<$i>" "<$(echo $i | cut -d'=' -f1,3)>"; done
<ch01=Beginning Shell Scripting=JP.odt> <ch01=JP.odt>
<ch02=Standard Output=CA.odt> <ch02=CA.odt>
<ch03=Standard Input=CA.odt> <ch03=CA.odt>
<ch04=Executing Commands=CA.odt> <ch04=CA.odt>
[...]

# Even more testing
$ set -x

$ for i in *.odt; do echo "<$i>" "<$(echo $i | cut -d'=' -f1,3)>"; done
++xtrace 1: echo ch01=Beginning Shell Scripting=JP.odt
++xtrace 1: cut -d= -f1,3
+xtrace 535: echo '<ch01=Beginning Shell Scripting=JP.odt>' '<ch01=JP.odt>'
<ch01=Beginning Shell Scripting=JP.odt> <ch01=JP.odt>
++xtrace 1: echo ch02=Standard Output=CA.odt
++xtrace 1: cut -d= -f1,3
+xtrace 535: echo '<ch02=Standard Output=CA.odt>' '<ch02=CA.odt>'
<ch02=Standard Output=CA.odt> <ch02=CA.odt>
++xtrace 1: echo ch03=Standard Input=CA.odt
++xtrace 1: cut -d= -f1,3
+xtrace 535: echo '<ch03=Standard Input=CA.odt>' '<ch03=CA.odt>'
<ch03=Standard Input=CA.odt> <ch03=CA.odt>
++xtrace 1: echo ch04=Executing Commands=CA.odt
++xtrace 1: cut -d= -f1,3
+xtrace 535: echo '<ch04=Executing Commands=CA.odt>' '<ch04=CA.odt>'
<ch04=Executing Commands=CA.odt> <ch04=CA.odt>

$ set +x
+xtrace 536: set +x
```

We have for loops like this throughout the book since they're so handy. The trick here is plugging the right values into the arguments to *mv*, or *cp*, or whatever. In this case we'd already used the = as a delimiter, and all we cared about was the first field, so it was pretty easy.

To figure out the values you need, use the *ls* (or *find*) command to list the files you are working on and pipe them into whatever tool chain seems appropriate, often *cut*, *awk*, or *sed. bash* parameter expansion (Recipe 5.18, "Changing Pieces of a String") is also very handy here:

```
$ ls *.odt | cut -d'=' -f1
```

Hopefully, a recipe somewhere in the book will give you the details you need to come up with the right values for the arguments, then you just plug all the pieces in and go. Be sure to test using *echo* first and watch out for spaces or other odd characters in file names: they'll get you every time.

Don't name your script *rename*. We are aware of at least two different *rename* commands in major Linux flavors, and there are certainly many others. Red Hat's *util-linux* package includes a rename *from_ string to_string file_name* tool. Debian and derivatives include Larry Wall's Perl-based *rename* in their Perl packages, and have a related *renameutils* package. And Solaris, HP-UX and some BSD's document a rename system call, though that is not easily end-user accessible. Try the *rename* manpage on your system and see what you get.

See Also

- man mv
- man rename
- help for
- Recipe 5.18, "Changing Pieces of a String"
- Recipe 9.2, "Handling File Names Containing Odd Characters"
- Recipe 17.12, "Removing or Renaming Files Named with Special Characters"
- Recipe 19.13, "Debugging Scripts"

17.2   Using GNU Texinfo and Info on Linux

Problem

You are having trouble accessing documentation because much of the documentation for GNU tools on Linux are in Texinfo documents, the traditional manpages are just a stub, and the default *info* program is user-hostile (and you don't feel like learning yet another single-use program).

Solution

Pipe the *info* command into a useful pager, such as *less*.

```
$ info bash | less
```

Discussion

info is basically a stand-alone version of the Emacs info reader, so if you are an Emacs fan, maybe it will make sense to you. However, piping it into *less* is a quick and simple way to view the documentation using a tool with which you're already familiar.

The idea behind Texinfo is good: generate various output formats from a single source. It's not new, since many other mark-up languages exist to do the same thing; we even talk about one in Recipe 5.2, "Embedding Documentation in Shell Scripts." But if that's the case, why isn't there a TeX to *man* output filter? Perhaps because manpages follow a standard, structured, and time-tested format while Texinfo is more free form.

There are other Texinfo viewers and converters if you don't like *info*, such as *pinfo*, *info2www*, *tkman*, and even *info2man* (which cheats and converts to POD and then to manpage format).

See Also

- man info
- man man
- *http://en.wikipedia.org/wiki/Texinfo*
- Recipe 5.2, "Embedding Documentation in Shell Scripts"

17.3 Unzipping Many ZIP Files

Problem

You want to unzip many ZIP files in a directory, but unzip `*.zip` doesn't work.

Solution

Put the pattern in single quotes:

```
unzip '*.zip'
```

You could also use a loop to unzip each file:

```
for x in /path/to/date*/name/*.zip; do unzip "$x"; done
```

or:

```
for x in $(ls /path/to/date*/name/*.zip 2>/dev/null); do unzip $x; done
```

Discussion

Unlike many Unix commands (e.g., *gzip* and *bzip2*), the last argument to *unzip* isn't an arbitrarily long list of files. To process the command unzip `*.zip`, the shell expands the wildcard, so (assuming you have files named *zipfile1.zip* to *zipfile4.zip*) unzip `*.zip` expands to unzip `zipfile1.zip zipfile2.zip zipfile3.zip zipfile4.zip`. This command attempts to extract *zipfile2.zip*, *zipfile3.zip*, and *zipfile4.zip* from *zipfile1.zip*. That command will fail unless *zipfile1.zip* actually contains files with those names.

The first method prevents the shell from expanding the wildcard by using single quotes. However, that only works if there is only one wildcard. The second and third methods work around that by running an explicit *unzip* command for each ZIP file found when the shell expands the wildcards, or returns the result of the *ls* command.

The *ls* version is used because the default behavior of *bash* (and *sh*) is to return unmatched patterns unchanged. That means you would be trying to unzip a file called */path/to/date*/name/*.zip* if no files match the wildcard pattern. *ls* will simply return null on STDOUT, and an error that we throw away on STDERR. You can set the shopt -s nullglob option to cause filename patterns that match no files to expand to a null string, rather than themselves.

See Also

- man unzip
- *http://www.info-zip.org/pub/infozip*
- Recipe 15.13, "Working Around "argument list too long" Errors"

17.4   Recovering Disconnected Sessions Using screen

Problem

You run long processes over SSH, perhaps over the WAN, and when you get disconnected you lose a lot of work. Or perhaps you started a long job from work, but need to go home and be able to check on the job later; you could run your process using *nohup*, but then you won't be able to reattach to it when your connection comes back or you get home.

Solution

Install and use GNU *screen*.

Using *screen* is very simple. Type screen or screen -a. The -a option includes all of *screen*'s capabilities even at the expense of some redraw (thus bandwidth) efficiency. Honestly, we use -a but have never noticed a difference.

When you do this, it will look like nothing happened, but you are now running inside a screen. echo $SHLVL should return a number greater than one if this worked (see also :L$SHLVL in Recipe 16.2, "Customizing Your Prompt"). To test it, do an ls -la, then kill your terminal (do not exit cleanly, as you will exit *screen* as well). Log back into the machine and type screen -r to reconnect to *screen*. If that doesn't put you back where you left off, try screen -d -r. If that doesn't work, try ps auwx | grep [s]creen to see if *screen* is still running, and then try man screen for troubleshooting information—but it should just work. If you run into problems with that *ps* command on a system other than Linux, see Recipe 17.19, "Finding Out Whether a Process Is Running."

Starting *screen* with something like the following will make it easier to figure out what session to reattach to later if necessary: screen -aS "$(whoami).$(date '+%Y-%m-%d_%H:%M:%S%z')". See the *run_screen* script in Recipe 16.20, "Getting Started with a Custom Configuration."

To exit out of *screen* and your session, keep typing exit until all the sessions are gone. You can also type Ctrl-A Ctrl-\ or Ctrl-A **:quit** to exit *screen* itself (assuming you haven't changed the default meta-key of Ctrl-A yet).

Discussion

According to the *screen* web site:

> Screen is a full-screen window manager that multiplexes a physical terminal between several processes (typically interactive shells). Each virtual terminal provides the functions of a DEC VT100 terminal and, in addition, several control functions from the ISO 6429 (ECMA 48, ANSI X3.64) and ISO 2022 standards (e.g., insert/delete line and support for multiple character sets). There is a scrollback history buffer for each virtual terminal and a copy-and-paste mechanism that allows moving text regions between windows.

What that means is you can have more than one session in a single SSH terminal (think DeskView on i286/386). But it also allows you to SSH into a machine, start a process, disconnect your terminal and go home, then reconnect and pick up—not where you left off, but where the process has continued to. And it allows multiple people to share a single session for training, troubleshooting, or collaboration (see Recipe 17.5, "Sharing a Single bash Session").

Caveats

screen is often installed by default on Linux but rarely on other systems. The *screen* binary must run SUID root so it can write to the appropriate *usr/dev* pseudoterminals (tty). If *screen* doesn't work, this is a likely reason why (to fix it, enter chmod u+s /usr/bin/screen as *root*).

screen interferes with in-line transfer protocols like *zmodem*. Newer versions of *screen* have configuration settings that deal with this; see the manpages.

Configuration

The default Emacs mode of *bash* command-line editing uses Ctrl-A to go to the start of the line. That's also the *screen* command mode, or metakey, so if you use Ctrl-A a lot like we do, you may want to add the following to your *~/.screenrc* file:

```
# Sample settings for ~/.screenrc
# Change the C-a default to C-n (use C-n n to send literal ^N)
escape ^Nn

# Yes annoying audible bell, please
vbell off

# detach on hangup
autodetach on

# make the shell in every window a login shell
shell -$SHELL
```

See Also

- screen manpage
- *http://www.gnu.org/software/screen*
- *http://en.wikipedia.org/wiki/GNU_Screen*
- *http://jmcpherson.org/screen.html*
- *http://aperiodic.net/screen*
- Recipe 16.2, "Customizing Your Prompt"
- Recipe 16.20, "Getting Started with a Custom Configuration"
- Recipe 17.5, "Sharing a Single bash Session"
- Recipe 17.6, "Logging an Entire Session or Batch Job"
- Recipe 17.9, "Creating an Index of Many Files"
- Recipe 17.18, "Grepping ps Output Without Also Getting the grep Process Itself"

17.5 Sharing a Single bash Session

Problem

You need to share a single *bash* session for training or troubleshooting purposes, and there are too many people for "over the shoulder" to work. Or you need to help someone who's located somewhere else, and you need to share a session across a network.

Solution

Use GNU *screen* in multiuser mode. The following assumes that you have not changed the default metakey from Ctrl-A as described in Recipe 17.4, "Recovering Disconnected Sessions Using screen." If you have, then use your new metakey (e.g., Ctrl-N) instead.

As the host do the following:

1. screen -S *session_name* (no spaces allowed); e.g., screen -S training.
2. Ctrl-A :addacl *usernames* of accounts (comma delimited, no spaces!) which may access the display; e.g., Ctrl-A **:addacl alice,bob,carol**. Note this allows full read/write access.
3. Use the Ctrl-A **:chacl *usernames permbits list*** command to refine permissions if needed.
4. Turn on multiuser mode: Ctrl-A **:multiuser on**.

As the viewer, do this:

1. Use `screen -x` *user*/*name* to connect to a shared screen; e.g., `screen -x host/training`.

2. Hit Ctrl-A K to kill the window and end the session.

Discussion

See Recipe 17.4, "Recovering Disconnected Sessions Using screen," for necessary details.

For multiuser mode, */tmp/screens* must exist and be world-readable and executable.

screen versions 3.9.15-8 to 4.0.1-1 from Red Hat (i.e., RHEL3) are broken and should not be used if you want multiuser mode to work. Version 4.0.2-5 or later should work; for example, *http://mirror.centos.org/centos/4.2/os/i386/CentOS/RPMS/screen-4.0.2-5.i386.rpm* (or later) works even on RHEL3. Once you start using the new version of *screen*, existing *screen* sockets in *$HOME/.screen* are not found and are thus orphaned and unusable. Log out of all sessions, and use the new version to create new sockets in */tmp/screens/S-$USER*, then remove the *$HOME/.screen* directory.

See Also

- man screen
- *http://www.gnu.org/software/screen*
- Recipe 9.11, "Finding a File Using a List of Possible Locations"
- Recipe 16.20, "Getting Started with a Custom Configuration"
- Recipe 17.4, "Recovering Disconnected Sessions Using screen"
- Recipe 17.6, "Logging an Entire Session or Batch Job"

17.6   Logging an Entire Session or Batch Job

Problem

You need to capture all the output from an entire session or a long batch job.

Solution

There are many ways to solve this problem, depending on your needs and environment.

The simplest solution is to turn on logging to memory or disk in your terminal program. The problems with that are that your terminal program may not allow that, and when it gets disconnected you lose your log.

The next simplest solution is to modify the job to log itself, or redirect the entire thing to *tee* or a file. For example, one of the following might work:

```
$ long_noisy_job >& log_file
$ long_noisy_job 2>&1 | tee log_file

$ ( long_noisy_job ) >& log_file
$ ( long_noisy_job ) 2>&1 | tee log_file
```

The problems here are that you may not be able to modify the job, or the job itself may do something that precludes these solutions (e.g., if it requires user input, it could get stuck asking for the input before the prompt is actually displayed). That can happen because STDOUT is buffered, so the prompt could be in the buffer waiting to be displayed when more data comes in, but no more data will come in since the program is waiting for input.

There is an interesting program called *script* that exists for this very purpose and it's probably already on your system. You run *script*, and it logs everything that happens to the logfile (called a *typescript*) you've given it, which is OK if you want to log the entire session—just start *script*, then run your job. But if you only want to capture part of the session, there is no way to have your code start *script*, run something to log it, then stop *script* again. You can't script *script* because once you run it, you're in a subshell at a prompt (i.e., you can't do something like script *file_to_log_to some_command_to_run*).

Our final solution uses the terminal multiplexer *screen*. With *screen*, you can turn whole session logging on or off from inside your script. Once you are already running *screen*, do the following in your script:

```
# Set a logfile and turn on logging
screen -X logfile /path/to/logfile && screen -X log on

# your commands here

# Turn logging back off
screen -X log off
```

Discussion

We suggest you try the solutions in order, and use the first one that meets your needs. Unless you have very specific needs, *script* will probably work. But just in case, it can be handy to know about the *screen* option.

See Also

- man script
- man screen
- Recipe 17.5, "Sharing a Single bash Session"

17.7 Clearing the Screen When You Log Out

Problem

You use or administer some systems that do not clear the screen when you log out, and you'd rather not leave the tail end of whatever you were working on visible, since that could be an information leak.

Solution

Put the *clear* command in your *~/.bash_logout:*.

```
# ~/.bash_logout

# Clear the screen on exit from the shell to prevent information leaks,
# if not already set as an exit trap in bash_profile
[ "$PS1" ] && clear
```

Or set a trap to run *clear* on shell termination:

```
# ~/.bash_profile
# Trap to clear the screen on exit from the shell to prevent
# information leaks, if not already set in ~/.bash_logout
trap ' [ "$PS1" ] && clear ' 0
```

Note that if you are connecting remotely and your client has a scroll-back buffer, whatever you were working on may still be in there. *clear* also has no effect on your shell's command history.

Discussion

Setting a trap to clear the screen is probably overkill, but could conceivably cover an error situation in which *~/.bash_logout* is not executed. If you are really paranoid you can set both, but in that case you may also wish to look into TEMPEST and Faraday cages.

If you skip the test to determine whether the shell is interactive, you'll get errors like this under some circumstances:

```
# e.g., from tput
No value for $TERM and no -T specified

# e.g., from clear
TERM environment variable not set.
```

See Also

- *http://en.wikipedia.org/wiki/TEMPEST*
- *http://en.wikipedia.org/wiki/Faraday_cag*
- Recipe 16.20, "Getting Started with a Custom Configuration"

17.8 Capturing File Metadata for Recovery

Problem

You want to create a list of files and details about them for archive purposes, for example, to verify backups, re-create directories, etc. Or maybe you are about to do a large chmod -R and need a back-out plan. Or perhaps you keep /etc/* in a revision control system that does not preserve permissions or ownership.

Solution

Use GNU *find* with some *printf* formats:

```
#!/usr/bin/env bash
# cookbook filename: archive_meta-data

printf "%b" "Mode\tUser\tGroup\tBytes\tModified\tFileSpec\n" > archive_file
find / \( -path /proc -o -path /mnt -o -path /tmp -o -path /var/tmp \
  -o -path /var/cache -o -path /var/spool \) -prune \
  -o -type d -printf 'd%m\t%u\t%g\t%s\t%t\t%p/\n' \
  -o -type l -printf 'l%m\t%u\t%g\t%s\t%t\t%p -> %l\n' \
  -o         -printf  '%m\t%u\t%g\t%s\t%t\t%p\n' >> archive_file
```

Note that the -printf expression is in the GNU version of *find*.

Discussion

The (-path /foo -o -path ...) -prune part removes various directories you probably don't want to bother with, e.g., -type d is for directories. The *printf* format is prefixed with a d, then uses an octal mode, user, group, and so forth. -type l is for symbolic links and also shows you where the link points. With the contents of this file and some additional scripting, you can determine at a high level if anything has changed, or re-create mangled ownership or permissions. Note that this does not take the place of more security-oriented programs like Tripwire, AIDE, Osiris, or Samhain.

See Also

- man find
- Chapter 9
- *http://www.tripwiresecurity.com*
- *http://sourceforge.net/projects/aide*
- *http://osiris.shmoo.com*
- *http://la-samhna.de/samhain/index.html*

17.9 Creating an Index of Many Files

Problem

You have a number of files for which you'd like to create an index.

Solution

Use the *find* command in conjunction with *head*, *grep*, or other commands that can parse out comments or summary information from each file.

For example, if the second line of all your shell scripts follows the format "name—description" then this example will create a nice index:

```
$ for i in $(grep -El '#![[:space:]]?/bin/sh' *); do head -2 $i | tail -1; done
```

Discussion

As noted, this technique depends on each file having some kind of summary information, such as comments, that may be parsed out. We then look for a way to identify the type of file, in this case a shell script, and grab the second line of each file.

If the files do not have easily parsed summary information, you can try something like this and manually work through the output to create an index:

```
for dir in $(find . -type d); do head -15 $dir/*; done
```

 Watch out for binary files!

See Also

- man find
- man grep
- man head
- man tail

17.10 Using diff and patch

Problem

You can never remember how to use *diff* to create patches that may later be applied using *patch*.

Solution

If you are creating a simple patch for a single file, use:

```
$ diff -u original_file modified_file > your_patch
```

If you are creating a patch for multiple files in parallel directory structures, use:

```
$ cp -pR original_dirs/ modified_dirs/

# Make changes here

$ diff -Nru original_dirs/ modified_dirs/ > your_comprehensive_patch
```

To be especially careful, force *diff* to treat all files as ASCII using -a, and set your language and timezone to the universal defaults as shown:

```
$ LC_ALL=C TZ=UTC diff -aNru original_dirs/ modified_dirs/ > your_comprehensive_patch

$ LC_ALL=C TZ=UTC diff -aNru original_dirs/ modified_dirs/
diff -aNru original_dirs/changed_file modified_dirs/changed_file
--- original_dirs/changed_file   2006-11-23 01:04:07.000000000 +0000
+++ modified_dirs/changed_file   2006-11-23 01:04:35.000000000 +0000
@@ -1,2 +1,2 @@
 This file is common to both dirs.
-But it changes from one to the other.
+But it changes from 1 to the other.
diff -aNru original_dirs/only_in_mods modified_dirs/only_in_mods
--- original_dirs/only_in_mods   1970-01-01 00:00:00.000000000 +0000
+++ modified_dirs/only_in_mods   2006-11-23 01:05:58.000000000 +0000
@@ -0,0 +1,2 @@
+While this file is only in the modified dirs.
+It also has two lines, this is the last.
diff -aNru original_dirs/only_in_orig modified_dirs/only_in_orig
--- original_dirs/only_in_orig   2006-11-23 01:05:18.000000000 +0000
+++ modified_dirs/only_in_orig   1970-01-01 00:00:00.000000000 +0000
@@ -1,2 +0,0 @@
-This file is only in the original dirs.
-It has two lines, this is the last.
```

To apply a patch file, *cd* to the directory of the single file, or to the parent of the directory tree and use the *patch* command:

```
cd /path/to/files
patch -Np1 < your_patch
```

The -N argument to *patch* prevents it from reversing patches or re-applying patches that have already been made. -p *number* removes *number* of leading directories to allow for differences in directory structure between whoever created the patch and whoever is applying it. Using -p1 will often work; if not, experiment with -p0, then -p2, etc. It'll either work or complain and ask you what to do, in which case you cancel and try something else unless you really know what you are doing.

Discussion

diff can produce output in various forms, some of which are more useful than others. Unified output, using -u, is generally considered the best because it is both reasonably human-readable yet very robust when used with *patch*. It provides three lines of context around the change, which allows a human reader to get oriented and allows the *patch* command to work correctly even if the file to be patched is different than the one used to create the patch. As long as the context lines are intact, *patch* can usually figure it out. Context output, using -c, is similar to -u output, but is more redundant and not quite as easy to read. The *ed* format, using -e, produces a script suitable for use with the ancient *ed* editor. Finally, the default output is similar to the *ed* output, with a little more human-readable context.

```
# Unified format (preferred)
$ diff -u original_file modified_file
--- original_file     2006-11-22 19:29:07.000000000 -0500
+++ modified_file     2006-11-22 19:29:47.000000000 -0500
@@ -1,9 +1,9 @@
-This is original_file, and this line is different.
+This is modified_file, and this line is different.
 This line is the same.
 So is this one.
 And this one.
 Ditto.
-But this one is different.
+But this 1 is different.
 However, not this line.
 And this is the last same, same, same.


# Context format
$ diff -c original_file modified_file
*** original_file     Wed Nov 22 19:29:07 2006
--- modified_file     Wed Nov 22 19:29:47 2006
***************
*** 1,9 ****
! This is original_file, and this line is different.
  This line is the same.
  So is this one.
  And this one.
  Ditto.
! But this one is different.
  However, not this line.
  And this is the last same, same, same.

--- 1,9 ----
! This is modified_file, and this line is different.
  This line is the same.
  So is this one.
  And this one.
  Ditto.
! But this 1 is different.
  However,
```

```
# 'ed' format
$ diff -e original_file modified_file
6c
But this 1 is different.
.
1c
This is modified_file, and this line is different.
.


# Normal format
$ diff original_file modified_file
1c1
< This is original_file, and this line is different.
---
> This is modified_file, and this line is different.
6c6
< But this one is different.
---
> But this 1 is different.
```

The -r and -N arguments to *diff* are simple yet powerful. -r means, as usual, recursive operation though the directory structure, while -N causes *diff* to pretend that any file found in one directory structure also exists in the other as an empty file. In theory, that has the effect of creating or removing files as needed; however, in practice -N is not supported on all systems (notably Solaris) and it may end up leaving zero-byte files lying around on others. Some versions of *patch* default to using -b, which leaves lots of *.orig* files laying around, and some versions (notably Linux) are less chatty than others (notably BSD). Many versions (not Solaris) of *diff* also support the -p argument, which tries to show which C function the patch affects.

Resist the urge to do something like diff -u prog.c.orig prog.c. This has the potential to cause all kinds of confusion since *patch* may also create *.orig* files. Also resist the urge to do something like diff -u prog/prog.c new/prog/prog.c since *patch* will get very confused about the unequal number of directory names in the paths.

See Also

- man diff
- man patch
- man cmp
- *http://directory.fsf.org/GNU/wdiff.html*
- *http://furius.ca/xxdiff/* for a great GUI *diff* (and more) tool

17.11 Counting Differences in Files

Problem

You have two files and need to know about how many differences exist between them.

Solution

Count the *hunks* (i.e., sections of changed data) in *diff*'s output:

```
$ diff -C0 original_file modified_file | grep -c "^\*\*\*\*\*\*"
2

$ diff -C0 original_file modified_file
*** original_file        Fri Nov 24 12:48:35 2006
--- modified_file        Fri Nov 24 12:48:43 2006
***************
*** 1 ****
! This is original_file, and this line is different.
--- 1 ----
! This is modified_file, and this line is different.
***************
*** 6 ****
! But this one is different.
--- 6 ----
! But this 1 is different.
```

If you only need to know whether the files are different and not how many differences there are, use *cmp*. It will exit at the first difference, which can save time on large files. Like *diff* it is silent when the files are identical, but it reports the location of the first difference if not:

```
$ cmp original_file modified_file
original_file modified_file differ: char 9, line 1
```

Discussion

Hunk is actually the technical term, though we've also seen hunks referred to as *chunks* in some places. Note that it is possible, in theory, to get slightly different results for the same files across different machines or versions of *diff*, since the number of hunks is a result of the algorithm *diff* uses. You will certainly get different answers when using different *diff* output formats, as demonstrated below.

We find a zero-context contextual *diff* to be the easiest to use for this purpose, and using -C0 instead of -c creates fewer lines for *grep* to have to search. A unified *diff* tends to combine more changes than expected into one hunk, leading to fewer differences being reported:

```
$ diff -u original_file modified_file | grep -c "^@@"
1

$ diff -u original_file modified_file
--- original_file       2006-11-24 12:48:35.000000000 -0500
+++ modified_file       2006-11-24 12:48:43.000000000 -0500
@@ -1,8 +1,8 @@
-This is original_file, and this line is different.
+This is modified_file, and this line is different.
 This line is the same.
 So is this one.
 And this one.
 Ditto.
-But this one is different.
+But this 1 is different.
 However, not this line.
 And this is the last same, same, same.
```

A normal or *ed* style *diff* works too, but the *grep* pattern is more complicated. Though not shown in this example, a multiline change in normal *grep* output might look like 2,3c2,3, thus requiring character classes and more typing than is the case using -C0:

```
$ diff -e original_file modified_file | egrep -c '^[[:digit:],]+[[:alpha:]]+'
2

$ diff original_file modified_file | egrep -c '^[[:digit:],]+[[:alpha:]]+'
2

$ diff original_file modified_file
1c1
```

```
< This is original_file, and this line is different.
---
> This is modified_file, and this line is different.
6c6
< But this one is different.
---
> But this 1 is different.
```

See Also

- man diff
- man cmp
- man grep
- *http://en.wikipedia.org/wiki/Diff*

17.12 Removing or Renaming Files Named with Special Characters

Problem

You need to remove or rename a file that was created with a special character that causes *rm* or *mv* to behave in unexpected ways. The canonical example of this is any file starting with a dash, such as *-f* or *--help*, which will cause any command you try to use to interpret the filename as an argument.

Solution

If the file begins with a dash, use -- to signal the end of arguments to the command, or use a full (*/tmp/-f*) or relative (*./-f*) path. If the file contains other special characters that are interpreted by the shell, such as a space or asterisk, use shell quoting. If you use filename completion (the Tab key by default), it will automatically quote special characters for you. You can also use single-quotes around the troublesome name.

```
$ ls
--help                        this is a *crazy* file name!

$ mv --help help
mv: unknown option -- -
usage: mv [-fiv] source target
       mv [-fiv] source ... directory

$ mv -- --help my_help

$ mv this\ is\ a\ \*crazy\*\ file\ name\! this_is_a_better_name

$ ls
my_help                  this_is_a_better_name
```

Discussion

To understand what is actually being executed after shell expansion, preface your command with *echo*:

```
$ rm *
rm: unknown option -- -
usage: rm [-f|-i] [-dPRrvW] file ...

$ echo rm *
rm --help this is a *crazy* file name!
```

See Also

- *http://www.gnu.org/software/coreutils/faq/coreutils-faq.html#How-do-I-remove-files-that-start-with-a-dash_003f*
- Sections 2.1 and 2.2 of *http://www.faqs.org/faqs/unix-faq/faq/part2/*
- Recipe 1.6, "Using Shell Quoting"

17.13 Prepending Data to a File

Problem

You want to prepend data to an existing file, for example to add a header after sorting.

Solution

Use *cat* in a subshell.

```
temp_file="temp.$RANDOM$RANDOM$$"
(echo 'static header line1'; cat data_file) > $temp_file \
  && cat $temp_file > data_file
rm $temp_file
unset temp_file
```

You could also use *sed*, the streaming editor. To prepend static text, note that backslash escape sequences are expanded in GNU *sed* but not in some other versions. Also, under some shells the trailing backslashes may need to be doubled:

```
# Any sed, e.g., Solaris 10 /usr/bin/sed
$ sed -e '1i\
> static header line1
> ' data_file
static header line1
1 foo
2 bar
3 baz

$ sed -e '1i\
> static header line1\
> static header line2
```

```
> ' data_file
static header line1
static header line2
1 foo
2 bar
3 baz


# GNU sed
$ sed -e '1istatic header line1\nstatic header line2' data_file
static header line1
static header line2
1 foo
2 bar
3 baz
```

To prepend an existing file:

```
$ sed -e '$r data_file' header_file
Header Line1
Header Line2
1 foo
2 bar
3 baz
```

Discussion

This one seems to be a love/hate kind of thing. People either love the *cat* solution or love the *sed* solution, but not both. The *cat* version is probably faster and simpler, the *sed* solution is arguably more flexible.

You can also store a *sed* script in a file, instead of leaving it on the command line. And of course you would usually redirect the output into a new file, like sed -e '$r *data*' *header* > *new_file*, but note that will change the file's inode and may change other attributes such as permissions or ownership. To preserve everything but the inode, use -i for in-place editing if your version of *sed* supports that. Don't use -i with the reversed header file prepend form shown previously or you will edit your header file. Also note that Perl has a similar -i option that also writes a new file like *sed*, though Perl itself works rather differently than *sed* for this example:

```
# Show inode
$ ls -i data_file
509951 data_file

$ sed -i -e '1istatic header line1\nstatic header line2' data_file

$ cat data_file
static header line1
static header line2
1 foo
2 bar
3 baz
```

```
# Verify inode has changed
$ ls -i data_file
509954 data_file
```

To preserve everything (or if your *sed* does not have -i or you want to use the prepend file method mentioned earlier):

```
# Show inode
$ ls -i data_file
509951 data_file

# $RANDOM is bash only, you can use mktemp on other systems
$ temp_file=$RANDOM$RANDOM

$ sed -e '$r data_file' header_file > $temp_file

# Only cat if the source exists and is not empty!
$ [ -s "$temp_file" ] && cat $temp_file > data

$ unset temp_file

$ cat data_file
Header Line1
Header Line2
1 foo
2 bar
3 baz

# Verify inode has NOT changed
$ ls -i data_file
509951 data
```

Prepending a header file to a data file is interesting because it's rather counterintuitive. If you try to read the *header_file* file into the *data_file* file at line one, you get this:

```
$ sed -e '1r header_file' data_file
1 foo
Header Line1
Header Line2
2 bar
3 baz
```

So instead, we simply append the data to the header file and write the output to another file. Again, don't try to use sed -i or you will edit your header file.

Another way to prepend data is to use *cat* reading from STDIN with a here-document or a here-string. Note that here-strings are not available until *bash* 2.05b or newer, and they don't do backslash escape sequence expansion, but they avoid all the *sed* version issues.

```
# Using a here-document
$ cat - data_file <<EoH
> Header line1
```

```
> Header line2
> EoH
Header line1
Header line2
1 foo
2 bar
3 baz


# Using a here-string in bash-2.05b+, no  backslash escape sequence expansion
$ cat - data_file <<<'Header Line1'
Header Line1
1 foo
2 bar
3 baz
```

See Also

- man cat
- man sed
- *http://sed.sourceforge.net/sedfaq.html*
- *http://sed.sourceforge.net/sed1line.txt*
- *http://tldp.org/LDP/abs/html/x15507.html*
- Recipe 14.11, "Using Secure Temporary Files"
- Recipe 17.14, "Editing a File in Place"

17.14 Editing a File in Place

Problem

You want to edit an existing file without affecting the inode or permissions.

Solution

This is trickier than it sounds because many tools you might ordinarily use, such as *sed*, will write to a new file (thus changing the inode) even if they go out of their way to preserve other attributes.

The obvious solution is to simply edit the file and make your updates. However, we admit that that may be of limited use in a scripting situation. Or is it?

In Recipe 17.13, "Prepending Data to a File," you saw that *sed* writes a brand new file one way or another; however, there is an ancestor of *sed* that doesn't do that. It's called, anticlimactically, *ed*, and it is just as ubiquitous as its other famous descendant, *vi*. And interestingly, *ed* is scriptable. So here is our "prepend a header" example again, this time using *ed*:

```
# Show inode
$ ls -i data_file
306189 data_file

# Use printf "%b" to avoid issues with 'echo -e' or not.
$ printf "%b" '1\ni\nHeader Line1\nHeader Line2\n.\nw\nq\n' | ed -s data_file
1 foo

$ cat data_file
Header Line1
Header Line2
1 foo
2 bar
3 baz

# Verify inode has NOT changed
$ ls -i data_file
306189 data_file
```

Discussion

Of course you can store an *ed* script in a file, just as you can with *sed*. In this case, it might be useful to see what that file looks like, to explain the mechanics of the *ed* script:

```
$ cat ed_script
1
i
Header Line1
Header Line2
.
w
q

$ ed -s data_file < ed_script
1 foo

$ cat data_file
Header Line1
Header Line2
1 foo
2 bar
3 baz
```

The 1 in the *ed* script means to go to the first line. i puts us into insert mode, and the next two lines are literal. A single . all by itself on a line exits insert mode, w writes the file and q quits. The -s suppresses some output, specifically for use in scripts, but you can see from the 1 foo that not everything is suppressed; of course, ed -s *data_file < ed_script >* /dev/null takes care of that.

One disadvantage to *ed* is that there isn't that much documentation for it anymore. It's been around since the beginning of Unix, but it's not commonly used anymore even though it exists on every system we checked. Since both *vi* (via *ex*) and *sed* (spiritually at least[*]) are descended from *ed*, you should be able to figure out anything you might want to do. Note that *ex* is a symbolic link to *vi* or a variant on many systems, while *ed* is just *ed*.

Another way to accomplish the same effect is to use *sed* or some other tool, write the changed file into a new file, then *cat* it back into the original file. This is obviously inefficient. It is also easier to say than to do safely because if the change fails for any reason you could end up writing nothing back over the original file (see the example in Recipe 17.13, "Prepending Data to a File").

See Also

- man ed
- man ex
- ls -l `which ex`
- *http://sed.sourceforge.net/sedfaq.html*
- Recipe 17.13, "Prepending Data to a File"

17.15 Using sudo on a Group of Commands

Problem

You are running as a regular user and need to *sudo* several commands at once, or you need to use redirection that applies to the commands and not to *sudo*.

Solution

Use *sudo* to run a subshell in which you may group your commands and use pipelines and redirection:

```
sudo bash -c 'command1 && command2 || command3'
```

This requires the ability to run a shell as *root*. If you can't, have your system administrator write a quick script and add it to your *sudo* privilege specification.

Discussion

If you try something like sudo *command1* && *command2* || *command3* you'll find that *command2* and *command3* are running as you, not as *root*. That's because *sudo*'s influence only extends to the first command and *your* shell is doing the redirection.

Note the use of the -c argument to *bash*, which causes it to just execute the given commands and exit. Without that you will just end up running a new interactive

---

[*] *http://www.columbia.edu/~rh120/ch106.x09*

root shell, which is probably not what you wanted. But as noted above, with -c you are still running a (non-interactive) root shell, so you need to have the *sudo* rights to do that. Mac OS X and some Linux distributions, such as Ubuntu, actually disable the *root* user to encourage you to only log in as a normal user and *sudo* as needed (the Mac hides this better) for administration. If you are using an OS like that, or have rolled your own *sudo* setup, you should be fine. However, if you are running a locked-down environment, this recipe may not work for you.

To learn whether you may use *sudo* and what you are and are not allowed to do, use sudo -l. Almost any other use of *sudo* will probably trigger a security message to your administrator tattling on you. You can try using sudo sudo -V | less as a regular user or just sudo -V | less if you are already *root* to get a lot of information about how *sudo* is compiled and configured on your system.

---

su and sudo

It's always been a best practice to run as a regular user and only use *root* privileges when absolutely necessary. While the *su* command is handy, many argue that *sudo* is better. For example:

- It takes more work to get *sudo* working properly (in other words, locked down rather than just "ALL=(ALL) ALL") and it can be slightly less convenient to use, but it can also foster more secure work-practices.
- You can forget that you have *su*'d to *root* and do something unfortunate.
- Having to type *sudo* all the time makes you think about what you are doing a little more.
- *sudo* allows delegation of individual commands to other users without sharing *root*'s password.

Both commands can incorporate logging, and there are some tricks that can make each command work very much like the other; however, there are still some significant differences. The two most important are that with *sudo* you enter your own password to confirm your identity before being allowed to execute a command. Thus, *root*'s password is not shared if more than one person needs some root privileges. Which brings us to the second difference; *sudo* can be very specific about what commands a given user can and cannot execute. That restriction can be tricky, since many applications allow you to shell out and do something else, so if you are able to *sudo* into *vi*, you can shell out and have an unrestricted root prompt. Still, used carefully *sudo* is an excellent tool.

See Also

- man su
- man sudo
- man sudoers
- man visudo
- sudo
- *https://help.ubuntu.com/community/RootSudo*
- Recipe 14.15, "Writing setuid or setgid Scripts"
- Recipe 14.18, "Running As a Non-root User"
- Recipe 14.19, "Using sudo More Securely"
- Recipe 14.20, "Using Passwords in Scripts"

17.16 Finding Lines in One File But Not in the Other

Problem

You have two data files and you need to compare them and find lines that exist in one file but not in the other.

Solution

Sort the files and isolate the data of interest using *cut* or *awk* if necessary, and then use *comm*, *diff*, *grep*, or *uniq* depending on your needs.

comm is designed for just this type of problem:

```
$ cat left
record_01
record_02.left only
record_03
record_05.differ
record_06
record_07
record_08
record_09
record_10

$ cat right
record_01
record_02
record_04
record_05
record_06.differ
record_07
record_08
record_09.right only
record_10
```

```
# Only show lines in the left file
$ comm -23 left right
record_02.left only
record_03
record_05.differ
record_06
record_09

# Only show lines in the right file
$ comm -13 left right
record_02
record_04
record_05
record_06.differ
record_09.right only

# Only show lines common to both files
$ comm -12 left right
record_01
record_07
record_08
record_10
```

diff will quickly show you all the differences from both files, but its output is not terribly pretty and you may not need to know all the differences. GNU *grep*'s -y and -w options can be handy for readability, but you can get used to the regular output as well. Some systems (e.g., Solaris) may use *sdiff* instead of diff -y or have a separate binary such as *bdiff* to process very large files.

```
$ diff -y -W 60 left right
record_01                       record_01
record_02.left only      |      record_02
record_03                |      record_04
record_05.differ         |      record_05
record_06                |      record_06.differ
record_07                       record_07
record_08                       record_08
record_09                |      record_09.right only
record_10                       record_10

$ diff -y -W 60 --suppress-common-lines left right
record_02.left only      |      record_02
record_03                |      record_04
record_05.differ         |      record_05
record_06                |      record_06.differ
record_09                |      record_09.right only

$ diff left right
2,5c2,5
< record_02.left only
< record_03
< record_05.differ
< record_06
---
```

```
> record_02
> record_04
> record_05
> record_06.differ
8c8
< record_09
---
> record_09.right only
```

grep can show you when lines exist only in one file and not the other, and you can figure out which file if necessary. But since it's doing regular expression matches, it will not be able to handle differences within the line unless you edit the file that becomes the pattern file, and it will also get very slow as the file sizes grow.

This example shows all the lines that exist in the file *left* but not in the file *right*:

```
$ grep -vf right left
record_03
record_06
record_09
```

Note that only "record_03" is really missing; the other two lines are simply different. If you need to detect such variations, you'll need to use *diff*. If you need to ignore them, use *cut* or *awk* as necessary to isolate the parts you need into temporary files.

uniq -u can show you only lines that are unique in the files, but it will not tell you which file the line came from (if you need to know that, use one of the previous solutions). uniq -d will show you only lines that exist in both files:

```
$ sort right left | uniq -u
record_02
record_02.left only
record_03
record_04
record_05
record_05.differ
record_06
record_06.differ
record_09
record_09.right only

$ sort right left | uniq -d
record_01
record_07
record_08
record_10
```

Discussion

comm is your best choice if it's available and you don't need the power of *diff*.

You may need to *sort* and/or *cut* or *awk* into temporary files and work from those if you can't disrupt the original files.

See Also

- man cmp
- man diff
- man grep
- man uniq

17.17 Keeping the Most Recent N Objects

Problem

You need to keep the most recent *N* logfiles or backup directories, and purge the remainder, no matter how many there are.

Solution

Create an ordered list of the objects, pass them as arguments to a function, shift the arguments by *N*, and return the remainder:

```
# cookbook filename: func_shift_by

# Pop a given number of items from the top of a stack,
# such that you can then perform an action on whatever is left.
# Called like:  shift_by <# to keep> <ls command, or whatever>
# Returns:  the remainder of the stack or list
#
# For example, list some objects, then keep only the top 10.
#
# It is CRITICAL that you pass the items in order with the objects to
# be removed at the top (or front) of the list, since all this function
# does is remove (pop) the number of entries you specify from the top
# of the list.
#
# You should experiment with echo before using rm!
#
# For example:
#     rm -rf $(shift_by $MAX_BUILD_DIRS_TO_KEEP $(ls -rd backup.2006*))
#
function shift_by {

# If $1 is zero or greater than $#, the positional parameters are
# not changed.  In this case that is a BAD THING!
if (( $1 == 0 || $1 > ( $# - 1 ) )); then
    echo ''
else
    # Remove the given number of objects (plus 1) from the list.
    shift $(( $1 + 1 ))
```

```
    # Return whatever is left
    echo "$*"
  fi
}
```

 If you try to shift the positional parameters by zero or by more than the total number of positional parameters ($#), shift will do nothing. If you are using shift to process a list then delete what it returns, that will result in you deleting everything. Make sure to test the argument to shift to make sure that it's not zero and it is greater than the number of positional parameters. Our shift_by function does this.

For example:

```
$ source shift_by

$ touch {1..9}

$ ls ?
1 2 3 4 5 6 7 8 9

$ shift_by 3 $(ls ?)
4 5 6 7 8 9

$ shift_by 5 $(ls ?)
6 7 8 9

$ shift_by 5 $(ls -r ?)
4 3 2 1

$ shift_by 7 $(ls ?)
8 9

$ shift_by 9 $(ls ?)

# Keep only the last 5 objects
$ echo "rm -rf $(shift_by 5 $(ls ?))"
rm -rf 6 7 8 9

# In production we'd test this first!  See discussion.
$ rm -rf $(shift_by 5 $(ls ?))

$ ls ?
1 2 3 4 5
```

Discussion

Make sure you fully test both the argument returned and what you intend to do with it. For example, if you are deleting old data, use *echo* to test the command that would be performed before doing it live. Also test that you have a value at all, or else you could end up doing rm -rf and getting an error. Never do something like rm -rf /$variable, because if $variable is ever null you will start deleting the root directory, which is particularly bad if you are running as *root*!

```
$files_to_nuke=$(shift_by 5 $(ls ?))
[ -n $files_to_nuke ] && rm -rf "$files_to_nuke"
```

This recipe takes advantage of the fact that arguments to a function are affected by the shift command inside that function, which makes it trivial to pop objects off the stack (otherwise we'd have to do some fancy substring or for loop operations). We must shift by *n*+1 because the first argument ($1) is actually the count of the items to shift, leaving $2..N as the objects in the stack. We could also write it more verbosely this way:

```
function shift_by {
    shift_count=$1
    shift

    shift $shift_count

    echo "$*"
}
```

It's possible you may run afoul of your system's ARG_MAX (see Recipe 15.13, "Working Around "argument list too long" Errors," for details) if the paths to the objects are very long or you have a very large number of objects to handle. In the former case, you may be able to create some breathing room by changing directories closer to the objects to shorten the paths, or by using symbolic links. In the latter case, you can use this more complicated for loop:

```
objects_to_keep=5
counter=1

for file in /path/with/many/many/files/*e*; do
    if [ $counter -gt $objects_to_keep ]; then
        remainder="$remainder $file"
    fi
    (( counter++ ))
done

[ -n "$remainder" ] && echo "rm -rf $remainder"
```

A common method of doing a similar operation is a trickle-down scheme such as the following:

```
rm -rf backup.3/
mv      backup.2/ backup.3/
mv      backup.1/ backup.2/
cp -al backup.0/ backup.1/
```

This works very well in many cases, especially when combined with hard links to conserve space while allowing multiple backups (see Rob Flickenger's *Linux Server Hacks*, Hack #42 [O'Reilly]). However, if the number of existing objects fluctuates or is not known in advance, this method won't work.

See Also

- help for
- help shift
- *Linux Server Hacks*, Hack #42, by Rob Flickenger (O'Reilly)
- Recipe 13.5, "Parsing Output with a Function Call"
- Recipe 15.13, "Working Around "argument list too long" Errors"

17.18 Grepping ps Output Without Also Getting the grep Process Itself

Problem

You want to *grep* output from the *ps* command without also getting the *grep* process itself.

Solution

Change the pattern you are looking for so that it is a valid regular expression that will not match the literal text that *ps* will display:

```
$ ps aux | grep 'ssh'
root    366  0.0  1.2  340  1588 ?? Is    20Oct06  0:00.68 /usr/sbin/sshd
root  25358  0.0  1.9  472  2404 ?? Ss    Wed07PM  0:02.16 sshd: root@ttyp0
jp    27579  0.0  0.4  152   540 p0 S+     3:24PM  0:00.04 grep ssh

$ ps aux | grep '[s]sh'
root    366  0.0  1.2  340  1588 ?? Is    20Oct06  0:00.68 /usr/sbin/sshd
root  25358  0.0  1.9  472  2404 ?? Ss    Wed07PM  0:02.17 sshd: root@ttyp0
```

Discussion

This works because [s] is a regular expression character class containing a single lowercase letter s, meaning that [s]sh will match ssh but not the literal string grep [s]sh that *ps* will display.

The other less efficient and more clunky solution you might see is something like this:

```
$ ps aux | grep 'ssh' | grep -v grep
```

See Also

- man ps
- man grep

17.19 Finding Out Whether a Process Is Running

Problem

You need to determine whether a process is running, and you might or might not already have a process ID (PID).

Solution

If you don't already have a PID, *grep* the output of the *ps* command to see if the program you are looking for is running. See Recipe 17.18, "Grepping ps Output Without Also Getting the grep Process Itself," for details on why our pattern is [s]sh.

```
$ [ "$(ps -ef | grep 'bin/[s]shd')" ] && echo 'ssh is running' || echo 'ssh not
running'
```

That's nice, but you know it's not going to be that easy, right? Right. It's difficult because *ps* can be wildly different from system to system.

```
# cookbook filename: is_process_running

# Can you believe this?!?
case `uname` in
    Linux|AIX) PS_ARGS='-ewwo pid,args'    ;;
    SunOS)     PS_ARGS='-eo pid,args'      ;;
    *BSD)      PS_ARGS='axwwo pid,args'    ;;
    Darwin)    PS_ARGS='Awwo pid,command' ;;
esac

if ps $PS_ARGS | grep -q 'bin/[s]shd'; then
    echo 'sshd is running'
else
    echo 'sshd not running'
fi
```

If you do have a PID, say from a lock file or an environment variable, just search for it. Be careful to match the PID up with some other recognizable string so that you don't have a collision where some other random process just happens to have the stale PID you are using. Just obtain the PID and use it in the *grep* or in a -p argument to *ps*:

```
# Linux
$ ps -wwo pid,args -p 1394 | grep 'bin/sshd'
 1394 /usr/sbin/sshd

# BSD
$ ps ww -p 366 | grep 'bin/sshd'
366 ?? Is    0:00.76 /usr/sbin/sshd
```

Discussion

The test and *grep* portion of the solution requires a little explanation. You need " " around the $( ) so that if *grep* outputs anything, the test is true. If the *grep* is silent because nothing matches, then the test is false. You just have to make sure your *ps* and *grep*s do exactly what you want.

Unfortunately, the *ps* command is one of the most fragmented in all of Unix. It seems like every flavor of Unix and Linux has different arguments and processes them in different ways. All we can tell you is that you'll need to thoroughly test against all systems on which your script will be running.

You can easily search for anything you can express as a regular expression, but make sure your expressions are specific enough not to match anything else. That's why we used bin/[s]shd instead of just [s]shd, which would also match user connections (see Recipe 17.18, "Grepping ps Output Without Also Getting the grep Process Itself"). At the same time, /usr/sbin/[s]shd might be bad in case some crazy system doesn't use that location. There is often a fine line between too much and not enough specificity. For example, you may have a program that can run multiple instances using different configuration files, so make sure you search for the config file as well if you need to isolate the correct instance. The same thing may apply to users, if you are running with enough rights to see other users' processes.

 Watch out for Solaris since its *ps* is hard-coded to limit arguments to only 80 characters. If you have long paths or commands and still need to check for a config filename, you may run into that limit.

See Also

- man ps
- man grep
- Recipe 17.18, "Grepping ps Output Without Also Getting the grep Process Itself"

17.20 Adding a Prefix or Suffix to Output

Problem

You'd like to add a prefix or a suffix to each line of output from a given command for some reason. For example, you're collecting *last* statistics from many machines and it's much easier to *grep* or otherwise parse the data you collect if each line contains the hostname.

Solution

Pipe the appropriate data into a while read loop and *printf* as needed. For example, this prints the $HOSTNAME, followed by a tab, followed by any nonblank lines of output from the *last* command:

```
$ last | while read i; do [[ -n "$i" ]] && printf "%b" "$HOSTNAME\t$i\n"; done

# Write a new logfile
$ last | while read i; do [[ -n "$i" ]] && printf "%b" "$HOSTNAME\t$i\n"; done >
last_$HOSTNAME.log
```

Or you can use *awk* to add text to each line:

```
$ last | awk "BEGIN { OFS=\"\t\" } ! /^\$/ { print \"$HOSTNAME\", \$0}"

$ last | awk "BEGIN { OFS=\"\t\" } ! /^\$/ { print \"$HOSTNAME\", \$0}" \
    > last_$HOSTNAME.log
```

Discussion

We use [[-n "$i"]] to remove any blank lines from the *last* output, and then we use *printf* to display the data. Quoting for this method is simpler, but it uses more steps (*last*, while, and read, as opposed to just *last* and *awk*). You may find one method easier to remember, more readable, or faster than the other, depending on your needs.

There is a trick to the *awk* command we used here. Often you will see single quotes surrounding *awk* commands to prevent the shell from interpreting *awk* variables as shell variables. However in this case we *want* the shell to interpolate $HOSTNAME, so we surround the command with double quotes. That requires us to use backslash escapes on the elements of the command that we do *not* want the shell to handle, namely the internal double quotes and the *awk* $0 variable, which contains the current line.

For a suffix, simply move the $0 variable:

```
$ last | while read i; do [[ -n "$i" ]] && printf "%b" "$i\t$HOSTNAME\n"; done

$ last | awk "BEGIN { OFS=\"\t\" } ! /^\$/ { print \"$HOSTNAME\", \$0}"
```

You could also use Perl or *sed* (note the → denotes a literal *tab* character, typed by pressing Ctrl-V then Ctrl-I):

```
$ last | perl -ne "print qq($HOSTNAME\t\$_) if ! /^\s*$/;"

$ last | sed "s/./$HOSTNAME → &/; /^$/d"
```

In the Perl command, we use qq( ) instead of double quotes to avoid having to escape them. The last part is a regular expression that matches a line containing either nothing or only whitespace, and $_ is the Perl idiom for the current line. In the *sed* command we replace any line containing at least one character with the prefix and the character that matched (&), then delete any blank lines.

See Also

- *Effective awk Programming* by Arnold Robbins
- *sed & awk* by Arnold Robbins and Dale Dougherty
- Recipe 1.6, "Using Shell Quoting"
- Recipe 13.14, "Trimming Whitespace"
- Recipe 13.17, "Processing Files with No Line Breaks"

17.21 Numbering Lines

Problem

You need to number the lines of a text file for reference or for use as an example.

Solution

Thanks to Michael Wang for contributing the following shell-only implementation and reminding us about cat -n. Note that our sample file named *lines* has a trailing blank line:

```
$ i=0; while IFS= read -r line; do (( i++ )); echo "$i $line"; done < lines
1 Line 1
2 Line 2
3
4 Line 4
5 Line 5
6
```

Or a useful use of *cat*:

```
$ cat -n lines
     1  Line 1
     2  Line 2
     3
     4  Line 4
     5  Line 5
     6
```

```
$ cat -b lines
     1  Line 1
     2  Line 2

     3  Line 4
     4  Line 5
```

Discussion

If you only need to display the line numbers on the screen, you can use less -N:

```
$ /usr/bin/less -N filename
      1 Line 1
      2 Line 2
      3
      4 Line 4
      5 Line 5
      6
lines (END)
```

 Line numbers are broken in old versions of *less* on some obsolete Red Hat systems. Check your version with less -V. Version 358+iso254 (e.g., Red Hat 7.3 & 8.0) is known to be bad. Version 378+iso254 (e.g., RHEL3) and version 382 (RHEL4, Debian Sarge) are known to be good; we did not test other versions. The problem is subtle and may be related to an older *iso256* patch. You can easily compare last line numbers as the *vi* and Perl examples are correct.

You can also use *vi* (or *view*, which is read-only *vi*) with the :set nu! command:

```
$ vi filename
      1 Line 1
      2 Line 2
      3
      4 Line 4
      5 Line 5
      6
~
:set nu!
```

vi has many options, so you can start *vi* by doing things like vi +3 -c 'set nu!' *filename* to turn on line numbering and place your cursor on line 3. If you'd like more control over how the numbers are displayed, you can also use *nl*, *awk*, or *perl*:

```
$ nl lines
      1  Line 1
      2  Line 2

      3  Line 4
      4  Line 5


$ nl -ba lines
      1  Line 1
      2  Line 2
      3
      4  Line 4
      5  Line 5
      6
```

```
$ awk '{ print NR, $0 }' filename
1 Line 1
2 Line 2
3
4 Line 4
5 Line 5
6

$ perl -ne 'print qq($.\t$_);' filename
1 → Line 1
2 → Line 2
3 →
4 → Line 4
5 → Line 5
6 →
```

NR and $. are the line number in the current input file in *awk* and Perl respectively, so it's easy to use them to print the line number. Note that we are using a → to denote a Tab character in the Perl output, while *awk* uses a space by default.

See Also

- man cat
- man nl
- man awk
- man less
- man vi
- Recipe 8.15, "Doing More with less"

17.22 Writing Sequences

Problem

You need to generate a sequence of numbers, possibly with other text, for testing or some other purpose.

Solution

Use *awk* because it should work everywhere no matter what:

```
$ awk 'END { for (i=1; i <= 5; i++) print i, "text"}' /dev/null
1 text
2 text
3 text
4 text
5 text

$ awk 'BEGIN { for (i=1; i <= 5; i+=.5) print i}' /dev/null
```

```
1
1.5
2
2.5
3
3.5
4
4.5
5
```

Discussion

On some systems, notably Solaris, *awk* will hang waiting for a file unless you give it one, such as */dev/null*. This has no effect on other systems, so it's fine to use everywhere.

Note that the variable in the print statement is i, not $i. If you accidentally use $i it will be interpolated as a field from the current line being processed. Since we're processing nothing, that's what you'll get if you use $i by accident (i.e., nothing).

The BEGIN or END patterns allow for startup or cleanup operations when actually processing files. Since we're not processing a file, we need to use one of them so that *awk* knows to actually do something even though it has no normal input. In this case, it doesn't matter which we use.

There is a GNU utility called *seq* that does exactly what this recipe calls for, but it does not exist by default on many systems, for example BSD, Solaris, and Mac OS X. It offers some useful formatting options and is numeric only.

Thankfully, as of *bash* 2.04 and later, you can do arithmetic integer for loops:

```
# Bash 2.04+ only, integer only
$ for ((i=1; i<=5; i++)); do echo "$i text"; done
1 text
2 text
3 text
4 text
5 text
```

As of *bash* 3.0 and later, there is also the {*x..y*} brace expansion, which allows integers or single characters:

```
# Bash 3.0+ only, integer or single character only
$ printf "%s text\n" {1..5}
1 text
2 text
3 text
4 text
5 text

$ printf "%s text\n" {a..e}
a text
b text
c text
d text
e text
```

See Also

- man seq
- man awk
- *http://www.faqs.org/faqs/computer-lang/awk/faq/*

17.23 Emulating the DOS Pause Command

Problem

You are migrating from DOS/Windows batch files and want to emulate the DOS pause command.

Solution

To do that, use the read -p command in a function:

```
pause ()
{
    read -p 'Press any key when ready...'
}
```

Discussion

The -p option followed by a string argument prints the string before reading input. In this case the string is the same as the DOS pause command's output.

See Also

- help read

17.24 Commifying Numbers

Problem

You'd like to add a thousands-place separator to long numbers.

Solution

Depending on your system and configuration, you may be able to use *printf*'s ' format flag with a suitable local. Thanks to Chet Ramey for this solution, which is by far the easiest if it works:

```
$ LC_NUMERIC=en_US.UTF-8 printf "%'d\n" 123456789
123,456,789

$ LC_NUMERIC=en_US.UTF-8 printf "%'f\n" 123456789.987
123,456,789.987000
```

Thanks to Michael Wang for contributing the following shell-only implementation and relevant discussion:

```
# cookbook filename: func_commify

function commify {
    typeset text=${1}

    typeset bdot=${text%%.*}
    typeset adot=${text#${bdot}}

    typeset i commified
    (( i = ${#bdot} - 1 ))

    while (( i>=3 )) && [[ ${bdot:i-3:1} == [0-9] ]]; do
        commified=",${bdot:i-2:3}${commified}"
        (( i -= 3 ))
    done
    echo "${bdot:0:i+1}${commified}${adot}"
}
```

Discussion

The shell function is written to follow the same logical process as a person using a pencil and paper. First you examine the string and find the decimal point, if any. You ignore everything after the dot, and work on the string before the dot.

The shell function saves the string before the dot in $bdot, and after the dot (including the dot) in $adot. If there is no dot, then everything is in $bdot, and $adot is empty. Next a person would move from right to left in the part before the dot and insert a comma when these two conditions are met:

- There are four or more characters left.
- The character before the comma is a number.

The function implements this logic in the while loop.

Tom Christiansen and Nathan Torkington's *Perl Cookbook*, Second Edition (O'Reilly), Recipe 2.16 also provides a string processing solution:

```
# cookbook filename: perl_sub_commify

#++++++++++++++++++++++++++++++++++++++++++++++++++++++++++++++++++++++++++++++
# Add comma thousands separator to numbers
# Returns:  input string, with any numbers commified
# From Perl Cookbook2 2.16, pg 84
sub commify {
    @_ == 1 or carp ('Sub usage: $withcomma = commify($somenumber);');

    # From _Perl_Cookbook_1 page 64, 2.17 or _Perl_Cookbook_2 page 84, 2.16
```

```
my $text = reverse $_[0];
$text =~ s/(\d\d\d)(?=\d)(?!\d*\.)/$1,/g;
return scalar reverse $text;

}
```

 The United States uses a comma as the thousands separator, but many
other countries use a period.

See Also

- *http://sed.sourceforge.net/sedfaq4.html#s4.14*
- *Perl Cookbook*, Second Edition, Recipe 2.16, by Tom Christiansen and Nathan Torkington (O'Reilly)
- Recipe 13.18, "Converting a Data File to CSV"

## CHAPTER 18

Working Faster by Typing Less

Despite all the improvements in processor speed, transmission rates, network speed, and I/O capabilities, there is still a limiting factor in many uses of *bash*—the typing speed of the user. Scripting has been our focus, of course, but interactive use of *bash* is still a significant part of its use and usefulness. Many of the scripting techniques we have described can be used interactively as well, but then you find yourself faced with a lot of typing, unless you know some shortcuts.

Now "back in the day," when Unix was first invented, there were teletype machines that could only crank out about 10 characters per second, and a good touch typist could type faster than the keyboard could handle it. It was in this milieu that Unix was developed and some of its terseness is likely due to the fact that no one wanted to type more than absolutely necessary to get across their command.

At the other end of the historical perspective (i.e., now) processors are so fast that they can be quite idle while waiting for user input, and can look back through histories of previous commands as well as in directories along your $PATH to find possible commands and valid arguments even before you finish typing them.

Combining techniques developed for each of these situations, we can greatly reduce the amount of typing required to issue shell commands—and not just out of sheer laziness. Rather, you may quickly find that these keystroke-saving measures are so useful because of the increased accuracy they provide, the mistakes they help you avoid, and the backups that you don't need to reload.

18.1 Moving Quickly Among Arbitrary Directories

Problem

Do you find yourself moving frequently between two or more directories? Are you changing directories to here, then there, and then back again? Do you tire of always typing long path names since the directories never seem to be close by?

Solution

Use the *pushd* and *popd* built-in commands to manage a stack of directory locations, and to switch between them easily. Here is a simple example:

```
$ cd /tmp/tank
$ pwd
/tmp/tank

$ pushd /var/log/cups
/var/log/cups /tmp/tank

$ pwd
/var/log/cups

$ ls
access_log   error_log   page_log

$ popd
/tmp/tank

$ ls
empty   full

$ pushd /var/log/cups
/var/log/cups /tmp/tank

$ pushd
/tmp/tank /var/log/cups

$ pushd
/var/log/cups /tmp/tank

$ pushd
/tmp/tank /var/log/cups

$ dirs
/tmp/tank /var/log/cups
```

Discussion

Stacks are *last in, first out* mechanisms, which is how these commands behave. When you *pushd* to a new directory, it keeps the previous directory on a stack. Then when you *popd*, it pops the current location off of the stack and puts you back in that first location. When you change locations using these commands, they will print the values on the stack, left to right, corresponding to the top-to-bottom ordering of a stack.

If you *pushd* without any directory, it swaps the top item on the stack with the next one down, so that you can alternate between two directories using repeated *pushd* commands with no arguments. You can do the same thing using the cd - command.

You can still *cd* to locations—that will change the current directory, which is also the top of the directory stack. If you can't remember what is on your stack of directories, use the *dirs* command to echo the stack, left-to-right. For a more stack-like display, use the -v option:

```
$ dirs -v
 0  /var/tmp
 1  ~/part/me/scratch
 2  /tmp
$
```

The tilde (~) is a shorthand for your home directory. The numbers can be used to reorder the stack. If you *pushd +2* then *bash* will put the #2 entry on the top of the stack (and *cd* you there) and push the others down:

```
$ pushd +2
/tmp /var/tmp ~/part/me/scratch
$ dirs -v
 0  /tmp
 1  /var/tmp
 2  ~/part/me/scratch
$
```

Once you get a little practice with these commands, you will find it much faster and easier to move repeatedly between directories.

See Also

- Recipe 1.2, "Showing Where You Are"
- Recipe 14.3, "Setting a Secure $PATH"
- Recipe 16.5, "Setting Your $CDPATH"
- Recipe 16.13, "Creating a Better cd Command"
- Recipe 16.20, "Getting Started with a Custom Configuration"

18.2   Repeating the Last Command

Problem

You just typed a long and difficult command line, one with long pathnames and complicated sets of arguments. Now you need to run it again. Do you have to type it all again?

Solution

There are two very different solutions to this problem. First, just type two exclamation marks at the prompt, and *bash* will *echo* and repeat the previous command. For example:

```
$ /usr/bin/somewhere/someprog -g -H -yknot -w /tmp/soforthandsoon
...
```

```
$ !!
/usr/bin/somewhere/someprog -g -H -yknot -w /tmp/soforthandsoon
...
```

The other (more modern) solution involves using the arrow keys. Typing the up-arrow key will scroll back through the previous commands that you have issued. When you find the one you want, just press the Enter key and that command will be run (again).

Description

The command is echoed when you type !! (sometimes called *bang bang*) so that you can see what is running.

See Also

- Recipe 16.8, "Adjusting readline Behavior Using .inputrc"
- Recipe 16.12, "Setting Shell History Options"

18.3 Running Almost the Same Command

Problem

After running a long and difficult-to-type command, you get an error message indicating that you made one tiny little typo in the middle of that command line. Do you have to retype the whole line?

Solution

The !! command that we discussed in Recipe 18.2, "Repeating the Last Command" allows you to add an editing qualifier. How good are your *sed*-like skills? Add a colon after the bang-bang and then a *sed*-like substitution expression, as in the following example:

```
$ /usr/bin/somewhere/someprog -g -H -yknot -w /tmp/soforthandsoon
Error: -H not recognized.  Did you mean -A?

$ !!:s/H/A/
/usr/bin/somewhere/someprog -g -A -yknot -w /tmp/soforthandsoon
...
```

You can always just use the arrow keys to navigate your history and commands, but for long commands on slow links this syntax is great once you get used to it.

Discussion

If you're going to use this feature, just be careful with your substitutions. If you had tried to change the -g option by typing !!:s/g/h/ you would have ended up changing the first letter g, which is at the end of the command name, and you would be trying to run /usr/bin/somewhere/someproh.

The comparison with *sed* is apt here because the substitution is applied successively to each word in the command line. That means that the expressions that you use for substitutions *cannot* cross word boundaries. You could not, for example, use:

    s/-g -A/-gA/

as a command, since the -g and -A are separate words to *bash*.

But that doesn't mean that your changes can't effect the whole line. If you want to change all occurrences of an expression in a command line, you need to precede the s with a g (for global substitution), as follows:

    $ /usr/bin/somewhere/someprog -g -s -yknots -w /tmp/soforthandsoon
    ...

    $!!:gs/s/S/
    /usr/bin/Somewhere/Someprog -g -S -yknotS -w /tmp/SoforthandSoon
    ...

Why does this g have to appear before the s and not after it, like in *sed* syntax? Well, anything that appears after the closing slash is considered new text to append to the command—which is quite handy if you want to add another argument to the command when you run it again.

See Also

- Recipe 16.8, "Adjusting readline Behavior Using .inputrc"
- Recipe 16.12, "Setting Shell History Options"
- Recipe 18.2, "Repeating the Last Command"

18.4   Substituting Across Word Boundaries

Problem

The !!:s/a/b/ syntax is restricted to substitutions within a word; what if you need to make a substitution that crosses word boundaries?

Solution

Use the caret (^) substitution mechanism:

    $ /usr/bin/somewhere/someprog -g -A -yknot -w /tmp/soforthandsoon
    ...

    $ ^-g -A^-gB^
    /usr/bin/somewhere/someprog -gB -yknot -w /tmp/soforthandsoon

You can always just use the arrow keys to navigate your history and commands, but for long commands on slow links this syntax is great once you get used to it.

Discussion

Write the substitution on the command line by starting with a caret (^) and then the text you want replaced, then another caret and the new text. A trailing (third) caret is needed only if you want to add more text at the end of the line, as in:

```
$ /usr/bin/somewhere/someprog -g -A -yknot
...

$ ^-g -A^-gB^ /tmp^
/usr/bin/somewhere/someprog -gB -yknot /tmp
```

If you want to remove something, substitute an empty value; i.e., don't put anything for the new text. Here are two examples:

```
$ /usr/bin/somewhere/someprog -g -A -yknot /tmp
...
$ ^-g -A^^
/usr/bin/somewhere/someprog -yknot /tmp
...
$ ^knot^
/usr/bin/somewhere/someprog -gA -y /tmp
...
$
```

The first example uses all three carets. The second example leaves off the third caret; since we want to replace the "knot" with nothing, we just end the line with a newline (the Enter key).

The use of the caret substitution not only spans word boundaries, it's just plain handy. Many *bash* users find it easier to use than `!!:s/.../.../` syntax. Wouldn't you agree?

See Also

- Recipe 16.8, "Adjusting readline Behavior Using .inputrc"
- Recipe 16.12, "Setting Shell History Options"

18.5 Reusing Arguments

Problem

Reusing the last command was easy with `!!` but you might not want the whole command. How can you reuse just the last argument?

Solution

Use !$ to indicate the last command. Use !:1 for the first argument on the command line, !:2 for the second, and so on.

Discussion

It is quite common to hand the same filename to a series of commands. One of the most common occurrences might be the way a programmer would edit and then compile, edit and then compile…. Here, the !$ comes in quite handy:

```
$ vi /some/long/path/name/you/only/type/once
...
$ gcc !$
gcc /some/long/path/name/you/only/type/once
...
$ vi !$
vi /some/long/path/name/you/only/type/once
...
$ gcc !$
gcc /some/long/path/name/you/only/type/once
```

Get the idea? It saves a lot of typing but it also avoids errors. If you mistype the filename when you compile, then you are not compiling the file that you just edited. With !$ you always get the name of the file on which you just worked. If the argument you want is buried in the middle of the command line, you can get at it with the numbered "bang-colon" commands. Here's an example:

```
$ munge /opt/my/long/path/toa/file | more
...
$ vi !:1
vi /opt/my/long/path/toa/file
```

You might be tempted to try to use !$, but in this instance it would yield more, which is not the name of the file that you want to edit.

See Also

- The *bash* manpage to read about "Word Designators"

18.6   Finishing Names for You

Problem

Some of these path names are pretty long. This is a computer that *bash* is running on… can't it help?

Solution

When in doubt, press the Tab key. *bash* will try to finish the pathname for you. If it does nothing, it may be because there are no matches, or because there is more than one. Press the Tab key a second time and it will list the choices and then repeat the command up to where you stopped typing, so that you can continue. Type a bit more (to disambiguate) then press the Tab key again to have *bash* finish off the argument for you.

Discussion

bash is even smart enough to limit the selection to certain types of files. If you type "unzip" and then the beginning of a pathname, and then you press the Tab key, it will only finish off with files that end in *.zip* even if you have other files whose names match as much as you have typed. For example:

```
$ ls
myfile.c      myfile.o      myfile.zip
$ ls -lh myfile<tab><tab>
myfile.c      myfile.o      myfile.zip
$ ls -lh myfile.z<tab>ip
-rw-r--r--    1 me mygroup 1.9M 2006-06-06 23:26 myfile.zip
$ unzip -l myfile<tab>.zip
...
```

See Also

- Recipe 16.8, "Adjusting readline Behavior Using .inputrc"
- Recipe 16.17, "Improving Programmable Completion"

18.7   Playing It Safe

Problem

It is so easy to type the wrong character by mistrake (see!). Even for simple *bash* commands this can be quite serious—you could move or remove the wrong files. When pattern matching is added to the mix, the results can be even more exciting, as a typo in the pattern can lead to wildly different-than-intended consequences. What's a conscientious person to do?

Solution

You can use these history features and keyboard shortcuts to repeat arguments without retyping them, thereby reducing the typos. If you need a tricky pattern match for files, try it out with *echo* to see that it works, and then when you've got it right use !$ to use it for real. For example:

```
$ ls
```

```
ab1.txt  ac1.txt  jb1.txt  wc3.txt
$ echo *1.txt
ab1.txt ac1.txt jb1.txt
$ echo [aj]?1.txt
ab1.txt ac1.txt jb1.txt
$ echo ?b1.txt
ab1.txt jb1.txt
$ rm !$
rm ?b1.txt
$
```

Discussion

The *echo* is a way to see the results of your pattern match. Once you're convinced it gives you what you want, then you can use it for your intended command. Here we remove the named files—not something that one wants to get wrong.

Also, when you're using the history commands, you can add a :p modifier and it will cause *bash* to print but not execute the command—another handy way to see if you got your history substitutions right. From the Solution's example, we add:

```
$ echo ?b1.txt
ab1.txt jb1.txt

$ rm !$:p
rm ?b1.txt
$
```

The :p modifier caused *bash* to print but not execute the command—but notice that the argument is ?b1.txt and not expanded to the two filenames. That shows you what will be run, and only when it is run will the shell expand that pattern to the two filenames. If you want to see how it will be expanded, use the *echo* command.

See Also

- The *bash* manpage on "Modifiers" for more colon (:) modifiers that can be used on history commands
- "Command-Line Processing Steps" in Appendix C

CHAPTER 19

Tips and Traps: Common Goofs for Novices

Nobody's perfect. We all make mistakes, especially when we are first learning something new. We have all been there, done that. You know, the silly mistake that seems so obvious once you've had it explained, or the time you thought for sure that the system must be broken because you were doing it exactly right, only to find that you were off by one little character, one which made all the difference. Certain mistakes seem common, almost predictable, among beginners. We've all had to learn the hard way that scripts don't run unless you set execute permissions on them—a real newbie kind of error. Now that we're experienced, we never make those mistakes anymore. What, never? Well, hardly ever. After all, nobody's perfect.

19.1 Forgetting to Set Execute Permissions

Problem

You got your script all written and want to try it out, but when you go to run the script you get an error message:

```
$ ./my.script
bash: ./my.script: Permission denied
$
```

Solution

You have two choices. First, you could invoke *bash* and give it the name of the script as a parameter:

```
$ bash my.script
```

Or second (and better still), you could set the execute permission on the script so that you can run it directly:

```
$ chmod a+x my.script
$ ./my.script
```

Discussion

Either method will get the script running. You'll probably want to set the execute permissions on the script if you intend to use it over and over. You only have to set the permissions once, thereafter allowing you to invoke it directly. With the permissions set it feels more like a command, since you don't have to explicitly invoke *bash* (of course behind the scenes *bash* is still being invoked, but you don't have to type it).

In setting the execute permissions, we used a+x to give execute permissions to all. There's little reason to restrict execute permissions on the file unless it is in some directory where others might accidentally encounter your executable (e.g., if as a system admin you were putting something of your own in /usr/bin). Besides, if the file has read permissions for all then others can still execute the script if they use our first form of invocation, with the explicit reference to *bash*. Common permissions on shell scripts are 0700 for the suspicious/careful folk (giving read/write/execute permission to only the owner) and 0755 for the more open/carefree folk (giving read and execute permissions to all others).

See Also

- man chmod
- Recipe 14.13, "Setting Permissions"
- Recipe 15.1, "Finding bash Portably for #!"
- Recipe 19.3, "Forgetting That the Current Directory Is Not in the $PATH"

19.2 Fixing "No such file or directory" Errors

Problem

You've set the execute permission as described in Recipe 19.1, "Forgetting to Set Execute Permissions," but when you run the script you get a "No such file or directory" error.

Solution

Try running the script using *bash* explicitly:

```
$ bash ./busted
```

If it works, you have some kind of permissions error, or a typo in your shebang line. If you get a bunch more errors, you probably have the wrong line endings. This can happen if you edit the file on Windows (perhaps via Samba), or if you've simply copied the file around.

To fix it, try the *dos2unix* program if you have it, or see Recipe 8.11, "Converting DOS Files to Linux Format." Note that if you use *dos2unix* it will probably create a new file and delete the old one, which will change the permissions and might also change the owner or group and affect hard links. If you're not sure what any of that means, the key point is that you'll probably have to *chmod* it again (Recipe 19.1, "Forgetting to Set Execute Permissions").

Discussion

If you really do have bad line endings (i.e., anything that isn't ASCII 10 or hex 0a), the error you get depends on your shebang line. Here are some examples for a script named *busted*:

```
$ cat busted
#!/bin/bash -
echo "Hello World!"

# This works
$ ./busted
Hello World!


# But if the file gets DOS line endings, we get:
$ ./busted
: invalid option
Usage:  /bin/bash [GNU long option] [option] ...
[...]


# Different shebang line
$ cat ./busted
#!/usr/bin/env bash
echo "Hello World!"

$ ./busted
: No such file or directory
```

See Also

- Recipe 8.11, "Converting DOS Files to Linux Format"
- Recipe 14.2, "Avoiding Interpreter Spoofing"
- Recipe 15.1, "Finding bash Portably for #!"
- Recipe 19.1, "Forgetting to Set Execute Permissions"

19.3 Forgetting That the Current Directory Is Not in the $PATH

Problem

You've got your script all written and want to try it out—you even remembered to add the execute permissions to the script, but when you go to run the script you get an error message:

```
$ my.script
bash: my.script: command not found
$
```

Solution

Either add the current directory to the $PATH variable, which we do not recommend, or reference the script via the current directory with a leading ./ before the script name, as in:

```
$ ./my.script
```

Discussion

It is a common mistake for beginners to forget to add the leading ./ to the script that they want to execute. We have had a lot of discussion about the $PATH variable, so we won't repeat ourselves here except to remind you of a solution for frequently used scripts.

A common practice is to keep your useful and often-used scripts in a directory called *bin* inside of your home directory, and to add that *bin* directory to your $PATH variable so that you can execute those scripts without needing the leading ./.

The important part about adding your own *bin* directory to your $PATH variable is to place the change that modifies your $PATH variable in the right startup script. You don't want it in the *.bashrc* script because that gets invoked by every subshell, which would mean that your path would get added to every time you "shell out" of an editor, or run some other commands. You don't need repeated copies your *bin* directory in the $PATH variable.

Instead, put it in the appropriate login profile for *bash*. According to the *bash* manpage, when you log in *bash* "looks for ~/.bash_profile, ~/.bash_login, and ~/.profile, in that order, and reads and executes commands from the first one that exists and is readable." So edit whichever one of those you already have in your home directory or if none exists, create ~/.bash_profile and put this line in at the bottom of the file (or elsewhere if you understand enough of what else the profile is doing):

```
PATH="${PATH}:$HOME/bin"
```

See Also

- Recipe 4.1, "Running Any Executable"
- Recipe 14.3, "Setting a Secure $PATH"
- Recipe 14.9, "Finding World-Writable Directories in Your $PATH"
- Recipe 14.10, "Adding the Current Directory to the $PATH"
- Recipe 15.2, "Setting a POSIX $PATH"
- Recipe 16.3, "Change Your $PATH Permanently"
- Recipe 16.4, "Change Your $PATH Temporarily"
- Recipe 16.9, "Keeping a Private Stash of Utilities by Adding ~/bin"
- Recipe 16.18, "Using Initialization Files Correctly"

19.4 Naming Your Script Test

Problem

You typed up a *bash* script to test out some of this interesting material that you've been reading about. You typed it exactly right, you even remembered to set the execute permissions on the file and put the file in one of the directories in $PATH, but when you try to run it, nothing happens.

Solution

Name it something other than *test*. That name is a shell built-in command.

Discussion

It is natural enough to want to name a file *test* when you just want a quick scratch file for trying out some small bit of code. The problem is that *test* is a shell built-in command, making it a kind of shell *reserved word*. You can see this with the type command:

```
$ type test
test is a shell builtin
$
```

Since it is a built-in, no adjusting of the path will override this. You would have to create an alias, but we strongly advise against it in this case. Just name your script something else, or invoke it with a pathname, as in: ./test or /home/path/test.

See Also

- "Built-in Commands and Reserved Words" in Appendix A

19.5 Expecting to Change Exported Variables

Problem

A common beginner mistake is to treat exported shell variables like globals in a programming environment. But exported variables are only one way: they are included in the environment of the invoked shell script, but if you change their values, those changes are not seen by the calling script.

Here is the first of two scripts. This one will set a value, invoke a second script, and then display the value after the second script completes, so as to see what (if anything) has changed:

```
$ cat first.sh
#
# a simple example of a common mistake
#
# set the value:
export VAL=5
printf "VAL=%d\n" $VAL
# invoke our other script:
./second.sh
#
# now see what changed (hint: nothing!)
printf "%b" "back in first\n"
printf "VAL=%d\n" $VAL
$
```

The second script messes with a variable named $VAL, too:

```
$ cat second.sh
printf "%b" "in second\n"
printf "initially VAL=%d\n" $VAL
VAL=12
printf "changed so VAL=%d\n" $VAL
$
```

When we run the first script (which invokes the second one, too) here's what we get:

```
$ ./first.sh
VAL=5
in second
initially VAL=5
changed so VAL=10
back in first
VAL=5
$
```

Solution

The old joke goes something like this:

> Patient: "Doctor, it hurts when I do this."
>
> Doctor: "Then don't do that."

The solution here is going to sound like the doctor's advice: don't do that. You will have to structure your shell scripts so that such a hand-off is not necessary. One way to do that is by explicitly echoing the results of the second script so that the first script can invoke it with the $( ) operator (or `` for the old shell hands). In the first script, the line ./second.sh becomes VAL=$(./second.sh), and the second script has to echo the final value (and only the final value) to STDOUT (it could redirect its other messages to STDERR):

```
$ cat second.sh
printf "%b" "in second\n"              >&2
printf "initially VAL=%d\n" $VAL       >&2
VAL=12
printf "changed so VAL=%d\n" $VAL      >&2
echo $VAL
$
```

Discussion

Exported environment variables are *not* globals that are shared between scripts. They are a one-way communication. All the exported environment variables are marshaled and passed together as part of the invocation of a Linux or Unix (sub) process (see the fork(2) manpage). There is no mechanism whereby these environment variables are passed back to the parent process. (Remember that a parent process can fork lots and lots of subprocesses...so if you could return values from a child process, *which* child's values would the parent get?)

See Also

- Recipe 5.5, "Exporting Variables"
- Recipe 10.4, "Defining Functions"
- Recipe 10.5, "Using Functions: Parameters and Return Values"

19.6 Forgetting Quotes Leads to "command not found" on Assignments

Problem

Your script is assigning some values to a variable, but when you run it, the shell reports "command not found" on part of the value of the assignment.

```
$ cat goof1.sh
#!/bin/bash -
# common goof:
#  X=$Y $Z
# isn't the same as
#  X="$Y $Z"
#
OPT1=-1
```

```
OPT2=-h
ALLOPT=$OPT1 $OPT2
ls $ALLOPT .
$
$ ./goof1.sh
goof1.sh: line 10: -h: command not found
aaa.awk  cdscript.prev  ifexpr.sh  oldsrc  xspin2.sh
$
```

Solution

You need quotes around the righthand side of the assignment to $ALLOPT. What is
written above as:

```
ALLOPT=$OPT1 $OPT2
```

really should be:

```
ALLOPT="$OPT1 $OPT2"
```

Discussion

It isn't just that you'll lose the embedded spaces between the arguments; it is pre-
cisely because there are spaces that this problem arises. If the arguments were combined with an intervening slash, for example, or by no space at all, this problem
wouldn't crop up—it would all be a single word, and thus a single assignment.

But that intervening space tells *bash* to parse this into two words. The first word is a
variable assignment. Such assignments at the beginning of a command tell *bash* to set
a variable to a given value just for the duration of the command—the command
being the word that follows next on the command line. At the next line, the variable
is back to its prior value (if any) or just not set.

The second word of our example statement is therefore seen as a command. That
word is the command that is reported as "not found." Of course it is possible that
the value for $OPT2 might have been something that actually was the name of an exe-
cutable (though not likely in this case with *ls*). Such a situation could lead to very
undesirable results.

Did you notice, in our example, that when *ls* ran, it didn't use the long format output even though we had (tried to) set the -l option? That shows that $ALLOPT was no
longer set. It had only been set for the duration of the previous command, which was
the attempt to run the (nonexistent) -h command.

An assignment on a line by itself sets a variable for the remainder of the script. An
assignment at the beginning of a line, one that has an additional command invoked
on that line, sets the variable only for the execution of that command.

It's generally a good idea to quote your assignments to a shell variable. That way you
are assured of getting only one assignment and not encountering this problem.

See Also

- Recipe 5.9, "Handling Parameters with Blanks"

19.7   Forgetting That Pattern Matching Alphabetizes

Warning—*bash* will alphabetize the data in a pattern match:

```
$ echo x.[ba]
x.a x.b
$
```

Even though you specified b then a in the square brackets, when the pattern matching is done and the results found, they will be alphabetized before being given to the command to execute. That means that you don't want to do this:

```
$ mv x.[ba]
$
```

thinking that it will expand to:

```
$ mv x.b x.a
```

Rather, it will expand to:

```
$ mv x.a x.b
```

since it alpha-sorts them before putting them in the command line, which is exactly the opposite of what you intended!

19.8   Forgetting That Pipelines Make Subshells

Problem

You have a script that works just fine, reading input in a while loop:

```
COUNT=0
while read PREFIX GUTS
do
    # ...
    if [[ $PREFIX == "abc" ]]
    then
        let COUNT++
    fi
    # ...
done
echo $COUNT
```

and then you change it to read from a file:

```
cat $1 | while read PREFIX GUTS
do
    # ...
```

only now it no longer works…`$COUNT` keeps coming out as zero.

Solution

Pipelines create subshells. Changes in the `while` loop do not effect the variables in the outer part of the script, as the `while` loop is run in a subshell.

One solution: don't do that (if you can help it). In this example, instead of using *cat* to pipe the file's content into the `while` statement, you could use I/O redirection to have the input come from a redirected input rather than setting up a pipeline:

```
COUNT=0
while read PREFIX GUTS
do
    # ...

done < $1

echo $COUNT
```

Such a rearrangement might not be appropriate for your problem, in which case you'll have to find other techniques.

Discussion

If you add an *echo* statement inside the `while` loop, you can see `$COUNT` increasing, but once you exit the loop, `$COUNT` will be back to zero. The way that *bash* sets up the pipeline of commands means that each command in the pipeline will execute in its own subshell. So the `while` loop is in a subshell, not in the main shell. If you have exported `$COUNT`, then the `while` loop will begin with the same value that the main shell script was using for `$COUNT`, but since the `while` loop is executing in a subshell there is no way to get the value back up to the parent shell.

Depending on how much information you need to get back to the parent shell and how much more work the outer level needs to do after the pipeline, there are different techniques you could use. One technique is to take the additional work and make it part of a subshell that includes the `while` loop. For example:

```
COUNT=0
cat $1 | ( while read PREFIX GUTS
do
  # ...
done
echo $COUNT )
```

The placement of the parentheses is crucial here. What we've done is explicitly delineated a section of the script to be run in a subshell. It includes both the while loop and the other work that we want to do after the while loop completes (here all we're doing is echoing $COUNT). Since the while and the echo statements are not a pipeline, they will both run in the same subshell created by virtue of the parentheses. The $COUNT that was accumulated during the while loop will remain until the end of the subshell—that is, until the end-parenthesis is reached.

If you do use this technique it might be good to format the statements a bit differently, to make the use of the parenthesized subshell stand out more. Here's the whole script reformatted:

```
COUNT=0
cat $1 |
(
    while read PREFIX GUTS
    do
        # ...
        if [[ $PREFIX == "abc" ]]
        then
            let COUNT++
        fi
        # ...
    done
    echo $COUNT
)
```

We can extend this technique if there is much more work to be done after the while loop. The remaining work could be put in a function call or two, again keeping them in the subshell. Otherwise, the results of the while loop can be echoed (as is done here) and then piped into the next phase of work (which will also execute in its own subshell), which can read the results from the while loop:

```
COUNT=0
cat $1 |
(
    while read PREFIX GUTS
    do
        # ...
        if [[ $PREFIX == "abc" ]]
        then
            let COUNT++
        fi
        # ...
    done
    echo $COUNT
) | read COUNT
# continue on...
```

See Also

- *bash* FAQ #E4 at *http://tiswww.tis.case.edu/~chet/bash/FAQ*
- Recipe 10.5, "Using Functions: Parameters and Return Values"
- Recipe 19.5, "Expecting to Change Exported Variables"

19.9   Making Your Terminal Sane Again

Problem

You have aborted an SSH session and now you can't see what you are typing. Or perhaps you accidentally displayed a binary file and your terminal window is now gibberish.

Solution

Type `stty sane` and then the Enter key, even if you can't see what you are typing, to restore sane terminal settings. You may want to hit Enter a few times first, to make sure you don't have anything else on your input line before you start typing the *stty* command.

If you do this a lot, you might consider creating an *alias* that's easier to type blind.

Discussion

Aborting some older versions of *ssh* at a password prompt may leave terminal echo (the displaying of characters as you type them, not the shell *echo* command) turned off so you can't see what you are typing. Depending on what kind of terminal emulation you are using, displaying a binary file can also accidentally change terminal settings. In either case, *stty*'s sane setting attempts to return all terminal settings to their default values. This includes restoring echo capability, so that what you type on the keyboard appears in your terminal window. It will also likely undo whatever strangeness has occurred with other terminal settings.

Your terminal application may also have some kind of reset function, so explore the menu options and documentation. You may also want to try the *reset* and *tset* commands, though in our testing `stty sane` worked as desired while *reset* and *tset* were more drastic in what they fixed.

See Also

- man reset
- man stty
- man tset

19.10 Deleting Files Using an Empty Variable

Problem

You have a variable that you think contains a list of files to delete, perhaps to clean up after your script. But in fact, the variable is empty and Bad Things happen.

Solution

Never do:

```
rm -rf $files_to_delete
```

Never, ever, *ever* do:

```
rm -rf /$files_to_delete
```

Use this instead:

```
[ "$files_to_delete" ] && rm -rf $files_to_delete
```

Discussion

The first example isn't too bad, it'll just throw an error. The second one is pretty bad because it will try to delete your root directory. If you are running as a regular user (and you should be, see Recipe 14.18, "Running As a Non-root User"), it may not be too bad, but if you are running as *root* then you've just killed your system but good. (Yes, we've done this.)

The solution is easy. First, make sure that there is some value in the variable you're using, and second, never precede that variable with a /.

See Also

- Recipe 14.18, "Running As a Non-root User"
- Recipe 18.7, "Playing It Safe"

19.11 Seeing Odd Behavior from printf

Problem

Your script is giving you values that don't match what you expected. Consider this simple script and its output:

```
$ bash oddscript
good nodes: 0
bad nodes: 6
miss nodes: 0
GOOD=6 BAD=0 MISS=0
$
$ cat oddscript
#!/bin/bash -
```

```
badnode=6
```

```
printf "good nodes: %d\n" $goodnode
printf "bad nodes: %d\n" $badnode
printf "miss nodes: %d\n" $missnode
printf "GOOD=%d BAD=%d MISS=%d\n" $goodnode $badnode $missnode
```

Why is 6 showing up as the value for the good count, when it is supposed to be the value for the bad count?

Solution

Either give the variables an initial value (e.g., 0) or put quotes around the references to them on printf lines.

Discussion

What's happening here? *bash* does its substitutions on that last line and when it evaluates $goodnode and $missnode they both come out null, empty, not there. So the line that is handed off to *printf* to execute looks like this:

```
printf "GOOD=%d BAD=%d MISS=%d\n" 6
```

When *printf* tries to print the three decimal values (the three %d formats) it has a value (i.e., 6) for the first one, but doesn't have anything for the next two, so they come out zero and we get:

```
GOOD=6 BAD=0 MISS=0
```

You can't really blame *printf*, since it never saw the other arguments; *bash* had done its parameter substitution before *printf* ever got to run.

Even declaring them as integer values, like this:

```
declare -i goodnode badnode missnode
```

isn't enough. You need to actually assign them a value.

The other way to avoid this problem is to quote the arguments when they are used in the printf statement, like this:

```
printf "GOOD=%d BAD=%d MISS=%d\n" "$goodnode" "$badnode" "$missnode"
```

Then the first argument won't disappear, but an empty string will be put in its place, so that what *printf* gets are the three needed arguments:

```
printf "GOOD=%d BAD=%d MISS=%d\n" "" "6" ""
```

While we're on the subject of *printf*, it has one other odd behavior. We have just seen how it behaves when there are too few arguments; when there are too many arguments, *printf* will keep repeating and reusing the format line and it will look like you are getting multiple lines of output when you expected only one.

Of course this can be put to good use, as in the following case:

```
$ dirs
/usr/bin /tmp ~/scratch/misc
$ printf "%s\n" $(dirs)
/usr/bin
/tmp
~/scratch/misc
$
```

The *printf* takes the directory stack (i.e., the output from the dirs command) and displays the directories one per line, repeating and reusing the format, as described earlier.

Let's summarize:

1. Initialize your variables, especially if they are numbers and you want to use them in *printf* statements.

2. Put quotes around your arguments if they could ever be null, and especially when used in *printf* statements.

3. Make sure you have the correct number of arguments, especially considering what the line will look like after the shell substitutions have occurred.

4. If you don't need the special formatting that *printf* offers (e.g., %05d), consider using a simple *echo* statement.

See Also

- *http://www.opengroup.org/onlinepubs/009695399/functions/printf.html*
- Recipe 2.3, "Writing Output with More Formatting Control"
- Recipe 2.4, "Writing Output Without the Newline"
- Recipe 15.6, "Using echo Portably"
- "printf" in Appendix A

19.12 Testing bash Script Syntax

Problem

You are editing a *bash* script and want to make sure that your syntax is correct.

Solution

Use the -n argument to *bash* to test syntax often, ideally after every save, and certainly before committing any changes to a revision control system:

```
$ bash -n my_script
$

$ echo 'echo "Broken line' >> my_script
```

```
$ bash -n my_script
my_script: line 4: unexpected EOF while looking for matching `"'
my_script: line 5: syntax error: unexpected end of file
```

Discussion

The -n option is tricky to find in the *bash* manpage or other reference material since it's located under the *set* built-in. It is noted in passing in bash --help for -D, but it is never explained there. This flag tells *bash* to "read commands but do not execute them," which of course will find *bash* syntax errors.

As with all syntax checkers, this will not catch logic errors or syntax errors in other commands called by the script.

See Also

- man bash
- bash --help
- bash -c "help set"
- Recipe 16.1, "bash Startup Options"

19.13 Debugging Scripts

Problem

You can't figure out what's happening in your script and why it doesn't work as expected.

Solution

Add set -x to the top of the script when you run it. Or use set -x to turn on *xtrace* before a troublesome spot and set +x to turn it off after. You may also wish to experiment with the $PS4 prompt (Recipe 16.2, "Customizing Your Prompt"). *xtrace* also works on the interactive command line (Recipe 16.2, "Customizing Your Prompt"). Here's a script that we suspect is buggy:

```
#!/usr/bin/env bash
# cookbook filename: buggy
#

set -x

result=$1

[ $result = 1 ] \
    && { echo "Result is 1; excellent."  ; exit 0;    } \
    || { echo "Uh-oh, ummm, RUN AWAY! "  ; exit 120; }
```

Now we invoke this script, but first we set and export the value of the PS4 prompt. *bash* will print out the value of PS4 before each command that it displays during an execution trace (i.e., after a set -x):

```
$ export PS4='+xtrace $LINENO:'
$ echo $PS4
+xtrace $LINENO:

$ ./buggy
+xtrace 4: result=
+xtrace 6: '[' = 1 ']'
./buggy: line 6: [: =: unary operator expected
+xtrace 8: echo 'Uh-oh, ummm, RUN AWAY! '
Uh-oh, ummm, RUN AWAY!

$ ./buggy 1
+xtrace 4: result=1
+xtrace 6: '[' 1 = 1 ']'
+xtrace 7: echo 'Result is 1; excellent.'
Result is 1; excellent.

$ ./buggy 2
+xtrace 4: result=2
+xtrace 6: '[' 2 = 1 ']'
+xtrace 8: echo 'Uh-oh, ummm, RUN AWAY! '
Uh-oh, ummm, RUN AWAY!

$ /tmp/jp-test.sh 3
+xtrace 4: result=3
+xtrace 6: '[' 3 = 1 ']'
+xtrace 8: echo 'Uh-oh, ummm, RUN AWAY! '
Uh-oh, ummm, RUN AWAY!
```

Discussion

It may seem odd to turn something on using - and turn it off using +, but that's just the way it worked out. Many Unix tools use *-n* for options or flags, and since you need a way to turn -x off, +x seems natural.

As of *bash* 3.0 there are a number of new variables to better support debugging: $BASH_ARGC, $BASH_ARGV, $BASH_SOURCE, $BASH_LINENO, $BASH_SUBSHELL, $BASH_EXECUTION_STRING, and $BASH_COMMAND. This is in addition to existing *bash* variables like $LINENO and the array variable $FUNCNAME.

Using *xtrace* is a very handy debugging technique, but it is not the same as having a real debugger. See The Bash Debugger Project (*http://bashdb.sourceforge.net/*), which contains patched sources to *bash* that enable better debugging support as well as improved error reporting. In addition, this project contains, in their words, "the most comprehensive source-code debugger for *bash* that has been written."

See Also

- help set
- man bash
- Chapter 9 in Cameron Newham's *Learning the bash Shell* (O'Reilly), which includes a shell script for debugging other shell scripts
- Recipe 16.1, "bash Startup Options"
- Recipe 16.2, "Customizing Your Prompt"
- Recipe 17.1, "Renaming Many Files"

19.14 Avoiding "command not found" When Using Functions

Problem

You are used to other languages, such as Perl, which allow you to call a function in a section of your code that comes before the actual function definition.

Solution

Shell scripts are read and executed in a top-to-bottom linear way, so you must define any functions before you use them.

Discussion

Some other languages, such as Perl, go through intermediate steps during which the entire script is parsed as a unit. That allows you to write your code so that main( ) is at the top, and function (or subroutines) are defined later. By contrast, a shell script is read into memory and then executed one line at a time, so you can't use a function before you define it.

See Also

- Recipe 10.4, "Defining Functions"
- Recipe 10.5, "Using Functions: Parameters and Return Values"
- Appendix C

19.15 Confusing Shell Wildcards and Regular Expressions

Problem

Sometimes you see .* sometimes just *, and sometimes you see [a-z]* but it means something other than what you thought. You use regular expressions for *grep* and *sed* but not in some places in *bash*. You can't keep it all straight.

Solution

Relax; take a deep breath. You're probably confused because you're learning so much (or just using it too infrequently to remember it). Practice makes perfect, so keep trying.

The rules aren't that hard to remember for *bash* itself. After all, regular expression syntax is only used with the =~ comparison operator in *bash*. All of the other expressions in *bash* use shell pattern matching.

Discussion

The pattern matching used by *bash* uses some of the same symbols as regular expressions, but with different meanings. But it is also the case that you often have calls in your shell scripts to commands that use regular expressions—commands like *grep* and *sed*.

We asked Chet Ramey, the current keeper of the *bash* source and all-around *bash* guru, if it was really the case that the =~ was the only use of regular expressions in *bash*. He concurred. He also was kind enough to supply a list of the various parts of *bash* syntax that use shell pattern matching. We've covered most, but not all of these topics in various recipes in this book. We offer the list here for completeness.

Shell pattern matching is performed by:

- Filename globbing (pathname expansion)
- == and != operators for [[
- case statements
- $GLOBIGNORE handling
- $HISTIGNORE handling
- ${*parameter*#[#]*word*}
- ${*parameter*%[%]*word*}
- ${*parameter*/*pattern*/*string*}
- Several bindable readline commands (glob-expand-word, glob-complete-word, etc.)

- `complete -G` and `compgen -G`
- `complete -X` and `compgen -X`
- The *help* built-in's `pattern` argument

Thanks, Chet!

See Also

- Learn to read the manpage for *bash* and refer to it often—it is long but precise. If you want an online version of the *bash* manpage or other *bash*-related documents, visit *http://www.bashcookbook.com* for the latest *bash* information.
- Keep this book handy for reference, too.
- Recipe 5.18, "Changing Pieces of a String"
- Recipe 6.6, "Testing for Equal"
- Recipe 6.7, "Testing with Pattern Matches"
- Recipe 6.8, "Testing with Regular Expressions"
- Recipe 13.14, "Trimming Whitespace"

APPENDIX A

Reference Lists

This appendix collects many tables of values, settings, operators, commands, variables, and more in one place for easy reference.

bash Invocation

Here are the options you can use when invoking current versions of *bash*. The multi-character options must appear on the command line before the single-character options. Login shells are usually invoked with the options -i (interactive), -s (read from standard input), and -m (enable job control).

In addition to these listed in Table A-1, any *set* option can be used on the command line; see the "set Options" section later in this chapter. In particular, the -n option is invaluable for syntax checking, see Recipe 19.12, "Testing bash Script Syntax."

Table A-1. Command-line options to bash

Option	Meaning
-c *string*	Commands are read from *string*, if present. Any arguments after *string* are interpreted as positional parameters, starting with $0.
-D	A list of all double-quoted strings preceded by $ is printed on the standard output. These are the strings that are subject to language translation when the current locale is not C or POSIX. This also turns on the -n option.
-i	Interactive shell. Ignores signals TERM, INT, and QUIT. With job control in effect, TTIN, TTOU, and TSTP are also ignored.
-l	Makes *bash* act as if invoked as a login shell.
-o *option*	Takes the same arguments as set -o.
-O, +O *shopt-option*	*shopt-option* is one of the shell options accepted by the *shopt* built-in. If *shopt-option* is present, -O sets the value of that option; +O unsets it. If *shopt-option* is not supplied, the names and values of the shell options accepted by *shopt* are printed on the standard output. If the invocation option is +O, the output is displayed in a format that may be reused as input.

Table A-1. Command-line options to bash (continued)

Option	Meaning
-s	Reads commands from the standard input. If an argument is given to *bash*, this flag takes precedence (i.e., the argument won't be treated as a script name and standard input will be read).
-r	Restricted shell.
-v	Prints shell input lines as they're read.
-	Signals the end of options and disables further option processing. Any options after this are treated as filenames and arguments. - - is synonymous with -.
--debugger	Arranges for the debugger profile to be executed before the shell starts. Turns on extended debugging mode and shell function tracing in *bash* 3.0 or later.
--dump-strings	Does the same as -D.
--dump-po-strings	Does the same as -D but the output is in the GNU *gettext* portable object (po) file format.
--help	Displays a usage message and exits.
--login	Makes *bash* act as if invoked as a login shell. Same as -l.
--noediting	Does not use the GNU *readline* library to read command lines if interactive.
--noprofile	Does not read the startup file */etc/profile* or any of the personal initialization files.
--norc	Does not read the initialization file *~/.bashrc* if the shell is interactive. This is on by default if the shell is invoked as *sh*.
--posix	Changes the behavior of *bash* to follow the POSIX standard more closely where the default operation of *bash* is different.
--quiet	Shows no information on shell startup. This is the default.
--rcfile *file*, --init-file *file*	Executes commands read from *file* instead of the initialization file *~/.bashrc*, if the shell is interactive.
--verbose	Equivalent to -v.
--version	Shows the version number of this instance of *bash* and then exits.

Prompt String Customizations

Table A-2 shows a summary of the prompt customizations that are available. The customizations \[and \] are not available in *bash* versions prior to 1.14. \a, \e, \H, \T, \@, \v, and \V are not available in versions prior to 2.0. \A, \D, \j, \l, and \r are only available in later versions of *bash* 2.0 and in *bash* 3.0.

Table A-2. Prompt string format codes

Command	Meaning	Added
\a	The ASCII bell character (007).	bash-1.14.7
\A	The current time in 24-hour HH:MM format.	bash-2.05
\d	The date in "Weekday Month Day" format.	

Command	Meaning	Added
\D {*format*}	The format is passed to *strftime*(3) and the result is inserted into the prompt string; an empty format results in a locale-specific time representation; the braces are required.	bash-2.05b
\e	The ASCII escape character (033).	bash-1.14.7
\H	The hostname.	bash-1.14.7
\h	The hostname up to the first " . ".	
\j	The number of jobs currently managed by the shell.	bash-2.03
\l	The basename of the shell's terminal device name.	bash-2.03
\n	A carriage return and line feed.	
\r	A carriage return.	bash-2.01.1
\s	The name of the shell.	
\T	The current time in 12-hour HH:MM:SS format.	bash-1.14.7
\t	The current time in HH:MM:SS format.	
\@	The current time in 12-hour a.m./p.m. format.	bash-1.14.7
\u	The username of the current user.	
\v	The version of *bash* (e.g., 2.00).	bash-1.14.7
\V	The release of *bash*; the version and patchlevel (e.g., 3.00.0).	bash-1.14.7
\w	The current working directory.	
\W	The basename of the current working directory.	
\#	The command number of the current command.	
\!	The history number of the current command.	
\$	If the effective UID is 0, print a #, otherwise print a $.	
nnn	Character code in octal.	
\\	Print a backslash.	
\[	Begin a sequence of nonprinting characters, such as terminal control sequences.	
\]	End a sequence of nonprinting characters.	

ANSI Color Escape Sequences

Table A-3 shows the ANSI color escape sequences.

Table A-3. ANSI color escape sequences

Code	Character attribute	FG code	Foreground color	BG code	Background color
0	Reset all attributes	30	Black	40	Black
1	Bright	31	Red	41	Red
2	Dim	32	Green	42	Green

Table A-3. ANSI color escape sequences (continued)

Code	Character attribute	FG code	Foreground color	BG code	Background color
4	Underscore	33	Yellow	43	Yellow
5	Blink	34	Blue	44	Blue
7	Reverse	35	Magenta	45	Magenta
8	Hidden	36	Cyan	46	Cyan
		37	White	47	White

Built-in Commands and Reserved Words

Table A-4 shows a summary of all built-in commands and reserved words. The letters in the Type column of the table have the following meanings: R = reserved word, blank = built-in.

Table A-4. Built-in commands and reserved words

Command	Type	Summary
!	R	Logical NOT of a command exit status.
:		Do nothing (just do expansions of any arguments).
.		Read file and execute its contents in current shell.
alias		Set up shorthand for command or command line.
bg		Put job in background.
bind		Bind a key sequence to a readline function or macro.
break		Exit from surrounding for, select, while, or until loop.
builtin		Execute the specified shell built-in.
case	R	Reserved word. Multi-way conditional construct.
cd		Change working directory.
command		Run a command bypassing shell function lookup.
compgen		Generate possible completion matches.
complete		Specify how completion should be performed.
continue		Skip to next iteration of for, select, while, or until loop.
declare		Declare variables and give them attributes. Same as typeset.
dirs		Display the list of currently remembered directories.
disown		Remove a job from the job table.
do	R	Part of a for, select, while, or until looping construct.
done	R	Part of a for, select, while, or until looping construct.
echo		Output arguments.
elif	R	Part of an if construct.
else	R	Part of an if construct.
enable		Enable and disable built-in shell commands.

Table A-4. Built-in commands and reserved words (continued)

Command	Type	Summary
esac	R	End of a case construct.
eval		Run the given arguments through command-line processing.
exec		Replace the shell with the given program.
exit		Exit from the shell.
export		Create environment variables.
fc		Fix command (edit history file).
fg		End background job in foreground.
fi	R	Part of an if construct.
for	R	Looping construct.
function	R	Define a function.
getopts		Process command-line options.
hash		Full pathnames are determined and remembered.
help		Display helpful information on built-in commands.
history		Display command history.
if	R	Conditional construct.
in	R	Part of a case construct.
jobs		List any background jobs.
kill		Send a signal to a process.
let		Arithmetic variable assignment.
local		Create a local variable.
logout		Exit a login shell.
popd		Remove a directory from the directory stack.
pushd		Add a directory to the directory stack.
pwd		Print the working directory.
read		Read a line from standard input.
readonly		Make variables read-only (unassignable).
return		Return from the surrounding function or script.
select	R	Menu-generation construct.
set		Set options.
shift		Shift command-line arguments.
suspend		Suspend execution of a shell.
test		Evaluate a conditional expression.
then	R	Part of an if construct.
time	R	Run command pipeline and print execution times. The format of the output can be controlled with TIMEFORMAT.
times		Print the accumulated user and system times for processes run from the shell.

Table A-4. Built-in commands and reserved words (continued)

Command	Type	Summary
trap		Set up a signal-catching routine.
type		Identify the source of a command.
typeset		Declare variables and give them attributes. Same as declare.
ulimit		Set/show process resource limits.
umask		Set/show file permission mask.
unalias		Remove alias definitions.
unset		Remove definitions of variables or functions.
until	R	Looping construct.
wait		Wait for background job(s) to finish.
while	R	Looping construct.

Built-in Shell Variables

Table A-5 shows a complete list of environment variables available in *bash* 3.0. The letters in the Type column of the table have the following meanings: A = Array, L = colon-separated list, R = read-only, U = unsetting it causes it to lose its special meaning.

Note that the variables beginning BASH_ and beginning COMP, as well as the variables DIRSTACK, FUNCNAME, GLOBIGNORE, GROUPS, HISTIGNORE, HOSTNAME, HISTTIMEFORMAT, LANG, LC_ALL, LC_COLLATE, LC_MESSAGE, MACHTYPE, PIPESTATUS, SHELLOPTS, and TIMEFORMAT are not available in versions prior to 2.0. BASH_ENV replaces ENV found in earlier versions.

Table A-5. Built-in shell environment variables

Variable	Type	Description
*	R	A single string containing the positional parameters given to the current script or function, separated by the first character of $IFS (e.g., arg1 arg2 arg3).
@	R	Each of the positional parameters given to the current script or function, given as a list of double-quoted strings (e.g., "arg1" "arg2" "arg3").
#	R	The number of arguments given to the current script or function.
-	R	Options given to the shell on invocation.
?	R	Exit status of the previous command.
_	R	Last argument to the previous command.
$	R	Process ID of the shell process.
!	R	Process ID of the last background command.
0	R	Name of the shell or shell script.
BASH		The full pathname used to invoke this instance of *bash*.
BASH_ARGC	A	An array of values, which are the number of parameters in each frame of the current *bash* execution call stack. The number of parameters to the current subroutine (shell function or script executed with . or source) is at the top of the stack.

Table A-5. Built-in shell environment variables (continued)

Variable	Type	Description
BASH_ARGV	A	All of the parameters in the current *bash* execution call stack. The final parameter of the last subroutine call is at the top of the stack; the first parameter of the initial call is at the bottom.
BASH_COMMAND		The command currently being executed or about to be executed, unless the shell is executing a command as the result of a trap, in which case it is the command executing at the time of the trap.
BASH_EXECUTION_STRING		The command argument to the -c invocation option.
BASH_ENV		The name of a file to run as the environment file when the shell is invoked.
BASH_LINENO	A	An array whose members are the line numbers in source files corresponding to each member of @var{FUNCNAME}. ${BASHLINENO[$i]} is the line number in the source file where ${FUNCNAME[$i + 1]} was called. The corresponding source filename is ${BASHSOURCE[$i + 1]}.
BASH_REMATCH	AR	An array whose members are assigned by the =~ binary operator to the [[conditional command. The element with index 0 is the portion of the string matching the entire regular expression. The element with index *n* is the portion of the string matching the *n*th parenthesized subexpression.
BASH_SOURCE	A	An array containing the source filenames corresponding to the elements in the $FUNCNAME array variable.
BASH_SUBSHELL		Incremented by 1 each time a subshell or subshell environment is spawned. The initial value is 0. A subshell is a forked copy of the parent shell and shares it's environment.
BASH_VERSION		The version number of this instance of *bash*.
BASH_VERSINFO	AR	Version information for this instance of *bash*. Each element of the array holds parts of the version number.
CDPATH	L	A list of directories for the *cd* command to search.
COMP_CWORD		An index into ${COMPWORDS} of the word containing the current cursor position. This variable is available only in shell functions invoked by the programmable completion facilities.
COMP_LINE		The current command line. This variable is available only in shell functions and external commands invoked by the programmable completion facilities.
COMP_POINT		The index of the current cursor position relative to the beginning of the current command. If the current cursor position is at the end of the current command, the value of this variable is equal to ${#COMPLINE}. This variable is available only in shell functions and external commands invoked by the programmable completion facilities.
COMP_WORDBREAKS	U	The set of characters that the Readline library treats as word separators when performing word completion. If COMP_WORDBREAKS is unset, it loses its special properties, even if it is subsequently reset.
COMP_WORDS	A	An array of the individual words in the current command line. This variable is available only in shell functions invoked by the programmable completion facilities.
COMPREPLY	A	The possible completions generated by a shell function invoked by the programmable completion facility.
DIRSTACK	ARU	The current contents of the directory stack.
EUID	R	The effective user ID of the current user.

Variable	Type	Description
FUNCNAME	ARU	An array containing the names of all shell functions currently in the execution call stack. The element with index 0 is the name of any currently-executing shell function. The bottom-most element is "main." This variable exists only when a shell function is executing.
FCEDIT		The default editor for the *fc* command.
FIGNORE	L	A list of names to ignore when doing filename completion.
GLOBIGNORE	L	A list of patterns defining filenames to ignore during pathname expansion.
GROUPS	AR	An array containing a list of groups of which the current user is a member.
IFS		The Internal Field Separator: a list of characters that act as word separators. Normally set to space, tab, and newline.
HISTCMD	U	The history number of the current command.
HISTCONTROL		A list of patterns, separated by colons (:), which can have the following values: ignorespace: lines beginning with a space are not entered into the history list; ignoredups: lines matching the last history line are not entered; erasedups: all previous lines matching the current line to are removed from the history list before the line is saved; ignoreboth: enables both ignorespace and ignoredups.
HISTFILE		The name of the command history file.
HISTIGNORE		A list of patterns to decide what should be retained in the history list.
HISTSIZE		The number of lines kept in the command history.
HISTFILESIZE		The maximum number of lines kept in the history file.
HISTTIMEFORMAT		If set and not null, its value is used as a format string for *strftime*(3) to print the time-stamp associated with each history entry displayed by the *history* built-in. If this variable is set, timestamps are written to the history file so they may be preserved across shell sessions.
HOME		The home (login) directory.
HOSTFILE		The file to be used for hostname completion.
HOSTNAME		The name of the current host.
HOSTTYPE		The type of machine *bash* is running on.
IGNOREEOF		The number of EOF characters received before exiting an interactive shell.
INPUTRC		The *readline* startup file.
LANG		Used to determine the locale category for any category not specifically selected with a variable starting with LC_.
LC_ALL		Overrides the value of $LANG and any other LC_ variable specifying a locale category.
LC_COLLATE		Determines the collation order used when sorting the results of pathname expansion.
LC_CTYPE		Determines the interpretation of characters and the behavior of character classes within pathname expansion and pattern matching.
LC_MESSAGES		This variable determines the locale used to translate double-quoted strings preceded by a $.
LC_NUMERIC		Determines the locale category used for number formatting.
LINENO	U	The number of the line that just ran in a script or function.
MACHTYPE		A string describing the system on which *bash* is executing.

Table A-5. Built-in shell environment variables (continued)

Variable	Type	Description
MAIL		The name of the file to check for new mail.
MAILCHECK		How often (in seconds) to check for new mail.
MAILPATH	L	A list of filenames to check for new mail, if $MAIL is not set.
OLDPWD		The previous working directory.
OPTARG		The value of the last option argument processed by getopts.
OPTERR		If set to 1, display error messages from getopts.
OPTIND		The number of the first argument after options.
OSTYPE		The operating system on which *bash* is executing.
PATH	L	The search path for commands.
PIPESTATUS	A	An array variable containing a list of exit status values from the processes in the most recently executed foreground pipeline.
POSIXLY_CORRECT		If in the environment when *bash* starts, the shell enters posix mode before reading the startup files, as if the --posix invocation option had been supplied. If it is set while the shell is running, *bash* enables posix mode, as if the command set -o posix had been executed.
PROMPT_COMMAND		The value is executed as a command before the primary prompt is issued.
PS1		The primary command prompt string.
PS2		The prompt string for line continuations.
PS3		The prompt string for the *select* command.
PS4		The prompt string for the *xtrace* option.
PPID	R	The process ID of the parent process.
PWD		The current working directory.
RANDOM	U	A random number between 0 and 32767 ($2^{15} - 1$).
REPLY		The user's response to the *select* command; result of the *read* command if no variable names are given.
SECONDS	U	The number of seconds since the shell was invoked.
SHELL		The full pathname of the shell.
SHELLOPTS	LR	A list of enabled shell options.
SHLVL		Incremented by 1 each time a new instance (not a subshell) of *bash* is invoked. This is intended to be a count of how deeply your *bash* shells are nested.
TIMEFORMAT		Specifies the format for the output from using the *time* reserved word on a command pipeline.
TMOUT		If set to a positive integer, the number of seconds after which the shell automatically terminates if no input is received.
UID	R	The user ID of the current user.
auto_resume		Controls how job control works (values are exact, substring, or something other than those keywords).
histchars		Specifies what to use as the history control characters. Normally set to the string !^#.

set Options

The options in Table A-6 can be turned on with the set -arg command. They are all initially off except where noted. Full names, where listed, are arguments to *set* that can be used with set -o. The full names braceexpand, histexpand, history, keyword, and onecmd are not available in versions of *bash* prior to 2.0. Also, in those versions, hashing is switched with -d.

Table A-6. set options

Option	Full name (-o)	Meaning
-a	allexport	Export all subsequently defined or modified variables.
-B	braceexpand	The shell performs brace expansion. This is on by default.
-b	notify	Report the status of terminating background jobs immediately.
-C	noclobber	Don't allow redirection to overwrite existing files.
-E	errtrace	Any trap on ERR is inherited by shell functions, command substitutions, and commands executed in a subshell environment.
-e	errexit	Exit the shell when a simple command exits with nonzero status. A simple command is a command not part of a while, until, or if; nor part of a && or || list; nor a command whose return value is inverted by !.
	emacs	Use Emacs-style command-line editing.
-f	noglob	Disable pathname expansion.
-H	histexpand	Enable ! style history substitution. On by default in an interactive shell.
	history	Enable command history. On by default in interactive shells.
-h	hashall	Enable the hashing of commands.
	ignoreeof	Disallow Ctrl-D to exit the shell.
-k	keyword	All arguments in the form of assignment statements are placed in the environment for a command, not just those that precede the command name.
-m	monitor	Enable job control (on by default in interactive shells).
-n	noexec	Read commands and check syntax but do not execute them. Ignored for interactive shells.
-P	physical	Do not follow symbolic links on commands that change the current directory. Use the physical directory.
-p	privileged	Script is running in suid mode.
	pipefail	The return value of a pipeline is the value of the last (rightmost) command to exit with a nonzero status, or zero if all commands in the pipeline exit successfully. This option is disabled by default.
	posix	Change the default behavior to that of POSIX 1003.2 where it differs from the standard.
-T	functrace	Any trap on DEBUG is inherited by shell functions, command substitutions, and commands executed in a subshell environment.
-t	onecmd	Exit after reading and executing one command.
-u	nounset	Treat undefined variables as errors, not as null.
-v	verbose	Print shell input lines before running them.

Table A-6. set options (continued)

Option	Full name (-o)	Meaning
	vi	Use *vi*-style command-line editing.
-x	xtrace	Print commands (after expansions) before running them.
-		Signals the end of options. All remaining arguments are assigned to the positional parameters. -x and -v are turned off. If there are no remaining arguments to *set*, the positional arguments remain unchanged.
--		With no arguments following, unset the positional parameters. Otherwise, the positional parameters are set to the following arguments (even if they begin with -).

shopt Options

The *shopt* options are set with shopt -s *arg* and unset with shopt -u *arg* (see Table A-7). Versions of *bash* prior to 2.0 had environment variables to perform some of these settings. Setting them equated to shopt -s. The variables (and corresponding *shopt* options) were: allow_null_glob_expansion (nullglob), cdable_vars (cdable_vars), command_oriented_history (cmdhist), glob_dot_filenames (dotglob), no_exit_on_failed_exec (execfail). These variables no longer exist.

The options extdebug, failglob, force_fignore, and gnu_errfmt are not available in versions of *bash* prior to 3.0.

Table A-7. shopt options

Option	Meaning if set
cdable_vars	An argument to *cd* that is not a directory is assumed to be the name of a variable whose value is the directory to change to.
cdspell	Minor errors in the spelling of a directory supplied to the *cd* command will be corrected if there is a suitable match. This correction includes missing letters, incorrect letters, and letter transposition. It works for interactive shells only.
checkhash	Commands found in the hash table are checked for existence before being executed and nonexistence forces a $PATH search.
checkwinsize	Checks the window size after each command and, if it has changed, updates the variables $LINES and $COLUMNS accordingly.
cmdhist	Attempt to save all lines of a multiline command in a single history entry.
dotglob	Filenames beginning with a . are included in pathname expansion.
execfail	A noninteractive shell will not exit if it cannot execute the argument to an *exec*. Interactive shells do not exit if *exec* fails.
expand_aliases	Aliases are expanded.
extdebug	Behavior intended for use by debuggers is enabled. This includes: the -F option of *declare* displays the source filename and line number corresponding to each function name supplied as an argument; if the command run by the DEBUG trap returns a nonzero value, the next command is skipped and not executed; and if the command run by the DEBUG trap returns a value of 2, and the shell is executing in a subroutine, a call to return is simulated.

Table A-7. shopt options

Option	Meaning if set
extglob	Extended pattern matching features are enabled.
failglob	Patterns that fail to match filenames during pathname expansion result in an expansion error.
force_fignore	The suffixes specified by the $FIGNORE shell variable cause words to be ignored when performing word completion even if the ignored words are the only possible completions.
gnu_errfmt	Shell error messages are written in the standard GNU error message format.
histappend	The history list is appended to the file named by the value of the variable $HISTFILE when the shell exits, rather than overwriting the file.
histreedit	If *readline* is being used, the opportunity is given for re-editing a failed history substitution.
histverify	If *readline* is being used, the results of history substitution are not immediately passed to the shell parser. Instead, the resulting line is loaded into the *readline* editing buffer, allowing further modification.
hostcomplete	If *readline* is being used, an attempt will be made to perform hostname completion when a word beginning with @ is being completed.
huponexit	*bash* will send SIGHUP to all jobs when an interactive login shell exits.
interactive_comments	Allows a word beginning with # and all subsequent characters on the line to be ignored in an interactive shell.
lithist	If the cmdhist option is enabled, multiline commands are saved to the history with embedded newlines rather than using semicolon separators where possible.
login_shell	If *bash* is started as a login shell. This is a read-only value.
mailwarn	If the file being checked for mail has been accessed since the last time it was checked, the message "The mail in *mailfile* has been read" is displayed.
no_empty_cmd_completion	If *readline* is being used, no attempt will be made to search the PATH for possible completions when completion is attempted on an empty line.
nocaseglob	*bash* matches filenames in a case-insensitive fashion when performing pathname expansion.
nullglob	Cause patterns that match no files to expand to null strings rather than to themselves.
progcomp	Programmable completion facilities are enabled. Default is on.
promptvars	Prompt strings undergo variable and parameter expansion after being expanded.
restricted_shell	Set if the shell is started in restricted mode. The value cannot be changed.
shift_verbose	The *shift* built-in prints an error if it has shifted past the last positional parameter.
sourcepath	The *source* built-in uses the value of $PATH to find the directory containing the file supplied as an argument.
xpg_echo	*echo* expands backslash-escape sequences by default.

Adjusting Shell Behavior Using set, shopt, and Environment Variables

Table A-8 combines Tables A-5, A-6, and A-7 and provides a quick way to look for what you can configure and which of the three mechanisms you use to configure it. The options are loosely grouped according to function or purpose, but it's worthwhile to scan the entire table to get an overall sense of what you can configure.

The "Set option" column contains the options that can be turned on with the set -*arg* command. All are initially off except where noted. Items in the "Set full name" column, where listed, are arguments to *set* that can be used with set -o. The full names braceexpand, histexpand, history, keyword, and onecmd are not available in versions of *bash* prior to 2.0. Also, in those versions, hashing is switched with -d.

The "Shopt option" column shows the options set with shopt -s *arg* and unset with shopt -u *arg*. Versions of *bash* prior to 2.0 had environment variables to perform some of these settings. Setting them equated to shopt -s. The variables (and corresponding *shopt* options) were: allow_null_glob_expansion (nullglob), cdable_vars (cdable_vars), command_oriented_history (cmdhist), glob_dot_filenames (dotglob), no_exit_on_failed_exec (execfail). These variables no longer exist.

The options extdebug, failglob, force_fignore, and gnu_errfmt are not available in versions of *bash* prior to 3.0.

The "Environment variable" column lists environment variables that affect *bash* configuration and operation. The letters in the Type column of the table have the following meanings: A = Array, L = colon-separated list, R = read-only, U = unsetting it causes it to lose its special meaning.

Note that the variables beginning BASH_ and beginning COMP, as well as the variables DIRSTACK, FUNCNAME, GLOBIGNORE, GROUPS, HISTIGNORE, HOSTNAME, HISTTIMEFORMAT, LANG, LC_ALL, LC_COLLATE, LC_MESSAGE, MACHTYPE, PIPESTATUS, SHELLOPTS, and TIMEFORMAT are not available in versions prior to 2.0. BASH_ENV replaces ENV found in earlier versions.

Table A-8. Adjusting shell behavior using set, shopt, and environment variables

Set option	Set full name	Shopt option	Environment variable	Env. var. type	Description
			COMP_CWORD		An index into ${COMPWORDS} of the word containing the current cursor position. This variable is available only in shell functions invoked by the programmable completion facilities.
			COMP_LINE		The current command line. This variable is available only in shell functions and external commands invoked by the programmable completion facilities.

Set option	Set full name	Shopt option	Environment variable	Env. var. type	Description
			COMP_POINT		The index of the current cursor position relative to the beginning of the current command. If the current cursor position is at the end of the current command, the value of this variable is equal to ${#COMPLINE}. This variable is available only in shell functions and external commands invoked by the programmable completion facilities.
			COMP_WORDBREAKS	U	The set of characters that the Readline library treats as word separators when performing word completion. If COMP_WORDBREAKS is unset, it loses its special properties, even if it is subsequently reset.
			COMP_WORDS	A	An array of the individual words in the current command line. This variable is available only in shell functions invoked by the programmable completion facilities.
			COMPREPLY	A	The possible completions generated by a shell function invoked by the programmable completion facility.
			FIGNORE	L	A list of names to ignore when doing filename completion.
		force_ fignore			The suffixes specified by the FIGNORE shell variable cause words to be ignored when performing word completion even if the ignored words are the only possible completions.
		hostcomple te			If *readline* is being used, an attempt will be made to perform hostname completion when a word beginning with @ is being completed.
			HOSTFILE		The file to be used for hostname completion.
		no_empty_ cmd_ completion			If *readline* is being used, no attempt will be made to search the PATH for possible completions when completion is attempted on an empty line.
		progcomp			Programmable completion facilities are enabled. Default is on.
			INPUTRC		The *readline* startup file.

Table A-8. Adjusting shell behavior using set, shopt, and environment variables (continued)

Set option	Set full name	Shopt option	Environment variable	Env. var. type	Description
-C	noclobber				Don't allow redirection to overwrite existing files.
-t	onecmd				Exit after reading and executing one command.
-P	physical				Do not follow symbolic links on commands that change the current directory. Use the physical directory.
		restricted _shell			Set if the shell is started in restricted mode. The value cannot be changed.
			SHELLOPTS	LR	A list of enabled shell options.
		sourcepath			The source built-in uses the value of $PATH to find the directory containing the file supplied as an argument.
			BASH_ARGC	A	An array of values, which are the number of parameters in each frame of the current bash execution call stack. The number of parameters to the current subroutine (shell function or script executed with . or source) is at the top of the stack.
			BASH_ARGV	A	All of the parameters in the current *bash* execution call stack. The final parameter of the last subroutine call is at the top of the stack; the first parameter of the initial call is at the bottom.
			BASH_ COMMAND		The command currently being executed or about to be executed, unless the shell is executing a command as the result of a trap, in which case it is the command executing at the time of the trap.
			BASH_LINENO	A	An array whose members are the line numbers in source files corresponding to each member of @var{FUNCNAME}. ${BASHLINENO[$i]} is the line number in the source file where ${FUNCNAME[$i +1]} was called. The corresponding source filename is ${BASHSOURCE[$i + 1]}.
			BASH_SOURCE	A	An array containing the source filenames corresponding to the elements in the $FUNCNAME array variable.

Table A-8. Adjusting shell behavior using set, shopt, and environment variables (continued)

Set option	Set full name	Shopt option	Environment variable	Env. var. type	Description
-E	errtrace				Any trap on ERR is inherited by shell functions, command substitutions, and commands executed in a subshell environment.
		extdebug			Behavior intended for use by debuggers is enabled. This includes: the -F option of *declare* displays the source filename and line number corresponding to each function name supplied as an argument; if the command run by the DEBUG trap returns a non-zero value, the next command is skipped and not executed; and if the command run by the DEBUG trap returns a value of 2, and the shell is executing in a subroutine, a call to return is simulated.
			FUNCNAME	ARU	An array containing the names of all shell functions currently in the execution call stack. The element with index 0 is the name of any currently-executing shell function. The bottom-most element is "main." This variable exists only when a shell function is executing.
-T	functrace				Any trap on DEBUG is inherited by shell functions, command substitutions, and commands executed in a subshell environment.
			LINENO	U	The number of the line that just ran in a script or function.
-n	noexec				Read commands and check syntax but do not execute them. Ignored for interactive shells.
-v	verbose				Print shell input lines before running them.
-x	xtrace				Print commands (after expansions) before running them.
			BASH_SUBSHELL		Incremented by 1 each time a subshell or subshell environment is spawned. The initial value is 0. A subshell is a forked copy of the parent shell and shares it's environment.

Table A-8. Adjusting shell behavior using set, shopt, and environment variables (continued)

Set option	Set full name	Shopt option	Environment variable	Env. var. type	Description
			SHLVL		Incremented by 1 each time a new instance (not a subshell) of *bash* is invoked. This is intended to be a count of how deeply your *bash* shells are nested.
-a	allexport				Export all subsequently defined or modified variables.
			BASH_ENV		The name of a file to run as the environment file when the shell is invoked.
			BASH_EXECUTION_STRING		The command argument to the -c invocation option.
			BASH_VERSINFO	AR	Version information for this instance of *bash*. Each element of the array holds parts of the version number.
			BASH_VERSION		The version number of this instance of *bash*.
			-	R	Options given to the shell on invocation.
-					Signals the end of options. All remaining arguments are assigned to the positional parameters. -x and -v are turned off. If there are no remaining arguments to *set*, the positional arguments remain unchanged.
		gnu_errfmt			Shell error messages are written in the standard GNU error message format.
			HOME		The home (login) directory.
			HOSTNAME		The name of the current host.
			HOSTTYPE		The type of machine bash is running on.
		huponexit			*bash* will send SIGHUP to all jobs when an interactive login shell exits.
--					With no arguments following, unset the positional parameters. Otherwise, the positional parameters are set to the following arguments (even if they begin with -).
			IFS		The Internal Field Separator: a list of characters that act as word separators. Normally set to space, tab, and newline.

Table A-8. *Adjusting shell behavior using set, shopt, and environment variables (continued)*

Set option	Set full name	Shopt option	Environment variable	Env. var. type	Description
-k	keyword				Place keyword arguments in the environment for a command.
			LANG		Used to determine the locale category for any category not specifically selected with a variable starting with LC_.
			LC_ALL		Overrides the value of $LANG and any other LC_ variable specifying a locale category.
			LC_COLLATE		Determines the collation order used when sorting the results of pathname expansion.
			LC_CTYPE		Determines the interpretation of characters and the behavior of character classes within pathname expansion and pattern matching.
			LC_MESSAGES		This variable determines the locale used to translate double-quoted strings preceded by a $.
			LC_NUMERIC		Determines the locale category used for number formatting.
		login_ shell			If *bash* is started as a login shell. This is a read-only value.
			MACHTYPE		A string describing the system on which *bash* is executing.
			PATH	L	The search path for commands.
			SECONDS	U	The number of seconds since the shell was invoked.
-B	braceexpand				The shell performs brace expansion. This is on by default.
		dotglob			Filenames beginning with a . are included in pathname expansion.
		expand_ aliases			Aliases are expanded.
		extglob			Extended pattern matching features are enabled.
		failglob			Patterns that fail to match filenames during pathname expansion result in an expansion error.
			GLOBIGNORE	L	A list of patterns defining filenames to ignore during pathname expansion.

Set option	Set full name	Shopt option	Environment variable	Env. var. type	Description
		nocaseglob			*bash* matches filenames in a case-insensitive fashion when performing pathname expansion.
-f	noglob				Disable pathname expansion.
		nullglob			Cause patterns that match no files to expand to null strings rather than to themselves.
		checkhash			Commands found in the hash table are checked for existence before being executed, and nonexistence forces a $PATH search.
-h	hashall				Disable the hashing of commands.
		cmdhist			Attempt to save all lines of a multiline command in a single history entry.
		histappend			The history list is appended to the file named by the value of the variable $HISTFILE when the shell exits, rather than overwriting the file.
			histchars		Specifies what to use as the history control characters. Normally set to the string !^#.
			HISTCMD	U	The history number of the current command.
			HISTCONTROL		A list of patterns, separated by colons (:), which can have the following values. ignorespace: lines beginning with a space are not entered into the history list. ignoredups: lines matching the last history line are not entered. erasedups: all previous lines matching the current line to are removed from the history list before the line is saved. ignoreboth: enables both ignorespace and ignoredups.
-H	histexpand				Enable ! style history substitution. On by default in an interactive shell.
			HISTFILE		The name of the command history file.
			HISTFILESIZE		The maximum number of lines kept in the history file.
			HISTIGNORE		A list of patterns to decide what should be retained in the history list.

Table A-8. Adjusting shell behavior using set, shopt, and environment variables (continued)

Set option	Set full name	Shopt option	Environment variable	Env. var. type	Description
	history				Enable command history. On by default in interactive shells.
		histreedit			If *readline* is being used, the opportunity is given for re-editing a failed history substitution.
			HISTSIZE		The number of lines kept in the command history.
			HISTTIMEFORMAT		If set and not null, its value is used as a format string for *strftime*(3) to print the timestamp associated with each history entry displayed by the *history* built-in. If this variable is set, timestamps are written to the history file so they may be preserved across shell sessions.
		histverify			If *readline* is being used, the results of history substitution are not immediately passed to the shell parser. Instead, the resulting line is loaded into the *readline* editing buffer, allowing further modification.
		lithist			If the cmdhist option is enabled, multiline commands are saved to the history with embedded newlines rather than using semicolon separators where possible.
			IGNOREEOF		The number of EOF characters received before exiting an interactive shell.
	ignoreeof				Disallow Ctrl-D to exit the shell.
		cdable_vars			An argument to *cd* that is not a directory is assumed to be the name of a variable whose value is the directory to change to.
			CDPATH	L	A list of directories for the *cd* command to search.
		cdspell			Minor errors in the spelling of a directory supplied to the *cd* command will be corrected if there is a suitable match. This correction includes missing letters, incorrect letters, and letter transposition. It works for interactive shells only.

Table A-8. Adjusting shell behavior using set, shopt, and environment variables (continued)

Set option	Set full name	Shopt option	Environment variable	Env. var. type	Description
		checkwinsize			Checks the window size after each command and, if it has changed, updates the variables $LINES and $COLUMNS accordingly.
			DIRSTACK	ARU	The current contents of the directory stack.
	emacs				Use Emacs-style command-line editing.
			FCEDIT		The default editor for the *fc* command.
		interactive_comments			Allows a word beginning with # and all subsequent characters on the line to be ignored in an interactive shell.
			OLDPWD		The previous working directory.
			PROMPT_COMMAND		The value is executed as a command before the primary prompt is issued.
		promptvars			Prompt strings undergo variable and parameter expansion after being expanded.
			PS1		The primary command prompt string.
			PS2		The prompt string for line continuations.
			PS3		The prompt string for the select command.
			PS4		The prompt string for the *xtrace* option.
			PWD		The current working directory.
		shift_verbose			The shift built-in prints an error if it has shifted past the last positional parameter.
			TIMEFORMAT		Specifies the format for the output from using the *time* reserved word on a command pipeline.
			TMOUT		If set to a positive integer, the number of seconds after which the shell automatically terminates if no input is received.
			_	R	Last argument to the previous command.
	vi				Use *vi*-style command-line editing.

Table A-8. Adjusting shell behavior using set, shopt, and environment variables (continued)

Set option	Set full name	Shopt option	Environment variable	Env. var. type	Description
			auto_resume		Controls how job control works (values are exact, substring, or something other than those keywords).
-m	monitor				Enable job control (on by default in interactive shells).
-b	notify				Report the status of terminating background jobs immediately.
			MAIL		The name of the file to check for new mail.
			MAILCHECK		How often (in seconds) to check for new mail.
			MAILPATH	L	A list of file names to check for new mail, if $MAIL is not set.
		mailwarn			If the file being checked for mail has been accessed since the last time it was checked, the message "The mail in *mailfile* has been read" is displayed.
		pipefail			The return value of a pipeline is the value of the last (rightmost) command to exit with a nonzero status, or zero if all commands in the pipeline exit successfully. This option is disabled by default.
			PIPESTATUS	A	An array variable containing a list of exit status values from the processes in the most recently executed foreground pipeline.
		posix			Change the default behavior to that of POSIX 1003.2 where it differs from the standard.
			POSIXLY_CORRECT		If in the environment when *bash* starts, the shell enters posix mode before reading the startup files, as if the --posix invocation option had been supplied. If it is set while the shell is running, *bash* enables posix mode, as if the command set -o posix had been executed.
		xpg_echo			*echo* expands backslash-escape sequences by default.

Set option	Set full name	Shopt option	Environment variable	Env. var. type	Description
			BASH_REMATCH	AR	An array whose members are assigned by the =~ binary operator to the [[conditional command. The element with index 0 is the portion of the string matching the entire regular expression. The element with index *n* is the portion of the string matching the *n*th parenthesized subexpression.
			0	R	Name of the shell or shell script.
			*	R	A single string containing the positional parameters given to the current script or function, separated by the first character of $IFS (e.g., arg1 arg2 arg3).
			@	R	Each of the positional parameters given to the current script or function, given as a list of double-quoted strings (e.g., "arg1" "arg2" "arg3").
			BASH		The full pathname used to invoke this instance of *bash*.
			$	R	Process ID of the shell process.
-e	errexit				Exit the shell when a simple command exits with nonzero status. A simple command is a command not part of a while, until, or if; nor part of a && or | | list; nor a command whose return value is inverted by !.
			EUID	R	The effective user ID of the current user.
			!	R	Process ID of the last background command.
		execfail			A noninteractive shell will not exit if it cannot execute the argument to an *exec*. Interactive shells do not exit if *exec* fails.
			GROUPS	AR	An array containing a list of groups of which the current user is a member.
-u	nounset				Treat undefined variables as errors, not as null.
			OPTARG		The value of the last option argument processed by getopts.
			OPTERR		If set to 1, display error messages from getopts.

Set option	Set full name	Shopt option	Environment variable	Env. var. type	Description
			OPTIND		The number of the first argument after options.
			OSTYPE		The operating system on which *bash* is executing.
			#	R	The number of arguments given to the current script or function.
			PPID	R	The process ID of the parent process.
-p	privileged				Script is running in *suid* mode.
			?	R	Exit status of the previous command.
			RANDOM	U	A random number between 0 and 32767 (2^{15} - 1).
			REPLY		The user's response to the select command; result of the read command if no variable names are given.
			SHELL		The full pathname of the shell.
			UID	R	The user ID of the current user.

Test Operators

The operators in Table A-9 are used with *test* and the [...] and [[...]] constructs. They can be logically combined with -a ("and") and -o ("or") and grouped with escaped parenthesis (\(...\)). The string comparisons < and > and the [[...]] construct are not available in versions of *bash* prior to 2.0, and =~ is only available in *bash* version 3.0 and later as noted.

Table A-9. Test operators

Operator	True if
-a *file*	*file* exists, deprecated, same as -e
-b *file*	*file* exists and is a block device file
-c *file*	*file* exists and is a character device file
-d *file*	*file* exists and is a directory
-e *file*	*file* exists; same as -a
-f *file*	*file* exists and is a regular file
-g *file*	*file* exists and has its *setgid* bit set
-G *file*	*file* exists and is owned by the effective group ID
-h *file*	*file* exists and is a symbolic link, same as -L
-k *file*	*file* exists and has its sticky bit set
-L *file*	*file* exists and is a symbolic link, same as -h

Table A-9. Test operators (continued)

Operator	True if
-n *string*	*string* is non-null
-N *file*	*file* was modified since it was last read
-O *file*	*file* exists and is owned by the effective user ID
-p *file*	*file* exists and is a pipe or named pipe (FIFO file)
-r *file*	*file* exists and is readable
-s *file*	*file* exists and is not empty
-S *file*	*file* exists and is a socket
-t N	File descriptor N points to a terminal
-u *file*	*file* exists and has its *setuid* bit set
-w *file*	*file* exists and is writeable
-x *file*	*file* exists and is executable, or *file* is a directory that can be searched
-z *string*	*string* has a length of zero
fileA -nt *fileB*	*fileA* modification time is newer than *fileA*
fileA -ot *fileB*	*fileA* modification time is older than *fileA*
fileA -ef *fileB*	*fileA* and *fileB* point to the same file
stringA = *stringB*	*stringA* equals *stringB* (POSIX version)
stringA == *stringB*	*stringA* equals *stringB*
stringA != *stringB*	*stringA* does not match *stringB*
stringA =~ *regexp*	*stringA* matches the extended regular expression regexp[a]
stringA < *stringB*	*stringA* sorts before *stringB* lexicographically
stringA > *stringB*	*stringA* sorts after *stringB* lexicographically
exprA -eq *exprB*	Arithmetic expressions *exprA* and *exprB* are equal
exprA -ne *exprB*	Arithmetic expressions *exprA* and *exprB* are not equal
exprA -lt *exprB*	*exprA* is less than *exprB*
exprA -gt *exprB*	*exprA* is greater than *exprB*
exprA -le *exprB*	*exprA* is less than or equal to *exprB*
exprA -ge *exprB*	*exprA* is greater than or equal to *exprB*
exprA -a *exprB*	*exprA* is true and *exprB* is true
exprA -o *exprB*	*exprA* is true or *exprB* is true

[a] Only available in *bash* version 3.0 and later. May only be used inside [[...]].

I/O Redirection

Table A-10 is a complete list of I/O redirectors. Note that there are two formats for specifying STDOUT and STDERR redirection: &>*file* and >&*file*. The second of these (which is the one used throughout this book) is the preferred way.

Table A-10. Input/output redirection

Redirector	Function
cmd1 | *cmd2*	Pipe; take standard output of *cmd1* as standard input to *cmd2*.
> *file*	Direct standard output to *file*.
< *file*	Take standard input from *file*.
>> *file*	Direct standard output to *file*; append to *file* if it already exists.
>| *file*	Force standard output to *file* even if noclobber is set.
n>| *file*	Force output to *file* from file descriptor n even if noclobber is set.
<> *file*	Use *file* as both standard input and standard output.
n<> *file*	Use *file* as both input and output for file descriptor *n*.
<< *label*	Here-document.
n> *file*	Direct file descriptor *n* to *file*.
n< *file*	Take file descriptor *n* from *file*.
n>> *file*	Direct file descriptor *n* to *file*; append to *file* if it already exists.
n>&	Duplicate standard output to file descriptor *n*.
n<&	Duplicate standard input from file descriptor *n*.
n>&*m*	File descriptor *n* is made to be a copy of the output file descriptor m.
n<&*m*	File descriptor *n* is made to be a copy of the input file descriptor m.
&>*file*	Directs standard output and standard error to *file*.
<&-	Close the standard input.
>&-	Close the standard output.
n>&-	Close the output from file descriptor *n*.
n<&-	Close the input from file descriptor *n*.
n>&*word*	If *n* is not specified, the standard output (file descriptor 1) is used; if the digits in word do not specify a file descriptor open for output, a redirection error occurs; as a special case, if *n* is omitted, and *word* does not expand to one or more digits, the standard output and standard error are redirected as described previously.
n<&*word*	If *word* expands to one or more digits, the file descriptor denoted by *n* is made to be a copy of that file descriptor; if the digits in word do not specify a file descriptor open for input, a redirection error occurs; if word evaluates to -, file descriptor *n* is closed; if *n* is not specified, the standard input (file descriptor 0) is used.
n>&*digit*-	Moves the file descriptor digit to file descriptor *n*, or the standard output (file descriptor 1) if *n* is not specified.
n<&*digit*-	Moves the file descriptor digit to file descriptor *n*, or the standard input (file descriptor 0) if *n* is not specified; digit is closed after being duplicated to *n*.

echo Options and Escape Sequences

echo accepts a number of arguments (see Table A-11).

Table A-11. echo options

Options	Function
-e	Turns on the interpretation of backslash-escaped characters
-E	Turns off the interpretation of backslash-escaped characters on systems where this mode is the default
-n	Omits the final newline (same as the \c escape sequence)

echo accepts a number of escape sequences that start with a backslash.

These sequences in Table A-12 exhibit fairly predictable behavior, except for \f, which on some displays causes a screen clear while on others it causes a line feed, and it ejects the page on most printers. \v is somewhat obsolete; it usually causes a line feed.

Table A-12. echo escape sequences

Sequence	Character printed
\a	Alert or Ctrl-G (bell)
\b	Backspace or Ctrl-H
\c	Omit final newline
\e	Escape character (same as \E)
\E	Escape character
\f	Formfeed or Ctrl-L
\n	Newline (not at end of command) or Ctrl-J
\r	Return (Enter) or Ctrl-M
\t	Tab or Ctrl-I
\v	Vertical Tab or Ctrl-K
\n*nnn*	The eight-bit character whose value is the octal (base-8) value *nnn* where *nnn* is 1 to 3 digits
\0*nnn*	The eight-bit character whose value is the octal (base-8) value *nnn* where *nnn* is 0 to 3 digits
\x*HH*	The eight-bit character whose value is the hexadecimal (base-16) value *HH* (one or two digits)
\\	Single backslash

The \n, \0, and \x sequences are even more device-dependent and can be used for complex I/O, such as cursor control and special graphics characters.

printf

The *printf* command, available in *bash* since version 2.02, has two parts (beyond the command name): a format string and a variable number of arguments:

```
printf format-string [arguments]
```

format-string describes the format specifications; this is best supplied as a string constant in quotes. *arguments* is a list, such as a list of strings or variable values that correspond to the format specifications.

The format is reused as necessary to use up all of the arguments. If the format requires more arguments than are supplied, the extra format specifications behave as if a zero value or null string, as appropriate, had been supplied.

A format specification is preceded by a percent sign (%), and the specifier is one of the characters described below. Two of the main format specifiers are %s for strings and %d for decimal integers (see Table A-13).

Table A-13. printf format specifiers

Format character	Meaning
%c	ASCII character (prints first character of corresponding argument)
%d, %i	Decimal (base 10) integer
%e	Floating-point format ([-]d.*precision*e[+-]dd)—see the text after the table for the meaning of *precision*
%E	Floating-point format ([-]d.*precision*E[+-]dd)
%f	Floating-point format ([-]ddd.*precision*)
%g	%e or %f conversion, whichever is shorter, with trailing zeros removed
%G	%E or %f conversion, whichever is shortest, with trailing zeros removed
%o	Unsigned octal value
%s	String
%u	Unsigned decimal value
%x	Unsigned hexadecimal number; uses a-f for 10 to 15
%X	Unsigned hexadecimal number; uses A-F for 10 to 15
%%	Literal %

The *printf* command can be used to specify the width and alignment of output fields. A format expression can take three optional modifiers following % and preceding the format specifier:

```
%flags width.precision format-specifier
```

The width of the output field is a numeric value. When you specify a field width, the contents of the field are right-justified by default. You must specify a flag of - to get left-justification (the rest of the flags are shown in the table). Thus, %-20s outputs a left-justified string in a field 20-characters wide. If the string is less than 20 characters, the field is padded with whitespace to fill. In the following examples, we put our format specifier between a pair of | in our format string so you can see the width of the field in the output. The first example right-justifies the text:

```
printf "|%10s|\n" hello@
```

It produces:

```
|     hello|
```

The next example left-justifies the text:

```
printf "|%-10s|\n" hello
```

It produces:

```
|hello     |
```

The precision modifier, used for decimal or floating-point values, controls the number of digits that appear in the result. For string values, it controls the maximum number of characters from the string that will be printed.

You can even specify both the width and precision dynamically, via values in the *printf* argument list. You do this by specifying asterisks in the format expression, instead of literal values:

```
$ myvar=42.123456
$ mysig=6
$ printf "|%*.*G|\n" 5 $mysig $myvar
|42.1235|
```

In this example, the width is 5, the precision is 6, and the value to print comes from the value of $myvar. The precision is optional and its exact meaning varies by control letter, as shown in Table A-14.

Table A-14. Meaning of "precision" based on printf format specifier

Format	What "precision" means
%d, %I, %o, %u, %x, %X	The minimum number of digits to print. When the value has fewer digits, it is padded with leading zeros. The default precision is 1.
%e, %E	The minimum number of digits to print. When the value has fewer digits, it is padded with zeros after the decimal point. The default precision is 10. A precision of 0 inhibits printing of the decimal point.
%f	The number of digits to the right of the decimal point.
%g, %G	The maximum number of significant digits.
%s	The maximum number of characters to print.
%b	[POSIX Shell—may be nonportable to other versions of *printf*.] When used instead of %s, expands *echo*-style escape sequences in the argument string (see Table A-15).
%q	[POSIX Shell—may be nonportable to other versions of *printf*.] When used instead of %s, prints the string argument in such a way that it can be used for shell input.

%b and %q are additions to *bash* (and other POSIX compliant shells) which provide useful features at the expense of nonportability to versions of the *printf* command found in some other shells and in other places in Unix. Here are two examples to make their functions a little clearer:

%q shell quotes:

```
$ printf "%q\n" "greetings to the world"
greetings\ to\ the\ world
```

%b *echo*-style escapes:

```
$ printf "%s\n" 'hello\nworld'
hello\nworld
$ printf "%b\n" 'hello\nworld'
hello
world
```

Table A-15 shows the escape sequences that will be translated in a string printed with the %b format.

Table A-15. printf escape sequences

Escape sequence	Meaning
\e	Escape character
\a	Bell character
\b	Backspace character
\f	Form-feed character
\n	Newline character
\r	Carriage return character
\t	Tab character
\v	Vertical tab character
\'	Single-quote character
\"	Double-quote character
\\	Backslash character
nnn	8-bit character whose ASCII value is the 1, 2, or 3 digit octal number *nnn*
xHH	8-bit character whose ASCII value is the 1 or 2 digit hexadecimal number *HH*

Finally, one or more flags may precede the field width and the precision in a *printf* format specifier. We've already seen the - flag for left-justification. The rest of the flags are shown in Table A-16.

Table A-16. printf flags

Character	Description
-	Left-justify the formatted value within the field.
space	Prefix positive values with a space and negative values with a minus.

Character	Description
+	Always prefix numeric values with a sign, even if the value is positive.
#	Use an alternate form: %o has a preceding 0; %x and %X are prefixed with 0x and 0X, respectively; %e, %E and %f always have a decimal point in the result; and %g and %G do not have trailing zeros removed.
0	Pad output with *zeros*, not spaces. This only happens when the field width is wider than the converted result. In the C language, this flag applies to all output formats, even non-numeric ones. For *bash*, it only applies to the numeric formats.
'	Format with thousands' grouping characters if %i, %d, %u, %f, %F, %g, or %G (although this is POSIX, it's still not always implemented).

Examples

These examples for *printf* use some shell variables, assigned as follows in Table A-17:

```
PI=3.141592653589
```

Table A-17. printf examples

printf statement	Result	Comment
printf '%f\n' $PI	3.141593	Note the default rounding.
# not what you want printf '%f.5\n' $PI	3.14.5	A common mistake—the format specifier should be on the other side of the %f; since it isn't, the .5 is just appended like any text.
printf '%.5f\n' $PI	3.14159	Gives five places to the right of the decimal point.
printf '%+.2f\n' $PI	+3.14	Leading + sign, only two digits to the right of the decimal point.
printf '[%.4s]\n' s string	[s] [stri]	Truncates to four characters; with only one character, we get only one character-wide output, not reuse of format string.
printf '[%4s]\n' s string	[s] [string]	Assures us of a minimum four-character field width, right-justified; doesn't truncate, though.
printf '[%-4.4s]\n' s string	[s] [stri]	Does it all—minimum width of four, maximum width of four, truncating if necessary, and left justifies (due to the minus sign) if shorter than four.

Here is one more example that will not display well in the table. The traditional way to write *printf* statements is to embed all formatting, including things like newlines, in the format string. This is shown in the table. That is encouraged, but you don't have to do it that way, and sometimes it's easier if you don't. Note the → denotes a Tab character in the output:

```
$ printf "%b" "\aRing terminal bell, then tab\t then newline\nThen line 2.\n"
Ring terminal bell, then tab → then newline
Then line 2.
```

See Also

- *http://www.opengroup.org/onlinepubs/009695399/functions/printf.html*

Date and Time String Formatting with strftime

Table A-18 shows common date and time string formatting options. Consult your system's manpages for *date* and *strftime*(3), as both the options and what they mean vary from system to system.

Table A-18. strftime format codes

Format	Description
%%	A literal %.
%a	The locale's abbreviated weekday name (Sun..Sat).
%A	The locale's full weekday name (Sunday..Saturday).
%B	The locale's full month name (January..December).
%b or %h	The locale's abbreviated month name (Jan..Dec).
%c	The locale's default/preferred date and time representation.
%C	The century (a year divided by 100 and truncated to an integer) as a decimal number (00..99).
%d	The day of the month as a decimal number (01..31).
%D	The date in the format %m/%d/%y (MM/DD/YY). Note that the United States uses MM/DD/YY while everyone else uses DD/MM/YY, so this format is ambiguous and should be avoided. Use %F instead, since it's a recognized standard and it sorts well.
%e	The day of month as a blank padded decimal number (1..31).
%F	The date in the format %Y-%m-%d (the ISO 8601 date format: CCYY-MM-DD); except when it's the full month name, as on HP-UX.
%g	The two-digit year corresponding to the %V week number (YY).
%G	The four-digit year corresponding to the %V week number (CCYY).
%H	The hour (24-hour clock) as a decimal number (00..23).
%h or %b	The locale's abbreviated month name (Jan..Dec).
%I	The hour (12-hour clock) as a decimal number (01..12).
%j	The day of the year as a decimal number (001..366).
%k	The hour (24-hour clock) as a blank padded decimal number (0..23).
%l	The hour (12-hour clock) as a blank padded decimal number (1,12).
%m	The month as a decimal number (01..12).
%M	The minute as a decimal number (00..59).
%n	A literal newline.
%N	Nanoseconds (000000000..999999999). [GNU]
%p	The locale's equivalent of either "AM" or "PM".
%P	The locale's equivalent of either "am" or "pm". [GNU]

Table A-18. strftime format codes (continued)

Format	Description
%r	The locale's representation of 12-hour clock time using AM/PM notation (HH:MM:SS AM/PM).
%R	The time in the format %H : %M (HH:MM).
%s	The number of seconds since the Epoch, UTC (January 1, 1970 at 00:00:00).
%S	The second as a decimal number (00..61). The range of seconds is (00-61) instead of (00-59) to allow for the periodic occurrence of leap seconds and double leap seconds.
%t	A literal tab.
%T	The time in the format %H : %M : %S (HH:MM:SS).
%u	The weekday (Monday as the first day of the week) as a decimal number (1..7).
%U	The week number of the year (Sunday as the first day of the week) as a decimal number (00..53).
%v	The date in the format %e - %b - %Y (D-MMM-CCYY). [Not standard]
%V	The week number of the year (Monday as the first day of the week) as a decimal number (01..53). According to ISO 8601 the week containing January 1 is week 1 if it has four or more days in the new year, otherwise it is week 53 of the previous year, and the next week is week 1. The year is given by the %G conversion specification.
%w	The weekday (Sunday as the first day of the week) as a decimal number (0..6).
%W	The week number of the year (Monday as the first day of the week) as a decimal number (00..53).
%x	The locale's appropriate date representation.
%X	The locale's appropriate time representation.
%y	The year without century as a decimal number (00..99).
%Y	The year with century as a decimal number.
%z	The offset from UTC in the ISO 8601 format [-] hhmm.
%Z	The time zone name.

Pattern-Matching Characters

The material in this section is adapted from the Bash Reference Manual (*http://www.gnu.org/software/bash/manual/bashref.html*; see Table A-19).

Table A-19. Pattern-matching characters

Character	Meaning
*	Matches any string, including the null string.
?	Matches any single character.
[...]	Matches any one of the enclosed characters.
[! ...] or [^ ...]	Matches any character not enclosed.

The following POSIX *character classes* may be used within [ ], e.g., [[:alnum:]]; consult the *grep* or *egrep* manpage on your system for more details.

```
[[:alnum:]]    [[:alpha:]]    [[:ascii:]]    [[:blank:]]    [[:cntrl:]]    [[:digit:]]
[[:graph:]]    [[:lower:]]    [[:print:]]    [[:punct:]]    [[:space:]]    [[:upper:]]
[[:word:]]     [[:xdigit:]]
```

The word character class matches letters, digits, and the character _.

[=c=] matches all characters with the same collation weight (as defined by the current locale) as the character c, while [.*symbol*.] matches the collating symbol *symbol*.

These character classes are affected by the locale setting. To get the traditional Unix values, use LC_COLLATE=C or LC_ALL=C.

extglob Extended Pattern-Matching Operators

The operators in Table A-20 apply when using shopt -s extglob. Matches are case-sensitive, but you may use shopt -s nocasematch (*bash* 3.1+) to change that. This option affects case and [[commands.

Table A-20. extglob extended pattern-matching operators

Grouping	Meaning
@(...)	Only one occurrence
*(...)	Zero or more occurrences
+(...)	One or more occurrences
?(...)	Zero or one occurrences
!(...)	Not these occurrences, but anything else

tr Escape Sequences

Table A-21. tr escape sequences

Sequence	Meaning
\ooo	Character with octal value ooo (1-3 octal digits)
\\	A backslash character (i.e., escapes the backslash itself)
\a	"Audible" bell, the ASCII BEL character (since "b" was taken for backspace)
\b	Backspace
\f	Form feed
\n	Newline
\r	Return
\t	Tab (sometimes called a horizontal tab)
\v	Vertical tab

Readline Init File Syntax

The GNU Readline library provides the command line on which you type to communicate with *bash* and some other GNU utilities. It is amazingly configurable, but most people are not aware of this.

Tables A-22, A-23, and A-24 are a subset of what is available to work with. See the Readline documentation for the full details.

The following is adapted directly from Chet Ramey's documentation (*http://tiswww. tis.case.edu/~chet/readline/readline.html*).

You can modify the run-time behavior of Readline by altering the values of variables in Readline using the *set* command within the *init* file. The syntax is simple:

```
set variable value
```

Here, for example, is how to change from the default Emacs-like key binding to use *vi* line-editing commands:

```
set editing-mode vi
```

Variable names and values, where appropriate, are recognized without regard to case. Unrecognized variable names are ignored.

Boolean variables (those that can be set to on or off) are set to on if the value is null or empty, on (case-insensitive), or 1. Any other value results in the variable being set to off.

Table A-22. Readline configuration settings

Variable	Description
bell-style	Controls what happens when Readline wants to ring the terminal bell. If set to none, Readline never rings the bell. If set to visible, Readline uses a visible bell if one is available. If set to audible (the default), Readline attempts to ring the terminal's bell.
bind-tty-special-chars	If set to on, Readline attempts to bind the control characters treated specially by the kernel's terminal driver to their Readline equivalents.
comment-begin	The string to insert at the beginning of the line when the insert-comment command is executed. The default value is #.
completion-ignore-case	If set to on, Readline performs filename matching and completion in a case-insensitive fashion. The default value is off.
completion-query-items	The number of possible completions that determines when the user is asked whether the list of possibilities should be displayed. If the number of possible completions is greater than this value, Readline will ask the user whether he wishes to view them; otherwise, they are simply listed. This variable must be set to an integer value greater than or equal to 0. A negative value means Readline should never ask. The default limit is 100.
convert-meta	If set to on, Readline will convert characters with the eighth bit set to an ASCII key sequence by stripping the eighth bit and prefixing an Esc character, converting them to a meta-prefixed key sequence. The default value is on.

Variable	Description
disable-completion	If set to on, Readline will inhibit word completion. Completion characters will be inserted into the line as if they had been mapped to self-insert. The default is off.
editing-mode	The editing-mode variable controls which default set of key bindings is used. By default, Readline starts up in Emacs editing mode, where the keystrokes are most similar to Emacs. This variable can be set to either emacs or vi.
enable-keypad	When set to on, Readline will try to enable the application keypad when it is called. Some systems need this to enable the arrow keys. The default is off.
expand-tilde	If set to on, tilde (~) expansion is performed when Readline attempts word completion. The default is off.
history-preserve-point	If set to on, the history code attempts to place the point (the current cursor position) at the same location on each history line retrieved with previous-history or next-history. The default is off.
horizontal-scroll-mode	This variable can be set to either on or off. Setting it to on means that the text of the lines being edited will scroll horizontally on a single screen line when they are longer than the width of the screen, instead of wrapping onto a new screen line. By default, this variable is set to off.
input-meta	If set to on, Readline will enable eight-bit input (it will not clear the eighth bit in the characters it reads), regardless of what the terminal claims it can support. The default value is off. The name meta-flag is a synonym for this variable.
isearch-terminators	The string of characters that should terminate an incremental search without subsequently executing the character as a command. If this variable has not been given a value, the characters Esc and C-J will terminate an incremental search.
keymap	Sets Readline's idea of the current keymap for key binding commands. Acceptable keymap names are emacs, emacs-standard, emacs-meta, emacs-ctlx, vi, vi-move, vi-command, and vi-insert. vi is equivalent to vi-command; emacs is equivalent to emacs-standard. The default value is emacs. The value of the editing-mode variable also affects the default keymap.
mark-directories	If set to on, completed directory names have a slash appended. The default is on.
mark-modified-lines	This variable, when set to on, causes Readline to display an asterisk (*) at the start of history lines that have been modified. This variable is off by default.
mark-symlinked-directories	If set to on, completed names which are symbolic links to directories have a slash appended (subject to the value of mark-directories). The default is off.
match-hidden-files	This variable, when set to on, causes Readline to match files whose names begin with a . (hidden files) when performing filename completion, unless the leading . is supplied by the user in the filename to be completed. This variable is on by default.
output-meta	If set to on, Readline will display characters with the eighth bit set directly rather than as a meta-prefixed escape sequence. The default is off.
page-completions	If set to on, Readline uses an internal *more*-like pager to display a screenful of possible completions at a time. This variable is on by default.
print-completions-horizontally	If set to on, Readline will display completions with matches sorted horizontally in alphabetical order, rather than down the screen. The default is off.
show-all-if-ambiguous	This alters the default behavior of the completion functions. If set to on, words that have more than one possible completion cause the matches to be listed immediately instead of ringing the bell. The default value is off.

Variable	Description
show-all-if-unmodified	This alters the default behavior of the completion functions in a fashion similar to show-all-if-ambiguous. If set to on, words that have more than one possible completion without any possible partial completion (the possible completions don't share a common prefix) cause the matches to be listed immediately instead of ringing the bell. The default value is off.
visible-stats	If set to on, a character denoting a file's type is appended to the filename when listing possible completions. The default is off.

emacs Mode Commands

The material in this section also appears in *Learning the bash Shell* by Cameron Newham (O'Reilly).

Table A-23 is a complete list of readline Emacs editing mode commands.

Table A-23. emacs mode commands

Command	Meaning
Ctrl-A	Move to beginning of line.
Ctrl-B	Move backward one character.
Ctrl-D	Delete one character forward.
Ctrl-E	Move to end of line.
Ctrl-F	Move forward one character.
Ctrl-G	Abort the current editing command and ring the terminal bell.
Ctrl-J	Same as Return.
Ctrl-K	Delete (kill) forward to end of line.
Ctrl-L	Clear screen and redisplay the line.
Ctrl-M	Same as Return.
Ctrl-N	Next line in command history.
Ctrl-O	Same as Return, then display next line in history file.
Ctrl-P	Previous line in command history.
Ctrl-R	Search backward.
Ctrl-S	Search forward.
Ctrl-T	Transpose two characters.
Ctrl-U	Kill backward from point to the beginning of line.
Ctrl-V	Make the next character typed verbatim.
Ctrl-V Tab	Insert a Tab.
Ctrl-W	Kill the word behind the cursor, using whitespace as the boundary.
Ctrl-X /	List the possible filename completions of the current word.
Ctrl-X ~	List the possible username completions of the current word.

Table A-23. emacs mode commands (continued)

Command	Meaning
Ctrl-X $	List the possible shell variable completions of the current word.
Ctrl-X @	List the possible hostname completions of the current word.
Ctrl-X !	List the possible command name completions of the current word.
Ctrl-X (	Begin saving characters into the current keyboard macro.
Ctrl-X)	Stop saving characters into the current keyboard macro.
Ctrl-X e	Re-execute the last keyboard macro defined.
Ctrl-X Ctrl-R	Read in the contents of the *readline* initialization file.
Ctrl-X Ctrl-V	Display version information on this instance of *bash*.
Ctrl-Y	Retrieve (yank) last item killed.
Delete	Delete one character backward.
Ctrl-[	Same as Esc (most keyboards).
Esc-B	Move one word backward.
Esc-C	Change word after point to all capital letters.
Esc-D	Delete one word forward.
Esc-F	Move one word forward.
Esc-L	Change word after point to all lowercase letters.
Esc-N	Nonincremental forward search.
Esc-P	Nonincremental reverse search.
Esc-R	Undo all the changes made to this line.
Esc-T	Transpose two words.
Esc-U	Change word after point to all uppercase letters.
Esc-Ctrl-E	Perform shell alias, history, and word expansion on the line.
Esc-Ctrl-H	Delete one word backward.
Esc-Ctrl-Y	Insert the first argument to the previous command (usually the second word) at point.
Esc-Delete	Delete one word backward.
Esc-^	Perform history expansion on the line.
Esc-<	Move to first line of history file.
Esc->	Move to last line of history file.
Esc-.	Insert last word in previous command line after point.
Esc-_	Same as above.
Tab	Attempt filename completion on current word.
Esc-?	List the possible completions of the text before point.
Esc-/	Attempt filename completion on current word.
Esc-~	Attempt username completion on current word.
Esc-$	Attempt variable completion on current word.
Esc-@	Attempt hostname completion on current word.

Command	Meaning
Esc-!	Attempt command name completion on current word.
Esc-Tab	Attempt completion from text in the command history.
Esc-~	Attempt tilde expansion on the current word.
Esc-\	Delete all the spaces and Tabs around point.
Esc-*	Insert all of the completions that would be generated by Esc-= before point.
Esc-=	List the possible completions before point.
Esc-{	Attempt filename completion and return the list to the shell enclosed within braces.

vi Control Mode Commands

The material in this section also appears in *Learning the bash Shell* by Cameron Newham (O'Reilly).

Table A-24 shows a complete list of readline *vi* control mode commands.

Table A-24. vi mode commands

Command	Meaning
h	Move left one character.
l	Move right one character.
w	Move right one word.
b	Move left one word.
W	Move to beginning of next nonblank word.
B	Move to beginning of preceding nonblank word.
e	Move to end of current word.
E	Move to end of current nonblank word.
0	Move to beginning of line.
.	Repeat the last a insertion.
^	Move to first nonblank character in line.
$	Move to end of line.
i	Insert text before current character.
a	Insert text after current character.
I	Insert text at beginning of line.
A	Insert text at end of line.
R	Overwrite existing text.
dh	Delete one character backward.
dl	Delete one character forward.
db	Delete one word backward.

Table A-24. vi mode commands (continued)

Command	Meaning
dw	Delete one word forward.
dB	Delete one nonblank word backward.
dW	Delete one nonblank word forward.
d$	Delete to end of line.
d0	Delete to beginning of line.
D	Equivalent to d$ (delete to end of line).
dd	Equivalent to 0d$ (delete entire line).
C	Equivalent to c$ (delete to end of line, enter input mode).
cc	Equivalent to 0c$ (delete entire line, enter input mode).
x	Equivalent to dl (delete character forwards).
X	Equivalent to dh (delete character backwards).
k or -	Move backward one line.
j or +	Move forward one line.
G	Move to line given by repeat count.
/*string*	Search forward for *string*.
?*string*	Search backward for *string*.
n	Repeat search forward.
N	Repeat search backward.
f*x*	Move right to next occurrence of *x*.
F*x*	Move left to previous occurrence of *x*.
t*x*	Move right to next occurrence of *x*, then back one space.
T*x*	Move left to previous occurrence of *x*, then forward one space.
;	Redo last character finding command.
,	Redo last character finding command in opposite direction.
\	Do filename completion.
*	Do wildcard expansion (onto command line).
\=	Do wildcard expansion (as printed list).
~	Invert (twiddle) case of current character(s).
\	Append last word of previous command, enter input mode.
Ctrl-L	Start a new line and redraw the current line on it.
#	Prepend # (comment character) to the line and send it to history.

Table of ASCII Values

Many of our favorite computer books have an ASCII chart. Even in the era of GUIs and web servers you may be surprised to find that you still need to look up a character every now and then. It's certainly useful when working with *tr* or finding some special sequence of escape characters.

Int	Octal	Hex	ASCII	Int	Octal	Hex	ASCII
0	000	00	^@	31	037	1f	^_
1	001	01	^A	32	040	20	
2	002	02	^B	33	041	21	!
3	003	03	^C	34	042	22	"
4	004	04	^D	35	043	23	#
5	005	05	^E	36	044	24	$
6	006	06	^F	37	045	25	%
7	007	07	^G	38	046	26	&
8	010	08	^H	39	047	27	'
9	011	09	^I	40	050	28	(
10	012	0a	^J	41	051	29	)
11	013	0b	^K	42	052	2a	*
12	014	0c	^L	43	053	2b	+
13	015	0d	^M	44	054	2c	,
14	016	0e	^N	45	055	2d	-
15	017	0f	^O	46	056	2e	.
16	020	10	^P	47	057	2f	/
17	021	11	^Q	48	060	30	0
18	022	12	^R	49	061	31	1
19	023	13	^S	50	062	32	2
20	024	14	^T	51	063	33	3
21	025	15	^U	52	064	34	4
22	026	16	^V	53	065	35	5
23	027	17	^W	54	066	36	6
24	030	18	^X	55	067	37	7
25	031	19	^Y	56	070	38	8
26	032	1a	^Z	57	071	39	9
27	033	1b	^[	58	072	3a	:
28	034	1c	^\	59	073	3b	;
29	035	1d	^]	60	074	3c	<
30	036	1e	^^	61	075	3d	=

Int	Octal	Hex	ASCII	Int	Octal	Hex	ASCII
62	076	3e	>	95	137	5f	_
63	077	3f	?	96	140	60	`
64	100	40	@	97	141	61	a
65	101	41	A	98	142	62	b
66	102	42	B	99	143	63	c
67	103	43	C	100	144	64	d
68	104	44	D	101	145	65	e
69	105	45	E	102	146	66	f
70	106	46	F	103	147	67	g
71	107	47	G	104	150	68	h
72	110	48	H	105	151	69	i
73	111	49	I	106	152	6a	j
74	112	4a	J	107	153	6b	k
75	113	4b	K	108	154	6c	l
76	114	4c	L	109	155	6d	m
77	115	4d	M	110	156	6e	n
78	116	4e	N	111	157	6f	o
79	117	4f	O	112	160	70	p
80	120	50	P	113	161	71	q
81	121	51	Q	114	162	72	r
82	122	52	R	115	163	73	s
83	123	53	S	116	164	74	t
84	124	54	T	117	165	75	u
85	125	55	U	118	166	76	v
86	126	56	V	119	167	77	w
87	127	57	W	120	170	78	x
88	130	58	X	121	171	79	y
89	131	59	Y	122	172	7a	z
90	132	5a	Z	123	173	7b	{
91	133	5b	[	124	174	7c		
92	134	5c	\	125	175	7d	}
93	135	5d	]	126	176	7e	~
94	136	5e	^	127	177	7f	^?

APPENDIX B
Examples Included with bash

The *bash* tarball archive includes an examples directory that is well worth exploring (after you've finished reading this book, of course). It includes sample code, scripts, functions, and startup files.

Startup-Files Directory Examples

The *startup-files* directory provides many examples of what you can put in your own startup files. In particular, *bash_aliases* has many useful aliases. Bear in mind that if you copy these files wholesale, you'll have to edit them for your system because many of the paths will be different. Refer to Chapter 16 for further information on changing these files to suit your needs.

The *functions* directory contains many function definitions that you might find useful. Among them are:

basename
> The *basename* utility, missing from some systems

dirfuncs
> Directory manipulation facilities

dirname
> The *dirname* utility, missing from some systems

whatis
> An implementation of the Tenth Edition Bourne shell *whatis* built-in

whence
> An almost exact clone of the Korn shell *whence* built-in

If you come from a Korn shell background, you may find *kshenv* especially helpful. This contains function definitions for some common Korn facilities such as *whence*, *print*, and the two-parameter *cd* built-ins.

The *scripts* directory contains many examples of *bash* scripts. The two largest scripts are examples of the complex things you can do with shell scripts. The first is a (rather amusing) adventure game interpreter and the second is a C shell interpreter. The other scripts include examples of precedence rules, a scrolling text display, a "spinning wheel" progress display, and how to prompt the user for a particular type of answer.

Not only are the script and function examples useful for including in your environment, they also provide many alternative examples that you can learn from when reading this book. We encourage you to experiment with them.

Table B-1 is an index of what you will find as of *bash* 3.1 or newer.

Table B-1. Paths for bash 3.1 and newer

Path	Description	X-ref
./bashdb	Deprecated sample implementation of a *bash* debugger.	
./complete	Shell completion code.	
./functions	Example functions.	
./functions/array-stuff	Various array functions (`ashift`, `array_sort`, `reverse`).	
./functions/array-to-string	Convert an array to a string.	
./functions/autoload	An almost *ksh*-compatible 'autoload' (no lazy load).	ksh
./functions/autoload.v2	An almost *ksh*-compatible 'autoload' (no lazy load).	ksh
./functions/autoload.v3	A more *ksh*-compatible 'autoload' (with lazy load).	ksh
./functions/basename	A replacement for *basename*(1).	basename
./functions/basename2	Fast *basename*(1) and *dirname*(1) functions for *bash/sh*.	basename, dirname
./functions/coproc.bash	Start, control, and end co-processes.	
./functions/coshell.bash	Control shell co-processes (see *coprocess.bash*).	
./functions/coshell.README	*README* for `coshell` and `coproc`.	
./functions/csh-compat	A C-shell compatibility package.	csh
./functions/dirfuncs	Directory manipulation functions from the book *The Korn Shell*.	
./functions/dirname	A replacement for *dirname*(1).	dirname
./functions/emptydir	Find out if a directory is empty.	
./functions/exitstat	Display the exit status of processes.	
./functions/external	Like `command`, but forces the use of external command.	
./functions/fact	Recursive factorial function.	
./functions/fstty	Front-end to sync TERM changes to both *stty*(1) and *readline* 'bind'.	stty.bash
./functions/func	Print out definitions for functions named by arguments.	
./functions/gethtml	Get a web page from a remote server (*wget*(1) in *bash*).	
./functions/getoptx.bash	*getopt* function that parses long-named options.	

Path	Description	X-ref
./functions/inetaddr	Internet address conversion (*inet2hex* and *hex2inet*).	
./functions/inpath	Return zero if the argument is in the path and executable.	inpath
./functions/isnum.bash	Test user input on numeric or character value.	
./functions/isnum2	Test user input on numeric values, with floating point.	
./functions/isvalidip	Test user input for valid IP addresses.	
./functions/jdate.bash	Julian date conversion.	
./functions/jj.bash	Look for running jobs.	
./functions/keep	Try to keep some programs in the foreground and running.	
./functions/ksh-cd	*ksh*-like *cd*: cd [-LP] [dir [change]].	ksh
./functions/ksh-compat-test	*ksh*-like arithmetic test replacements.	ksh
./functions/kshenv	Functions and aliases to provide the beginnings of a *ksh* environment for *bash*.	ksh
./functions/login	Replace the *login* and *newgrp* built-ins in old Bourne shells.	
./functions/lowercase	Rename files to lowercase.	rename lower
./functions/manpage	Find and print a manpage.	fman
./functions/mhfold	Print MH folders, useful only because *folders*(1) doesn't print mod date/times.	
./functions/notify.bash	Notify when jobs change status.	
./functions/pathfuncs	Path related functions (no_path, add_path, pre-path, del_path).	path
./functions/README	*README*	
./functions/recurse	Recursive directory traverser.	
./functions/repeat2	A clone of the C shell built-in *repeat*.	repeat, csh
./functions/repeat3	A clone of the C shell built-in *repeat*.	repeat, csh
./functions/seq	Generate a sequence from *m* to *n*; *m* defaults to 1.	
./functions/seq2	Generate a sequence from *m* to *n*; *m* defaults to 1.	
./functions/shcat	Readline-based pager.	cat, readline pager
./functions/shcat2	Readline-based pagers.	cat, readline pager
./functions/sort-pos-params	Sort the positional parameters.	
./functions/substr	A function to emulate the ancient *ksh* built-in.	ksh
./functions/substr2	A function to emulate the ancient *ksh* built-in.	ksh
./functions/term	A shell function to set the terminal type interactively or not.	
./functions/whatis	An implementation of the 10th Edition Unix *sh* built-in *whatis*(1) command.	
./functions/whence	An almost *ksh*-compatible *whence*(1) command.	
./functions/which	An emulation of *which*(1) as it appears in FreeBSD.	
./functions/xalias.bash	Convert *csh* alias commands to *bash* functions.	csh, aliasconv

Path	Description	X-ref
./functions/xfind.bash	A *find*(1) clone.	
./loadables/	Example loadable replacements.	
./loadables/basename.c	Return nondirectory portion of pathname.	basename
./loadables/cat.c	*cat*(1) replacement with no options—the way *cat* was intended.	cat, readline pager
./loadables/cut.c	*cut*(1) replacement.	
./loadables/dirname.c	Return directory portion of pathname.	dirname
./loadables/finfo.c	Print file info.	
./loadables/getconf.c	POSIX.2 *getconf* utility.	
./loadables/getconf.h	Replacement definitions for ones the system doesn't provide.	
./loadables/head.c	Copy first part of files.	
./loadables/hello.c	Obligatory "Hello World" / sample loadable.	
./loadables/id.c	POSIX.2 user identity.	
./loadables/ln.c	Make links.	
./loadables/logname.c	Print login name of current user.	
./loadables/Makefile.in	Simple makefile for the sample loadable built-ins.	
./loadables/mkdir.c	*Make* directories.	
./loadables/necho.c	*echo* without options or argument interpretation.	
./loadables/pathchk.c	Check pathnames for validity and portability.	
./loadables/print.c	Loadable *ksh-93* style *print* built-in.	
./loadables/printenv.c	Minimal built-in clone of BSD *printenv*(1).	
./loadables/push.c	Anyone remember TOPS-20?	
./loadables/README	*README*	
./loadables/realpath.c	Canonicalize pathnames, resolving symlinks.	
./loadables/rmdir.c	Remove directory.	
./loadables/sleep.c	Sleep for fractions of a second.	
./loadables/strftime.c	Loadable built-in interface to *strftime*(3).	
./loadables/sync.c	Sync the disks by forcing pending filesystem writes to complete.	
./loadables/tee.c	Duplicate standard input.	
./loadables/template.c	Example template for loadable built-in.	
./loadables/truefalse.c	True and false built-ins.	
./loadables/tty.c	Return terminal name.	
./loadables/uname.c	Print system information.	
./loadables/unlink.c	Remove a directory entry.	
./loadables/whoami.c	Print out username of current user.	

Path	Description	X-ref
./loadables/perl/	Illustrates how to build a Perl interpreter into *bash*.	
./misc	Miscellaneous	
./misc/aliasconv.bash	Convert *csh* aliases to *bash* aliases and functions.	csh, xalias
./misc/aliasconv.sh	Convert *csh* aliases to *bash* aliases and functions.	csh, xalias
./misc/cshtobash	Convert *csh* aliases, environment variables, and variables to *bash* equivalents.	csh, xalias
./misc/README	*README*	
./misc/suncmd.termcap	SunView TERMCAP string.	
./obashdb	Modified version of the Korn Shell debugger from Bill Rosenblatt's *Learning the Korn Shell*.	
./scripts.noah	Noah Friedman's collection of scripts (updated to *bash* v2 syntax by Chet Ramey).	
./scripts.noah/aref.bash	Pseudo-arrays and substring indexing examples.	
./scripts.noah/bash.sub.bash	Library functions used by *require.bash*.	
./scripts.noah/bash_version. bash	A function to slice up $BASH_VERSION.	
./scripts.noah/meta.bash	Enable and disable eight-bit *readline* input.	
./scripts.noah/mktmp.bash	Make a temporary file with a unique name.	
./scripts.noah/number.bash	A fun hack to translate numerals into English.	
./scripts.noah/PERMISSION	Permissions to use the scripts in this directory.	
./scripts.noah/prompt.bash	A way to set PS1 to some predefined strings.	
./scripts.noah/README	*README*	
./scripts.noah/remap_keys. bash	A front end to *bind* to redo *readline* bindings.	readline
./scripts.noah/require.bash	Lisp-like require/provide library functions for *bash*.	
./scripts.noah/send_mail. bash	Replacement SMTP client written in *bash*.	
./scripts.noah/shcat.bash	*bash* replacement for *cat*(1).	cat
./scripts.noah/source.bash	Replacement for source that uses current directory.	
./scripts.noah/string.bash	The *string*(3) functions at the shell level.	
./scripts.noah/stty.bash	Front-end to *stty*(1) that changes *readline* bindings too.	fstty
./scripts.noah/y_or_n_p. bash	Prompt for a yes/no/quit answer.	ask

Table B-1. Paths for bash 3.1 and newer (continued)

Path	Description	X-ref
./scripts.v2	John DuBois' *ksh* script collection (converted to *bash* v2 syntax by Chet Ramey).	
./scripts.v2/arc2tarz	Convert an *arc* archive to a compressed *tar* archive.	
./scripts.v2/bashrand	Random number generator with upper and lower bounds and optional seed.	random
./scripts.v2/cal2day.bash	Convert a day number to a name.	
./scripts.v2/cdhist.bash	*cd* replacement with a directory stack added.	
./scripts.v2/corename	Tell what produced a core file.	
./scripts.v2/fman	Fast *man*(1) replacement.	manpage
./scripts.v2/frcp	Copy files using *ftp*(1) but with *rcp*-type command-line syntax.	
./scripts.v2/lowercase	Change filenames to lowercase.	rename lower
./scripts.v2/ncp	A nicer front end for *cp*(1) (has -i, etc)..	
./scripts.v2/newext	Change the extension of a group of files.	rename
./scripts.v2/nmv	A nicer front end for *mv*(1) (has -i, etc)..	rename
./scripts.v2/pages	Print specified pages from files.	
./scripts.v2/PERMISSION	Permissions to use the scripts in this directory.	
./scripts.v2/pf	A pager front end that handles compressed files.	
./scripts.v2/pmtop	Poor man's *top*(1) for SunOS 4.x and BSD/OS.	
./scripts.v2/README	*README*	
./scripts.v2/ren	Rename files by changing parts of filenames that match a pattern.	rename
./scripts.v2/rename	Change the names of files that match a pattern.	rename
./scripts.v2/repeat	Execute a command multiple times.	repeat
./scripts.v2/shprof	Line profiler for *bash* scripts.	
./scripts.v2/untar	Unarchive a (possibly compressed) tarfile into a directory.	
./scripts.v2/uudec	Carefully *uudecode*(1) multiple files.	
./scripts.v2/uuenc	*uuencode*(1) multiple files.	
./scripts.v2/vtree	Print a visual display of a directory tree.	tree
./scripts.v2/where	Show where commands that match a pattern are.	
./scripts	Example scripts.	
./scripts/adventure.sh	Text adventure game in *bash*!	
./scripts/bcsh.sh	Bourne shell's C shell emulator.	csh
./scripts/cat.sh	Readline-based pager.	cat, readline pager
./scripts/center	Center a group of lines.	
./scripts/dd-ex.sh	Line editor using only /bin/sh, /bin/dd, and /bin/rm.	
./scripts/fixfiles.bash	Recurse a tree and fix files containing various bad characters.	
./scripts/hanoi.bash	The inevitable Towers of Hanoi in *bash*.	

Path	Description	X-ref
./scripts/inpath	Search $PATH for a file the same name as $1; return TRUE if found.	inpath
./scripts/krand.bash	Produces a random number within integer limits.	random
./scripts/line-input.bash	Line input routine for GNU Bourne Again Shell plus terminal-control primitives.	
./scripts/nohup.bash	*bash* version of *nohup* command.	
./scripts/precedence	Test relative precedences for && and || operators.	
./scripts/randomcard.bash	Print a random card from a card deck.	random
./scripts/README	*README*	
./scripts/scrollbar	Display scrolling text.	
./scripts/scrollbar2	Display scrolling text.	
./scripts/self-repro	A self-reproducing script (careful!).	
./scripts/showperm.bash	Convert *ls*(1) symbolic permissions into octal mode.	
./scripts/shprompt	Display a prompt and get an answer satisfying certain criteria.	ask
./scripts/spin.bash	Display a spinning wheel to show progress.	
./scripts/timeout	Give *rsh*(1) a shorter timeout.	
./scripts/vtree2	Display a tree printout of the direcotry with disk use in 1k blocks.	tree
./scripts/vtree3	Display a graphical tree printout of dir.	tree
./scripts/vtree3a	Display a graphical tree printout of dir.	tree
./scripts/websrv.sh	A web server in *bash*!	
./scripts/xterm_title	Print the contents of the *xterm* title bar.	
./scripts/zprintf	Emulate *printf* (obsolete since *printf* is now a *bash* built-in).	
./startup-files	Example startup files.	
./startup-files/Bash_aliases	Some useful aliases (written by Fox).	
./startup-files/Bash_profile	Sample startup file for *bash* login shells (written by Fox).	
./startup-files/bash-profile	Sample startup file for *bash* login shells (written by Ramey).	
./startup-files/bashrc	Sample Bourne Again Shell *init* file (written by Ramey).	
./startup-files/Bashrc.bfox	Sample Bourne Again Shell *init* file (written by Fox).	
./startup-files/README	*README*	
./startup-files/apple	Example startup files for Mac OS X.	
./startup-files/apple/aliases	Sample aliases for Mac OS X.	
./startup-files/apple/bash.defaults	Sample User preferences file.	
./startup-files/apple/environment	Sample Bourne Again Shell environment file.	
./startup-files/apple/login	Sample login wrapper.	

Table B-1. Paths for bash 3.1 and newer (continued)

Path	Description	X-ref
./startup-files/apple/logout	Sample logout wrapper.	
./startup-files/apple/rc	Sample Bourne Again Shell config file.	
./startup-files/apple/README	*README*	

APPENDIX C
Command-Line Processing

Throughout the book we've seen a variety of ways in which the shell processes input lines, especially using read. We can think of this process as a subset of the things the shell does when processing command lines. This appendix provides a more detailed description of the steps involved in processing the command line and how you can get *bash* to make a second pass with *eval*. The material in this appendix also appears in *Learning the bash Shell* by Cameron Newham (O'Reilly).

Command-Line Processing Steps

We've touched upon command-line processing throughout this book; we've mentioned how *bash* deals with single quotes (' '), double quotes (""), and backslashes (\); how it separates characters on a line into words, even allowing you to specify the delimiter it uses via the environment variable $IFS; how it assigns the words to shell variables (e.g., $1, $2, etc); and how it can redirect input and output to/from files or to other processes (pipeline). In order to be a real expert at shell scripting (or to debug some gnarly problems), you might need to understand the various steps involved in command-line processing—especially the order in which they occur.

Each line that the shell reads from STDIN or from a script is called a *pipeline* because it contains one or more *commands* separated by zero or more pipe characters (|). Figure C-1 shows the steps in command-line processing. For each pipeline it reads, the shell breaks it up into commands, sets up the I/O for the pipeline, then does the following for each command.

1. Splits the command into tokens that are separated by the fixed set of metacharacters: space, tab, newline, ;, (,), <, >, |, and &. Types of tokens include words, keywords, I/O redirectors, and semicolons.

2. Checks the first token of each command to see if it is a keyword with no quotes or backslashes. If it's an opening keyword such as if and other control-structure openers, function, {, or (, then the command is actually a *compound command*. The shell sets things up internally for the compound command, reads the next

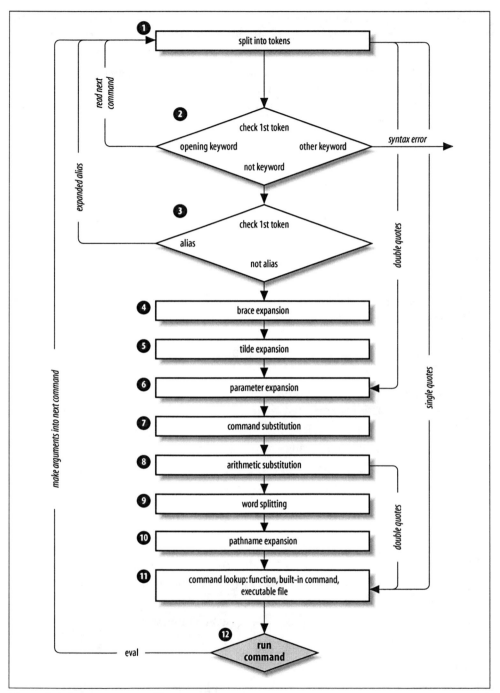

Figure C-1. Steps in command-line processing

command, and starts the process again. If the keyword isn't a compound command opener (e.g., it is a control-structure "middle" like then, else, or do; an "end" like fi or done; or a logical operator), the shell signals a syntax error.

3. Checks the first word of each command against the list of aliases. If a match is found, it substitutes the alias' definition and goes back to Step 1; otherwise, it goes on to Step 4. This scheme allows recursive aliases. It also allows aliases for keywords to be defined, e.g., alias aslongas=while or alias procedure=function.

4. Performs brace expansion. For example, a{b,c} becomes ab ac.

5. Substitutes the user's home directory ($HOME) for tilde if it is at the beginning of a word.

6. Substitutes user's home directory for ~user.

7. Performs parameter (variable) substitution for any expression that starts with a dollar sign ($).

8. Does command substitution for any expression of the form $(*string*).

9. Evaluates arithmetic expressions of the form $((*string*)).

10. Takes the parts of the line that resulted from parameter, command, and arithmetic substitution and splits them into words again. This time it uses the characters in $IFS as delimiters instead of the set of metacharacters in Step 1.

11. Performs pathname expansion, a.k.a. wildcard expansion, for any occurrences of *, ?, and [/] pairs.

12. Uses the first word as a command by looking up its source in the following order: as a function command, then as a built-in, then as a file in any of the directories in $PATH.

13. Runs the command after setting up I/O redirection and other such things.

That's a lot of steps—and it's not even the whole story! But before we go on, an example should make this process clearer. Assume that the following command has been run:

```
alias ll="ls -l"
```

Further assume that a file exists called *.hist537* in user *alice*'s home directory, which is */home/alice*, and that there is a double-dollar-sign variable $$ whose value is 2537 (remember $$ is the process ID, a number unique among all currently running processes).

Now let's see how the shell processes the following command:

```
ll $(type -path cc) ~alice/.*$(($$%1000))
```

Here is what happens to this line:

1. ll $(type -path cc) ~alice/.*$(($$%1000)) splits the input into words.

2. ll is not a keyword, so Step 2 does nothing.

3. `ls -l $(type -path cc) ~alice/.*$(($$%1000))` substitutes `ls -l` for its alias `ll`. The shell then repeats Steps 1 through 3; Step 2 splits the `ls -l` into two words.

4. `ls -l $(type -path cc) ~alice/.*$(($$%1000))` does nothing.

5. `ls -l $(type -path cc) /home/alice/.*$(($$%1000))` expands *~alice* into */home/alice*.

6. `ls -l $(type -path cc) /home/alice/.*$((2537%1000))` substitutes 2537 for $$.

7. `ls -l /usr/bin/cc /home/alice/.*$((2537%1000))` does command substitution on `type -path cc`.

8. `ls -l /usr/bin/cc /home/alice/.*537` evaluates the arithmetic expression 2537%1000.

9. `ls -l /usr/bin/cc /home/alice/.*537` does nothing.

10. `ls -l /usr/bin/cc /home/alice/.hist537` substitutes the filename for the wild-card expression `.*537`.

11. The command *ls* is found in */usr/bin*.

12. */usr/bin/ls* is run with the option -l and the two arguments.

Although this list of steps is fairly straightforward, it is not the whole story. There are still five ways to modify this process: quoting; using `command`, `builtin`, or `enable`; and using the advanced command `eval`.

Quoting

You can think of quoting as a way of getting the shell to skip some of the 12 steps described earlier. In particular:

- Single quotes (`''`) bypass everything from Step 1 through Step 10—including aliasing. All characters inside a pair of single quotes are untouched. You can't have single quotes inside single quotes—even if you precede them with back-slashes.

- Double quotes (`""`) bypass Steps 1 through 4, plus Steps 9 and 10. That is, they ignore pipe characters, aliases, tilde substitution, wildcard expansion, and split-ting into words via delimiters (e.g., blanks) inside the double quotes. Single quotes inside double quotes have no effect. But double quotes do allow parame-ter substitution, command substitution, and arithmetic expression evaluation. You can include a double quote inside a double-quoted string by preceding it with a backslash (\\). You must also backslash-escape $, ` (the archaic command substitution delimiter), and \\ itself.

Table C-1 has simple examples to show how these work; they assume the statement `person=hatter` was run and user *alice*'s home directory is */home/alice*.

If you are wondering whether to use single or double quotes in a particular shell programming situation, it is safest to use single quotes unless you specifically need parameter, command, or arithmetic substitution.

Table C-1. Examples of using single and double quotes

Expression	Value
$person	hatter
"$person"	hatter
\$person	$person
`$person'	$person
"'$person'"	'hatter'
~alice	/home/alice
"~alice"	~alice
`~alice'	~alice

eval

We have seen that quoting lets you skip steps in command-line processing. Then there's the eval command, which lets you go through the process again. Performing command-line processing twice may seem strange, but it's actually very powerful: it lets you write scripts that create command strings on the fly and then pass them to the shell for execution. This means that you can give scripts "intelligence" to modify their own behavior as they are running.

The eval statement tells the shell to take eval's arguments and run them through the command-line processing steps all over again. To help you understand the implications of eval, we'll start with a trivial example and work our way up to a situation in which we're constructing and running commands on the fly.

eval ls passes the string "ls" to the shell to execute; the shell prints a list of files in the current directory. Very simple; there is nothing about the string "ls" that needs to be sent through the command-processing steps twice. But consider this:

```
listpage="ls | more"
$listpage
```

Instead of producing a paginated file listing, the shell will treat | and more as arguments to *ls*, and *ls* will complain that no files of those names exist. Why? Because the pipe character appears as a pipe in Step 6 when the shell evaluates the variable, which is *after* it has actually looked for pipe characters. The variable's expansion isn't even parsed until Step 9. As a result, the shell will treat | and more as arguments to *ls*, so that *ls* will try to find files called | and *more* in the current directory!

Now consider eval $listpage instead of just $listpage. When the shell gets to the last step, it will run the command eval with arguments ls, |, and more. This causes the shell to go back to Step 1 with a line that consists of these arguments. It finds | in Step 2 and splits the line into two commands, *ls* and *more*. Each command is processed in the normal (and in both cases trivial) way. The result is a paginated list of the files in your current directory.

Now you may start to see how powerful eval can be. It is an advanced feature that requires considerable programming cleverness to be used most effectively. It even has a bit of the flavor of artificial intelligence, in that it enables you to write programs that can "write" and execute other programs. You probably won't use eval for everyday shell programming, but it's worth taking the time to understand what it can do.

APPENDIX D
Revision Control

Revision control systems are a way to not only travel back in time, but to see what has changed at various points in your timeline. They are also called *versioning* or *version control* systems, which is actually a more technically accurate name. Such a system allows you to maintain a central *repository* of files in a project, and to keep track of changes to those files, as well as the reason for those changes. Some revision control systems allow more than one developer to work concurrently on the same project, or even the same file.

Revision control systems are essential to modern software development efforts, but they are also useful in many other areas, such as writing documentation, tracking system configurations (e.g., */etc*), and even writing books. We kept this book under revision control using Subversion while writing it.

Some of the useful features of revision control systems include:

- Making it very difficult to lose code, especially when the repository is properly backed up.
- Facilitating change control practices, and encourage documenting why a change is being made.
- Allowing people in multiple locations to work together on a project, and to keep up with others' changes, without losing data by saving on top of each other.
- Allowing one person to work from multiple locations over time without losing work or stepping on changes made at other locations.
- Allowing you to back out changes easily or to see exactly what has changed between one revision and another (except binary files). If you follow effective logging practices, they will even tell you why a change was made.
- Allowing, usually, a form of *keyword* expansion that lets you embed revision metadata in nonbinary files.

There are many different free and commercial revision control systems, and we would like to strongly encourage you to use one. If you already have one, use it. If you don't, we'll briefly cover three of the most common systems (CVS, Subversion, and RCS), all of which either come with or are available for every major modern operating system.

Before using a revision control system, you must first decide:

- Which system or product to use
- The location of the central repository, if applicable
- The structure of the projects or directories in the repository
- The update, commit, tag, and branch polices

This only scratches the surface; see O'Reilly's *Essential CVS* by Jennifer Vesperman and *Version Control with Subversion* by Ben Collins-Sussman et al. for more in-depth introductions to revision control and complete details on their respective systems. Both have excellent treatments of the general concepts, although the Subversion book covers repository structure in more detail due to its more fluid nature.

Both also cover revision control policy. If your company has change control or related policies, use them. If not, we recommend you commit and update early and often. If you are working as a team, we strongly recommend reading one or both of the books and carefully planning out a strategy. It will save vast amounts of time in the long run.

CVS

The Concurrent Versions System (CVS) is a widely used and mature revision control system, with command-line tools for all major modern operating systems (including Windows), and GUI tools for some of them (notably Windows).

Pros

- It is everywhere and is very mature.
- Many Unix system administrators and virtually every open source or free software developer is familiar with it.
- It's easy to use for simple projects.
- It's easy to access remote repositories.
- It's based on RCS, which allows for some hacking of the central repository.

Cons

- Commits are not atomic, so the repository could be left in an inconsistent state if a commit fails half-way through.
- Commits are by file only; you must also tag if you need to reference a group of files.

- Directory structure support is poor.
- Does not allow easy renaming of files and directories while retaining history.
- Poor support for binary files, and little support for other objects such as symbolic links.
- Based on RCS, which allows for some hacking of the central repository.

 CVS tracks revisions by file, which means that each file has its own internal CVS revision number. As each file is changed, that number changes, so a single project can't be tracked by a single revision number, since each file is different. Use tags for that kind of tracking.

Example

This example is not suitable for enterprise or multiuser access (see the "More Resources" section in the Preface). This is just to show how easy the basics are. This example has the EDITOR environment variable set to *nano* (export EDITOR='nano --smooth --const --nowrap --suspend'), which some people find more user-friendly than the default *vi*.

The cvs command (with no options), the cvs help command (where help is not a valid argument, but is easy to remember and still triggers a useful response), and the cvs --help *cvs_command* command are very useful.

Create a new repository for personal use in a home directory:

```
/home/jp$ mkdir -m 0775 cvsroot
/home/jp$ chmod g+srwx cvsroot
/home/jp$ cvs -d /home/jp/cvsroot init
```

Create a new project and import it:

```
/home/jp$ cd /tmp

/tmp$ mkdir -m 0700 scripts

/tmp$ cd scripts/

/tmp/scripts$ cat << EOF > hello
> #!/bin/sh
> echo 'Hello World!'
> EOF

/tmp/scripts$ cvs -d /home/jp/cvsroot import scripts shell_scripts NA

  GNU nano 1.2.4                    File: /tmp/cvsnJgYmG

Initial import of shell scripts
CVS: -----------------------------------------------------------------------
CVS: Enter Log.  Lines beginning with `CVS:' are removed automatically
```

```
CVS:
CVS: ------------------------------------------------------------------

                             [ Wrote 5 lines ]

    N scripts/hello

    No conflicts created by this import
```

Check out the project and update it:

```
/tmp/scripts$ cd
/home/jp$ cvs -d /home/jp/cvsroot/ checkout scripts
cvs checkout: Updating scripts
U scripts/hello

/home/jp$ cd scripts

/home/jp/scripts$ ls -l
total 8.0K
drwxr-xr-x  2 jp jp 4.0K Jul 20 00:27 CVS/
-rw-r--r--  1 jp jp   30 Jul 20 00:25 hello

/home/jp/scripts$ echo "Hi Mom..." >> hello
```

Check the status of your sandbox. The second command is a hack to give you a short summary status since the real status command is a little verbose:

```
/home/jp/scripts$ cvs status
cvs status: Examining .
===================================================================
File: hello             Status: Locally Modified

   Working revision:    1.1.1.1 Thu Jul 20 04:25:44 2006
   Repository revision: 1.1.1.1 /home/jp/cvsroot/scripts/hello,v
   Sticky Tag:          (none)
   Sticky Date:         (none)
   Sticky Options:      (none)

/home/jp/scripts$ cvs -qn update
M hello
```

Add a new script to revision control:

```
/home/jp/scripts$ cat << EOF > mcd
> #!/bin/sh
> mkdir -p "$1"
> cd "$1"
> EOF

/home/jp/scripts$ cvs add mcd
cvs add: scheduling file `mcd' for addition
cvs add: use `cvs commit' to add this file permanently
```

Commit changes:

```
/home/jp/scripts$ cvs commit
cvs commit: Examining .

  GNU nano 1.2.4                        File: /tmp/cvsY1xcKa

* Tweaked hello
* Added mcd
CVS: -----------------------------------------------------------------------
CVS: Enter Log.  Lines beginning with `CVS:' are removed automatically
CVS:
CVS: Committing in .
CVS:
CVS: Modified Files:
CVS:    hello
CVS: Added Files:
CVS:    mcd
CVS: -----------------------------------------------------------------------

                         [ Wrote 12 lines ]

/home/jp/cvsroot/scripts/hello,v  <--  hello
new revision: 1.2; previous revision: 1.1
/home/jp/cvsroot/scripts/mcd,v  <--  mcd
initial revision: 1.1
```

Update the sandbox, make another change, then check the difference:

```
/home/jp/scripts$ cvs update
cvs update: Updating .

/home/jp/scripts$ vi hello

/home/jp/scripts$ cvs diff hello
Index: hello
===================================================================
RCS file: /home/jp/cvsroot/scripts/hello,v
retrieving revision 1.2
diff -r1.2 hello
3c3
< Hi Mom...
---
> echo 'Hi Mom...'
```

Commit the change, avoiding the editor by putting the log entry on the command line:

```
/home/jp/scripts$ cvs -m '* Fixed syntax error' commit
/home/jp/cvsroot/scripts/hello,v  <--  hello
new revision: 1.3; previous revision: 1.2
```

See the history of the file:

```
/home/jp/scripts$ cvs log hello
```

```
RCS file: /home/jp/cvsroot/scripts/hello,v
Working file: hello
head: 1.3
branch:
locks: strict
access list:
symbolic names:
        NA: 1.1.1.1
        shell_scripts: 1.1.1
keyword substitution: kv
total revisions: 4;     selected revisions: 4
description:
----------------------------
revision 1.3
date: 2006-07-20 04:46:25 +0000;  author: jp;  state: Exp;  lines: +1 -1
* Fixed syntax error
----------------------------
revision 1.2
date: 2006-07-20 04:37:37 +0000;  author: jp;  state: Exp;  lines: +1 -0
* Tweaked hello
* Added mcd
----------------------------
revision 1.1
date: 2006-07-20 04:25:44 +0000;  author: jp;  state: Exp;
branches:  1.1.1;
Initial revision
----------------------------
revision 1.1.1.1
date: 2006-07-20 04:25:44 +0000;  author: jp;  state: Exp;  lines: +0 -0
Initial import of shell scripts
=============================================================================
```

Add some revision metadata that is automatically kept up-to-date by the revision control system itself. Commit it and examine the change:

```
/home/jp/scripts$ vi hello

/home/jp/scripts$ cat hello
#!/bin/sh
# $Id$
echo 'Hello World!'
echo 'Hi Mom...'

/home/jp/scripts$ cvs ci -m'* Added ID keyword' hello
/home/jp/cvsroot/scripts/hello,v  <--  hello
new revision: 1.4; previous revision: 1.3

/home/jp/scripts$ cat hello
#!/bin/sh
# $Id: hello,v 1.4 2006/07/21 08:57:53 jp Exp $
echo 'Hello World!'
echo 'Hi Mom...'
```

Compare the current revision to r1.2, revert to that older (broken) revision, realize we goofed and get the most recent revision back:

```
/home/jp/cvs.scripts$ cvs diff -r1.2 hello
Index: hello
===================================================================
RCS file: /home/jp/cvsroot/scripts/hello,v
retrieving revision 1.2
retrieving revision 1.4
diff -r1.2 -r1.4
1a2
> # $Id$
3c4
< Hi Mom...
---
> echo 'Hi Mom...'

/home/jp/scripts$ cvs update -r1.2 hello
U hello

/home/jp/scripts$ cat hello
#!/bin/sh
echo 'Hello World!'
Hi Mom...

/home/jp/cvs.scripts$ cvs update -rHEAD hello
U hello

/home/jp/cvs.scripts$ cat hello
#!/bin/sh
# $Id: hello,v 1.4 2006/07/21 08:57:53 jp Exp $
echo 'Hello World!'
echo 'Hi Mom...'
```

See Also

- man cvs
- man rcs2log
- man cvs-pserver
- The official CVS web site, at *http://www.nongnu.org/cvs/*
- CVS Docs and Cederqvist manual, at *http://ximbiot.com/cvs/manual/*
- Windows shell extention for CVS, at *http://www.tortoisecvs.org/*
- "Introduction to CVS," at *http://linux.oreillynet.com/lpt/a/1420*
- "CVS Administration," at *http://linux.oreillynet.com/lpt/a/1421*
- "Tracking Changes in CVSm," at *http://linux.oreillynet.com/lpt/a/2443*
- "CVS Third-Party Tools," at *http://www.onlamp.com/lpt/a/2895*
- "Top 10 CVS Tips," at *http://www.oreillynet.com/lpt/a/2015*

- "CVS Branch and Tag Primer," at *http://www.psc.edu/~semke/cvs_branches.html*
- "CVS Best Practices," at *http://www.tldp.org/REF/CVS-BestPractices/html/index.html*
- *Essential CVS* by Jennifer Vesperman
- Recipe 16.14, "Creating and Changing into a New Directory in One Step"

Subversion

According to the Subversion web site, "The goal of the Subversion project is to build a *version control system* that is a compelling replacement for CVS in the open source community." Enough said.

Pros

- Newer than CVS and RCS.
- Simpler and arguably easier to understand and use than CVS (less historical baggage).
- Atomic commits means the commit either fails or succeeds as a whole, and makes it easy to track the state of an entire project as a single revision.
- Easy to access remote repositories.
- Allows easy renaming of files and directories while retaining history.
- Easily handles binary files (no native diff support) and other objects such as symbolic links.
- Central repository hacking is more officially supported, but less trivial.

Cons

- Not 100 percent CVS compatible for more complicated projects (e.g., branching and tagging).
- Can be more complicated to build or install from scratch due to many dependencies. Use the version that came with your operating system if possible.

 SVN tracks revisions by repository, which means that each commit has its own internal SVN revision number. Thus consecutive commits by a single person may not have consecutive revision numbers since the global repository revision is incremented as other changes (possibly to other projects) are committed by other people.

Example

This example is not suitable for enterprise or multiuser access (see the "More Resources" section in the Preface). This is just to show how easy the basics are. This example also has the EDITOR environment variable set to *nano* (export EDITOR='nano --smooth --const --nowrap --suspend'), which some people find more user-friendly than the default *vi*.

The svn help and svn help help commands are very useful.

Create a new repository for personal use in a home directory:

```
/home/jp$ svnadmin --fs-type=fsfs create /home/jp/svnroot
```

Create a new project and import it:

```
/home/jp$ cd /tmp

/tmp$ mkdir -p -m 0700 scripts/trunk scripts/tags scripts/branches

/tmp$ cd scripts/trunk

/tmp/scripts/trunk$ cat << EOF > hello
> #!/bin/sh
> echo 'Hello World!'
> EOF

/tmp/scripts/trunk$ cd ..

/tmp/scripts$ svn import /tmp/scripts file:///home/jp/svnroot/scripts

  GNU nano 1.2.4                   File: svn-commit.tmp

Initial import of shell scripts
--This line, and those below, will be ignored--

A    .


                                        [ Wrote 4 lines ]

Adding         /tmp/scripts/trunk
Adding         /tmp/scripts/trunk/hello
Adding         /tmp/scripts/branches
Adding         /tmp/scripts/tags

Committed revision 1.
```

Check out the project and update it:

```
/tmp/scripts$ cd

/home/jp$ svn checkout file:///home/jp/svnroot/scripts
A  scripts/trunk
A  scripts/trunk/hello
A  scripts/branches
```

```
A  scripts/tags
Checked out revision 1.

/home/jp$ cd scripts

/home/jp/scripts$ ls -l
total 12K
drwxr-xr-x  3 jp jp 4.0K Jul 20 01:12 branches/
drwxr-xr-x  3 jp jp 4.0K Jul 20 01:12 tags/
drwxr-xr-x  3 jp jp 4.0K Jul 20 01:12 trunk/

/home/jp/scripts$ cd trunk/

/home/jp/scripts/trunk$ ls -l
total 4.0K
-rw-r--r--  1 jp jp 30 Jul 20 01:12 hello

/home/jp/scripts/trunk$ echo "Hi Mom..." >> hello
```

Check the status of your sandbox. Note how the svn status command is similar to our cvs -qn update hack in the "CVS" section earlier in this appendix:

```
/home/jp/scripts/trunk$ svn info
Path: .
URL: file:///home/jp/svnroot/scripts/trunk
Repository UUID: 29eeb329-fc18-0410-967e-b075d748cc20
Revision: 1
Node Kind: directory
Schedule: normal
Last Changed Author: jp
Last Changed Rev: 1
Last Changed Date: 2006-07-20 01:04:56 -0400 (Thu, 20 Jul 2006)

/home/jp/scripts/trunk$ svn status -v
                1        1 jp        .
M               1        1 jp        hello

/home/jp/scripts/trunk$ svn status
M      hello

/home/jp/scripts/trunk$ svn update
At revision 1.
```

Add a new script to revision control:

```
/home/jp/scripts/trunk$ cat << EOF > mcd
> #!/bin/sh
> mkdir -p "$1"
> cd "$1"
> EOF

/home/jp/scripts/trunk$ svn st
?      mcd
M      hello
```

```
/home/jp/scripts/trunk$ svn add mcd
A         mcd
```

Commit changes:

```
/home/jp/scripts/trunk$ svn ci

  GNU nano 1.2.4                      File: svn-commit.tmp

* Tweaked hello
* Added mcd
--This line, and those below, will be ignored--

M    trunk/hello
A    trunk/mcd


                              [ Wrote 6 lines ]

Sending        trunk/hello
Adding         trunk/mcd
Transmitting file data ..
Committed revision 2.
```

Update the sandbox, make another change, then check the difference:

```
/home/jp/scripts/trunk$ svn up
At revision 2.

/home/jp/scripts/trunk$ vi hello

/home/jp/scripts/trunk$ svn diff hello
Index: hello
===================================================================
--- hello       (revision 2)
+++ hello       (working copy)
@@ -1,3 +1,3 @@
 #!/bin/sh
 echo 'Hello World!'
-Hi Mom...
+echo 'Hi Mom...'
```

Commit the change, avoiding the editor by putting the log entry on the command line:

```
/home/jp/scripts/trunk$ svn -m '* Fixed syntax error' commit
Sending        trunk/hello
Transmitting file data .
Committed revision 3.
```

See the history of the file:

```
/home/jp/scripts/trunk$ svn log hello
------------------------------------------------------------------------
r3 | jp | 2006-07-20 01:23:35 -0400 (Thu, 20 Jul 2006) | 1 line

* Fixed syntax error
```

```
-----------------------------------------------------------------------
r2 | jp | 2006-07-20 01:20:09 -0400 (Thu, 20 Jul 2006) | 3 lines

* Tweaked hello
* Added mcd

-----------------------------------------------------------------------
r1 | jp | 2006-07-20 01:04:56 -0400 (Thu, 20 Jul 2006) | 2 lines

Initial import of shell scripts

-----------------------------------------------------------------------
```

Add some revision metadata, and tell the system to expand it. Commit it and examine the change:

```
/home/jp/scripts/trunk$ vi hello

/home/jp/scripts/trunk$ cat hello
#!/bin/sh
# $Id$
echo 'Hello World!'
echo 'Hi Mom...'

home/jp/scripts/trunk$ svn propset svn:keywords "Id" hello
property 'svn:keywords' set on 'hello'

/home/jp/scripts/trunk$ svn ci -m'* Added ID keyword' hello
Sending        hello

Committed revision 4.

/home/jp/scripts/trunk$ cat hello
#!/bin/sh
# $Id: hello 5 2006-07-21 09:09:34Z jp $
echo 'Hello World!'
echo 'Hi Mom...'
```

Compare the current revision to r2, revert to that older (broken) revision, realize we goofed and get the most recent revision back:

```
/home/jp/scripts/trunk$ svn diff -r2 hello
Index: hello
===================================================================
--- hello        (revision 2)
+++ hello        (working copy)
@@ -1,3 +1,4 @@
 #!/bin/sh
+# $Id$
 echo 'Hello World!'
-Hi Mom...
+echo 'Hi Mom...'

Property changes on: hello
_____
```

```
Name: svn:keywords
   + Id

/home/jp/scripts/trunk$ svn update -r2 hello
UU hello
Updated to revision 2.

/home/jp/scripts/trunk$ cat hello
#!/bin/sh
echo 'Hello World!'
Hi Mom...

/home/jp/scripts/trunk$ svn update -rHEAD hello
UU hello
Updated to revision 4.

/home/jp/scripts/trunk$ cat hello
#!/bin/sh
# $Id: hello 5 2006-07-21 09:09:34Z jp $
echo 'Hello World!'
echo 'Hi Mom...'
```

See Also

- man svn
- man svnadmin
- man svndumpfilter
- man svnlook
- man svnserve
- man svnversion
- The Subversion web site at *http://subversion.tigris.org/*
- TortoiseSVN: Simple SVN frontend for Explorer (cool!), at *http://tortoisesvn. tigris.org/*
- *Version Control with Subversion*, at *http://svnbook.red-bean.com/*
- SVN static builds for Solaris, Linux, and Mac OS X at *http://www.uncc.org/ svntools/clients/*
- "Subversion for CVS Users," at *http://osdir.com/Article203.phtml*
- Version control system comparison, at *http://better-scm.berlios.de/comparison/ comparison.html*
- Recipe 16.14, "Creating and Changing into a New Directory in One Step"

RCS

RCS was a revolution in its time, and is the underlying basis for CVS.

Pros

- It's better than nothing.

Cons

- Does not allow concurrent access to the same file.
- Does not have the inherent concept of a central repository, though you can go out of your way to create one using symbolic links.
- No concept of remote repositories.
- Only tracks changes to files, and does not store or consider directories at all.
- Poor support for binary files, and no support for other objects such as symbolic links. Unlike CVS or SVN, which have a single main end-user binary, RCS is a collection of binaries.

Example

Create a new script directory for personal use in a home directory:

```
/home/jp$ mkdir -m 0754 bin
```

Create some scripts:

```
/home/jp$ cd bin

/tmp/scripts/bin$ cat << EOF > hello
> #!/bin/sh
> echo 'Hello World!'
> EOF

/home/jp/bin$ ci hello
hello,v  <--  hello
enter description, terminated with single '.' or end of file:
NOTE: This is NOT the log message!
>> Obligatory Hello World
>> .
initial revision: 1.1
done

/home/jp/bin$ ls -l
total 4.0K
-r--r--r--  1 jp jp 228 Jul 20 02:25 hello,v
```

Huh? What happened? It turns out that if a directory called *RCS* does not exist, the current directory is used for the RCS file. And if the -u or -l switches are not used, the file is checked in and then removed. -l causes the file to be checked back out and locked so you can edit it, while -u is unlocked (that is, read-only). OK, let's try that again. First, let's get our file back, then create an *RCS* directory and check it in again.

```
/home/jp/bin$ co -u hello
hello,v --> hello
revision 1.1 (unlocked)
done

/home/jp/bin$ ls -l
total 8.0K
-r--r--r--  1 jp jp  30 Jul 20 02:29 hello
-r--r--r--  1 jp jp 228 Jul 20 02:25 hello,v

/home/jp/bin$ rm hello,v
rm: remove write-protected regular file `hello,v'? y

/home/jp/bin$ mkdir -m 0755 RCS

/home/jp/bin$ ci -u hello
RCS/hello,v  <-- hello
enter description, terminated with single '.' or end of file:
NOTE: This is NOT the log message!
>> Obligatory Hello World
>> .
initial revision: 1.1
done

/home/jp/bin$ ls -l
total 8.0K
drwxr-xr-x  2 jp jp 4.0K Jul 20 02:31 RCS/
-r--r--r--  1 jp jp   30 Jul 20 02:29 hello

/home/jp/bin$ ls -l RCS
total 4.0K
-r--r--r--  1 jp jp 242 Jul 20 02:31 hello,v
```

Note that our original file is now read-only. This is to remind us to check it out using co -l before working on it. Let's do that:

```
/home/jp/bin$ co -l hello
RCS/hello,v  --> hello
revision 1.1 (locked)
done

/home/jp/bin$ ls -l
total 8.0K
drwxr-xr-x  2 jp jp 4.0K Jul 20 02:39 RCS/
-rw-r--r--  1 jp jp   30 Jul 20 02:39 hello

/home/jp/bin$ echo "Hi Mom..." >> hello
```

Commit changes, but keep a copy locked for editing:

```
/home/jp/bin$ ci -l hello
RCS/hello,v  <-- hello
new revision: 1.2; previous revision: 1.1
enter log message, terminated with single '.' or end of file:
>> * Tweaked hello
```

```
>> .
done

/home/jp/bin$ ls -l
total 8.0K
drwxr-xr-x  2 jp jp 4.0K Jul 20 02:44 RCS/
-rw-r--r--  1 jp jp   40 Jul 20 02:39 hello
```

Make another change, then check the difference:

```
/home/jp/bin$ vi hello

/home/jp/bin$ rcsdiff hello
===================================================================
RCS file: RCS/hello,v
retrieving revision 1.2
diff -r1.2 hello
3c3
< Hi Mom...
---
> echo 'Hi Mom...'
```

Commit the change, and keep an unlocked copy for actual use:

```
/home/jp/bin$ ci -u -m'* Fixed syntax error' hello
RCS/hello,v  <--  hello
new revision: 1.3; previous revision: 1.2
done

/home/jp/bin$ ls -l
total 8.0K
drwxr-xr-x  2 jp jp 4.0K Jul 20 02:46 RCS/
-r--r--r--  1 jp jp   47 Jul 20 02:45 hello
```

See the history of the file:

```
/home/jp/bin$ rlog hello

RCS file: RCS/hello,v
Working file: hello
head: 1.3
branch:
locks: strict
access list:
symbolic names:
keyword substitution: kv
total revisions: 3;     selected revisions: 3
description:
Obligatory Hello World
----------------------------
revision 1.3
date: 2006/07/20 06:46:30;  author: jp;  state: Exp;  lines: +1 -1
* Fixed syntax error
----------------------------
revision 1.2
date: 2006/07/20 06:43:54;  author: jp;  state: Exp;  lines: +1 -0
```

```
* Tweaked hello
----------------------------
revision 1.1
date: 2006/07/20 06:31:06;  author: jp;  state: Exp;
Obligatory Hello World
=============================================================================
```

Add some revision metadata, and tell the system to expand it. Commit it and examine the change:

```
/home/jp/bin$ co -l hello
RCS/hello,v  -->  hello
revision 1.3 (locked)
done

/home/jp/bin$ vi hello

/home/jp/bin$ cat hello
#!/bin/sh
# $Id$
echo 'Hello World!'
echo 'Hi Mom...'

/home/jp/bin$ ci -u -m'Added ID keyword' hello
RCS/hello,v  <--  hello
new revision: 1.4; previous revision: 1.3
done

/home/jp/bin$ cat hello
#!/bin/sh
# $Id$
echo 'Hello World!'
echo 'Hi Mom...'
```

Compare the current revision to r1.2, revert to that older (broken) revision, realize we goofed and get the most recent revision back:

```
/home/jp/bin$ rcsdiff -r1.2 hello
===============================================================
RCS file: RCS/hello,v
retrieving revision 1.2
diff -r1.2 hello
1a2
> # $Id$
3c4
< Hi Mom...
---
> echo 'Hi Mom...'

/home/jp/bin$ co -r hello
RCS/hello,v  -->  hello
revision 1.4
writable hello exists; remove it? [ny](n): y
done
```

```
/home/jp/bin$ cat hello
#!/bin/sh
# $Id$
echo 'Hello World!'
echo 'Hi Mom...'
```

Workon Script

Here is a script that may make life with RCS a little easier. It facilitates using an RCS "repository" and automates much of the process of checking files in and out to work on them, hence the name. We recommend that you use Subversion or CVS if possible, but if you must use RCS you may find this helpful:

```
#!/usr/bin/env bash
# cookbook filename: workon
# workon--Work on a file in RCS

# Set a sane/secure path and export it
PATH=/usr/local/bin:/bin:/usr/bin
export PATH

VERSION='$Version: 1.4 $' # JP Vossen
COPYRIGHT='Copyright 2004-2006 JP Vossen (http://www.jpsdomain.org/)'
LICENSE='GNU GENERAL PUBLIC LICENSE'

CAT='/bin/cat'
if [ "$1" = "-h" -o "$1" = "--help" -o -z "$1" ]; then
    ${CAT} <<-EoN
    Usage: $0 {file}

    Work on a file in RCS.  Create the RCS subdirectory if necessary.
    Do the initial checkin if necessary, prompting for a message.
    Must be in the same directory as the file to be worked on.
EoN
    exit 0
fi

# Use a pseudo central repository
RCSHOMEDIR='/home/rcs'

# Make sure $VISUAL is set to something
[ "$VISUAL" ] || VISUAL=vi

####################################################################
# Start of Main program

# Make sure RCS Home Dir exists
if [ ! -d $RCSHOMEDIR ]; then
    echo "Creating $RCSHOMEDIR..."
    mkdir -p $RCSHOMEDIR
fi

# Make sure there is no local RCS directory
```

```
if [ -d RCS -a ! -L RCS ]; then
    echo "Local 'RCS' already exists--exiting!"
    exit 2
fi

# Make sure the destdir exists
if [ ! -d $RCSHOMEDIR$PWD ]; then
    echo "Creating $RCSHOMEDIR$PWD..."
    mkdir -p $RCSHOMEDIR$PWD
fi

# Make sure the link exists
if [ ! -L RCS ]; then
    echo "Linking RCS --> $RCSHOMEDIR$PWD."
    ln -s $RCSHOMEDIR$PWD RCS
fi

if [ ! -f "RCS/$1,v" ]; then
    # If the file is not ALREADY in RCS add it as v1.0.

    echo 'Adding "Initial Revision/Default" of file to RCS...'

    # Get input
    echo -n 'Describe this file: '
    read logmsg

    # Check in v1.0
    ci -u1.0 -t-"$logmsg" -m'Initial Revision/Default' $1

else
    # If the file is in RCS, work on it.

    # Checkout the file in locked mode for editing
    co -l $1

    # Edit the file locally
    $VISUAL $1

    # Check the file back in, but keep a read-only copy out for use
    ci -u $1
fi
```

See Also

- man ci
- man co
- man ident
- man merge
- man rcs
- man rcsclean

- man rcsdiff
- man rcsmerge
- man rlog
- man rcsfreeze
- *Applying RCS and SCCS,* Chapter 3, by Tan Bronson and Don Bolinger (O'Reilly)
- "BSD Tricks: Introductory Revision Control," at *http://www.onlamp.com/lpt/a/428*

Other

Finally, it is worth noting that some word processors, such as OpenOffice.org Writer and Microsoft Word, have three relevant features: document comparison, change tracking, and versions.

Document Comparison

Document Comparison allows you to compare documents when their native file format makes use of other *diff* tools difficult. You would use this when you have two copies of a document that didn't have change tracking turned on, or when you need to merge feedback from various sources.

While it is trivial to *unzip* the *content.xml* file from a given OpenDoc file, the result has no line breaks and is not terribly pretty or readable. See Recipe 12.5, "Comparing Two Documents" for a *bash* script that will do this low-level kind of difference.

Refer to the table below for information on how to access the built-in GUI comparison function, which is much easier than trying to do it manually.

Change Tracking and Versions

The change-tracking feature saves information about changes made to a document. Review mode uses various copyediting markup on the screen to display who did what, when. This is obviously useful for all kinds of creation and editing purposes, but please read our warnings.

The versions feature allows you to save more than one version of a document in a single file. This can be handy in all sorts of odd ways. For example, we've seen router configurations copied and pasted from a terminal into different versions inside the same document for archival and change control purposes.

The change tracking and versions features will cause your document to continually grow in size, since items that are changed are still kept and deleted items are not really deleted, but only marked as deleted.

If accidentally turned on, change tracking and versions can be very dangerous information leaks! For example, if you send similar proposals to competing companies after doing a search and replace and other editing, someone at one of those companies can see exactly what you changed and when you changed it. The most recent versions of these tools have various methods that attempt to warn you or clear private information before a given document is converted to PDF or emailed.

Take a look at any word processor attachments you receive in email, especially from vendors. You may be surprised.

Accessing These Features

Table D-1. Word processor functions

Feature	Writer menu option	Word menu option
Document comparisons	Edit → Compare Document	Tools → Compare and Merge Documents
Change tracking	Edit → Changes	Tools → Track Changes
Versions	File → Versions	File → Versions

Building bash from Source

In this appendix we'll show you how to get the latest version of *bash* and install it on your system from source, and we'll discuss potential problems you might encounter along the way. We'll also look briefly at the examples that come with *bash* and how you can report bugs to the *bash* maintainer. The material in this appendix also appears in *Learning the bash Shell* by Cameron Newham (O'Reilly).

Obtaining bash

If you have a direct connection to the Internet, you should have no trouble obtaining *bash*; otherwise, you'll have to do a little more work. The *bash* home page is located at *http://www.gnu.org/software/bash/bash.html* and you can find the very latest details of the current distribution and where to obtain it from there.

You can also get *bash* on CD-ROM by ordering it directly from the Free Software Foundation, either via the web-ordering page at *http://order.fsf.org* or from:

The Free Software Foundation (FSF)
59 Temple Place – Suite 330
Boston, MA 02111-1307 USA
Phone: +1-617-542-5942
Fax: +1-617-542-2652
Email: *order@fsf.org*

(Valid as of Thursday April 20, 2006 11:45:40 PDT.)

Unpacking the Archive

Having obtained the archive file by one of the above methods, you need to unpack it and install it on your system. Unpacking can be done anywhere—we'll assume you're unpacking it in your home directory. Installing it on the system requires you to have root privileges. If you aren't a system administrator with root access, you can still compile and use *bash*; you just can't install it as a system-wide utility. The first thing to do is uncompress the archive file: `gunzip bash-3.1.tar.gz`. Then you need to *untar* the archive: `tar -xf bash-3.1.tar`. The `-xf` means "extract the archived material from the specified file." This will create a directory called *bash-3.1* in your home directory. If you do not have the *gunzip* utility, you can obtain it in the same way you obtained *bash* or simply use `gzip -d` instead.

The archive contains all of the source code needed to compile *bash* and a large amount of documentation and examples. We'll look at these things and how you go about making a *bash* executable in the rest of this appendix.

What's in the Archive

The *bash* archive contains a main directory (*bash-3.1* for the current version) and a set of files and subdirectories. Among the first files you should examine are:

CHANGES
: A comprehensive list of bug fixes and new features since the last version

COPYING
: The GNU Copyleft for *bash*

MANIFEST
: A list of all the files and directories in the archive

NEWS
: A list of new features since the last version

README
: A short introduction and instructions for compiling *bash*

You should also be aware of two directories:

doc
: Information related to *bash* in various formats

examples
: Examples of startup files, scripts, and functions

The other files and directories in the archive are mostly things that are needed during the build. Unless you are going to go hacking into the internal workings of the shell, they shouldn't concern you.

Documentation

The *doc* directory contains a few articles that are worth reading. Indeed, it would be well worth printing out the manual entry for *bash* so you can use it in conjunction with this book. The *README* file gives a short summary of the files.

The document you'll most often use is the manpage entry *bash.1*. The file is in *troff* format—the same format used by the manpages. You can read it by processing it with the text-formatter *nroff* and piping the output to a pager utility; e.g., `nroff -man bash.1 | more` should do the trick. You can also print it off by piping it to the line-printer (*lp*). This summarizes all of the facilities your version of *bash* has and is the most up-to-date reference you can get. This document is also available through the *man* facility once you've installed the package, but sometimes it's nice to have a hardcopy so you can write notes all over it.

Of the other documents, *FAQ* is a Frequently Asked Questions document with answers, *readline.3* is the manual entry for the *readline* facility, and *article.ms* is an article about the shell that appeared in *Linux Journal*, and was written by the current *bash* maintainer Chet Ramey.

Configuring and Building bash

To compile *bash* "straight out of the box" is easy—you just type `./configure` and then **make**! The *configure* script attempts to work out whether you have various utilities and C library functions, and their location on your system. It then stores the relevant information in the file *config.h*. It also creates a file called *config.status*, which is a script you can run to recreate the current configuration information. While *configure* is running, it prints out information on what it is searching for and where it finds it.

The *configure* script also sets the location that *bash* will be installed; the default is the */usr/local* area (*/usr/local/bin* for the executable, */usr/local/man* for the manual entries, etc). If you don't have root privileges and want it in your own home directory, or you wish to install *bash* in some other location, you'll need to provide *configure* with the path you want to use. You can do this with the `--exec-prefix` option. For example:

```
$ configure --exec-prefix=/usr
```

specifies that the *bash* files will be placed under the */usr* directory. Note that configure prefers option arguments be given with an equals sign (=).

After the configuration finishes and you type **make**, the *bash* executable is built. A script called *bashbug* is also generated, which allows you to report bugs in the format the *bash* maintainers want. We'll look at how to use it later in this appendix.

Once the build finishes, you can see if the *bash* executable works by typing `./bash`.

To install *bash*, type **make install**. This will create all of the necessary directories (*bin*, *info*, *man* and its subdirectories) and copy the files to them.

If you've installed *bash* in your home directory, be sure to add your own *bin* path to your PATH and your own *man* path to MANPATH.

bash comes preconfigured with nearly all of its features enabled, but it is possible to customize your version by specifying what you want with the `--enable` *feature* and `--disable` *feature* command-line options to *configure*. Table E-1 provides a list of the configurable features and a short description of what those features do.

Table E-1. bash configurable features

Feature	Description
alias	Support for aliases.
arith-for-command	Support for the alternate form of the *for* command that behaves like the C language `for` statement.
array-variables	Support for one-dimensional arrays.
bang-history	C-shell-like history expansion and editing.
brace-expansion	Brace expansion.
command-timing	Support for the *time* command.
cond-command	Support for the [[conditional command.
cond-regexp	Support for matching POSIX regular expressions using the =~ binary operator in the [[conditional command.
directory-stack	Support for the *pushd*, *popd*, and *dirs* directory manipulation commands.
disabled-builtins	Whether a built-in can be run with the *builtin* command, even if it has been disabled with `enable -n`.
dparen-arithmetic	Support for ((...)).
help-builtin	Support for the *help* built-in.
history	History via the *fc* and *history* commands.
job-control	Job control via *fg*, *bg*, and *jobs* if supported by the operating system.
multibyte	Support for multibyte characters if the operating system provides the necessary support.
net-redirections	Special handling of filenames of the form */dev/tcp/HOST/PORT* and */dev/udp/HOST/PORT* when used in redirections.
process-substitution	Whether process substitution occurs, if supported by the operating system.
prompt-string-decoding	Whether backslash escaped characters in PS1, PS2, PS3, and PS4 are allowed.
progcomp	Programmable completion facilities. If *readline* is not enabled, this option has no effect.
readline	*readline* editing and history capabilities.
restricted	Support for the restricted shell, the -r option to the shell, and *rbash*.
select	The `select` construct.
usg-echo-default xpg-echo-default	Make *echo* expand backslash-escaped characters by default, without requiring the -e option. This sets the default value of the xpg_echo shell option to *on*, which makes *bash's echo* behave more like the version specified in the Single Unix Specification, Version 2.

The options `disabled-builtins` and `xpg-echo-default` are disabled by default. The others are enabled.

Many other shell features can be turned on or off by modifying the file *config-.top.h*. For further details on this file and on configuring *bash* in general, see *INSTALL*.

Finally, to clean up the source directory and remove all of the object files and executables, type `make clean`. Make sure you've run `make install` first; otherwise, you'll have to rerun the installation from scratch.

Testing bash

There are a series of tests that can be run on your newly built version of *bash* to see if it is running correctly. The tests are scripts that are derived from problems reported in earlier versions of the shell. Running these tests on the latest version of *bash* shouldn't cause any errors.

To run the tests just type `make tests` in the main *bash* directory. The name of each test is displayed, along with some warning messages, and then it is run. Successful tests produce no output (unless otherwise noted in the warning messages).

If any of the tests fail, you'll see a list of things that represent differences between what is expected and what happened. If this occurs, you should file a bug report with the *bash* maintainer; see the "Reporting Bugs" section later in this appendix for information on how to do this.

Potential Problems

Although *bash* has been installed on a large number of different machines and operating systems, there are occasionally problems. Usually the problems aren't serious and a bit of investigation can result in a quick solution.

If *bash* didn't compile, the first thing to do is check that *configure* guessed your machine and operating system correctly. Then check the file *NOTES*, which contains some information on specific Unix systems. Also look in *INSTALL* for additional information on how to give *configure* specific compilation instructions.

Installing bash as a Login Shell

See Recipe 1.9, "Setting bash As Your Default Shell."

Examples

See Appendix B for examples included with *bash*.

Who Do I Turn To?

No matter how good something is or how much documentation comes with it, you'll eventually come across something that you don't understand or that doesn't work. In such cases it can't be stressed enough to *carefully read the documentation* (in more casual computer parlance: RTFM). In many cases, this will answer your question or point out what you're doing wrong.

Sometimes you'll find this only adds to your confusion or confirms that there is something wrong with the software. The next thing to do is to talk to a local *bash* guru to sort out the problem. If that fails, or there is no guru, you'll have to turn to other means (currently only via the Internet).

Asking Questions

If you have any questions about *bash*, there are currently two ways to go about getting them answered. You can email questions to *bash-maintainers@gnu.org* or you can post your question to the USENET newsgroup *gnu.bash.bug*.

In both cases either the *bash* maintainer or some knowledgeable person on USENET will give you advice. When asking a question, try to give a meaningful summary of your question in the subject line (see *http://www.catb.org/~esr/faqs/smart-questions.html*).

Reporting Bugs

Bug reports should be sent to *bug-bash@gnu.org*, and include the version of *bash* and the operating system it is running on, the compiler used to compile *bash*, a description of the problem, a description of how the problem was produced, and, if possible, a fix for the problem. The best way to do this is with the *bashbug* script, installed with *bash*.

Before you run *bashbug*, make sure that you've set your EDITOR environment variable to your favorite editor and have exported it (*bashbug* defaults to Emacs, which might not be installed on your system). When you execute *bashbug* it will enter the editor with a partially blank report form. Some of the information (*bash* version, operating system version, etc.) will have been filled in automatically. We'll take a brief look at the form, but most of it is self-explanatory.

The From: field should be filled out with your email address. For example:

From: *confused@wonderland.oreilly.com*

Next comes the Subject: field; make an effort to fill it out, as this makes it easier for the maintainers when they need to look up your submission. Just replace the line surrounded by square brackets with a meaningful summary of the problem.

The next few lines are a description of the system and should not be touched. Then comes the `Description:` field. You should provide a detailed description of the problem and how it differs from what is expected. Try to be as specific and concise as possible when describing the problem.

The `Repeat-By:` field is where you describe how you generated the problem; if necessary, list the exact keystrokes you used. Sometimes you won't be able to reproduce the problem yourself, but you should still fill out this field with the events leading up to the problem. Attempt to reduce the problem to the smallest possible form. For example, if it was a large shell script, try to isolate the section that produced the problem and include only that in your report.

Lastly, the `Fix:` field is where you can provide the necessary patch to fix the problem if you've investigated it and found out what was going wrong. If you have no idea what caused the problem, just leave the field blank.

 If the maintainer can easily reproduce and then identify the problem, it will be fixed faster. So make sure your `Repeat-By` (and ideally `Fix`) sections are as good as you can make them. Reading *http://www.catb.org/ ~esr/faqs/smart-questions.html* is also encouraged.

Once you've finished filling in the form, save it and exit your editor. The form will automatically be sent to the maintainers.

Index

Numbers and Symbols

- dash, 392
! exclamation point, 11
- operations, 298
!! double exclamation point (bang bang), 150, 456
!$ exclamation, dollar sign, 459
" double quotes, 12, 30, 254
pound, 82
pound, trailing, 4
#!, and finding bash, 321
#!/bin/sh, 321
$ dollar sign, 29, 81, 109, 153
$ dollar sign, trailing, 4
$- syntax, lists current shell option flags, 15
$$ double dollar sign, 243
$( ) (see also ``), 147
$( ) dollar sign, parentheses, 46
$(( )) expression, 108
$* dollar, asterisk, 91
$? dollar sign, question mark, 74
$@ dollar, at sign, 94
${!prefix*}, for parameters programmable completion, 287
${!prefix@}, 287
${#} dollar sign, bracket, pound sign, bracket, 96, 248
${#VAR}, 97
${:=} syntax, 101
${:?} syntax, 103
${:-} syntax, 99
${1:0:1} syntax, 248
${parameter#[#]word}, 480
${parameter%[%]word}, 480
${parameter/pattern/string}, 480
${VAR#alt}, 97
${variable/pattern/replacement}, 195
$0 variable, 236
$COMP_WORDS, 393
$COMPREPLY, 393
$cur variable, 393
$FUNCNAME, 206
$HISTCONTROL, 378
$HISTFILE, 378
$HISTFILESIZE variable, 378
$HISTIGNORE, 378
$HISTSIZE, 378
$HISTTIMEFORMAT, 378
$i, don't use (see also $x), 85
$i, use of, in awk, 157
$IFS (bash Internal Field Separator), 287
$IFS=':', 196
$include (readline), 201, 373
$INPUTRC, 371
$LESS variable, 182
$LESSCLOSE, 182
$LESSOPEN, 182
$PASSWD, 65
$PATH, 6, 68, 195, 283, 361, 362–366
$PROMPT_COMMAND, 359
$PS1, 353, 357, 410
$PS2, 353, 374
$PS3, 357, 374
$PS4, 357, 376
$PWD, 358
$RANDOM, 292
$REPLY, 64

We'd like to hear your suggestions for improving our indexes. Send email to *index@oreilly.com*.

$result, 341
$SCRIPT, 79
$SSH_ID, 341
$SSH_USER, 341
$STAT, 70
$temp_dir, 293
$TMOUT variable, 318
$UMASK variable, 288
$UNZIP, 78
$VERBOSE, 98
$x, don't use (see also $i), 85
$ZIP, 78
% percent sign, 31
& ampersand, 72
&& double-ampersands, 72
&> ampersand, greater than sign, 38
'{}', holds filenames during command
        execution, 193
( ) parentheses, 42, 190
(( )) double parentheses, 127
(-) dash, 40
* asterisk, 9, 10, 121
** double asterisk, 109
*.pub public key, 309
*.txt, for pattern matching, 11
+ operations, 298
+ plus sign, 40
, comma operator, 110
. dot, 68, 201
. dot files, 11
. period, 152
.* period, asterisk, 10, 152
./ leading dot
    slash character, 7
./ leading dot and slash character, 69
.[!.]*, 11
.bash.0, 27
.deb files (see also .rpm), 173
.FAQ, 26
.html, 27
.INTRO, 26
.jpg, 121
.ps, 27
.rbash.0, 27
.rpm (see also .deb files), 173
/ slash, 35, 105
/ slash with -F, 9
/bin/bash, 370
/dev/nul, 148
/etc/bash.bashrc, 395
/etc/bash_completion, 395
/etc/bashrc, 395, 401

/etc/inputrc, 395
/etc/passwd file, 16
/etc/profile, 395, 400
/etc/shells, 20
/etc/shells, list of valid shells, 16
/proc/core for accessing passwords, 65
/sbin/ifconfig -a, 338
/tmp for scratch directory, 35
/tmp/ls, 292
/usr partition, 17
/usr/bin/env command, 321
:- assignment operator, 101
: colons, 68
:+ variable operator, 203
:= colon, equal sign, 102
; semicolon, 72, 112
< less than symbol, 55
<<- syntax, 59
<= greater than, equal sign, 240
<a> tags, 253
= (or ==), for string comparisons, 119
= equal sign, 81, 109
== double equal signs, 240
> greater than sign, 33, 48, 55
>& greater than sign, ampersand, 38
>> double greater than, 39, 115
>outputfile, 29
? question mark, 121
?, shell pattern matching operator, 11, 514
@ at sign, 9, 203
[[ ]] double bracket, 121
[ ] single brackets, 10, 126, 152
[bracket, 10
\ backslash, 152, 153
\ leading backslash, 285
\; backslash, semicolon, 193
\<inputfile, omitting allows output to go
        anywhere, 29
\{n,m\}, for repetition (regular
        expressions), 153
\c, for echo escape sequence, 33
\unalias -a command, 285
\w, 358
\W, to print basename, 358
^ caret, 11, 153
_mcd_command_failed_, 382
_signals, 393
_struct, 385
`` backward quotes (see also $( )), 46
{ } braces, 42
{{ }} double braces, code block, 341
{x..y} brace expansion, 449

| (vertical bar) pipe
  ' single quote, 12, 30, 152, 254, 535
  || double pipes, 77
  pipe characters (|), 532
  pipe symbol (|)
  pipeline, 532
~ tilde, 4
~/.bash_history, 395
~/.bash_login, 395
~/.bash_logout, 395
~/.bash_profile, 395
~/.bashrc, 395
~/.inputrc, 396
~/.profiles, 395
~/bin directory, 373
0m, clears all attributes and set no color, 360
-1 option, 9

A

-a flag, 6
-a operator, 9, 115
-A option (mkisofs), 244
absolute pathname, 35
absolute paths, hardcoding, 284, 362
accessing data, on remote machines, 307
accounts, shared, 302
Add/Remove Applications, 19
adding directories, 362
Advanced Bash-Scripting Guide, 27
AIDE, 282
AIX, 22
aliases
  avoiding, 213
  clearing, 285
  commands, redefining with, 211
  expand_aliases, 370
  expansion, suppressing with \ leading
    backslash, 285
  Host_Alias, 306
  malicious, 285
  processing on command line, 534
  ' (single quote) with, 212
  recursive, 534
  \unalias -a command, 285
  User_Alias, 306
ampersand (&) to run commands in the
    background, 72
AND (-a), 117
AND constructs, 190
ANSI color escape sequences, 484
ANSI escape sequence, 355, 359

AppArmor, 304
application directories, 362
Application Software for NetBSD, 20
apropos, searches manpage for
    expressions, 7
archives, 22, 388
  ar archives, 173
  Archive Center, 22
  archiving data, 421
  untaring, 175
ARG_MAX, 344
arguments
  ${ } syntax for variables, 105
  $VERBOSE, 98
  breaking up, 343
  cd (current directory) command, 368
  counting, 96
  getopts, 249–252
  insufficient, 104
  list too long error, 343
  looping over, 91
  options with, 98, 249
  parsing, 134, 231, 248
  positional parameters, 101
  quotes, around file, 411
  real arguments, 98
  repeat without retyping, 460
  reusing, 458
  -v argument, 98
arithmetic
  $ (dollar sign), 109
  $(( )) expression, 108
  ** (double asterisk), for raising to a
    power, 109
  assignment operators, 109
  comma operator (,), 110
  dates and times, 225
  equal sign (=), 109
  expansion, 103
  integer expressions, 108
  integer for loops, 449
  let statement, 108
  operators, 109
  spaces, 109
  while looping construct, 126
arithmetic expressions
  evaluation of, 534
arrays
  initialization of, 107, 255
  output, parsing into, 255
  single-dimension, 106
  variables, using, 106, 123

article.ms, bash article, 26
assignment operators, 109
associative arrays (hashes in awk), 159
asterisk
  *dollar, asterisk, 91
  in strings, 10
  match any number of characters, 121
  means file is executable, 9
  means to repeat zero or more
    occurrences, 152
at sign (@), 9, 203
attacker, non-root, 293
attacks, man in the middle, 315
automating processes, 348–351
available space, tracking on MP3
    players, 238
awk
  awk command, 265
  awk program, 157
  awk utility, 155
  to split on multiples of whitespace, 265

B

backslash (\), 12, 153
backslash, semicolon (\;), 193
backup directories, 439–442
backward quotes (``) (see also $( )), 46
bad line endings, 464
Barrett, Daniel, 308, 316
basename command, 136
bash, 16
  bash --version, checks for bash
    installation, 16
  built-in umask, 288
  documentation, 25
  environment replication, 398
  functions, 203
  installation instructions, 26
  Ramey, Chet, 21, 25
  redirector, 39
  session, sharing a single, 417
  tarballs, 297
  version 3.0, for pattern matching, 123
  version 3.1+, for changing case
    sensitivity, 124
bash $IFS (Internal Field Separator), 254,
    258, 268, 270
bash invocation, 482
bash.1, manpage, 26
bashbug.0, manpage formatted, 27
bashbug.1, bashbug manpage, 26
bash-completion library, list of modules, 390

bashgetopt.h, 387
bash_logout, sample of, 408
bash_profile, sample of, 401
bashrc, sample of, 403
bashref, Bash Reference Guide, 27
bashref.info, reference manual by
    makeinfo, 26
bashref.texi, reference manual, 26
bashtop, 25
batch job, logging, 418
bdiff, 437
Beagle, desktop search engine, 194
Beebe, Nelson H.F., 281
BEGIN keyword (awk), 158
bg, to unpause the job, 73
bin directory, 69
bind commands, 372
bit buckets, 148
bits, take away from default
    permissions, 288
blank spaces, 109
blanks, embedded, 92
blocks, 192
Boolean flags, 202
Bourne shells, /etc/profile, global login
    environment file, 395
brace expansion, 534
braces ({ }), 42, 87, 91
bracket ([), in strings, 10
branching construct, 111
branching, multiway, 132
Browser Appliance v1.0.0, 326
browser, viewing photos with, 233
BSD, 20, 325
buffer overflows, 282
built-in commands
  bash, network redirection feature, 345
  BUILTIN_ENABLED, 385
  builtin_name, 385
  builtins.0, built-ins manpage, 27
  builtins.1, 26
  builtins.h, 387
  C code, 385
  commands, replacing, 13
  turn off commands, 14
  description structure, 385
  enable -a, lists commands, 14
  enable command, 14
  enable -n, turns off shell commands, 14
  ./examples/loadables/, 384
  help command, 14
  loadables, 384

loading, 385
memory and conserving when
     loading, 389
popd command, 454
pushd command, 454
pwd (print working directory
     command), 5
shell cd, using, 382
shell functions and aliases, ignoring, 213
shift command, 135
test command, 118
textual completion, extending, 391
tty command, 385
unmask, 288
writing, 385
bytes, 192
bzip2, file compression, 172

C

C header files, 387
-c option (grep), 146
cached SSH keys, flushing, 313
call by value, 88
canonical portable syntax for bash $IFS, 287
caret (^), 11, 153
case, identify options, 248
case-insensitive search, 57, 149
case sensitivity, 133, 177
case statement, 132, 232, 250, 349
cat command, 34, 72, 236
cat program, 244
cdAnnotation, 244
cd (current directory) command, 42, 74,
     214, 368, 380–381
cdrecord, 242
CDs, burning, 242
CentOS, 19, 170
CHANGES, bash change history, 26
changing command names, 369
changing directories, 381
changing the exported value, 88
characters
     asterisk (*), match any number of, 121
     backslash (\), matches special, 153
     caret (^), to negate character class, 11
     counting, 180
     -d option (cut), specify delimiters, 178
     -d option (tr), for deleting, 178
     default, for paper and screen, 85
     exclamation point (!) to negate class, 11
     for enclosed non-printing, 355
     leading with, other than a tab, 60

odd characters in file names, 186
parsing one at a time, 260
patterns for matching, 152
pound (#), 82
question mark (?), for matching a single
     character, 121
renaming or removing files with
     special, 428
space characters, 92
tabs, 59
tr command, for translation of, 176
translation of, 176
unprintable, 333
whitespace, 333
chmod, 298
choice function, prompts for and verify a
     package date, 62
chpass -s shell, changes default shell, 16
chroot command, 303
chroot Jails, 303
chroot, and system recovery, 304
chsh -l, lists valid shells, 16
chsh -s /bin/bash, makes bash default
     shell, 16
chsh -s, changes default shell, 16
chsh, opens editor, 16
Classic Shell Scripting (O'Reilly), 25, 281
--clean option, flushes cached SSH keys, 313
clear command, 420
clear, using with traps, 410
clobber a file, 53
cmdhist, 379
Cmnd_Alias (sudo), 306
cmp, 427
code, running interactively, 15
colon, equals sign (:=), 102
colons (:), to separate directories, 68
color escape sequence, and trailing m, 360
comm, 438
comma operator (,), 110
Comma Separated Values (CSV), 277
command
     changing a typo in, 456
     command, 197, 213, 324, 382
     eval command, 536
     exit status ($?), 70
     for compiling and linking, 388
     hash, 286
     line calculator, 142
     lines, repeating, 455
     names, changing or shortening, 369
     not found errors, 204, 468, 479

command (*continued*)
    number, 359
    -p, 324
    quoting affecting, 535
    redefine with alias, 211
    run several in sequence, 71
    running in the background, 73
    separating with semicolons, 72
    substitution, 103, 340
    using sudo on several, 434
    verify success of, 69, 74
command-line processing
    repeating, 536
commas, as the thousands separator, 452
comments, 82, 97, 309
comparison operators, 120
COMPAT, compatibility issues, 26
compgen, 392, 393, 481
complete command, 391, 481
completion strings, viewing, 392
compound commands, 114
compressed archives, uncompressing, 391
compressed files, 154, 172
compression algorithms, 173
config.h, 387
configuration and customization
    $CDPATH directories, 367–368
    $COMP_WORDS, 393
    $COMPREPLY, 393
    $cur variable, 393
    $HISTCONTROL, 378
    $HISTFILE, 378
    $HISTFILESIZE variable, 378
    $HISTIGNORE, 378
    $HISTSIZE, 378
    $HISTTIMEFORMAT, 378
    $include, 373
    $INPUTRC, 371
    $PATH, 362–366
    $PATH, change permanently, 361
    $PROMPT_COMMAND, 359
    $PS1, command prompt, 353, 357
    $PS1, errors with, 410
    $PS2, 353, 374
    $PS3, select prompt, 357, 374
    $PS4 prompt, 376
    $PWD, to print entire CWD, 358
    /etc/bash.bashrc (Debian), global
        environment file, 395
    /etc/bash_completion, for programmable
        completion library, 395

/etc/bashrc (Red Hat), bash sub-shells
    global environment file, 395
/etc/bashrc, for system-wide environment
    settings, 401
/etc/inputrc, for global GNU Readline
    configuration, 395
/etc/profile, Bourne shells global login
    environment file, 395
/etc/profile, system-wide profile
    settings, 400
\W, to print basename, 358
\w, to print entire path, 358
_mcd_command_failed_, 382
_signals, 393
_struct, 385
~/.bash_history, command history
    default storage file, 395
~/.bash_login, for Bourne login shells
    personal profile files, 395
~/.bash_logout, 395
~/.bash_profile, for bash login shells
    personal profiles, 395
~/.bashrc, for bash sub-shells personal
    environment files, 395
~/.inputrc, for GNU Readline
    customizations, 396
~/.profile, for Bourne logging shells
    personal profile files, 395
~/bin directory, 373
0m, clears all attributes and set no
    color, 360
absolute paths, hardcoding, 362
alias, 369
ANSI, 359
ANSI escape sequence, 355
application directories, 362
archive, 388
bash -c help, 353
bash-completion library, list of
    modules, 390
bash environment, replication, 398
bashgetopt.h, 387
bash --help, 353
bash login rc files, 396
bash_logout, sample of, 408
bash_profile, sample of, 401
bashrc, sample of, 403
bash -x, 353
bind commands, 372
built-in
    commands, 382
    list of loadables, 385

memory and conserving when
loading, 389
textual completion, extending, 391
writing, 385
BUILTIN_ENABLED, 385
builtin_name, 385
builtins.h, 387
C code, 385
C header files, 387
cd argument, 368
clear, using with traps, 410
cmdhist, 379
command
command, 382
names, changing or shortening, 369
number, 359
compgen, 392, 393
complete command, 391
completion strings, viewing, 392
compressed archives, uncompressing, 391
config.h, 387
configuration files, using in bash
scripts, 202
configure script, 388
Ctrl-X P, displays $PATH, 362
beginning custom configuration, 400
CWD (current working directory), 358
description structure, for built-ins, 385
directories, creating and changing in one
step, 381
directories, using find command in many
levels, 383
downloads for this book, 356
dynamic shared objects, 388
echo statements, care when using, 399
egrep pattern, 363
enable built-in, 385
enclosed non-printing characters, 355
environment settings, system-wide, 401
erasedups, 378
error messages, identifying, 366
EX_USAGE, 386
./examples/loadables/, for pre-written
built-ins, 384
EXECUTION_FAILURE, 387
EXECUTION_SUCCESS, 387
exit code, 363
exit status ($?), 354
expand_aliases, 370
export command, 357
Fedora Core 5, 353
function-name, 385

functions, 369
grep -l PATH ~/.[^.]*, 361
gunzip utility, 391
hello.c, 384
help_array, 385
histappend, 379
history, between sessions and
synchronization, 376
history command, 376
history number, 359
history options, setting, 377
history sharing, automation of, 377
if command, 363
ignoreboth, 378
ignoredups, 378
ignorespace, 378
improving cd commands, 380
.inputrc, 371
inputrc, sample of, 407
internal_getopt, 387
jobs, number being currently
managed, 354
kill command, 392
leading dots in filenames, 398
libraries, third-party, 389
lithist, 379
loadable built-ins, 384
loptend, 387
macros, for shell interaction
documentation, 362
Makefile, 384
Meta Ctrl-V, displays variable for
editing, 362
mkdir command, 382
no_options(list), 386
NULL, 387
options, 353
PATH="$PATH:newdir", 362
paths, 361, 362, 366
personal utilities, 373
POSIX mode, 368
profile settings, system-wide, 400
programmable completion, 389
prompts, 353, 355, 359
prompt strings, 357
promptvars shell option, 357
PTY, pseudo-terminal number, 354
RC (initialization) files, 394, 398–400
readline, 362, 371
reset_internal_getopt, 387
root, set paths, 361

configuration and customization (*continued*)
  run_screen, sample of, 408
  -s option (example loadable built-in), 385
  secondary prompts, 374
  select statement, 374
  settings subdirectory, 398
  set +x, 353
  shell.h, 387
  shells, levels of, 354
  signal names, 392
  startup options, 353
  stdio.h, 387
  strftime, 378
  symbolic links, 370
  trailing m, indicates color escape
     sequence, 360
  tty built-in, 385
  ttyname, 387
  unalias, 369
  usage, short form of help, 386
  WORD_LIST, 386
  world-writable directory, avoid in root's
     path, 361
  xterms, 355, 359
  xtrace, for debugging prompt, 357
configuration files, 200–203
configure script, 388
continue statement, 163
converters, for documents, 414
converting dates and times to Epoch
    seconds, 222
converting Epoch seconds to human-readable
    dates and times, 223
Conway, Damian, 84
Copernic Desktop Search, 194
core dumps, 65, 287
CPIO files, 173
creating directories, 381
creating RC files, 398–400
cron, 228, 347
cron jobs, and passwords, 308
cross-platform scripts, 326
crypt hashes, 307
CS_PATH, 323
C strftime( ) function (man 3 strftime), for
    formatting options, 217
CSV (Comma Separated Values), 277, 278
Ctrl-A K, to kill the window and end the
    session, 418
Ctrl-X P, displays $PATH, 362
cur_weekday, 222
curl, 336

current working directory, 358
custom configuration, introduction to, 400
cut command, 170, 264
CWD (current working directory), 358
Cygwin, 23
cygwin1.dll, 23

D

D/M/YY formats, avoid, 218
-d option (date)
  -d option, 170, 219, 221
  -d option (cut) specify delimiters, 178
  -d option (tr), 178
daemon, 199
dash (-), 40, 392
dash, shell, 324
dashes, print a line of, 230
data
  accessing on remote machines, 307
  archiving, 421
  files, updating specific fields, 266
  fixed-length, 273
  fixed-width, 273
  isolating fields, 264
  numeric, 166
  prepending, 429–432
  subsets, 170
  validation, 282
databases, setup with MySQL, 262
dates and times
  %z format, 218
  arithmetic, 225
  C strftime( ) function (man 3 strftime), for
    formatting options, 217
  converting to specific day and time, 223
  crons, 228
  crontab, 228
  cur_weekday, 222
  -d option, 219, 221
  D/M/YY formats, avoid, 218
  date command, 216
  date ranges, automating, 220
  DAY, caution using, 221
  Daylight Saving Time, 227
  day, ranges, 229
  day of week for the given day, 222
  DD/MM/YY formats, avoid, 218
  default dates, 218
  end of month of the given month, 222
  end_month, 222
  Epoch seconds, 222, 223, 227
  formatting options, 217

gawk, 216
getdate, 220
GNU date command, 216, 219, 221, 224
ISO 8601, displays dates and times, 218
leap years, 226, 227
Linux Vixie Cron, 228
M/D/YY formats, avoid, 218
MM/DD/YY formats, avoid, 218
NTP (Network Time Protocol), 226
number of days between two dates, 222
Perl, 223, 224, 227
pn_day, 222
pn_day_nr, 222
pn_month, 222
pn_weekday, 222
previous and next x days of the given
        day, 222
previous and next x months, 222
scripts, running on Nth day, 228
seconds, 226, 227
SQL query, 219
strftime format specification, 217
string formatting with strftime, 513
this week, caution using, 221
time zones, 218, 226
tomorrow's, 224
Unix command, omits the year, 226
UnixReview, 221
DAY, caution using, 221
Daylight Saving Time, 227
day of week for the given day, 222
DD/MM/YY formats, avoid, 218
Debian, 17, 173, 183, 197
DEBUG signal, 210
debugging, and core dumps, 287
declare option, 210
default dates, 218
default values, 99, 100
deleting characters, 178
delimiters, 170
description structure, for built-ins, 385
desktop search engine, 194
developerWorks (IBM), 313
diff, 246, 422–425, 437
digit octal modes, 298
direct parsing, ${#} dollar sign, bracket,
        pound sign, bracket, 248
directories, 361
    $CDPATH directories, 368
    $PATH errors, 465
    add or remove, 362

adding current to $PATH, 291
application, 362
backups of, 439–442
colons (:), to separate, 68
creating and changing in one step, 381
find command, using in many levels, 383
moving among arbitrary ones, 453
names, parsing off, 175
photos, viewing, 232
relative, 173
tar archives, 175
temporary, 282
world-writable, 289–291, 361
disconnected sessions, 415
display variables for editing, 362
divert output, 47
documentation, 25, 83, 362
documents, comparing, 244
dollar sign ($), 29, 81, 109, 153
    variable substitution, 534
dollar sign, brace, pound sign, brace
        (${#}), 96
dollar sign, parentheses ($( )), for command
        substitution, 46
dollar, asterisk ($*), 91
dollar, at sign ($@), 94
DOS
    carriage returns (\r), deletion, 178
    endlines, converting to Unix, 173
    files, convert to Linux, 178
    pause command, 450
dos2unix, 464
dot (.) files, 10, 11, 201
dot directory, 68
double asterisk (**), for raising to a
        power, 109
double braces ({{ }}) code block, 341
double bracket compound statement
        ([[ ]]), 121
double dollar sign variable ($$), 243
double equals signs (==), 240
double exclamation point (!!) history
        operator, 150
double greater than operator (>>), 115
double parentheses ((( ))) construct, 127
double quotes ("), 30, 254, 535
double-ampersands (&&), 72
downloads for this book, 356
duplicate lines, removing, 171
dynamic shared objects, 388

E

-e option, escape sequence (echo), 33
echo *, ls command substitute, 11
echo command, 29, 32, 70, 214, 329–331
echo options and escape sequences, 508
echo portability, 329
echo statements, care when using, 399
ed script, 433
egrep, 265, 363
egress filtering, 337
elif, 111
else clause, 111
else-if (elif), 111
Emacs and vi, allow shell escapes, 303
Emacs mode commands, 518
email, sending, 345–348
embedded blanks, 92
embedding documentation, in shell
    scripts, 83
EMIT function, 236
empty variables, 474
enable -a, lists built-in commands, 14
enable built-in, 385
enable command, 14
enable -n, turns off shell built-in
    commands, 14
end of month, 222
END keyword (awk), 158
end_month, 222
endlines, converting to Unix to DOS, 173
end-user documentation, 83
env (export -p), 88
env command, 321
environment settings, system-wide, 401
EOF (end-of-input word), 237
end-of-input word (EOP), 237
Epoch seconds, 222, 223, 227
eq operator, 120
-eq operator, for numeric comparisons, 119
equal sign (= sign), 109
erasedups, 378
ERR signal, 210
error messages, 37, 77, 103, 251, 366
errors, and core dumps, 287
ERROUT function, 236
escape sequences, 33, 179
eval command, 536
EX_USAGE., 386
./examples/loadables/, 384
exclamation point (!) to negate character
    class, 11
-exec, 185

exec command, 335, 342
exec option, 193
executables
    $PATH, 68
    $SCRIPT, 79
    $STAT, 70
    . (dot) with ls, supersedes normal ls
        command, 68
    ./ (leading dot and slash character), 69
    || syntax, for error/debug messages, 77
    ampersand (&) to run commands in the
        background, 72
    asterisk (*), 9
    bg, to unpause the job, 73
    bin directory, 69
    cd command, 74
    colons (:), to separate directories, 68
    commands, 69, 71, 72, 74
    conditional execution, of if statement, 75
    dot directory, 68
    double-ampersands (&&), to run the next
        program, 72
    echo command, 70
    error messages, 77
    executePermissions, forgetting to set, 462
    exit, 70
    exit status ($?), 70, 74
    fg command, reconnects to a background
        job, 73
    file permissions, 69
    for looping, 67
    hangup (hup) signal, 76
    if statement, 71, 74, 75
    if/then/else branching, 67
    InfoZip, 78
    job number, 73
    jobs, running unattended, 76
    kill command, 76
    locate executables, 68
    nohup command, 76
    Permissions, forgetting to set
        execute, 462
    PID (process ID, $$), 73
    rm command, 74
    run a command, 67
    scripts, running a series of, 79
    set -e flag, 76
    variable names, use with care, 78
    variables, running commands from, 78
    while loops, 75
EXECUTION_FAILURE, 387
EXECUTION_SUCCESS, 387

exglob extended pattern-matching
    operators, 515
exit, 70, 350
exit 0, 84
exit code, 363
exit status ($?), 74, 354
expand_aliases, 370
export command, 357
exported environment variables, 468
exported value, changing, 88
exported variables, 87, 467
expressions, short-circuited, 117
ext script, 57
external commands, 13
extglob option (extended pattern
    matching), 122

F

-f option (awk) counting string values, 160
-F option (awk) to delineate fields, 155
-F option (ls), shows type of file with trailing
    designators, 9
-F switch (tail), 39
-f switch (tail), 39
FC (see Fedora Core)
feature creep, 230
Fedora Core
    'ps' command, 170
    bash login rc files, 396
    customize the $PS1 and $PS2
        variables, 353
    Red Hat distributions, 19
fg command, reconnects to a background
    job, 73
field delimiter, 272
field separator, 168, 254, 272
fields, 170, 264, 266
FIELDWIDTHS, 273
FILE1 -ef FILE2, for locating identical
    files, 116
FILE1 -nt FILE2, checks modification
    date, 116
FILE1 -ot FILE2 , for locating "is older than
    dates", 116
filenames
    $( ) dollar sign, parentheses, for filenames
        on command lines, 147
    ${ } argument, 105
    '{}', holds names during command
        execution, 193
    .jpg, 121
    = (equal) symbols in, 81

delimit substitutions, 105
delimit the reference, 105
file characteristics, testing, 114
filename expansion, 10
finding, 186
for loop, 105
ls, shows names of, 9
mv command, 105
odd characters in, 186
operators, string-manipulation, 106
and quotes, 93
random, for security, 293
renaming, 105, 411
searches, 147
slash (/), 105
use of meaningful ones, 294
files
    $( ) dollar sign, parentheses, for filenames
        on command lines, 147
    .[!.]*, for filename expansion patterns, 11
    .0, for formatted manual pages, 27
    .html, for HTML versions, 27
    .ps, for postscript versions, 27
    /etc/passwd file, 16
    = (equals) symbols, in filenames, 81
    AND (-a), 117
    batch job, logging, 418
    characteristic, testing for more than
        one, 117
    compression, 172
    converting to CSV, 277
    counting differences of, 426
    CSV data file, parsing, 278
    data files, compare and find lines in, 436
    deleting using an empty variable, 474
    descriptor, 38
    editing in place, 432
    expression, short-circuited, 117
    extensions, 174
    extensions, uncompressing, 174
    file characteristics, testing, 114
    file command, 175
    file handles, 335
    FILESIZE function, 240
    finding by content, 192
    finding by date, 189
    finding by size, 192
    finding by type, 191
    finding content quickly, 194
    finding existing files quickly, 194
    finding with list of locations, 195
    for information on specific files, 8

files (*continued*)
    index for several, 422
    info, 413
    info command, 413
    info program, 413
    line breaks, eliminate, 275
    ls -l, provides file details, 9
    ls options, 9
    metadata recovery, 421
    -mtime predicate to find, 190
    naming, 173
    operations, speeding up resulting, 187
    OR (-o), 117
    overwrite, 172
    permissions, 69
    quotes, around file arguments, 411
    Red Hat, util-linux package, 413
    rename commands, 413
    rename from_string to_string file_
        name, 413
    renaming, 411
    sessions, logging, 418
    -size predicate to find, 192
    symbolic links, 188
    system-level, 287
    tar command, 172
    temporary files, and security, 282, 292
    test options, 116
    testing, 117
    Texinfo, 413
    Unix permissions, 300
    unzipping, 246
    updating specific fields, 266
    ZIP, 246, 414
find command
    find utility, 185
    finding by file content, 192
    finding by file date, 189
    finding by file size, 192
    finding by file type, 191
    finding existing files quickly, 194
    finding file by content quickly, 194
    finding files with list of locations, 195
    finding IP addresses, 335–338
    listing files, 145
    Metadata, capturing for recovery, 421
    MP3 files, locating, 239
    phrases, searching for, 163
    printf formats, 421
    xargs command, 343
fingerprints, 315

Firefox 1.0.7, 326
fixed-length data (fixed-width), 273
fixed-width data, 273
flags, 163, 249
floating-point values, 131
fmt command, 181
-follow predicate to find, 188
FollowMeIP, 337
for loop, 67, 85, 91, 130, 157, 327, 343, 449
for syntax, for looping with a count, 130
forced commands, SSH, 316
Fox, Brian, 1
FreeBSD, 20, 183, 197
FREESPACE function, 239
frequently asked questions
    .FAQ, 26
    awk program, 155
    bash default shell, 17
    bash official documentation, 25
    BSD syslog protocol, 335
    chmod command, 53
    counting string value, 161
    current directory to the $PATH,
        avoiding, 292
    data as histograms, 162
    data, discarding portions of, 155
    DOS pause command, 450
    editing a file in place, 432
    file permissions, 53
    finding bash for #!, 322
    free shell accounts, 25
    hidden (.) dot files, 12
    interpreter spoofing attacks, 283
    IP addresses, finding, 340
    noclobber option, 53
    pipelines and subshells, 473
    prepend data to a file, 429
    removing or renaming files named with
        special characters, 428
    reversing word order, 158
    RFC 3164, 335
    spoofing attacks, avoiding, 283
    summing a list of numbers, 159
    testing scripts, 325
    text paragraphs after a found phrase, 164
    Unix shell differences, 27
    writing sequences, 448
    xargs, "argument list too long"
        errors, 343
Friebel, Wolfgang, 183
Friedman, Noah, 297

function
   arguments, 369
   avoiding, 213
   call, 256
   definitions, 204
   function-name, 385
   parameters, 205
   values, 205

G

gawk, 216
getconf ARG_MAX command, 344
getconf utility, 284, 323
getdate, 220
getline command, 159
getopts, 134, 249, 249–252
globbing (extended pattern matching), 10, 122
Gnome 2.12.1, 326
gnome-apt, 19
GNU
   /etc/inputrc, for global Readline configuration, 395
   ~/.inputrc, 396
   date command, 216, 219, 221, 224
   find, 344, 421
   grep, 437
   Linux, 324
   long options, 325
   Readline customizations, 396
   Readline library, 373
   run_screen, sample of, 408
   screen, installation, 415
   sed utility, 429
   seq utility, 449
   tar utility, 173
   Texinfo, 413
   Text Utils, 23
   xargs, 344
Google Desktop Search, 194
GOTO, 348
greater than sign (>) redirect output, 48
greater than, equal sign (<=), 240
grep, 254, 262
   awk, outputting to, 159
   -c option, 427
   -c, created fewer lines to search for, 427
   complex pattern searches, 152
   compressed files, 154
   egrep, 265, 363
   ext script, for parameterization, 57
   filename output, 262

find command, 383, 421
grep '<a', 254
grep command, 56
grep -l PATH ~/.[^.]*, 361
grep -o, 265
grep -v, 151
gzcat, 154
-h switch, 146
-i option, 149
-i option, (grep), makes search case-insensitive, 57
-l option, 147
output, 442
pipelines, 150
ps command, 442
-q (quiet) option, 148
regular expression, 152
single quote ('), 254
supply with a source of input, 146
text-related utilities, 144
variables, to find specific, 90
vary output with options, 146
zgrep, 154
groff -Tascii, 27
Groupe Bull, 22
gsub, 272
guest users, restricting, 301
GUI, 19
GUI Rpmdrake, 19
gunzip utility, 391
gzip, file compression, 172

H

-h for getting help, 6, 14
-H option (grep), 193
-h switch (grep), 146
hangup (hup) signal, 76
hash -r command, 286
hash, one-way, 307
hashes, 159, 307
head commands, 39
header lines, 40
hello.c, 384
help_array, 385
help command, 6, 14
here-document, 56
   <<- for indenting, 59
   << syntax, 56
   data kept with script, 56
   HTML in scripts, 236
   indenting for readability, 59
   odd behavior in, 57

Hex, viewing output, 333
hexdump, 333
hidden (dot) files, 10
histappend, 379
history
    !! (double exclamation point)
        operator, 150
    ~/.bash_history, for default storage
        file, 395
    CHANGES, to change bash, 26
    histogram, 161
    history command, 376
    history number, 359
    setting shell options, 377
    sharing, automation of, 377
    synchronization between sessions, 376
Host_Alias, 306
host, external, 336
host restriction, 317
.html for versions, 27
HTML, parsing, 253
hunks, sections of changed data, 426

I

-i option (xargs), 187
-i option, (grep), makes search
        case-insensitive, 57
I/O redirection, 506
IBM, 22
if command, 363
if list, 112
if statement, 71, 74, 75, 100, 111, 240
if test, 97
if/then, to identify options, 248
if/then/else branching, 67
ifconfig, 336
ignoreboth, 378
ignoredups, 378
ignorespace, 378
-iname predicate to find, 189
indenting for readability, 59
index, for several files, 422
info command, 413
info2man, Texinfo viewer and converter, 414
info2www, Texinfo viewer and
        converter, 414
InfoZip, 78, 285
initialization (rc) files, 394
input
    $INPUTRC, for readline, 371
    $PASSWD, 65
    $REPLY, 64

$THISPACKAGE, 62
/etc/inputrc, for readline, 395
/proc/core, for accessing passwords, 65
<< syntax, for here-documents, 56
<<- syntax, for indenting
        here-documents, 59
choice function, prompts for and verify a
        package date, 62
command filename, 55
core dumps, accessing passwords, 65
EOF (end-of-input word), 237
getting input, from other machines, 340
grep command, 56
here-document, indenting for
        readability, 59
inputrc, sample of, 407
leading characters, 60
-p option (read), 60, 65
password prompt, 65
preprocessors, 182
printf, 65
read statement, 60
redirection, (< less than symbol), 55
REPLY, 60
root, 65
-s option (read), 65
select, 64
SSH certificates, 65
stty sane, to fix echo, 66
stty sane, to restore echo, 66
tab character, 59
user input, 60
validation, 296
whitespace, trailing, 59
yes or no input, 61
.inputrc, 371
inputrc, sample of, 407
INSTALL, bash installation instructions, 26
integer expressions, 108
Internal Field Separator (bash $IFS), 254,
        268, 270, 287
internal_getopt, 387
IP address, 167, 335–338
ireset_internal_getopt, 387
ISO 8601, displays dates and times, 218

J

-j, for bzip2, 173
job number, 73
jobs, 76, 354

K

k (kilobytes), 192
KDE-based desktop distribution, 326
Kernighan, Brian, 320
key pair, creation, 309
keychain, 308, 313–315
keyphrase, 163
keyword command, 214
keywords, processing on command line, 532
kill command, 76, 392
kill -l, 207, 211
Knoppix, 19
kpackage, 19

L

-l chpass, changes bash default shell, 16
-l option (grep), 147
-L option (ls), for linked file information, 9
-l option (ls), for long listing, 9
-l option (unzip), to convert Unix end
        lines, 173
-L, (pwd, cd) displays logical path, 5
last in, first out mechanisms, 454
leading characters, 60
leading dot and slash (./), for accessing
        current directory, 7
leading dots in filenames, 398
leading, trim, 268–271
leap years, 226, 227
Learning the bash Shell, 25, 301, 384, 389
lefthand side (LHS), 277
less command, 44, 155, 182
less utility, 155
less -V, 447
lesspipe*, 182
lesspipe.sh, 183
let statement, 108
LHS (lefthand side), 277
libraries, third-party, 389
line breaks, eliminate, 275
line counting, 180
lines, numbering, 446
lines, removing duplicates, 171
links, symbolic, 188, 237
Linux
        $PATH, changing, 397
        /bin/bash, 370
        /etc/apt/sources.list, 19
        /etc/profile, 363

Add/Remove Applications, 19
application installation, 17
application upgrades, 17
bash versions, 17
CentOS, 19
crontab, 228
Debian, 17
DOS files, convert to Linux, 178
error message, 19
FC (Fedora Core), 19
gnome-apt, 19
GUI Rpmdrake, 19
info, 413
Knoppix, 19
kpackage, 19
Linux API emulation, 23
Linux API functionality, 23
Mandrake, 19
Mandriva, 19
MEPIS, 19
Red Hat, 363
Red Hat Enterprise Linux (RHEL), 19,
        197
root, 17
sort comparisons, 169
SUSE, 19, 183
Synaptic, 19
tarball.tar.gz, 172
Ubuntu, 326
Vixie Cron, 228
YaST, 19
Linux Security Cookbook, 308
listing, of all built-ins commands, 14
lithist, 379
Live CDs, 19
-ll option, (unzip), convert DOS end lines to
        Unix, 173
loadable built-ins, 384
locale setting, when sorting, 168
locate, 7, 194
locating identical files, 116
locating "is older than" dates, 116
log messages, eliminating by error, 151
logger, 335, 345
logging, 418
logmsg, 350
looping, 130
loptend, 387
ls -a, shows all files, 10
ls command, shows filenames, 7
ls -d, 10

ls -l, 9, 156
ls options, 9
ls, shows filenames, 9
lynx, 336

M

m (trailing), indicates color escape
        sequence, 360
MAC (Mandatory Access Controls), 304
Mac OS X
    /bin/sh, 21
    10.4, and curl, 336
    bash-2.05, 21
    bash versions, 21
    BSD, 325
    chsh, opens editor, 16
    cut command, garbles output, 170
    Darwin, 21
    DarwinPorts, 21
    default user shell, 3
    Fink, 21
    HMUG, 21
    Mac OS 10.2 (Jaguar), 21
    Mac OS 10.4 (Tiger), 21
    source bash, 21
    sudo, 435
Macdonald, Ian, 389
macros, for shell interaction
        documentation, 362
mail, 346
Mail User Agent (MUA), 348
mail*, 347
MAILTO variable, 347
mailx, 346
Makefile, 384
malicious script, /tmp/ls, 292
man command, 6
man in the middle attacks, 315
man sudoers, 306
Mandatory Access Controls (MAC), 304
Mandrake, 19
Mandriva, 19
manpages, 6, 27
manual pages, formatting, 27
Mastering Regular Expressions, 266
M/D/YY formats, avoid, 218
meaningful_prefix, and security, 294
menus, 137
MEPIS, 19
Message Transfer Agent (MTA), 346
metacharacters, 532

Meta Ctrl-V, displays variable for
        editing, 362
meta key (screen command mode), 416
Microsoft Services for Unix, 24
Midnight Commander, 292
MIME-aware update, to mail, 347
mkdir command, 382
mkdir -p -m 0700 $temp_dir, avoids race
        condition, 293
mkisofs, 242
mktemp, 293
MM/DD/YY formats, avoid, 218
modification dates, 116
MP3 files
    $$ (double dollar sign) variable, 243
    <= (greater than, equals sign), 240
    == (double equals signs), 240
    -A option (mkisofs), 244
    available space, tracking when
            loading, 238
    cat program, 244
    cdAnnotation, 244
    cdrecord, 242
    CDs, burning, 242
    FILESIZE function, 240
    find command, 239
    FREESPACE function, 239
    if statements, 240
    loading, tracking available space
            automatically, 238
    mkisofs, 242
    MP3 player, 237, 238
    -p option (mkisofs), 244
    REDUCE function, 240
    -V parameter (mkisofs), 244
    while loop, 239
MP3 player, loading, 237
mpack, 347
-mtime predicate to find, 190
MUA (Mail User Agent), 348
multiplication symbol, 143
mysql command, 263
MySQL, databases setup with, 262

N

N log files, 439–442
-n option (sort), for sorting numbers, 166
-name '*.txt', to narrow searches using
        find, 193
-name predicate to find, 185
NetBSD, 20, 169
Netcat, 334, 345

Net-redirection, 334
network redirection feature, 345
network traffic, 334
new line with echo, -n option, 32
NEWS, changes to versions of bash, 25
NF variable (awk), 156, 160
no command-line tools, 336
No such file or directory error, 463
no_options(list), 386
noclobber option, 52
nohup command, 76, 200
NOPASSWD option, 307
NOT constructs, 190
NOTES, configuration and operation
        notes, 26
NSA's Security Enhanced Linux
        (SELinux), 304
NSF, to store test scripts and data, 326
NTP (Network Time Protocol), 216, 226
null, 101, 387
null strings, and shopt -s nullglob
        option, 344
number of days between two dates, 222
-number switch (head, tail), changes number
        of lines, 39
numbering line, 446
numbers, 158, 450
numeric data, sorting, 166

0

-o options (recipe 6.4), 243
octal dump command (od), 333
octal modes, 298
od (octal dump command), 333
ODF (Open Document Format), 245, 275
OFS (awk output field separator), 272
one file per line option (ls -1), 9
online references, shell security, 281
Open Document Format (ODF), 245, 275
OpenBSD, 20, 280
OpenSSH, 280, 308, 318
operations, speeding up resulting, 187
operators
    !! (double exclamation point) history, 150
    *.txt, for pattern matching, 11
    :- assignment operator, 101
    :+ variable operator, 203
    ?, shell pattern matching operator, 11,
        514
    -a operator, 115
    assignment, 109

comma operator (,), 110
comparison, 120
double greater than operator (>>), 115
eq operator, 120
-eq operator, for numeric
        comparisons, 119
extended pattern-matching, 10
Perl, 120
redirection, 38
string-manipulation, 106
option filename, 116
options
    and arguments, 249
    filename, 116
    history options, 377
    promptvars shell option, 357
    -s option (example loadable builtin), 385
    setting on startup, 353
    standalone, 249
    turn off interactively, 353
OR (-o), 117
OR constructs, 190
Outlook, 347
output
    $( ) (dollar sign, parentheses), for
        command substitution, 46
    &> (ampersand, greater than sign), sends
        STDOUT and STDERR to same
        file, 38
    /dev/null, 41
    > (greater than sign) redirect output,
        33, 35, 48
    >& (greater than sign, ampersand), sends
        STDOUT and STDERR to same
        file, 38
    >> (double greater than), append the
        output, 39
    | (pipe symbol)
    -1 (ls minus one) option, 36
    adding prefix or suffix to, 444
    bit bucket, 41
    braces ({ }), for grouping output, 42
    buffered, 49
    -C option, (ls), redirects output, 35
    clobber a file, 53
    control over placement of, 31
    display beginning of file, 39
    display end of file, 39
    divert output, 47
    double quotes ("), to preserve spacing, 30
    dump unwanted data, 41

output (*continued*)
  echo command, 29
  eliminating output, 41
  file descriptor, 38
  formatting control, 31
  function call, 256
  grouping from several commands, 41
  head commands, 39
  header lines, 40
  header lines, skipping, 40
  less command, 44
  line output, keeping selected
            portions, 156
  ls command, 35
  messages.out, 37
  -n option, new line with echo, 32
  newline default, 32
  noclobber option, 52
  -number switch (head, tail), changes
            number of lines, 39
  OFS (awk field separator), 272
  output messages, redirect to different
            files, 37
  overwriting, 52
  parentheses ( ), redirects subshell's
            execution, 42
  parsing into an array, 255
  partial elimination, 155
  pathnames, for redirecting output, 34
  piped I/O, 44
  plus (+) sign for offsetting top of the
            file, 40
  printf, 31
  programs, connecting two, 43, 46
  redirect messages, 37, 48, 342
  redirection operators, 38
  reserved words, 42
  rm command, 46
  save to other files, 34
  saving from a command, 33
  single quote ('), to preserve spacing, 30
  sorted, 165
  split, 332
  STDERR (>&2), 38
  STDIN (standard in), 49
  STDOUT (standard output), 37, 49, 50
  tail commands, 39
  tee command, 45, 50
  unbuffered, 49
  using as input, 43
  viewing, in Hex, 333

P
-p option (mkisofs), 244
-p option (read), 60, 65
-p option (trap), 210
package dates, verification, 62
paragraphs, rewrapping, 181
parameters
  $* (unquoted), 95
  $@ (unquoted), 95
  ${!prefix*}, for programmable
            completion, 287
  ${!prefix@}, for expansion, 287
  ${parameter#[#]word}, 480
  ${parameter%[%]word}, 480
  ${parameter/pattern/string}, 480
  embedded blanks, 92
  errors in, 94
  errors using $*, 94
  expansion of, 103
  function parameters, 205
  positional arguments, 101
  quotes, around, 93
  unsetting of, 103
  -V parameter (mkisofs, 244
parentheses ( ), 42, 190
parsing
  ${#}, for direct parsing, 248
  arguments, 231, 248
  characters, one at a time, 260
  command-line arguments, 134
  CSV data file, 278
  directory names, 175
  HTML, 253
  output into an array, 255
  output, with a function call, 256
  with read into an array, 258
  text, with a read statement, 257
passphrase, changing and protection, 308
passwd, changes bash default shell, 16
passwords, 65, 299, 307, 308
patch, 422–425
path, security, 283
PATH="$PATH:newdir", 362
PATH="newdir:$PATH", 362
pathnames
  absolute, 176
  expansion of, 534
  using Tab key to finish the name, 459
paths
  absolute, 284
  modifying, 366

permanently change, 361
setting explicit, 362
updates, 361
pattern matching
  ${parameter/pattern/string}, 480
  ${variable/pattern/replacement}, 195
  *.txt, 11
  .jpg, 121
  ?, shell pattern matching operator, 11,
    514
  asterisk (*), match any number of
    characters, 121
  bash alphabetizes, 470
  bash version 3.0, 123
  case sensitivity, 122
  double bracket compound statement
    ([[ ]]), for matches on righthand
    side of equals operator, 121
  egrep, 363
  extglob option, for extended
    matching, 122
  globbing (extended pattern
    matching), 122
  patterns, strings containing an asterisk (*),
    exclamation sign (!), or bracket
    ([), 10
  question mark (?), for matching a single
    character, 121
  and regular expressions, 152
  searches, ignoring case, 149
  searching with complex patterns, 152
  symbols, grouping, 122
  symbols to use for, 480
  testing strings with, 121
pattern-matching characters, 514
pause command (DOS), 450
PC-BSD, 326
PCRE (Perl Compatible Regular
  Expressions), 266
percent sign (%) to format specifications, 31
period (.), 152
period, asterisk (.*), with file wildcards, 10
Perl, 84, 120, 224, 227, 266
Perl Best Practices, 84
Perl Cookbook, 451
Perl's date and time data structure, 223
Permission denied, error message, 462
permission information storage, 7
permissions, 298
personal utilities, 373
phases, 348

phone-number lookups script, 56
photo albums, 233–237
photos, 232, 233
phrases, searching for, 163
PID (process ID, $$), 73, 443
pinfo, Texinfo viewer and converter, 414
piped I/O, 44
pipeline searches, 149
pipelines, subshell creation, 470
pkg_add (bash installation/update), 20
pkg_add -vr, 20
plural function, 260
plural noun, 259
pn_day, 222
pn_day_nr, 222
pn_month, 222
pn_weekday, 222
POD (Plain Old Documentation), 84
pod2* programs, 84
Polar Home, 24
popd built-in commands, 454
POSIX, 168, 211, 284, 321, 322, 368
postscript file versions (.ps), 27
pound (#) character, 82
pr command, 181
Practical UNIX & Internet Security
  (O'Reilly), 281
predicates, 185
prepend data, 429–432
previous and next x days of the given
  day, 222
previous and next x days of the given day,
  non-recursive, 222
previous and next x months, 222
-print condition (find), 185
-print0 (find, xargs -0), 186
printf, 31, 65, 135, 329, 474, 509
private key, 309
problems, portability, 284
processes
  automating, 348–351
  verify it is running, 443
profile settings, system-wide, 400
programmable completion, 287, 389
prompt string customizations, 483
prompts
  # (pound) trailing prompt means root, 4
  $ dollar sign, trailing, means logged as a
    regular user, 4
  $PROMPT_COMMAND, 359
  $PS1, command prompt, 357

prompts (*continued*)
    $PS2 (secondary prompt string), 374
    $PS3, select prompt, 357, 374
    $PS4, 376
    ~ (tilde), default for home directory, 4
    0m, clears all attributes and set no
        color, 360
    basic examples of, 353
    changing, on simple menus, 138
    choice function, 62
    customizing, 353
    default prompts, 4
    directory location, 5
    downloads for this book, 356
    find and run particular commands, 6
    keep short and simple, 359
    -L, (pwd, cd) displays logical path, 5
    password prompt, 65
    printing strings, with -p option (read),
        60, 65
    promptvars shell option, 357
    pwd (print working directory) built-in
        command, 5
    root, 5
    secondary, 374
    to show everything, 355
    strings, 357
    su command, 5
    sudo command, 5
    who did what, when, and where, 355
    xtrace, 357
ps, showing passwords on command
    line, 299
PTY, pseudo-terminal number, 354
public key, 309, 310
pushd built-in commands, 454
pwd (print working directory) built-in
    command, 5

Q

-q (quiet) option (grep), 148
-Q option (ls), for quote names, 9
question mark (?), 10, 121
quoting
    " double quotes, 12
    $* (unquoted), 95
    $@ (unquoted), 95
    $VAR expression, 119
    ' (single quote), 12, 30, 152, 212
    \ (backslash), 12
    in arguments, 32
    backward quotes (``) (see also $( )), 46

command not found errors, 468
command-line, 12, 535
double quotes ("), to preserve output
    spacing, 30
filenames, 93
parameters, 93
-Q option (ls), for quote names, 9
quotes, 411, 468
smart quotes, removing, 179
trailing spaces, 12
unquoted text, 12
variable references, 93

R

-r option (ls), for reverse sort order, 9
-R option (ls), to recurse though
    subdirectories, 9
-r options, 245
r00t, 282
race condition, 282, 293
Ramey, Chet
    =~, and use of regular expressions in
        bash, 480
    bash web site, 21, 25
    for loops, 344
    input validation, 297
    Mac OS 10.2 (Jaguar), 21
    Mac OS 10.4 (Tiger), 21
    using printf with a suitable local, 450
rbash.1, for shell manpage, 26
RC (initialization) files, 394
RC files, creating portable files, 398–400
RE (regular expression), 145, 152, 159
RE (regular expressions), for pattern
    matching, 122
read statement, 60, 129, 257, 258
readability, indenting for, 59
readline, 201, 362, 371
readline.3, readline manpage, 26
README, bash description, 25
real arguments, 98
reconnect to a background job, 73
recovering sessions, 415
Red Hat, 183, 196, 304, 321, 413
Red Hat Enterprise Linux (RHEL), 19, 197
redirecting operator (>), 200
redirection operators, 38
REDUCE function, 240
regular expressions (RE), confusing with shell
    wildcards, 480
relative directory, 173
relative pathname, 35

removing directories, 362
rename commands, 413
rename from_string to_string file_name, 413
rename, Perl-based, 413
repetition mechanism, for searches
        (\{n,m\}), 153
replace, and search globally, 254
REPLY, 60, 268–271
reserved words, 42
RETURN signal, 210
RHS (righthand side), 277
rm command, 46, 74
Robbins, Arnold, 281
Robbins, Daniel, 313, 314
root account, 4, 16, 65, 361
ROT13, 307
ROT47, 308
RPM (Red Hat Package Manager), 22, 173
RPN (postfix) notation, 140
RPN calculator, 139
rsh (Remote Shell), 303
rssh, 318
rsync, 317
run commands from variables, 78
run commands in the background, 72
run several commands at once, 72
run several commands in sequence, 71
run the next program, 72
run_screen, sample of, 408
running scripts, several at one time, 79

S

-s option (example loadable built-in), 385
-S option (ls), to sort by file size, 9
-s option (read), 65
-S, turns off stable sort on NetBSD, set buffer
        size otherwise (sort), 168
Schneier, Bruce, 280
scp, using without a password, 308
screen command mode (meta key), 416
screen
    caveats, 416
    for sharing a single bash session, 417
    clearing when logging out, 420
script-kiddies, 280
scripts, 203, 419
    " (double quotes), 254
    # pound, 82
    $ (*dollar, asterisk), 91
    $* (unquoted), 95
    $@ (unquoted), 95
    ${#}, 96

${#}, for direct parsing, 248
${#VAR}, 97
${:=} operator, 101
${:?} syntax, 103
${:-} syntax, 99
${1:0:1} syntax, tests 1st character of 1st
        argument, 248
${VAR#alt}, 97
$0 variable, 236
$i variable, don't use (see also $x), 85
$include, 201
$VERBOSE, 98
$x syntax, 85
' (single quote), 254
.bad, 105
/tmp/ls, and malicious, 292
:- assignment operator, 101
:+ variable operator, 203
:= (colon, equals sign), 102
<a> tags, 253
@ (at sign), 203
~/bin directory, collecting in, 373
-a operator, 115
arguments, 91, 96, 104, 231, 248
arithmetic expansion, 103
array, 106, 107, 255
awk script, 175
basename command, 136
bash $IFS (Internal Field Separator), 258
bash functions, 203
behavior, changing, 125
bit placement, 85
braces ({ }), 87, 91
branching construct, 111
breaking a line, 86
browser, viewing photos with, 233
call by value, 88
case statement, 250
case, identify options, 248
cat command, 236
character default, for paper and
        screen, 85
characters, one at a time, 260
colon (:), 83
command not found error, 204
command substitution, 103
comments, 82
compound commands, 114
configuration files, 200–203
configure script, 388
daemon, 199
data validation, 282
DEBUG signal, 210

scripts (*continued*)
  debugging, 477
  default values, 99, 100
  delimit substitutions, 105
  diff, to compare content of two
      documents, 246
  directory, 232, 291
  documentation, 82
  documents, comparing, 244
  dot (.), 201
  double greater than operator (>>), 115
  double parentheses ((( ))) construct, 127
  ed script, 433
  else clause, 111
  else-if (elif), 111
  EMIT function, 236
  end-user documentation, 83
  env (export -p), 88
  EOF (end-of-input word), 237
  error messages, 103, 251
  ERROUT function, 236
  exit 0, 84
  exported value, changing, 88
  extglob option (extended pattern
      matching), 122
  feature creep, 230
  field separator, 254
  file characteristics, testing, 114
  file test options, 116
  FILE1 -ef FILE2, for locating identical
      files, 116
  FILE1 -nt FILE2, checks modification
      date, 116
  FILE1 -ot FILE2, for locating is "older
      than dates", 116
  flags, 249
  for loop, 85, 91, 105
  function call, parsing output, 256
  function definitions, 204
  function parameters, 205
  functions, 85
  function values, 205
  getopts, 134, 249–252
  grep, 90, 254
  here-document, 83, 236
  HTML, parsing, 253
  if list, 112
  if statement, 100, 111
  if test, 97
  if/then, to identify options, 248
  indentation, 85
  keychain, 313

kill -l, 207, 211
line breaks, 85
log messages, eliminating by error, 151
mv command, 105
nohup command, 200
NOPASSWD option, 307
null, 101
ODF (Open Document Format), 245
opening comments, 97
operators, string-manipulation, 106
option arguments, 98
options, standalone, 249
options, with arguments, 249
output, parsing into an array, 255
output, writing across several
    statements, 32
-p option (trap), 210
parameters, 90, 92, 101, 103
passwords, 307
pattern matching, case sensitivity, 122
Perl, 84
photo albums, 233–237
plural function, 260
plural noun, 259
POD (Plain Old Documentation), 84
print a line of dashes, 230
printf, 135
quotes, around parameters, 93
RE (regular expressions), for pattern
    matching, 122
read statement, parsing, 257, 258
readability, 85
readline, 201
redirecting operator (>), 200
redirections, 125
RETURN signal, 210
root account, 4
running a series of, 79
running on Nth day, 228
scp, using without a password, 308
search and replace, globally, 254
searches, complex, 152
searches, narrowing, 151
security problems with, 282
semicolon (;), 112
set command, 89
setgid, 300
setuid, 300
shell scripting, 3
shift built-in command, 135
shift statement, 250
signal handlers, 208

signal number, 208
slash (/), 105
sourcing, 201
space characters, 92
square brackets ([ ]), 126
STDERR (>&2), 200
STDIN (standard input), 200
STDOUT (standard output), 200
string constants, using for default, 102
substring function, 260
symbolic links, 237
syntax, verifying correctness of using
        bash, 476
test command, 113
test -t option, 125
test, avoid naming as, 466
then (if), 112
tilde (~), for expansion, 103
trap interrupts, 207
trap signals, 207
trap utility, 207
trapping, 207–211
tty, 199
unzipping files, 246
USAGE function, 236
-v argument (for verbose), 98, 347
variable errors, 94
variable names, 85, 86
variable reference, use full syntax, 87
variables, 87, 89, 478
while loop, 126, 128
while read, 127
whitespace, 85
word content, document
        comparison, 245
write only syntax, 82
xtrace, for debugging, 478
zero returns, 127
ZIP files, 246
scripts, writing advanced
    #!/bin/sh, avoid using, 321
    $result, 341
    $SSH_ID, 341
    $SSH_USER, 341
    /sbin/ifconfig -a, 338
    /usr/bin/env command, 321
    { } braces, 341
    ARG_MAX, 344
    ARG_MAX, limits in bytes, 344
    arguments, breaking up, 343
    arguments, list too long error, 343
    bash portables, finding, 321

bash, built-in network redirection
        feature, 345
Browser Appliance v1.0.0, 326
BSD, 325
case statement, 349
characters, unprintable, 333
command command, 324
command -p, 324
command substitution, 340
cron, 347
cross-platform scripts, 326
cross-platform scripts, avoid, 324
CS_PATH, 323
curl, 336
echo, 329–331
echo portability, 329
egress filtering, 337
email, sending, 345–348
env command, 321
exec command, 335, 342
exit, 350
file handles, 335
find command, 343
Firefox 1.0.7, 326
FollowMeIP, 337
for loop, 343
for loop portables, 327
getconf ARG_MAX command, 344
getconf utility, 323
Gnome 2.12.1, 326
GNU long options, 325
GOTO, 348
hexdump, 333
host, external, 336
ifconfig, 336
input, getting from other machines, 340
IP address, external and routable, 336
IP addresses finding, 335–338
KDE-based desktop distribution, 326
logger, 345
logger utility, 335
logmsg, 350
lynx, 336
Mac OS X, 325
Mac OS X 10.4, and curl, 336
mail, 346
mail*, 347
mailto, 346
MAILTO variable, 347
mailx, 346
MIME-aware update, to mail, 347
mpack, 347

scripts, writing advanced (*continued*)
   MTA (Message Transfer Agent), 346
   MUA (Mail User Agent), 348
   Netcat, 334, 345
   Net-redirection, 334
   network traffic, 334
   no command-line tools, 336
   NSF, to store test scripts and data, 326
   od (octal dump command), 333
   Outlook, 347
   output, redirect for entire script, 342
   output, split, 332
   output, viewing in Hex, 333
   PC-BSD, 326
   phases, 348
   POSIX, 321
   POSIX $PATH, setting, 322
   printf "%b", 329
   processes, automating, 348–351
   Red Hat, 321
   script testing in VMware, 326
   shell scripts, portable, 324
   shopt -s nullglob option, expands files to a
      null string, 344
   Solaris, 325, 333
   split command, 332
   SSH, with public keys, 340
   syslog messages, 335
   syslog priority value, 335
   syslog, log to, 345
   Thunderbird, 347
   Ubuntu Linux 5.10, 326
   UDP, 335
   uuencode, 346
   -v argument (for verbose), 347
   virtual machines, prebuilt, 326
   virtualization packages, getting free, 326
   VMware, 325
   VMware player, 326
   VMware Server, 326
   VNC-based VMware Console, 326
   wget, 336
   whitespace, 333
   writing portable scripts, 320
   x86 architecture, 326
   xargs command, 343
   xpg_echo, 329
sdiff, 437
searches
   ${variable/pattern/replacement}, 195

$IFS=':', 196
$PATH, 195
\{n,m\}, repetition mechanism, 153
AND constructs, 190
apropos, searches manpage for
   expressions, 7
Beagle, desktop search engine, 194
-c, created fewer lines to search for
   (diff), 427
command command, 197
complex, 152
Copernic Desktop Search, 194
desktop search engines, 194
files, 194, 195
finding by file content, 192
finding by file date, 189
finding by file size, 192
finding by file type, 191
-follow predicate to find, 188
for filenames, 147
Google Desktop Search, 194
-i option, (grep), makes search
   case-insensitive, 57
-iname predicate to find, 189
-l option, with grep, 147
locate, 194
-mtime predicate to find, 190
-name '*.txt', to narrow searches using
   find, 193
narrowing, 151
NOT constructs, 190
OR constructs, 190
phrases, searching for, 163
pipeline, 149
repetition mechanism for, 153
search and replace, globally, 254
-size predicate to find, 192
slocate, 194
Social Security Number, 153
source command, 195
Spotlight, desktop search engines, 194
true or false, 148
-type d (find directories), 191
type -P, 195
-type predicate to find, 191
-v option (grep), 151
secondary prompt string ($PS2), 374
seconds, 226, 227
secure paths, 283
secure shell programming techniques, 281

security
  $IFS (bash Internal Field Separator), 287
  $PATH, 283
  $RANDOM, 292
  $temp_dir, 293
  $TMOUT variable, 318
  $UMASK variable, 288
  *.pub (public key), 309
  /tmp/ls, malicious script, 292
  \unalias -a command, 285
  ~/bin, security problems, 374
  absolute paths, 284
  accessing data, on remote machines, 307
  accounts, shared, 302
  AIDE, 282
  aliases, clearing, 285
  aliases, malicious, 285
  AppArmor, 304
  attacker, non-root, 293
  Bourne shell, 303
  buffer overflows, 282
  canonical portable syntax for bash
    $IFS, 287
  chroot command, 303
  chroot Jails, 303
  --clean option, flushes cached SSH keys
    (keychain), 313
  command hash, 286
  comments, changing, 309
  common problems with, 282
  core dumps, 287
  cron jobs, using without a password, 308
  crypt hashes, 307
  data validation, 282
  debugging, and core dumps, 287
  directories, temporary, 282
  Emacs and vi, allow shell escapes, 303
  filenames, use of meaningful ones, 294
  files, temporary, 292
  fingerprints, 315
  from host restriction, 317
  getconf utility, 284
  guest users, restricting, 301
  hash -r command, 286
  Host_Alias, 306
  input, validation, 296
  key pair, creation, 309
  keychain, 308, 313–315
  leading backslash, supress alias
    expansion, 285
  MAC (Mandatory Access Controls), 304

  man in the middle attacks, 315
  man sudoers, 306
  meaningful_prefix, 294
  mkdir -p -m 0700 $temp_dir, avoids race
    condition, 293
  mktemp, 293
  NOPASSWD option, 307
  one-way hash, 307
  online references, shell security, 281
  OpenSSH Restricted Shell, 318
  passphrase, 308
  passwords, 299, 307
  permissions, setting, 298
  policy, 304
  POSIX, 284
  private key, 309
  problems, portability, 284
  ps, showing passwords on command
    line, 299
  public key, 310
  r00t, 282
  race condition, 282, 293
  and random filenames, 293
  rbash, restricting login shells, 302
  Red Hat Linux, 304
  restricted shell, 302
  ROT13, 307
  ROT47, 308
  rsh (Remote Shell), 303
  rssh, 318
  rsync, 317
  scp, using without a password, 308
  secure paths, 283
  secure shell programming
    techniques, 281
  SELinux (NSA's Security Enhanced
    Linux), 304
  sessions, inactive, 318
  setgid, 300
  setuid, 300
  setuid root spoofing, 283
  shebang line, 283
  SSH commands, 308, 316–318
  ssh-add command, 312
  ssh-agent, 308
  ssh-keygen (ssh-keygen2), 309
  sudo bash, 305
  sudoers, 306
  system integrity, securing of, 282
  temporary files and, 282
  trap, setting, 293

security (*continued*)
    Tripwire, 282
    Trojan horse, 282
    trojaned utilities, 282
    ulimit, 287
    umask, secure, 288
    Unix, file permissions, 300
    Unix groups, 300
    unprivileged users, 282
    urandom, 293
    user, non-root, 305
    User_Alias, 306
    users, inactive, 318
    vi and Emacs, allow shell escapes, 303
    visudo, for editing, 306
    world-writable directories, 289–291
sed, 277
select prompt ($PS3), 64, 137, 357, 374
SELinux (NSA's Security Enhanced
    Linux), 304
semantic differences, with parentheses, 42
semicolon (;), 72, 112
separators for numbers, 450
seq command, to generate floating-point
    values, 131
sequences, writing, 448
sessions, 318, 376, 415, 418
set, 371, 482
set command, 89
set -e, 76
set -o functrace option, 210
set -o posix, 211
setgid, 300
settings subdirectory, 398
setuid, 300
setuid root spoofing, 283
SGI, 22
shebang line, 283
shells
    $- syntax, lists current option flags, 15
    $IFS (bash Internal Field Separator), 268
    .rbash.0 , for restricted manpage, 27
    /dev/nul for portable scripts, 148
    /etc/bash.bashrc (Debian) global
        environment file, subshell
        environment file, 395
    /etc/bashrc (Red Hat), bash subshells
        global environment file, 395
    /etc/shells, 20
    /etc/shells, list of valid, 16
    ~/.bash_login, for Bourne login personal
        profile files, 395

~/.profile, for Bourne logging personal
    profile files, 395
backslash (\), for expansion of, 12
bash $IFS (bash Internal Field
    Separator), 254
bash $IFS (Internal Field Separator), 270
bash shell, 16
Bourne shell (sh), 1, 3, 303, 395
built-in commands, to ignore functions
    and aliases, 213
C Shell (csh), 1
cd command, 382
changing root shell on Unix, 17
chpass -s shell, changes default shell, 16
chsh -l, lists valid, 16
chsh -s /bin/bash, makes bash default, 16
chsh -s, changes default, 16
chsh, changes setting in, 16
Cygwin, 3
Emacs, allow shell escapes, 303
embedding documentation in scripts, 83
enable -n, turns off commands, 14
environment adjustment, 371
expand_aliases, 370
free accounts, 24
functions, 203, 221
history options, setting, 377
history, between sessions and
    synchronization, 376
Korn shell (ksh), 1
-l option, 16
levels of, 354
Linux default user shell, 3
Mac OS X default user shell, 3
macros, for interaction
    documentation, 362
online references, for security, 281
OpenBSD, 280
OpenSSH, 280
OpenSSH Restricted Shell, 318
parentheses ( ), redirects subshell's
    execution, 42
passwd -e, changes bash default, 16
passwd, changes bash default, 16
pipelines, subshell creation, 470
promptvars option, 357
rbash, restricting login, 302
restricted, 302
rsh (Remote Shell), 303
script security, 280
script testing in VMware, 326
scripting (programming), 3

secure shell programming techniques, 281
set, 371, 482
shell.h, 387
shopt, 371
shopt -s command, turns on shell options, 122
standard shell, 1
subshells, 42
Unix shell, 2
usermod -s /usr/bin/bash, changes default, 16
variables, testing for equal, 119
vi and Emacs, allow shell escapes, 303
wildcards, confusing with regular expressions, 480
writing portble scripts, 324
Writing Shell Scripts, documentation for, 27
shift, 231
shift built-in command, 135
shift statement, 250
shopt, 371
shopt -s command, turns on shell options, 122
shopt -s nocasematch, changes case sensitivity, 124
shopt -s nocasematch, for bash versions 3.1+, 133
shopt -s nullglob option, expands files to a null string, 344
short form of help, usage, 386
short-circuited expressions, 117
signal handlers, 208
signal names, 392
signal number, 208
Silverman, Richard, 308, 316
single brackets ([ ]), 10, 153
-size predicate to find, 192
slash (/), 35, 105
slocate, 7, 194
smart quotes, removing, 179
Social Security number searches, 153
Software Porting, 22
Solaris, 325
    2.x, 22
    7, 22
    8, 22
    cut command, 170
    less, 183
    sort comparisons, 169
    virtual environments, 325

sort
    command, 167
    comparisons, 169
    IP addresses, 167
    numeric data, 166
    options, 166
    pre-sorting, 167
    stable, 168
    utility, 165
source code, for bash, 26
source command, 195, 201
source tree, 261
sourcing, scripts, 201
space characters, 92
Spafford, Gene, 281
split command, 332
spoofing, setuid root, 283
Spotlight, desktop search engines, 194
SQL query, 219
square brackets ([ ]), 126
SSH
    $SSH_ID, 341
    $SSH_USER, 341
    certificates, 65
    commands, disable, 317
    fingerprint support, 315
    forced commands, 316
    host restriction, 317
    how the ssh command works, 318
    OpenSSH, 308
    OpenSSH Restricted Shell, 318
    password, without using a, 308
    public keys, 340
    rssh, 318
    SSH commands, restricting, 316–318
    SSH Communications Security, 308
    SSH forced commands, 316
    ssh -v, to locate problems with, 318
    ssh-add command, 312
    ssh-agent, 308
    ssh-keygen (ssh-keygen2), 309
stacks, 454
startup options, 353
STDERR (>&2), 38, 50, 200, 247
STDIN (standard input), 49, 200
stdio.h, 387
STDOUT (standard output), 37, 49, 50, 200
strftime, 378
strftime format specification, 217
strings
    $-, list current shell option flags, 15
    ${parameter/pattern/string}, 480

strings (*continued*)
    $PS2 (secondary prompt string), 374
    * (asterisk), matches file patterns, 10
    = (or ==), for string comparisons, 119
    ? question mark, 10
    [bracket, 10
    associative arrays (hashes in awk), 159
    asterisk (*), 121
    built-in test command, 118
    characteristics, testing, 118
    characters, parsing, one at a time, 260
    completion strings, viewing, 392
    constant strings, using for default, 102
    double bracket compound statement
        ([[ ]]), 121
    embedded spacing, 32
    -f option (awk) for counting values, 160
    filenames, renaming, 105, 411
    find all occurrences, 145
    first digits, 31
    left-align strings, 31
    max specifiers, 31
    min specifiers, 31
    negative sign on specifier, 31
    NF variable, for counting string values
        (awk), 160
    null strings, 344
    operators, for string-manipulation, 106
    output, variations, 146
    -p option (read), for printing a prompt
        string, 60, 65
    pattern matches, 121
    question mark (?), match single
        character, 121
    quotes, 32, 119
    rename from_string to_string file_
        name, 413
    searches, ignoring case, 149
    second digit, 31
    shopt -s nullglob option, expands files to a
        null string, 344
    single brackets ([), in, 10
    substring function, 260
    values, counting, 159
stty sane, to fix or disable echo, 473
stty sane, to restore echo, 66
su command, 5, 435
sub-expressions, to populate array
    variables, 123
subsets, data, 170
subshells, 42
substitutions, across boundaries, 457

substring function, 260
Subversion, 128, 261, 538
sudo, 5, 17, 435
sudo bash, 305
sudo security, 305
sudoers, 306
Sunfreeware, 22
SUSE, 19
svn command, 128
svn status command, 261
symbolic links, 188, 237, 370
Synaptic, 19
syntactic differences, with parentheses, 42
syntax, canonical portable for bash $IFS, 287
syntax, verifying correctness of using
    bash, 476
syslog, 335, 345
system integrity, securing of, 282
system-wide environment settings, 401
system-wide profile settings, 400

T

-t option (sort), 168
tab character, 59, 170, 271
Tab key, 460
table of contents, view with tar -t, 175
tail commands, 39
tar archives, checking unique
    directories, 175
tar command, 172
tar -t, view table of contents, 175
tarball, 172, 297
tee command, 45, 50
temporary file security, 282
terminal window, viewing gibberish, 473
test command, 113
test operators, 505
test -t option, 125
Texinfo, 413, 414
text-related utilities
    !! (double exclamation point) history
        operator, 150
    $ (dollar sign), 153
    $( ) dollar sign, parentheses, for filenames
        on command lines, 147
    $LESS variable, 182
    $LESSCLOSE, 182
    $LESSOPEN, 182
    ' single quote, for searches, 152
    . period (in regular expressions), 152
    .deb files, 173

/dev/nul (for portable shell scripts), 148
[ ] single brackets, 153
\ (backslash), in searches, 152
\{n,m\}, repetition mechanism, 153
^ (caret), matches beginning of line, 153
^total, 159
absolute pathnames, 176
ar archives, 173
associative arrays (hashes in awk), 159
asterisk (*), 152
awk program, 144, 157
awk utility, 155
backslash (\), matches special
        characters, 153
BEGIN keyword (awk), 158
bit buckets, 148
bzip2, file compression, 172
-c option (grep), 146
case sensitivity, eliminating, 177
case-insensitive search, 149
character translation, 176
compressed files, grepping, 154
compression algorithms, 173
continue statement, 163
CPIO files, 173
cut command, 170
-d option (cut), specify delimiters, 178
-d option (tr), delete characters, 178
-d option, specify delimiters, 170
data subsets, 170
delimiters, 170
directories, and tar archives, 175
directory names, parsing off, 175
DOS carriage returns (\r), deletion, 178
DOS files, convert to Linux, 178
duplicate lines, removing, 171
END keyword (awk), 158
escape sequences, 179
extensions, uncompressing, 174
-f option (awk) counting string
        values, 160
-F option (awk), to delineate fields, 155
field separator, 168
fields, 170
file command, 175
file compression, 172
file extensions, 174
files, naming, 173
files, overwriting, 172
flags, turning off, 163
fmt command, 181
for loop, 157

getline command, 159
GNU tar, 173
grep compressed files, 154
grep program, 144
gzcat, 154
gzip, file compression, 172
-h switch (grep), to grep, 146
histogram, 161
input preprocessors, 182
input source, with grep, 146
IP addresses, sorting, 167
-j, for bzip2, 173
keyphrase, 163
-l option (unzip), to convert Unix end
        lines, 173
-l option, with grep, 147
less manpage, 182
less pager, 182
less utility, 155
lesspipe*, 182
lesspipe.sh, 183
line output, keeping selected
        portions, 156
-ll option, (unzip) convert end lines to
        Unix, 173
locale setting, when sorting, 168
log messages, eliminating by error, 151
ls -l command, keeping selected portions
        of line output, 156
-n option (sort), for sorting numbers, 166
NetBSD, stable sorts, 168
NF variable (awk), 156, 160
numbers, summing a list, 158
numeric data, sorting, 166
options (with grep), 146
output, partial elimination, 155
output, variations, 146
paragraphs, rewrapping, 181
phrases, searching for, 163
pipeline searches, 149
POSIX, 168
pr command, 181
pre-sort, 167
-q (quiet) option (grep), 148
RE (regular expression), 152, 159
relative directory, 173
repetition mechanism, for searches, 153
return value of 0, 148
RPM (Red Hat Package Manager), 173
-S, turns off stable sort on NetBSD, set
        buffer size otherwise (sort), 168
searches, 149, 151, 152, 153

text-related utilities (*continued*)
    sed program, 144
    smart quotes, removing, 179
    sort comparisons, 169
    sort options, 166
    sort utility, 165
    stable sort, 168
    string values, counting, 159
    -t option (sort), 168
    tab character, 170
    tar command, 172
    tar -t, view table of contents, 175
    tarball, 172
    tarball.tar.gz, 172
    tarball.tar.Z, 172
    textutils, 275
    tr command, character translation, 176
    tr utility, 179
    true or false searches, 148
    -u option (sort), to remove duplicates
        when sorting, 167
    uniq, viewing duplicate lines, 171
    -v option (grep), for searches, 151
    wc (word count) command, 180
    words, reversing order of, 157
    write only expressions, 153
    -Z, for compress using GNU tar, 173
    -z, for gzip using tar, 173
    zcat, 154
    zgrep, 154
then (if), 112
third-party libraries, 389
this week, caution using, 221
thousands-place separator, 450
Thunderbird, 347
tilde (~), 4, 103
time zones, 218, 226
tkman, Texinfo viewer and converter, 414
tokens, processing on command line, 532
tomorrow's date, getting with Perl, 224
tr command, character translation, 176
tr escape sequences, 515
tr utility, 179
trailing m, indicates color escape
    sequence, 360
translation of characters, 176
trap interrupts, 207
trap utility, 207
trapping, 207–211, 293
tree, filesystem hierarchy, 35
Tripwire, 282
Trojan horse, 282

trojaned utilities, 282
Tru64 Unix, 22
true or false searches, 148
tty, 199
tty built-in, 385
ttyname, 387
turn off built-in commands, 14
txt versions (ASCII text), 27
type command, 13, 213
-type d (find directories), 191
type -P, 195
-type predicate to find, 191

U

u option (sort), to remove duplicates when
    sorting, 167
Ubuntu
    6.10, bash login rc files, 396
    cut command, 170
    Debian-derived systems, 19
    lesspipe, 183
    Linux 5.10, 326
    sudo, 435
    using dash, 21, 321, 324, 329, 368, 400
UCLA, 22
UDP, 335
ulimit, 287
umask, secure, 288
unalias, 369
uncompressing compressed archives, 391
uncompressing files, 174
uniq, viewing duplicate lines, 171
Unix
    $PATH, changing, 397
    bash versions, 22
    BSD Unixes, 17
    date command, 216
    dates and times, commands omit the
        year, 226
    file permissions, 300
    groups, 300
    -l option, to convert end lines to
        DOS, 173
    -ll option, (unzip) convert DOS end lines
        to, 173
    Microsoft Services, 24
    root shells, changing, 17
    shell, 1
    tarball.tar.gz, 172
    tarball.tar.Z, 172
    UnixReview, 221

unprivileged users, 282
unzip files, 246, 414
updates, to paths, 361
urandom, 293
USAGE function, 236
usage message, 203
usage, short form of help, 386
user
    documentation, 83
    inactive, 318
    non-root, 305
    unprivileged, 282
    usermod -s /usr/bin/bash, changes default
        shell, 16
user directories, 362
user input, 60
utilities, personal, 373
uuencode, 346

V

-v argument (for verbose), 98, 347
-v option, for searches, 151
-V parameter (mkisofs), 244
values, counting, 159
variables
    $ (dollar sign), 81
    $* (errors using), 94
    $* (unquoted), 95
    $@, 94
    $@ (unquoted), 95
    $0 variable, 236
    $HIST* variables, 377
    $HISTFILE, 378
    $HISTFILESIZE variable, 378
    $HISTTIMEFORMAT, 378
    $LESSCLOSE, 182
    $LESSOPEN, 182
    $PS1, 353, 357, 410
    $PS2, 353
    $PS3, 64, 137, 357, 374
    $PS4, 357, 376
    = (equals) symbols, in commands, 81
    array variable, 106, 123
    arrays, 255
    braces ({ }), 87
    call by value, 88
    commands, distinguish between variables
        and, 81
    env (export -p), 88
    -eq operator, for numeric
        comparisons, 119

errors in, 94
exported value, changing, 88
exporting, 87
grep command, 90
MAILTO, 347
name=value syntax, 80
names, 78, 80, 86
reference, use full syntax, 87
running commands from, 78
R-value syntax, 81
set command, 89
spell out names of, 85
syntax, 80
testing for equal shells, 119
values, viewing of, 89
vi, 447
vi and Emacs, allow shell escapes, 303
vi control mode commands, 520
viewers, for documents, 414
viewing completion strings, 392
viewing photos, with a browser, 233
viewing, output in Hex, 333
view command, to verify password file
    consistency, 16
virtual machines, prebuilt, 326
virtualization packages, getting free, 326
visudo, for editing, 306
VMware, 325
VMware player, 326
VNC-based VMware Console, 326

W

Wall, Larry, 413
Wang, Michael, 446, 451
wc (word count) command, 180
wdiff, 426
wget, 336
which command, 6, 13
which utility, 196
while loop, 75, 126, 128, 239
while read, 127
whitespace, 59, 268–271, 333
wildcards, 10, 480
Windows
    bash, 23
    Cygwin, 23
    GNU Text Utils, 23
    Linux-like environment, 23
word content, document comparison, 245
word counting, 180
WORD_LIST, 386

words, reversing order of, 157
world-writable directories, 289–291, 361
write only expressions, 124, 153

X

x86 architecture, 326
xargs command, 186, 343
xpg_echo, 329
xterm, 355, 359
xtrace, 357, 478

Y

YaST, 19
yes or no input, 61
yesterday's date, getting with Perl, 224

Z

-Z, for compress using GNU tar, 173
-z, for gzip using tar, 173
zcat, 154
zero returns, 127
zeroth, 123, 206
zgrep, 154
ZIP files, 246, 414

About the Authors

Carl Albing is a veteran Java, C, and bash programmer, having worked with Linux and Unix since his days at St. Olaf College in the mid-1970s. An author and teacher as well, he has made technical presentations for conferences and corporations in the U.S., Canada, and Europe. With a Bachelor's degree in Mathematics and a Master's in International Management, he continues to pursue his studies. He currently works as a software engineer for the supercomputer company Cray, Inc. and as an independent consultant. Carl is co-author of *Java Application Development on Linux* from Prentice Hall PTR. He can be reached via his web site *www.carlalbing.com* or by visiting *www.oreilly.com* and searching for *Albing*.

JP Vossen has been working with computers since the early 1980s and has been in the IT industry since the early 90s, specializing in information security since the late 90s. He's been fascinated with scripting and automation since he first understood what an *autoexec.bat* was, and he was delighted to discover the power and flexibility of bash and GNU on Linux in the mid-90s. He has previously written for *Information Security Magazine* and SearchSecurity.com, among others. On those few occasions when he's not in front of a computer, he is usually taking something apart, putting something together, or both.

Cameron Newham is an information technology developer living in the United Kingdom. Originally from Australia, Cameron completed a Bachelor of Science degree in Information Technology and Geography at the University of Western Australia. In his spare time, he can be found working on his project to digitally record buildings of architectural interest in England. He also has more than a passing interest in a diverse range of subjects including photography, space science, digital imaging, ecclesiology, and architectural history. He is co-author of *Learning the bash Shell* from O'Reilly.

Colophon

The animal on the cover of *bash Cookbook* is a wood turtle (*Glyptemys insculpta*) and is named so because its shell looks like it was carved from wood. The wood turtle can be found in forests and is very common in North America, particularly in Nova Scotia through to the Great Lakes region. The wood turtle is an omnivorous and lazy eater; it will eat whatever crosses its path, including plants, worms, and slugs (a favorite). But this isn't to say wood turtles are slow—in fact, they can be quite agile and quick to learn. Some researchers have seen wood turtles stamping on the ground to mimic the sound of raindrops, which lures worms out to their certain death.

Wood turtles are threatened by human expansion into their territories. They nest on the sandy banks of rivers, streams, and ponds, which are prone to erosion, damming, and use by outdoor enthusiasts. Roadside fatalities, toxic pollution, and the pet trade have also taken a toll on the wood turtle population, so much so that in many states and provinces, they are considered a threatened species.

The cover image is from Dover Pictoral Archive. The cover font is Adobe ITC Garamond. The text font is Linotype Birka; the heading font is Adobe Myriad Condensed; and the code font is LucasFont's TheSans Mono Condensed.

CPSIA information can be obtained at www.ICGtesting.com
Printed in the USA
LVOW09s0447250913

353926LV00017B/807/P